Gerald L. Hocker

June 11, 1988

Moberly, Missouri

KENTUCKY PIONEER AND COURT RECORDS

ABSTRACTS OF
EARLY WILLS, DEEDS AND MARRIAGES FROM COURT HOUSES

and
Records of

OLD BIBLES, CHURCHES, GRAVE YARDS, AND CEMETERIES

Copied by American War Mothers

GENEALOGICAL MATERIAL

Collected From Authentic Sources

Records from

Anderson, Bourbon, Boyle, Clark, Estill, Fayette, Garrard, Harrison, Jessamine, Lincoln, Madison, Mercer Montgomery, Nicholas and Woodford Counties

---

Compiled by

MRS. HARRY KENNETT McADAMS

GENEALOGICAL PUBLISHING CO., INC.
BALTIMORE   1975

Originally Published
Lexington, 1929

Reprinted
Genealogical Publishing Co., Inc.
Baltimore, 1967

Baltimore, 1975

Library of Congress Catalogue Card Number 67-28612
International Standard Book Number 0-8063-0217-8

INDEX TO COUNTY RECORDS

FOREWORD

Records, like people, grow old and are lost or destroyed. and it is a vital necessity that they be preserved in a compact form for historical research.

Others have gone before us in this work, others will follow; yet, to none will it be a greater inspiration or work of love. The proceeds from the sale of this book is to be donated to the Kentucky Chapter, American War Mothers.

As descendants turn these pages they will walk with their hardy pioneer forebears, and read their preparation for death in wills, taking thought of loved ones.

The quaint spelling of the old records has been very carefully copied, in many cases family names have been spelled differently in the same will.

We hope that this book will prove a valuable "link in the chain," to all those doing historical research.

EDNAH WILSON McADAMS.

309 North Broadway,
    Lexington, Ky.

ANDERSON COUNTY, KENTUCKY

(Copied by Mrs. George R. Mastin)

FIRST ORDER BOOK, PAGE 1

The Justices of County Court, Anderson County, met at house of William Hudgins, in the Town of Lawrenceburg, on Monday the fifth day of February in the year of Christ, one thousand eight hundred and twenty-seven, in 35th year of Commonwealth of Kentucy; and proceeded to constitute and organize the County of Anderson, according to Act of Assembly creating and establishing the County of Anderson out of parts of the counties of Franklin, Washington and Mercer. Approved 7th day of January, 1827.

Following gentleman Justicies of County Court, appeared with Certificates of having taken Oath * * page 2. Took seats according to seniority: James McBrayer, Dixon G. Dedman, John Wash, Andrew McBrayer, John Busey, Christopher Lillard, Reuben Boston, John C. Richardson ,Thomas Philips. Signed, Jesse Guess, presiding Justice.

David White, Jr., appointed Clerk * * * signed David White, Jr., John T. Davis, Wm. Hudgins, Thomas Tripplett, Wm. Robison. Atteste, Jesse Guess, Presiding Judge.

John F. Blackwell * * * appointed Sheriff, January 10, 1827, and took proper Oath of office. Robert Blackwell, Andrew McBrayer, Thomas Philips and Wm. Lawrence, are bound for $3,000 for John F. Blackwell Sheriff's bond.

On motion of George Morris, he is appointed Jailer * * *.

On motion of Epraim Lillard, Esq. * * * appointed Coroner * * February 10, 1827.

Court met February 6, 1827. Justices present, James McBrayer, Dixon T. Dedman, John Wasg, Andrew McBrayer, John Busey, Christopher Leeland, Reuben Boston and Thomas Philips, Esquires.

ANDERSON COUNTY, WILL ABSTRACTS, BOOK A

ALLEN, MEMUCM—Will—Page 17—Names, wife, Polly. Sons, Joseph and Charles. Grandson, Washington Dale, son of my daughter, Sally Allen, late Sally Dale, deceased. Daus., Susannah Stotts, Elizabeth Hank and Polly Stott. Executors, Sons, Joseph and Charles Allen. Written Sept. 28, 1832. Witnesses, Jordan H. Walker and Eli Penney. Rec. Aug. Court 1833.

BOND, JAMES S.—Will Book A, page 10—Names wife. Son, David, Brother, Anthony Bond. Robert McMichael. Written Jan. 11, 1831. Witnesses, Joshua McMichael and Joseph McMichael. Probated Oct., 1831.

BRUIN, SUSANNAH—Will Book A, page 35—Written Dec. 24, 1835. Names, 2 dau's., Martha and Jane Bruin. Names, Prior Bruin, Martha Bruin, Jane Bruin, James and William Bruin. Witnesses, Samuel P. Mayell and Henry W. Norton. Recd. Mch 16, 1836.

BURRIS, SAMUEL—Will—Page 172—Date May 7, 1846. Names son, James R. Burris, Dau., Jane Morgan. Children of my son Thomas Burris, deceased. Children of my dau., Elizabeth Petty. Son, John Burris. Dau., Mary Travis. Dau., Catherine Shouse. Children of dau., Nancy Richey. Son, Samuel Burris. Children of my son, Monroe Burris, deceased. Son, Alfred Burris. Sons-in-law, Moses Travis and Henry Richey. Exec's., Son, John Burris, Alvin Herndon and Robert Elliott. Witnesses, Presley F. Herndon, Wm. H. Thomas and Ronsey P. Herndon. Probated Nov. 13, 1855.

CARR, PETER—Will Book A, page 36—Dated Oct. 29, 1835. Names my daughters, Rachell Watts, wife of Thurman Watts, and her heirs. My dau., Sally Watts, wife of Felix Watts, dau., Polly Elliott, wife of Robert Elliott. Exec., Felix Watts. Probated Sept. 19, 1836. Test., Jordan H. Walker and Randolph Walker.

CARTER, JOHN, SENIOR—Will Book A, page 34—Dated June 1, 1835. "My dau., Mary Waterfield, sole legatee and executor. Atteste, Jordan H. Walker, Turner Hanks, and Henry N. Thompson. Probated Sept. 19, 1835. Jordan H. Walker, County Clerk.

CARTER, JOSHUA—Will—Page 15—Dated June 28, 1833. Names wife, Molly. Children, Providence Smith, his dau., and her heirs Dau's., Sarah Boggess, and Katherine Parker. Sons, Isaah G. (?) and William Carter. Atteste, Chichester Hanks and Johua McMichael. Probated July 8, 1833.

CATLETT, FRANCES—Will—Page 35—Names wife, Elizabeth. Written Aug. 30, 1832. Witnesses, Anthony Lang, Henry Lang and Peyton Spears. Rec. Mch. 16, 1836.

CORBAN, JOHN—Will—Page 4—Names wife, Mary. 4 daughters, Son, John. Written Dec. 3, 1836. Witnesses, F. S. Carmar and Jeremiah Ford. Prob. Sept. 20, 1838.

CRUTCHFIELD, JOHN—Spottsylvania Co., Va.—Will Book A, page 2 —Anderson Co., Ky. Names wife. Son, William. Dau's., Mildred Crutchfield and Mary B. Burk. Brother, Robert Crutchfield, executor. Written Jan. 8, 1819. Witnesses, Stephen J. Bayles, Rawling Puliam and Oscar M. Crutchfied. Probated Feb. Court 1819.

DOWNEY, JAMES, of Mercer County, Ky.—Will—Page 1—Written May 31, 1825. Names sons, Joseph A., John, James, Jr., and my dau., Martha Morris. Wife, Martha Downey. Dau., Nancy Oate (or Outes). Son, James as trustee for my dau; Nancy and her heirs, free from control of her husband. Son, Joel and his heirs. Exec., Son, James. Witnesses, Robert B. McAfee, Susan J. Boyce, Sally C. McAfee. Will of James Downey, deceased proved on oaths of Robert B. McAfee and Sally C. McAfee. Sept. 3, 1827.

DRISKELL, DENNIS—Will—Page 32—Dated Apr. 12, 1834. Names wife, Barbara. Sons, Jesse Driskell, John, Wm., David, Thomas P., James H., and Dennis C. Driskell. Dau's., Frances Brack and Sally Bowman. Atteste, Richard Paxton, James Paxton and Wm. D. Sale. Probated July 17, 1835.

FINCH, JEREMIAH—Will—Page 9—Dated May 2, 1831. Names wife, Lydia Ann Finch. Witnesses, Dedman and J. B. Bush. Probated June Court 1831.

FISHER, WILLIAM—Will—Page—Noncupative—Dated July 14, 1833. "Merit Fisher must pay debts that Jacob Fisher owes in Versailles. Provides for Mother; sell effects and use for own benefit." Atteste, Joel Medley and John Witherspoon. Probated Aug. Court 1833.

FORTUNE, ZACHARIAH—Will—Page 23—Dated Oct. 9, 1833. Names wife, Elizabeth. Sons, Thomas, John B., Zachariah, Richard F. Fortune. Dau., Patty T. Alexander, wife of James Alexander. Dau., Sally, wife of John Alexander, and her son, Zachariah Alexander. Dau., Jinetty Willis S. Penney. Son, Elisha Fortune, son, Benjamin Fortune, son, Edmund Fortune. Atteste, Jesse Guess and John Lynn. Probated Nov. 12, 1833.

6

GILL, JAMES L.—Will—Page 39—Names wife, Martha Gill. 3 children, William, George and James. Exec's., Wife, Martha, Samuel W. Chambers and Gideon Mitchell. Written, Nov. 18, 1836. Witnesses, J. H. Waler and James D. Hardin. Probated Dec. Court, 1836.

GREEN, ZACHARIAH—Will—Page 1—Date. Oct. 10, 1826. Names wife, Eleanor Harris Green. Probated Mch., 1827.

HALEY, BENJAMIN—Will—Page 42—Date July 27, 1835. Names wife, Judith Haley. To be equally divided between James, the son of my wife, and John Haley, my son. Atteste, John Dycke, Wm. Dycke and Peggy Dycke. Probate Apr. 26, 1837.

HUTTON, JAMES—Will—Page 14—Names wife, Hannah Hutton. Dau., Elizabeth Reed, formerly Elizabeth Miller, at present a resident of Ohio, and her children, Jane Miller and James H. Miller. Dau., Sarah Mastin, son, Henry Hutton, at present a resident of Ohio. Dau., Mary Swingle. Dau., Nancy Brown, at present a resident of Missouri, Exec's., sons-in-law, John G. Mastin, John Swingle, and Jeremiah Buckley. Will of James Hutton, deceased, probated July Court 1833. Written Jan. 3, 1832.

JACKSON, ANN—Will—Page 7—Written Feb. 2, 1831. Names eldest dau., Ellander Jackson. Son, William Jackson. Son-in-law, Charles Rice. Grandson, John Hathaway and Harriett, infant children of John Hathaway. My dau., Tabitha Hathaway, now Tabitha Rice. Exec's., son, Wm. Jackson and dau., Ellander. Witnesses, J. H. Walker, and Joseph Allen. Probated Apr. 11, 1831.

LANE, EDWARD—Will—Page 6—Names Grand-children, heirs of son, Garland Lane, deceased, viz., Lucinda, Permelia, Louisa, Rhod and Betsy. Garland's wife, Betsy Lane. Son, Felix Lane. Son, Hayston Lane. Dau., Nancy Stansberry, dau., Alpha Watts; grand-dau., Julia Lane, late Julia Thurman. Exec's., Son, Felix Lane and Elijah Thurman. Witnesses, Jordan H. Walker, Elijah Thurman and Hayston Lane. Written May 23, 1830. Probated Mch. 14, 1831.

LEATHERS, NICHOLAS—Will—Page 44—Dated (?) 1838. Names wife, Fanny Leathers. Son, Alfred. "The rest of my children. Exec., John Leathers. Atteste, John Bunny and Jeremiah Anderson. Probated June 13, 1838.

McBRAYER, HIRAM—Will—Page 33—Names Mother, Jane McBrayer. Wm. C. Twyman, heir of sister, Nancy Twyman. Rachel Hanberry, to have lot of land given me by Commissioners appointed. Brother, James' two daughters. C. McBrayer. Susan and Alexander McBrayer's children. Exec., Alvin Herndon. Witnesses, James McBrayer and Alvin Herndon. Rec., July Court 1835.

McBRAYER, MARTHA—Will—Page 11—Names sister, Nancy S. Twyman. Two children, Wm. Clark Twyman and Martha Jane Twyman. Brother, Hiram McBrayer. Written Mch. 8, 1831. Teste, Alvin Herndon, James Hawthorn and Wm. McBrayer. Proved Dec. Court 1831.

McGINNIS, JAMES—Will—Page 47—Names dau's., Polly Slayton, Nancy Stout, and Elizabeth Haynes and her husband, John Haynes. To children of my late dau., Jane, which she had by William

Haynes. Dau., Ann Haynes. Son, Samuel McGinnis. Dau., Frances Gilpin. Dau., Sally Stout. Exec's., Son, Samuel and friend, Jordan H. Walker. Written June 12, 1833. Witnesses, David White, Henrietta M. White. Rec. Sept. Court 1838

MADISON, JAMES—Will—Page 5—Written Jan. 21, 1820. Of Hanover County, Va. Names Brother, Lewis Madison. Exec., Brother, Lewis Madison. Witnesses, Robert W. Tompkins and Archibald Mathews. Will recorded in Carolina Co., Jan. 11, 1830. Will recorded in Anderson Co., Ky., Apr. 20, 1830.

MARSHALL, WILLIAM—Will—Page 29—Written Mch. 17, 1834. Names son, George Wm. Jordan Marshall (one name). Names nephew, Wm. Marshall, son of Charles Marshall. Samuel Ayers and Ephraim A. Smith, Trustees, Names friend, James Harland, Exec. Witnesses, James Harland, Merit Fisher, Powhatan B. Darr. Codicil, Apr. 28, 1834. Niece, Ann Maria Wallace. Brother, Charles Marshall. Codicil, Oct. 15, 1834. Jeremiah P Lancaster. Signed, Joel Medley and Merit Fisher. Will with 2 Codicils, recorded Mch. 13, 1835.

MILLS, JOHN J. T.—Will—Page 28—Dated Dec. 8, 1834. Names wife, Maria Mills. "My children." Exec's., Wife, Maria Mills and friend, Allen Rowlands. "I was 43 years old on the 8th of Feb. last." Atteste, Allen Rowland and B. W. Rhoton and D. G. Dedman. Probated Jan. 12, 1835

MOSBY, THOMAS—Will—Page 23—Names Elizabeth, Devenport, of County of Woodford, Ky Richard Dawson, Anderson Co., Ky., whom I esteem my best friend. Exec., Richard Dawson. Written 1833. Witnesses, Wm. Rece, Jeremiah Hanks. Proved Nov. Court 1833.

MOTHERSHEAD, JOHN—Will—Page 26—Names wife, Susannah Motherhead. Children all equal. Son, John. Daus., Polly Vance, Elizabeth Dawson, William Mothershead, Nathaniel Mothershead, Elijah Mothershead, Susannah Cornell (Or Comell) and John Mothershead. Exec's., Hankerson Reed and Henry Story. Written, Oct. 5, 1833. Witnesses, Hankerson Reed and Henry Story, and J. H. Walker. Probated Jan. 13, 1834.

OLIVER, PLEASANT—Will—Page 21—Written Aug. 15, 1833. Names wife, Sarah. Dau., Polina, who married H. H. Buntain. Son, John. Codicil, Names wife, Sarah. Son, James B. Oliver. Exec's., John Busey and John Olive. Witnesses, Thomas H White and T. B. Petty. Rec. Oct. 14, 1833.

PENNY, JOHN—Will—Pages 18 and 19—Date Feb. 9, 1829. Names wife, Fanny. Grand-dau., Sally Penny, dau. of Thomas Penny, deceased. Grand-dau., Sally Penny, dau. of Phillip Penny, deceased. Grand-children, Fanny, Clement and Elizabeth, of John Lillard, deceased. Dau., Elizabeth, wife of Will James, formaly Elizabeth Lillard, wife of John Lillard, deceased. Dau., Polly Freeman, wife of Charles Y. Freeman. Sons, Wm. W. Penny, Eli Penny and James Penny. Exec's., Sons, Eli, James and Wm. W. Penny. Witnesses, David White, J. McBrayer, J. H. Walker and Randall Walker. Probated Aug. Court 1833.

POSEY, JEREMIAH B.—Will—Page 51—Names two children, Mary Walker Posey, James Monroe Posey, under age. Brother, Thomas

8

B. Posey, of Henry Co. Exec., Written Aug., 1838. Witnesses, Jeremiah Buckley, John Mothershead, Elijah Mothershead. Probated Dec. 1, 1838.

RANDLE, WALKER—Will—Page 42—Names wife, Polly Walker. Children, Marier, Moses, Randol, Artemisia, Sally, Porter and Monroe Walker. Grand-son and Grand-dau., children of my dau., Lucretia, deceased. Exec's., Sons, Moses and Randol. Written, June 37, 1837. Witnesses, Jordan H. Walker, Allen Rowland and John Dawson. Rec. Oct. Court 1837.

RILEY, EDWARD, of Mercer Co., Ky.—Will—Page 49—Names wife, Polly, Sons, Sanders and Daniel Riley. Son, William, deceased and his son, Edward W. Riley. Emma Riley, wife of William, deceased. Dau., Polly Riley; daus., Sally McGinnis, Elizabeth Settles, Nancy Nichols. Exec's., John McGinnis and James Downey, Jr. Written Mch. 10, 1828. Witnesses, Robert Breckinridge, Arthur Edbert, and D. L. Slaughter. Rec. Nov. 19, 1838.

ROUTE, JOSHUA K.—Will—Page 38—Names wife. Dau., Willalmona, my brother, John Route, Jr. Teste, D. G. Dedman, A. R. Hann and John Route. Probated Nov. 16, 1836.

SEARCY, DUDLEY—Will—Page 9—Names wife, Sally Searcy. Dau., Lucy Searcy. "My brother and sister." Exec's., Wife, Sally and Reuben Morton. Written Mch. 2, 1831. Witnesses Elijah Morton and William J. Burford. Proved Aug. Court 1831.

SCOTT, JOHN—Will—Page 26—Dated Oct. 19, 1833. Names children, in North Carolina, Lucy Scott, Jesse Scott, John Scott, Milly Scott, Betsy Scott, Sarah Scott and Mary Scott. Teste, Andrew McBrayer. Probated, Nov. 15, 1833.

SEARCY, HENRY—Will—Page 20—Dated June 17, 1833. Names wife, Elizabeth. Son, Edmund Searcy's heirs, and his widow, Winny Searcy. Deceased son, Dudley's widow, Sally Searcy and her dau., Lucy Ann Searcy. Son, James Searcy and his heirs. Dau., Patsy Green and her heirs. Attest, Allen Rowlands, Argyle Boggess and Wade Wall. Probated Aug. Court 1833.

SLAUGHTER, DANIEL S.—Will—Page 31—No natural heirs. Leaves all to slaves, to be emancipated as they reach the age of 21. Witnesses, Jordan H. Walker and John O'Dell. Rec. July Court 1835.

SLAUGHTER, FRANCES L.—Will—Page 12—Names wife, Dolly Slaughter. Son, Lewis, son, Elias Slaughter. Heirs of dau., Jemima Harris, late wife of Webb Harris viz; Thomas Slaughter Harris and Zerelda Engleton Harris (under age). Written Dec. 26, 1831. Witnesses, L. J. Witherspoon, and Leroy D. Stephens. Probated March, 1832.

SLAYTON, ARTHUR—Will—Page 45—Names wife, Lucy, Niece, Mahala Clark. Brother, Joseph Slayton. Nephew, James Watts, by Marnago and Mahala Clark my niece. Exec's., Joseph Slayton and James Watts. Written May 8, 1838. Rec. July Court 1838. Witnesses, Robert McMichael and Joseph Biles.

STOTT, GEORGE—Will—Page 37—Names wife, Polly. Children, Jane, Elizabeth, John, America, Mary and George Stott. Written, Nov. 6, 1833. Witnesses, R. Walker and Lewis S. Walker. Rec. Sept. Court 1836.

TASH, KATHERINE—Will—Page 40—Dated Mch. 25, 1831. Names Polly Watts, infant dau. of Thurman Watts. Katherine Watts, dau. of Thurman Watts. Jane Watts, infant dau. of Felix Watts. Rhoda Watts, dau. of Felix Watts. Lucy Ann, infant dau. of Thurman Watts. My living sisters. Exec., J. H. Walker. Teste, Wm. T. Stone, Elija Thurman and James Hunter. Probated March 16, 1837.

WALKER, JOHN, SENIOR—Will—Page 22—Dated Oct. 1833. Names wife, Elizabeth. Sons, Jordan H. Walker, Randolph Walker, James S. Walker, John Walker, Jr., Lewis S. Walker, Lucinda Walker (late Lucinda Haynes), Arameans Walker, Katherine Walker (late Katherine Mozner), Elizabeth Walker, Harriett Walker (late Harriett Mozner). Atteste, Randolph Walker.

WALLACE, WILLIAM B.—Will—Page 12—Names son, Wm. B. Wallace, James B. Wallace, daus., Fanny Hudgins, Eliza Dedman, and Ann Daviess. Mentions land part of Patent granted Dr. James Wallace, on Ohio River, opposite Hurricane Island, in County of Levington. Fielding L. Cannon, and Jordan H. Walker, Trustees of my dau., Eliza Dedman and her 3 sons by Dickson G. Dedman. Written May 31, 1833. Names brother, Gustavius. Mentions deed Partition between Mary Bede (?) and Lucinda Wallace. Recorded in Court of Levington. Will rec. Anderson Co., June, 1833, on oath of Dickson D, Dedman, Administrator. Teste, J. H. Walker, Clerk.

WATSON, JOHN—Will—Page 52—Names sons, Westley and Richard Watson. "Ballance of my sons and daughters not here mentioned." Exec's., Sons, Wm. P. and Westley Watson. Written Mch. 20, 1838. Witnesses, Jordan H. Walker, and John Dawson. Proved July 8, 1839.

WATTS, JEREMIAH—Will—Page 53—Names dau., Eliza Watts. Written June 3, 1837. Witnesses, B. F. Major, John Droffin, R. C. McBrayer, Lucinda Watts. Proved July Court 1839.

ANDERSON COUNTY, FIRST ORDER BOOK

PENNY, ELI—Order Book, page 54—Date Jan. 12, 1828. On motion of Eli Penny, letters of administration granted him on Estate of Phillip M. Penny, deceased, Margaret Penny, widow gives her consent. Bond $2000. Eli Penny took oath prescribed by law.

PENNY, PHILLIP—Page 39—Phillip Penny against Ramey, date Sept. 1827.

PENNY, ELI—Date Sept. 3, 1827. On motion of Eli Penny, he is appointed guardian to Catherine Rucker, James and Ezekiel Rucker, infants of Wisdom Rucker, who has abandoned them. Eli Penny executed bond for $2000 together with Phillip Penny.

CARDWELL—Page 68—Elvira and Louisa Cardwell, children of John B. Cardwell, deceased, came into Court and chose Alvin Herndon, for guardian, bond $1000, with Archibald Elliott and Thompson Thomas, security. Date Mch. 15, 1828.

TAYLOR, GRAYSON B.—Appointed Constable in place of James Hawkins, resigned.

ELI PENNY AND MARK LILLARD, sworn in as Justices. Page 98.

LILLARD, FRANCES—Page 96—Frances Lillard, infant orphan of John Lillard, deceased, over 14 and under 21, came into Court and chose Charles Y. Freeman for guardian. Bond $2000 with John Penny ,security. Feb. 1829.

DEED BOOK B

TAYLOR, ARGYLE—Page 27—Argyle Taylor of Anderson Co., Ky., to James McConnell of Woodford Co., land in Anderson Co. on Gilberts Creek. Date July 11, 1831.

PENNY, WM. W.—Deed Book A—Wm. W. Penny and Mary, to Wm. Patterson. Date Apr. 15, 1829.

PENNY, ELI—Deed Book B, page 361—Eli Penny and Polly, to John Rout, of Garrard Co. Teste, C. H. Fenwick. Sept. 5, 1833.

BURRIS, SAMUEL AND ALFRED—Deed Book D, page 246—Alfred and Samuel Burris contract to pay debt to Wm. W. George. Date Mch. 26*, 1838.

BURRIS, JOHN—Deed Book G, page 231—Date Oct. 14, 1848. John Burris and Polly of Nelson Co., Ky. to Robert Houchens of Anderson Co.

BOURBON COUNTY RECORDS

(Donated by Mrs. B. F. Buckley, Lexington, Ky.)

ABSTRACT OF COURT ORDER

JACOB LEER—Power of Attorney to Jacob Leer, from Ann, widow of Henry Leer, and other heirs:
   "To all to whom these presents shall come we, Aaron Smedley and Rebecca, his wife, David Lear, Abraham Lear, John Lear, Mary Lear and Anne Lear, widow, children and kins of Henry Lear, deceased, all of the county of Bourbon and State of Kentucky, send greeting: Whereas the said Henry Lear in his lifetime was sized and possesed of one lot in the town of Liberty in the state of Maryland, on Main St., with sundry valuable improvements thereon and whereas: the said Henry departed this life intestate, leaving the above named Anne Lear, his widow, and Rebecca who has intermarried with Aaron Smedley, David Lear, Abraham Lear, John Lear and Mary Lear, his children and kins and representatives. Now know ye by the presents that we the said Aaron Smedley and Rebecca his wife, David Lear, Abraham Lear, John Lear, Mary Lear and Ann Lear, have this day for good and valuable considerations is hereunto moving, made, ordained constituted and appointed Jacob Lear, of the aforesid County of Bourbon and State of Kentucky, our true and lawful attorney, for us and in our names to make sale of the aforesaid lot of ground with the improvements thereon and every advantage thereunto pertaining to such person or persons and for such price or sum of money * * * our said attorney * * * per * * * such sale in our names to make and execute * * * deed or deeds of conveyance with such clauses of warranty therein contained as shall be deemed proper for the absolute conveyance thereof and of every part thereof to such purchaser or purchasers, his or their kins or assigns, Hereby ratifying for valid whatsoever, said attorney shall lawfully do or cause to be, the premises by virtue of these presents as; we were personally present and done the same.
   In witness thereof we have hereunto set our hands and af-

fixed our seals, this 25th day of August one thousand eight hundred and two."

Signed * * * *

		In presence of:
Benjamin Williams	Abraham Lear	(Seal)
Benjamin Williams	David Lear	(Seal)
Benjamin Williams	Anney Leer	(Seal)
Benjamin Williams	Mary Leer	(Seal)
	Aaron Smedley	(Seal)
	John Leer	(Seal)
	Rebecca Smedley	(Seal)

Bourbon County Act:

Before the subscriber, a justice of the peace, for the county aforesaid, personally came Benjamin Williams a subscribing witness to the annexed letter of attorney and being duly sworn upon the holy Evangelists of Almighty God, did dispose and say, that Abraham Lear, David Lear, Ann Lear, Mary Lear did severally in his presence acknowledge the said letter of attorney to Jacob Lear to be their act and deed.

Given under my hand this 25th day of August, 1802.

THOMAS HUGHES (Seal)

Kentucky Act:

"I, Thomas Arnold, clerk of the County Court of Bourbon, do certify that Thomas Hughes, Gent, whose signature is annexed to the certificate of probate of the within letter of attorney, was at the time thereof an acting justice of the peace in and for county aforesaid, duly commissioned and sworn, and that to such certificates and official acts, full faith and credit is due and ought to be had and given as well in courts of justice thereof.

In testimony whereof I have hereunto set my * * and affixed the seal of my office, this 25th day of August, eighteen hundred and two."

THOMAS ARNOLD.

WILL ABSTRACTS

WRIGHT, WILLIAM, of Bourbon County, Ky.—Will written Oct. 7, 1802. Mentions wife, Martha. Sons, James Wright, William Wright, Robert Wright, John Wright, and Hugh Wright. Dau's., Hannah Melvin, oldest dau., Mary Stewart, Margaret Hendrix, Elizabeth Leer, Sally Hannah and Jean Champ. Exec's., David Leer and Joseph Hanna. Mentions Samuel and Thomas Wright. Probated July Court. (This is a copy of a "Certified" copy, does not give witnesses.)

KENNEY, JAMES, of Bourbon Co.—(Will copy certified by Thos. P. Smith, D. C. B. C. and donated by Mrs. B F. Buckley, Lexington). Written Mch. 12, 1814. Names wife, Peggy Sons, John, Victor, Joseph, Moses, Napoleon Dau's., Maria, Abbe, Helena, Cordee, and Peggy. Dau's., Sally Barnett, Elizabeth Trotter, Nancy Rhodes, and Polly Hildreth. Exec's., Wife, Peggy Kenney, James Hughes and John Barnett. Witnesses, Thos. Rogers, Josiah McDowell and Alexander Barnett. Will of James Kenney, deceased, proved June Court 1814.

McCONNELL, MARTHA—Wlil Book E, page 38—Martha McConnell, widow of Archibald McConnell, Sr., of Bourbon Co., Ky. Names children, James, Samuel, John, Archibald, Jr., Catherine, Sampson, Martha, and Joseph. Probated May Court 1814. Also Deed Book K, page 196. Archibald McConnell, Jr., and wife, Sarah (McCracken) of Clark Co., Ky., made deed the 30th of April, 1814 to

Sampson McConnell (brother), for land in Bourbon Co. granted to Wm. Hord, Mch. 1784.

SUTTON, NATHANIEL—Will Book F, page 348—Bourbon Co. Date June, 1820. Names children by first wife, James, Nancy, Betsy, Lucy Anna, Mary and Sally. Children by second wife, Sarah, Rowland. William, Clary, Frances, John, Amos, Talifaro.

BOYLE COUNTY, KY., DANVILLE

WILL ABSTRACTS

(Copied by Mrs. Joseph Beard, Sr.)

LETITIA BARBOUR—Will Book 1, page 23—Names sons, James and Ambrose. To daughters, Catherine and Martha, to son, Lewis. Written Aug. 31, 1844. Witnesses, Wm. Craig, Peachy Johnston, George P. Berger, Wm. B. Craig. Probated Oct. Court 1844.

MARY BURCH—Will Book 1, page 28—Of Mercer Co., Ky. To only surviving child, James K. Burch. Exec., James K. Burch. Written Nov. 3, 1835. Witnesses, Charles Henderson, D. N. Donegly. Probated Jan., 1845.

DREAD BOLLING—Will Book 1, page 50—Names wife, Mary E. Bolling. Children, Silas, John, Thomas, P. M., and George Washington Bolling. To two youngest daughters, Mary E. Bolling and Rachel Ann Bolling, when 21 years old. Son, Jeremiah. To following named children, Elizabeth Greenwood, Nancy R. Curry, John Kimberland, grand-father of children. Exec., John A. Burton. Written Dec. 12, 1845. Witnesses, O. Clemmons, Sr., E. Bottom, Elihu Booth, Jeremiah Briscoe. Probated Jan., 1846.

DRURY CLARKSTONE—Will Book 1, page 32—Names daughters, Martha, Nancy, Roberts and Happy. Written May, 1845. Witnesses, John Durham, Isaac Lavier, Addison Durham. Probated June 16, 1845.

THOMAS COWAN—Will Book 1, page 19—Names nephews, William W. Wallace of Pittsburgh, to my brother, to my niece, Mary, daughter of my late brother, John Cowan. To children of nephew, John Wallace of Pittsburgh. To children of Joseph Jackson, to my sister, Mary Ann Young. Exec's., Joshua Bell. (My nephew, Alexander Wallace and Rev. Thomas Sproule and Rev. Samuel Wells and my niece, his wife, get no portion of estate). Written Jan. 25, 1844. Witnesses, John Exum and Thomas Collins. Probated Apr., 1844.

BAKER F. EWING—Will Book 1, page 27—Names wife, Sarah M. Ewing. My children. Grand-daughter, Frances L. Lapsley. Exec's., Maj. Andrew Knox, Rev. James L. Lapsley. Written July 8, 1844. Witnesses, Nelson Mays, John Jennings and Thomas Ewing. Probated Dec. Court 1844.

HENRY FIELDS—Will Book 1, page 23—Names wife, Susan. Daughter, Sally C. Wright. Daughter, Mary M. Durham. Sons, William, Frederick, and youngest son, Smith. Exec's., Frederick Ripperdan, James Fields, Henry I. Cowan, James P. Mitchell. Written May 8, 1837. Witnesses, D. A. Russell and Charles Henderson. Probated Nov. Court 1844.

13

ELIAS FISHER—Will Book 1, page 30—Names wife, Sarah. Sons, Charles B. Fisher and James D. Fisher. To Nancy Christopher. To Hunter Southworth. My six first children, Nancy Byers (husband, Edmund Byers). Polly Williams, Thursey Fisher, wife of Stephen Fisher. Sarah Doors, Susan Doors, and Elias Fisher, Jr. To Amanda Wilhite and Cynthia Deer. Exec's., John Whelan and Charles B. Fisher. Written June 15, 1844. Witnesses S. D. Montgomery and Thomas T. Daviess, Garrett Coovert, Thomas Doke. Probated Apr. Court 1845.

EZEKIAL GAINES—Will Book 1, page 37—To daughters, Ellen McRoberts, Susan Gaines, Emily M. Gaines, Almira Gaines and my grand-daughters, Susan E. Balling and Tabitha Balling, children of deceased daughter, Eveline Balling. To wife, Susan Gaines, sons, Benjamin W. Gaines, Ezekiel Gaines. To daughters, Ellen McKaber, Susan Gaines, Elinor Gaines, Emily M. Gaines. Exec's., Haydon I. McRoberts and Jerry T. Boyle. Written Mch. 21, 1845. Witnesses, N. Rice, James Hutchings, Joseph Smith, Samuel Ayres. Probated July Court 1845.

JOHN GRANT—Will Book 1, page 25—To Amelia Ann Grant, daughter of brother, William Grant. To Lugena Griffin, daughter of brother Wm. Grant. To William May, Sr., brother of late wife. To John Grant Black, son of Robert Black. To niece, Susan Sutherland, wife of Robert Southerland. To Charles and James Southerland, children of niece, Susan. To John Grant Harlan, son of John Harlan. To John Harlan and wife, Clarissa, who is my niece. Exec's., Jehu Harlan, Wm. May, Sr., and James P. Mitchell. Written Apr. 25, 1843. Witnesses, Wm. R. McGrath, and A. G. Kyle. Probated Nov. Court 1844.

ROBERT GRAY—Will Book 1, page 45—To sister, Jane Gray. Exec's., Seneca W. Wade and James H. Rochester. Written Jan. 14, 1845. Witnesses, Wm. Wade, George B. Webb. Probated Aug. Court 1845.

DAVIS C. HARLAN—Will Book 1, page 44—Names wife, Marty C. Harlan. To son, James H. Harlan. To heirs of brother, James Harlan. Father-in-law, Henry Prewett of Scott Co., Ky., to hold in trust. Written May 12, 1845. Witnesses, H. Goodloe, John Pitman, W. R. McGrath. Codicil appoints Henry H. Prewett and brother, James Harlan Executors. Probated July Court 1845.

ELIJAH HARLAN—Will Book 1, page 14—Names wife, Sally and unmarried children, namely, Emaline, Isabella, James, John and Sophia. Daughter, Elizabeth Gray and child. Married daughters, Sally Ann, wife of John B. Hughes, Martha C., wife of Andrew Grafton. To J. S. Hopkins. Exec's., Andrew W. Kyle and Thomas Pitman. Written Nov. 17, 1843. Witnesses, Wm. Pauling, S. W. Caldwell. Probated Dec. Court 1843.

MARY HARLAN—Will Book 1, page 85—To my husband, Silas Harland. Betsy Ann Lillard, wife of Barret Lillard. To Patsy Pancake, wife of Argalles Pancake. To John Neff (raised by Mr. Harlan and myself). A. G. Kyle, trustee for my husband, Silas Harlan. Written Aug. 18, 1848. Witnesses, A. G. Kyle, R. N. Bolling, F. Frost. Probated Jan. Court 1849.

SARAH HAMNER—Will Book 1, page 48—To William M. Hamner, Edmund D. Hamner and Sarah Hamner and Martha Jane Hamner, the four youngest children of my son, William. To children of my daughter, Lucy Clarkson. Written Mch. 14, 1844. Witnesses, B. D. Williams and J. L. Bolling. Probated Mch. Court 1845.

ANN HARROD—Will Book 1, page 9—Names grand-daughters, Mary Ann Ray and Eliza Davis. To great grand-sons, John H. Fauntleroy, Jr. and Edwin Moore. To grand-daughter, Nancy Fauntleroy. To grand-son, Griffin T. Fauntleroy. To grand-son, James H. Fauntleroy. To great-grand-daughter, Elizabeth Ray. Other grand-children; namely, John H. Fauntleroy, David E. Fauntleroy, Maria W. Mastin, Margaret Becket, Robert Fauntleroy, and Samuel Fauntleroy. Exec's., W. H. Martin and grand-son, John H. Fauntleroy. Written Nov. 24, 1842. Witnesses, John D. Terhune and William M. Brown. Probated May Court 1843.

ELIABETH HENDERSON—Will Book 1, page 18—To Esther Duncan. Daughters, Nancy McGill, Polly Caldwell, Dicy Johnson. The children of deceased daughter, Phebe Caldwell, viz: Betsy Rice, Ann Pritchett. The children of deceased daughter, Margaret Robertson, viz: Priscilla Gordon and Sally Parks. Witnesses, Wm. Caldwell. and John Henderson. Probated Mch. Court 1844.

MICHAEL HOPE—Will Book 1, page 40—Names wife. Daughters, Martha and Cynthiana. Son, Michael, when of age. To daughter, Ellen Hoagland. To daughter, Isabella Batterton. Grand-son, James F. Hall. Son, Robert James Hope. Exec's., Son-in-aw, Wm. W. Batterton and brother-in-law, Alexander Sneed. Written Sept. 16, 1834. Witnesses, M. G. Youce, R. D. Crutchfield and John F. Warren. Probated Nov. Court 1845.

ABSOLOM LYLE IRVINE—Will Book 1, page 45—To brother, James H. Irvine. My daughter, Letitia Reed, under 21. Brother-in-law, Samuel K. Hughes. To Edward Vontress. Exec's., James S. Hopkins, Thomas B. Hughes, and James H. Irvine. Written Aug. 12, 1845. Witnesses, Joseph Weisiger, James Barbour and Charles Henderson. Codicil. Brother-in-law, Abram Irvine. Probated Sept. Court 1845.

JAMES ISOM—Will Book 1, page 6—Names wife, Nancy. Sons: James, John. Daughters, Tabitha Gardner, Ursly Hamilton, Lucy Grady, Susannah Agerton. Son, Michael Isom. Daughter, Polly Gardner's children, viz; James, Price Gardner, and Sally Thompson. Daughter, Matilda Gardner. Daughter, Sally Frost. Grand-daughter, Spicy Gray. Exec., Jacob Goodnight. Written Sept. 9, 1842. Witnesses, Benjamin Chatham, James H. McGinnis and John C. Russell. Probated Jan., 1843.

CHARLES KIRKLAND—Will Book 1, page 1—Names wife, Elizabeth. Children, viz: Son, Thomas, daughter, Lettice Elder, son, George L. Daughter-in-law, Fanny Kirkland. Daughter, Ann Philips. Exec's., Sons, Thomas and George L. Kirkland. Written Feb. 15, 1842. Witnesses, J. A. Lewis, R. P. Guthrie. Probated Mch. Court 1842.

ROBERT KNOX—Will Book 1, page 8—Names wife, Elizabeth. Two name-sakes, Robert K. Philips, son of my wife's sister, Catherine, and Robert K. Spears, son of John and Marthy Spears, now of Indiana. Exec., Wife, Elizabeth. Written Oct. 7, 1838. Witnesses, C. Raines and John Harlan. Codicil. To Mary Bilbo. Exec's., John Harlan and James P. Mitchell in conjunction with wife. Written Apr. 15 ,1843. Witnesses, Elijah Harlan, A. D. Myer. Probated May Court 1843.

GABRIEL LACKEY—Will Book 1, page 49—Names wife, Paulina. My children by last wife. Daughter, Martha Grimes, by first wife. My daughter, Paulina Lackey. Exec's., Samuel O. Middleton, and Henry Owsley. Written, Oct. 23, 1845. Witnesses, Wm. Pawlings, J. I. McCormick, Wm. D. Kerr. Probated Nov. 17, 1845.

JEREMIAH LAWS—Will Book 1, page 46—Names wife, Susanna. My children. To son-in-law, Jacob Busey. To son-in-law, James Long, ton son-in-law, Amos Hill, his wife Sarah Laws. Son-in-law, George McCastlin. To son-in-law, Gabriel Rice. To son, Williams Laws, for use of his wife and children. To daughter, Matilda Wilkerson. To daughter, Priscilla Wright. To daughter, Frances Russell. To son, Jeremiah Laws. To Frances Laws a daughter of son, John Laws. To Elmira Laws, daughter of son, James M. Laws. To James M. L. Whoberry. Exec's., Son, Jeremiah Laws and son-in-law, Jacob Busey. Written Aug. 4, 1842. Witnesses, J. P. Mitchell, and J. D. Mitchell. Probated Oct. Court 1845.

JESSE McGINNIS—Will Book 1, page 10—Names son, James H. Mc-Ginnis. To Jesse McGinnis, son of James. To son, Benjamine L. McGinnis, and Jesse S. McGinnis. Son, J. B. McGinnis. All my children. Deceased daughter, Patsy's children, youngest child, Patsy, daughter of Patsy. Daughter, Peggy. My daughter, Agnes. Daughter, Sally and her husband and chldren. Daughter, Nancy Morrison, deceased, late Nancy McGinnis. Exec's., Sons, James H., William R. and John R. McGinnis. Written Nov. 10, 1841. Witnesses, J. A. Burton, C. F. Burton and Wm. Rains. Probated May Court 1843.

ISAAC MONTGOMERY, of Mercer Co., Ky.—Will Book 1, page 52—Names wife, Nancy. My children, already some have received their portion. My Mothers Dower land. Exec's., Wife and son, Levy. Written Oct., 1835. Witnesses, Wm. Wade and Obediah Brumfield. Codicil, My daughter, Sally Piper (husband,Morris Piper), my son, Elias Montgomery, to be added to Executors. Codicil added to body of Will, Aug. 1, 1840. Witnesses, Wm. Wade, G. S. Cardwell, Jacob Crow. Probated Dec. Court 1840.

MARGARET MOORE—Will Book 1, page 4—To grand-children, John Moore, Margaret Moore, Mary Ann Moore, children of son, James A. Moore. Written Mch. 7, 1842. Witnesses, H. Goodloe, James Barnett. Probated Apr. Court 1842.

SAMUEL L. MOORE—Will Book 1, page 20—Names wife, Mary Moore. All my children. Grand-child, Sarah Ann L. Durham. To sons, William, Benjamin, Simeon, Samuel. Daughter, Elizabeth Weeden and children. Son, John. To Eliza Weeden. Exec's., J. S. Hopkins and son, Simeon. Written June 21, 1844. Witnesses, Benjamin Crow, Wm. Craig, L. B. Taylor and Wm. B. Taylor. Probated Sept. Court 1844.

GEORGE R. NIELD—Will Book 1, page 12—Names wife, Elizabeth. Son, Henry Nield. Daughter, Harriet Neal. To son, Daniel. Daughter, Elizabeth Ann, daughter, Emiline, son, George R. Nield, son, Pembroke S. Nield. Exec's., C. H. Mays, Angelus Pancke and Elizabeth Nield. Written Aug. 19, 1843. Teste, George W. French, Bennett Ball, C. H. May Probated Oct. Court 1843.

MAXON OWEN—Will Book 1, page 1—Names wife, Phebe and children. Exec., Wife, Phebe Owens. Written Feb. 22, 1840. Witnesses, J. P. Mitchell, Wm. H. Mitchell. Probated Apr. Court 1842.

MARTHA A. PREWETT—Will Book 1, page 3—Names sister, Elizabeth Prewett. To Mrs. Tilford and two sons, Hancy and George. To Pamelia Gregory To Mary E. Tilford, Susannah Tilford. Written Sept. 28, 1841. Witnesses, James Brumfield and James H. Davenport. Probated Apr. Court 1842.

CARTER TADLOCK—Will Book 1, page 16—Of County of Oldham. Names all my children. When youngest comes of age. Wife, Cinthia Tadlock. Exec's., D. Walker, Isaac Philips, of Boyle Co., Robert King and Samuel Ewing, of Mercer Co. Written Aug. 18, 1843. Witnesses, Peter Cinder, and Albert W. Ballard. Probated Feb. Court 1844.

WILLIAM TAYLOR—Will Book 1, page 3—Of Mercer Co., Ky. Names wife, Nancy. Children, Julet Herrington. Heirs to Clayton Taylor. Heirs to Henry Taylor. Heirs to William Taylor. Daughters, Ann Shin, Judith Cox, Isabel Cox, Haney Taylor, and Nancy Tinkhorn, Letty Ilsairy, Simon Taylor. Exec., Rice Cox. Written Jan. 31, 1842. Witnesses, Mark Purdon, Silas Taylor, J. J. Polk. Probated Mch. Court 1842.

JEREMIAH WADE—Will Book 1, page 29—Names wife, Mary. My children, when they come of age. Exec's., William and Seneca W. Wade. Written, Dec. 14, 1844. Witnesses, Nelson A. Thomson, J. S. Caldwell, John Parr. Probated Jan. Court 1845.

CLARK COUNTY, WINCHESTER
WILL ABSTRACTS

(Copied by Mrs. Joseph Beard, Sr.)

PAMELIA ALLEN—Will Book 1, page 102—Pamelia Allen, wife of Richard Allen. Pamelia heir of William McCracken, deceased.

ISAAC BAKER—Will Book 1, page 1—Names Elizabeth Walker, Robert McFarling, Mericum Baker, daughter of John Baker. Brothers, John and Joshua Baker Executors. Written Sept. 24, 1792. Witnesses, Samuel Plummer, Robert McDaniel and James Huls. Probated Mch. 26, 1793

JOHN BAKER—Will Book 1, page 302—Names son, Joshua Baker. Peter Fontain. Son, John. Daughters, Mariam Baker and Elizabeth Baker. Sons, Isaac Shelby Baker and Cuthbert Bullett Baker, Cythe Baker and Nancy Baker. Wife, Polly. Exec's., James Sympson and Thomas Scott. Written Mch. 11, 1803. Probated May 2, 1803 on oath of John Ward and Thomas Hind.

JOHN BLEDSOE—Will Book 1, page 195—Names daughter, Elizabeth Adams. Son, Thomas Bledsoe, son, Lewis Bledsoe, son, William Bledsoe, daughter, Sally Bledsoe, son, John Bledsoe. Wife. Exec's., Thomas Burris, Dillard Collins. Written Dec. 26, 1799. Witnesses, James Duncan and Wm. Calloway and John Williams. Probated July Court 1800.

JAMES BODKIN—Will Book 2, page 6—Names wife, Dinah Bodkin. Sons, George, John Thomas, William and James. Daughters, Margaret Benson, Sarah Barnor, Rachel Duglas and Betsy, Mary, Ginney Ann Wise. Exec's., Wife and son, George. Written Aug. 18, 1804. Witnesses, Wm. Morris, Mathew Patton,, John Patton. Codicil, Names Richard Wise. Probated Aug. 27, 1804.

MARTHA BOONE—Will Book 1, page 7—Names son, George Boone. Daughters, Charity Elledge, Jane Morgan, Mary Scholl. Son, Joseph Boone. Daughter, Sarah Hunter and her son, Joseph Hunter. Exec., John Morgan, Jr. Written May 10, 1793. Teste, John Morgan, Wm. Craycroft, John Stilwell. Probated July 23, 1793.

JOHN WASHINGTON BUCKNER, deceased—Estate—Book 1, page 177—Appraised Jan. 28, 1800 by Wm. Bronaugh, H. Taylor, Jacob Fishback, John Martin and Mary Ann Buckner.

ZACHARIAH BUNCH—Will Book 1, page 21—Names wife, Saby. Sons, Henry and Mark Bunch. Daughters, Milly and Mourning. Grand-son, James Cubbage. Youngest daughters Anna and Lucy. Exec's., Elijah Summers and wife, Saby. Witnesses, John Summers, Sr., Peter Dewitt, Jr., Peter Dewitt, Sr. Oct. 28, 1794.

DANIEL CLIFTON—Book 1, page 19—Verbal will of Daniel Clifton, killed by Indians, Apr. 2, 1794. Names wife, Margaret, to have all Estate. Teste, Samuel Downey and Thomas Minor. Probated May 27, 1794.

JAMES CHEATHAM—Will Book 1, page 79—Names wife. Eldest son, James. Only daughter, Polly, under 18 years old. Sons, Edmund (as soon as he comes of age) and John. Exec's., Thomas Dawson, and Thomas Scott. Written Oct. 12, 1796. Witnesses, Wm. Knox, Joshua Stamper, Wm. Hill. Probated Dec. 27, 1796. Page 95, Book 1. Ann Cheatham, widow of James Cheatham. Mch. 28, 1797.

VIVIAN DANIEL—Will Book 1, page 270—Names daughter, Margaret. Sons, John, Peter, daughter, Jane, wife of George Quisenberry. Daughter, Frances Deale's 3 children viz: Elizabeth Deale, Daniel Deale and Janet Deale. Daughter, Nan Oldham. Wife, Nancy. Exec's., Dillard Collins and David Bullock. Written June 25, 1802. Witnesses, Robert Steel, Isabella Steel, Samuel Steel. Probated Feb. 7, 1803.

MARTHA DOWNEY—Will Book 1, page 202—Written Jan. 20, 1801. Names two sons, Samuel and William Downey. Daughters, Marian and Rebecca, Janet and Margaret, Elizabeth and Rachel. Exec., Sons, Samuel and William. Witnesses, John Stevenson, Samuel Stevenson, and Reason Beall. Probated Jan. Court 1801.

ARCHIBALD EDMONDSON—Will Book 1, page 206—Names wife, Sinay, land left him by James Edmondson (Sept. 4, 1777). Sons, James and Thomas. Daughters, Patsy, Polly, Sucky, Margery and Debby Jordon. Exec's., Wife, Sinay and friend Aron Lacklen. Written Nov. 3, 1800. Witnesses, W. McMillan and Azariah Prather. Probated Mch. Court 1801.

JAMES ELKIN, Sr.—Will Book 8, page 534—Names wife, Martha. Son, James Elkin, Jr. To other children, to wit: Mary Richerson, Martha Richerson, Jane Barnes, Rhoda Crow, Nancy Crow. Son, Zachariah Elkin, Subrina Richerson and Elizabeth Crow, being my lawful heirs. Exec., James Wood, Sr. Written Apr. 20, 1836.

Witnesses, James H. Allen and Abell Watts. Probated July Court 1836.

JAMES ELKIN, Jr.—From Book 1855-1885, page 327—Names wife, Lucinda Elkin and all my children. Exec's., Sons, Z. F. Elkin and Silas A. Elkin and son-in-law, John W. Dawson. Written Apr. A. D., 1876. Witnesses, Joseph Adair and Thomas J. Bush. Probated Sept. 23, 1878.

JACOB EMBREE—Will Book 1, page 99—Names brothers and sisters. Step Mother. Exec's., Brother Wm. Embree and brother, Thomas Embree. Written Feb. 23, 1797. Witnesses, Michael Stoner and Joseph Embree. Probated July 25, 1797.

SARY EMMETTS—Will Book 1, page 40—Names son-in-law, John Gordon. Grand-daughter, Anna Stone. Exec's., John Gordon. Written Mch. 20, 1795. Witnesses, James Ramey, Wm. Kindred, Amelia Downes. Probated July 28, 1795.

WILLIAM EMERSON, deceased—Estate—Will Book 5, page 180-182—Wife, Polly Ann (Tuggle) Emerson. Approved May Court 1822.

HARVEY FIELDER and AMANDA EMERSON, daughter of William Emerson, married Nov. 23, 1830. Clark Co. marriage records, Winchester C. H.

DANIEL EWING—Will Book 2, page 35—Names wife, Elenor. Also following persons, Mary Halsy, daughter of my brother, William Ewing, deceased. Patrick Gelespe, son of Wm. Gelespe. Eleanor and Nancy Nunley, daughters of Buckner Nunley. Exec's., Wm. Gelespe and Wm. Robinson. Written Sept. 27, 1804. Witnesses, John Lyle, James Kenney. Probated Feb. 24, 1805.

RICHARD EVANS—Will Book 2, page 45—Names children, Mayberry Evans, Mary Waddell, Elizabeth Stinson, Susannah Waddell, James Evans, Ann Bell. Youngest daughter, Sarah Evans. Exec., Daughter, Sarah Evans. Written Feb. 27, 1797. Witnesses, Paul Huls, Robert Walker and John Huls. Probated May 27, 1805.

JOHN GORDON, of Goochland Co., Va., registered in Clark Co., Ky.—Will Book 1, page 349—Names wife, Judith. Children, Elizabeth, Mary, John, Lucy, Judith, William, Frances, Nancy and Benjamin. Exec's., Sons, John and William. Written July 18, 1803. Witnesses, David Utley, John Utley, Josiah Woodson. Probated Dec. 9, 1803, in Goochland Co., Va. J. Hopkins, J. P.

DAVID HAMPTON, Sr.—Will Book 4, page 534—Written Aug. 18, 1819. Names wife, Sarah. Daughter, Sally. Sons, Wade, George, Wilson, Jesse, James, William and Joseph Hampton. Daughter, Esther Daniel. Witnesses, Thomas Scott, John Daniel, James Adams, Marshall Jordan. Probated Oct. 25, 1819.

THOMAS HARRIS—Will Book 1, page 100—Written Mch. 9, 1793. Names wife, Mary. Sons, Joshua and Caleb. Four daughters. Exec's., Wife, Mary and eldest son, Joshua. Witnesses, Daniel Ramey, James McMeekan, Wm. Bush. Probated Aug. 22, 1797.

JAMES HARROW—Will Book 1, page 50—Names son, Daniel. Daughter, Sarah Harrow. Sons, Samuel, William, Charles, John and James. To Daniel Hacket, son of Nelson and Elizabeth Hacket. To Daniel Harrow, son of William. To Daniel Harrow, son of

James. To Daniel Harrow, son of John. Exec's., Guy and Samuel Harrow. Written Aug. 12, 1795. Witnesses, Wm. Sudduth, Sanos (?) Sudduth, Samuel Arnett. Probated Jan. 26, 1796.

CHARLES HAZELRIGG—Will Book 1, page 59—Names eldest brother, John Hazelrigg. To Nancy Clements, daughter of Sarah Clements. To Green Clements and Fielding Clements, sons of Sarah Clements. To Charles Oldfield, son of Sarah Hatton. Graham Nelson, son of Elizabeth Nelson. Given to them when they come of age. Exec's., Friends, Isaac Hulbert, and Graham Hazelrigg. Written Oct. 19, 1795. Witnesses, George Winn, Laurence Daly and Thomas Winn. Probated Apr. 26, 1796.

HENRY HUKEL—Will Book 1, page 125—Names 2 sons, James Foster Hukel and Henry Brevard Hukel. Harman Foster, of State of Maryland. Wife, Elizabeth. Exec., Wife, Elizabeth. Written Mch. 4, 1798. Witnesses, Thomas Owens, Richard Hukel, Edward Roberts. Probated, July 24, 1798. On page 119. Estate of Henry Hukel, deceased. Appraised Aug. 28, 1798.

WILLIAM LEDGERWOOD—Will Book 1, page 14—Of Fayette Co., Ky. Names wife, Rebecca. Son, Samuel. Daughters, Isabel, Margaret and Mary. Son, James. Exec's., Sons, James and Samuel. Written May 7, 1792. Witnesses, James McMillan, R. McMillan, Allen Neil. Probated Jan. 28, 1794.

ROBERT LEWIS—Will Book 1, page 142—To John Lewis Martin. To James Taylor Martin. To Robert B. Martin. To Sally Rowland, daughter of Thomas Rowland. To Polly Lewis, daughter of Jesse Lewis, of Albermarl Co., Va. The two eldest sons of my brother, John Lewis. Two eldest sons of my brother, Charles Lewis. Two eldest sons of brother, Henry Lewis. Exec's., Jacob Fishback, John Martin, John L. Martin, and James T. Martin. Written Feb. 20, 1799. Witnesses, John Martin, John Fishback, Thomas Martin and Mathew Anderson. Codicil, Names Elizabeth Martin, wife of John Martin. To Frank and Peter Hernsley. Probated July 23, 1799.

THOMAS MARTIN—Will Book 2, page 40—Names brother, George Martin. Sister, Eliza Martin. Mother, Elizabeth Martin Written Dec. 24, 1804. Witnesses, Jacob Fishback. Samuel Lyon, John Summer. Probated May 27, 1805.

MARY McCREARY—Book 1, page 65—By order of Court, dower of Mary McCreary relict of Robert McCreary, deceased, allotted Mch. 19, 1790. Signed H. Taylor, J. Martin, Jacob Fishback, John Morgan.

ANDREW McCLURE—Will Book 1, page 136—Names son, John McClure. Andrew and Elizabeth McClure. Son, Samuel. Daughters, Margaret and Elizabeth McClure. Exec's., James McMillan, Wm. Ralston and John McClure. Written June 28, 1799. Witnesses, Archibald Edmundson, George Ritchie, and James McMillan. Probated Jan. 22, 1799.

FRANCIS McCLURE—Will Book 1, page 347—Names children, Sophia, John, Caleb, Richard, Lydia, Fanny, Kitty and Betsy, when she becomes of age. Exec., ————. Written Nov. 8, 1803. Witnesses, Margaret Calloway, Eliza Calloway, Theodore Combs. Probated Feb. Court 1804.

JAMES McMILLAN, Sr., of Fayette Co., Ky.—Book 1, page 166—

Names eldest son, Robert. Son, James. Daughter, Elizabeth. James, the eldest son of Robert. To John, son of my son, James. To son, William. To daughter, Mary. Exec., eldest surviving son. Written Jan. 23, 1793. Witnesses, Jacob Armstrong and Elias Browning. Probated Oct., 1799.

LEMUEL McMURRY, deceased—Book 1, page 62—Appraisement of estate, by Josiah Hart and William Craig. Date Mch. 22, 1796.

JOHN McPHEETERS—Will Book 1, page 75—Names wife, Elizabeth. Son, Charles. Daughters, Mary, Sarah and Jenny. Exec's., Wife, Elizabeth, Charles McPheeters, James Crawford, and William McPheeters. Written Oct. 29, 1796. Witnesses, James Wardlow, James Wardlow, Jr. and Martha Wardlow. Probated Dec. 27, 1796.

PETER NOE—Will Book 1 ,page 266—Names wife, Mary. Eldest son, James. Father and Mother. Pryor Noe. James Noe to be guardian of Pryor Noe. To daughters, Sarah Tracy, Sibba Tracy, Elizabeth Kinkead and Bytha Noe and Quelse Noe. Exec's., Wife, Mary and son, James. Written Jan. 16, 1802. Witnesses, Samuel McKee, Paul Huls, Joseph Clark. Probated Nov. 22, 1802.

PATRICK O'HARROW—Will Book 1, page 43—Names elder sister, Sarah O'Harrow. Nephew, Patrick O'Harrow, son of John O'Harrow. Exec's., Simon Adams, and John O'Harrow. Written July 1, 1795. Witnesses, John Williams, Mary Ann O'Harrow, Malcolm Wood. Probated July 28, 1795.

WILLIAM OSBORNE—Will Book 7, page 687—Names wife, Kesiah. Children, Lucinda Elkin, Tempy Walls, Caty, Benjamin, Ceny, Elizabeth, Matilda, John, Solomon, Mary, Sally and Milly. Son, Mathias. Children by first wife well fixed. Others mostly infants and of tender years. Exec's., James Elkin and Solomon Dumford. Written Jan. 30, 1830. Witnesses, John Rice, Jr. and David White. No date for probate.

MATHEW PATTON—Will Book 1, page 315—Names wife. Sons, Mathew, Jr., Roger and William. Daughter, Sarah and 4 small children. Exec's., Roger and William Patton. Written May 2, 1803. Witness, James Crocket. Probated June 6, 1803.

WILLIAM PETTY—Will Book 2, page 41—Names wife, Lettiss Petty. Youngest son, Thomas. Son, Francis. Daughters, Rhoda Cast, Elizabeth Dodson, Rachel Russell, Hannah Ward, Zachariah Petty, Randall Petty, John Petty, James Petty, Sara Stevens, Leas Petty. Exec's., Wife, Lettiss and son, Thomas. Written May 3, 1804. Witnesses, Charles Tracy, Sarah Tracy. Probated May 27, 1805.

NANCY PLUMMER—Book 1, page 85—Allotment of dower to Nancy Plummer, late Nancy McCracken, widow of William McCracken, deceased. Jan. 24, 1797.

JANE RICHIE—Will Book 1, page 140—Names sons, Alexander and George. Daughter, Violette. Exec's., Two sons and Mr. James Cardwell. Witnesses, Wm. McMillan and Frederick Couchman. Probated May Court 1799.

DANIEL SWANEY—Will Book 1, page 158—Names wife, Sarah Swaney. Son, William. Daughter, Elizabeth Green. Son, John Swaney. Daughter, Mary Swaney. Son, Robert Swaney. Daughter, Catherine Swaney. Son, James Swaney. Exec's., Wife, Sarah and son, James. Written May 21, 1799. Witnesses, David Scott, James McLeland, Paul Haff, Richard Wharton, George Sharp and H. Moreland. Probated Nov. Court 1799.

BAPTIST SCOTT—Will Book 1, page 273—Date Dec. 5, 1801. Names eldest son, Robert. 2nd. son, George. Eldest daughter, Sally Scott. Sons, Levi, Elisha, Elijah, daughter, Kesiah. Wife, Nancy. Youngest son, Baptist Scott. To John Fouquor. Exec's., Wife, Nancy and Dillard Collins and Edward Hocady. Probated May 2, 1803. Witnesses, Edward Summers, Philip Ballow, Nancy Stripling.

JOSEPH SMITH—Will Book 1, page 63—Names wife, Nancy. Children. Written Nov. 28, 1795. Witnesses, Daniel Holmes, Enoch Smith, Mary E. Smith, Aaron Green. Probated June 28, 1796. No Exec.

JONATHAN TAYLOR—Will Book 1, page 319—Names children. Nephew, George G. Taylor. Married children have received their part. My wife. Unmarried children. Son, George Taylor, Brother, Frances Taylor. Exec's., Wife, sons, Wm. and George. Written Feb. 9, 1802. Witnesses, Thomas Martin, Phebe Fishback, Hannah Taylor. Probated Sept. 5, 1803.

DAVID TINSLEY, deceased—Book 1, page 117—Estate. May 22, 1798.

JAMES TOWNSEN—Will Book 1, page 27—Names wife. My child, Rhoda Townsin. Son, Garrett Townsin. Exec's., Wife and Markham Ware. Written Dec. 6, 1796. Witnesses, Peter Goosey, Caleb Ware, Benjamin Duniway, Samuel Varson. Probated Dec. 23, 1794.

WILLIAM TUGGLE—Will Book 8, page 211—Names wife, Nancy. Chidlren, Betsy Lane, deceased wife of James Lane. Polly Emerson, wife of William Emerson, deceased. Son, Charles Tuggle. Daughter, Nancy Emerson, wife of James. Sons, John and William. Daughter, Milly Rout, wife of Richard Rout. Daughter, Fanny Railsback, wife of Edward Railsback. Sons, James and Thomas A. Tuggle. Exec's., David Hampton, and Achilles Taggle. Witnesses, A. H. Hampton, and George W. Hampton. Written Jan. 11, 1834. Probated July Court 1834.

GEORGE WADDE (OR WADDLE)—Will Book 1, page 183—Names wife, Mary. Sons, John and Daniel. Young children, viz: Betsy, Nancy, Becky, Peggy. Married daughters, Susanna, Mary, Sarah. Exec's., Wife, Mary, sons, John and Daniel. Written Feb. 7, 1800. Witnesses, John Baker, Peter School. Probated May Court 1800.

JONATHAN WHITE—Will Book 1, page 339—Names sons, John, Frances. Daughters, Elizabeth White, Polly White, Susanna White. Sons, William, Richard, Joel. Daughter, Nanny White. Son, Daniel White. Wife, Elizabeth White. Exec., Wife, Elizabeth. Written Nov. 14, 1802. Witnesses, Andrew Hardy and Rawley Corbin. Probated Dec. 5, 1803.

WILLIAM WHITE—Will Book from 1855-1802, page 328—Names wife, Elizabeth. Children, Sarah Lilly, Milly Lowry, Allen White, Catherine Spry, Dianthe Stone, Winfield White, Henry White,

Solomon White, John White, Martha Curtis and Francis White, the three children by my first wife. Written Mch. 31, 1874. Witnesses, G. W. Lowry and Silas A. Elkin. Probated Oct. 28, 1878.

FREDERICK W. WILLS—Book 1, page 47—Names Francis Wills. Daughter, Sarah when 21 years old. My children, sons, William, John and Richard. Son, Derrit Wills. Exec's., Son, John and son-in-law, Dick Hood and son, Richard. Written Dec. 20, 1795. Witnesses, James Harris, A. W. Sudduth. Probated Jan. 26, 1796.

RICHARD WRIGHT—Will Book 2, page 1—Names wife, Frances. Son, John. Daughters, Nancy Johnson, Frances Hazelrigg, son, William, daughters, Elizabeth Penill, Isabel Miller. Exec's., Wife, Frances and son, John Wright, and Joshuay Hazelrigg. Written May 16, 1804. Witnesses, D. Hampton, Samuel Reed, Joseph Reed. Probated Aug. 27, 1804.

FAYETTE COUNTY, KENTUCKY

(Donated by Mrs. Jos. Beard, Lexington, Ky.)

WILL BOOK C

CATHERINE CADE—Will—Page 520—Signed Nov. 2, 1807. Mentions, Massey Coulter, Jeremiah Hay, Margaret Thomas, wife of David Thomas, Mary Hay, Catherine Hay. Children of John Hay, Mary, Catherine, Charles, Nathaniel, Elizabeth, Mariah Ellen. Witnesses, James Whaley, Sr., Isaac Johnston, Horatio Johnston and John Hay. Exec., John Hay. Probated Dec. Court 1815.

CARSTAPHRON, ROBERT—Will—Page 135—Names, son, James. Goodman Marshall, husband of dau., Sally Marshall. Children, Joel, Robert, Ana, and Betsy Richmond. Grandson, Chappell Carstaphron. Exec's., Ezra Richmond, and Ana Carstaphron. Witnesses, James Innes and Will Hicks. Will signed Feb. 12, 1814. Proved Apr. Court 1814.

CAVE, SUSANNAH—Will—Page 261—Mentions, friend and brother, William Grant Sr. Exec., Wm. Grant, Sr. Witnesses, John C. Richardson and Beckley Lemon. Will signed Feb. 25, 1805. Proved Aug. Court 1814.

CAVIN, ED.—Will—Page 102—Signed Mch. 18, 1814. Names daughters, Sally, Jane, and Polly. Son, Absalom. Three younger sons, Wm. Ignacious and John. Exec's., Benjamin Cromwell and Absalom Cavins. Witnesses, James McDowell, Joseph Simpson and Thomas Gosham. Proved Apr. Court 1814.

DUDLEY, WILLIAM—Will—Page 17—Names wife, Lucy and children under age. Son, Robert Garland. Exec's., Wife, Lucy and son, Robert Garland, Wm. Boon, and Asey Thompson. Witnesses, Robert Prewett, John Darnaby and James Darnaby. Will signed Mch. 24, 1813. Proved Oct. Court 1813.

DUNLAP, WILLIAM—Will—Page 553—Written Mch. 1, 1816. Names wife, Rebecca, son, John R. Dunlap. Dau's., Rebecca Downing, Elizabeth Dunlap, Patsey Dunlap. Son, William Dunlap. Son-in-law, Francis Downing. Son, Alexander, son, James, son, George. Exec's., Wm. Dunlap, John R. Dunlap and Francis Downing. Witnesses, Waller Bullock, Patsey Dunlap, Richard Downing, Jr., George Hunt and Elizabeth Dunlap. Proved Apr. Court 1816.

DOOLIN, THADDEUS—Will—Page 365—Written Dec. 5, 1814. Names, wife, Elizabeth. Daughters, Frances Green, Winefred James. Son, Edward Doolin. Dau's., Anne Frances, Lydia Whaley and Susannah Winn, Jane Presley, that was Jane Jenkins, and Lindy McDaniel. Exec's., wife, Elizabeth, sons-in-law, John Winn and Wm. James. Witnesses, Linchfield Burbridge, John McCall, Thomas Burbridge. Probated Dec. Court 1814.

ELLIOTT, GEORGE—Will—Page 297—Written Oct. 17, 1814. Names wife, Nancy and John Prather to be sole heirs. Exec's., wife, Nancy and John Prather. Witnesses, Wm. Allen and Betsy Allen. Proved Oct. Court 1814.

FRAZIER, GEORGE—Will—Page 373—Written Sept. 3, 1814. Names wife, Sarah. Sons, George Patrick Frazier and Charles C. Frazier. Dau's., Polly Campbell, Elizabeth Farris and Clementine. Exec's., Wife, Sarah, son, Charles C. Frazier and John Frances. Witnesses, Jonathan Lamme, Daniel Barton and Isaac McIsaac. Probated Dec. Court 1814.

GOODWIN, JAMES COLEMAN—Will—Page 153—Signed July 10, 1812. Names, wife, Nancy C. Goodwin. Eldest dau., Sally C. Flournoy, husband, Francis Flournoy. Eldest son, Joseph Graves Goodwin. Youngest son, Loyd K. Goodwin. Youngest dau., Polly. Exec's., Wife, Nancy, brother-in-law, John C. Graves, Loyd K. Goodwin and Polly C. Goodwin. Witnesses, Julius C. Goodwin and Polly C. Coleman. Probated May Court 1814.

GRANT, WILLIAM, SR.—Will—Page 349—Signed Aug. 18, 1803. Names wife, Elizabeth. Dau., Rebecca Lemmon, wife of James Lemmon. Grandson, William Grant, son of John. Sons, John Wm. and Squire. Daus., Mary Mitchell, Sarah Sanders, Elizabeth Mosby. Grand children, sons and daughters of Israel Grant, deceased. Grand children, Elizabeth and Betsy Grant, children of son, Samuel, deceased. Exec's., Wife, Elizabeth, son, William and John C. Richardson. Witnesses, Francis Browning and Wm. Caldwell. Probated July Court 1804. Codicil, 1804. Witnesses to Codicil, James Kay, Wm. Grant, E. Kay and Becky Lemmon.

GRANT, WILLIAM, JR.—Will—Page 131—Signed Apr. 1814. Names, Son-in-law, John Moore. Dau., Keturah Grant. Dau., Eliza Grant. Sons, Squire, James M. and William Grant. Youngest, son, Samuel Grant. Mother. Elizabeth and Susannah Cave. Exec., not named. Witnesses, John C. Richardson and Charles Smith. Probated May Court 1814.

GRAVES, ROBERT—Will—Page 419—Signed Sept. 14, 1814. Mentions, brothers, David Thomas and John. Sisters, Mary and Sarah. Exec's., Cousin, James A. Richardson, brothers, David, Thomas and John. Witnesses, Mary M. Edmiston, Martha L. Richardson. Probated Apr. Court 1815.

HALL, JOHN—Will—Page 335—Signed Sept. 15, 1814. Names, 2nd. wife, Jane Hall. Son, Robert Miller Hall. Children of 1st. wife, George Hall, John Hall, Moses Hall, Samuel Hall, and Peggy Hall Nicholas. Exec., not named. Witnesses, Thomas Watkins, Alexander Hall and Mashack Vaughn. Probated Nov. Court 1814.

HUMPHREYS, JONATHAN—Will—Page 14—Signed Sept. 7, 1813. Names, daus., Catherine and Martha. Grandson, James Banford.

Exec's., Henry McDonald and Thomas Ferguson. Witnesses, James Whaley, Robert Marshall and George C. Muir. Probated Oct. Court 1813.

HUTCHISON, MARGARET—Will—Page 412—Signed Sept. 18, 1814. Names, Joseph P. Cunningham, son of Robert Cunningham. Polly Alexander, Ann Robinson. Exec., not given. Will noncupative. Probated Feb. Court 1815, by oaths of Edward Welsh and Robert M. Cunningham.

JOHNSTON, ELIZABETH—Will—Page 152—Signed Apr. 16, 1814. Names, children of sister, Mary Garrett, wife of Henry Garrett. Nephew, Thomas Garrett, Nephews, Ashton and Peter Garrett. Niece, Clarissa Garrett. Nieces, Nancy Garrett and Susan Davenport. Nephew, Francis Garrett. Exec., Thomas I. Garrett. Witnesses, Charles R. Thompson, C. B. Grimes, Elizabeth Grimes, and Jane Grimes. Probated, May Court 1814.

McCLAIN, JAMES—Will—Page 133—Signed Nov. 26, 1806. Names, wife, Sally. Son, William, daughters, Polly Vegus and Betsey. Son, John. Exec's., Wife, Sally and son, Wm. Witnesses, Christopher Irwine, John Pace and Rosanna Hardin. Probated May Court 1814.

McCOY, HUGH—Will—Page 123—Signed Mch. 6, 1814. Names, wife, Elizabeth. Son, Samuel Love McCoy. Exec., Mathew Flournoy. Witnesses, John Graves and John Dickey. Probated May Court 1814.

McCRARY, MARTHA—Will—Page 507—Signed Apr. 23, 1814. Names, Hiram, Wm. Thomas and Margaret Phemster, children of brother John Phemster. Jane Bradshaw, Margaret Chambers, Martha Newton, and Rachel Morgan, children of' brother, William Phemster. Andrew Littleton, son of Robert Littleton. Elizabeth Bratton. Samuel and John Carlisle, sons of sister, Rachel Carlisle. Polly Kenny and Robert McCreary, son of Wm. McCreary of Clark Co. Exec's., Mathew Kenny and William Prewitt. Witnesses, Wharton Schooler, Wm. M. Kenny and Robert P. Kenny. Probated Oct. Court 1815.

McDANIEL, ENOCH—Will—Page 467—Signed May 29, 1815. Names, Mother, Mary McDaniel. No. exec. Witnesses, George Clark, Wm. Atchison and Boon McDaniel.

MARSHALL, ROBERT—Will—Page 299—Signed July 30, 1814. Names, wife, Mary Ann Marshall. Children, Robert, Cynthia, America, Dorinda, Calista, Daughters, Elizabeth Hill, Susannah Berton, Nancy Oldham, Polly Simpson, Malinda Marshall, Peggy Marshall, son, Robert Marshall. Exec's., Wife, Mary Ann, William Collins and Wm. Davenport. Witnesses, Thomas Ferguson, Christy Epperson and Henry Walker. Probated Oct. Court 1814.

McKEE, JOHN—Will—Page 298—Signed Sept. 16, 1814. Names, sister, Elizabeth Hunter. Exec., Brother-in-law, George Hunter. Witnesses, Wm. Boon and Robert P. Kenny. Probated Oct. Court 1814.

McKEE, SAMUEL—Will—Page 24—Signed Sept. 2, 1813. Names, Daughter, Polly. Sons, John and James. Grand daughters, Martha Story and Clara McKee, dau's. of son, Wm. McKee, deceased. Exec's., Elijah Poage, son Archabald McKee. Witnesses, Nancy

Poage, Elizabeth Poage and Elijah Poage. Probated Nov. Court 1813.

MOORE, JOHN—Will—Page 371—Signed Jan. 29, 1809. Names, daughter, Mary. Sons, James, Joseph, John. Daughter, Jenny. Exec's., Sons, James and Joseph Moore. Witnesses, Robert Stewart and Caly Moore. Probated Dec. Court 1814.

MONTGOMERY, ALEXANDER—Will—Page 125—Signed Feb. 3, 1814. Names, wife, Elizabeth. Sons, Robinson, Elijah, Williams, and John. Daughters, Elizabeth R. Coleman, and Malinda Montgomery. Exec's., Wife, Elizabeth, son, William, son-in-law, George Coleman and Wm. C. Prewett. Witnesses, Walter Preston, Abraham Estes and James C. Robinson. Probated May Court 1814.

PAYNE, JENNY O.—Will—Page 428—Signed Apr. 11, 1815. Names, children, daughter, Edward Ann Payne, son, Orlanda Payne and George R. Payne. Nephew, Hugh Payne. Father, Edward Payne. Exec's., Brothers, Henry Payne, Wm. Payne, Edward Payne, and Jilson Payne. Witnesses, Gabriel Tandy and John Marsh. Proved, May Court 1815.

PIATT, SALEM—Will—Page 51—(No date). Names, Kitty Peel, John Bodley, Eldest dau. of John Bodley. James Shely. No. exec. Witnesses, Samuel Q. Richardson, W. Montgomery and David Stee. Proved Jan. Court 1814.

POAGE, JOHN—Will—Page 522—Signed Dec. 12, 1815. Names, wife, Sarah Poage. Youngest son, John Campbell Poage. Youngest dau., Julia. Exec's., Wife, Sarah Poage and Charles Mc-Pheeters. Witnesses, Isaac Johnston, Horatio Johnston, James Johnston and Amos Johnston. Proved, Jan. Court 1816.

REDMON, WILLIAM—Will—Page 512—Signed Mch 3, 1814. Names, Sons, Levi and Chukerberry (or Cheekerberry). Daughter, Letty Page. Grand children, Wm. and Jane Redmon, son and dau. of Benjamin Redmon, deceased. No. exec. Witnesses, Tandy K. Perry and Daniel Moore Proved Nov. Court 1815.

RUCKER, JOHN—Will—Page 137—Signed June 18, 1812. Names, daughters, Rachel Rucker, deceased. Milly Rucker. Sons, Benjamin and Lewis. Wife, Patty. Children, Ahmed, Barnett, Wm., James, Joshua, Isaac Rucker. No exec. Witnesses, Robert Chambers, Thomas B. Young and Joseph Chambers. Proved May Court 1814.

SCOTT, JAMES—Will—Page 50—Signed Dec. 30, 1811. Names wife, Jenet. Children, Robert, James, Thomas, William and John. Grand dau., Jenny Milligan. Son, Andrew Scott. Exec's., Sons, James and Thomas Scott. Witnesses, Gilson Berryman and Wm. Rice. Proved Jan. Court 1814.

SIMPSON, ROBERT—Will—Page 38—Signed Nov. 26 ,1813. Names, wife, Elizabeth. Children, John G. Simpson, James Simpson and Martha Simpson. Exec's., Andrew M. Campbell, and Wm. Simpson. Witnesses, John Q. Dabney and Samuel Laird. Proved Dec. Court 1813.

SMITH, DAVID—Will—Page 339—Signed Feb. 11, 1811. Names, son of brother, Joseph Smith. Brother, John Smith. Brother, James Smith. Exec's., Asa Farrow and Ebenezer Sharp. Witnesses, James Blythe and Enoch M. Smith. Proved Apr. Court 1814.

TINSLEY, WILLIAM—Will—Page 430—Signed Jan. 30, 1815. Names wife, Mary. Daughter, Nancy. Other children. Exec's., Samuel Boone, Belair P. Evans, and wife, Mary Tinsley. Proved May Court 1815.

TROTTER, GEORGE—Will—Page 510—Written Apr. 1, 1807. Names wife, Eliza Trotter. Son, John Pope Trotter. Mother. Brothers, Samuel and Gabriel, also James Gabriel Trotter. Father, James Trotter. John Pope, Esq. to be guardian of children. Exec's., Wife, Eliza. Father, Col. James Trotter, and John Pope, Esq. Test. Robert Scott. Probated Nov. 1815.

WALLACE, JOHN—Will—Page 92—Written June 20, 1813. Names, wife, Jane. Son, John. Four younger children to be apprenticed, James T. Wallace, Abraham Hill Wallace, Andrew S. Wallace, Joseph. Dau's., Jane, Margaret, Martha, Mary Hill, Peggy Wallace. Exec., John Wallace. Witnesses, Wm. Alexander and Charles Campbell. Probated Apr. 1814.

WILL BOOK D.

(Donated by Mrs. Joseph Beard, Lexington, Ky.)

ALEXANDER, WILLIAM—Will—Page 404—Written Apr. 8, 1818. Names, wife, Agnes. Sons, Robert, and Henry. Children, James, Polly, William, Rachel, John and James Brewster. Executors, wife, Agnes, sons; James, Wm. and John Alexander. Witnesses, Robert W. Ricketts and Thomas Hunter. Probated, August Court 1818.

ARMITAGE, SAMUEL—Will—Page 281—Mentions Jacob Peyton. Written Oct. 8, 1817. Witnesses, Wm. R. Parker, Wm. Cox and Daniel McIntosh. Proved, Dec. Court 1817.

BALL, DRUCILLA—Will—Page 205—Written April 7, 1817. Names daughter, Nanny W. Fauntleroy and her husband, Wm. M. Fauntleroy. Son, John Ball. Grand-dau., Betty Fauntleroy and Drucilla Fauntleroy. Nephew, Wm. Jones. Witnesses, John C. Alberti, Lucy C. Webb and Francis Jones. Proved, May Court 1817. Executors, Brother, Isaac Webb and son, John W. Ball.

BENTLEY, JAMES—Will—Page 390—Written, May 2, 1818. Names, wife, Frances. Daughter, Rebecca Keithly. Sons, Washington, Reuben and Bartley. Mentions "7 children." Executors, Bailey and Reuben Bentley. Witnesses, David Morton, Wm. Curran, Wm. Cotton and Eli Cleveland. Proved July Court 1818.

BERRYMAN, SARAH—Will—Page 280—Written June 21, 1817. Names daughter, Ann W. Berryman. Son-in-law, Gilson Berryman. Grand children; Henrietta N. Berryman, Harriet W. Berryman, Thomas Berryman and Sarah Ann Berryman. Executors, George Webb and Wm. N. Lane. Proved Nov. Court 1817. Witnesses, Thomas B. Pinckard and Wm. Thomas.

BOBB, JACOB—Will—Page 253—Mentions, Sister-in-law, Polly Bobb, wife of brother, John Bobb. Nephew, Wm. Bobb. Witnesses, Abraham Howe, John Runnell and James Vincent. Signed Aug. 23, 1817. Proved Oct. Court 1817.

BOSWELL, GEORGE—Will—Page 178—Signed June 20, 1805. Names, son, George F. Boswell. Grandson, Wm. E., Son of Wm. E. Boswell. Son, Wm. E. Boswell. Grandson, George, son of Wm. E. Boswell, and grand dau., Nancy, dau. of Wm. E. Boswell Son, John Boswell, also "son of John." Two grand daughters. Daughter "Swanny" Warren. Son, Joseph Boswell and son, Bushrod and son, Thomas E. Boswell. Wife, Judith Boswell. Executors, Sons, Wm. and Joseph Boswell. Witnesses, Robert Prewitt and Wm. C. Prewitt. Proved Apr. Court 1817.

BOYD, JOHN—Will—Page 527—Signed Nov. 3, 1810. Names, wife, Martha. Dau's., Martha McIsaac, Mary and Agnes Boyd, Heirs of son, Robert, heirs of son, John. Son, Samuel Boyd, son, Hugh Boyd, son, Rowling. Daughter, Jenet Brown. Executors, Isaac McIsaac and Joseph Frazier. Witnesses, David Downton and G. Frazier. Proved Feb. Court 1816.

BROCKMAN, AARON—Will—Page 464—Written Dec. 15, 1818. Names, wife, Lydia Brockman. Sons, John and James. 4 daughters, Cynthia Cox, Elizabeth Brockman, Polly and Henico Brockman. Executors, Roger Quarles and James Wood. Witnesses, Wm. Quillan and James Wood, Jr. Probated Feb. 1819.

BRUMAGER, PATRICK—Will—Page 481—Written Feb. 5, 1819. Mentions wife. Executors, Alexander Edger and James Gibson. Witnesses, William Gibson and Thomas Harris. Probated Mch. Court 1819

CAMPBELL, ELIABETH—Will—Page 86—Written May 24, 1816. Widow of Robert Campbell, willed to emancipate negro Suckey but died before it was carried out. The heirs of Robert and Elizabeth agreed to carry out her wishes. Signed Arthur and James Campbell. Witnesses, Samuel Ayres and Elizabeth Nixon. Proved July Court 1816.

CARSON, JAMES—Will—Page 335—Written Jan. 12, 1818. Names, wife, Isabella. Son (oldest), James. Children, Patsy Stone, Nancy Carson, Peggy Carson, Elizabeth Carson, James Carson, Polly Keller, Willis Carson, Joseph Carson, Sallie Carson, Matilda Carson. Executors, George Berry and Lewis Bryant. Witnesses, James Daley and Thomas Nutall. Probated April Court, 1818.

CHOWNING, CHARLES—Will—Page 204—Written Mch. 21, 1817. Names wife, Milly Chowning. Children, Charles, Robert, Milly Tap, Betsey Kemper; grand children, Milly, Lucinda, Mahaly and Thursey Stephens, children of daughter, Lucy Stephens, Ann Vaughn and Sally Fass (or Tap). Two daughters in Virginia. Executors, Abraham Ferguson and John Barton. Witnesses, Leonard Young, Wm. Bowlin and H. Hardesty. Probated May Court, 1817.

CORDERY, JOHN—Will—Page 463—Written Dec. 30, 1818. Names wife, Polly. Nephew, John Cordery. Children, Hallim, Sally and Mary Ann. Executrix, wife, Polly. Witnesses, Thos. Outten, Thos. H. Stout, Ann F. Outten. Probated Feb. 1819.

COTTON, JOHN—Will—Page 326—Written Feb. 20, 1818. Names sister, Frances Spurr. Nephew, William Cotton. Executors, Nephew, Wm. Cotton, Jr. and nephew, Wm. C. Spurr. Witnesses, Lewis Hickman, Samuel Duncan and Samuel Blythe. Probated April Court 1818.

CRAIG, JOSEPH—Will—Page 478—Written Sept. 7, 1818. Mentions, son, Joseph Craig. Wife, Sarah. Daughter, Salley Allen, deceased, her part to her 7 children. Had 9 living children and 1 dead. Executors, Wife, Sally, and sons, Reuben, James, Samuel, Joseph Craig. Witnesses, Anny Pilcher, Lewis Pilcher and Wills Jenkins. Probated March Court 1819.

DALE, NANCY—Will—Page 98—Mentions Children of Jamse A. Richardson. Names daughters, Nancy Allen and Martha L. Richardson. Witnesses, Wm. Robinson, Jr. and John Nichols. Proved Aug. term 1816. Settlement Dec. 24, 1818.

DOWNTON, RICHARD, SR.—Will—Page 96—Written Nov. 13, 1812. Names Sons, Wm. Thrift Downton, Richard Downton and Thomas Downton. Grand-dau., Nancy Adams, when 18 yrs. old. Granddaus., Maria Gilliam and Nancy Gilliam. Daughter, Polly Dunlap, wife of George. Daughter, Sally, wife of Wm. Grubbs. Executors, sons, Richard, Jr. and Thomas Downton. Witnesses, Chas. R. Thompson, Ann Thompson, James Trotter, Sr. and John Tilford. Probated Aug. Court 1816.

DUNN, JOHN—Will—Page 335—Written June 24, 1817. Names wife, Urnney. Son, James Dunn. Daughter, Patsey Page. Executors, Wife, Urnney and son, James, and Charles Patrick. Witnesses, George M. Patrick, Charles Patrick and Thomas Pitts. Probated Apr. Court 1818.

EDWARDS, JOHN—Will—Page 303—Written May 12, 1817. Names, wife, Patsey. Chilrden, William, John, Sally, Julyann, and Nancy. Witnesses, Wm. B. Price and Walker Butler. Probated Feb. Court 1818.

FRIER, ROBERT—Will—Page 305—Names, wife, Jane Frier. Sons, Robert and David. Dau's., Nancy Arnold and Elizabeth Arnold. and Thomas Welch, and Polly, his wife. Son, James Frier. Dau.. Peggy Vallandingham, dau., Parthena Eastin, dau., Lear Miller, dau., Jane Reed. Exec's., Wife, Jane and two sons, Robert and James Frier. Witnesses, Wm. B. Summers, Curtis Ballard and James Reeds. Written June 9, 1816. Probated Feb. 1818

FOLEY, JOHN—Will—Page 337—Written Jan. 27, 1818. Names wife, Jenny. Sons, Thomas, Lorenzo Dow and Gabriel Foley. Daughters, Polly, Sarah, Letitia, Margaret, Jane, and Julianne Foley. Exec's., Wife, Jenny, brother, William Foley and James Mars. Witnesses, Lewis Falconer, Benjamin Tutt and Wm. Alfred. Probated Apr. Court 1818.

FRAZER, WILLIAM—Will—Page 501—Written Aug. 11, 1818. Names wife, Philadelphia. Dau's., Rebecca, Mary, Martha, and sons, David and William, (lawful age.) Exec's., Wife and children. Witnesses, Will Frazer, Jr. and Robert Frazer. Probated April Court 1819.

GARRARD, DAVID—Will—Page 83—Written Feb. 15, 1816. Names wife, Elizabeth. Several children (no names.) Exec's., William Shreve, of Jessamine, and Ambrose Young. Witness, David Hudson. Probated July Court 1816.

GRAVES, BENJAMIN—Will—Page 492—Written Aug. 13, 1812. Names wife, Polly Graves. Mother, Brother, Thomas C. Graves,

Charles Tunning. Any children, after wife's death, all surviving and rest to heirs of those dead. Exec's., Wife, Polly, Brothers, John C. Graves and George Graves, and wife's brother, James Dudley. Probated April Court 1819.

HALEY, SUSANNA—Will—Page 176—Written Jan. 9, 1817. Names, daughter, Catey Haley and son, Larkin Haley. Exec., Samuel Ayres. Witnesses, Thomas G. Richardson, John Richardson and Abner Cornelius. Probated Feb. Court 1817.

HAPPY, JAMES—Will—Page 223—Names, three daughters, Polly Barnett, Nancy Dunn, Betsy Stivers. Son, Enoch. Wife, Mary. Daughter, Lydia Pemberton. Witnesses, George Hunter, and Elisha Metcalf. Probated July Court 1817. Codicil, gives Mary Boyd. Will written May 8, 1814.

KEENE, FRANCIS—Will—Page 307—Written Oct. 11, 1816. Names, wife, Mary Keene. Son, Sanford Keene. Son-in-law, Thomas H. Berryman. Daughters, Betsy Keene and Ellen Payne. Children of Ellen Payne, Hugh Payne. Dau., Margaret Price, son, Edward Payne, dau., Sinai Hicks, Mary Price, Sally Payne, Nancy Payne, son, Sandford Payne, son, Silas Payne, dau., Ellen Payne. Son-in-law, John Blakemore, dau., Sinai Blakemore, son, Oliver Keen, son John Keen. Witnesses, J. T. Threshley, Ben W. Dudley. Probated Feb. 18, 1818.

KERNS, JAMES, formally of Ireland—Will—Page 253—Written (no date). Names Nephew, Henry Wats. Nieces, Mary Ann, Jane, Amelia. Nephew, James Kerns, son of brother, Hugh Kerns. Exec., Cornelius Coyle. Witnesses, Spencer Cooper and J. Bell. Probated Oct. Court 1817.

LONG, WILLIAM—Will—Page 392—Names, wife, Agnes. Son, William, dau., Elizabeth, dau., Rebecca Smith. Sons, Robert, Isaac, Samuel, Alexander. Exec's., Sons, Robert and William Long. Witnesses, John White and Randolph Harris. Will written April 8, 1818. Probated Aug. Court 1818.

LYDIG, JACOB—Will—Page 38—Names, wife, Barbara. Son-in-law, Jacob Sidener and other children. Executrix, Wife, Barbara. Witnesses, David Smith, George P. Sidener and Bennett Fryer. Will written July 16, 1810. Probated April Court 1814

WILL BOOK F

(Copied by Mrs. H. K. McAdams, Notary Public. Wills and Estates)

ALEXANDER ATCHISON—Will—Will Book F, page 231—Names, wife, Mary Atchison, son, James and grand-daughter, Jane Clark. Executors, Samuel Blain and Elijah McClannehan. Will dated Oct. 20, 1823. Witnesses, John McNair, John Clark and Alexander Clark. Proved Dec. Court 1823.

RICHARD ALLEN—WILL—Page 167—Names wife, Anna Allen. Daughters, Polly Lamme, Sally Higgins, and Fanny Curd. Sons, John Allen and Francis Allen, grand-children, Madison and Richard Allen, sons of Francis Allen. Daughter-in-law, Elizabeth Allen. Executors, Richard Higgins and William Gist and John Allen. Witnesses, Jos. Boswell, E. Yeiser and L. Young. Will dated Aug. 8, 1821. Proved Feb. Court 1824.

THOMAS BARR, JR.—Estate—Will Book F, page 236—Sale. Dec. 2, 1823. Administrator, Marthey Barr. Recorded Jan. Court 1824. Inventory. Page 215.

ABRAHAM STOUT BARTON—WILL—Will Book F, page 263—Names, wife, Sarah Hart Barton Children, Abraham and John Barton. Friend Doc't. Elisha Warfield. Partner, Andrew McClure. Father, John Barton. Wife's father, Benjamin Merrell. Uncle, David Barton. Executors, John M. Hunt, Elisha I. Winter, Abram. Barton and Mathew T. Scott. Dated Dec. 29, 1823. Witnesses, Charles Wilkins, J. Posthlethwaite and Andrew McClure. Proved Feb. Court 1824.

CHARLES BRADFORD—Estate—Will Book, page 213—Administratrix, Maryann Bradford. Rec. Nov. Court 1823.

FRANCIS BROWN—Will Book F, page 129—Wife, Juliet. Executrix, wife, Juliet, together with Michael Clarke, Executor. Dated Apr. 8, 1812. Witnesses, W. Macbean, Peter I. Robert, J. McIlvain. Recorded Aug. Court 1823. Witnesses, W. Macbean and Charles Humphreys.

CHARLES BURLINGAME—Estate—Page 277—Jesse Bunnell, Administrator. Sale Nov. 16, 1822, account recorded Feb. Court 1824. Also page 284. Settlement. Feb. 9, 1824.

ELIZABETH BYRNES—Estate—Will Book F, page 203—Aug. 21, 1823. Appraisors, John W. Moore, John Hurst and Newbald Crockett. Nov. term Court 1823.

ELIZA BYRNES—Estate—Will Book F, page 203—Appraisers, Jno. W. Moore, John Hurst and Newbald Crockett. Aug. 21, 1823. Recorded Nov. Court 1823.

JOHN D. CLIFFORD—Estate—Page 286—John S. Snead, Executor. Account Jan. 13, 1824. Commissioners, Alex. Parker, W. W Worsley and R. Higgins. Rec. Feb. Ct. 1824.

HENRY COONS—Will Book F, page 135—Mentions wife, Mary, son, Samuel Coons and his infant children, Pauline, Henry and Thomas M. Coons. Son, John Coons, deceased and heirs Jemima, Molly, Joshua, Susan, James, Martin and Betsy. Executors, son, Joshua Coons, James Coons, and Martin Coons. Witnesses, Jas. Darnaby, John Darnaby. June 5, 1821. Codicil, Mentions Mary, widow of John Coons, deceased. Elijah, Joshua, Henry, Marianne, John, Samuel, and Peter Coons, heirs of John Coons. Witnesses, James and John Darnaby. Will and Codicil recorded Aug. Court 1823.

CORNELIUS COYLE—Estate—Page 290—Com's., A. LeGrand, Jas McKane and Henry Wier. Inv., Rec. Feb. Court 1824.

WILLIAM DAVIS—Estate—Will Book F, page 246—Inventory. Appraisers, John Barton, George Ware, and James Weathers. Sept. 12, 1823. Recorded Jan. Court 1824 Sale on page 247

WILLIAM DUDLEY—Estate—Will Book F, page 142—Executrix, Lucy Dudley, and Wm, Boon, Asa Thomson, and Robert Dudley, executors. Witness, E. Darnaby, Jas. Darnaby, John Darnaby, Jno. Boyd. Aug. 23, 1823. Recorded Sept. Court 1823.

JOHN ELDERS—Estate—Page 271—Administrators, Matthew Elder and Robert Grinstead Witness, Mrs. Anna Elders. Commissioners, George Robinson, and M. Fishel. Acct. rendered Aug. 29, 1818. Rec. Feb. Court 1824.

JOSEPH R. FARROW—Inventory of Estate—Wlil Book F, page 204— Administrator, Leslie Combs. Witnesses, Will Morton, A. Le Grand and Jas. W. Palmer. Recorded Nov. Court 1823.

BRYANT FERGUSON—Estate Inventory—Will Book F, page 209— Nov. 6, 1823. Executor, Nathaniel Ferguson. Mentions Nathaniel as son of Bryant Ferguson. Rec. Nov. Court 1823.

JOHN FRANK—Estate—Page 276—Comm. appointed Jan. Court 1824 to settle with Nancy Riley, late Nancy Frank, administratrix of Estate of John Frank. Acct. given Feb. 6, 1824, names guardian of heir, Henry Roberts. Comm's., John G. Parks, W. McClanahan and John Campbell. Rec. Feb. Court 1824.

JANE FREER—Estate—Will Book F, page 134—Appraisers, B. Abernathy, Archid McNeil, Thomas Baxter. Aug. 11, 1823. Administrator, George Vallandigham.

JANE FRIER—Estate—Page 269—George Vallandigham, Administrator. Commissioners, Wm. B. Summers and A. Young. Dec. 31, 1823. Recorded Feb. Court 1824.

GEORGE ALEXANDER GILLISPIE—Will—Will Book F, page 227— Mentions Brothers, Wm., John and Angel Gillispie. Sisters, Patsey Cravens, Peggy Hampton. Executor, brother, William Gillispie. Date Sept. 16, 1823. Witnesses, J. Stonestreet, Lucy Schooler, Henry Sanders. Proved Dec. Court 1823.

WILLIAM GILLISPEE—Estate—Will Book F, page 187—Administrator, Wm. Boon. Recorded Sept. Court 1823. Witnesses, Waller Bullock and John Todd, and James Minter.

GEORGE GRAY—Will—Page 357—Mentions wife, Mary Gray. 8 sons and 3 daughters. Sons, Joseph, Isaac, George, James Jonathan, Wm. S., James and Benj. T. Gray. Dau., Hannah Benning, Sarah Travers, Martha Grimes. Written Nov. 30, 1818. Proved July CT. 1824.

HEZEKIAH HARRISON—Estate—Will Book F, page 212—Mentions Will examined. Wife, Jane, son, John. Commissioners, Wm. Boon, Richard Hunter, and James Criner. Rec. Nov. Court 1823. Also page 255 to 262 account of Ambrose Young, Executor. Rec. Jan. Court 1824.

JOHN HIGBEE—Estate Inventory—Will Book F, page 195—Appraisers, Elijah Carmell, Wm. Gish and Elisha Meredith. Recorded Oct. Court, 1823.

SANDFORD KEEN—Will—Will Book F, page 197—Mentions wife, Martha N. Keen, Executrix and Doc't. Benjamine W. Dudley, Wm. G. Wilson, Richard H. Chinn and Upshaw Berryman, Executors. Dated Sept. 29, 1823. Witnesses, R. Wickliffe, R. Higgins, and I C. Richardson, Jr. Probated Oct. Court 1823.

FRANCIS HODGES—Will—Page 381—Written June 9, 1821. Mentions sons, Daniel, Galin Hodges, heirs of dau., Mary Ann (deceased), heirs of son, Francis Hodges (deceased). Executors, sons, Daniel and Galin Hodges, and friend, Leonard Young. Witnesses, A. W. Burrows, John Ferguson, Oliver Beasley and J. L. Detiste. Probated July Court 1824. Probated again Sept. term 1824.

REUBEN HUDSON—Allotment of Dower—Page _411—Mentions Nancy Hudson, Widow, of Reuben. Rec. Oct. Ct. 1824. Estate Page 355. Appraisers, Nathaniel Winn, James Whaley, Jr., and James Grimes. Nov. 22, 1823. Rec. June CT. 1824. Page 274. Inventory of Sale. Dec. 11, 1823. Administrators, Jesse Hudson and Frederic B. Nichols. Recorded Feb. Court 1824.

JOSHUA HUMPHREYS—Will—Will Book F, page 229—Names, wife, Mary T. Humphreys and two children, Larry T. and Hetty W. Humphreys. Wife, Mary, Executrix and brother Charles Humphreys, Executor. Names nephew, Kames H. Humphreys of Harrodsburg, Ky. Will dated Nov. 4, 1823. Witnesses, E. M. Patterson and L. W. Combs, and Notley Conn. Proved Dec. Court 1823.

HUNT AND FLETCHER—Division of Mansfield—Will Book F, page 194—Commissioners, Richard Darinton, George Dunlap, James Trotter, Sen. James Gibson, Richard Higgins and Thomas Wallace, to divide tract of land called "Mansfield" between John W. Hunt and Thomas Fletcher. Recorded Oct. Court 1823.

JOHN HUTSELL—Estate—Page 296—Administrator, George Hutsell. Inventory returned, Dec. Court, 1822, additional Invent'., Jan. Court 1824. Commissioners, James Darnaby, Wm. Scott and John Hedges. Rec. Feb. Court 1824. Division of Estate of John Hutsell, Page 298, mentions 10 heirs. Henry Liter intermarried with Polly Hutsell. Also Vincent Scott, who intermarried with Ann Hutsell. Rec. Feb. Court 1824.

JOSEPH INNSKEEP—Sale—Will Book F, page 217—Oct. 8, 1823. Administrator, Samuel M. Grant. Inventory, page 224. Rec. Dec. Court 1823.

WILLIAM JENKINS—Estate Settlement—Page 409—Son, John S. Jenkins, Administrator. Rec. Oct. Ct. 1824.

HENRY JOHNSON—Estate—Will Book F, page 134—Henry Johnson, who died in 1821. Appraised by Wm. McConnell, Thomas Stephenson and Allen Davis, on Aug. 11, 1823, before John Bradford. Recorded Aug. Court, 1823.

SANFORD KEEN—Estate—Page 321—Inventory by Commissioners, R. Higgins, David Megowan and Joseph Logan. Mch. 19, 1824. Rec. Apr. Ct. 1824.

JONATHAN LAMME—Estate—Page 331—Commissioners, John Allen, Wm. Gest, and William Sullivan. Mch. term Court 1823. Mentions, Widow and 10 heirs. Wm. Gray, guardian for Adison Lamme. Milton Lamme, Hervey Lamme, Jane Lamme, Jonathan Lamme, Jr., Polly Lamme, Nathan Lamme, Julian Lamme, Maria Gray, Sally Kay, Wm. Kay. Rec. Apr. Ct. 1824.

JAMES LEMMON—Estate—Will Book F, page 199—Samuel M. Grant, administrator. Probated Sept. Court 1823. Commissioners, Jno. W. Moore and Wm. Fisher.

AUGUSTUS P. LEVETT—Will—Will Book F, page 199—Dated Nov. 8, 1823. Witnesses, Wm. Challen, Jno. Lockwood and Thomas J. Skilman. Rec. Sep. Court 1823.

ELIJAH McCROSKY—Will Book F, page 137—Mentions sister, Sally Blackwood, Mary Nealy, and Ann Spires. Brothers, David Mc-Crosky, Levi McCrosky. Nephews, Anderson Blackwood and Hiram McCrosky. Executors, David McCrosky, and Noah Spires. Dated July 22, 1823. Witnesses, John Hendley, Arch'd McIlvain, Jr., Benj. S. Cockrill. Probated Sept. Court, 1823.

WILLIAM MANUEL—Will Book F, page 128—Mentions wife, Sterling, and children, not named. Executor, John W. Moore. Written Apr. 14, 1823. Witnesses, James S. Gray and John Devore. Recorded, Aug. Court 1823.

FRANCES MARSHALL—Inventory—Page 360—Appraisers, Saml. Trotter, Thomas Anderson, and Asa Blanchard. Mentions Widow, Eliza Marshall. Rec. July Ct. 1824.

MICAJAH MASON—Estate—Page 410—Appraisers, Elijah Cartmell, Larken Gatewood, and Benjamin White. Rec. Oct. Ct. 1824.

JOHN MEEKINS—Will Book F, page 129—Mentions Sarah Meekins, his wife. Executors, John H. Lusby, and Arter Brewar. Witnesses, Elizabeth Humphreys, and Michael Kiblar. Recorded Aug. Court, 1823.

WILLIAM MILES—Will—Page 322—Written Nov. 1817. Mentions being broken-up for the third time, housekeeping. Mentions 6 brothers (one named Thomas) and one sister, if alive. Brother-in-law, John F. Greenwood, and his daughter, Jane Greenwood. Proved Aug. Ct. 1824.

JAMES MORRISON—Sales and Accounts—Pages 366-381—Oct. 21, 1823. Part of Estate, Carlisle farm. Legatees mentioned, Mrs. E. Morrison, Miss Edmiston, Robert Scott, M. Montgomery, F. Dewees' wife. Wife of Richard Haws, Jr., J. M. Holmes, Morrison Bosworth, and M. Pindell. H. Clay, Executor. Settlement recorded Aug. Ct. 1824.

JOHN MORRISON—Estate—Will Book F, page 231—June 9, 1823. Robert Scott. Agent for H. Clay, only executor. Schedule of Bonds and Notes on page 233. Recorded Dec. Court 1823.

WILLIAM J. R. MOSELEY—Estate—Wlil Book F, page 245—Appraisers, Thomas I. Dickison, Sampson Oates and Thomas M. Merchant. Dec. 10, 1823. Recorded Jan. Court 1824.

THOMAS MOXLEY—Estate—Will Book F, page 251—Names Elizabeth Moxley, Christopher Moxley, and Nancy Voirs (late Nancy Moxley). Maryann Moxley, Milly Moxley, Thomas Moxley, William Moxley, Perry Moxley, Penelope, widow of deceased Thomas Moxley. Commissioners, George Ware, Wm. Scott, and David Barton. Recorded Jan. Court 1824.

FREDERICK NICHOLS—Will—Page 358—Written Nov. 4, 1816. Mentions, Elizabeth Nichols and 8 children. Sons, George, Wm., Robert, Frederick B., and James Nichols. Dau., Frances Whaley, Catherine Childs and Elizabeth Reid. Son, George Nichols, executor with wife, Elizabeth Nichols Executrix. Proved July Ct. 1824.

JAMES NICHOLS—Division—Page 314—Account with James Ewing and Elizabeth Conner, Administratrix. Commissioners, Edward C. Payne, Wm. Boon and Clement Smith. Heirs, Phoebe Ann Livingston, Adilla Nichols, Antinoney Nichols and Desdemona Nichols. Rec. March Court, 1824.

SUSANNA NOE—Estate—Page 413—Rec. Oct. Ct. 1824.

MICHAEL J. NOUVELL—Estate—Will Book F, page 151—Inventory, Mch. 12, 1823. Commissioners, Thos. Curry, Leonard Wheeler, James M. Kane. Administrators, Wm. Pritchartt and Sandford Keen. Sept. Court 1823. Page 176, sale by Thomas Anderson.

THOMAS NUTTLE—Estate—Page 363—Adms., Nancy Nuttle, Moses H. Walls and Robert P. Penniston. Oct. 4, 1822. Sale. Rec. Aug. Ct. 1824.

JOHN POWER—Estate—Will Book F, page 148—Elizabeth Power, deceased, Executrix with E Bryan, administrator. Witnesses, Wm. Boon, James Darnaby. Waller Bullock. Sept. Court.

ELIZABETH POWER—Estate—Legatees, William Power, Mary Bryant, Patsey Power, Susan Power, Thomas Power, dec'd. John Power and Rebecca Coppage. July 26, 1823. Commissioners, Wm. Boon, Waller Bullock and James Darnaby.

HUGH PRICE—Estate—Page 303—Administrator, Bird Price. Inv. Comm's., Enoch Bryan and George W. Clark. Rec. March Court 1824.

JOSEPH ROBINSON—Will—Will Book F, page 202—Mentions wife, Moley Robinson. Two sons, John and Dudley Robinson. Dated Oct. 27, 1819. Witness, Wm. Whiting, James Wilson and Abner Wilson, Sen. Probated Nov. Court 1823.

BENJAMINE F. ROGERS—Will—Page 266—Dated Dec. 27, 1823. Names brothers, Barnard Rogers, Elijah Rogers, and Coleman Rogers. Father, Joseph Rogers. Nephew, William Rogers. Witnesses, Jeremiah Vardeman, Polly Coons, and John C. Richardson, Sen. Proved Feb. Court 1824.

BENJAMIN ROGERS—Estate—Page 320—Inventory by Commissioners, Jno. C. Richardson, Samuel Smith, and James Munday. Rec. Apr. Ct. 1824.

JOSEPH ROGERS—Bond—Mentions sons, Benjamin F. Rogers, Elijah Rogers and William Rogers. Son, Barnet Rogers. Written Mch. 24, 1824. Witnesses, John C. Richardson, Sr., Samuel Smith and James Munday. Rec. April Ct. 1824.

JACOB SAGASER—Will—Page 354—Written July 24, 1821. Witnesses, John Hall, Waller Rodes, and Asa Hall. Mentions Mary Ann Troutman, Fanny (?) Troutman and Elizabeth Troutman. Heirs of Mary Ann Troutman, desc'd. Leonard Troutman, Barbery Baker, Frederick Seckester, Jacob Seckester, Elizabeth Arnspiker, Daniel Seckester and Nancy Hardestey. Exects., Sons, Frederick and Jacob Sickester. Rec. June Ct. 1824.

WILLIAM SANDERSON, SR.—Will—Page 362—Written July 5, 1824. Mentions, wife, Lucy. Son, Robert Sanderson (deceased). Heirs,

Son, Wm. E. Sanderson, Mary Thompson, Catherine Simmerson, Jane Beatty, Sally Haze, Matty Hamilton, Barbara Rankin, Ann Sanderson. Executor, Samuel Devore. Rec. Aug. Ct. 1824.

WHARTON SCHOOLER—Will—Page 341—Written June 7, 1819. Mentions, wife, Margaret Schooler, executrix, with son, Lewis and son-in-law, Robert D. Schooler, executors. Mentions, daughters, Patsey Allen, Polly Schooler, Sarah Adams, Beulah Estes, Betsey Schooler and Peggy (no surname). Proved May Ct. 1824. Witnesses, Wm. C. Prewitt, Thos. Ellis and Lloyd K. Goodwin.

WHARTON SCHOOLER—Estate—Inventory—Page 385—June 3, 1824. Appraisers, James True, Jr., Lewis C. Ellis, Thos. Ellis, and Wm. C. Prewett. Rec. Sept. Ct. 1824

CONRAD SIDENER—Will—Page 408—Written Aug. 22, 1823. Mentions sons, John, William, and Gwynn R. Tompkins. Dau., Powell and other children, but no names. Proved Oct. Ct. 1824.

ABRAHAM SIMPSON—Will—Will Book F, page 190—Mentions daughter, Nancy, Sally and Delia. Son, Jordon. Dated Aug. 7, 1823. Witnesses, Wm. Dykes and John Seiders. Probated Oct. Court 1823.

ABRAHAM SIMPSON—Estate—Page 346—Appraisers Nathaniel Winn, James Grimes, and Charles Clarke. Rec. May Court 1824.

JOSEPH SINGER—Inventory, Estate—Will Book F, page 228—Oct. 27, 1823. Rec. Dec. Court 1823.

BENJAMINE SMITH AND NANCY SMITH—Estate—Page 273—Edward Wm. Smith, gave account of increase, Dec. 4, 1823. Commissioners, James Munday, Samuel Smith and Edward Herndon. Rec. Feb. Court 1824.

BENJAMIN SMITH—Estate—Page 387-395—Sale Jan. 27, 1824. And Nancy Smith, Estate. Account with William Smith, Executor of Benjamin and Nancy Smith. Recorded Sept. Court 1824. Will Book F, page 206. Inventory. Rec. Nov. Court 1823.

BENJAMIN SMITH—Estate. Inventory—Will Book F, page 207—Executor, Wm. Smith. Appraisers, Samuel Smith, James Munday, and Ed. H. Herndon. Rec. Nov.Court 1823.

RICE SMITH—Will—Will Book F, page 200—Mentions, wife Margaretta. 4 grand-daughters, Betsy Julia Johnson, Louisa Evelina Flournoy, Martha Matilda Flournoy, and Emily Flournoy. 2 grand-sons, Claudius Marcella Flournoy and Victor Monroe Flournoy. Emily, wife of Mathews Flournoy, Esq. Executrix, Wife, Margaretta, with Mathew Flournoy, Benjamin Smith, and John Graves, Sen., Executors. Witnesses, W. Henry, Gideon Gaines, Francis F. Wells and Wm. Smith,Jr. Probated,Nov. Court, 1823. Estate, page 279. Inventory Jan. 22, 1824. Executor, M. Flournoy. Appraisers, Moses Randolph, Wm. Patterson and Edw. Maguire. Rec. Feb. Court 1824.

WILLIAM SMITH—Estate—Will Book F, page 144—Samuel Smith, executor. May 1, 1822. Recorded Sept. Court, 1823.

WILLIAM SMITH—Estate Division—Page 317—Commissioners, Mathew Kenney, Asa Thompson, James Rogers and James Darnaby. Mentions 4 youngest daughters, Polly Smith (now Polly Boice), Juliet Smith (now Juliet Dudley, Martha and Margaret Smith. Recorded April Court 1824,

JOHN STARK—Estate—Page 416—Oct. 4, 1824. Commissioners, George Dunlap, Archibald McKee, Richard Downton and R. G. Dudley. Rec. Oct. Ct. 1824.

ELIZABETH STEPHENS—Estate—Will Book F, page 139—Appraisers, Jacob Cassell, M. Fishel and John Wirt. July 8, 1823. Administrator, John McCalla. Witnesses, Thos. Tibbatts, W. Gilliam, Josh. Humphreys. Recorded Sept. 1823.

JAMES STEWART—Estate—Will Book F, page 239—Inventory, Dec. 29, 1823. Appraisers, John Pollock, M. Fishel and Jacob McConothy. Administrator, Nancey Stewart. Sale Jan. 2, 1824. Recorded Jan. Court 1824.

JOAB STOUT—Estate—Page 318—Oct. Court 1823. Commissioners, Wm. C. Counette, Wm. Akin and Reuben Houghton. Admin., Azariah S. Higgins. Rec. April Court 1824.

DANIEL TALBOT—Estate—Page 270—B. Stout, Administrator. Commissioners, R. Higgins, Abrm. S. Drake and James Beach. Account rendered Feb. 1, 1824. Recorded Feb. Court 1824.

JOHN TRUE—Appraisement—Page 302. Inventory. Commissioners, Edward Carter, Dudley Shipp and Wm. E. True. Feb. 23, 1824. Rec. March Court 1824.

LEWIS TURNER—Estate—Page 280—Inventory. Appraisers, Wm. Pollock, Richard Gray and Nathan Payne. Oct. 20, 1823. Rec. Nov. Court 1824.

LEWIS E. TURNER—Sale—Page 395—Dr. Asa Payne, Administrator. Account page 402. Recorded Sept. Ct. 1824.

JOHN WAINWRIGHT—Estate—Will Book F, page 130—Administrator, J. Maslin Smith. Aug. 9, 1823. Appraisers, Jas. W. Palmer, Robert Frazer, James Wier. Recorded Aug. Court 1923.

MARY WASON—Estate—Page 289—Commissioners appointed Jan. Court 1824. J. Worley, Wm. B. Price, Jno. Steele and George F. Muldrow. Administrators, James and Thomas Wason. Rec. Feb. Court 1824.

LUCY WEST—Will—Page 342—Mentions husband, William West. Son, Francis George West. Dau., Allice Francis West. Son, Augustine Moore West. Grandfather, John Robinson. Executors, husband, Wm. West and son, Francis G. West. Written Jan. 20, 1824. Witnesses, George T. Chapman, Charles Humphreys, Francis Scott. Proved May Ct. 1824.

JESSE D. WINN—Estate—Page 305—Appraisers, Abrm. Jones, Abrm. Farguson, James Grant, Wm. Scott. Jan. 13, 1824. Rec. March Court 1824. Legatees, Fanny Combs, Richard A. G. Winn, Nancy Sinclair, Dolly Beachamp, Phillip B. Winn, Lucy C. Gatewood, Stephen I. Winn, Clary Combs, Braxton B. Winn, Kitty Gray and Jesse D. Winn, Jr. Jan. 1824. Division Recorded, Mch. Court 1824. Page 310 to 314, Division of land. Rec. Mch. Court 1824.

JAMES VANCE—Will—Page 351—Mentions wife, Margaret Vance. Sons, Wm. James, Samuel, John, Alexander and Montgomery Vance. Daughters, Nancy McDowell, Jane Vance, Sally Vance, Mary Vance, and Marthy Ann Vance. Executors, George W. Botts, Samuel Scott and son, Wm. S. Vance. Witnesses, D. I.

Williams, Samuel Clew and Maxwell Chambers. Will written, May 5, 1824. Proved June Ct. 1824.

VANPELT ESTATE—Sale—Will Book F, page 132—Apr. 3, 1822. Recorded Aug. Court 1823.

WILL BOOK G

ADAMS, ABSALOM—Deceased—Estate—Page 35—Inventory, sale on Dec. 26, 1823. Administrator, Abner Alilson. Rec. Dec. Court 1824. Page 47. Appraisers, James Weathers, Abraham Farguson, D. Barton. Rec. Nov. 9, 1924.

ALLEN, JOSEPH—Will—Page 74, 147—Will written May 16, 1824. Names, wife, Nancy, and 6 children, Buford Allen, Eliza C. Elly, Polly C. Downton, Simeon B. Allen, Greenby D. Allen, Sally M. Prewett. Grand-daughters, Zorilda Barbee and Lucinda Prewett. Erecutors, Simeon B. Allen, Greenby M. Allen and Wm. Boon. Witnesses, John Hendly, W. Hayes, and Hezekiah Ellis. Proved Feb. Court 1825.

ASHBY, NATHANIEL—Deceased—Estate—Page 211—Executor, M. Q. Ashby. Commiss., W. W. Worsley, John Brand, Thomas Anderson. Rec. Sept. Court 1825.

BIRD, ABRAHAM—Will Book E, page 149—Names wife, Rachael, sons; Abraham, Mark, and George. Daughters; Magdelane, Elizabeth, Mary, Catherine and Margaret. Executors; sons, Abraham Bird and Wm. I. Russell. Written 1808. Witnesses; Joseph Jay, Wm. Manuel and David Coffman. Proved Mch. Ct. 1820. Will Book G, page 217 give legatees; Rachel Bird, No. 3. Catherine Thomas, No. 4. Page 426, gives legatees; Joseph Hawins, No. 1. Magadaline Allen, No. 2.

BARR, THOMAS, SR.—Deceased—Inv. and appraisement, page 51. Estate, page 81. Apprs., Enoch Bryan and James Gibson. Executors, W. Barr and Archibald McKee. Rec. Feb. Court 1825.

BARR, THOMAS TILTON—Will—Page 54—Names brother, Robert Ross Barr. Sole executor, Robert Ross Barr. Written Sept. 1, 1823. Witness, John Lowrey. Proved on oath of Ashton Garnet, John Lowrey and James C. Rodes. Proved Jan. Court 1825.

BARKER, ANN—Deceased—Will—Page 193—Written June 26, 1825. Names, daughter, Mary Hatton and her daughter, Ann Finsley. Son, Joseph Barker. Grand-daughters, Sarah Summers, Ann Barker, the dau. of my son, Thomas Barker. Executor, Son, Joseph Barker. Witnesses, P. B. Evans, Wall (?) Barker, Milton Bradley. Proved July Court 1825. Page 279. Sale Aug. 5, 1825. Rec. Mch. Court 1826. Page 420. Estate settled, recorded Nov. Court 1826. Commissrs., J. Parrish, Belain P. Evans, and Jas. Eastham.

BRAND, I. W.—Deceased—Estate—Page 133—Settlement of Thomas Smith, Exectr'. Commsrs., Thomas Anderson, David ——— and Bird Smith. Rec. Apr. 11, 1825.

BRIDGES, JNOS.—Deceased—Estate—Page 22—Nov. 8, 1824. Apprs., W. Connel, John Coldwell, and Francis Kerigle. Administratrix, Elizabeth Bridges. Rec. Nov. Court 1824.

BRIGGS, E. L.—Page 274—Allotment of Dower to widow of E L.

Briggs, Mrs. Margaret Briggs. To Miss Juliet E. Briggs, to E. L. Briggs, to E. F. Briggs, to J. W. Briggs, to T. H. Briggs, to S W. Briggs. Recorded on oaths of John Norton, Alex. Parker, and Thos. Nelson. Jan. 9, 1826.

BRUMBARGER, SUSAN—Deceased—Page 153—Settlement of estate. Adm'n., Benjamin Dawns. Commissrs., Nathaniel Ferguson, W. Price, and John Steele. Rec. Nov. Court 1825.

BOYCE, WILLIAM—Deceased—Estate—Page 7—Dec. 1 and 1, 1812. Exec., Gerard McKenney, and Elizabeth, his wife, and John Boyce. Rec., Oct. Court 1824. Page 12. Settlement, Names, John Boyce, Wm. Boyce, Gerard McKenney and wife, as guardians of Daniel, Emily, Peggy and Carolina Boyce. Extracts, "That the Executors were compelled to go to Ohio, several times, 3 times to Va." "Once from Va. to North Carolina." "The business being in Surrey, Isle of Wight, Southhampton and so forth." Commsrs., Lindsay Coleman, John Bradford and Wm. West. Rec. Oct. Court, 1824.

BRYANT, JOSEPH—Deceased—Page 184—July 11, 1825. Appraisers, David Sutton, Thomas Stevenson and James Wilson. Rec. July Court 1825. Page 253. Proved in Dec. Court.

GARRARD COUNTY, KENTUCKY

(Copied by Mrs. H. K. McAdams)

WILL ABSTRACTS, BOOK A

LINN BANKS—Book A, page 24—Names wife, Sarah. Children, William Banks, Leanna Pollard, Sarah Poindexter, Lucy Marksberry, Mary Mayfield, John Banks, Cevina Taylor, Susannah Nanks, Nancy Wilson, Garrard Banks. Grand-son, Arasha Hudson, daughter, Sophia, grand-son, Linn Banks, son of William Banks. Exec's., Sons, William, John and Garrard Banks. Written Dec. 27, 1799. Witnesses, John Bryant, Wm. Steen, Isaac Marksberry. No date for probate.

JOSHUA BLANTON—Will Book A, page 4—Garrard Co., Ky. Joshua Blanton, of Mercer Co., Ky. Names wife, Sary Blanton. Sons, Jesse, Joshua, Billy, land in Jefferson Co., Ky. Son, Elijah, son, John, daughters, Polly, Deny, Betsy, Fanny, Nancy, Patsy. Exec's., wife, Sary, son, Joshua, friends, Lewis Hawks, James Speed. Witnesses, Polly S. Hopkins, Cumberland Hart, Henry Speed. Written July 21, 1796. Probated Aug. 7, 1796.

ZOPHER CARPENTER, of Madison Co., Ky.—Will Book A, page 6—Names son, Robert Carpenter, son, Zuris Carpenter, son, Rusus Carpenter. Witnesses, John Manier, John Courtney. Written Sept. 24, 1794. Estate appraised Apr. 23, 1798.

ZACHARIAH COMPTON—Will Book A, page 179—Names wife, Catherine. Daughter, Betsy Ison, son Heli Compton, son, Burras Compton. Daughters, Sally Peter, Betsy Ison. Exec's., William Peter and son, Burras Compton. Written June 25, 1804. Witnesses, Charles Spilman, James Ison, Hugh Turpin. Probated Nov. Court 1804.

MATTHEW COWDEN, of Madison Co., Ky.—Will Book A, page 18—

Names step-father, Joshua Nichols. Brothers, John and William Cowden. Land in Carolina. Two sisters, Elizabeth and Martha. Exec's., Hugh Andrew and brother, John Cowden. Written Mch. 4, 1793. Witnesses, Alex Denny, Samuel Woods, John Martin. Probated Mch. 27, 1795.

MATTHEW COWDEN—North Carolina, May session Court, 1799. Will of Matthew Cowden, of Madison Co., Ky., executed on oath of Hugh Andrews and John Cowden, executors.

MOSES CUMMINS—Will Book A, page 142—Names brothers and sisters. Sons, Daniel and Stephens. Children, Elizabeth Sord, Moses Cummins, Hannah Cummins, Cealah Cummins, Polly Cummins, Thomas Cummins, Daily Cummins. Exec's., Sons, Daniel and Stephens. Witnesses, Susannah Brady, John Williams, Walter Williams. Written Sept. 15, 1803. Probated Aug., 1803.

BENJAMIN DICKENS—Will Book A, page 195—Names wife. Children. Daughter, Jenny Dickens, under 16 years of age. Dau., Susannah Dickens. Three smallest children by first wife. Mary and Elizabeth Fisher, to care for Fanny, Jenny and Sally Dickens. Daughter, Smith. Exec's., Friends, Jesse Smith, Benjamin Fisher, and John Dunklin. Written Apr. 19, 1804. Probated June, 1804. Witnesses, Stephen Fisher, Joshua Davis and James Davis.

JOHN HOGAN, of Garrard Co., Ky.—Will Book A, page 8—Names wife, Elizabeth and children. Exec's., Jacob Black, Daniel Brown, and wife, Elizabeth. Witnesses, Nicholas Lloyd, Robert McKay, Lewis Hogan. Written Dec. 18, 1797. Probate not given.

FREDERICK HUFFMAN—Will Book A, page 200—Names wife, Mary. Children and Grand-children, Henry Huffman, John Huffman, Mary Caise, Elizabeth Craig and Frederick Craig. Two sons, Frederick Huffman and William Huffman. Exec's., Frederick Huffman and son-in-law, John Craig. Witnesses, Randolph Hale, Zachariah Ray, Nicholas Smith. Written Mch. 17, 1804. Probated Feb. 19, 1805.

JAMES MACKLIN, of Garrard Co., Ky.—Will Book A, page 111—Names sons, William and Henry Macklin. Daughter, Elizabeth Macklin. Dolly Macklin, sons, Joseph and Fethwick Macklin. Daughter, Nancy Mackin and son, John Macklin. Exec's., John Edmonson, John Jones, John Floyd. Written Dec. 15, 18——. No probate date. Witnesses, Charles Craig, Isaac Roach, John Huffman, Samuel Mullins.

AMBROSE NELSON, of Mercer Co., Ky.—Will Book A, page 1—Names wife, Rhoda. Son, Daniel. Daughter, Elizabeth Blanton. Other children, Mathers, Thomas, Polly, Martha, Judith, Susannah, Ambrose. Exec's., Wife, Rhoda, son, Daniel and Joshua Blanton. Written Jan. 29, 1797. Probated Aug. 7, 1797. Witnesses, Elijah Garrott, Jacob Garrott, Loving Garrott.

MICHAEL NICKUM—Will Book A, page 22—Names wife, Susannah. Children, son, John Nickum. Exec's., Wife, Susannah and son, John, Nickum. Witness, Benedick Swope. Written Jan. 23, 179——. No date for probate.

ROBIN POOR—Will Book A, page 104—Names sons, John and Thomas. Daughter, Susannah Felite. Son, William, dau., Mary Pollock, Hope Bradshaw, Elizabeth Taylor, Nancy Croucher, Sally

Lewis. Grand-son, Robert Poor, son of William Poor. Written July 20, 1801. Witnesses, Wm. Egerton, Benjamin Perkins, Jr., Benjamin Perkins, Sr., Jeremiah Turpin. No probate.

SAMUEL SCOTT, of Mercer Co., Ky.—Will Book A, page 147—Names son, John Scott, of Fayette Co., Ky., and John Scotts' children by first wife, viz: Samuel, Thomas, Brown, Sarah Scott, Robert and William Scott, land in York Co., Pa., lying by land of Wm. Read and Thomas Shannon. Also money coming from Thomas Patterson of York Co., Pa. Son, Joseph Scott and Joseph Scott's children. Son, Robert Scott's chidlren of York Co., Pa., widow of. Robert, Jane Scott. Widow of Wm. Scott, deceased and his children. Daughter, Isabella Brown, deceased. Daughter, Mary Craig's children. Daughter, Jane Rarity's children. Son-in-law, William Brown. Son-in-law, Robert Craig, son-in-law, Timothy Rarity. Exec's., Son, John Scott of Fayette Co., Ky. Son-in-law, William Brown, of Mercer Co., Ky. Witnesses, Ambrose Garrott, Enoch Kamper, John Stephens, Richard Roser. Written May 20, 1796. Probated Jan. Court 1804.

JAMES SMITH—Will Book A, page 9—Names son, James, under 21 years of age. Son, Edwin. Daughter, Elizabeth, who is also under 21 years, son, Henry, under 21 yrs., daughter, Sally, under 16 yrs. of age, son, William, land in Mason Co., Ky. Daughters, Nancy and Patty, land in Mason Co. Betsy Jeffries, daughter of Daniel and Patsy Jeffries. To wife. Son, Christopher. Exec's., Davis Finley, Joshua Burdet, John Floyd, Alexander Collier, Col. George Thompson, and son, William Smith. Witnesses, Capt. Wm. Smith, Alexander Collier, John Todd, and William Sparks. Probated June Court 1798.

BISHOP TONEY—Will Book A, page 15—Names sons, Alexander, John, Jesse, daughters, Mary, Agnes. Wife. Grand-son, James Alford. Written June 22, 1798. Witnesses, William Davis, Hanna Davis, John Seffrett. Exec's., Son, Alexander Toney and John Seffrett. No probate date.

GOLSON STAPP—Will Book A, page 101—Names wife, Rachael and children, Polly, John, Rachael and James Stapp. Written Dec. 7, 1802. Witnesses, John Boyle and William Lair. No probate.

RACHAEL STAPP—Will Book A, page 202—Her "one-eighth part of Gholson Stapp's estate, to be divided among 4 children of Rachael, viz: William, Sally, Rachael and James: Betsy, all under 21 years of age. Exec., John Jones. Written Dec. 21, 1804. Witnesses, William Lair, John Queen and Abner Littul. Probated Jan. Court 1805.

ROWLAN SUTTON—Will Book A, page 145—Names wife, Jane. Sister, Sucky Sope (or Pope). Estate of Christopher Sutton. Rowlan, son of John Sutton. Exec's., Wife, Jane, friend Elemander Pope. Written July 12, 1795. Witnesses, Wm. Flack and James Kirkpatrick. No probate.

WILLIAM WOOLEY—Will Book A, page 192—Names children, William, Crisley, Henry and Peter Wooley, Mary Hambleton, Michael Wooley's heirs, John Wooleys heirs, David Wooley and daughter, Margaret Wooley. Exec's., Crisley Wooley, Henry Wooley and William Hambleton. Written Mch. 6, 1797. Probated Sept. Court 1804. Witnesses, Alex Cains, James Guthrie and William Wooley.

WILLIAM ASKINS—Will Book B, page 52—Names wife, Patsey C. Askins. Children, daughters, Betsy Franklin and Nancy Washington. Son, Charles Askins. Exec., Brother, John Askins. Written June 1, 1811. Probated Dec. Court 1811. Witnesses, William Tracy, Thomas Tracy, and Pheneas G. Rice.

WILLIAM M. BLEDSOE—Book B, page 11—Names wife, Patience, infant chidlren, Adam and Jesse. Son, Joseph Bledsoe, land in Knox Co., Ky. Son, Moses. Grand——, Craig. Written ——. Exec's., Wife, Patience and William Owsley, Sr., and son, Moses Bledsoe. Witnesses, B. Letcher, H. P. Buford, Samuel Gill, James Aldridge. Probated Aug. Court 1811.

SAMUEL BLACK—Book B, page 53—Names wife, Polly Black. To William Jeffries. Half-brother, Andrew Hickenbottom, land in Montgomery Co., Va. To half-brother, Emanuel Hickenbottom. Six nephews, Samuel Turpin, Samuel Kenon, Samuel Hickenbottom, son of Joseph. Samuel Hickenbottom, son of Samuel. Samuel Hickenbottom, son of Andrew. Samuel Hickenbottom, son of James. Oldest sister, Magdalene Turpin. Exec's., Augustine Smith, and Robert Brank. Written Aug. 8, 1812. Witnesses, Charles Baker, Richard Randals, Charles D. Butcher, James W. Butcher. Probated Oct. Court 1812.

JAMES DISMUKES—Book B, page 25—Names wife, Geny. Daughter, Amy (or Anny) Compton. Sons, William and Joseph Dismukes. Daughter, Polly Smith's four daughters, viz: Nancy, Egletina, America and Levisa. Daughter, Sally Smith. Exec's., Wife, Genny Dismukes and Burris Compton. Written Feb. 8, 1810. Witnesses, Charles Spilman, John Wild, Henry Thompson. No probate date.

WILLIAM FINNELL—Book B, page 69—Dated Mch. 9, 1811. "My mother to have all my property." Witnesses, Clary Finnell, Susannah Finnell. Probated Nov. Court 1813.

JOHN FLEET—Will Book B, page 19—Names wife, Drusilla Fleet. My brothers, James Fleet, of Orange Co., Va. Brother, Lellice Fleet. Friend, Joel Noel, of Lincoln Co., Ky. Widow Bourn, Exec., Joel Noel. Brother, James to be guardian of brother, Filly. Written Aug. 31, 1809. Probated Nov. 1809. Witnesses, John Bryant, David White and James Thompson.

GEORGE GIBSON—Book B, page 67—Names sister, Katy Gibson of Fauquier Co., Va. Sister, Sally Gibson, of same Co. Sister, Ruthy. My aunt, Peggy Askins and her children, John Askins, son of Aunt Peggy. Exec., John Askins. Witnesses, Charles Spilman, Benjamin Wilds and John Wilds. Written Oct. 20, 1813. Probated Nov. Court 1813.

GARRARD GREEN—Book B, page 44—Names children, Catherine Allenbaugh, Barbara Meddey, Mary Gramer, Anne Poulton and Henry Green. Exec., John Gramer. Written Oct. 3, 1810. Witnesses, Garrard Gramer, Abraham Burton, John White and Sherwood Burton. Probated Oct. 1810.

JAMES HOGAN—Book B, page 41—Names son, James, daughter, Betsey. Daughter, Rebecca, deceased. Daughter Caty's four children, land in Scott Co., Ky. Mason Moss' children, land. Sally, the youngest, when becomes 18 years old. William Moss, eldest, Jamey

Moss, John Moss and Sally Moss, my four grand children. Daughter Polly, wife, Elizabeth. Four youngest children, viz: Sally, John, Samuel and William Hogan. Exec's., John Bryant, Samuel Mullins, Benjamin Dunn. Written, Feb. 13, 1811. Probated Apr., 1811. Witnesses, John A. Pulliam, Edward Smith, William Hogan.

EDWARD HOMES—Book B, page 71—Names John, Edward, Samuel, Isaac, Selay, Jacob, Joseph and George Homes, Sarah Homes, Wesley Homes. Daughter, Sally. Grand-son, Wesley. Exec., Sons, Edward and Samuel Homes. Written Mch. 19, 1813. Witnesses, William Oswley, Thomas Oswley. Probated Aug., 1813.

JOHN JONES—Book B, page 33—Names Elizabeth Jones, with whom I now live. To Thomas Kennedy, to William Oswley, to John Boyle, Jr. and Sr. To Edney Kennedy, wife of Thomas. To Elizabeth Jones Kennedy, daughter of Edna. To James Adams, son of William, when 21 years old. Gabriel Jones Salter, son of Michael Salter, under 21 years. Robert Stevens. Exec's., John Boyle, Sr. and John Boyle, Jr. Written Nov. 12, 1811. Witnesses, Henry Mangum, Nancy Duncan and Elizabeth Pope. Probated Feb., 1812.

JOHN HURD—Book B, page 17—Names oldest son, George Hurd, and George's oldest son, John. Son, John, son, William Hurd and William's son, John. Wife, Susannah. Four daughters, Anna Harris, Margaret Rogers, Elizabeth Harris, Susannah Harris. Son, John Hurd, executor. Written Mch. 7, 1812. Witnesses, Samuel Arbuckle, Thad Harmoth and Wm. Sublett.

JAMES LEAVELL, of Spottsylvania Co., Va.—Will Book B, page 204—To Mother. To sister, Nancy Pemberton. Brother, John Leavell. To John Leavell's children, and Edward Leavell. To my brother, William Leavell. Friend, William Pemberton to be executor. Written Oct. 17, 1775. Witness, Henry Pemberton. Proved and recorded, Spottsylvania Co., Va. Court held Aug. 21, 1783. Teste, John Waller, clerk. Robert Chew, clerk of Spottsylvania Co. Court July 27, 1813, certifies the foregoing to be the Will of James Leavell .

ARON LOSSON—Book B, page 70—Names wife, Elizabeth. Non-cupative Will. Probated Oct. Court 1811. Witnesses, James Garrison, Levicy Lawson and David Lawson.

SAMUEL MARKESBERRY—Book B, page 57—Names wife, Isabella. Sons, Isaac, William, John, Samuel Marksberry. Daughters, Rachel Banks, Nancy Fugate, Jane Banks, Milly Franks, and Deliah Hogan. Exec's., Sons, John, Isaac and William Marksberry. Written Dec. 29, 1812. Probated July, 1813. Witnesses, Anna Huffman, Arthur Steen and Patsey Marksberry.

JAMES MONTGOMERY—Book B, apge 50—Names wife, Jane. My children, Stephen Montgomery, Margaret Crow. Exec's., Wife, Jane Montgomery and John Rout. Written Aug. 16, 1811. Witnesses, Henry Speed, George Allen, Lavina Black, and Betsy Speed. Probated July, 1813.

HENRY PAWLING—Book B, page 75—Names wife, Elizabeth Pawling. To Eleanor Watkins, to Polly Watkins, dau. of Eleanor, under age. Exec's., John Boyle, Jr., James Thompson, Samuel McKee. Written Mch. 9, 1812. Witnesses, John Alderson, Joshua Jacobs,

John L. Pawling, Noah Brannon, Benjamin Alderson, William Dunn, William Sampson, Samuel Johnson, A. Jennings. Amendment Mch. 19, 1812. Probated Apr., 1814.

GRIFFIN POND—Book B, page 61—Names wife's son, Dillard Schooler. Wife, Caty Pond. Son, John Pond, under 16 years of age. Daughters, Nancy Stewart, Jenny Brown. Son, Joseph R. Pond. Dau., Massa Harnshall. Exec., Joseph R. Pond. Written Oct. 14, 1813. Witnesses, William Rayston, Timothy Logan, Dicy Clark, and Absolom Hughes. Probated Oct. Court 1813.

JOEL ROBINSON—Names wife, Marget Roberson. Son, Joel Robinson. My heirs, Robert, Jack, John, and George. Daughters, Sarah, Margaret and Jane. Exec's., Sons, Robert and Jack Roberson. Written May 14, 1812. Witnesses, James Steel (or Sleet), Sr., Reuben Sleet, James Coyle. Probated Apr. Court 1813.

PATSEY THORNTON, widow of Caleb Thornton, of Virginia, now of Garrard Co., Ky.—Book B, page 73—Names son, John Thornton. Daughter, Isabell, balance of children, Catherine, Joseph, Nancy and Sarah. Son, Joseph under 21 years of age. Exec., John Thornton. Written Feb. 22, 1814. Witnesses, Agatha Doty and Mary Ford. Probated Apr., 1814.

THOMAS WHEELER—Book B, page 64—Names wife, Clary. My children and Thaddeus Warmath. William Wheeler, and Benjamin Wheeler, Executors. Written Mch. 25, 1813. Witnesses, Tebiller Stone, Ann Taylor. Probated Oct., 1813.

VINCENT WREN—Book B, age 46—Names three eldest children, Sally McMurtry, Woodson Wren and Polly Spillman, daughter, Temperance Wren, son, Thomas Wren. Grand-son, Vincent Wren McMurtry. Wife, Tabitha Wren. Exec's., Wm. Brown, Sr., and Alexander McMurtry. Written Mch. 14, 1810. Witnesses, Wm. Lobb, Nathan Pulliam, Robert Pulliam. Probated Aug. Court 1810.

ESTATE PAPERS

NANCY DENTON—Estate papers, package 331, date Oct. 15, 1821. John Denton, deceased, widow, Nancy Denton, appointed guardian of infant children, Paulina, Polly and James Thompson Denton. Witnesses, Nancy Denton, John Arnold and John Denton.

THOMAS ASHLEY—Bond as guardian for Francis M. Ashley, infant son of William Ashley, deceased and who is devised of Francis Moredend, deceased, of North Carolina. Signed, Thomas M. Ashley and John Faulkner. (This bond was among the marriage bonds).

HARRISON COUNTY, KENTUCKY

ORIGINAL LOT OWNERS. TOWN OF CYNTHIANA, KY.

1796	John Anderson.	1795	Samuel Jameson.
1796	Andrew Cogswell.	1795	Isaac Jameson.
1795	Benjamin Harrison.	1795	William E. Coleman.
1795	George Hamilton.	1795	Robert McBride.
1795	Nicholas Harrison.	1795	James Mitchell.

1795	John McLaughlin.	1798	W. A. Vance.
1795	Lewis Marshall.	1798	Andrew Harrison.
1795	Thomas Nailor.	1799	Samuel Cook.
1795	Ralph Nailor.	1799	Jonathan Jaquess.
1795	James Nailor.	1799	Gavin Morrison.
1795	John Nailor.	1799	William Montjoy.
1795	Aaron Pickens.	1799	James Sharp.
1795	Hugh Stephenson.	1799	E. Warfield.
1796	James Ferguson.	1799	Robert Wilson.
1796	Robert Hinkson.	1800	Samuel Ayres.
1796	Charles Kelso.	1800	James Bliss.
1796	Victor Larimore.	1800	Richard Henderson.
1796	William Moore.	1800	Isaac Miller.
1796	Peter McArthur.	1804	William Ross.
1796	Onner Powell.	1808	John Pickett.
1796	Jerry Shannon.	1808	Garret Burnes.
1796	John Veatch.	1815	Robert Rankin.
1796	Josiah Walker.	1816	John Trimble.
1796	Lewis Timberlake.	1818	R. Harrison.
1797	Reuben Anderson.	1818	Alexander Downing.
1797	James Coleman.	1818	John B. Long.
1797	James Chambers.	1818	John Huddleson.
1797	Robert Forbes.	1819	William Brown.
1797	Horatio Hall.	1819	James Morrison.
1797	Abijah North.	1819	Jerry Robison.
1797	Henry Coleman.	1819	M. Shannon.
1797	Samuel Sharp.	1819	William Stewart.
1797	Thomas Hamilton.	1824	John Douglas.
1797	Joseph Hunter.	1826	Robert Houston.
1798	William Garmony.	1830	Edward Lamb.
1798	John Johnson.	1830	Thomas Odor.
1798	Samuel Lamme.	1838	A. Broadwell.
1798	Andrew Lawell.	1842	T. B. Woodyard.

HARRISON COUNTY WILL AND ESTATES ABSTRACTS

ABDILL, GEORGE—Will Book D, page 336—Written Feb. 1840. Names wife, Abagail. After her death, land equally divided between, Benjamin N. Mullin, infant son of Wm. O. Mullin, deceased and Ann Mariah Wright and Polly Wright, infant daughters of Wellington Wright, deceased. Names Nancy Wright and her children. Executor, Jacob Sodusky, of Bourbon Co. Witnesses, Jackson Hicks and Elizabeth Debruler. Proved Sept. Court 1840.

AKLER (EKLER), JACOB—Will Book D, page 456—Written May 15, 1837. Names wife, Susanna. 4 children, Son, Jacob, Dau's., Catherine and Susanna, son, George. Executors, My trusty friends, Thomson Conrad and George Ecklar. Witnesses, David and George Lemmon. Recorded Jan. 18, 1840.

BARNES, JOHN—Will Book D, page 333—Written May 19, 1836. Names, wife, Milly Barnes. 2 daughters, Sarey and Elizabeth. 8 sons, James, Oliver, William, John W., Daniel, Delany B., Amsterd, and Samuel Barnes. Exec., son, Amsterd Barnes. Witnesses, N. H. Matthews and James Baird. Proved Aug. Court 1840.

BENNETT, ZENAS—Will Book D, page 80—Written Nov. 20, 1836. Names wife, Elizabeth. Children, Nancy, Joel, James, Eliza, Sarah, Martha, Thomas, Carolina, Eleanor and William. Exec's., Wife, Elizabeth, and sons, Joel and James. Witnesses, James McMurtry and Peter Carder. Proved Aug. Court 1837.

BOYD, ALLICE M.—Division of Estate—Will Book D, page 284—Dec. Court, 1839. 3 Heirs-at-Law, Ann Boyd, John S. Boyd and Montgomery W. Boyd. Admrt., J. B. Righter, Hugh Levi and Hugh Frazier. Recorded Jan. Court 1840.

BROMELEY, JOHN—Will Book D, page 250—Noncupative Will— Names wife, Matilda Bromeley. Written Nov. 8, 1839. Witnesses, Catherine Bromeley, Joseph Brumley, Elizabeth Clark and George M. Clark. Proved by oaths of Joseph Bromley and George M. Clark. Nov. 21, 1839.

BROWN, SAMUEL—Will Book D, page 401—Names wife, Dorcas Brown. Children, James Brown, Nancy Tisdale, William Brown, Hiram Brown, Elizabeth Brown, John W. Brown, Mary E. Brown, and Franklin Brown. Extrx., Wife, Dorcas Brown, and Executor, Benjamin Branson. Witnesses, Thomas January and Abraham Warth. Will written Mch. 2, 1841. Proved June 18, 1841.

AMMERMAN, DANIEL—Will Book E, page 182—Names wife, Zuba Ammerman. "All my children." Sons, James, William, Joel, Amos; daughters, Rebecca,Tabitha. Executrix, wife, Zuba. Will written Oct. 16, 1844. Proved Nov. 21, 1844. Witnesses, J. R. Curry and G. C. Frazier.

ANDERSON, ISAAC NEWTON—Will Book E, page 497—"To my mother, Mary Vanfansen To Telitha Shawhan. To brother, John Anderson. Exec., John Shawhan. Written June 30, 1847. Teste, J. C. Frazer and Abram Keller. Probated Aug. 9, 1847.

BARNETT, PETER—Will Book E, page 439—Names children of Enoch McGilton, children of Thomas Philips, dau., Margaret Barnett, grand-dau's., Nancy Tilton and Nancy Heddleson, son, Lucas Barnett. Exec's., Sons, Lucas and Wesley Barnett. Written, May 1842. Probated Jan. 1847. Teste, Andrew Moore and Stephen Harber.

BREWSAUGH—Will Book E, page 48—Names Richard, John James and Berton Brewsaugh. Dau., Margaret. Teste, Moss Monson and Joseph W. Tate. Written Oct. 16, 1842. Probated Nov. 1842.

BROOKS, WILLIAM—Will Book E, page 179—Names son, Paschal Brooks. Wife, Margaret Brooks. Youngest chillren under age to equal older children. Dau., Angeline Brooks. Exec's., Sons, Paschal, Wm. M., and Colby Brooks. Written Sept. 6, 1844. Probated Oct. 1844. Teste, James Henry, W. W. Steward and Robert Biggers.

BOYERS, JACOB, SR.—Will Book E, page 76—Names wife, Dorithy. Dau., Milly, "rest of my daughters." Exec., Son, John. Written Sept. 25, 1833. Probated June 1843. Teste, Samuel Endicott.

BUMBARGER, MICHAEL—Will Book E, page 218—Names wife, Catherine. Dau., Mary Delf, formally Mary Bumbarger. Son, William, son, John. Exec's., Sons, John and William Bumbarger. Teste, W. Moore, Daniel Ammerman and Andrew Scott. Written Dec. 26, 1842. Probated Dec. 1844.

CRAGMYLES, JAMES—Will Book E, page 176—Son, Washington, Alexander, son of Washington. Son, Enoch and Enoch's children namely James W., William, dau., Susan and son, John. Witnesses,

Hugh Newell, Abel Pulliam. Written, Sept. 23, 1844. Probated Oct. 1844.

OLD DEEDS, HARRISON COUNTY, KENTUCKY

(Copied by Mrs. H. K. McAdams and Mrs. Joseph Beard, Sr.)

1795. Deed Book 1, page 40. Indenture between, Benjamin Harrison, Morgan Vanmeter, Jeremiah Robinson, John Wall, Sr. and Henry Coleman, Trustees of Town of Cynthiana, of one part; and George Hamilton, of other part.

1794. Deed Book 1, page 36. Deed between Christopher Shuck, one part, and Francis Hestler and Mary, his wife, of other part. Signed, Francis Hestler, Mary Hestler. Witnesses, John Cook, Jacob Latherman and Henry Gray.

ORDER BOOK, 1796

Court for Harrison Co., held Tuesday, April 5, 1796. Present, Samuel McIlvain, Wm. E. Boswell, Robert Hinkson, Esq. George Reading and Samuel McMillan, qualified as Justices of the County of Harrison. On motion of Samuel McMillan, ordered that Will E. Boswell, Thomas Craig and Joseph Ward, be appointed Commissioners, under act of Assembly, to ascertain the boundaries of land to establish the beginning of an entry of 5000 acres in the names of Thomas Holt and Samuel McMillan, on South fork of Mill Creek.

Tavern licence granted Adam Zumalt, who gave bond with George Huffman, security.

Robert Ellison, appointed guardian to James Curry, Betsy Curry and John Curry, infants of John Curry, deceased, who gave bond with Thomas Martin security.

Benjamin Goodwin, appointed Constabe, with Mooses Goodwin his security.

Inventure and Appraisement of Estate of Samuel Turnan, deceased.

Deed from Jas. Trabue, to Elkanah Jennings, proved.

Deed from Trustees of Cynthiana to Samuel Tharp.

Administration of Estate of William Thompson, deceased, granted to David Shields, with Samuel Shields, security.

Appointed Appraisers, Joseph Bell, Lemuel Barritt, Hugh Bell and Samuel Herons, of estate William Thompson, deceased.

Deed from William Little to Robert Ellison. Proved by Thomas Martin and Jacob Martin .

1796. June Court. A bill of Sale from Nancy Robinson, wife of W. Robinson, to Leonard Stump.

George Rees, appointed guardian of Davis Rees, infant of Joel Rees, deceased, and gave bond with Peter Barret, security.

Deed from Benjamin Harrison to Robert Griffith.

Deed from James Parberry to Wm. Campbell.

Deed from John Smith, attorney in fact for William Woods, to Samuel McElvain, proved by John McElvain, witness.

Inventory and appraisement of estate of Daniel Rankin, deceased, recorded.

Deed from Josiah Watson, by John Taylor, attorney in fact, to Gerrard Green, proved.

Same from same to Thomas Green, proved. Same from James Thomas, to Robert Lowry, proved. Same from Josiah Watson, by John Taylor, attorney in fact, to Samuel McMillen. Proved by H. Colman.

Tavern licence granted William Stafford.

LINCOLN COUNTY, STANFORD COURT HOUSE

(Copied by Mrs. Joseph Beard, Sr.)

ABSTRACTS OF WILLS AND DEEDS

JAMES ALLIN—Will Book B, page 255—To son, Hartwell Allin. To dau., Lucy Giles. My children, viz: James, Churchwell, Thomas, Rebecca, Gabriel R., and Ludwell Allin. Exec., Son, Hartwell Allin. Written July 28, 1804. Witnesses, Joseph Ballinger, David Simpson, Daniel Hudgeons. Probated Oct. 8, 1804.

WILLIAM BAKER—Book C, page 39—Names wife, Patsy. My children. My father-in-law, Sowell Woolfolk. Exec's., Wife, Patsy, Pierce Wade and John Warren. Written Dec. 2, 1806. Witnesses, John Welsh, Wm. Wade, John Wade, Sr., Charles Worthington. Probated Dec. 2, 1806

EDWARD BALL—Book A, page 159—Children, William, Elizabeth, Shadrack Chave. Execs., Wife and son, William. Witnesses, Joseph Helm, Wm. Marshall and David White. Written Sept. 29, 1788. Probated Oct. 21, 1788.

JOHN BARNETT, Jr.—Book B, page 272—To children of half-sister, Polly, wife of Elisha Moore. To Anna Barnett, daughter of Robert Barnett. To William McNeely, of Montgomery Co., Ky. To Wm. McNeely's daughter, Polly. To children of my brother, James Barnett. To chidlren of Joseph Hall and my sister, Anna Hall, his wife. Execs., Joseph Hall and John Welsh. Written ———. Witnesses, Joseph Welsh, Gabriel Lackey, and Andrew Hall. Probated Apr. 8, 1805.

JAMES BERRY—Book A, page 9—Daughter, Elizabeth. Wife, Christina and unborn child. Step-son, John Wilson. Execs., Wife and Ebenezer Miller, and John Smith. Witnesses, John Kearriel, Samuel Dennis, Thomas Denton. Written Mch. 10, 1781. Probated Jan. 15, 1782.

JOHN BERRY—Book A, page 189—Names two sons, James and William. Daughters, Betsy, Polly, Hannah, Sally, Peggy and Jane. Two sons, Joseph and John. Wife, Hannah. Executrix Wife. Witnesses, James Piggot, James Kerr and Isaac Fallis. Written Aug. 10, 1789. Probated July 20, 1790.

ALEXANDER BLAIN—Book C, page 54—To wife, Hannah. To Nancy Shackleford, James Blain and Hannah McKinley. To son, John. To daughter, Sarah Murrel. Execs., Hannah Blain and James Blain. To son, George Blain. To legatees, Margaret Gay, Jean Montgomery, Nancy Shackleford, Alcy Hundly and Sarah Murrel. Written Apr. 10, 1807. Witnesses, Ezra Morrison, Adam Carpenter, Conrad Carpenter. Probated Mch. 10, 1806.

SAMUEL BOWDERY—Book A, page 191—Names wife, Elizabeth. Two youngest daughters, Jemimah and Martha. Execs., Son, James and wife, Elizabeth. Witnesses, John Bailey and Francis Cutting. Written May 1, 1790. Probated Dec. 21, 1790.

JOHN BOWMAN—Book A, page 72—Names wife, Elizabeth. Son, John. Brothers, Abraham and Isaac. Sisters, Mary Stephens,

Elizabeth Ruddle, Sarah Wright, Reginer Durley and Rebecca Brinker. Exec's., Wife and brothers, Abraham and Isaac. Witnesses, Joseph Love, James Cox, Richard Foley and Wilson Maddox. Written Feb. 5, 1784. Probated Aug. 17, 1784.

ROY BRASSFIELD—Book B, page 163—Of Mercer Co., Ky. Names, wife, Mary. Children, James, Elizabeth and Leonard Brassfield. Exec's., Friend, John Edwards and my wife, Mary. Written Apr. 4, 1791. Witnesses, Reuben Baker, Robert Baker. Probated Oct. 18, 1796.

SAMUEL BRIGGS—Book B, page 52—To wife, Mary. To sons, Benjamin and Joseph. Daughters, Jean Todd and Elizabeth. To children, Margaret Drake, Elizabeth Briggs, Hannah, Rachel and Joseph Briggs, under 21 years of age. Elizabeth, Hannah and Rachel are youngest daughters. Exec's., Wife, Mary and son, Benjamin. Written May 27, 1792. Witnesses, John Magill, Hugh Logan and Benjamin Logan. Probated Oct. 16, 1792.

WILLIAM BUCHANAN—Book C, page 107—Names wife, Isabel. Sons, John, Andrew, William. Daus., Betsy, Polly, Agnes. Exec's., Wife, Isabel and son, John. Written Jan. 6, 1804. Witnesses, Moses McCarley and Daniel Persire. Probated Sept. 14, 1807.

EDWARD BULGER—Book A, page 99—Names brother, Daniel Bulger. Friend, Joseph Jones. Friend, Abram James, Capt. John Smith, Jonathan Drake, Thomas Guess. Witnesses, John Reed, Henry French and William Crowl. Written Aug. 21, 1782. Probated Jan. 21, 1783.

BENJAMIN BURCH—Book B, page 90—To wife, Jane. Children, namely, Thomas, Sarah, William, Elizabeth, Benjamin, Mozy, John, Mary, Jane Cheadle, and Hannah Burch. Exec's., Wife, Jane and son, Benjamin. Witnesses, John Cook, John Burch and William Mode. Written Feb. 21, 1794. Probated May 20, 1794.

JEREMIAH BYARS—Book B, page 170—Estate of Jeremiah Byers, deceased. Between wife and 3 children. To widow, Elizabeth. To Edmund Byers, son of Jeremiah Byers, deceased. To Nancy Smith, wife of Jesse Smith. To John Byers, son of Jeremiah Byers, deceased. Nov. 18, 1796. By James Thompson and Wm. Bryant. Recorded Mch. 15, 1797.

JOHN CALDWELL—Book B, page 111—To mother. To brother, Andrew. Written ——. Witnesses, James Davis and John Batiste. Probated Mch. 7, 1795.

ISAAC CAMPBELL—Book B, page 59—To brothers, Charles, James and younger brother, William. To sister, Betsy. If brother, William moves to Kentucky this fall. Exec's., Brothers, Charles and James. Witnesses, John Hall, Peter Hegins, William Hall and A. Schedeele. Codicil. Mother is mentioned. Written Apr. 17, 1783. Probated Feb. 21, 1792.

JOHN CARPENTER—Book A, page 83—Names wife, Elizabeth. Son, George, daughters, Margaret and Mary. My three children. Brothers, Adam and George. Exec's., Wife and Conrod Carpenter and Adam Carpenter. Witnesses, James Coppedge, John Litter and Isaac Shelby. Written Nov. 19, 1784. Probated Feb. 15, 1785.

JOHN CASSEY—Book A, page 189—Names wife, Margaret. Children,

William, James, Agnes and Marthew. Exec's., friend, Hugh Logan. Witnesses, John Magill, Hannah Barry and Esther Dougherty. Written Apr. 28, 1790. Probated July 20, 1790.

EDWARD CHAPMAN—Book A, page 158—Names four children, viz: Edward, William, Lewis and Sally. Wife. Exec., ————. Witnesses, Isaac Farris, Benjamin Talbert, Jerusha Lovas and Daniel Chapman. Written July 26, 1788. Probated Sept. 16, 1788.

JAMES CLOYD—Book B, page 242—To wife. To Aggy, Polly and Nancy Nash, daughters of sister, Peggy. To Thomas and Tramp Nash, sons of sister, Peggy. To Charles Lockridge, sister Polly's son, To Polly Hood, sister Polly's daughter. To John and James Lockridge and oldest living daughter of Nancy Robertson, my sister Polly's daughter. Exec's., William and Benjamin Logan. Written Apr. 10, 1804. Witnesses, James Dunn, Solomon Laurence, Jas. Cloyd. Probated May 14, 1804.

WILKENSON CONNELLY—Book B, page 167—Inventory of estate of Wilkenson Connelly, deceased, returned and recorded Oct. 18, 1796.

WILLIAM CONWELL—Book C, page 42—Names wife, Esther. Eldest son, Isaac Conwell. Youngest son, William. Daughter, Peggy Conwell. Executrix, Wife, Esther. Written Nov. 23, 1803. Witnesses, John Davis, John Conwell, Thomas Royall, John Chance. Probated Dec. 12, 1803.

ANN COWAN—Book M, page 14—Names son, Samuel Moor. Daughters, Peggy McRoberts, Polly Ann Blanks. Exec's., Anareal McRoberts, Willis Blanks, Joseph Sprowl. Written Apr. 25, 1822. Witnesses, William Farris, and Thomas Price. Probated Apr. Court 1829.

JOHN CRAIG—Book C, page 60—To William Craig, son of John. To his brother, John Craig. To David, James and Charles. To son, James Craig and his brother, William. To son-in-law, Samuel Beard. To daughters, Sarah Beard, and Mary Cowan. To John Cowan. To youngest son, John Craig. To William Craig, son of James, when of age. Exec's., Son, John Craig and son-in-law, Samuel Beard. Written Jan. 22, 1800. Witnesses, George Weatherford, and Andrew Shanklin. Probated Nov. 8, 1802.

SAMUEL CRAIG—Book B, page 156—Estate of Samuel Craig, deceased. Appraised Nov., 1795. Recorded July 19, 1795.

SAMUEL CRAIG, Sr.—Book B, page 268—Land of Samuel Craig, Sr., deceased, divided as follows, to Zachariah Tucker and Polly, his wife, late Polly Craig. To Pleasant Tucker and Sally, his wife, late Sally Craig. To Samuel Craig. To John Craig. July 9, 1804. By John Gilbert, James Logan and James ————.

JAMES COX—Book B, page 148—Inventory of estate of James Cox, deceased. June 3, 1796.

JOHN CROW—Book C, page 27—Names eldest daughter, Elizabeth Messick. To daughters, Martha Jaeson and Mary Flack. To sons, William Crow and Abraham Crow. To two daughters, Sarah and Ann Crow. Exec's., Son, Abraham and daughters, Sarah and Ann Crow. Written July 10, 1793. Witnesses, Morias Hansbrough, Henry Orkes and William Crow. Probated Aug. 10, 1801.

WILLIAM CROW—Book H, page 140—Names wife, Patience. Sons, Walter and James Crow. To son, Benjamin. To daughters, Elizabeth Pierce and Rachel Hambleton. To Ann Givings. To Mary Moore. To Sarah Cooke. To Margaret Hopper. To Maria Bledsoe. To Matilda Letcher. Exec's., George Givings, Samuel Moore, William Cook, Thomas Hambleton, Joseph Hopper, Willis Bledsoe and Stephens Letcher. Written Sept. 16, 1820. Probated Feb. 21, 1821. Witnesses, E. McDowell, and Joshua Barber.

SAMUEL DAVIS—Book B, page 211—One-third part of estate of Samuel Davis, deceased, allotted to Jane Davis, widow. To John Davis. To Patsy Davis, wife of William Owsley. To Jinny Davis. To Polly Davis. To Samuel Davis. To Betsy Davis. To Joseph Davis. Signed, Jonathan Forbis, John James, William Owsley and John Hargrove. Recorded May 8, 1798. Teste, Willis Green, C. C.

ANDREW DODD—Book B, page 233—To brother, John. To wife, Sarah. Executrix, Wife, Sarah. Written Sept. 5, 1798. Witnesses, Christopher Greenup, Samuel P. Duvall and John Mansfield. Probated Nov. 13, 1798.

CHARLES DONNELLY—Book B, page 151—To wife, for raising children. Written Feb. 25, 1796. Witnesses, Wm. Nash, John McKenney, Thomas McMurray. Probated July 19, 1796.

ANDREW DUNCAN—Book A, page 130—Names sister, Elizabeth Buchanan's son, Andrew. Sister, Mary Craig's son, Andrew. Sister, Jean McKenney's daughter, Jenny. Exec's., Brothers-in-law, John Edmiston and John McKenney. Witnesses, William Edmiston, Robert Harreld and John Buchanan. Written Mch. 25, 1784. Probated Feb. 21, 1786.

JOHN DUGEAN—Book B, age 274—Names wife. Sons, William and John. To other beloved son and daughter and sons-in-law, Armstrong Kerr and John Rogers and my daughters, Polly Dugean and Peggy Dugean and my son, Sublett Dugean. To daughter, Patsy Dugean. Executrix, Wife. Written Apr. 10, 1804. Witnesses, Wm. Shanks, James Henderson and John Shanks. Probated June 10, 1805.

JAMES ESTILL—Book B, page 242—To wife, Rachel. To Benjamin, Walles, James, and Jonathan Estill. Witnesses, David Gass, Samuel Estill. Written May 4, 1781. Probated Jan. 22, 1783.

NATHAN FARRIS—Book B, page 176—Estate of Nathan Farris, deceased, appraised and recorded May 9, 1797. By John Wilkenson, John McQuerry and John Caldwell.

DAVID FLOYD—Book A, page 165—Names wife, Sarah. Sons, Benjamin, George, John, David. Two daughters, Mary and Gracy. Grand-daughter, Mary Singleton, daughter of my daughter, Sally Singleton, deceased. Exec's., Sons, Benjamin, George and John. Witnesses, John Bryant, Robert Singleton, and Nathan Lamme. Written Sept. 12, 1787. Probated Dec. 16, 1788.

WILLIAM FORD—Book C, page 1—To wife, Sarah. To son, William. To Charles Ford. To James Tinsley. To Daniel McElroy in part of his wife, my daughter, Sally Ford. Written July 5, 1801. Exec's., Sons, William and Charles, James Tinseley, Daniel McElroy. Witness ————. Probated Oct. 10, 1803.

PAUL FROMAN—Book A, page 46—Names wife, Elizabeth. Sons, Paul and Jacob. My daughters. My daughters, who are deceased, to their husbands or children. Exec., Son, Jacob. Witnesses, John Gritton, John Summut, John Woolman and Christian Samet. Written Apr. 28, 1783. Probated May 20, 1783.

THOMAS GAY—Book C, page 52—Names sons, Thomas, Samuel, James, daughter, Patsy, sons, John and Alexander Gay, Hannah Bailey, Elizabeth Briggs and Sarah Huston. Written Apr. 14, 1806. Witnesses, John Blain, William Tate and James Barnett. Probated Dec. 13, 1806. Exec's., Sons, Alexander and John Gay and John Blane.

JOHN GIBSON—Book B, page 113—Estate of John Gibson, deceased, divided May 19, 1795.

WILLIAM GILES—Book C, page 43—Names wife, Lucy. Brother, Ephraim Giles. Written July 5, 1805. Witnesses, Isaac Blain, Anne Blain, John Bailey. Probated Aug. 8, 1803.

WILLIAM GILLAS—Book A, page 64—Names brother, Thomas. William, son of Thomas Gillas. Elizabeth Cathers, Edward Cathers. Exec., ————————. Witnesses, John Jameson, and James Scott. Written Apr. 2, 1783. Probated Apr. 21, 1784.

JAMES GILMORE—Book C, page 47—Names wife, Jinney Gilmore. My half-brother, Robert Logan. To John Gilbert. To Samuel Porter. Written Sept. 2, 1801. Witnesses, James Logan and James Tinsley. Probated Mch. 14, 1803.

JAMES GIVENS—Book C, page 33—To son Samuel. Sons, Robert, James, John, Benjamin. To wife, Martha. To daughters, Sally Campbell and Martha Givens. Written May 1, 1801. Witnesses, George Givens, Isaac Shelby. Probated July 15, 1801.

MARTHA GIVENS, widow of James Givens, deceased—Book C, page 76—Exec's., Sons, Benjamin and Samuel. Written Aug. 18, 1802. Witnesses, Arthur M. Smith and John Givens. Probated Apr. 11, 1803.

JOHN GIVENS—Book B, page 95—To wife, Rebecca. To two oldest sons, Samuel and John Givens. To my sons, Robert, James and Allen. To my son, Eliezer. To son, Robert's daughter, Sarah Mitchell Givens. Exec's., Sons, Robert and Eliezer. Written Apr. 19, 1794. Witnesses, John Magill, Wm. Magill, Sarah Campbell. Probated July 15, 1794.

JOHN GOOD—Book C, page 23—Names wife, Jinny. To my son, Timothy. To daughters, Nancy and Ellender. Father, Thomas Good. Exec's., Major Joseph Gray of Washington Co., Ky., and Thomas Hutchins of Lincoln Co., Ky., and my wife. Written Apr. 6, 1800. Witnesses, William Cooley, Joseph Ayre, John Cooley. Probated July 8, 1800.

JAMES GORDON—Book A, page 104—Names wife and all my children. Exec's., Wife, Martin Nall and Edward Darnaby. Witnesses, Edmund Ware, Henry Nixon, Seuky Ware and Edward Darnaby. Written Nov. 16, 1784. Probated July 19, 1785.

JOHN GORDON—Book B, page 201—Estate of John Gordon, deceased, appraised. Elizabeth Davis, late widow of John Gordon, deceased, allotted her part. Teste, John Thompson, Newton Curd, Jacob Woodson. Date Oct. 10, 1797. To Ambrose Gordon. To John and James Gordon. To Elizabeth and Janetta Gordon. To William Gordon. To Mary Gordon, now wife of Paulser Smelser. To Nancy Gordon, wife of Abner Martin. Date Oct., 1797.

ANN GRAVES—Book B, age 106—Dower allowed to Ann Graves from husband, William Graves, deceased estate. Dec. 16, 1794. Signed Wm. Manifee, Daniel Ousley, Charles Warren.

ALEXANDER HANNAH—Book A, page 191—Names wife, Isable. Sisters, Elizabeth Wylie, Jean Moffet, Margaret Galbraith. Children. Brother, John Hanna. Exec's., Wife and Robert Moffett. Witnesses, James Davis, Hugh Galbraith, and Robert Moor. Written July 21, 1785. Probated Sept. 21, 1790.

SILAS HARLAN—Book A, page 2—Names brother, Jehu Harlan. Brothers, Elijah and James. "Due me from Stephen Harlan of father's estate." Exec., brother, James. Written Jan. 7, 1780. Witnesses, Jeremiah Briscoe, Charles Farguson and Jacob Harlan. Probated Jan. 22, 1783.

NATHANIEL HART, of Lincoln Co., Va.—Book A, page 4—Names wife, Sarah and my two sons, Simpson and Nathaniel Hart, and my two brothers, David and Thomas to be executors. To each of my nine children to wit: Keziah Thompson, Susannah Hart, Simpson Hart, Nathaniel Hart, John Hart, Mary Ann Hart, Cumberland Hart, Chinai Hart, Thomas Richard Green Hart and unborn child. Land not to exceed 1000 acres each. Witnesses, Wm. Calk, Nicholas George and Nicholas Anderson. Written June 27, 1782. Probated Jan. 22, 1783. (Note, Collins history of Ky., Vol. 1—Page 512, about Col. Hart and family).

WILLIAM HENDERSON—Book B, page 255—Names wife, Mary Henderson. Exec's, Samuel Beard, my wife and John Craig. Written Dec. 8, 1804. Witnesses, William Davis, David Thompson, Peter Bainbridge. Probated Dec. 10, 1804.

JOHN HENRY, of Sullivant Co., N. C.—Book A, page 66—Names my five children, Samuel, Thomas, James, Jesse and John. Wife, Mary. Land I received for service as soldier in Illinois in 1778. Exec's., Brother, Hugh Henry. Witnesses, Ben Porter, David Gwin and David Henry. Written Dec. 13, 1779. Probated Aug. 19, 1783.

MICHAEL HESS—Book B, page 100—Inventory of estate of Michael Hess, deceased, on June 27, 1794. Appraisers, Stephenson Huston, Christopher Rice, William Dinwiddie. Recorded Nov. 18, 1794.

WILLIAM HICKS—Book A, page 10—Names odlest son, John, second son, William, wife, Agnes and rest of my children. Exec's., Wife and William Cleery. Witnesses, James Davis, William Young and Samuel Gordon. Written Aug. 4, 1780. Probated May 15, 1781.

JOSEPH JACKSON—Book B, page 188—To children of my eldest daughter Writter Houneler, Polly and James Houneler. To daughter, Frances Levi's two children, Jean and Betsy Levi. To daughter, Elizabeth Brunson. To daughter, Polly Lee. To daughter, Jean Ewing. My son, Ephraim Jackson. Exec's., Son, Ephraim and Zachariah Shackleford. Written May 18, 1797. Witnesses, Zachariah Shackleford, David Logan, David Arnett. Probated Oct. 10, 1797.

NOEL JOHNSON—Book C, page 37—Names wife, Tabitha and my children, namely: Tandy, Thomas, David, Benjamin, Susannah, Mary Sweeny, Patsy Rice, Nancy Alcorn and Matilda Johnson. Son, John. Exec's., Sons, Tandy, Benjamin, and David. Written July 15, 1802. Witnesses, Val Peyton, John McAnelly and Jesse Carter. Probated Jan. 10, 1803.

JACOB JONES—Book B, page 146—Names sons, Abram, Thomas. Daughters, Mary Knots, Elizabeth Jones, Sarah Jones. To son, Moses Jones. To wife, Elizabeth. Executrix, Wife, Elizabeth. Written May 19, 1780. Witnesses, John Milner and Reuben Harrison. Probated Mch. 15, 1796.

JOHN JOSLING—Book B, page 92—To my seven children, John, William, Daniel, Benjamin, Elizabeth Evans, Molly Evans, Sally Whittle (or Whitley). Two grand-children, James and Lucy Joslin, children of James Joslin. Exec's., Edmund Powell and William Patton. Written June 29, 1793. Witnesses, Edmund Powell, William Patton and Jane Patton. Probated July 15, 1794.

JOSEPH LANKFORD—Book A, page 106—Names wife and my children, Joseph, youngest daughter, Sarah and my other children. Exec's., Wife and James Brown. Witnesses, James Curry, Daniel Brown and Edward Taylor. Written Sept. 1, 1783. Probated July 20, 1785.

JOSEPH LINDSAY—Book A, page 6—Names wife, Ann. To Joseph Lindsay, Jr., my son. To Fulton Lindsay, Jr., when 21 years old. To heirs of William Poge, deceased. To Lindsay Thompson. To brother, Arthur Lindsay. Execs., Wife, Ann and brother, William Lindsay. Written July 11, 1782. Witnesses, John Kennady, John Ray. Probated Jan. 21, 1783.

NATHAN LINN—Book B, page 78—Estate of Nathan Linn settled by Ozeas Welch and Hannah, his wife, Administrators. Nov. 19, 1793.

JAMES LOGAN—Book A, page 156—Names wife, Martha. Children, James Mathew, Hugh, David, Jonathan, Charles, Martha, son, Robert Allison. Friend, Benjamin Logan. Witnesses, Alexander Gaston, William Main, and Mary Gaston. Written May 23, 1787. Probated July 15, 1788.

WILLIAM LOGAN—Book B, age 154—To wife. To daughter, Margaret Forbis. To sons, Hugh, James, William, and Benjamin when 21 years old. To daughters, Jean, Nancy Jerusha and Catherine. Exec's., Wife and William Hamilton and Hugh Logan. Witnesses, Philip Lumpkin, James McCown and John Bird. Probated July 19, 1796.

WILLIAM McBRIDE—Book A, page 7—Names wife, Martha. Sons, William, Lapsley, daughters, Sarah, Martha, Elizabeth, Mary. Exec's., Wife, John Lapsley and James Davis. Written Oct. 3, 1781. Probated Jan. 21, 1783. Book B, page 81. Estate of Wm. Bride recorded Nov. 13, 1790.

JOHN McMURTRY, of Kentucky County—Book A, page 35—Names land at Spring, called Wm. McMurtry's. Son, James, land at Holston, Va. Sons, Samuel, William under age. Wife, Mary. Witnesses, John Hutton, James Hutton, William McMurtry. Written July 7, 1780. Probated Feb. 18, 1782.

ALXEANDER MANNERS—Book C, page 11—Wife, Millender and children, when of age. Written Feb. 18, 1807. Witnesses, John, Warren, Hezekiah Perdun. Probated Mch. 9, 1807.

ANN MARSHALL—Book B, page 247—Dower allotted to Ann Marshall, widow of Markham Marshall, by Wm. Patton and Wm. Warren. July 22, 1803. To John Marshall. To Wm. Marshall. To Bailey Marshall, Charles Marshall, and James Marshall, legatees of Markham Marshall, deceased. May 11, 1804.

MARKHAM MARSHALL—Book C, page 25—To daughters, Mary Powell, Anne Green, Elizabeth Montgomery, Jane Marshall. Son, Charles. Son, James. My wife. Sons, John, William, Bailey and James. Exec's., Sons, John, and Bailey Marshall and my wife. Written Oct. 17, 1801. Witnesses, Jane Marshall, Charles Marshall, James Alcorn, George Helm. Probated July 11, 1813.

ISAAC MAYFIELD—Book B, page 129—To son, Isaac. To my wife, Jean Mayfield. My children. Grand-son, James Parks Mayfield, son of my daughter, Susannah Mayfield. Exec's., Two sons, George and Isaac. Written Mch. 17, 1795. Witnesses, Joseph Hicks and Henry Huffman. Probated Aug. 12, 1795.

JOHN MILLER—Book B, page 142—Inventory of John Miller, deceased, estate Mch. 15, 1796 (or 5). Henry Ortkes, Thomas Bale, William Crow.

JOHN MILNER—Book B, page 231—Names wife, Sarah and small chidlren. To sons, Mark, Luke, John, Beverly, and Robert Dudley Milner. Alice Lacey, Peggy Bates, children of my first wife. Mark Milner's part, if he should die, to be divided between last wife, Sarah and her children. Ten last children begotten by Sarah. Written 1798. Teste, Joseph Glover, Wm. Glover and Isabel Glover. Probated May 14, 1799.

EDWARD MOORE—Book B, page 49—Names wife. Sons, William, Samuel, George, Jonathan, Joshua. Isaac, son of Edward Moore, deceased. Daughters, Maryanne, Sally Anne. Exec's., Sons, William and Samuel. Witnesses, Jonathan Forbis, William Magill and Hugh Logan. Written May 20, 1792. Probated Oct. 16, 1792.

ROBERT MONTGOMERY—Book A, page 183—Wife, Mary. John Simpson. Sons, Joseph, James, William, Thomas, Samuel and Robert. Exec's., Sons, James, William and Samuel. Witnesses, John Montgomery, Nathaniel Evins, Samuel Montgomery. Written May 15, 1789. Probated Mch. 16, 1790.

WILLIAM MOODY—Book B, page 172—Noncupative will of Wm. Moody, who deceased in Pittsylvania Co., Va., Oct. 22, 1794. To wife, Judith. To sister, Mary Moody. To mother, Elizabeth Moody. My sisters and brothers and my two daughters, Elizabeth Buford Moody and Mary Moody. Exec., Father-in-law, William Buford. Committed to writing and proven in Pittsylvania Co. Apr. 20, 1795 on oaths of Blanks Moody, William Easly and Littleberry Wells. Recorded Aug. 17, 1795, in Lincoln Co., Ky.

ROBERT MOORE—Book B, page 280—Names wife, Anne Moore, and three children, son, Samuel. Daughters, Margaret and Polly Ann Moore. Written June 25, 1805. Execs., Wife, Ann and son, Samuel Moore. Witnesses, John Wilkerson, James Davis and Wm. Farris. No probate.

WILLIAM MORGAN—Book B, page 190—To wife. Son, Joseph. My five children, James, William, Joseph, Daniel and Sally and my daughter, Hannah Bruce's children. To daughter, Mary Settle. To daughter, Elizabeth McCormick. To son, Charles. To daughter, Phebe Fishback. To daughter, Alice Fishback. To daughter, Rosamond Settle. To Polly Settle, daughter of Rosamond Settle. To William Bruce. To James Withers, husband of my daughter, Frances Withers. Exec's., Sons, James, William, Joseph and Daniel. Written Apr. 29 ,1797. Witnesses, William Spillman, John Dodds, and Luke Robinson. Probated Oct. 10, 1797.

JACOB MYERS—Book B, page 287—Mentions Lewis Myers. Brother, Christian Myers. My Brother's children, Valentine, Peter and Jacob Myers. Rebecca Myers, daughter of Jacob Myers. Exec's., Lewis Myers, James Thompson of Lincoln Co., Ky. and David Shearer of Frederick Co., Md. Written Oct. 1, 1796. Witnesses, John Reid, Enoch Burdell and Margaret Ellison. Probated Nov. 8, 1802.

JAMES NICHOLSON—Book C, page 22—Dated Apr. 19, 1797. Names wife, Sarah. To son, Robert. Son, William. Son, James. To Betsy Robertson. Execs., William Owsley and Francis Davis. Witnesses, George Reed, Richard Morris, Nancy Reed, William Owsley, Thomas Davis. Probated July 8, 1800.

JOHN POTTS—Book A, page 98—Names wife, Naomi. Son, David. Daughter, Sarah Burks. Grand-son, John, son of Amos Potts. Exec's., Son, David and friend, Thomas Harbison. Witnesses, James McCullock, Margaret Harbison and William Shaw. Written Oct. 28, 1783. Probated June 21, 1785.

JOHN PRESTON—Book C, page 24—My children. Daughter, Jane. To William, son of Jane. Written July 28, 1800. Witnesses, Wm. Graves, Christian Perkins. Probated Mch. 9, 1801.

ABRAHAM PRICE—Book B, page 225—To daughter, Rebecca Price. To wife, Sarah. My eight children, namely, Moses, Sarah, Manafee, Samuel, Susannah Clarey, Elizabeth, Meguamy Rebecca Price, Isaac Price, Marah Evans. To heirs of son, Benjamin. Exec's., Wife, Sarah and son, Isaac Price. Written July 29, 1797. Witnesses, Daniel Owsley, Henry Ousley, and Wm. Manafee. Probated July 10, 1798.

MICAJAH PROCTOR—Book C, page 44—Names wife, Elizabeth. 3 sons, Robert, Jeremiah and Micajah. Daughters, Sarah Proctor, Polly Nichols, Martha, Betsy, Jinny, Phanny. To grand-son, Micajah Proctor. Exec's., Wife, Elizabeth and son, Robert and Robert Brank. Written May 20, 1800. Witnesses, Robert Brank, Robert Henery, Robert Proctor. Probated Oct. 12, 1801.

WILLIAM RAMSEY—Book B, page 136—Wm. Ramsey, now of Lincoln Co., Ky., and late of Philadelphia, Pa. To James McFerren. Exec., James McFerren. Written Oct. 16, 1795. Witnesses, Edward Young, Polly Young, Thomas Montgomery. Probated Dec. 15, 1795.

CHARLES RADCLIFFE—Book A, page 9—Names wife and three children. Exec., Daniel Radcliffe. Witnesses, Azor Rees, Thomas Moore and Joseph Scott. Written Nov. 13, 1780. Probated Feb. 20, 1781,

JOHN REED—Book C, page 104—John Reed the elder. To wife, Elizabeth. To children, William, John, Johathan, Thomas. To Mary Rall. To Sarah Green. To Lettice Hughes. Exec's., Son, John Reed and son-in-law, Willis Green. Written Nov. 1, 1806. Witnesses, Walter Crow, David Myers, John Withers, Garland Withers. Codicil, mentions grand-children, James Birney and Nancy Birney, chidlren of late daughter, Martha Birney. Witnesses to Codicil, Anne Reed, Susannah Robison and Aaron Wilhoit. Probated Oct. 12, 1807.

HANNAH ROBERTSON—Book B, page 67—To son, Luke Robison. To daughters, Hannah and Nelly. To children of my daughter, Nelly and my daughter, Kitty's four children. Exec's., Son, Luke and Wm. Fields. Written Oct. 20, 1792. Witnesses, Morrias Hansbrough, James Thompson, Mary M. Fields. Probated July 16, 1793.

THOMAS SHARPE SPENCER—Book B, page 101—Dated Oct. 26, 1793. Leaves negro slave in care of John Hansbrough. When he dies to go to sister, Elizabeth Spencer. Witnesses, John, Sarah and George Hansbrough. Proved Nov. 18, 1794.

HUGH SHIELL—Book A, page 121—Names wife, Anne. Friend, John Hunter. My daughter, Catherine Harris, born on 19 of month. My wife's father, John Harris, Esq., deceased, of Buck's Co., Pa. Executrix Wife. Witnesses, George Muter, Mary W. Faunt LeRoy, Thomas Lowrie. Written Aug. 24, 1782. Probated Nov. 15, 1785.

JOHN SLOAN—Book B, page 255—Names wife, Polly. Two daughters, Margaret and Elizabeth. Written Aug. 5, 1804. Witnesses, Daniel McCormick, Thomas Shannon, James Jameson. No probate date.

MARGARET SLOAN—Book B, page 15—Names son, Thomas. 3 daughters, Margaret, Betsy and Anna Sloan. Exec., James Davis. Witnesses, Agnes Sloan, Abraham Miller, and Margaret Wilkins. Written Aug. 14, 1791. Probated Nov. 15, 1791.

HENRY SMITH—Book A, page 178—Names sons, Henry and Liberty. Wife, Margaret. Daughters, Elizabeth, Letty Duff, Sarah S——tour. Step-son, Henry Garret. Daughter, Chloe Deal. Exec's., Samuel Taylor, Edmund and Christopher Smith. Witnesses, John Bryant, George Douglas and Ezekiel Lacefield. Written Dec. 9, 1788. Probated Sept. 15, 1789.

JOHN SMITH—Book B, page 199—To wife and children. Exec., John Jackman. Teste, Daniel Duncan, Nancy Duncan, Elizabeth Duncan, Wm. Jackman. Written July 30, 1793. Probated Oct., 1797.

URIAH SOUTHERLAND—Book B, page 253—To wife. My children, Daniel, Ruth, Hannah and Thomas. Exec's., Abraham Riffe and wife, Rebecca Southerland. Written Apr. 13, 1804. Witnesses, John Dillingham, John Kenedy and John Riffe. Inventory Rec. Aug. 22, 1804.

WILLIAM SOUTHERLAND—Book B, page 251—Dated June 20, 1803. To son, Fendle. To sons, William, Owen, George. My wife, Mary. To daughter, Thursy Hawkins. To daughter, Milly Goldsmith. To daughter, Susannah Harper. To daughter, Polly Jones. To daughters, Jenny and Nancy. Exec., Jabez Jones. Witnesses, Edmund Farris, Sr., Edmund Farris. No probate date.

PHILIP SPOONAMORE—Book C, page 46—Names wife, Magdalene. Exec., ————. Written May 17, 1803. Witnesses, Benedick Swope, David Logan and Reuben Emerson. Probated Mch. 10, 1806.

JOHN STUART—Book C, page 35—To sons, Robert, James Stuart, Charles Stuart, Clement Stuart. Lida Davis. Son, Ayres. Wife, Mary. Sons, William, Jiles, Washington, when of age. Son, John. Two sons, Milton and Gibson, when of age. Exec's., Sons, William and Washington Stuart. Written Apr. 18, 1801. Witnesses, Wm. Ousley, Anthony Ousley, and Wm. Ousley, Jr. Probated Aug. 10, 1801.

STEPHEN SLADE—Book A, page 170—Names wife, Anne. Daughters, Margaret and Mary. Exces., Wife and William Walton of Cumberland. Witnesses, I. Manire, Andrew Oliver and Joseph Horn. Written Feb. 26, 1789. Probated Apr. 21, 1789.

WILLIAM STEWART—Book A, page 19—To father. To brother, Robert Stewart. To sisters, Hanna and Mary. Exec's., James Hinton, John Smith, and Wm. McBride. Witnesses, Clough Overton, Ebenezer Miller and Francis McBride. Written Aug. 20, 1781. Probated Jan. 21, 1783.

JOHN SWAN—Book A, page 11—Sons, John, Joel, Thomas, posthumous child, daughters, Elizabeth, Lettis. Wife. Exec's., Wife, Richard Swan, Jacob VanMetree. Witnesses, Mary Hinton, Rebecca Rowling and Margaret Haycraft. Written July 12, 1780. Probated Feb. 18, 1783.

FOUSHEE TEBBS—Book C, page 132—To wife, Hanna Willcocks Tebbs, my whole estate. Friend, Wm. Warren and Thomas Ball executors and my wife, Hanna, Executrix. Written Sept. 5, 1786. Teste, John Young, Even C. Kelbreath, and Wm. Renick. Probated Dec. 14, 1807.

JOHN TUCKER—Book B, page 74—To wife and 5 children, when the youngest becomes of age. Exec's., Wife, Edmund Powell and Wm. Patton. Witnesses, John Deaver, Mary Payton and Sarah Josling. Written Aug. 9, 1790. Probated Oct. 15, 1793.

DAVID WALKER—Book B, page 63—To wife, Elizabeth. To two sons, Jesse and David Walker. To daughters, Polly, Betsy and Susanna. To 2 youngest daughters, Phoebe and Rhoda Walker. Exec's., Sons, Jesse and David. Witnesses, John Chiles, Marvell Nash, John Embree. Probated July 16, 1793.

SAMUEL WALLIS—Book B, page 127—To son, Andrew. To son-in-law, Henry Pawling and Elizabeth (my daughter). To son, Caleb. Exec's., Son, Caleb Wallis and son-in-law, Henry Pawling and Elizabeth Pawling. Written Apr. 24, 1794. Witnesses, Wm. Pawling, John Ewing, Samuel Gill. Codicil. To all my other children. Probated Aug. 18, 1795.

WILLIAM WARREN—Book G, page 41—To son, John. To children of son, William. Sons, Samuel, William, James and Thomas B. Warren. To daughters, Frances Burch, and Polly Taylor. To Lettice Ewing, John Warren. The children of Ann Stephens. Wm. Warren, Elizabeth Kennedy, James Warren, Thomas B. Warren, Samuel W. Warren, and Polly Taylor, to be divided in 9 equal parts, deducting for Frances Burch and Winifred Ewing. Exec's., Sons, John, Wm., James, Thomas B. and Samuel. Written May 17, 1817. Witnesses, Samuel Moore, I. Shelby, Jr., Even Shelby. Probated Oct. 11, 1819.

GILES WILLIAMS—Book A, page 152—To wife, Sarah and three children, Sarah, Nancy and Lizzie Williams. Execs., John Jones, George Stowbald Smith. Witnesses, William Hamilton, Philip Thurman and John Fields. Written Nov. 28, 1787. Probated June 17, 1788.

GEORGE WILSON—Book C, page 48—To my daughter, Mary Hocker. Sons, John, and Thomas. Wife, Rebecca Wilson. Exec., Friend, Hugh Magill. Written June 25, 1800. Witnesses, Wm. Magill, Hugh Logan, Wm. Dougherty, Sr. Probated July 12, 1802.

EDWARD WORTHINGTON—Book B, page 282—Estate of Edward Worthington, deceased. Appraised July 16, 1805, by Samuel Johnson, George Givens, James Tinsley.

JOHN WRIGHT—Book C, page 9—Will dated June 26, 1805. Names wife, Any Right. To Sally Stokes, my daughter. Exec's., Wife, Any Right and Joel Stokes. Witnesses, Reuben Bailey, Samuel Coleman, Abram Kenrick. No probate date.

JACOB YANTIS—Book B, page 275—To wife, Ruth. My children, as they come of age. Children already married. Exec's., Wife and son, John. Written Nov. ——, 1804. Witnesses, Wm. Hamilton, Samuel Duderar. Probated June 10, 1805.

MATHIAS YOAKUM—Book A, page 148—Names wife, Eleanor. Son, Felty Yoakum's oldest son, George. Other children married. Youngest son, George, unmarried. Execs., Wife and son, George. Witnesses, William Walton, Peter Deyerle, and Peter Keeny. Written Jan. 29, 1780. Probated Feb. 18, 1783.

JOHN WILLEY—Book B, page 18—Names 3 sons, Peter, Alexander, and Thomas. Eldest son, John. Exec., Son, John. Witnesses, James Davis, Wm. C. Perrin (or Perrn), John Wylie. Written Jan. 3, 1792. Probated Nov. 20, 1792.

MADISON COUNTY, KENTUCKY

WILL AND DEED ABSTRACTS

(Donated by Mrs. Joseph Beard)

KAVANAUGH, CHARLES—Will Book A, page 125—Names wife, Ann. Children, Mary, William, Charles (III), Jael, Sarah Ann. Heirs of son, Philimon, deceased. James Mills Moore and his children, Charles K. Moore and Elizabeth Moore. Witnesses, I Hocaday and William Fox. Exec's., William and Charles Kavanaugh, and Peter Woods. Written Oct. 13, 1795. Probated Oct. 4, 1796.

KAVANAUGH, WILLIAM—Will Book E, page 21—Names wife, Ruth. Children, Archibald, Charles, Philemon. Dau's., Susanna Duncan, Ann Briscoe, Polly Oldham, Sally English. Witnesses, Henry Goodloe, John Harish, John Robertson and Thomas Warren. Exec's., Son, Charles Kavanaugh and William Goodloe. Written Mch. 15, 1825. Probated Nov. 2, 1829.

KAVANAUGH, PHILEMON—Will Book D, page 548—Appraisement, May term of Court 1829.

WOOD, JAMES—Will Book E, page 213—Names son, Dudley and other children. Produced in Court Oct. 1831, and proven on oath of son, Dudley Wood and Notty M. Conn.

WOOD, ADAM, SR.—Deed Book X, page 463—Dated Oct. 15, 1825. Adams Wood, Sr. to George Fox, land * * * being part of Christopher Irvine, deceased, preemption.

WOOD, PATRICK and FANNY—Deed Book R, page 240—Patrick and Fanny Wood, of county of Howard, Missouri, of one part and Michael Baker, of Shelby Co., Ky., of other part, land formally part of 1000 acres that Hart sold to Coopers Woods and others. Aug. 4, 1826. State of Missouri and county of Howard. Deed Book R. This day, personally appear before me, George Jackson and A. C. Woods, two acting Justices of the peace, for said county, took oath * * * and for said Patrick and Fanny, his wife, as to Patrick and Fanny Woods signiture.

WOODS, ADAM, JR.—Deed Book X, page 19—Aug. 16, 1823. Indenture * * between Adam Woods, Jr. and Polly, his wife, of Madison Co., Ky., of one part and Robert Caldwell of same county and state, of the other part * * land * * for sum of $1875, containing 77 acres. * * Said 77 acres conveyed to Adam Woods, Jr., by Adam Woods and Anna, his wife, by deed, bearing date May 5, 1809, and now of Madison Co., Ky. * * * The said Adam Woods and Polly, his wife, sole owners, do covenant with said Robert Caldwell * * *.

WOODS, ARCHIBALD, SR.—Will Book F, page 241—Dated Mch. 17, 1836. Names wife, Elizabeth L. Woods. Children, Archibald, Lucy Caperton, William W., Susannah Goodloe, Anna Miller, Mourning Miller, Mary Collins, deceased. Exec., Grand-son, Archibald W. Goodloe. Witnesses, James Estill, Sr. and Mary E. Estill. Clerk, David Irvine.

WOODS, ADAM, Sr.—Deed Book G, page 134—Dated May 6, 1809. Adam Woods and Anna, his wife, to Patrick Woods, of Madison Co., Ky. * * and natural affection and friendship I bear to said Patrick Woods.

WOODS, ADAM—Deed Book—Date Nov. 3, 1803. From Commissioners, Richard Calloway, Robert Caldwell, appointed in behalf of infant heirs, of Christopher Irvine, deceased, of one part and Adam Woods, other part, land on Tates Creek, in Madison Co., Ky. * * * Witnesses, Josiah Phelps, Martin Hardin, Richard P. Fox.

WOOD, WILLIE—Madison Co., Ky. Written Jan. 12, 1855. Names wife. Children, Starling Wood, deceased, Tilitha Wood, Sally Buchanon, Parolee Gordon, Anderson Wood, Green Wood and Schuyler Wood. Witnesses, Jefferson Williams, C. S. Wilmore. Exec's., Anderson and Schuyler Wood. Probated Sept. 29, 1858.

WOODS, ADAM, JR.—Deed Book G, page 344—Adam Woods, Jr. to George Shackleford one acre of land for $11.75 * * between Hart's settlement and preemption, and that of Christopher Irvine. Witnesses, William Williams, John Woods and Tyree Harris. Monday, Feb. 5, 1810.

WOODS, ADAM—Deed Book N, page 244—Dated Feb. 4, 1819. Adam Woods to Samuel Estill, 300 acres entered and patented in Woods' name on Otter Creek.

WOODS, MICHAEL—Of County of Scott, State of Va. Sells to Elias Barker, for 300 pounds, land lying on Muddy Creek, joining Lackey land in Madison Co., Ky. Date, Mch. 27, 1789.

WOODS, PATRICK—Deed Book L, page 320—Dated Sept. 23, 1813. Patrick Woods, of Madison Co., Ky., being about to move to Territory of Louisanna, appoints Archibald Woods of Madison Co. Ky., his lawful attorney, in conveying lands and * * *. Page 333. Deed Book L. Patrick Woods and Frances, his wife, to Daniel Maupin. * * This land was in dispute as result of Joseph Delaney, Sr.'s will, giving dau., Frances less than he gave son, Joseph Delaney, Jr., to satisfyWood, Joseph Delaney, Jr. agreed to pay $95 to Woods to relinguish all claim to land, he had sold to Maupin. Sept. 21, 1816.

WOOD, JAMES—Deed Book E, page 278—Dated Mch. 1, 1802. James Wood and Sally, his wife, of Madison Co. Ky., to David Seery, of same county, 80 acres on Ky. river.

WOODS, ADAM—Deed Book F, page 312—Jan. 28, 1807. Adam and Anna Woods, deed to Ebenezer Dickey * * land on waters of Tates Creek, part of land Woods purchased from Christopher Irvine.

WOODS, MICHAEL—Deed Book E, page 930—Madison Co. Ky. Michael and Hannah Woods, sold land to John Quisenbery, land on Muddy Creek in Madison Co. part of Woods survey of 1000 acres. Feb. 20, 1783.

WOODS, WILLIAM—Wm. Woods to Patrick Woods, Mch. 6, 1806. Personal property.

WOODS, MICHAEL—Deed Book F, page 18—Nov. 4, 1805. Michael and Hannah Woods to McGuire land, part of 1,000 acres pre-emption. Same to Tinchner, Mch. 4, 1805.

WOODS, PATRICK—Deed Book L, page 298—Sept. 1, 1816. Patrick Woods and Fanny, his wife, of Madison Co. Ky., to John Jarman, of same Co., * * being part of Christopher Irvins settlement and pre-emption, and part of land sold by C. Irvine to Adam Woods and by said Adam conveyed by deed to Patrick Woods, as will appear deed May 6, 1809. * *.

WOOD, JOHN—Madison Co. Ky. John and Keziah Wood. Page 177, Book F. Sold land, * * *. Same, to McQuinn, page 50, Book F. Nov. 30, 1805.

WILL ABSTRACTS

(Donated by Mrs. B. F. Buckley)

BERRY, JAMES—Of Madison Co., Ky. Written Feb. 22, 1822. Names daus.,Nancy Berry, Susannah Parrish, Elizabeth Berry, Anna Turner. Sons, William and James H. Berry. Wife, Sarah. Executors, Wm. Stone, Humphrey Jones and son, James H. Berry. Witnesses, James Stone, Caleb Stone, Anthony Phelps. Probated, Monday, Apr. 1, 1822.

HOBBS, JOSEPH—Will written Oct. 25, 1809. Will Book B, page 201. Names Sons, Thomas Hobbs and his wife, Urith. Zachariah Hobbs, of Washington Co., Ky. Nathan Hobbs, of Nelson Co., Ky. Daughters, Sarah Dorsey, wife of Greenberry Dorsey, Rachel Hobbs, wife of Joshua Hobbs, Jr., Susanna Stone, Mary Tevis, of Madison Co., Ky. Husband, Robert Tevis, Debora Fontain, of Jefferson Co., Ky., husband, James Fontain, Elizabeth Waddy, of Shelby Co., Ky., husband, Sam Waddy. Exec's., William Stone, son-in-law, Nathan Hobbs, son. Witnesses, S. H. Hubbard, Solomon Bishop, David Houston, Benjamin Houston, Thomas Bishop. Codicil dated Feb. 7, 1810. Names Nathaniel Parker and Susanna Powell, son and dau. of my dau., Mary Tevis, formally Mary Parker. Witnesses, A. H. Hubbard, Solomon Bishop, Thomas Bishop, Joshua Hobbs, Jr., Jack Hobbs. Probated, 1810, on oaths of Thomas Bishop and Solomon Bishop. Test., Ben Grayson, C. C.

TEVIS, ROBERT—Of Madison Co., Ky. Names wife, Polly. Eldest dau, Matilda Ann Tribble, dau., Harriott F. Miller, sons, Cyrus C. Tevis, Napoleon O. Tevis, Joseph H. Tevis. Written Mch. 17, 1823. Attest, Sam Havin, John Bennett, Thomas Tevis. Codicil added May 13, 1823. Witnesses, Samuel, Austin, Daniel Johns, and John Bennett. Probated, Nov. 3, 1823. On oaths of John Bennett and Thomas Tevis and Sam Austin.

TEVIS, NATHANIEL—Dated Aug. 21, 1798. Names sons, Nathaniel Tevis, Robert Tevis, Jeremiah Tevis. Dau's., Peggy Tevis, and Susannah Wheeler. Witnesses, John Sappington, Robert Rebum and Edward Davis. Exec's., Son, Robert Tevis, and son-in-law, John Wheeler. Probated, Tuesday Oct. 2, 1798. On oaths of John Sappington, Robert Rebumand Edward Davis.

TURNER, THOMAS—Names Squire Leavell and Martin Turner, trustees for daughter, Sarah Ann Baker, husband, Jonah Baker. Dau., Rebecca S. Turner, son, James Turner, guardian of Rebecca. Wife, Elizabeth Turner. Witnesses, Robert Jennings and Jesse Jennings. Probated Madison Co. Ky. Dec. 4, 1848. On oaths of John Stone, Jesse Jennings and Robert Jennings.

Note—Thomas, John and Phillip Turner came from North Carolina to Madison Co. Ky., where they resided. John died in Madison Co. Ky., where his will is on record.

TURNER, JOHN—Of Madison County, Ky. (Copy donated by Mrs. B. F. Buckley, Lexington, Ky., and sent to her by R. M. Turner, of El Paso, Texas). Will written Jan. 3, 1813. Names first wife, Rebecca and their 8 children, viz.: Andrew, Thomas, Edward, John, Conelius, Amy, Sarah and Charity. 2nd. wife, Jane, and their children, viz.: James, Mildred, Philip, Barnett, Jesse, Jonathan, Elinor, Jane, William. Dau., Catherine Patterson. Exec's., Brother, Philip Turner, my son, Barnett and James Berry. Witnesses, Robert Harris, John Harris and Nathan Roberts. Probated Jan. 3, 1814.

MERCER COUNTY, KENTUCKY
HARRODSBURG COURT HOUSE

(Copied by Mrs. Joseph Beard, Sr. and Mrs. H. K. McAdams)

JOHN BREWER—Order Book 1, page 190—John Brewer, appointed guardian to Daniel, Cornelius, Anne and Sarah Cozine, orphans of Cornelius Cozine, deceased. Mch. 25, 1788. Abraham Banta and Samuel Cemeree, their securities.

JOSEPH DICKEN—Order Book 1, page 471—Joseph Dicken, appointed guardian to Daniel, Winniford, and Lott Dicken, orphans of Christopher Dicken, deceased. With Wm. Kennedy, John Lillard and Robert Sutton, secureties. Feb. 23, 1790.

MATHEW ENGLISH, deceased—Inventory recorded Mch. Court, 1794. Book 1, page 156.

DOMINACK FLANNAGAN, deceased—Estate recorded Feb. Court 1790. Will Book 1, page 77.

THOMAS FREEMAN—Order Book 1, page 100—Thomas Freeman appointed guardian to Margaret, Thomas, Eliner, Stephen and Elizabeth Prather, orphans of Thomas Prather, deceased. Henry Mather, security. June 26, 1787.

ELIZABETH KING—Order Book 1, page 372—Elizabeth King, orphan of Nimrod King, deceased, came into court and made choice of John Yocum, as her guardian. Security, Caleb Donally. Aug. 25, 1789.

GEORGE McAFEE—Order Book 1, page 229—George McAfee came into Court and made oath that Ann, Margaret and Mary McAfee are the heirs of William McAfee, deceased, and, on motion of said George, the same is ordered to be certified to the Register of the Land Office. May 28, 1788.

JAMES McAFEE—Order Book 1, page 101—James McAfee appointed guardian of John, Nancy, Billy and Betsy Woods, orphans of David Woods, deceased. Samuel McAfee, security. June 26, 1787.

WILLIAM McBRAYER—Order Book 1, page 352—Wm. McAfee, appointed guardian of Alexander, Robert and Sarah Walker, orphans of John Walker, deceased. Samuel McAfee, security. June 23, 1789.

JAMES PRIESTLY—Order Book 1, page 459—James Priestly, appointed guardian (instead of John Gilmore, deceased) to William, and Lapsley McBride, orphans of William McBride, deceased, and also to Martha McBride, orphan of said William McBride, deceased. James Lapsley, security. Jan. 6, 1790.

ELIZABETH ROBARDS—Order Book 1, page 57—Elizabeth Robards, orphan of William Robards, deceased, being of lawful age for that purpose, made choice of Jesse Robards for her guardian. Robert Mosby, security.

WILL BOOK 1

WILLIAM ADAMS—Will Book 1, page 205—Of County of Lincoln, Commonwealth of Virginia. Names sons: William Adams, Samuel and David Adams. Daughters, Jennet Adams, Anne Adams, Margaret Curry and Mary Willson. Exec's., Sons, Samuel, and David Adams. Written July 29, 1789. Witnesses, Elizabeth Thomas, Wm. Stewart, John Stewart. Proved July Court 1795.

MARY ARMSTRONG—Will Book 1, page 103—Written Dec. 13, 1792.

Names daughter, Elizabeth. Sons, William, Abel, Richard. Grandsons, Wm. Armstrong, son of Abel, and John Armstrong, son of Richard. Grand-daughters, Jean Steel, dau. of my son, James and Mary Armstrong, dau. of my son, James. Exec., Son, Richard Armstrong. Witnesses,. Nunan Steel, John Bunton. Proved May Court 1793.

STEPHEN ARNOLD—Page 159, Will Book 1—Names wife, Jane. Sons: Stephen, John, James. Daughters, Sarah, Elizabeth and Jane. Sons-in-law, Alexander Armstrong, and Thomas Wilson. Granddaughter, Jenny Arnold, dau. of Abegale. Written Dec. 1793. Witnesses, Wm. Steel and Staley McClure. Proved Mch. Court 1794.

JOHN BEAMAN, deceased—Inventory recorded July 24, 1787—**Book 1, page 14.**

HENRY BOLLING, deceased—**Book 1, page 4**—Inventory recorded Jan. 2, 1787.

ALEXANDER BOWLING, deceased—**Book 1, page 57**—Recorded inventory Aug. Court 1791.

JOHN BERRY—Will Book 1, page 214—Names wife, Anne. Children, Peggy, and Rachel, when they come of age. Exec's., Rachel Berry and Robert Mitchael. Written Oct. 8, 1795. Witnesses, Thomas Gash, Richard Berry, Elizabeth M. Ewing and Polly Berry. Codicil, names James B. Sparrow and wife, to use certain land during his life time. Proved Oct. Court 1795.

JOSEPH BOHANNON, deceased—Inventory recorded Mch. Court. 1796. Will Book 1, page 202.

ROBERT BRUMFIELD—Will Book 1, page 183—Names daughter, Tabitha Brumfield. To Mary McCastin. Sons, Job, Wm. and James Brumfield. Daughters, Edah Prewitt, Susan Richardson and Rachel Minor. Exec's., Son, James and son-in-law, John Richardson. Written Feb. 7, 1790. Witnesses, Vincent Wren, Cloe Latimore, Agnes McLaughlin. Proved Oct. Court 1794.

DANIEL BROWER—Will Book 1, page 49—Names eldest son, Abraham Brower, son, Daniel Brower, daughter, Leah Stagg, wife of James Stagg. Dau., Susannah Demaree, wife of Samuel Demaree. Dau., Rachel Commings, wife of Henry Commings. Dau., Mary Demaree, wife of Samuel Demaree, Jr. Son, John Brower. Dau., Phebe Demaree, wife of Cornelius Demaree. Exec's., Sons, Abraham and John Brower, and Samuel Demaree, Sr. Written Jan. 15, 1791. Witnesses, Peter Demaree, Frances Monfort and John Demaree. Proved Feb. 22, 1791.

REBECCA BROWN, late Rebecca McAfee—**Book 1, page 80**—Dower in lands of late husband, William McAfee. Witnesses, John Thomas, Stephen Ashby, Daniel Ashby. Written Feb. 17, 1792. Recorded Feb. 28, 1792.

GEORGE BUCHANNON—Account as "late guardian" to Polly McAfee. Will Book 1, page 21.

JAMES CAMPBELL, deceased—**Book 1, page 30**—Inventory recorded Nov. 24, 1788.

RACHEL CANADY—Will Book 1, page 34—Names son, Jeremiah

Laws. Son, Samuel Canady. Daughters, Rachel Underwood, and Elizabeth Canady. Exec's., Friends, Morias Hansbrough and William Crow. Witnesses, John Underwood, George Hansbrough, and Manah Hansbrough. Written Nov. 18, 1789. Probated Apr. Court 1790.

SETH CASON, deceased—Will Book 1, page 190—Estate. Recorded Dec., 1794.

REUBEN COOLEY, deceased—Will Book 1, page 204—Inventory. Court 1795.

CORNELIUS COZINE—Will Book 1, page 12—Written Feb. 9, 1787. Names wife, Mary. Eldest son, Daniel. Son, Cornelius. Daughters, Anney and Sarah. Exec's., Samuel Demeree and Abraham Banta. Witnesses, John Banta, Simon Vanosdol (Vanarsdale), Albert Vorhis and Luke Vorie. Probated May 23, 1787. Inventory page 14.

DANIEL COZINE, deceased—Will Book 1, page 210—Inventory July 10, 1795.

JOSEPH DAVIS—Will Book 1, page 220—Written May 13, 1795. Names wife, Jennet. Children, John, Jenny, William. Sons, James, Robert, Joseph. Exec's., Wife, Jennet, sons, Robert and Joseph Davis. Witnesses, Wm. Gales, James Gates and Joseph Davis. Proved Nov. Court 1795.

DANIEL DICKEN—Book 1, page 74—Names younger brothers and sisters. Brothers, Charles, Winneford and Lot Dicken. Exec's., Friends, Christopher Dicken and Isaac Dicken. Witnesses, William and Joseph Dicken, and William Batton. Proved Feb. 28, 1792.

WILLIAM DOWNING, deceased—Book 1, page 86—Inventory recorded Dec. Court 1792.

ABRAHAM ESTES—Book 1, page 17—Written May 23, 1788. Names wife, Kesiah. Son, Henry and Joel. Daughters, Lucy, Rachel, Betty Ward, Jemimah, Frankey. Exec's., William Rice, my wife, Keziah and Robert Childers, and Henry Estes. Witnesses, Joseph Robinson, Joseph Lawrence and Robert Lawrence. Probated Sept. 23, 1788.

ISAAH FOSTER—Will Book 1, page 200—Names friend, Absolom Froman. To Miss Susannah Froman. Friend Michael Tothers. My sister, Rebecchah Craesap. My brother, Job Foster. Friend Abraham Froman. To my well beloved friend and companion, Jacob Froman. Written Nov. 29, 1794. Witnesses, Peter Reiley, Emanuel Vantress. Proved Dec. Court 1794.

JOHN GILL—Will Book 1, page 36—Of Mercer Co., Virginia, District of Kentucky. Names wife, Margaret. Mentions my executors in South Carolina, Wm. Bishop, Richard Ellis and Robert Lethgan. My executors in Kentucky, Brother, Wm. Gill and John and Thomas Pelham. Written Sept. 26, 1788. Witnesses, Wm. McGowen, and Wm. Sanders. "State of South Carolina, Richland County. True copy taken from Book B, folio 52, Oct. 9, 1789." Probated Mercer Co., June 22, 1790.

SAMUEL GIVENS—Will Book 1, page 210—Names wife, Martha. Martha Reed, Jr., daughter of Jonathan Reed, deceased. Nephew,

Robert Givens. Exec's., Robert Caldwell, Sr. and David Gillispie. Written Dec. 29, 1794. Witnesses, David Gillispie, Stephen Collett and Josiah Grover. Proved Aug. Court 1795.

JOHN GORDON, deceased—Book 1, page 78—Inventory recorded Feb. Court 1792.

BENJAMIN GRAHAM—Book 1, page 41—Names wife, Faithful. 4 daughters, Alice, Elizabeth, Mary and Jane. Alice to live with my brother, Samuel. Mary to live with my brother James' widow, until they arrive at full age. Elizabeth and Jane to remain with my wife, Faithful. Exec's., Brother, Samuel Graham and friend, Elisha Thomas. Written Aug. 2, 1790. Witnesses, Joshua Podson, and Wm. M'Achron. Proved Sept. Court 1790.

SAMUEL GRIXON—Estate. Page 81—Inventory recorded July Court 1792.

ANN HALE, deceased—Will Book 1, page 195—Widow of Joseph Hale, deceased. Settlement of estate. To schooling and boarding three children 3 years. Administrators, Thomas Freeman, James Hanna, Joseph Willis. Recorded Oct. Court 1794.

JOBE HALE—Book 1, page 109—Names wife, Hannah. Eldest son, Isaac. Son, Johnny, when sons are of age. 3 daughters, Betsy, Nancy and Sally. Exec's., Friends, John Chiles and Capt. John Lillard. Written July 17, 1790. Witnesses, John Daly and John P. Steele and Wm. Huff. Proved May Court 1793.

JOSEPH HALE, deceased—Inventory recorded Jan. Court 1793.

JOHN HARBISON, deceased—Inventory recorded Mch. 2, 1787. Book 1, page 11.

WILLIAM HARRIS—Will Book 1, page 126—Names wife, Henrietta. Daughters, Ann Harris, when 16 years old and Bradbourn. Exec's., Wife, Henrietta, and friend, George Thompson. Written May 8, 1792. Witnesses, James Taylor, Jr., Wm. Clark, Zacks Field, George Thompson, Jr., and G. Thompson. Proved July Court 1793.

JAMES HARROD—Will Book 1, page 144—Names wife, Ann Harrod. Daughter, Margaret Harrod. Exec's., Wife, Ann Harrod and Wm. Moor, of Mercer Co., Ky. and John Hardin, of Nelson Co., Ky. Witnesses, John Winn, John Young, Israel Donalson, Thomas Banfield and Samuel Naylor. Written Nov. 28, 1791. Proved Dec. Court 1793. Inventory page 146. Recorded Mch. Court 1794.

THOMAS HARTLEY—Will Book 1, page 27—William Binney. To John Binney, son of William Binney. To Isaac Coffman. To George Miles, eldest son of John Miles. To Jean Binney. To Ann Binney. To Wm. Binney, Sr. Exec's., William Binney, Sr., and John Binney. Written May 15, 1789. Witnesses, Vincent Wren, James Harlan, Daniel and Thomas Thornberry. Probated June 23, 1789. Inventory page 31.

ALEXANDER HOLLAN, deceased—Book 1, page 85—Inventory recorded Sept., 1792.

ALEXANDER HOLLAND, deceased—Book 1, page 91—Inventory recorded Oct., 1792.

GEORGE HOLLOWAY—Will written, no date—Book 1, page 95—Names wife, Mary. Sons, Samuel, James and John. Daughters, Mary McGill, Charlotte Goodwin. 2 grand-children, children of my son, Clayton Holloway, deceased. Exec's., Wife, Mary, friend, Thomas Allen. Witnesses, John Thomas, Peter Banta, Samuel Holloway. Proved Mch. Court 1793.

ABRAHAM JAMES—Will Book 1, page 52—Written Mch. 30, 1791. Names wife, Mary. Son, George, when he comes of age. All my children as they come of age. Daughters, Sarah and Leah. Exec's., Wife, Mary, William Crow, Robert Mosby. Witnesses, Wm. Rice, Philip Fulkerson and Frances Monfort. Proved May 24, 1791.

MATTHEW J. JEFFRIES—Will Book 1, page 63—Names wife, Isabell. Sons, William and John, when they come of age. Daughter, Agnes. Names Mrs. Hinkston. Exec's., Son, Wm. Jeffries, Capt. John Smith and Thomas Allen. Written Dec. 3, 1788. Witnesses, Thomas Berry, Na Hart, Horatio Petty. Proved June Court 1791.

RACHEL KENNEDY, deceased—Will Book 1, page 77—Inventory rec. May Court 1790.

JOHN LITTLE—Will Book 1, page 187—Names Miss Molly Smith, daughter of Colonel John Smith. To Peggy Smith, Betsy Smith, Patsy Smith, Jenny Smith, Sally Smith, John Smith and his brother, William, sons of John Smith. To Samuel Daugherty. Exec's., Colonel John Smith and Robert Mosby. Written July 7, 1794. Witnesses, James M. Graham, Andrew B. Shilidey, Samuel Graham. Proved Nov. Court 1794.

ISAAC LONGLY, deceased—Inventory rec. Mch. Ct. 1794.

PATRICK LOWRY—Will Book 1, page 202—Names 3 sons, John, James and Melvin Lowry. Daughters, Margaret, Hannah, Betty, Mary, Jane Todd. Wife and "expected child." Written July 25, 1781. Witnesses, John Triggs, Elmer Frakes, Mary Conaway, Elizabeth Grundy. Proved Mch. Court 1795.

ROBERT McAFEE—Will Book 1, page 218—Written Feb. 28, 1795. Names children, Margaret, Janat, Sarah, Samuel, Mary Ann. Youngest sons, Robert and John. To my children that are married and not named. Exec's., John Brackinridge and James McCoun, Jr. Witnesses, Joseph Adams and Samuel Woods. Codicil. Proved Oct. Court 1795.

JAMES McCOUN—Will Book 1, page 44—Names wife, Ann. Sons, James, John and David. Daughters, Elizabeth, Ann, Margaret and Mary. Exec's., Sons, James and John McCoun. Written Aug. 1, 1790. Witnesses, John Armstrong, Ann McAfee, James Ledgerwood. Robert Armstrong. Probated Dec. Court 1790.

STEPHEN McKENNY, deceased—Inventory recorded Jan. Court 1793.

JOHN McMURTRY—Will Book 1, page 52—Mercer Co., State of Virginia. Names Sons, James, Alexander, William, John, Joseph. Daughter, Mary, "Till Joseph is of age." Wife, Mary. Executrix, Wife, Mary. Written Sept. 6, 1790. Witnessees, Wm. McKee, Wm. Gordon, Henry Bishong. Proved Apr. Court 1791.

HANNAH MILLER—Will Book 1, page 157—Hannah Miller, widow of John Miller, names son-in-law and friend, William Fields and daughter, Hannah Robinson. Exec's., Daughters, Elizabeth, Jamine Thomas, Hannah and Mary. Witnesses, John Crow, Elener Wright, Jean Owens. Written Aug. 16, 1786. Proved Mch. Court 1795.

ROBERT MITCHELL, deceased—Book 1, page 87—Inventory recorded Dec. Court 1792.

BENJAMIN NEELD—Will Book 1, page 181—Names brothers, Nathan and Robert Neeld. Nathan's daughter, Sarah. My sister, Jenny Steen. Exec's., Friends, Augustus Passmore, Peter Casey, and Nathan Neeld. Written July, 1794. Witnesses, John Steen, Robert Brown, John Daily. Proved Oct. Court 1794.

THOMAS NOEL—Will Book 1, page 24—Names wife, Drucillar. Children, Elizabeth, Garnet, Musker, John, Ann, Cancy, Lette, Benjamin, Beckey, Moses, Toby, and Sally. Exec's., Wife, Drucillar, John Chiles, Sr., and Garnet Noel. Witnesses, David Chiles, Henry Chiles and Elizabeth Chiles. Probated June 23, 1789.

JAMES OVERTON—Will Book 1, page 46—Divided between "My brothers and sisters." Exec's., Walter Overton, Thomas Overton, and John Overton, Jr. Written (?) 18, 1785. Witnesses, Wm. Petters, Edward Eggleston, Sarah Micher. Copy of Will of James Overton, deceased, together with certificate of the Clerk of Louisa Co., where it has been recorded. Recorded Mercer Co., Ky. Jan. 25, 1791.

GEORGE POFF—Will Book 1, page 217—Names friend, John Willis. Exec., John Willis. Witnesses, Edward Willis, Samuel Devine, Mary Devine. Proved Oct. Court 1795.

THOMAS PRATHER, deceased—Estate—Account with Thomas Freeman, guardian of children, Betsy, Stephen and Nelly Prather, orphans of Thomas Prather, deceased. 1794-1795.

THOMAS PRATHER—Will Book 1, page 1, records—Will of Thomas Prather, "of the Parish of Ky., and County of Lincoln." Names, Theophilus Phillips. Wife, Mary. Executrix, Wife, Mary. Written May 16, 1786. Witnesses, Ja Speed, Maliolin Worley, Thomas Speed, John Speed. Codicil, June 25, 1786. James Cobum and Henry Prather, to be executors with wife, Mary. Witnesses, James Harrod, Ja Speed, John Chiles, Jr. Probated Aug. 1, 1786.

JAMES QUIGLY, deceased—Inventory recorded Mch. Court 1793.
ROBERT ROBARDS, deceased—Inventory recorded Nov. Court 1793.

JAMES ROBERTSON—Will Book 1, page 193—Names wife, Sarah. Daughter, Mary. My Mother. Witness, William Day. Proved on oath of William Day and Samuel Laurence. Proved Dec. Court 1794.

WILLIAM ROBERTSON, deceased—Inventory recorded June 22, 1790.

GEORGE SILVERTOOTH, deceased—Inventory recorded Oct. Court 1793.

ADAM SMITH—Will Book 1, page 98—Names wife, Elizabeth. Sons, Ezekiel, Benjamin. Daughter, Elizabeth. Exec's., Wife, Elizabeth and sons, Ezekiel and Solomon. Witnesses, Zachariah Smith, John

Smith, and John Samuel Mow. Written Aug. 11, 1792. Proved, Mch Court 1793.

GEORGE WILLIAM STEPHENS—Will Book 1, page 21—"Of Lincoln County Virginia." Names mother, Mary Stephens. Brothers, Jacob, Isaac, Joseph, Laurence and Bryan Martin Stephens. Half-brothers, Peter and John Stephens. Sisters, Mary Earnest and Sarah Bowman. Exec's., Mother, Mary Stephens, brothers, Joseph, Laurence Stephens. Witnesses, Watson Henry, P. Hite, Abraham Bowman, Robert Craige, James Bryan. Probated Apr. 28, 1789. Written Dec. 27, 1784.

ROBERT SUTTON—Will Book 1, page 198—Names wife, Anne. Three daughters. Daughter, Anne. Exec's., Friend, Benjamin Beall, Joseph Dickens and wife, Anne Sutton. Witnesses, Wm. Kennedy, Jannette A. Beall, Mary M. Fields. Written Dec. 28, 1794. Proved Jan. Court 1795.

DAVID TAYLOR, deceased—Inventory recorded July 27, 1790. Book 1, page 38.

DAVID THOMAS, deceased—Inventory Will Book 1, page 124—Recorded Oct. Court 1793.

ELIZABETH THOMPSON—Will Book 6, page 18—Widow of James Thompson. Allotment. Commissioners, Archibald Bilbo, Richard Huff, and Cornelius Cozine. Feb. Court 1817.

FOSTER THOMPSON—Will Book 6, page 113—Names wife, Polly. Children when they come of age. Names wife's father, David Williams. Executrix, Wife, Polly. Written July 27, 1818. Witnesses, George W. Thompson and Samuel Taylor. Proved Aug. Court 1818.

GEORGE C. THOMPSON, guardian of Ann G. Thompson, Eliza M. Thompson, Joseph Thompson and Margaret Thompson, infant heirs of Joseph Thompson, deceased. Since last account, Ann G. Thompson (one of the wards) has married Thomas B. Hood, in June last. Submitted to Court Oct. 6, 1817 and recorded in Book 6, page 52. On page 137. Book 6, account gives "on July 2, 1818, Elizabeth Thompson (one of the wards) married Dr. John A. Tomlinson. Recorded Oct. Court 1818. Page 311, Book 6. Account of George C. Thompson, guardian of Joseph A. Thompson and Mary M. Thompson." No further division of estate. Recorded Sept. Court 1820.

JAMES THOMPSON, deceased—Book 5, page 324—Inventory. Recorded Court, 1816. Book 6, page 67. Estate, administrator, James Thompson, Jr. Mentions eleven heirs and widow, Elizabeth, administratrix. Rec. Aug. 13, 1817.

JAMES THOMPSON—Will Book 12, page 148—Written Feb. 19, 1844. Names wife, Abbigil. Five children. Sons, James H. Elias, Henry, Samuel. Daughter, Mary Rebecca Thompson. Exec., Friend, James Turner. Witnesses, Elijah Thompson, Garrett Bohon and Elijah Thompson Dean. Probated June Court 1844.

JOHN THOMPSON—Will Book 1, page 100—Written Aug. 20, 1792. Names wife, Pricella. Sons, John and Even Thompson. Exec's., Wife, Pricella, Even Thompson. Witnesses, John Wilcoxson, Daniel Bennet. Proved Mch. Court 1793.

JOSEPH THOMPSON, deceased—Estate—Administrator, Elizabeth Thompson. Recorded Apr. 17, 1815. Book 5, page 320.

RICHARD THOMPSON—Will Book 12, page 473—Written Apr. 14, 1847. Names wife, Lucy A. Thompson. Son, James E. Thompson. Executrix, Wife, Lucy A. Thompson. Witness, George Thompson. Probated Mch. Court 1849.

MOSES THRELKELD, deceased—Will Book 1, page 25—Inventory, recorded June 23, 1789.

THOMAS THRELKELD—Will Book 1, page 32—County of Mercer, State of Virginia. Names wife, Nelly. George and Daniel, sons of my brother, John Threlkeld. Thomas and William, sons of Moses Threlkeld. Daniel Threlkeld McKonky, Armstead Long. Mary Buckley Threlkeld and Rachel Threlkeld, daughters of my brother, Henry. Exec's., Wife, Nelly, brother, John Threlkeld and John Waggoner. Written Jan. 31, 1790. Witnesses, Robert Pogue, Ezek Kennedy. Probated Mch. 23, 1790.

DAVID TILFORD—Will Book 1, page 177—Names Mother. Brother, Andrew Tilford. Sisters, Peggy Ewing, Polly Cull and Rachel Cloyd. Nephew, Samuel Tilford, son of my brother, Samuel. Remaining brothers and sisters. Exec's., Brother, Jeremiah Tilford, and nephew, James McCoun. Written July 23, 1794. Witnesses, Joseph Davis, Jeremiah Tilford and Ja. McCown. Proved Aug. Court 1794.

WILLIAM VANCLEVE—Will Book 1, page 75—Names wife, Abigail Children, Elizabeth, Jane, Mary, John, Ebenezer and William. Son. Jonathan and his sister, Sarah, deceased. Daughter, Phebe Harris. Exec's., Friend, William Crow, and my wife, Abigail. Written Sept. 2, 1786. Witnesses, Thomas and William Gilmore, Rachel Vancleve and Katherine Anderson. Proved Feb. Court 1788.

DAVID WOODS—Will Book 1, page 3—Of Collony of Virginia, Court of Mercer County. Names wife, Mary. Deed of conveyence to Ann Jennings, wife of Jonathan Jennings. Mother, Ann Woods. Children, John, Nancy, Billy, and Betsy Woods. Exec's., Capt. Samuel McAfee and Capt. John Gilmore. Written Sept. 30, 1786. Witnesses, Bernard Noel, John Smith and Samuel Woods. Probated Dec. 5, 1786.

MARTHA ALEXANDER—Will Book 2, page 76—"To Maj. Gen. Samuel Hopkins. My dear friend Polly Hopkins. To Elizabeth Davis, wife of Charles. To brother, Robert Alexander. To half-brother, William Jones Alexander. To half-sister, Nancy Jones Alexander. My friend Catherine Hopkins. Executor Maj. Gen. Samuel Hopkins. Written May 1, 1798. Witnesses, E. McDowell and John O. Houseman. Probated July Court 1798.

JOHN ARMSTRONG—Will Book 2, page 244—Names wife, Priscilla. Sons, Robert, Abraham, William, Lanty and John. Daughters, Mary Lapsley, Prudence Irvine, Rebecca Buchannan, Priscilla, and Margaret. Exec's., Sons, Robert, William, John and Lanty. Written July 7, 1799. Witnesses, Wm. Mahan, Margaret McAfee and George McAfee, Jr. Probated July Court 1801.

HENRY ASHBY—Will Book 2, page 80—Names wife, Elenor. Daughter, Elizabeth. My three sons, Argyle, Robert and Bounds Ashby. My two grand-children, Mary and Matildy Ashby, heirs of Stephen Ashby, deceased. Grand-sons, Lewis and John Robason. Daughters, Mary Jones, Nancy Harrison. Son, George Ashby. Daughters, Sinai and Sarah. Exec's., Mason Jones and son, Bounds Ashby. Written Feb. 5, 1797. Witnesses, Dan Ashby, John Ashby and Stephen Ashby. Probated Aug. Court 1798.

STEPHEN ASHBY—Will Book 2, page 36—Stephen Ashby, Sr., names wife. Sons, John, Stephen, and Enos. Sons, Daniel, Absalom. Daughters, Lettice Neally, Rosa Timmons, Anna Prather. Exec., Sons, Daniel, Absalom, John and Stephen. Written May 19, 1797. Witnesses, Thomas Adams, John Waggoner, Moses Neal, Enos Haden, Gilson Harall and Mason Jones. Probated July Court 1797.

THOMAS BARBER—Will Book 2, page 31—Names my brother Joshua. To Benjamin Fields. To Elizabeth Barber, wife of my brother, Elias. To Mildred Field, wife of Benjamin. To brothers, John, Daniel and William. Exec., Brother Joshua. Written Feb. 7, 1797. Witnesses, Robert Craddock, E. McDowell, James G. Heniler and A. Rankin. Probated May Court 1797.

JOHN BOTTOM—Will Book 2, page 324—Names wife, Nancy. Sons, Robert, William and Merry Sanders Bottom. Daughters, Rebecca, Elizabeth, Nancy and Sally. Grand-children, Nancy, John and Elizabeth, and their brothers and sisters, children of son-in-law, William Sallee and my daughter, Polly Sallee. Nancy and Sally, under 15 years. To Merry Sanders, under 17 years. Exec's., James Clark, Wm. I. Sallee and Horatio Chandler. Written May 29, 1802. Witnesses, John Durham, John Lewelling, John Embree. Probated Sept. Court 1802.

ROBERT BRUSTON—Will Book 2, page 96—Written Feb. 8, 1798. Names "to two brothers children." Brothers, John and David, in County Derry Ireland. Witnesses, James Brown, John Pursley and John Dunn. Probated Oct. Court 1798.

PETER BRUNER—Will Book 2, page 241—Names son, Jacob. Son-in-law, John Thomas. Written July 7, 1801. Names 8 children: Jacob, Macey Vorhees, Elizabeth Thomas, Rachel Demaree, Lydia Bruner, Polly Bruner, Nancy and Fanny Bruner. Exec's., Capt. Robert Mosby and Capt. John Cowan. Witnesses, John George, Deliah George, and William Raines. Probated July, 1801.

JOB BRUMFIELD—Will Boop 2, page 106—Date Mch. 18, 1798. Names wife, Elizabeth and children. Exec's., William Brumfield, Samuel Latimore and John Latimore. Witnesses, James Mitchell, Samuel Daugherty and Thomas Whitwell. Probated Mch. Court 1798.

HENRY BUTT—Will Book 2, page 219—Names Wife, Betsy. Exec's., Wife, Betsy, Jacob Bruner and Peter Bruner. Written Dec. 7, 1800. Witnesses, J. Birney, E. McDowell, Thomas Hampton, James Maxwell, E. M. D. Smith and Frances Reed. Probated Dec., 1800.

WILLIAM CURRY—Will Book 2, page 263—Names wife, Sarah. Sons, John, William, James, Robert, Samuel. To each of my married daughters. To Jean. Exec's., Wife, Sarah, Son, John. Written Aug. 25, 1801. Witnesses, John Bigham and Beverly Mann. Probated Oct. Court 1801.

LAWRENCE DEMOTT—Will Book 2, page 143—Written Aug. 9, 1798. Names, daughter, Martha Bruce. Rachel Demott, under 18 years of age, daughter of Martha. Nicholas Bruce, husband of Martha. My children: Lawrence, Peter, Abraham, and John Demott, Mary Banta, and Deborah Van Nays. Grand-son, Lawrence Demott, son of Derrick Demott. Grand-son, Lawrence VerByke, my daughter, Sarah Hall. Exec's., Sons, Lawrence, Peter, Abraham and John Demott. Witnesses, Thomas Freeman, Peter Vanorsdale and Peter Van Nest. Probated May, 1799.

ANNE DERHAM—Book 2, page 21—Anne Derham, wife. Jacob Derham, and widow of John Berry. Right of Dower. Oct. 22, 1796. By commissioners, Arch. Bilbo, Wm. Bilbo and William Brumfield.

DAVID GILLISPIE, of the town of Danville, Mercer Co., Ky.—Will Book 2, page 247—Names wife, Mary. Sons, David and James. Brother, John. Exec's., Willis Green, clerk of Lincoln Co. and William McDowell, and John Rochester, Esq. of Mercer Co. Written Dec. 1, 1798. Witnesses, Jesse Smith, John Lewis, and Garret Darland. Probated July Court 1801.

THOMAS HARBISON—Will Book 2, page 83—Names wife, Nancy. Son, James. Daughters, Ruth, Mary, and Rachel Harbison. Witnesses, Wm. Thompson and Wm. McBrayer. Probated Aug. Court 1799.

JOHN HARRISON, Sr.—Will Book 2, page 11—Names wife, Mary. Grand-son, Reuben Smith. Sons, John and Richard Harrison. Exec's., Wife, Mary, sons, John and Richard, friends, Ambrose Barber, and David Walker. Written Oct. 1, 1795. Witnesses, David Walker and William Smith. Probated Aug. Court 1796.

JOHN HALE—Will Book 2, page 74—Names wife and infant children. Exec., Jesse Hale. Written Mch. 9, 1798. Witnesses, John Hungate, James Stevens and Thomas Stephens. Probated July Court 1798.

JAMES LAWRENCE—Will Book 2, page 290—Names son, Solomon Lawrence. Daughter, Elizabeth Arbuckle, wife of Thomas. Other children, viz: William, David, John, Isaac, Sarah Crow. Son-in-law, James Cloyd, heirs of son, Joseph, deceased. Heirs of son, Robert, deceased. Grand-son, James Lawrence, son of Robert, deceased. Son, Samuel, deceased, estate. Exec's., Son, John Lawrence and James Brown. Written Aug. 13, 1801. Witnesses, Samuel Dunn, Samuel Pursel and John Cowley. Probated Mch. Court 1802.

JOHN LILLARD—Will Book 2, page 260—Names wife, Ann. Children, Nancy Lillard, daughter son, Thomas, by his first wife, Elizabeth Chiles, John Lillard, Anna Pelham, Mary McGinnis, Susannah Jones, Joseph Lillard, Ephraim Lillard, James Lillard, Patsy McGinnis, Daniel and David Lillard. Exec's., John, Joseph and Ephriam Lillard and Thomas Freeman. Written Feb. 24, 1800. Witnesses, Joseph Willis, Jonathan Jenkins and Abel Jenkins. Probated Aug. Court 1801.

CHRISTOPHER LILLARD, deceased—Will Book 2, page 48—Written July 21, 1794. Wills to Elizabeth Chiles and children land. To brothers and sisters. Inventory of above estate. Dec. 27, 1794.

WILLIAM LOCKE—Will Book 2, page 188—Names wife, Elizabeth. Daughter, Polly Locke. Brother, Frank. To John Gibson. Exec's., Wife, Elizabeth and John Marshall. Written Feb. 8, 1800. Witnesses, George Robinson and John Jones. Probated July 1800.

GEORGE McAFEE—Will Book 2, page 339—Names son, George Mc-Afee, Jr. Daughter, Peggy. Sons, John and James. Daughter, Polly Armstrong have their share. Wife, Susannah. Written Mch. 21, 1803. Witnesses, John McKamey, Robert B. McAfee, Robert Rennick. Codicil, son, John, died in Charleston, S. C. and his property to go to son, James and his heirs. Probated Apr. Court 1803.

SAMUEL McAFEE—Will Book 2, page 252—Names wife, Hannah. Daughter, Anna McAfee, William McAfee, Hannah McAfee, Samuel McAfee and Polly McAfee. To sons, John and Robert McAfee, and daughter, Jenny McGoffin have given share of land. Exec., Wife, Hannah and sons, John and Robert. Written June 6, 1801. Witnesses, Thomas Essex, Alexander Buchannan and James McAfee. Probated Aug. Court 1801.

JAMES McCOUN—Will Book 2, page 199—Written Apr. 26, 1800. Names, son, John. Daughters, Mary and Ginney. James McCoun, son of my son, James, deceased. Grand-sons, Samuel Walker Kerr and Moses McCoun, grand-son, John McCoun, son of my daughter, Susannah, and grand-son, Samuel McAfee. To children of my daughter, Betsy. Exec's., son, John and grand-son, James McCoun. Witnesses, Robert Armstrong, John Armstrong and John Armstrong, Jr. Probated Oct. Court 1800. Written Apr. 26, 1800.

JAMES McCOUN—Will Book 2, page 216—Names son, Moses McCoun. Daughter, Margaret McCoun. Son, John. Daughters, Agnes Mc-Coun and Jane, when she comes of age. Sons, Alexander and Samuel. Exec's., Jordon Edward Smith and son, John McCoun. Written June 26, 1800. Witnesses, Andrew Wilson and Edward Smith. Probated Nov. Court 1800.

CHARLES McKINNEY—Will Book 2, page 61—Names son, Charles, of Charlotte Co., Va. Sons, William, Josiah and Abraham. Daughters, Elizabeth Lawrence, Judith Lawrence. Son, Thomas, Rane, Peter, and James, under age. Son, Daniel Fuquay, under age. Son, Abraham. Exec's., James Speed and sons, Rane and James Mc-Kinney. Written 1795. Witnesses, John Hopkins, Mathers Speed, Wm. Walker and Henry Speed. Proved May Court 1798.

WILLIAM MOORE—Will Book 2, page 298—Names brother, Aaron. Sisters, Dorcas and Sarah. To Daniel Morris' three orphan children, begot by my sister, Mary, 66 pounds due from Ann Harrod. To Ann Harrod. Exec's., Brother, Aaron Moore and Ann Harrod. Written Mch. 20, 1802. Witnesses, Lewis H. Smith, Daniel Lamb and Philip Fulkerson. Probated Apr. Court 1802.

EDMUND MUNDAY—Will Book 2, page 201—Names wife, Ruth. Son, Harrison. Daughter, Lucy Brown. Son, Thomas Munday. Daughter, Elizabeth. Sons, William, James and Reuben Munday. Dau., Sally Munday, when of age. Daughters, Polly and Nancy. Exec's., Thomas Sneed, Son, Harrison Munday and Scott Brown. Written July 1, 1800. Witnesses, Samuel Woods, Gideon Pulliam and James Samuel. Probated Oct. Court 1800

JAMES ROBERTSON—Will Book 2, page 125—Names wife, Sarah. Sons, George, Israel, James and Samuel. Daughters, Elizabeth, Mary and Anna. Grand-daughter, Sally Armstrong. Exec's., Wife, Sarah and sons, George and Israel Robertson. Written May 15, 1799. Witnesses, Robert Armstrong, David Williams, Susanna Jones. Probated May Court 1799.

JOHN ROGERS—Will Book 2, page 43—Wills estate to father, George Rogers. Written Jan. 15, 1791. Probated 1797. Witnesses, Hugh Roy and John Farish.

JOHN RYAN—Will Book 2, page 70—Names wife, Sarah. Sons, John, Solomon, Thomas and David. Daughters, Elizabeth, Sarah, Eleanor, Mary and Catherine. Exec's., Wife, Sarah and son, John and son-in-law, Robert Johnston. Written Apr. 2, 1798. Witnesses, David Williamson, John Jones and John Thomas. Probated May Court 1798.

JOHN STEEN—Will Book 2, page 149—Names wife, Jane. Sons, William, John, Jr. and Frederick. Daughters, Susannah, wife of Joseph Lathy. Daughters, Jane Haws and Margaret, wife of Robert Chamberlain. Daughter, Abigail, wife of Wm. McFartridge, deceased. Exec's., Wife, Jane and son, William. Written July 18, 1799. Witnesses, Abraham Chaplin, Thomas Owens,' and Aaron Hogue. Probated Oct. Court 1799.

BENONI SWEARENGEN—Will Book 2, page 120—Of Washington Co., State of Maryland, land in Kentucky and Virginia. Names wife, Hester, son, Henry Thomas Swearengen, when 18 years of age. Daughter, Sarah Blackford. Joseph Swearengen and Henry Bedinger, both of Berkley County, Va., to be guardian of Sarah Blackford and Henry Thomas Swearengen. Exec's., Joseph Swearengen, Henry Bedinger and Abraham Chapline, of Kentucky. Written Mch. 18, 1798. Witnesses, Wm. Chapline, Thomas Mugg, Walter B. Selby and Jacob Bysong. Probated July Court 1799.

JEREMIAH TILFORD—Will Book 2, page 352—Names sons, James, John, Robert and Wear Tilford. To____ Lamme, husband of daughter, Jane. To John Boyle, husband of daughter, Betsy. To Jacob Bowman, husband of daughter, Nelly. Wife, Sarah Tilford. Five grand-children: Sinclair, Robert, Jeremiah, James and America Travis, children of daughter, Polly Travis. Exec., Son, James. Written Mch. 22, 1802. Witnesses, David Tilford and Thomas Allin. Probated July Court 1803.

JOHN THRELKELD, Sr.—Will Book 2, page 292—Names wife, Margaret, sons, George, Daniel and John. Daughters, Judith Bohon, Sarah Bohon, Molly Burris. Grand-daughter, Peggy Russell, daughter of John Russell and Betty, his wife. Grand-daughter, Elly Russell and Betsy Russell. Exec's., Wife, Margaret and sons, George and Daniel Threlkeld. Written Jan. 23, 1797. Witnesses, Wharton Ransdal and Nathan Neeld. Probated Mch. Court 1802.

THOMAS TURPIN—Will Book 2, page 25—Names sons, Edmund, Josiah, Jeremiah, and Thomas Turpin. Wife, Averilor. Exec's., Son, Jeremiah and wife, Averilor. Written Nov. 20, 1796. Witnesses, Thomas Gill, John Calverd, Michael Mires and Wm. Mires. Probated Mch., 1797.

WILLIAM R. VANCE—Noncupative—Will Book 2, page 343—"To four sisters, brother, Robert, brother, James. Oldest sister, M. Vance. Teste: William McDowell and John Cowan. Probated June Court 1803.

PETER WALKER—Will Book 2, page 294—Names wife, Barbara. Written Jan. 30, 1802. Witnesses, David Hart, Wm. Peddoct, Charles Powell, Sr. Probated Mch. Court 1802.

RICHARD WEBSTER—Will Book 2, page 225—Names wife, Rebecca, and nine children. Exec's., Wm. Webster and Wm. Thompson. Written Nov. 26, 1800. Witnesses, Thomas Newgert and Humphreys May. Probated Jan., 1801.

JAMES WOODS, deceased—Book 2, page 227—To be divided among 6 heirs: Joseph, Mary, Archibald, Samuel, James and Elizabeth Woods. Consent of James Adams, husband of Peggy Woods, and guardian of the 6 legatees. Date Aug. 20, 1800. Signed James McAfee, Robert Armstrong, and Wm. Adams.

GEORGE ADAMS—Deceased, estate appraised by Samuel Graham, Wm. Shields, James Shields. Book 3, page 31. Aug. 11, 1803.

NANCY BOTTOM—Will Book 3, page 39.—Commissioners appointed by Court assign to Nancy Bottom, widow of John Bottom one-third part of estate. Jan. 11, 1804. Witnesses, Thomas Freeman, D. Knox and James Harland.

JOHN CHILES—Will Book 3, page 36—Names wife, Elizabeth. Children: William, Thomas, Susannah, Sally, John, Elizabeth and Polly. Deceased brother-in-law, Christopher Lillard. Exec's., Wife, Elizabeth and son, William. Written Dec. 19, 1803. Witnesses, Thomas Freeman, Wm. Gales and James Gales. Probated, no date.

FRANCIS CLARK—Will Book 3, page 1—Names wife, Dorcas. Son, Frances, to my son, Jas. Daughters, Sarah Mahan, Susannah Price and Mary Clark. Exec's., Wife, Dorcas, sons, James and Frances. Written June 8, 1796. Witnesses, Thomas Hicks, John Moss, Mathias Kelly and Martin Kelly. Probate, no date.

JOHN COONEY, deceased—Inventory Book 3, page 33—Ann Cooney Administrator. Recorded Dec. Court 1803.

JARAD COWON, deceased—Estate. Booke 3, page 14—Recorded Sept. Court 1803.

HANNAH McAFEE—Will Book 3, page 8—Hannah McAfee, guardian of William McAfee, Hannah, Samuel and Polly, orphans of Samuel McAfee. 1803.

SAMUEL MOONS, deceased—Book 3, page 34—Recorded Jan. Court 1804.

NATHAN NEELD, deceased—Account of George McAfee, guardian of Sally Neeld, orphan of Nathan Neeld. Recorded Sept. Court 1803.

JEREMIAH RILEY—Will Book 3, page 52—Names Son, Edward Riley. Five children: Elender, Mary, Elizabeth, Rasmus and Edward. Witnesses, Robert McGee, James Adams. Proved July Court 1804.

THOMAS SNEED, deceased—Inventory. Book 3, page 34—Recorded Jan. Court 1804. Sally Sneed, administratrix.

JEREMIAH TILFORD, deceased—Inventory. Book 3, page 11—Recorded Sept. Court 1803.

LAWRENCE VERBRYKE, deceased—Inventory. Book 3, page 10—Recorded Oct. Court 1803.

JOHN COWAN—Will Book 7, page 197—Names wife. Sons, William C. Cowan, Henry T., daughters, Betsy, Sally and Mary. Sons, John, David. Exec's., Sons, Wm. and Henry. Written May 8, 1819. Witnesses, David G. Cowan, Samuel Baird, Elizabeth Cowan, and Sarah Cowan. Codicil, July 18, 1819. Probated May Court 1823.

JOHN COCHRAN, deceased—Inventory. Will Book 9, page 322, and Book 8, page 257—Shows widow was Jane. Daughters, Sally, wife of Stephen Waller, and Betsy, wife of Mathew O'Brian. Wife, Jane. Son, Benjamin F. Cochran. July 14, 1825. Commissioners, Michael G. Youse, Joshua Barber, William Fields and F. Yeiser.

ANDREW HARBISON—Will Book 9, page 466—Division of estate, to Lydia Garr, relict of Andrew Harbison, deceased. Date Jan. 13, 1832. Commissioners, J. P. Mitchell, J. L. Ewing and Nelson Mays. Recorded Feb. Court 1832.

JOHN B. THOMPSON—Will Book 9, page 524—Names wife, Nancy P. Thompson, and my sons and daughters. Written Sept. 5, 1819. Executrix, Wife, Nancy. Codicil, Oct. 1833.

JOHN THOMPSON—Will Book 93, page 525—Names son, John B. Thompson. Daughter, Mary B. Allen. Sons, John B., Philip, George B. Thompson. Exec., John B. Thompson. Written June 2, 1833. Witnesses, H. T. Dewees, C. B. Bradshaw and Richard Thompson. Probated Aug. Court 1833.

ARCHIBALD THOMPSON—Will Book 9, page 219—Namse wife, Jane. Daughters, Margaret Thompson, Mary Jennings. Grandsons, John Jennings and Thompson Jennings. Exec's., Step-son, Samuel Ecles, son-in-law, Wm. Jennings and Wm. Nourse. Written Apr. 14, 1829. Witnesses, John Ecles and Thomas Gaunt. Probated July Court 1829. Inventory of estate taken July 16, 1829, by James Lillard, Jackson Mann and Joseph Wiggand. Recorded July, 1831.

GEORGE THOMPSON, Sr.—Book 9, page 538—To grand-son, Wm. Thompson. To grand-daughters, Mary and Rebecca Thompson, "when they marry or become 21 years of age." Son, George C. Thompson. Exec's., Son, George C. Thompson and nephew, John B. Thompson and grand-son, Wm. Thompson. Written June 30. Witnesses, James Gass, John A. Tomlinson and James Taylor. Probated Apr. Court 1834.

ANNE BURRIS—Will Book 11, page 27—Division of Anne Burris' land made Nov. Court 1841, by undersigned commissioners to Anna Mariah Connor, wife of Wm. G. Connor, late Anne Maria Lankford. To Ardenah Lankford and to Sarah Lankford. To Harriett Lankford from their grand-mother, Anne Burris (late Anne Littlepage and formally Anne Meaux). Signed James B. Westerfield, Richard Holman and James B. Irvine.

WILLIAM GIBSON—Will Book 11, page 285—Names wife, Malindy Gibson, and my child, Sara Ann Gibson. Exec., George F. Kerkham. Written Aug. 20, 1840. Witnesses, Henry Sheering, William Bolin, J. A. Lewis. Probated Sept., 1840

EDMUND BURRIS—Will Book 14, page 78—Edmund Burris, Sr. to son, Philip, son, Gabriel, and Stanfield Burris. To daughter, Polly Penny, to daughter, Jane Bell, deceased and children viz: Napoleon

Price, Susan Francis and Henry Clay Bell. To daughter, Mildred Paxton. To son, Wm. Burris. To son, Edmund Burris. Trustees to be sons, Gabriel and Stanfield Burris, and H. Walker. 1-4 acre of land, where beloved wife is buried, to be set aside for a family burying ground. Written Oct. 16, 1850. Witnesses, John Kennedy and Wm. N. Montgomery. Probated Jan. 1, 1853.

JAMES W. BURRIS—Will Book 15, page 141—Guardian to James E. Burris, infant son of John W. Burris, deceased. Jan. 1, 1854.

NATHANIEL BURRIS—Will Book 15, page 94—Nathaniel Burris, Sr., wills to daughters, Elizabeth Lyon, to Nancy Penny, to Susan Walker. To children of my dau., Polly Burton. To dau., Sally Slaughter's children in trust with son, Edward Burris, until children become 21 years old. Grand-dau., Sarah McAfee, the daughter of my deceased daughter, Margaret Penny. Trustee to be Jordon Walker. Grand-son, Hickerson Wayland. To my 3 grandsons, the children of my deceased dau., Dicy Lillard. To my dau., Fanny Black, land lying on Salt River in Anderson Co., Ky. Slaves not to be sold, but to be distributed at their value, as part of above legacies. To son, Edward. To children of my deceased daughters, Polly Burton and Sally Slaughter. Exec's., Three grand-sons, Edward Burris, Jr., Jesse L. Burris and Hickerson Wayland. Edward Burris to enclose 1-4 acres of land for family burying ground, for which executors will pay. Nov. 15, 1853.

PHILIP BURRIS—Will Book 15, page 39—Names wife, Catherine. 2 youngest children, Samuel and Lydia. To Mary Hale, wife of Thomas. To Harry J. Burris. To Lewis I. Burris. To John Burris. Daughter, Elizabeth Moore. To Samuel Burris. To Lydia Burris. My son, P. S. Burris. Grand-son, Thompson Burris, I give to his son, Philip Burris. Exec's., Sons, Harry J. and Lewis I. Burris. Written June 14, 1854. Witnesses, J. W. Bottom, John Sallee. Probated Nov. Court 1854.

WILLIAM P. BURRIS, deceased—Book 15, page 189—Inventory by Edmund Burris. Oct. 6, 1855.

EDMUND BURRIS, Sr., deceased—Inventory—To Mrs. Mary Burris, widow of said Edmund, Sr., by appraisers, J. B. Roach, Andrew Forsyth and Abraham Sharpe. Exec's., sons, Jesse and Edmund. Date Sept. 27, 1858. Debetors to Edmund Burris estate, namely James Burris, Thomas Penny, Jesse Burris. Jesse Burris to pay for land willed to him by his father, Edmund. Exec's., Son, Edmund and widow, Mary.

MISCELLANEOUS

WILL ABSTRACTS

(Donated by Mrs. Joseph Beard)

WILLSON, SAMPSON—Estill Co., Ky. Court Records—Will Book A—Written Aug. 9, 1827, and Probated Sept. 17, 1827. Mentions wife, Mourning. Children, Marshall M., Anderson S., America Ann, Polly W., Minitree I., Elizabeth E., Sampson, Jr., Augustine W. Execs., Elibabb Willson, wife, Mourning and Isaac Thornberg.

WILLSON, SAMUEL—Will written, Aug. 22, 1774. Augusta County,

Colony of Va. Names executors, wife, Mary and beloved friend, Thomas Hughart. Eldest son, Ralph, next eldest son, Elibabb, youngest son, Sampson. Dau., Ruth. Witnesses, John McCoy, Joseph Gamwell, and John Jordan. Probated, Augusta Co. Court Nov. 16, 1774. (Note: The above is an abstract of the Will of Captain Samuel Willson, who was killed at the Battle of Point Pleasant, Oct. 10, 1774).

WILLSON, ELIBABB—Estill Co., Ky. Court Records—Deed Book E, page 187-275—Date Mch. 9, 1832. Elibabb Willson and Nancy, his wife, Elizabeth Noland and Sarah Willson, heirs at law, of Ralph Willson, who died intestate, of first part, convey to Mourning Willson, widow of Sampson Wilson, deceased and children, Marshall M., Anderson S., America Ann, Polly W., Minitree I., Elizabeth E., Sampson, Jr., and Augustine W., heirs of Sampson Willson, deceased, and parties of second part, land including 250 acres which belonged to Ralph Willson, but now occupied by Sampson's heirs. Witnesses, Marshall Willson and Wiliam Skinner.

WOOD, JAMES—Estill Co., Ky. Court Records—Will Book B, page 254—Names wife, Nancy. Sons, Fielding and Simpson Wood, and children of wife, Nancy, by her first husband, namely: Hutson Vaughn, James Vaughn, and Mary Railsback, wife of David Railsback. Exec., Johnathan Nelson. Witnesses, Martin Brock and Henry Skinner. Written 1843. Probated 1843.

VIRGINIA, KENTUCKY AND MARYLAND

(Donated by Mrs. J. W. Marr, Lexington, Ky.)

MARR, JOHN—Fayette County, Ky.—Will Book S, page 274—Written Sept. 22, 1847. Mentions, children: Tazewell Marr, Madison Marr, Mildred Snyder, Jane Deavers, Susan Corsa, Francis Todd, Anne Williams, Martha White. Witnesses, Charles Talbutt and James D. France. Probated September, 1847.
(Note. Tazewell Marr was born Oct. 17th, 1812. Married Oct. 17th, 1833, to Eilza B. Rogers, dau. of Thomas Rogers (b. Dec. 13, 1754, and Rebecca Sphear (Sphar), b. 1771. (Thomas and Rebecca Rogers mar. Sept. 11, 1792. Rebecca Sphear was a dau. of Jacob Sphar, killed by Indians at Strodes' Station, Mch. 1, 1781).

CLARK, JAMES—Will—Augusta County, Va.—Will Book VI, page 4— Court House in Staunton, Va. Will dated Aug. 20, 1774. Proved Mch. 17, 1776. Names wife, Elizabeth. Chidlren, Jean Clark, Elizabeth, Sarah Clark, John, James Clark, William, Anne Dunlop, Alexander, Samuel, Robert, Margaret.

(Note. James Clark was a private in Co. No. 7, Augusta Co. Militia in 1742. Authority, "Drapers' Manuscript Hist. Society of Wisconsin).

CLARK, ELIZABETH—Will—Augusta Co., Va.—Will Book VI, page 208—Date. Oct. 8, 1781. Proved Nov. 20, 1781. Mentions, Jean Elliott's heirs, Elizabeth Breath, Sarah Elliott, Anne Dunlap, Margaret Clenkard, John Clark, Samuel Clark, James Clark, William Clarks' heirs, Alexander Clark and his wife, Robert Clark.

Note: Will in possession of Mrs. J. W. Marr; copy donated by her.

CLARK, JAMES—Will written in long hand by James Clark. Apr.

30, 1810. Mentions wife, Susanna Clark. Sons, John, Edmund, William, James, Hipkins, Thomas, Peter, Samuel and Sidney. Daughters, Lucy, Delphy, Betsey, and Susan (Soockey). Executrix, Susanna Clark with sons, John and Edmund, and William Ellis, executors. Probated July Court 1810.

(Note. James Clark, son of above James and Elizabeth Clark. See in list Saffell's Officers and Privates, James Clark, page 265. James Clark, b. Apr. 30, 1759 in Va. Died, 1810 in Fayette County, Ky.

GALE, MATHEW—Will—Spottsylvania Co., Va. Executors bond, dated Feb. 18, 1779, by wife, Judith Gale, John Gale, Mathew Gale, Jr., and Joseph Gale. Witnesses, Robert Dudley, James Smith, George Todd and Ambrose Dudley. Legatees, wife, Judith Gale, Mathew Gale, Jr., son, Joseph Gale and wife, Rachel. Sarah Edwards Deatherage, John Edwards Gale, son of Joseph Gale. Estate to be divided between my seven children, John Gale, Elizabeth Pool, Joyce Dudley, Judith Darnaby, Sarah Edwards Deatherage, Matthew Gale, Jr., and Joseph Gale. Recorded, Will Book E.
1772 to 1798, page 266, in Spottsylvania Co., Va.
Mathew Gayle (Gale) was evidently born in Gloucester Co., Va. as the following abstract from a deed on record in Spottsylvania Co., Va. will show "Matthew Gale, of Gloucester Co., Va. on May 17, 1733, for the sum of 50 pounds, paid to Ambrose Grayson, was deeded 300 acres of land in Spottsylvania Co., Va." Deed Book B, 1729 to 1734.

RICKS, NICHOLAS—Goochland Co., Va.—Deeb Book No. 18, page 34—
Power of Attorney from Nicholas Ricks to Gilbert Ricks was proved by the oaths of Wm. Johnson, Benjamin Hopkins and John Frank. Nicholas Ricks, names his son, Gilbert Ricks, his grandfather, Benjamin Ricks, Sr., deceased, his father, Nicholas Ricks, deceased, his mother Frances Wood, deceased. Written July 19, 1800. Proved July 21, 1800.

MARRIAGE RECORD—Deed Book No. 16, page 175—John Wood married to Susanna Ricks, Feb. 21st, 1793. Signed Hugh French. "At a court held in Goochland Co., Va. the 15th day of April, 1793. This list of marriages solemnized by the Rev. Hugh French, was returned to Court and ordered to be recorded." Teste, Wm. Miller, Clerk. Bondsmen, John Wood and Gilbert Ricks.

WOOD, WILLIAM—Will—Nicholas Co., Ky.—Will Book 3, page 364—
Written Feb. 20, 1852. Probated May Court, 1853. Mentions, "all my children." Names son, Caleb Wood and his 2nd. wife, Tessy Wood and children. George Carr, as Trustee for children of his daughter, Letitia (Tessy) Carr Wood. Executor, Hiram Norton. Witnesses, J. G. Parks and John W. Wood.

WOOD, JOHN—Estate—Will Book 3, page 451—Names children, Ursela (note, mar. John Payne or Pace), Delicia (note, mar. Wm. L. Campbell, Feb. 7, 1850), Caleb (note, mar. Hannah Maxwell, 2nd Letitia Carr), Hezekiah, Thirza, Nancy (note, mar. Joseph Frigate, Sept. 7, 1820), Polly, Nimrod (note, mar. Dryden Marsh, 2nd. mar. Margaret McClintock. Mentions A. G. Fisher and Wm. H. Evans, as beneficiaries.

WOOD, JOHN THOMAS—Henrico County, Va., Dec. 3rd, 1853—Page 284—Deed from Thomas Wood and wife, Martha, of Henrico Co., Va., to Jacob Age * *. Henrico Co., Va., Nov. 1, 1756, page 467.

Thomas Wood and wife, Martha of Varina Parish, Henrico, Co. to his son, Wm. Wood. * * Thomas Wood died intestate, appraisement filed Feb. 5, 1771. * * * John Wood, son of Thomas Wood, makes deed to Wm. DuVal, attorney, dated May 4, 1772. * * * John Wood, son of Thomas Wood died intestate, appraisement filed Dec. 15, 1784, by Drury Wood, administrator. Wm. Wood, son of Thomas Wood, removed to Louisa Co. Deed of Wm. Wood and Ursley Wood, his wife, of Louisa Co. to Turner Southall of Henrico, Mch. 13, 1787.

SPHEAR, JOHN ULRICH—Will—Frederick Co., Va. Written Sept. 2, 1769. Names wife, Margaret Sphear and 9 children. Sons, John Ulric Sphear, Jacob, Mathias, Haunse, Matharorns, Henry and Theodorus. Daughters, Barbara Sphear, otherwise Myers, Rebecca Sphear. Proved Mch. 6, 1770. Witnesses, Burkett Beager and John Drake. Executrix, Margaret Sphear, refused to serve, letters of administration then issued to two sons, John and Matthias Sphear, together with James Forman and Henry Pedinger.

SPHEAR, CATHERINE—Will—Frederick Co., Va. Written May 10, 1821. Mentions daughter, Elizabeth Kailer. Note of Jacob Sphear. Attest, John Anderson, Stewart Grant and Abraham Nulton. Proved Aug. 5th, 1823. No executor named, John Richardson with George Pelter entered bond. Will Book II, page 452.

ELLIS, WILLIAM—Will—Fayette Co., Ky.—Will Book A, page 1 to 3 inclusive—Names wife, Aggie Ellis. Daughter, Susanna Clark and her husband, Phebe McDonald (or McDaniel). Betsy Ellis, Nancy Ellis, Polly Ellis. Sons, John, Wm., Thomas, Charles Hezekiah and Walter. Excs., my wife, Aggie Ellis, my sons, John and Wm. Ellis, and my brother, John Ellis. Written Aug. 4, 1793. Witnesses, Wm. Ellis, Jr., Timothy Parrish, Richard Mitchell and Benjamin Robinson. Recorded Fayette Ct. Oct., 1793. Admitted to probate second time Feb. 10, 1803.

ELLIS, WILLIAM—Will Book D, page 241—Dated May 19, 1766. Probated Aug. 4, 1766. Spottsylvania Co., Va. (Note, Father of above). Names daughter, Mary Proctor. Son, William Ellis. Daughter, Elizabeth Hawkins and Ann O'Neal. Sons, Hezekiah. Son, John, when he arrives at age of 21. Dau., Agnes, when she is of age. If my wife dies or marries before Agnes is of age, Hezekiah is to be her guardian. Executors, Col. Jos. Brock, son, Hezekiah and son, Wm. Ellis. Witness, Wm. Wood.

CARR, WILLIAM—Will—Spottsylvania Co., Va.—Will Book B, page 497—Written Aug. 2, 1760. Probated Nov. 4, 1760. Names sons, Thomas, William, Walter Chiles Carr and Charles Brooks Carr. Daughters, Ann Carr, Elizabeth, Phoebe, Ann Brooks Carr. Son-in-law, Mordecai Hord. Witness, Wm. Ellis.

CARR, SUSANNA—Will Book B, page 502—Spottsylvania Co., Va., Nov. 6, 1760. Susanna Carr, appointed guardian of Charles Brooks Carr, Agnes Brooks Carr, Walter Chiles Carr, Phoebe Carr, Thomas Carr, orphans of Wm. Carr, deceased. Wm. Carr, gent., security.

DARNABY, JOHN—Spottsylvania Co., Va.—Deed Book 1, page 35—Sept. 14, 1774. Indenture for John Darnaby, son of Wm. Darnaby, deceased, of this County to Ambrose Dudley, with consent of his mother, Judith Darnaby, now Judith Smith, "to learn the art and mystery of joiner and house carpenter for a period of 5 years." Note: John Darnaby, b. at Fredericksburg, Va., June 27, 1760, married Elizabeth Alsop 1782. She was b. Feb. 23, 1757 and d. Jan. 24, 1832. Bureau of Pension records (F. S. C.—S file 16360) show John Darnaby served as private in Capt. Ambrose Dudley's Co., Col. Muhlenburg, State of Va., from Spring 1776-Spring 1777. Also from Fall of 1777-Oct. or Nov. 1781, as wagoner under Wm. Crittenden. Fayette Co., Ky., Will Book L, page 202. John Darnaby mentions wife, Elizabeth, sons; William, George W., James, John and Edward. Daughters; Judith Coons and Betsey Clark. Brother Edward. Executors, Sons, Wm., James and George W. Darnaby. Written Sept. 22, 1827. Proved Oct. Court 1833. Witnesses; Beverly A. Hicks and A. Thomson. Deed book 9, page 387. Marriage contract between John Darnaby and Elizabeth Pinkard. Nov. 10, 1832. (Note: John Darnaby d. Fayette Co., Ky., Sept. 21, 1833.)

MARSH, JOSHUA—Baltimore Co., Maryland—The 2nd. additional acacount of Joshua Marsh, administrator of Thomas Marsh, deceased. Mentions Sons, John, Joshua, Thomas, David, Benedict, Beale and Clement. Beneficiaries: James Bosley, James Enlows, Benjamin Hendon, James Stover, acting for their wives. Also statement "current money paid by these accountants to Thomas Winks, Joshua Winks, and John Buck, who intermarried with Sophia Winks." "Current money retained by this accountant Joshua, as guardian of Achsah Temperance, and John Winks." Recorded Oct. 5, 1803. Signed, Wm. Buchannan, Register of Wills.

MARYLAND CORBIN FAMILY

(Furnished by Mrs. Effie S. Honson, of Ventura, California, to

Mrs. J. W. Marr, Lexington, Ky.)

NICHOLAS CORBIN—Came to Baltimore Co., Md. in 1671. (Authority, "Early Maryland Settlers List." "Annapolis land office records. Vol. XVI., page 533." Alice, wife of Nicholas Corbin, 2nd., mar. John Barrot. (Annapolis Md. Inventories and Accounts, XX, page 47). Children of Nicholas and Alice Corbin, 1, Elizabeth (mar. Roberts); 2, Mary (mar. Gostwick); 3, Edward (mar. Jane Wilkinson, a daughter of Wm. Wilkinson, 1718). Children of Edward and Jane Corbin: 1, Nicholas; 2, William Wilkinson Corbin, died; 3, Abraham Corbin; 4, Phyllis Anna Corbin; 5, Providence Corbin; 6, Unity Corbin; 7, Edward Corbin, Jr.
Abraham Corbin, son of Edward and Jane, mar. Rachel Marshall. Abraham was born Sept. 7, 1722, St. Paul's Parrish, Baltimore, Co., Md. Married Dec. 4, 1766, (see rec. St. John's). Their children (Lib. W. G. No. 56, page 122. Mentions all these children and widow, Rachel): Abraham, Thomas, Nicholas, Nathan, Sarah (mar. Thomas Marsh, Jr.), Eleanor (mar. Beale Marsh). All six of these came to Kentucky.

MARSH, BEALE—Will Book J, page 389—Dated Nov. 4, 1831. Probated Dec. Court 1833. Mentions 6 children: Executors, friend, John B. Rains and my son, Nicholas C. Marsh. Sons, Nicholas C. Marsh, Benedict Marsh, Beale Marsh. Daughter, Rachel, chidlren of my deceased dau., wife of Drydon Wood. Brother-in-law,

Nicholas Corbin. Witnesses, Thomas P. Smith, Frances R. Smith and Mary T. Barbee.
(Note by family, "Thomas K. Marsh and Corbin Marsh are the other two children not mentioned by name.")
License number 187, in the City of Baltimore, State of Maryland, shows the marriage of Beal Marsh and Elinor Corbin, on 21st. of March, 1797, by the Rev. Mr. Richards. Attested copy July 3rd, 1926, by Stephen C. Little, Clerk.

MADISON COUNTY, KENTUCKY
(Donated by Mrs. B. F. Buckley)

TRIBBLE, DUDLEY, Sr.—Will dated April 26, 1872. Madison Co., Ky. Names daughter, Mary Jane Turner, deceased. Sons, Jas. P. Tribble and Robert G. Tribble. Son-in-law, J. F. Collier. Daughter, Nannie Collier. Other children. Witnesses, Cyrus T. Fox, Achilles Deatherage, Joe Phelps. Probated Aug. ——, 1878. On oaths Cyrus T. Fox, Joe Phelps and Achilles Deatherage.

ATTESTED WILLS
(Donated by Mrs. B. F. Buckley)

DAVIES, JAMES—Rowan Co., N. C.—Book A, page 35, 1765—Names son, James Davies. Son, John Davies. Son, Evan Davies. Wife, Elinor. Daughters, Mary Enoch, Ann Turner, Elinor Douthitt, Ruth Davies. Witnesses, Wm. Johnson, David Jones and Evan Ellis. Salisbury Court House, N. C.

TURNER, WILLIAM, Sr.—Written 1696. Albermarle, N. C. Names eldest son, William. Son, John Turner. Daughter, Sarah. Wife, Katherine.

TURNER, WILLIAM, II—Perguimans County, N. C., 1709. Names eldest son, William. Son, Edward. Wife, executrix.
(Note: John Turner, brother of William, died 1715, N. C.)

SMITH, ANDREW—Rowan, N. C. Parrish of St. Lukes, 1778. Names sons, Cornelius, Andrew, Thomas. Daughters, Catherine, Rebecca Turner. Grand-sons, John Bushall, James and Thomas Smith. Executors, Brothers, James and Thomas Smith. Book A, page 204.

HOBBS, JOSEPH—Will Book J. G. I., No. 36, folio 222—Of Ann Arundell County, Maryland. Planter. Names son, Noah Hobbs, son, Henry Hobbs. Son, Joseph Hobbs. Daughters, Rachel Bissitt, Hannah Spurrier and Elizabeth Hobbs. "That Major Harry Ridgely * * convey to my daughter, Hannah Spurier * * tract of land called Ridgleys Great Park * * paying him the cash rents due on said land * *." Executors and executrix, Sons, Thomas, Henry Cornelius, Joseph and Noah Hobbs, and daughters, Rachel Bissett, Hannah Spurrier and Elizabeth Hobbs. Witnesses, John Hood, Jr., Charles Poole, and Walter Pearce. Dated Mch. 19, 1791.

BOURBON COUNTY, KENTUCKY
(Donated by Miss Margaret Steele)

CUNNINGHAM, WALTER—Will—Jessamine Co., Ky. Written June 27, 1807. Names, Robert Lowrey and my daughter, Mary, his wife. Jean Cunningham, my wife. Son, John Cunningham. Grand-daughter, Sarah Cunningham Lamine. Wm. Drake and my dau., Agnes, his wife. Daughter, Jean, and dau., Isabella. Also "land

surveyed by John Lowry. Land whereon Thomas Whiten lives.
Land nigh to Jeremiah Penexes, including the spring near Mount
Moriah, meeting house. Thomas Kinkead, note. Deed of Warranty to David Steele. Land where John Ashford, blacksmith now
lives, same was some years ago surveyed for him by Samuel Lamine. Executors, Wm. Drake, Robert Lowrey, Jean Cunningham,
by wife, and my son, John. Witnesses, Gavid Steele, Jr., Enoch
Chamberd and Samuel C. Steele. Recorded Sept., 1809.

MONTGOMERY COUNTY

(Copied by Mrs. H. K. McAdams)

ABSTRACTS

WILL BOOK C, MT. STERLING COURT HOUSE

BLEDSOE, DULCINEA—Estage—Page 277—E. Stocton, guardian, of
Miss Dulcinea Bledsoe. Commsrs., Joseph Bondurant, Robert
Glover and Peter G. Glover. Dec. 4, 1826. Recorded Dec. Ct.
1826.

CALL, WILLIAM—Will—Page 243—Mentions, wife, Mary Call and
children, (not named). Written May 1, 1826. Proved Oct. Ct.
1826.

CHORNS, SAMUEL, guardian—Page 233—Guardian for, Elizabeth,
Cynthia, Avarilla and Absalom Chorn, infant children of Absalom
Chorn, deceased. Brought suit in Chancery against Nancy Chorn,
their mother. Account recorded Aug. Ct. 1826.

CLEMENTS, ELIZABETH—Estate—Page 226—Aug. 9, 1825. Executor, G. A. Clements. Appraisors, Philip Clements, Gustavos A.
Wilson and Roger Clements. Recorded July Court 1826.

DAVIS, JAMES—Will—Page 249—(also inventory page 263)—Mentions son, Samuel Davis, daughter, Sarah Mathew (or Matheer),
grandson, James Davis McClure and his sisters. Grandson, James
Davis Mathew (or Matheer), son, John Davis, his
wife and children. Son, Josiah Davis. Grand-daughter, Betsy
Davis, oldest daughter of son, Josiah Davis. 10 grand-daughters
and 2 grand-sons. 5 daughters of my daughter, Flora McClure,
and 2 oldest sons and 2 daughters of my daughter, Sarah Matheer
and 3 daughters of my son, Josiah Davis. Executor, son, Josiah
Davis. Written Oct. 1, 1825. Witnesses, Samuel Chorn, Wm. Me-
Kee and Melvin McKee. Proved Oct. Ct. 1826.

DOWNS, ROBERT—Estate—Page 274—Appraisers, John Fox, Robert
Trimble and Absalom Croswaite. Oct. 10, 1826. Sale bill page
275. Appraisement by Permelia Downs, Administratrix. Page 276.
Recorded Dec. Ct. 1826.

EPPERSON, ROBERT—Estate—Page 246—Commsrs., Thomas Howard,
Rawleigh Morgan and Abel Morgan. Rec. Oct. Ct. 1826.

FLETCHER, JESSE—Bill of Sale—Page 247—Appsrs., Gustavus Hefling, John Clarke and Peter Burch. Rec. Oct. Ct. 1826.

FORTNER, JONAS—Appraisers Bill—Page 235—May 6, 1826. Appraisers, John Fox, Jesse Coffee and W. H. Forkner. Recorded Aug. Ct. 1826.

GILLON, THOMAS B.—Estate—Page 142—Dec. 29, 1825. Commsrs., I. Creason, Aaron Masterson and John Clements. Rec. Oct. Ct. 1826.

GROOMS, ELIZABETH—Allotment—Page 279—Elizabeth Grooms, late Elizabeth Chorn, daughter of Absalom Chorn. Guardian, Samuel Chorn. Commsrs., Josiah Davis, John Treadway and Stephen French. Rec. Jan. Ct. 1827.

HAGAN, ALEXANDER—Will—Page 225—Written Oct. 5, 1824. Mentions sister, Peggy Hagan. Joint heirs, John Hagan of East Tennessee. Rachel Cooper and Nancy Adams. Mentions Miss Dunn and John Milton. Executrix, Peggy Hagan. Proved by Asa Carington, May Ct. 1826. Appraisers bill page 236.

HAWLEY, JUDA—Will—Page 235—Mentions three children, John Hawley, Fanny Hawley, late Fanny Benfield, Anne Hawley, late Anne Oldham. Administrator, John Hawley. Written Jan. 3, 1826. Proved Aug. Ct. 1826.

LACY, PHILEMON H.—Will—Page 269—Mentions, wife, Betsey. Children, Lucy Jane, John Marcus, Henry Bascom. Witnesses, Clement Conner and John Alexander. Executrix, wife, Betsy. Proved Nov. Ct. 1826.

LOCKRIDGE, ROBERT—Will—Page 241—Mentions, father and brother, John. Wife, Elizabeth. Son, Andrew and other children (but not named). Executors, Charles Glover and John H. Goodbar. Written Sept. 5, 1826. Proved Oct. Ct. 1826.

LOCKRIDGE, ROBERT—Inventory—Page 267 — Administrator, Charles Glover with Elizabeth Lockridge, Administratrix. Oct. 9, 1826. Appsrs., Chesley Glover, Daniel Harrah and Thomas Trimble. Rec. Nov. Ct. 1826.

PAYNE, GIBSON—Bill of Sale—Page 251 to 263—Executor, James Mason. Recorded Nov. Ct. 1826.

ROGERS, ATWELL L.—Estate—Page 248—Traverse Duncan, executor with Wm. Mitchell, Wm. A. Carter and Wm. Northcutt, and John Creason, commissioners. Rec. Oct. Ct. 1826.

ROGERS, JAMES—Estate—Page 246—Administrator, Thomas I. Rogers. Dec. 3, 1825. Rec. Oct. Ct. 1826.

SADDLERS, MARY—Will—Page 229—Mentions grandson, Lucien I. Feemster, heir and executor. Written Jan. 27, 1823. Witness, Joshua Barnes, and Wm. P. Reed. Recorded July Court 1826.

SMITH, MARY E.—Estate—Sale page 227—Feb. 11, 1826. Recorded July 1826.

TATMAN, JOHN, SEN.—Estate—Page 219—Executor, John Tatman, Jr. Administrator, James Mason and Archabald Hamilton. Mentions widow, Wm. Talman, heir. Ruth Tatman, and John Tatman, Jr., A Barrow, husband of Ruth Tatman. Commrs., A. S. Farrow, R. McDonald and Wen. Nelson. Recorded July Court 1826.

TATMAN, JOHN, JR.—Page 231—Appraisers bill. Apr. 12, 1825. Administrators, James Mason and A. Hamilton. Recorded July Ct. 1826.

THOMPSON, JOSEPH—Estate—Page 238—Commsrs. report and inventory. Enoch Thompson, Administrator. Recorded Aug. Ct. 1826.

THOMPSON, WILLIAM—Allotment—Page 280—William, son of Joseph Thompson, deceased. Commissioners, Robert Glover and Wm. Smart. Recorded Feb. Ct. 1827. Allotment to Elizabeth Thompson, widow of Joseph Thompson. Recorded Feb. Ct. 1827.

WELLS, JOHN—Page 213 to 222—Inventory. Sale page 222 to 224.

WHITE, JOHN—Will—Page 279—Mentions three sons, John, Frederick and Peter. Executor, Frederick White. Witnesses, Edward Sallee, and Joseph Bondurant. Recorded Jan. Ct. 1827.

VERT, JACOB—Appraisers Bill—Page 244—Wm. Ribelin, Henry Myers and Francis Myers. Rec. Oct. Ct. 1826.

MARRIAGES, ANDERSON COUNTY, KENTUCKY—1831-1835

(Copied by Mrs. B. F. Buckley, Lexington)

David Abbott-Anna Maria Barns, Aug. 7, 1832. Signed David Abbott and Wm. J. Buford. License granted on oath of Wm. J. Buford, that Ann Maria Barns is 21 yrs. old.

Yelverton Adkins-Lidia Ann French (widow) Apr. 23, 1833. Signed Yelverton Adkins and Preston McBrayer.

James Barnes-Sarah Barnes. Aug. 14, 1832. Signed James Barnes and Zachariah Barnes.

Elisha Beasley-Almeda Penney. Apr. 27, 1835. Signed Jordan Walker.

James M. Bell-Martha A. Penney. Mch. 19, 1835. By, Jordan Walker. Consent of Henry Bell, father of James M. and Mary Penny, mother of Martha A. Penney. Signed Elisha Beazley.

Richard B. Bickers-Elizabeth ————. Jan. 15, 1835. By Jordan H. Walker. Signed Richard Bickers and James R. Mizner.

David Blackwell-Susan Mountjoy. Mch. 5, 1832. Signed David Blackwell and Edward Mountjoy.

Argyle Boggess-Evy Carlisle Biles. Oct. 30, 1834. By Jordan H. Walker. Father security in bond.

Flemmon Boggess-Martha E. Philips. Oct. 18, 1833. By Jeremiah P. Lancaster. Signed Flemmon Boggess and W. B. Smith. License requested by Richard Philips.

James Bond-Malinda Fraizer, dau. of Robert Fraizer. Feb. 4, 1834. By Jordan H. Walker.

Merit M. Breckinridge-Eleanor Paxton. Aug. 13, 1832. Signed M. M. Breckinridge and Samuel Paxton. License granted on oath of Sam Paxton that Eleanor is 21 yrs. old.

Henry H. Bunton-Pauline (daughter of Pleasant Oliver). Sept. 26, 1831. Signed Henry H. Bunton and Pleasant Oliver.

Samuel Burgin-Philadelphia Moore. Feb. 14, 1835. Signed Samuel Burgin and James Moore, Jr.

Hazeal L. Butts-Mary Ann Rigg, dau. of David Rigg. Aug. 15, 1832. Signed Hazeal L. Butts and David Rigg.

Samuel M. Butts-Elizabeth Jane Fortune. Jan. 2, 1832. Signed Sam M. Butts and Thos.E. Fortune.

Basil O. Carlisle-Margaret E. Robertson, dau. of James Robertson. June 4, 1833. Signed B. O. Carlisle and F. Dillon. Married by Rev. Edward McMahon.

Cornelius Carter-Susan Utterbach, dau. of Charles Utterbach. May 13, 1833. Signed Cornelius Carter and Matthias Carter. Married by John T. Mills. Susan proved to be 21 yrs. old.

Charles Case-Mary Ellis. Oct. 15, 1831. Signed Charles Case and Seperate Case.

James Case-Arena Bryant. Feb. 1, 1833, by Benjamin H. Peck. Signed James Case and Seperate Case.

Robert Case-Caroline, dau. of Edward Harris. Oct. 9, 1832. By Jeremiah P. Lancaster.

Seperate Case-Lititia McKinney, dau. of John McKinney. July 31, 1833. Signed Seperate Case and John Case.

George Catlett and Nancy Cole, dau. of Elijah Cole. Signed George Catlett and Elijah Cole. Mar. Nov. 14, 1832.

Wilfred G. Chesher-America Heachley. Mar. Dec. 19, 1833. By Jeremiah P. Lancaster. Signed W. G. Chesher and C. N. Fenwick.

Robert E. Collins-Pamelia Lane. Mar. Mch. 12, 1835. By Jordan H. Walker. Signed Robert E. Collins and Preston McBrayer.

John Cook-Jaysia Hanchens. Jan. 21, 1834. Signed John Cook, Francis Hanchens. Written consent of Jesse Hanchens and James Cook, fathers of John Cook and Francis Hanchens.

Elias ,Cornell and Susannah Mothershead, dau. of John Mothershead. Mar. Sept. 2, 1833, by Rev. James Hawthorne. Signed Elias Cornell and Wm. Mothershead.

Edward Cox-Emerall Harris, dau. of Edward Harris. Oct. 21, 1832. Signed Edward W. Cox and Archer Harris.

George Cox-Emilia Bond. June 26, 1834, by Rev. Jeremiah P. Lancaster. Signed George Cox and Martha Marshall. Consent of Rebecca Bond.

Lindsey Craig-Mary Robertson. Mch. 26, 1834, by Jordan H. Walker. Consent of Wm. Robertson. Signed Lindsey Craig and Robert Robertson.

Lambert Darland-Mary Crab. Apr. 16, 1835, by Jordan H. Walker. Signed Lambert Darland and Zecharieh Barnes.

Bushrod T. Darr-Emily Darr. May 6, 1834, by Rev. Jeremiah P. Lancaster. Signed Bushrod T. Darr and Robert C. McBrayer. Consent of Powhattan B. Darr.

Anderson Davis-Betsy Poor. Nov. 6, 1834, by Rev. James Hawthorne. Signed by Anderson Davis, Jesse Reed and Ben N. Hickman.

John Dawson-Lydia Bond,dau.of Anthony Bond. Dec. 24, 1832. Signed John Dawson and Richard Dawson.

John Draffin-Mary Robertson. Nov. 14, 1833, by Jeremiah P. Lancaster. Mary, dau. of Jos.Robertson. Signed John Draffin and R. W. Sea.

Lewis Drew-Lorinda Pamers. Oct. 8, 1833. Signed Lewis Drew and Samuel Paxton. Married by J. J. Mills.

James Egbert-Mary Smith. May 20, 1835. Signed James Egbert and W. B. Smith.

Dillancy Egbert-Jane Ashford. Feb. 25, 1834, by Jordan H. Walker. Signed Dillancy Egbert and Tarlton Railey. Consent of John E. Ashford, father of Jane.

Robert Elliott-Polly McBrayer. Aug. 21, 1834, by Jordan H. Walker. Signed Robert Elliott and Allen A. Ryal. Certificate of Mary McBrayer.

Merritt Fisher-Jane Duvall. June 14, 1832. Signed Merit Fisher and Wm. Duvall.

George Fitzgerald-Cynthia Gill. Feb. 21, 1833, by Jeremiah P. Lancaster. Signed George Fitzgerald and M. M. Breckinridge.

William G. Foore and Emerine A. Richardson, dau. of Allen Richardson, deceased. Mar. Jan. 11, 1832. Signed Wm. G. Foore and Sam C. Payne.

Zachariah Ford-Malinda Bond. Apr. 18, 1831. Signed by Z. Ford and John Bond, father of Malinda.

Elisha Fortune-Haddapah Egbert. Mar. May 8, 1834, by Jordan H. Walker. Signed Elisha Fortune and Jas. Egbert. Consent of David Egbert, father of Haddapah.

Henry H. Frazer-Eliza Ann Boils. June 5, 1832. Signed Henry Frazer and Joseph Biles.

William Gillis-Fanny Hedges. Nov. 5, 1834, by Jordan H. Walker. Signed Wm. Gillis and Wm. Hedger, James Hedges, father of Fanny Hedges.

William Gilpin, Jr.-Frances M. C. McGuire. Jan. 29, 1831. Signed Wm. Gilpin and Abner W. Gilpin.

Harvey Gilman-Mary Catlett, dau. of Francis Catlett. Sept. 19, 1831. Signed Harvey Gilman and Francis Catlett.

Wakefield Glass-Rebecca Bussey. Aug. 15, 1831. Signed Wakefield Glass and John Bussey.

Sandford Gordon-Mary Melear, dau. of Philip Melear. Signed Sandford Gordon and Philip Melear. July 19, 1832.

Sineca Gregory-Rhoda Bell. Aug. 17, 1831. Signed Sineca Gregory and Wm. Patterson.

William Griffie-Mary Emily Butts. Jan. 3, 1832. Signed Wm. Griffey and Samuel M. Botts.

Joseph Griffey-Ann McMichael, dau. of R. McMichael. Joseph Griffey 21 yrs. old, bond issued Nov. 13, 1832, married by James Hawthorne, Nov. 15, 1832.

Richard Hackley-Sarah McBrayer. Nov. 1, 1831. Signed Richard Hackley and Abner W. Gilpin.

George Hammond-Mary Simpson. Aug. 4, 1834. Signed George Hammond and Thomas More, married Aug. 21, 1834.

John Hammonds-Susan Towsen. Mar. Mch. 21, 1833, by Rev. James Hawthorne. Signed John Hammond and Wm. Patterson.

Thomas C. Hancock-Eliza Settle, dau. of John Settle. Signed Thomas C. Hancock and John M. Settle. Aug. 31, 1831.

David Harris-Ann Leathers. Mar. May 3, 1831. Charles Leathers, father of Ann. Signed David Harris and Jesse Ellis. David Harris 21 yrs. of age.

Thomas S. Harriss-Mahala D. Redman, dau. of John Redman. Mar. Dec. 22, 1831. Signed Thomas S. Harriss and Wm. Haverin.

Henry Hardin-Cassey M. Manaway, dau. of Barbary Leathers. Signed Henry Hardin and Gabriel Deal.

Sheridan B. Hawkins-Mary Ann White, dau. of Presley White. Apr. 23, 1832. Signed Sheridan B. Hawkins and Luke Lillard. Consent of Presley White and her age proven by oath of L. Lillard.

David Hawthorne-Mary Bond. Mar. Dec. 27, by Rev. James Hawthorne. Signed David Hawthorne and D. J. Dedman.

Joseph Hawthorne-Sarah Ann Holeman, mar. Sept. 18, 1834, by Rev. James Hawthorne. Consent of the father, R. Holeman.

John R. Hedger-Stacy Ann Dawson. May 2, 1834, by J. H. Walker. Signed J. R. Hedger and John Dawson.

Lemuel C. Hedger-Polly Frazer. Mar. Oct. 21, 1834, by Jordan H. Walker. Signed Lemuel C. Hedger and Luke Lillard.

Adonijah Hill-Christiana Crafton, dau. of Anthony Crafton, mar. Apr. 1, 1835. Signed Adonijah Hill and James Searcy.

Ephraim Hogue-Jane Reynolds, dau. of Vincent Reynolds, Sr. July 12, 1831. Signed Ephraim Hogue and Vincent Reynolds, Jr.

James A. Hunter-Lucinda Lane. Mar. Jan. 22, 1835, by Jordan H. Walker. Signed James Hunter and Preston W. McBrayer.

James Hutton-Rebecca Griffin, dau. of John Griffin, mar. July 9, 1831. Signed James Hutton and Winston J. Griffin.

Edgar Jett-Elizabeth Hancock. Apr. 4, 1834. Signed Edgar Jett and Nathan Railsback.

John Walker Jett-Virginia Hancock, dau. of Frances Hancock. Oct. 1, 1832. Signed John W. Jett and Nathan Railsback.

William Jewell-Eleanor Cromwell (widow) mar. Oct. 22, 1831. Signed Wm. Jewell and John P. Sparks.

Isaac Jordon-Zerulda Searcy. Mar. Feb. 26, 1835, by Jordon Walker, Clerk. Signed Isaac Jordon and Bartlett Searcy. Consent of Bartlett Searcy, father of Zerulda Searcy.

John Kennedy-Sophia Searcy. May 17, 1835. Signed John Kennedy and Richard Searcy.

Samuel Lawrence-Emily Thompson. Mar. May 26, 1831. Signed Ellis Corn and Sam Lawrence. Nancy Hawkins (mother of Emily), wife of Andrew Hawkins. Proved by oath of Henry Thompson.

David R. Lewis-Mary Redding, dau. of Wm. Redding. Oct. 30, 1832. Signed David R. Lewis and Wm. Redding.

John C. Lillard-Frances Berchley. Mar. Aug. 14, 1834, by Rev. Wm. Hickman. Signed John C. Lillard and James G. White.

Stephen Lillard-Rosanna Hudgins, dau. of Wm. Hudgins. Sept. 18, 1832. Signed Stephen Lillard and Wm. Hudgins.

Robert Logan-Nancy Montgomery. Sept. 26, 1833. Bond signed Robert Logan and Caleb Montgomery. Mar .by Rev. James Hawthorne.

John McAlister-Marcissa Parker, dau. of Martin Parker, deceased. Mar. Dec. 12, 1833, by Jordon H. Walker. Signed John McAlister and David Parker.

William McCormick-Perlina Baker. Mar. Mch. 19, 1835, by Rev. James Hawthorne. Signed Wm. P. McCormick and Jeremiah Ford.

John McDaniels-Mary Wise. Aug. 15, 1831. Signed John McDaniels and Wm. Wise.

John L. McGinnis-Mildred Mountjoy. Mar. Feb. 10, 1834, by Rev. James Hawthorne. Signed John L. McGinnis and Thomas McGinnis.

William Marshall-Rachel Jordan. Sept. 29, 1831. Signed Wm. Martin and Leroy D. Stephens.

Clabourne Martin-Fanny Wirt (or Wurt), dau. of George. Oct. 15, 1833. Signed Clabourne Martin and John R. Martin.

John B. Martin-Elizabeth Ann Alexander, mar. Feb. 26, 1835, by Jordan H. Walker. Signed John B. Martin and James Alexander.

Obadiah Martin-Mary Prather. Jan. 12, 1835. Signed Obadiah Martin and James Prather, brother of Mary.

John G. Mastin-Jane Miller. Sept. 14, 1833. Bond as proven by oath of Wm. Toppass and James Miller, upon a written consent of Hannah Hutton, her father and mother being dead, as proved. Signed John G. Mastin and John Wash.

Westley Melear-Polly Coghill. Mar. June 4, 1835, by Jordan H. Walker. Signed Westley Melear and John P. George. Alvin Kenneday, guardian of Polly Coghill, consent of Philip Melear, father of Westley Melear.

Berryman R. Miller-Harriett .Mountjoy, dau. of W. Mountjoy. Mar. Dec. 24, 1833, by Jordan H. Walker. Signed by B. R. Miller and George Mountjoy.

James J. Morgan-Mary Crafton. Jan. 12, 1835. Signed James J. Morgan and J. W. Morgan.

William Morris-Martha Haverin. Sept. 3, 1832. Signed Wm. Morris and Benjamin Haverin.

Armsted Mosely-Nancy Driskill, dau. of Dennis Driskill. Oct. 10, 1832. Signed Armsted Mosely and Dennis Driskill.

Elijah Mothershead-Katherine McGuire. Apr. 24, 1834. Signed Elijah Mothershead and Henry Stacy, who raised Katherine McGuire.

John Mothershead-Alicy Boggess, mar. Sept. 12, 1834, by Jordan H. Walker. Signed John Motherhead and Vincent Boggess, father of Alicy.

William Mothershead-Elizabeth Reading. Mar. Sept. 11, 1834, by Rev. Wm. Hickman. Certificate of Nehemiah Reading, father.

Leroy Mountjoy-Louisianna Cardwell, dau. of John Cardwell, deceased. March 5, 1833, by Rev. Wm. Hickman. Signed Leroy Mountjoy and Alvin Herndon. Consent of guardian, Alvin Herndon.

Robert Mountjoy-Lucy Mountjoy. Mch. 5, 1832. Signed Robert Mountjoy and Edward Mountjoy.

Joseph Mullins-Ziulda E. Harris. Feb. 17, 1834. Signed Joseph Mullins and Thomas S. Harris. Consent of Will Harris, father.

Richard H. Mullins-Nancy Mullins. May 1, 1834, by Rev. Jeremiah P. Lancaster. Signed Richard H. Mullins and John Crossfield.

Jabez B. Noe-Adaline White. Nov. 13, 1834, by Rev. Jeremiah P. Lancaster. Signed John B. White, father of Adaline.

James B. Oliver-Mary Ann Hieatt, mar. Dec. 2, 1834, by Rev. Jeremiah P. Lancaster. Signed James P. Oliver and Meredith Hieatt.

John Parker, Jr.-Catherine Carter. Mar. Mch. 19, 1832. Signed John Parker and N. B. Smith. Proof of age by William Carter.

James Penney-Jannett W. S. Fortune, mar. Apr. 20, 1831. Signed James Penney and Thomas E. Fortune. Jannett is 21 yrs. old.

Isaac N. Prather-Maria Prather. Mar. June 2, 1832. Signed I. N. Prather and James Prather.

Albert Reed-Mary Samuel. Oct. 16, 1834, by Rev. Jeremiah P. Lancaster. Consent of Woodson Munday, guardian.

Zebulon Richards-Elizabeth Ann Ashford. Oct. 9, 1834, by Rev. Jeremiah P. Lancaster. Consent of John S. Ashford, father of Elizabeth Ann Ashford.

Sanders Riley-Joan Young. June 12, 1834, by Rev. Wm. Hickman. Signed Sanders Riley and Reuben Young. Certificate returned Nov. 23, 1834.

John Robertson-Nancy Hedger. Sept. 2, 1834. Signed John C. Robertson and Wm. Hedger. Certificate of Joseph Hedger.

James M. Rucker-Julila Kilbey. Jan. 5, 1832. Signed James M. Rucker and Adam B. Rains.

Allen A. Ryal-Sarah Buckley. Apr. 6, 1835, by Rev. Jeremiah P. Lancaster. Signed Jordan Walker, Clerk, Allen A. Ryal and George Bain.

James Saffield-Martha Haslette. Sept. 25, 1834, by Rev. Jeremiah P. Lancaster. Request of James White, brother-in-law of Martha Haslette.

Samuel Saffield-Sarah Woods, dau. of Joseph Woods. Nov. 2, 1831. Signed Samuel Saffield and J. P. Woods.

Austin Sea-Dicey Mosnone. Aug. 8, 1833, by Rev. Jeremiah P. Lancaster. Signed Austin Sea and Joseph Husband and John Sea.

Henry Searcy-Lucretia Snyder. Dec. 15, 1834. Signed Henry Searcy and James L. Tramer.

Jefferson Searcy-Amanda Zimmerman, dau. of Wm. Zimmerman. June 22, 1833. Signed Jefferson Searcy and Bartlett Searcy.

Henry Snider-Catherine Bowman. Aug. 1, 1831. Signed Henry Snider and William Case.

Bailey Southerland-Rachiel Taylor. Oct. 23, 1833. Signed Bailey Southerland and H. Southerland.

Zachariah Stallings-Rosanna Taylor. Apr. 11, 1835. Signed Zachariah Stallings, Zachariah Barnes. She being of age.

Jacob K. Starr-Nancy Hunt, dau. of Mary Hunt, widow. Jan. 9, 1832. Signed Jacob K. Starr and Dellancy Egbert.

James Stephens-Lucy Crossfield. Feb. 19, 1835, by Jordan H. Walker. Signed James Stephens and John Crossfield.

Marshall Stivers-Mary Ann Houchens, dau. of Jesse Houchens. Feb. 27, 1833. Signed Marshall Stivers and James Houchens. Mar. by Rev. Wm. Hickman. Feb. 28, 1833.

William Tinsley-Sarah Reeds. Mar. May 23, 1831. Wm. Tinsley, 21 yrs. of age. Armstead Reeds, father of Sarah.

Henry N. Thompson-Pamelia Waterfield, dau. of Widon Waterfield. July 30, 1833. Signed Henry N. Thompson and Mathias Carter.

James Lee Traiver-Eliza Snider. Mar. Aug. 1, 1831. Signed James Lee Traiver, Ellis H. Parris and Wm. Case.

William Travis-Elizabeth Bowman, dau. of John Bowman. Feb. 26, 1833. Signed Wm. Travis and Wm. Bowman.

William Tyre-Margaret Hunter. Feb. 9, 1833. Signed Wm. Tyre and Abner W. Gilpin.

Soloman Tyree-Elizabeth McAndy, dau. of Elizabeth McCurdy. Apr. 27, 1833. Signed Soloman Tyree and Jacob Tyree and Elizabeth McCurdy.

William Vardman-Lucretia Middleton. ——— 7, 1833, by Jeremiah P. Lancaster. Signed Wm. Vardman and James Middleton, father of Lucretia.

Randall Walker-Sarah Boggess, sister to Henry Boggess. Dec. 12, 1831. Signed Randolph Walker and Henry Boggess.

Robert Warford-Frances Blake. Apr. 8, 1833, by Wm. Penney. Signed Robert Warford, R. Walker and Reuben Baker.

Jesse C. Waterfield-Renor Rout. Oct. 17, 1833. Consent of Mary Waterfield, Jesse being under 21 yrs. of age. Signed Jesse Waterfield and John Carter.

Dudley George Watson-Jane Robison. Mar. June 24, 1834, by Rev. David Robinson. Signed Dudley G. Watson and David Robinson.

Shebbain Watts-Elizabeth Railsbach, mar. Feb. 19, 1834, by Jordan H. Walker. Signed Shebbain Watts and Nathan Railsbach. Consent of Mrs. Railsbach, mother of Elizabeth.

Henry Whitenach-Frances Griffy, mar. Feb. 20, 1834, by Jordan H. Walker. License issued by request of Joseph Griffy, father of Fanny Griffy.

James H. Whittington-Martha A. Lillard, dau. of John Lillard, mar. Dec. 5, 1831. Signed James H. Whittington and John Lillard.

Jacob Willard and Ducepha Murphy, sister of Fred Murphy. Jan. 27, 1832. Signed Jacob Willard and Fewell Murphy.

Alfred Williams-America Young, dau. of Elizabeth Young. Mar. May 17, 1833, by Rev. Wm. Hickman. Signed Alfred Williams and Merit Young.

William Wilson-Elizabeth Grace, dau. of Thomas Grace. Mar. Jan. 12, 1832. Signed Wm. Wilson and Thomas Grace.

John Woodsman-Sally Ann Browning, dau. of Wesley Browning. Signed John Woodsman and Wesley Browning.

Evan R. Wright-Susan Gray. Nov. 11, 1834. Signed Evan R. Wright and John Whip. John Whip, guardian.

BOYLE COUNTY, DANVILLE COURT HOUSE

MARRIAGE BONDS—1842

(Copied by Mrs. H. K. McAdams)

James I. Lapsley-Frances I. Ewing. Apr. 11, 1842.

Wm. Philips-Margaret Clemons. Apr. 12, 1842. (Dau. of Wm. Clemons on oath of Wm. Clemons, Jr., witness).

Richard Russell-Elizabeth Williams. Apr. 13, 1842. (Consent of mother, Mary Williams).

Wm. Eason-Clemance Bell. Apr. 3, 1842.

Scott Hankley-Lucy Dunkin. Age 23 yrs. Apr. 15, 1842.

John B. H. Latimer-Elizabeth M. Parks. Moses Parks, father. Apr. 18, 1842.

James Byars-Mary Jane Floyd. May 2, 1842.

John H. Butler-Mary Southerland. Age 21. May 5, 1842.

Wm. R. Davis-Mary H. Garnett. Age 21. May 23, 1842.

Robert Willis-Lucinda Gordon. Age 21. June 15, 1842.

Henry Whitehouse-Melissa Conder. Peter Conder, father. May 24, 1842.

Robert T. Stockton-Melinda Tadlock. Cynthia Tadlock, mother. July 4, 1842.

Wm. V. Nevins-Elizabeth Cook. July 5, 1842.

Aaron A. Hogue-Elizabeth Jane Gilkerson. July 12, 1842.

John B. Bergen-Jane Maria Stelle. July 23, 1842. Both legal age.

Edward I. Dodd-Mary E. Murphy. Aug. 4, 1842.

Joseph Biggers-Jane Sparrow. Aug. 9, 1842.

Zachariah Hargrove-Lucy Gray. Aug 24, 1842. (Proof by Mr. Kenley—that Mrs. Lucy Gray was lawful age).

Logan Myers-Ellen I. Nevins. John I. Nevins, father. Aug. 24, 1842.

Edward Hoch-Elizabeth Stout. Lawful age. Aug. 26, 1842.

John L. Crum-Elizabeth Jane Locker. Jesse L. Locker, father. Aug. 31, 1842.

George T. McRoberts-Ellen S. Gaines. Sept. 1, 1842.

Wm. M. Withers-Mary F. Engleman. Sept. 5, 1842.

Gabriel Pandergrass-Mickey Montgomery. Lawful age. Sept. 19, 1842.

Woodson Bowling-Sarah Owens. Sept. 22, 1842.

Wm. H. Skomp-Sarah L. Minor. Lawful age. Oct. 3, 1842.

John L. Taylor-Matlida S. Harrison. John M. Harrison, guardian. Oct. 3, 1842.

James P. Johnson-Susan Coleman. Oct. 7, 1842.

Richard Guthrie-Sarah Stewart. Oct. 10, 1842.

Alexander Van Arsdell-Ann Stone. Lawful age. Oct. 17, 1842.

Jeremiah Louis Kalfus-Sarah Ann Mock. Oct. 17, 1842.

Alexander B. Walker-Mary T. Sandifer. Oct. 21, 1842.

Alexander S. McGrarty-Rosa B. Yeizer. Oct. 22, 1842.

Philip Allgood-Hannah Clemmons. Oct. 26, 1842.

Tarelton Morton-Lucinda Pipes. Oct. 31, 1842.

Squire Hurst-Docia Jones. Lawful age. Nov. 2, 1842.

James W. Bates-Galriella Gaines. Guardian, Jesse Locker. Nov. 15, 1842.

James H. Davenport-Martha Sanderfir. Nov. 26, 1842.

Harry Paget-Goley Christeson. Over 14 years of age. Dec. 9, 1842.

W. M. Northcraft-Melissa S. Caldwell. Dec. 10, 1842.

Thompson Sutherland-Abigail I. Butler. Dec. 19, 1842.

Wm. Owens-Jane Cooper. Lawful age. Dec. 17, 1842.

Archibale Gray-Martha Montgomery. Jan. 30, 1843.

Wm. Martin-Sarah Hickman. Jan. 30, 1843.
Benjamin Wilmot-Marianne Bentley. Feb. 15, 1843.
Osburn Clemons-Elizabeth Lobb. 21 years old. Feb. 27, 1843.
George W. Latimer-Deborah A. Vanoy. Mch. 3, 1843.
Stephen R. Hurt-Angelina Jackman. Mch. 6, 1843.
Benjamin L. McGinnis-Francis Penny. Mch. 13, 1843.
Hugh M. Oldham-Rebecca Neviens. 21 years old. Apr. 3, 1843.
Washington Dunham-Sarah Ann L. Moore. Apr. 4, 1843.
Wm. D. Willis-Harriet A. Fulkerson. Apr. 19, 1843.
Robert A. Johnson-Ann Peachy Green. 21 years old. Apr. 26, 1843.
Wm. Gray-Mary Holland. May 8. 1843.
Peremiah Brescoe-Icyphenia Tarkington. 21 years old. May 11,
1843.
James S. Mosby-Paulina Walker. May 15, 1843.
Wm. M. Smith-Mary Ann Inman. 21 years. May 17, 1843.
David C. Wilson-Sarah Jane Walker. May 24, 1843.
Hiram Kenley-Nancy Gray. 21 years. June 27, 1843.
John Fry-Sarah A. Tilford. Aug. 2, 1843.
Wm. Henderson-Margaret Cook. Over 21. Aug. 7, 1843.
Jacob Paul-Rosella Mattingly. 21 years. Aug. 8, 1843.
George M. Proctor-Mary Tompkins. Aug. 8, 1843.
Jesse Y. Durham-Martha Tarkington. Aug. 28, 1843.
Andrew Grafton-Martha A. Harlan. Sept. 9, 1843.
Napoleon B. Price-Harriet A. Stewart. Sept. 23, 1843.
Thomas Gadburry-Nancy F. Goode. Oct. 4, 1843.
Wm. A. Wight-Sarah Ann Harrison. Guardian, John M. Harrison.
Oct. 11, 1843.
James Hoffner-Eliza Jane Gill. Oct. 19, 1843.
James N. Cocke-Lucy G. Cocke. Lawful age. Oct. 19, 1843.
John Depaw-Jane Mars. Oct. 23, 1843.
James Green-Elizabeth Asher. Guardian, James Asher. Oct. 24,
1843.
Israel Milbern-Eliabeth Bolling. Nov. 1, 1843.
John L. Bolling-Susan H. Mitchell. Nov. 6, 1843.
James W. W. Smith-Nancy C. Gover. Nov. 29, 1843.
Samuel W. Taylor-Maria C. Fisher. Dec. 5, 1843.
Morris L. Chatham-Kezziah Catherine Williams. Dec. 20, 1843.
Wm. Hudson-Mary Wigam. Dec. 7, 1843.
Wm. B. Nold-Nancy A. Frick. Dec. 27, 1843.
Horace May-Brunetta Vanarsdall. Dec. 22, 1843.
Anthony L. Woodson-Eliza B. Chapline. Dec. 30, 1843.
Wm. F. Clarkson-Bathshela Minor. Jan. 2, 1844.
James Richardson-Zurilda Holder. Jan. 9, 1844.
Augustus E. Morris-Ann Jane Johnson. Feb. 5, 1844.
Silas Boling-Juliana Russell. Guardian, Loronzo D. Goode. Feb.
10, 1844.
Robert Lambert-Ann Scott. Feb. 12, 1844.
Ambrose Hodges-Nancy Phillips. Feb. 12. 1844.
Wm. Owens-Eliza Jane Boswick. Feb. 19, 1844.
Austin Whitehouse-Mary Jane Cruize. Lawful age. Feb. 22, 1844.
John McClain-Elizabeth Knox. Lawful age. Feb. 27, 1844.
Wm. Semonis-Susan Leonard. Feb. 28, 1844.
Wm. R. Hines-Mary Tewney. Mch. 4, 1844.
Wm. Bowling-Sarah Gray. Mch. 4, 1844.
Henry H. Farnsworth-Martha L. Doneghy. 21 years. Mch. 6, 1844.
Allison H. Canton-Mary H. Kenley. Mch. 11, 1844.
James Barbour-Elizabeth G. Foster. Mch. 25, 1844.
Richard Emmet-Milah Pendergrass. 21 years. Apr. 13, 1844.
Daniel Swope-Matilda Walters. 21 years. Apr. 25, 1844.
Robert Morrison-Elizabeth I. Johnson. Apr. 30, 1844.
John Pipes-Lydia Morton.

Robert H. Gray-Emily M. J. Prewitt. Guardian, John Caldwell. May 20, 1844.

Caleb B. Wallace-Magdalin R. McDowell. Lawful age. May 28, 1844.

George W. Coulter-Priscilla Bennington. June 11, 1844.

John Jackson-Sarah Sanderfar. Father, Edmund Sanderfar. June 25, 1844.

George Hollon-Nancy Gray. July 8, 1844.

Nathaniel Robeson-Polly Lawhorn. Lawful age. Aug. 1, 1844.

Green T. Martin-Mrs. Anna M. Harrison. Aug. 8, 1844.

Hugh Minor-Lucendy Bodgett. Father, John R. Bodgett. Aug. 13, 1844.

Henry Pope, Jr.-Mary Elizabeth Broyles. Father, John Broyles. Aug. 19, 1844.

James K. Martin-Mary E. Marrs. Father, James Marrs. Aug. 20, 1844.

Jonas Durham-Eliza Turney. Father, Wm. W. Turney. Aug. 26, 1844.

Alexander Aldridge-America Proctor. Lawful age. Aug. 27, 1844.

George W. Prewitt-Sarah Amanda Randolph. Father, C. E. Randolph. Sept. 14, 1844.

Richard Daring-Hester Ann Broiles. Father, Monroe Broiles. Sept. 16, 1844.

James Taylor, son of John-Alvira Prall. Oct. 10, 1844.

Matthew W. Crowdus-Phebe E. Caldwell. Father, Wm. Caldwell. Oct. 15, 1844.

John M. Sneed-Mary Jane Stewart. Father, Wm. Stewart. Oct. 21, 1844.

Taylor Sevier-Sarah Vermilion. Father, Henderson Vermilion. Oct. 21, 1844.

Samuel E. Phillips-Harriet P. Calvert. Father, Isaiah Calvert. Oct. 21, 1844.

James Hutchings-Sally Margaret Mullens. Oct. 23, 1844.

Benjamin J. Borden-Sarah Geiser. Daniel Geiser, father. Oct. 28, 1844.

Burdett Wright-Louise Shannon. Nov. 4, 1844.

Robert J. Overstreet-Mary Frost. Joseph Frost, father. Nov. 4, 1844.

John J. Crowdis, 21 years old-Modocia Henley. H. Henley, father. Nov. 16, 1844.

James Jones-Elizabeth Webb. Nov. 18, 1844.

Micah T. Chrisman-Catharine J. McNeill. Dec. 3, 1844.

John M. Meyer-Mary R. McDowell, of Samuel McDowell. Dec. 9, 1844.

Andrew C. Martin, mother, Ann Martin-Minerva J. Tolley, mother, Jane Tolley. Dec. 21, 1844.

Jefferson Hocker-Nancy Ann Webster. John Webster, father. Dec. 27, 1844.

Richard G. Perry-Mary Jane Wilson. John Wilson, father. Dec. 30.

Arthur Norcutt-Polly Ann Shannon. Jan. 10, 1845.

Herod Jones-Emeline Crane. C. A. Crane, father. Jan. 21, 1845.

James P. Harlan-Lucinda Burton. Mother, Eliza Bryan. Jan. 27, 1845.

James Wilson-Eliza Jane Doneghy. Jan. 29, 1845.

John Pendergraff-Eliza Emmett. Richard Emmett, father. Mch. 26, 1845.

Thomas H. Ball-Susan C. Fisher. Apr. 2, 1845.

Solomon Jones-Elvira Crutchfield. Apr. 10, 1845.

Jordon Rowsey-Nancy Curry. Apr. 14, 1845.

Wilbur C. Snail-Margaret Fen. Apr. 16, 1845.

John Ludowick-Frances M. Davenport. Samuel Davenport. Apr. 21, 1845.

Mappalus Roberts-Nancy Clarkson, sister of Gerret Clarkson. Apr. 29, 1845.

James McGinnis-Lucy Sanderfur. Edmund Sanderfur, father. May 14, 1845.

—————— Robbins-Mary E. Tipton, dau.: of Agnes Tipton. May 21, 1845.

W. H. Ward-Amelia Williams. May 26, 1845.

Wm. H. McCabo-Elizabeth Anne Leslie. May 30, 1845.

Alfred Clemmons-Mary Anne Nixon. Wm. Nixon, father. June 9, 1845.

Wm. Parks-Emily Walker. June 18, 1845.

George Mankley-Mary Franklin. C. Franklin, father. June 19, 1845.

John Shaw-Sarah Hall. Tharp Hall, father. June 26, 1845.

Henry Baughman-Nancy P. Ball. July 9, 1845.

Wm. Whitehouse-Maranda W. Overstreet. Mother, Susanna Overstreet. July 16, 1845.

James Powell-Ellen Pherigo. July 16, 1845.

Finley L. McGinnis-Mary Jane Armstrong. James R. Armstrong, father. July 30, 1845.

Samuel Goode-Elizabeth L. Tuttle. Aug. 9.

Andrew Pope-Mary Ann Bryant. Aug. 11, 1845.

Wm. F. Graham-Catherine Prewitt. Aug. 13, 1845.

Sterling C. Vanarsdall-Eliza Ann Hickman of John W. Hickman. Aug. 25, 1845.

John B. Kearby-Eliza Jane Lander. Aug. 26, 1845.

Lewis Lancurt-Mary McGinnis. Sept. 2, 1845.

Wm. Rice-Maria Rice. Phemias Rice, father. Sept. 4, 1845. Married by Rev. N. S. Rise, of Presbyterian Church.

Wm. B. Watson-Annie Philips. John Philips, father. Sept. 6, 1845.

Henry I. Barker-Julia Ann Farnsworth. Samuel Farnsworth, father. Sept. 10, 1845

Charles H. May-Martha Ann Penny. Sept. 11, 1845.

Wm. Hatchett-Catherine Bottom. Sept. 13, 1845.

Thomas J. Doke-Susan Gaines. Sept. 15, 1845.

Samuel Dunn-Frances Shannon. Sept. 20, 1845.

Jessee W. Smith-Nancy B. Smith. Sept. 27, 1845.

Henry Duerson-Eliza I. Harrison. Sept. 29, 1845.

Harrey M. Robinson-Eva Ann Bentley. Oct. 6, 1845.

John W. Dick-Catherine Ann Barbour. Oct. 7, 1845.

Wm. G. Sweeney-Eliza Ann Frost. Oct. 8, 1845.

Moses J. Hodges-Elizabeth Taylor. Oct. 16, 1845.

John M. Armstrong-Eliza Ann Fields. Oct. 22, 1845.

V. C. Lasley-Margaret C. Mitchell. Oct. 27, 1845.

Jeremiah Fresh-Mrs. Isabella Hammer. Oct. 28, 1845.

Fielding Kenley-Mrs. Lucy Ann Marshall. Nov. 3, 1845.

George Porter-Sarah Ann Foster. Nov. 10, 1845.

P. W. Hall-Demina F. Williams. Nov. 13, 1845.

Robert H. Biswick-Ellen Helch. Nov. 20, 1845.

Charles Gray-Elizabeth Ann Biswick. Noc. 24, 1845.

Samuel Hart-Sarah B. Fulkerson. Dec. 6, 1845.

George A. Armstrong-Elizabeth P. McKinney. Dec. 10, 1845.

John Coulter-Elizabeth Temple. Dec. 11, 1845.

Thomas Elliott-Martha Clarkson. Dec. 15, 1845.

Joseph H. Davis-Emily Gaines. Dec. 18, 1845.

John C. Paddock-Mary L. Lewellin. Dec. 19, 1845.

Frederick Ripperdan, Jr.-Martha Ann Davenport. Dec. 20, 1845.

Edmund Ragland-Mary Gaines. Dec. 24, 1845.

MARRIAGES, CLARK COUNTY, KENTUCKY

(Donated by Mrs. Joseph Beard)

William Barnes-Jane Elkin, (daughter of James). Sept. 8, 1818.
Jeremiah Barnett-Betsy Dumford. Dec. 20, 1803. Verbal consent of Daniel Dumford, father of Betsy.
Charles Bowman-Betsy Wood. Oct. 17, 1814. Bondsman James Wood.
Joseph Boswell-Judith Bell Gist. Nov. 22, 1801.
John Bunch-Polly Oliver. Dec. 23, 1822.
Daniel Burch-Rebecca Hunter, widow. Apr. 20, 1795.
Tilman Bush-Sarah Elkin. Jan. 8, 1814.
John Bruner-Franky Quisenberry. Dec. 4, 1804.
John Bruner-Rebecca Blackburn. Jan. 1, 1811.
Clayburn Cox-Cynthia Hampton. Sept. 1914.
Abraham Conkwright-Nancy Jackson. Nov. 27, 1793. Consent of Jesse Jackson, father of Nancy.
Beverly Daniel-Easter Hampton. Aug. 15, 1813.
Jesse Devary-Mary Dumford, widow. Oct. 27, 1801.
Reuben Elkin-Sary Elkin. Dec. 12, 1802.
James Elkin, Jr.-Lucinda Osbourn. Dec. 9, 1822.
Smallwood Elkin-Lucinda Bush. 1827.
William Fletcher-Dully Elkin (sister of Malinda Elkin).
John Foster-Elizabeth Hill. Mch. 1809. Leonard Hill, father of Elizabeth.
James Gibson-Polly Hill. Aug. 9, 1804. Bond, Leonard Hill.
Richard Gordon-Nancy Hampton. July 11, 1824.
Burgess Griggs-Permela Hampton. July 18, 1824.
William Groom-Sallie Woods. Dec. 12, 1812.
David Hampton-Polly Johnson. April 24, 1819.
George Hampton-Caty Routt. Dec. 17, 1807.
Jesse Hampton-Sarah Haggard. Jan. 10, 1803.
Joseph Hampton-Sarah Lampton. Feb. 1, 1816.
Wilson Hampton-Susan Grigsby. Apr. 5, 1814.
Samuel Hally-Meriam Elkin. May 8, 1827.
Joseph Knott-Elizabeth Dumford. June 30, 1806. Consent of Daniel Dumford and Sary Dumford, parents of Elizabeth.
Jonathan Lemon-Nancy Hunter. July 22, 1800.
George Lennox-Lucy Osbourn. Mch. 6, 1825.
William Lenox-Mary Willson. Aug. 8, 1801.
Charles Lindsey-Malinda Elkin. Jan. 26, 1826.
Thomas Lyndsey-Betsy Elkin. Feb. 2, 1815.
Archibald McConnell-Sally McCracken. June 26, 1806.
John Mcguire-Fanny Holder. Widow. Dec. 13, 1802.
Caleb Masterson-Nancy Wills. Oct. 29, 1824.
Sid. Noland-Mary Babb Willson. Mch. 17, 1806.
Isaac Oliver-Hannah Woods. Jan. 18, 1818.
Joel Oliver-Polly Wood. Dec. 19, 1820.
William Osbourn-Sarah Grooms. Dec. 28, 1812.
William Pigg-Polly Hampton. Jan. 5, 1819.
Ebenezer S. Platt-Ann Foulger. June 19, 1794.
Robert Rankin-Matilda Dumford. Aug. 5, 1832.
Henry Reynolds-Debby Halsell. Sept. 22, 1806. Consent of Wm. Halsell.
William Richardson-Polly Elkin. Dec. 15, 1808.
Bradley Richardson-Patsey Elkin. Feb. 18, 1810.
Esom Vice-Polly Osbourn. Dec. —, 1809.
Simpson R. Viser-Nancy Hampton. July 29, 1828.
John Webber-Elizabeth Willson. Jan. 27, 1802.

Edward White-Polly Oliver. 1828.
Eli Babb Willson-Nancy Webber (2nd. wife). May 17, 1815.
Sampson Willson, Sr. (2nd. wife)-Mourning Webber. Feb. 28, 1812.
Fielding Wood-Patsy Tuggle, daughter of Wm. Tuggle.
Jacob Wood-Rachel Rainy. Oct. 25, 1808.
James Wood-Betsy Cook. Oct. 25, 1816.
James Wood-Nancy Vaughn. Aug. 10, 1818.
James Wood, Jr.-Elizabeth Willson. Jan. 7, 1828.
Jesse Wood-Elizabeth Stipp. Jan. 27, 1808. Conent of Michael Stipp, father of Elizabeth.
Jonathan Wooten-Nancy Hampton. June 6, 1824.
Joseph Wood-Rachel Gardner. Apr. 5, 1821.

FAYETTE COUNTY COURT

(List of Marriages solemnized by Adam Rankin in bond box, 1803-1850 and marked "recorded.")

1 7 9 6
Aug. 5. Thomas Thompson-Margaret Scott.
1 7 9 7
Jan. 8. Jacob Brassfield-Nancy Gillespie.
Sept. 4. Samuel Wilkison-Jane Williams.
Sept. 3. William Lester-Elizabeth Davis.
Oct. 2. William Logan-Anna Ryan.
Jan. 20. John Scroggin-Nancy Hall.
Jan. 30. William Hawkins-Jane Black.
1 7 9 9
Feb. 7. Thomas Cunningham-Nancy Black.
Mch. 15. John H. Williams-Jane Brothers.
Mch. 20. John Boggs-Polly Anderson.
Mch. 26. John Shaw-Jane Logan.
July 2. James Kennedy-Ester Crews.
Aug. 10. Daniel Havy (or Hany)-Catherine Murry.
Aug. 7. Alex. McCoy-Nancy Stewart.
Aug. 29. Brice Steele-Elizabeth Thornberry.
Sept. 4. John McClellen-Margaret Carethers.
Oct. 30. John Brown-Sarah Jameson.
May 20. Thos. Dougherty-Nancy Scott.
1 8 0 0
Feb. 11. Frances Underwood-Peggy Jervis.
Feb. 18. James Logan-Ester Fisher.
Feb. 3. Jesse Lawrence-Jane Tilford.
Apr. 22. Moses Wilson-Polly January.
May 25. William Simpson-Patsey Wardly.
June 10. Thos Waller-Betsey McFerland. (See book 1, page 26, given date as 1815).
Aug. John Atchison-Margaret Agnes (?).
Oct. Daniel Hook (?)-Patsey McBreer (or McBreen).
Oct. John Nelson-Peggy Davis.
Oct. John Smith-Phebe Rankin.
Nov. Thos. Steele-Margaret Morrison.
Dec. Alex ————————Polly Sack.
1 8 0 1
Feb. 16. Oliver Brown-Mary Garrett.
Feb. 27. Thos. Wallace-Elizabeth Hamilton.
Mch. 10. Robert Simpson and ————————.
Mch. 16. John Wright-Jane Corn.

Mch. 20. Andrew Woods-Jane Smith.
Mch. 20. Isaach McIsaach-Rebecca McMillen.
Apr. 16. William Bee-Isabella Davidson.
Sept. 22. William Logan-Molly Fisher.
Dec. 18. Martin Goodman-Elizabeth Rankin.
Marriages, before 1802, Fayette Co. Court Record, book 1, page 6.
1795. July 16. John Love-Elizabeth Ross, by H. Toulmon (?).
1795. Apr. 21. James Longhead-Mary Brown, by Robert Marshall.
1795. Dec. 31. Archibald Dinwiddle-Jenny Johnson, by Robert
Marshall.
1796. Jan. 20. William McClure-Patsey Steele, by Robert
Marshall.
1797. July 22. James Jameson-Rebecca Buchhannon, by Robert
Marshall.
1798. Apr. 18. Thomas Longdon-Anne Christian, by Robert
Marshall.
1798. Nov. 8. Caleb Kamper-Nancy Caldwell, by Robert Marshall.
1799. Mch. 2. John McAtee-Sarah Power, by Robert Marshall.
1799. Aug. 15. James Patterson-Jenny Lowrey, by Robert
Marshall.
1800. Mch. 28. Edward Little-Polly Bird by Robert Marshall.
1801. Apr. 9. John Gordon-Anne Armstrong, by Robert Marshall.

MARRIAGES SOLEMNIZED IN ST. PETER'S CATHOLIC CHURCH, LEXINGTON, KY.

(Copied by Miss Joe Nugent)

Matthews Alton-Elizam Jeter. Mch. 30, 1834. Witnesses, Jo-
seph S. Gardiner and Susanna Anna Jeter.
Joanum Burke-Saram Manly. Apr. 11, 1834. Witnesses, Edwardo
Kelly and America Uxore.
Richardum Watts-Rebeccom Epington. May 6, 1834. Witnesses,
Augustine Tracy and Clarissa Curry.
Celetina Roberts-Joanni Candy. ―― ―, 1834.
Josephus S. Gardiner-Susanna Anna Jeter. ―― ―, 1834.
Jacobus O'Brien-Eliza Geoghegan. Feb. 17, 1835. Witnesses, Ja-
cobo Bush and Lucia Hanley.
Sydnius Sherman-Isabella J. Cox. Apr. 27, 1835. Witnesses, An-
tonio Lockwood and Maria Mony.
H. Buchholts-Harietta Thwaits. Apr. 28, 1835.
Jacobus O'Reilly-Anna Sharp. June 2, 1835. Witnesses, Bernardo
Busby and Anna Rees.
Samuelis A. Young-Mario A. Morgan. Sept. 2, 1835. Witnesses,
Carmichaeli Wickliffe and Eliza Joannia Orr.
Thomas L. Worland-Maria Anna Blincoe. Sept. 8, 1835. Wit-
nesses, Roberto Worland and Maria Wist.
Septanum Bonner-Luciam M. Hanly. Oct. 22, 1835. Witnesses,
Manritio Byrne and Letitia Bonner.
Robertus H. Hanna-Louisa Thompson. Nov. 3, 1835. Witnesses,
Jocobo S. Douglas and Margarita Goddard.
Michaelem Davis-Hesterem Annam Keiser. Jan. 1, 1836. Wit-
nesses, Jacobo O'Mara and ―― Keiser.
Franciscum Dominicum Dabe-Elizabeth Loiseau. Jan. 13, 1836.
Witnesses, Ubert Clemont and Julia Loiseau.
Hennecus ――――Maria Lewis. June 2, 1836. Witnesses, R――
Joanno McGill and ――――.
Smith Laudeman-Susanna Climes. Nov. 8, 1836. Witnesses, Ri-
cardo Porter and Eliza Miller.
Joannum Heils-Angelicum Leid. Aug. 31, 1837. Witnesses, Mich-
ael Currun Hanly and Elizabeth A. O'Reilly.
Jacobum Rowan-Annam Covington. Oct. 10, 1837. Witnesses,
Ambrosio and Jemima Wagers.

Jacobum Collier-Rebecca R. Coyle. Oct. 6, 1837. Witnesses, Georgio N. Carnell and Maria Sheriff.

Thomam Green-Franciscam Scantland. Nov. 16, 1837. Witnesses, Michaele Healy and Anna McCabe.

Edwardum Durbin-Elvinam Kelly. Nov. 21, 1837. Witnesses, Joanne Durbin and Julia Molloy.

Jacobus Scully-Elizabeth Steel. Dec. 24, 1837.

Joannum Jackson-Annam Payne. Nov. 27, 1837.

Enoch Bacon-Maria E. Gill. Mch. 27, 1838. Witnesses, Jacob O'Mara and Elizabeth I. Barr.

Alexandri Roguskey-Elizabeth O'Neil. May 13, 1838. Witnesses, Jacobo and Anna O'Reilly.

Thomas M. Hickey-Catherinam A. Barry. May 20, 1838. Witnesses, Armstead Barry and Maria Joanna Hickey.

Mauretium Call-Elizabeth McGonnegil. Aug. 13, 1838. Witnesses, Antonio ————— and Maria Walker.

Bernardus O'Dougherty-Maria Anna O'Dougherty. Aug. 4, 1838. Witnesses, Gulielmo O'Dougherty and Sara Brenaugh.

Joannem Ubanks-Susannam Joannam Smith. Oct. 8, 1838. Witnesses, Moses A. and Joanna Anna Quigly.

Jacbus Goolrick-Anna Lancaster. Nov. 12, 1838. Witnesses, Roberto ————— and Eliza McCartney.

Thomas Butte (?)-Judith Barry. Date faded. Witnesses, Jacobo O'Mara and Maria O'Driscoll.

Joannum T. Washington-Adelaidam I. Tibbatts. Jan. 20, 1839. Witnesses, Leone Tibbatts and Cecilia Giron.

Edwardum Gibbon-Annam Ceciliam Conry. Apr. 25, 1839. Witness, Jacobo H. Rice and Julia Molloy.

Isaac C. Miller-Elizabeth I. Barr. Apr. 30, 1839. Witnesses, Henrico Flint and Elizabeth Howell.

Robertus Buckley-Margarita Picket. July 15, 1839. Witnesses, Joanum Byrne and Julia A. Mullen.

Garhardum Henricum Dallinghers-Mariam Annam Shrader. Aug. 7, 1839. Witnesses, Patricio Kelly and Francisca Geoghegan.

Michael McNamara-Joanum Walls. Aug. 26, 1839. Witnesses, Jacbo Walls and Catherine Cassell.

Jacobum Dolan-Saram Coll. Oct. 6, 1839. Witnesses, Jacobo Campbell and Isabella McGonegil.

Michael Morgan-Catherine Fitzpatrick. Jan. 27, 1840. Witnesses, Jacobo ————— and Margareta Hanly.

Marshall Sharpe-Elizabeth O'Reilly. May 12, 1840. Witnesses, F. S. Butt and Sara Gilert.

Edwardum Durbin-Paticutiam Lynch. June 3, 1840. Witnesses, Josepho and Margurita Lynch.

P. Durbin-Margarita Barber. Sept. 24, 1840. Witnesses, Joanne Durbin and Sara Anna Durbin.

Joannem Durbin-Judiam (?) Mann. Oct. 14, 1840.

Jas. Cally-Mary McCauliff. Dec. 5, 1854. County Cork, Ireland.

Michael Haggerty of County Call, Ireland-Catherine McCourt, age 19, County Waterford, Ireland. Nov. 26, 1854.

Cornelius O. Connell-Ellen Murphy, County Kerry, Ireland, ages 25 and 22. Jan. 12, 1855.

John Nevans-Eliza Reynolds, of County Rascommon, Ireland, ages 33 and 18. Jan. 15, 1855.

David Connor-Hanna Davine, of County Kerry, Ireland. Jan. 15, 1855.

John Brennau-Mary Murray, of County Rascommon, Ireland. Jan. 19, 1855.

Daniel Callahan-Bridget Guthrie, Co. Clare, Ire. Jan. 21, 1855.

James Smith, Co. Cavan, Ire., age 23-Mary Burnes, Co. Wexford, Ire. Age, 22. Jan. 28, 1855.

John Reynolds-Mary Gorman (By dispensation, 2nd cousins). Feb. 5, 1855.

Nicholas Moore-Ellen McQuinn. (5th and 6th cousins.) Feb. 6, 1855.

John Marney, age 23, Co. Derry, Ire.-Eliza Mallory, 21, Co. Tyrone, Ire. Mar. 4, 1855.

Hugh Rafferty, age 26, Co. Tyrone, Ire.-Annie Lyons, age 20, Co. Rascommon, Ire. Mar. 18, 1855.

James Ronan-Elizabeth O'Shea, of Co. Limerick, Ire. Apr. 14, 1855.

Daniel Slavin, Co. Derry, Ire.-Mary Shaughnessey Dolan, Co. Rascommon, Ire. Apr. 15, 1855.

Charles Cook, Co. Kilkenney, Ire., age 25-Mary Coughlin, Co. Cork, Ire., age 30. Apr. 16, 1855.

James Bradley-Catharine Henry of Co. Derry, Ire. May 7, 1855.

John Traner-Mary Shannon of Londonderry. June 5, 1855.

Thos. Mehy-Bridget Totten (or Sullon) of Harrison Co. ,Kentucky. June 26, 1855.

Phillip Cummins-Catherine Bouden of Ireland. June 6, 1855.

Patrick Foster-Mrs. Mary Donahoo of Bourbon Co. Aug. 1, 1855.

Robt. McGlone-Mrs. Jane Haggin (widow). Aug. 9, 1855.

Thos. Kane-Mary Murray of Ireland. Aug. 9, 1855.

James Curran-Mary Clancy of Ireland. Aug. 16, 1855.

Thos. Kelly-Julia Gibney of Ireland. Aug. 17, 1855.

Michael McAuliff-Margaret Ragan of Ireland. Aug. 23, 1855.

Timothy McAuliff-Senkas Catherine Riley of Ireland, July 8, 1855.

John Franklin-Mary Tobin of Ireland. July 17, 1855.

Dennis O'Regan-Johanna Fennessey. July 17, 1855.

Thos. Mullaly-Margaret Canning. July 14, 1855.

Patrick Shine-Margaret Reiley. July 22, 1855.

John Powell-Mary Keller. July 25, 1855.

Patrick Cashman-Rosanna Thompson. Sept. 28, 1855.

John Sullivan-Mrs. Bridgit McCarty. Oct. 17, 1855.

Patrick Shelly-Margaret Black. Oct. 23; 1855.

William O'Brien-Ellen Morrissey. Oct. 20, 1855.

Timothy McNamara-Elizabeth Fitzgerald. Nov. 17, 1855.

William Moloney-Catherine Cocarran. Nov. 20, 1855.

John McCarthy-Mary Hoy. Nov. 22, 1855.

Patrick Barrs-Mary A. Molloy. Nov. 24, 1855.

James Fitzgerald-Margaret Dalton. Nov. 26, 1855.

John Brennan-Mrs. Ellen Conner. Nov. 16, 1855.

Edward Roache-Anna Harnett. Nov. 2, 1855.

Thos. McNearney-Mrs. Bridget Lynch. Nov. 29, 1855.

John Murphy-Mary Murphy. Nov. 29, 1855.

Timothy Higgins-Mary Lynch. Dec. 8, 1855.

Cornelius Twomey-Anna Fealey. Dec. 10, 1855.

Thos. Jenkins-Elizabeth Flynn. Dec. ——, 1855.

Patrick Long-Ella Dramy (?). Dec. 26, 1855.

John Fealy-Mary O'Connell. Dec. 26, 1855.

Phillip Gormly-Anna Pray (?). Dec. 29, 1855.

Charlie Haney-Anna Goodwin. Dec. 31, 1855.

S. Grattan Hanly-Francis L. Daniels. Dec. 31, 1855.

GARRARD COUNTY, KENTUCKY
LANCASTER COURT HOUSE

MARRIAGE BONDS
(Copied by Mrs. B. F. Buckley and Mrs. H. K. McAdams)

Bazalell Brown-Susannah Gibbs. Jan. 12, 1798. Consent of father, John Gibbs.

Hezekiah Ford-Susannah Woodson (?). June 12, 1797.

Benj. Hiatt-Elizabeth Simpson. July 3, 1797.

James Morris-Polly Stevens. July 3, 1797. Consent of father, Abraham Stevens.

Jas. Tuley-Patsey McDonald. Aug. 7, 1797. Consent of Augustus (?) and Betsey McDonald, parents.

Matthew Hickson (Hixon)-Polly Kelly. Aug. 21, 1797.

William Woodson-Tabitha Nowlin. Aug. 21, 1797. Consent of James Nowlin.

James Bailey-Rebecca Anderson. Oct. 23, 1797.

Stephen Manire-Elizabeth Henderson. Oct. 23, 1797.

George Ewing-Elizabeth Wallace. Oct. 31, 1797.

David Gordon-Aley Edwards. Dec. 4, 1797.

John Pheamaster-Mary Kesiale (?). Dec. 9, 1797.

Burkitt Hughes-Sealey Mounce. Dec. 25, 1797. Mother, Mary Mounce.

John Cochraham-Susanah Ray. Dec. 28, 1797.

Will Chapline-Betsey Perkins. Jan. 1, 1798. Father, Benjamin Perkins.

Ebenezer Coal-Mary Rowman. Jan. 1, 1798.

James Aldridge-Casander Gill. Jan. 25, 1798.

James Finney-Sabra Hulloard. Jan. 19, 1798.

Dan'l Preston-Susanna Littrell. Feb. 7, 1798.

James Scott-Polly Crutchfield. Feb. 7, 1798.

William Wilson-Nanny Banks. Feb. 19, 1798. Linn Banks, father.

Enoch Kamper-Susanna Holschaw. Feb. 24, 1798. Father, Jacob Holsclaw.

Joel Kelley-Letty Doherty. Feb. 28, 1798.

Dan'l McCollurn-Polly Kirkendoll. Mar. 5, 1798.

Charles Younger-Nancy Loney. April 13, 1798. Joshua Younger, father.

Benjamin Lalyear-Nancy Bishop. March 26, 1798.

John Bowlin-Catherine Daugherty. April 1, 1798.

Charles Lounger-Nancy Loney. Ajril 13, 1798. Joshua Younger, father—Alexander Loney, father.

Lawrence Hutcherson-Sally Hopkins. April 18, 1797. Mother, Frances Hopkins.

George Simpson-Elizabeth Alexander. April 21, 1798. Mother, Sarah Alexander.

Edward Vest-Mary Ketchen. April 23, 1798.

Elijah Reeder-Elizabeth Davidson. April 25, 1798.

William Blanton-Fanny Blanton. May 2, 1798. Mother of Fanny is Lucy Blanton.

Havilah Crump-Sally Perkins. May 15, 1798.

Joseph Bigger-Jane Denny. May 20, 1798.

Jesse Keeny-Darkis Mobley. May 21, 1798.

Micajah Harbour-Jinny Boyle. May 28, 1798.

Samuel Forbes-Peggy Champ. June 12, 1798.

Robert Proctor-Sally Forbush. June 13, 1798. James Martin, brother-in-law, of Sally Forbush.

Jesse Walker-Polly Wallace. June 17, 1799.

Richard Sampson-Susannah Gaddey. June 21, 1798.

Wm. Champ-Susanna Daugherty. July 17, 1798.

Wm. Ellis-Martha Radcliff. July 19, 1798. Father, Richard Radcliff.

John Ember-Elisabeth Ember. July 23, 1798. Father of Elisabeth given is John Ember.

John Woodram-Marget Findley. Aug. 26, 1798.

Jesse Luttrell-Clary Shelton. Aug. 9, 1798. Father, James Shelton.

Absolom Renfro-Cloe Renfro. Aug. 28, 1798. Parents of Cleo—Mark and Naomy Renfro.

James Montgomery-Jane Lindsay. Sept. 3, 1898.

Thomas Turpin-Pheby Garrot. Sept. 7, 1798.
James Stephens-Sally Hale. Sept. 10, 1798.
Richard Slary-Susanna Mounts. Sept. 17, 1798.
Chapman Lobb-Polly Robertson. Sept. 19, 1798.
Robin Person-Hannah McWilliams. Sept. 27, 1798.
Joseph Clark-Polly Boyles. Oct. 3, 1798.
Abraham Hale-Martha Fitzgerald. Oct. 11, 1798.
Jennings McDaniel-Polly Singleton. Oct. 15, 1798.
John Ballinger-Hannah Jennings. Oct. 16, 1798.
Wm. Clarke-Mary Comely. Oct. 17, 1798.
Warren Boley-Polly Rice. Oct. 24, 1798.
Jno. Woolford-Jinny Lapsley. Nov. 8, 1798.
Zachariah Short-Sally Pettig. Nov. 12, 1798.
John Banks-Jenny Marksberry. Nov. 26, 1798.
Lewis Ball-Lucy Singleton. Nov. 28, 1798. Father, Christopher
Singleton.
John Proctor-Sally Elliott. Dec. 8, 1798. George Elliott, father.
William Sharren-Martha Wood. Dec. 1, 1798.
Daniel Ball-Susanna White. Dec. 23, 1798. Parents, David White
and Kazia White.
Bartrick Dohay-Milly Sidebottoms. Dec. 30, 1798.
Joseph Black-Nancy Brumet. Jan. 15, 1799.
Robt. Stewart-Ann Watson Pond. Jan. 22, 1799.
James L. White-Rachel Mounts. Feb. 7, 1799.
Joseph Harbour-Polly Stephens. Feb. 11, 1799.
Robt. Pope-Elliner Vance. Feb. 26, 1799. Father of Elliner,
Benjamin Leacher.
William McQuerry-Sarah Allcorn. Feb. 23, 1799.
Michael Lotter-Osee Reed. Feb. 25, 1799. Weeden Smith, guardian
of Osee Reed.
Nathaniel Turney-Elizabeth Pope. Feb. 26, 1799. Thomas Pope,
father of Elizabeth.
Daniel Duncan-Lucy Lee. Mar. 6, 1799. Signed by Stephen Lee.
John Brock-Patsy (Martha) Harbard. Mar. 19, 1799, of John
James Davis-Polly Whiteside. Mar. 12, 1799.
and Mary Harbard.
Sam Sellers-Sally Ellis. Mar. 20, 1799. Father, Joseph Ellis.
Jacob Miller-Betsey Sutton. April 3, 1799.
Stephen Harmon-Nancy Jostlin. April 5, 1799.
Ephraim Tunget-Nancy Marksberry. April 20, 1799. Parents,
Samuel and Isabella Marksberry.
John Hiatt-Polly Ashby. April 12, 1799.
Lewis Sasseen-Sally Phelps. May 2, 1799.
Christian Crall-Patty Nicum. May 7, 1799. Father, Michel
Nicum.
John Sanders-Sarah Wooley. May 16, 1799. Signed by Henry
Wooly.
William Martin-Rachel Lash. May 20, 1799.
George Tracy-Hiththy Burdett. June 2, 1799.
Thomas Allcorn-Caty Montgomery. July 8, 1799. Father, Sam'l
Montgomery.
James Baldock-Betsy Hogan. July 29, 1799. Father, James
Hogan.
George Brady-Milberry McFaddin. Aug. 2, 1799.
Thomas Rentfro-Betsy Kyler. July 20, 1799.
Jesse Liverston-Dicey Stoghill. Aug. 7, 1799.
Wm. Leister-Isabel Lapsley. Aug. 23, 1799. Father, James
Lapsley.
James Smith-Lidy Jeffries. Aug. 27, 1799.
Henry Hawhimer-Eliz. Sidebottom. Aug. 29, 1799.
Beverly Brown-Fanny Fletcher. Sept. 2, 1799.

Moses Cummins-Betsy Garrett. Sept. 3, 1799.
Abraham Bledso-Ruhannah Dryden, daughter of Wm. Dryden. Sept., 1799.
James Crawford-Sally Duggins. Sept. 12, 1799.
Thomas Brannan-Milly Huey. Sept. 7, 1799.
Richard Jones-Francis Turpin, of Hezekiah Turpin. Oct. 14, 1799.
James Rice-Polly England. Oct. 21, 1799.
Elbert I. Holcomb-Elizabeth Clarke, of John Clarke. Nov. 2, 1799.
John Maxwell-Polly Carns, of Alexander Carns. Nov. 11, 1799.
John Woods-Charity Dysert, of John Dysert. Nov. 18, 1799.
Joseph Pointer-Sarah Cottral. Nov. 19, 1799.
Benjamin Holsclaw-Sally Kemper, of John Kemper. Nov. 26, 1799.
John Stoker-Sally Campbell. Dec. 2, 1799.
Absolem Hughes-Rachael Sampson. Dec. 12, 1799.
Thos. Williams-Barbara Cromer. Dec. 16, 1799.
Gabriel Overstreet-Lucy Alford. Dec. 30, 1799.
Stephen M'Collum-Rachel Carpenter. (no month) 13, 1799.
William Wheeler-Sally Shrewsberry, of Nathaniel Shrewsberry, (no month), 1799.
Elijah Walden-Martha Nowland. Jan. 8, 1800.
Walter Adams-Judy Adams. Jan. 14, 1800.
Blanks Moody-Polly Sapsley. Jan. 18, 1800.
John Killam-Sally Shackleford, of Zachariah Shackleford. Jan. 26, 1800.
John Mason-Sally Stevens. Jan. 29, 1800.
Matthew Singleton-Nancy Brown. Feb. 3, 1800.
Amos Rawls-Lucy Scott. Feb. 7, 1800.
Thos, B. Boslee-Lucy Sutton. Feb. 7, 1800.
Sabrill (?) Coneley-Elizabeth Comely. Feb. 22, 1800.
Thomas M'Coy-Jenney Paul. Feb. 25, 1800.
Abner Bassett-Susannah Harbard. Mch. 4, 1800.
Joseph Baldwin-Patsy Clendennen, of James Clendennen. Mch. 9, 1800.
Thomas Livingston-Sarah Stephens of John and Lucy Stephens. Mch. 15, 1800.
George Gaston M'Henry-Polly Hubbard. Mch. 17, 1800. Consent of John Hubbard.
Benjamin Brown-Polly Poe. Mch. 19, 1880.
Frances Sasseen-Lucy Brown, of Absolom and Anna Brown. Mch. 26, 1800.
Alexander Jemmison-Henny Craig. Mch. 20, 1800.
James Miller-Betsy Proctor. Mch. 26, 1800.
Thomas Faulkner-Polly Renfrow. Mch. 30, 1800.
Joshua Short-Henrietta Jackson. Apr. 1, 1800.
John Dysert-Martha Woods. Apr. 1, 1800.
William Heard-Franky Adams. Apr. 5, 1800.
James Clay-Faithful Grimes. Apr. 9, 1800.
Moses Preston-Sally Ott. Apr. 10, 1800.
Richard Barton-Nancy Harris. May 2, 1800.
John M'Cord-Peggy Biggers. May 4, 1800.
John Burnsides-Nancy Smith. May 21, 1800.
Augustine Jennings-Polly Dunn. May 28, 1800.
William Thomas-Betsy Chance. May 29, 1800.
Washington Strange-Mary Copelin, of Jacob and Anne Copelin. June 5, 1800.
Roderick M'Donold-Isabel M'Coy. June 10, 1800.
Thos. Wheeler-Clary Harris, of Jonathan Harris. June ——, 1800.
Henry Smith-Elizabeth Laughlin. June 12, 1800.
John Woods-Jinney Brank, of Robert Brank. June 11, 1800.
John Saylor-Sarah Nicholson. June 15, 1800.
Erasmus Allen-Lucy Ballinger. June 24, 1800.

Thos. Coy-Anna Ford. June 30, 1800.

Jesse Thompson-Agnes Randels, of John Randels. July 1, 1800.

Thomas Brown-Caty Adams. July 5, 1800.

Ignatious Garrett-Elizabeth Crawford. July 10, 1800.

George Baker-Easther Robertson, of Samuel Robertson. July 13, 1800.

Robert Creath-Ann Crawford, of James Crawford. July 21, 1800.

John Stephens-Parthina Denton. July 21, 1800.

William M'Lean-Peggy Miller, of Wm. Miller. July 30, 1800.

Absolom Brown-Cile Kyler, of Joseph Kyler. Aug. 13, 1800.

Henry McManies-Bathsheba Stogdhill. Aug. 1, 1800.

Charles Brown-Jane Pond. Aug. 22, 1800.

John Banks-Dolly M. Land. Aug. 19, 1800.

Julius Burton-Lealia Wheelor, of B. Wheeler. Aug. 19, 1800.

Tobias Grider-Sally Hogan, of Wm. Hogan. Sept. 9, 1800.

Levi Lines-Nancy Jones. Sept. 18, 1800.

William Gully-Sary Burton, of Lucy Burton. Sept. ——, 1800.

Joseph Reed-Betsy Maxwell. Oct. 8, 1800.

Samuel Coy-Fanny Clark. Oct. 15, 1800.

Thomas Reynolds-Caty Willis. Oct. 27, 1800.

John Jones-Rachel Greene. Nov. 18, 1800. John Jones, son of George Jones.

George Bradley-Hannah Logston. Mar: Nov. 19, 1800, by Rev. Peter Bainbridge.

Daniel Laman-Susannah Gemblin. Nov. 25, 1800.

Garland Akin-Nancy Rattan. Sept. 15, 1800.

James Morrison-Polly W. Williams. Dec. 27, 1800.

William Kennedy-Dolly Thomson, of David Thomson. Dec. 24, 1800.

Elijah Carteel-Lucy Tunget, of Jeremiah Tunget. Dec. 29, 1800.

James Tarpin-Nelly Barnsides. Dec. 29, 1800.

William Walden-Polly Ingram. Dec. 30, 1800.

MISCELLANEOUS MARRIAGE BONDS

Stephen Defo-Mary Ann Campdeno (or Campdexo). Jan. 2, 1801.

James Anderson-Margaret Allcorn. Jan. 6, 1801.

Charles Burriss-Rosannah Lanfield. Jan. 7, 1801.

John Route-Fanny Kamper, of John Kamper. Jan. 28, 1801.

Davis Carns-Polly Selvin, of John Selvin. Feb. 7, 1801.

Mansfield Coon-Lena Green, of Zechariah Green. Feb. 13, 1801.

James Layer-Sally Hamilton, of Charles Hamilton. Feb. 14, 1801.

Armstead Redd-Lucy ——. Feb. 25, 1801.

Thomas Spillman-Alice Kemper. Apr. 8, 1801.

Daniel Hubbard-Betsy Manier, of John and Betsy Manier. Mch. 9, 1801.

Thomas Ballew-Fanny Hubbard. Apr. 9, 1801.

Berry Noell-Patsey Sutton. Apr. 20, 1801. Consent of Benjamin Sutton.

John Aldridge-Polly Gill. Apr. 28, 1801.

Francis Kennedy-Mary Brooks, of John Brooks. May 8, 1801.

Robert Dysert-Susannah Denny. May 11, 1801.

Edmond Smith-Jenny Ann Finley, of David Finley. May 13, 1801.

John Steel-Drucilla Nowell. June 8, 1801.

Stephens Cummins-Clary Dermin. June 11, 1801.

John Bourne-Elizabeth Arnold. July 25, 1801. Signed by Reuben Arnold.

James Hutchinson-Rebecca Weathers. July, 1801.

William Dorrill-Adsy Vickers. Aug. 27, 1801.

Samuel Douglass-Polly Outman. Sept. 2, 1801.

Elijah Holesclaw-Sally Collier. Sept. 15, 1801.

Travis Rogers-Peggy Adams. Sept. 29, 1801. Father, John Rodgers. Father, Luke Adams.

Fleming Jones-Polly Parks. Oct. 2, 1801.

William Clark-Sarah Crawford. Oct. 22, 1801.

Richard Barker-Sharlot Crocket. Oct. 26, 1801.

Robert Brinler-Sally Russ. Oct. 28, 1801.

John Burdett-Elizabeth Gooch. Oct. 29, 1801.

John Black-Janny enderson. Nov. 4, 1801. Father, Alexander Henderson.

Charles Hays-Kitty Holland. Nov. 11, 1801. Father, Wm. Holland.

William Banks-Elizabeth Brown. Dec. 5, 1801.

Alexander Jameson-Polly Moor. Dec. 10, 1801.

Zechariah Smith-Aggy Dicken. Dec. 22, 1801. Father, Benj. Dicken.

James Crump-Elizabeth Ballingr. Dec. 23, 1801.

Jesse Spraggens-Nancy Adkinson. Dec. 25, 1801.

John Marshall-Jane Haughman. Dec. 30, 1801.

John Schooler-Polly Pond. Jan. 2, 1802. Father, John Schooler.

John Menifee-Polly Faulkner. Jan. 4, 1802. Father, Isaac Rentfro. (?)

William Shackleford-Nancy Sheckley. Jan. 4, 1802.

Wm. Curby-Susanna Wiley. Jan. 7, 1802.

John Gromer-Jane Wagers. Jan. 18, 1802.

Jesse Smith-Prudy McGee. Jan. 7, 1802. John Thornberry guardian of Prudy McGee.

Joseph Fenton-Mary F. Terrill. Feb. 10, 1802.

Silas Enyart-Sealy Best. Feb. 15, 1802.

Anthony Franklin-Polly Nelson. Feb. 15, 1802.

James Barnes-Patsy Gatewood. Feb. 17, 1802.

John Quin-Lucy Hiat. Feb. 17, 1802.

James Oubay-Elis. Bright. Feb. 24, 1802.

James Gatliff-Polly Langford. Mar. 9, 1802.

Zachariah Short-Suky Walden. Mar. 15, 1802.

David Jenkins-Patsy Alford. Dec. 1, 1807. Consent of mother, Nancy Alford.

William Anderson-Lucy Stewart. Dec. 21, 1807.

Thomas Brown-Anky ————. Dec. 29, 1807.

Stephen Hopkins-Betsy Mason. Dec. 30, 1807.

John Snoddy-Synta (?) Miller. Dec. 30, 1807.

John Johnson-Dicey ————. Dec. 31, 1807.

William Adams-Elizabeth B. Steger. Apr. 9, 1808.

John Fennell-Sally Henderson. Apr. 12, 1808.

John Denton-Betsy Arnold. Apr. 27, 1808. Daughter of John and Betty Arnold.

Archibald Garvin-Peggy ————. Apr. 12, 1808.

Giles Allegy-Betsy Southern. May 3, 1808. Bond by Jesse Hill, that Betsy Southern was 21 years old.

Benjamin Alderman-Betsy ————. July 7, 1808.

James Wallace-Peggy Baker. Oct. 3, 1808.

Anthony Owsley-Tabitha Martin. Oct. 16, 1808.

Daniel Lee-Mary Myers. Oct. 26, 1808.

Thomas Reynolds-Sally Perkins. Dec. 3, 1808.

James Fisher-Polly Giles. Dec. 15, 1808. Polly is an orphan, but of age, scigned by William Wallace.

James Sadles-Dohesty Lawson. Dec. 20, 1808.

Henry Atkinson-Sally Inman. Dec. 29, 1808.

H. Ballinger-Lucy Jeffries. Feb. 9, 1809.

William Gutherie-Polly ————. Apr. 5, 1809.

Patten Denton-Mary Evans. Apr. 5, 1809. Daughter of John Evans.

William Austin-Sarah McLean.   Oct. 15, 1809.   Nathaniel Austin, father.

Thomas Denton-Betsy Barnett.   Dec. 29, 1818.
James Adams-Caroline Sartain.   Nov. 10, 1829.
Luke Adams-Elizabeth Parker.   Dec. 2, 1829.
Solomon Casey-Eliza Denton.   Feb. 20, 1843.
James Duncan-Mrs. Francis Dawson.   Mch. 14, 1843.
Elijah Lear-Juliana Sadler, daughter of Asa Sadler.   Oct. 10, 1843.

MARRIAGE INDEX—LINCOLN COUNTY

(Copied by Jewell McWilliams, Circuit Court Clerk)

William Alexander-Margaret Hog.   Nov. 28th, 1785.
Stephen Arnold-Sarah Jones.   Oct. 5th, 1782.
John Arnold-Jane Scott.   June 11, 1782.
William Anderson-Elizabeth Hingston.   May 27th, 1783.
Talbot Arthur-Mary Hancock.   March 10, 1786.
John Arbuckle-Hannah Payne.   May 4th, 1786.
Samuel Arbuckle-Barshabe Peyton.   June 23, 1787.
Matthew Adams-Esther Barnett.   April 1st, 1788.
David Andrews-Mary Cooley.   Feb. 6th, 1788.
Silas Ashby-Sarah Collett.   April 20, 1789.
John Allen-Elenor Lynch.   Feb. 17th, 1790.
James Andrews-Puscy Copten.   July 24, 1792.
Alexander Andrews-Ann Copelan.   April 13, 1792.
Charles Anderson-Sarah Manksfile.   May 28th, 1793.
Tobias Allen-Mary Poynter.   July 23, 1794.
Robert Ashmore-Margaret Bailey.   ————, 1795.
Daniel Allstott-Polly Devers.   Dec. 21, 1795.
Anderson Atkinson-Rhoda Carr.   May 31, 1796.
James Alcorn-Nancy Johnson.   May 10, 1797.
George Anderson-Charity Elliott.   April 3, 1797.
William Adams-Polly Long.   April 3, 1797.
James Arnett-Caty Lamb.   Oct. 15th, 1798.
James Aldridge-Anne Lease.   Aug. 14th, 1798.
Robert Allen-Nancy Christerson.   Oct. 22, 1798.
William Allen-Sukey Paine.   May 14th, 1798.
William Barbee-Mary Smith.   Feb. 20th, 1781.
Jeremiah Briscoe-Elizabeth Harlan.   Aug. 25, 1783.
Daniel Bonta-Anne Duree.   June 5th, 1784.
Joseph Bledsoe-Mary Sanders.   April 20, 1784.
Henry Bonta-Sarah Sogh.   June 5th, 1784.
John Beshong-Jannet Summers.   April 6th, 1784.
Henry Bright-Elizabeth Pope.   Jan. 7th, 1784.
James Bezley-Anny Shackleford.   Nov. 3, 1785.
John Beard-Polly Losson.   Sept. 23, 1785.
Benjamin Brown-Elizabeth Ross.   Aug. 8th, 1785.
John Bond-Margaret Adams.   Jan. 4th, 1785.
John Butler-Elanor Harbison.   June 6th, 1785.
Nathaniel Burros-Mary Threlkeld.   Mar. 7th, 1785.
James Butler-Mary Harbison.   Nov. 28th, 1785.
James Baxter-Deborah Westerfield.   June 17th, 1784.
William Barnett-Mary Bell.   Apr. 4th, 1785.
Wm. Bradshaw-Catherine Curd.   Dec. 31st, 1782.
John Barbee-Polly Gaines.   Jan. 21st, 1782.
Peter Bonta-Rachel Vancleave.   July 8, 1783.
William Baker-Ann Harbison.   April 21, 1788.
Elijah Baker-Elizabeth McClure.   Jan. 7th, 1788.
Solomon Brundage-Sarah McCarty.   Sept. 19th, 1788.

Jacob Bonta-Kissa Vorhis. Feb. 8th, 1786.
Wm. Bledsoe-Patience Owsley. Dec. 27th, 1786.
Peter Blair-Sarah Boyrey. Sept. 23rd, 1786.
John Bryant-Mary Owsley. May 16th, 1786.
Peter Bonta-Rachel Bonta. Jan. 11th, 1786.
Nathaniel Blackford-Mary McNeele. Dec. 13th, 1786.
John Burton-Margaret Eagin. Jan. 3rd, 1786.
Benjamin Boston-Sarah Looney. Oct. 13th, 1787.
Jeremiah Boone-Joyce Neal. May 8th, 1787.
Edward Bradley-Molly Duncan. August 30, 1787.
Henry Beckner-Charity Mannon. Apr. 28th, 1788.
John Berrell-Polly Floyd. May 8th, 1788.
James Bryant-Rossetta Wyley. Aug. 20th, 1788.
John Bright-Betsy May Hawkins. Dec. 7th, 1789.
Samuel Blankenbecker-Mary Tryer. Oct. 26th, 1789.
Bartlett Brown-Ann Bryant. May 10th, 1789.
John Brund-Nancy Ping. May 27th, 1789.
John Breader-Elizabeth Powell. Jan. 12th, 1789.
John Baliste-Hannah Shuck. April 7th, 1790.
William Banks-Rachel Marksbury. June 30th, 1790.
Benjamin Bush-Margaret McClure. Feb. 10, 1790.
Thomas Buckner-Hannah Burton. Apr. 10th, 1790.
Joshua Burdett-Gracy Floyd. Feb. 26th, 1790.
William Ball-Lettie Smith. April 10th, 1790.
Nicholas Burks-Polly Mason. May 13th, 1790.
Benjamin Bledsoe-Caty Jennings. Feb. 10th, 1791.
James Birney-Martha Reed. April 15th, 1791.
Benajah Brown-Judith Brown. Nov. 22, 1791.
Wm. Baker-Nancy Reed. July 30th, 1791.
Reuben Bird-Sarah Black. Mar. 28th, 1791.
Jacob Brite-Lidea Springate. Nov. 26th, 1791.
Thomas Bayne-Ann Middleton. Dec. 24th, 1791.
Charles Bland-Phillips Pope. January ——, 1791.
James Bondry-Lettie Perrin. Sept. 20, 1791.
Elijah Bailey-Sarah Jackman. March 3, 1791.
Richard Ballenger-Betsey Jennings. Aug. 21, 1792.
Squire Baker-Elizabeth Followay. January 24, 1792.
John Burnside-Mary Denton. April 13th, 1792.
Matthew Brown-Sarah Simpson. Oct. 1, 1792.
John Benedict-Hannah Phillips. Feb. 9th, 1792.
John Buford-Frances Banton. Dec. 18th, 1792.
Richard Bruch-Nancy Warren. March 21, 1792.
Thomas Bentley-Rode Hikeson. March 6th, 1793.
George Berry-Sarah Lapsley. Dec. 25th, 1794.
Thomas Berreman-Nancy Emmerson. Aug. 11, 1794.
Allen Burks-Sally Berry. July 21, 1794.
William Brown-Elenor East. Sept. 11, 1794.
Joseph Ballinger-Jane Logan. Jan. 9, 1794.
James Ball-Jane Denton. June 18, 1794.
James Brush-Mary Spratt. Dec. 7th, 1795.
Reuben Bailey-Martha Emmerson. Dec. 29, 1795.
Abraham Buford-Mary Moody. Jan. 17, 1795.
Jacob Blackledge-Charlotte Neavel. Nov. 31, 1795.
Levi Baldock-Sallie Edwards. Feb. 25, 1795.
William Berry-Amy Moore. Mar. 4th, 1795.
Samuel Brady-Nancy Culberson. May 9, 1795.
William Baxter-Elizabeth Brampton. July 16, 1795.
Jeremiah Black-Sally Neale. Dec. 2, 1795.
John Brown-Anne McPeake. June 3, 1795.
Henry Brown-Rebecca Noel. June 18, 1795.
James Bird-Susanna Farris. Dec. 18, 1796.

Taliford Bronaugh-Jenny Gilmore. Jan. 5, 1796.
Samuel Bishop-Fanny Conn. Dec. 12, 1796.
John Branham-Rachel Brown. Nov. 12, 1796.
Benjamin Burch-Anne Williams. April 26, 1796.
James Baxter-Lucy Stults. June 14, 1796.
Eddy Barnette-Jane Woodson. Jan. 20, 1796.
Abner Baker-Betsey Buford. Oct. 19, 1796.
Littleberry Blevins-Molly Riley. June 30, 1796.
Joseph Berry-Malsey Campbell. Sept. 5, 1796.
Andrew Buchanan-Nancy Prosith. Dec. 1st, 1797.
Thomas Buford-Betsey Speed. May 15th, 1797.
Adam Banks-Elizabeth Meek. Sept. 1st, 1797.
Robert Brenton-Sarah Brown. Sept. 16, 1797.
James Breeding-Peggy Simpson. Nov. 15, 1797.
Leonard Bearenger-Betsey Pulliner. Jan. 17, 1797.
John Peter Bondurant-Sussannah Damron. Sept. 28, 1797.
Joseph Black-Prudence Reed. Jan. 9th, 1797.
James Brown-Mary Harris. Jan. 25, 1797.
Frederick Baker-Polly Hetrick. Jan. 7, 1797.
Moza Burch-Eleanor Williams. March 6, 1797.
William Brown-Sarah Scott. July 7th, 1797.
William Brooks-Sarah Davis. Jan. 12, 1797.
Absolam Bridges-Jane Davis. May 26th, 1798.
Abraham Bosley-Rebecca Myers. Mar. 7, 1798.
Robert Barbee-Elizabeth Daugherty. Dec. 18, 1798.
John Boreing-Nancy Wood. Jan. 12, 1798.
Ebenezer Blackiston-Lettee Combs. July 2, 1798.
Benjamin Baker-Susan Warren. July 25, 1798.
Thomas Bird-Lavina Breeding. Sept. 19, 1798.
George Banks-Rhoda Emberson. May 5, 1798.
Abner Bembridge-Polly Williams. Feb. 25, 1798.
Elisha Brown-Fanny Singleton. April 7, 1798.
Henry Bonta-Willmoth Combs. July 6th, 1798.
Benjamin Benedict-Mary Richey. May 5th, 1798.
Wm. Bryant-Barbara Alspaugh. Mar. 13, 1799.
Wm. Bright-Jane McHatton. June 4th, 1799.
John Baker-Nancy Alcorn. May 18th, 1799.
Ezekiel Barbee-Polly Bryan. Sept. 11, 1799.
Zacharia Boyle-Elizabeth Christopher. Jan. 9, 1799.
John Bradley-Judith Stringer. Nov. 1, 1800.
John Brady-Elizabeth Lowe. Aug. 2, 1800.
Wm. Burke-Caty Ruby. Feb. 4th, 1800.
John Bly-Charity Adams. Sept. 25, 1800.
Michael Carvate-Caty Shad. Dec. 25, 1784.
Patrick Carmichael-Mary Arthur. Feb. 7th, 1784.
Henry Campbell-Rebeckah Connell. Aug. 5, 1784.
Nicholas Calsh-Barbara Dallinger. July 17, 1784.
James Cutting-Elizabeth Bowdry. Sept. 3, 1784.
Augustine Cumpton-Anne Threilkeld. June 14, 1784.
Elijah Chin-Betty Smith. Sept. 7, 1784.
Aquilla Carmack-Permery Carthright. Aug. 7, 1784.
Samuel Campbell-Mary Kennedy. Apr. 13, 1785.
James Crutcher-Nancy Poage. May 7, 1785.
James Clark-Lucy Ellis. Sept. 26, 1785.
Wm. Custer-Ann Smith. June 16, 1785.
Wm. Crowdus-Dolly Arnold. June 7, 1785.
Adam Carpenter-Mrs. Catherine Fry. March 9, 1785.
John Chiles-Eliza Lillard. Mar. 7, 1785.
John Childress-Sarah Green. Sept. 22, 1783.
John Cochran-Frances Scott. Aug. 20, 1783.
Wm. Crow-Sarah Lawrence. Nov. 22, 1781.

Samuel Craig-Mary Masterson. March 7, 1781.
Jacob Coffman-Mary Hendrix. Feb. 1, 1781.
Wm. Caldwell-Elizabeth Kennedy. Aug. 15, 1786.
Robert Cox-Jean Robinson. Aug. 1, 1786.
James Caldwell-Meeke Perrin. Nov. 27, 1786.
Thomas Chilton-Peggy Bledsoe. Dec. 20, 1786.
Daniel Cooley-Milly Ball. Jan. 10, 1786.
Jacob Crow-Eleanor Wright. April 28, 1787.
Henry Couts-Henny Freeman. Jan. 19, 1787.
John Cook-Margaret Forbes. Jan. 2, 1787.
Christ Clark-Elizabeth Adams. Dec. 23, 1788.
Elisha Chisum-Elizabeth Wallen. Jan. 30, 1787.
Alexander Crawford-Margaret McElwee. Jan. 21, 1787.
Benjamin Codington-Katy Hondershalt. June 20, 1788.
John Coffman-Peggy Boyle. Aug. 9, 1788.
Jessee Cravens-Anne McClure. Jan. 14, 1789.
James Craig-Mary Culberson. Sept. 2, 1689.
Robert Collier-Rebekah Campbell. Mar. 9, 1789.
Martin Cope-Caty Zachrence. July 4, 1789.
Richard Compton-Elizabeth Comers. Oct. 4, 1790.
Joseph Cook-Sally Boylls. Dec. 29, 1790.
Moses Collier-Elizabeth Spalden. Oct. 19, 1790.
Alexander Carson-Anna Hudgens. Feb. 11, 1790.
Abraham Crow-Mary Henderson. Feb. 20, 1790.
James Coppage-Nancy O'Bannon. Dec. 19, 1791.
Henry Creighton-Eliza Wiley. June 2, 1791.
Wm. Carr-Hannah Williams. Mar. 2, 1791.
John Clark-Anna Whitton. May 17, 1791.
Wm. Campbell-Rachel Robertson. Feb. 9, 1791.
Christopher Chronic-Elizabeth Spoonamore. Jan. 18, 1791.
James Clark-Sarah Ross. July 10, 1792.
Joshua Clark-Margaret Galbraith. May 18, 1792.
Thomas Coleman-Ruthy Cook. Mar. 20, 1792.
Richard Churchwell-Nancy Napper. June 9, 1792.
Charles Campbell-Phebe Taylor. Sept. 23, 1793.
Micajah Cole-Susanna Wiley. Jan. 23, 1793.
David Cloyd-Marjory Marshal. Mar. 12, 1793.
Thomas Campbell-Sarah Lynam. Sept. 3, 1793.
James Crawford-Martha Right. Mar. 12, 1793.
Travis Coppage-Elizabeth Helm. Mar. 13, 1793.
Moses Collier-Polly Mounce. Nov. 13, 1793.
Rankin Chandler-Catherine Worthington. Dec. 26, 1793.
Anthony Cook-Martha Gilbraett. Feb. 24, 1794.
Wm. Cook-Elizabeth Cook. Mar. 31, 1794.
David Cloyd-Nancy McFerran. Mar. 7, 1794.
Sterling Crowder-Mary Bowdry. June 15, 1795.
Frederic Crout-Barbara Allspaugh. Sept. 28, 1795.
Thomas Copeland-Nancy Montgomery. Dec. 25, 1795.
John Curran-Bathsheba Menefee. July 30, 1796.
Wm. Chapman-Mary Bird. June 1, 1796.
Abraham Cashwiller-Christena Balker. Feb. 8, 1796.
James Collier-Rachel Montgomery. March. 22, 1796.
Moses Campbell-Catherine Spratt. Sept. 20, 1796.
John Coplen-Polly Downing. May 31, 1796.
Henry Clay-Peggy Helms. Jan. 11, 1796.
Charles Cooley-Esther Thompson. Feb. 21, 1796.
James Collier-Nancy Bellow. Jan. 25, 1796.
Joel Crow-Jane Blankenship. Feb. 14, 1796.
James Craften-Mary Mankspile. Sept. 3, 1798.
Samuel Clark-Polly Williams. Sept. 3, 1798.
John Campbell-Rachel Ramsey. April 17, 1798.

Cornelius Cochran-Mrs. Betsy Upton. Feb. 26, 1798.
Geo. Campbell-Anna Adams. Apr. 27, 1799.
Thomas Cox-Ruth Boneham. Mar. 15, 1799.
Reuben Carrier-Polly Darnell. Jan. 26, 1799.
James Culton-Nancy Arthur. Feb. 12, 1799.
Thomas Christeson-Betsey Northcut. Feb. 11, 1799.
John Campbell-Rebecca Edward. Jan. 7, 1799.
James Conley-Hannah Thompson. Jan. 22, 1799.
William Colvin-Mary Perreman. Mar. 12, 1799.
James Cloid-Chanty Graham. Mar. ——, 1800.
Nimrod Canterberry-Molly Franklin. May 27, 1800.
James Clemons-Patsey Gilbert. Nov. 3, 1800.
Jacob Carpenter-Leah Fry. Sept. 9, 1800.
John Davison-Susanna Jackson. Jan. 22, 1784.
John Devine-Anne Davis. May 27, 1784.
Richmond Deadman-Caty Gatewood. Jan. 26, 1784.
David Dust-Rozella Holman. Jan. 14, 1784.
Joseph Dobson-Sarah Sloan. July 25, 1785.
Alexander Denney-Ann Adams. June 10, 1785.
John Downing-Jane Thompson. Jan. 2, 1783.
Joseph Davis-Elizabeth Gordon. Sept. 3, 1783.
Robert Daniels-Mary Trigg. Aug. 18, 1783.
Patrick Dorman-Elizabeth Goodnight. Jan. 29, 1783.
Leonard Dozier-Rebecca Evans. Mar. 27, 1786.
Thomas Davis-Susanna Johnson. Feb. 13, 1786.
Charles Duncan-Margaret Burnside. Jan. 27, 1787.
Robert Dean-Mary Rogers. Aug. 21, 1787.
James Dooley-Rachel Moore. Nov. 29, 1787.
Jessee Davis-Polly Chapman. May 2, 1787.
Joseph Dobson-Betty Matthews. July 25, 1788.
John Dillingham-Esther Chapman. May 26, 1789.
Wm. Dalton-Delilah Iverson. Jan. 16, 1789.
Geo. Duncan-Elizabeth Phillips. Apr. 6, 1790.
James Drummond-Susanna Joslin. Aug. 22, 1791.
John Davis-Elizabeth Wyley. July 2, 1791.
Henry Daugherty-Katherine French. May 21, 1792.
Abner Dooley-Nancy Douglass. Apr. 16, 1793.
Abraham Dyer-Esther Dillingham. May 9, 1795.
Wm. Daugherty-Anne McGill. May 20, 1794.
Rogers Devine-Jane Burch. Aug. 22, 1794.
James Denton-Sarah Clarkston. Jan. 21, 1794.
Claburn Duncan-Mittice Whittle. July 26, 1794.
John Dickens-Elizabeth Caldwell. June 26, 1795.
Benjamin Duncan-Christena Baughman. June 13, 1796.
Robert Davis-Sally Smith. Nov. 15, 1796.
Daniel Drake-Peggy Acres. Aug. 11, 1796.
Charles Datson-Jenny Sidebottom. July 9, 1796.
Nathan Douglass-Nelly Dunn. May 31, 1796.
Joshua Dillingham-Peggy Brasfiel. Oct. 26, 1796.
Reuben Dunbar-Lettie Mason. Oct. 3, 1796.
James Davis-Nancy Hawkins. March 28, 1796.
Wm. Dearman-Estha Trap. Nov. 30, 1797.
Charles Daugherty-Agnes Daugherty. Jan. 24, 1797.
John Davis-Keaty Antle. Nov. 28, 1797.
Jacob Danner-Caty Horine. Sept. 23, 1797.
Samuel Davidson-Sally Logan. Feb. 15, 1797.
Thomas Dowthett-Mary Jones. May 22, 1797.
Wm. Dougherty-Susanna McGill. Jan. 9, 1797.
Robert Davis-Patsey Solesberry. June 15, 1797.
James Dorrill-Molley Trap. Oct. 6, 1797.
John Dougherty-Mary Magil. Oct. 2, 1797.

Charles Duncan-Letler Shelton. Aug. 21, 1797.
John Dodds-Nancy Young. Apr. 29, 1797.
Carter Drake-Polly Josling. Jan. 16, 1797.
Frederic Dayhoff-Polly Yantis. Jan. 21, 1799.
———— Dillingham-Polly Bailey. Oct. 14, 1800.
John Davis-Caty Harris. May 27, 1800.
John Dodds-Mary Gary. Dec. 25, 1800.
Baker Ewing-Lettie Warren. Nov. 24, 1784.
North East-Karenhapuck Peyton. Mar. 14, 1786.
Abraham Estes-Margaret McCormack. Dec. 31, 1789.
John Evins-Nancy Talbot. Sept. 21, 1790.
James Ely-Sally Masterson. Dec. 19, 1790.
Simon Engleman-Polly Griggs. Mar. 25, 1790.
Young Ewing-Winney Warren. June 15, 1791.
Wm. Elliott-Margaret Arnold. Oct. 10, 1791.
Joseph Evans-Elizabeth Nash. Dec. 24, 1793.
Robert Ellison-Rebecca McClure. Nov. 13, 1794.
George Elliott-Francis Smith. May 5, 1794.
Samuel Ewing-Jane Jackson. Jan. 20, 1795.
Henry Edwards-Mary Cross. Jan. 13, 1796.
Benjamin Echols-Elizabeth Miller. Jan. 18, 1796.
John Elliott-Rachel Davisman. May 17, 1797.
Andrew Evans-Sarah Roberson. Nov. 27, 1797.
John Evans-Mary Price. Mar. 29, 1797.
Jacob Engleman-Anna Hill. Feb. 27, 1798.
Thomas Estes-Mrs. Elizabeth Cuttings. Feb. 28, 1798.
Elisha Embry-Polly McBride. Oct. 10, 1799.
Emeriah Edwards-Sally Northcutt. Mar. 18, 1799.
John Emerson-Jenny Dillingham. Mar. 6, 1800.
John East-Sophia Whittle. Sept. 24, 1800.
James French-Cassa Calloway. June 19, 1783.
Michael Fagan-Rachel Bland. Jan. 30, 1884.
David Floyd-Sarah Crutchfield. July 20, 1884.
John Francis-Nancy Mounts. May 12, 1884.
Elias Fisher-Gemmimah Butler. Oct. 24, 1885.
Samuel Flannory-Nancy Martin. June 17, 1885.
Geo. Finley-Polly Gaines. June 29, 1885.
Johnson Farris-Jenny Lankford. Aug. 13, 1887.
David Foreman-Elizabeth Horne. Apr. 18, 1888.
Robert Fletcher-Agnes Casay. Mar. 29, 1888.
Thos. Farris-Ruthy Moore. Apr. 22, 1888.
Thomas Fletcher-Elizabeth Hannson. May 22, 1789.
Nicholas Flourney-Elizabeth Warner. Oct. 30, 1789.
James Feland-Isabel Roberson. July 21, 1790.
Jonathan Forbes-Florence Montgomery. Oct. 26, 1790.
David Floyd-Caty Burdett. Dec. 17, 1790.
Robert Franklin-Fanny Crutchfield. April 21, 1790.
Robt. Frazier-Sukey Peyton. June 5th, 1790.
Wm. Ford-Sally Shackelford. Oct. 25, 1791.
Andrew Feland-Francis Mason. June 13, 1791.
John Ferrell-Kesia Cook. Aug. 1, 1791.
Caleb Frizby-Elizabeth Puckite. Sept. 28, 1792.
Micajah Farris-Nancy Chadwick. Sept. 18, 1792.
Abraham Fitsworth-Lydia Cumpton. Sept. 3, 1792.
Gilbert Farris-Dicey Farris. Feb. 8, 1798.
Wm. 'Feland-Sallie Culberson. Mar. 13, 1794.
Joseph Feland-Elizabeth Huston. Aug. 6, 1794.
Elisha Farris-Ann Lankford. June 24, 1794.
Francis Fresh-Lucy Burdette. Feb. 4, 1794.
John French-Levisa Harrington. July 18, 1795.
Lewis Farris-Rebeckah Robinson. March 25, 1795.

James Mc. Fair-Elizabeth May. 1796.
John Fitzgerald-Mary Farris. Dec. 20, 1796.
Nimrod Farris-Nancy Farris. Sept. 8, 1796.
John Farris-Polly Pennex. May 7, 1796.
Wm. Farris-Peggy Shannon. Oct. 3, 1796.
Wm. Farris-Jenny Wilkerson. Aug. 16, 1797.
Wm. Flack-Susanah Callerson. Mar. 15, 1797.
Henry Francis-Elizabeth Pearl. Jan. 2, 1798.
John Fox-Betsey Robertson. Aug. 19, 1799.
John Forsythe-Betsey Nelson. Dec. 18, 1799.
Vivian Goodloe-Dolly Tompkins. Aug. 5, 1784.
Thomas Graves-Mary Shelton. Aug. 23, 1785.
John Galloway-Darky Ray. May 30, 1785.
Samuel Gilmore-Elizabeth Modiloe. Sept. 21, 1785.
Thos. Gash-Martha Daugherty. Jan. 21, 1785.
Alexander Gillmore-Rebecca Smith. Oct. 18, 1791.
Patrick Gray-Margaret Woods. Sept. 19, 1785.
Wm. Goggin-Drusilla Jackman. Dec. 8, 1785.
Willis Green-Sarah Reed. Dec. 23, 1783.
Henry Grass-Mary Gray. Aug. 11, 1783.
Wm. Griffin-Molly Henry. July 10, 1782.
James Gilmore-Martha McKelsee. July 6, 1782.
Patrick Gallahan-Judith Noland. Aug. 20, 1785.
Barnabas Gilbert-Elizabeth Hellicost. Dec. 29, 1788.
Jeremiah Gibbs-Barbara Brown. Jan. 20, 1789.
James Gilmore-Susy Loden. Feb. 20, 1789.
Wm. Green-Anna Marshal. Aug. 19, 1790.
Wm. Graves-Nancy Owsley. Dec. 22, 1790.
Isaac Garvin-Jenny Huston. June 27, 1791.
James Givens-Jane Givens. July 27, 1791.
Ezekiel Gibbs-Martha Brown. Oct. 1, 1792.
Samuel Gibbs-Martha Logan. July 11, 1792.
Jesse Gooch-Elizabeth Owsley. April 14, 1792.
Wm. Graves-Lydia Williams. Apr. 30, 1793.
Samuel Givens-Hannah Miller. Aug. 8, 1793.
Abraham Goodnight-Mary Hannah. Jan. 22, 1794.
Eleazer Givens-Mary Campbell. Jan. 20, 1794.
Alexander Gilbrath-Nancy Baughman. Dec. 16, 1794.
John Griffin-Mary James. Mar. 25, 1794.
Robert Gilleland-Peggy Claunch. July 29, 1796.
Elizer Givens-Jenny Robertson. Aug. 27, 1796.
James Golston-Patsy Lewis. Feb. 4, 1796.
Uriah Gresham-Nancy Tayler. Feb. 10, 1796.
Luke Graham-Mary Huffman. March 22, 1796.
John Gary-Agnes McKee. Aug. 15, 1796.
John W. Gilbert-Mary Craig. Nov. 30, 1797.
Wm. Gooch-Mildred Atkinson. Aug. 9, 1797.
Fleming Good-Rhoda Peyton. Dec. 20, 1797.
John Gilbert-Eleanor Gilmore. Nov. 14, 1797.
Robert Givens-Mary Givens. Sept. 10, 1798.
Aaron Gill-Elizabeth Murphy. May 15, 1798.
James Gooding-Martha Alexander. June 5, 1799.
James Gilmore-Jenny Tinsley. Feb. 26, 1799.
Alexander Givens-Nancy Logan. June 19, 1799.
Joseph Glover-Betsey Chapman. July 23, 1800.
Daniel Guthrie-Nancy Shackleford. Nov. 26, 1800.
John Gibbs-Deliah Kelley. Dec. 27, 1800.
Wm. Greenwood-Elizabeth Evans. Dec. 2, 1800.
Cornelius Gatliff-Sally Lankford. Feb. 25, 1800.
Wm. Guthrie-Patsy Jackson. July 29, 1800.
Benjamin Givens-Hannah Riggs. Mar. 18, 1800.

Michael Hampton-Catherine Smith.   Apr. 19, 1788.
Samuel Harris-Elizabeth Van Cleve.   Oct. 25 ,1784.
Moses Hall-Isabell Stevenson.   Sept. 4, 1784.
Clement Hill-Mary Anne Douglas.   Mar. 19, 1784,
James Harlan-Sarah Caldwell.   May 15, 1784.
James Hays-Rebecca Hendrix.   May 10, 1784.
Samuel Hutton-Ruth Boghart.   July 12, 1784.
James Hutchison-Elizabeth Edwards.   May 8, 1784.
John Hart-Elizabeth Hall.   May 11, 1784.
Clayton Holloway-Nancy Washburn.   Feb. 9, 1784.
Charles Hounslin-Rittah Jackson.   Dec. 28, 1785.
Aaron Higgins-Ann Chapman.   June 2, 1785.
Benjamin Haggard-Polly Nokes.   July 21, 1785.
Joseph Hall-Ann Barnet.   Dec. 31, 1785.
John Hendrick-Mary Gibson.   Dec. 10, 1785.
Hendrick Hutton-Hannah Long.   Sept. 5, 1785.
Uriah Humble-Bridget Cain.   August 1, 1785.
Stephen Huston-Jane Feland.   Sept. 2, 1783.
Thomas Harrison-Nancy Walker.   Apr. 19, 1783.
Isaac Houghlan-Martha Hubbard.   July 14, 1782.
James Hord-Nancy Curd.   Mar. 23, 1782.
Geo. Helm-Francis Coppage.   Dec. 15, 1783.
Edward Hogan-Elizabeth Hendrix.   Mar. 5, 1783.
Richard Hope-Eliza Ewing.   Nov. 20, 1782.
Prossor Hogan-Mary Whooly.   May 27, 1786.
David Hogan-Elizabeth Whooly.   Jan. 2, 1786.
Andrew Harris-Ede Hart.   Nov. 28, 1786.
Wm. Harrison-Peggy Miller.   May 19, 1786.
Marcus Helm-Rebecca Cade.   Aug. 13, 1787.
Elijah Harbour-Hannah Bell.   Sept. 27, 1787.
Wm. Hamilton-Mary Baughman.   June 22, 1787.
Samuel Hind-Peggy Wells Arnold.   Oct. 29, 1787.
Israel Hart-Elizabeth Price.   Mar. 19, 1788.
James Hogan-Jean Rogers.   May 25, 1788.
Wm. Haggard-Rosanna Nowell.   Feb. 11, 1788.
Israel Harman-Kizea Thompson.   Mar. 19, 1788.
John Henderson-Nancy Singleton.   July 19, 1788.
Alexander Hamilton-Martha Smith.   Nov. 10, 1789.
James Hamilton-Cecilia Collier.   1789.
James Hogan-Polly Simpson.   Feb. 17, 1789.
Nathan Huston-Ann Montgomery.   Feb. 27, 1789.
Daniel Hudgeons-Dolly Menally.   Oct. 10, 1789.
James Hindman-Mary Brunts.   Oct. 12, 1790.
William Howse-Polly Wilcocks.   Apr. 25, 1790.
John Holland-Mary Turner.   Nov. 1, 1790.
Thomas Hardin-Mary Glover.   Feb. 2, 1790.
Hinson Hoobes-Mary Shipman.   July 20, 1790.
Wm. Hill-Nancy Mayfield.   July 17, 1790.
Wm. Henderson-Eleanor Clark.   July 10, 1790.
James Henderson-Lettie Rutherford.   Dec. 5, 1790.
Joseph Hiatt-Margaret Reid.   May 6, 1790.
Archabald Huston-Sally Gay.   July 9, 1792.
Thomas Holman-Mary Graham.   July 9, 1792.
James Haggard-Lucy Brown.   May 29, 1792.
John Isaacs-Polly Moore.   Oct. 28, 1783.
John Irvin-Prudence Armstrong.   May 29, 1786.
William Innes-Caty Poynter.   May 12, 1790.
Charles Alford-Sidney Jones.   Apr. 18, 1792.
Henry Innes-Ann Sheele.   Feb. 7th, 1792.
Benjamin Irvin-Polly Burrs.   Jan. 12, 1797.
John Jurney-Nancy McMullin.   Sept. 2, 1798.

Luke Johnston-Nancy Worthington. June 8, 1799.
Abraham James-Mary Holloway. June 28, 1784.
Robert Jammison-Isabelle Maehan. Jan. 10, 1784.
Joseph James-Elizabeth Garnett. Aug. 4, 1784.
John Jamison-Rhoda Buchanan. Oct. 10, 1782.
Jonathan Jennings-Ann Woods. June 27, 1786.
John Jones-Polly Floyd. Oct. 28, 1788.
Josiah Jones-Barbara Baxter. Aug. 30, 1788 .
James Jones-Elizabeth Spillman. June 24, 1789.
Wm. Johns-Mollie Thirmond. Feb. 25, 1790.
Peter Jump-Mrs. Katy Links. Apr. 1, 1790.
Joel Jackson-Nancy Caldwell. Dec. 17, 1791.
David Johnson-Polly Burch. Oct. 2, 1792.
John Jackman-Hannah VanMetre. Aug. 20, 1793.
Ephraim Jackson-Nancy Bird. May 7, 1793.
Francis Jordan-Mary Browning. Nov. 29, 1796.
Edward Johnson-Jenny Cook. Oct. 28, 1796.
Benjamin Johnson-Betsey Hawker. Dec. 13, 1796.
William Jones-Nancy Combs. Nov. 12, 1800.
Abraham Jones-Mary Inyart. Sept. 2, 1800.
Jacob Kauffman-Mary Hendricks. Jan. 1, 1781.
Chas. Kavanaugh-Francis Powell. July 6, 1784.
James Kincaid-Sarah Wilson. Feb. 4, 1784.
John King-Susana Davidson. Apr. 6, 1785.
John Kirkland-Mary Fally. May 14, 1783.
James Kelly-Mary Shelp. Dec. 17, 1783.
Christian Knary-Barbara Garshimler. July 19, 1787.
Henry Kilburn-Chairity Poynter. Aug. 19, 1788.
Joseph Kennedy-Patsy Perrin. Aug. 1, 1788.
David Kennedy-Elizabeth Thompson. Oct. 11, 1788.
James Kenly-Theodolia Thurmond. Jan. 21, 1788.
James Kennedy-Elizabeth Warren. Dec. 23, 1789.
John Kipinger-Sarah Middleton. July 14, 1789.
James Kare-Elizabeth Williams. July 23, 1790.
Michael Kenney-Susannah Rawls. May 14, 1790.
Daniel Kenny-Mary Ogletharp. Feb. 19, 1790.
Chas. Kavanaugh-Mary Gentry. April 12, 1791.
Thomas Key-Martha Davis. Jan. 6, 1791.
George Keys-Mary Huffman. April 4, 1795.
Chas. Kirkland-Elizabeth Thompson. Oct. 6, 1796.
John Killen-Sarah Dodds. Dec. 1, 1798.
Abner Key-Nancy Roberson. Feb. 14, 1798.
Lewis Kester-Rachel Zacheries. Dec. 16, 1798.
Elijah Kirtly-Polly Buford. Dec. 10, 1800.
Wm. King-Peggy McLain. Sept. 17, 1800.
Hugh Leeper-Martha Dawson. Sept. 27, 1784.
Solomon Lawrence-Ann McConnell. Jan. 21, 1784.
Joseph Lyons-Jenny McMillans. May 31, 1784.
Hugh Leeper-Martha Dawson. Sept. 27, 1784.
Samuel Lyons-Lydia Berrisford. April 2, 1784.
Samuel Lapsley-Peggy Irvin. Oct. 3, 1785.
John Lawrence-Elizabeth McKinney. Aug. 3, 1785.
James Ledgerwood-Elizabeth McConor. Dec. 29, 1781.
Joseph Lindsay-Ann Poage. June 18, 1781.
John Lally-Elenor Potts. Mar. 1, 1783.
John Liggett-Susan Backer. Feb. 22, 1786.
Jonathan Luney-Jane Harbson. Aug. 17, 1786.
James Leggett-Esther McClure. Dec. 22, 1786.
George Lair-Catherine Hogland. Sept. 1, 1787.
Samuel Lowe-Sarah Peters. Sept. 28, 1787.
Jeremiah Laws-Frances Durham. Nov. 24, 1787.

Soloman Levi-Frances Jackson. Jan. 1, 1787.
Nathaniel Logan-Judith Wilson. Jan. 16, 1787.
Benjamin Lankfort-Nancy Peyton. Feb. 21, 1787.
John Lewis-Hannah Stephens. Feb. 11, 1788.
Ezekiel Lyon-Martha Gill. Feb. 23, 1788.
Andrew Lyman-Elizabeth Green. Dec. 7, 1788.
David Lawson-Ann Richardson. Aug. 4, 1788.
Henry Link-Mary Moreton. Jan. 2, 1790.
David Logan-Nancy Thurmond. June 15, 1790.
Mather Logan-Dicy Thurmond. July 20, 1790.
John Logan-Dorcas McKinly. Feb. 25, 1791.
William Lee-Polly Jackson. Nov. 25, 1791.
John Leiver-Eve Weighley. July 20, 1791.
Benjamin Little-Mary Lowe. Sept. 25, 1792.
Jonathan Logan-Frances Thurmond. Sept. 24, 17 2.
James Logan-Mary Logan. Nov. 16, 1792.
John Logan-Eva Latherice. July 31, 1792.
James Lorrine-Mildred Arnold. Sept. 28, 1792.
Phillip Lemon-Nancy Goode. July 14, 1796.
George Lowe-Nancy Henry. March 2, 1796.
Benjamin Long-Nancy Menefee. Dec. 19, 1796.
John Lopsley-Caty Fermester. Dec. 28, 1796.
Edward Love-Mary Wright. Dec. 1, 1796.
Henry Locter-Barbara Rufner. Sept. 23, 1797.
Frederick Landberrier-Caty May. June 23, 1798.
Samuel Lawrence-Rachel Barnett. July 7, 1799.
Walker Lankford-Mary Warren. Sept. 9, 1800.
William Lawrence-Jane Barnett. Nov. 3, 1800.
David McFall-Phoebe Beler. Nov. 9, 1784.
Joseph McCan-Eliza Ellis. Apr. 30, 1784.
Robert Moore-Margaret Campbell. Dec. 7, 1784.
George Miller-Sarah Rice. Apr. 20, 1784.
Thos. McMurry-Catherine Robinson. Mar. 20, 1784.
John Martin-Mary Means. Feb. 14, 1784.
Wm. McBrayer-Jeannette Walker. Dec. 24, 1785.
Joseph McCormack-Peggy Stams. Aug. 23, 1785.
Robert McDonald-Phoebe Wells. Feb. 14, 1785.
Samuel McDowell-Ann Irvine. Oct. 3, 1785.
Thomas Mann-Elizabeth Jones. Aug. 29, 1785.
John Miller-Elizabeth Bright. Dec. 21, 1784.
Thomas Montgomery-Mary Montgomery. Nov. 10, 1785.
James McComb-Paty Woods. May 3, 1783.
Robert McMahan-Margaret Clark. June 29, 1785.
Stephen McKinney-Katherine Grigg. May 3, 1785.
John McComsey-Jane Foker. Sept. 1, 1785.
James Montgomery-Sarah Dozier. June 27, 1785.
Thomas Moore-Elizabeth Harbison. Mar. 21, 1783.
Wm. Mumony-Susannah Linn. Sept. 10, 1783.
Wm. McBrayer-Jane Phillips. Oct. 5, 1782.
Thomas McNeal-Elizabeth Swann. July 7, 1783.
John Martin-Nancy Berry. Jan. 17, 1781.
Charles McDougall-Elizabeth Garghan.(?) Nov. —, 1783.
John Mahan-Sarah Clark. Jan. 28, 1786.
Andrew McCala-Patsy Moore. Feb. 9, 1786.
Thos. McClannahan-Elizabeth Fields. March 13, 1786.
John McClure-Lucy Martin. Nov. 28, 1786.
George Mayfield-Hannah Burdette. Oct. 30, 1786.
Levi Myers-Elizabeth McKay. March 7, 1785.
John McNelly-Susannah Duncan. Mch. 6, 1787.
James Mason-Sally Feland. July 28, 1787.
Jared Menefee-Sarah Price. Jan. 30, 1787.

James McFadden-Martha Graham. Mch. 20, 1788.
John McQuery-Elizabeth Price. Feb. 6, 1788.
Robert McClure-Peggy Hinds. Mar. 29, 1788.
Hugh McCormack-Elizabeth Josling. April 5, 1788
Archibald McKinney-Jean McClure. May 7, 1788.
William Mitchell-Susana Davis. July 22, 1788.
Jacob Mann-Mary Arnold. Feb. 27, 1788.
Jesse May-Ann English. Sept. 10, 1788.
Samuel Moore-Polly Allen. Feb. 29, 1789.
John McKenzie-Mary Shackleford. Dec. 18, 1789.
John Morrison-Sally Layton. Aug. 18, 1789.
John Montgomery-Jane Elliott. Oct. 7, 1789.
Samuel McQuerry-Mary Young. Jan. 24, 1789.
John Morris-Mary Burd. Aug. 13, 1789.
Joseph McAdams-Nancy Bailey. July 15, 1789.
John Mansfield-Polly Crasher. April 20, 1789.
Samuel Marksbury-Lucy Banks. Nov. 15, 1790.
James Mckay-Sarah Sampson. Aug. 3, 1789.
John Mansfield-Rebecca Simmons. Apr. 14, 1789.
Isaac Mayfield-Mary Banks. Dec. 22, 1789.
James McMurry-Jane McElmore. Dec. 30, 1790.
Robert McBride-Isabel Young. Feb. 2, 1790.
Samuel Moore-Elizabeth Berry. Dec. 18, 1790.
Ezra Morrison-Elizabeth Carpenter. Sept. 30, 1791.
Wm. McElwee-Agnes McClure. Oct. 19, 1791.
Thomas McClure-Susanah Hines. July 27, 1791.
————— McMurtry-Isabel Hannah. Nov. 15, 1791.
Robert Maloney-Nancy Gibbs. Aug. 30, 1791.
Edward McKendry-Elizabeth Worthington. July 14, 1791.
George Mann-Mary Mansfile. Apr. 14, 1791.
Joseph McIntosh-Martha Bowdry. Apr. 9, 1791.
Samuel Montgomery-Hannah Copeland. Jan. 11, 1791.
Mathias Mounce-Mary Montgomery. Feb. 28, 1791.
William Moody-Judith Buford. Dec. ——, 1790.
James McAlister-Hannah Montgomery. Feb. 28, 1792.
John Miller-Betsy Antle. Sept. 10, 1792.
Armstead Milner-Jaminay Bright. July 23, 1792.
Michal Murrin-Jenny Cathy. Apr. 22, 1792.
Lawrence McGuire-Rose Wiley. Dec. 31, 1792.
James McDonell-Mary Wright. Aug. 2, 1792.
Thomas McMurry-Christena Rice Hesnor. July 14, 1792.
Moses McCarley-Elizabeth Potter. Jan. 24, 1792.
Wm. Mansfile-Catherine Feland. Nov. 27, 1793 .
Ezekiel Montgomery-Nancy Colvin. Feb. 1, 1793.
James McFerran-Elizabeth Young. —— ——, 1793.
Andres Mann-Rachel Tucker. May 12, 1793.
Richard Mason-Anny Davis. Mar. 26, 1793.
John Marksberry-Caty Fraiks. Feb. 4, 1793.
Archibald McCullon-Sarah Armstrong. Dec. 25, 1793.
John McKey-Susanna Farris. June 19, 1793.
Isaac Marksberry-Susana Radcliff. Jan. 27, 1794.
Samuel Means-Polly Nash. Nov. 27, 1794.
Abraham Miller-Sally Givens. Dec. 2, 1794.
Jonathan Moore-Sarah Berry. Jan. 27, 1794.
John Moffett-Betsey Sampson. June 30, 1794.
John Mann-Susanna Roundtree. June 1 ,1794.
Elisha Moore-Mary Barnett. June 9, 1794.
Collin McKinney-Amy Moore. Feb. 10, 1794.
Daniel McKinney-Margaret McClure. Apr. 2, 1794.
Mark McPherson-Mary Middleton. Nov. 25, 1795.
Henry Middleton-Anne Graves. Dec. 18, 1795.

George Moore-Polly McKinney. Feb. 10, 1795.
Elijah Mansfile-Susannah Pence. Jan. 3, 1795.
Abraham Miller-Martha Blevins. Oct. 27, 1795.
Enoch McKinney-Mary Feland. June 20, 1795.
Nicholas Myers-Rebecca Young. June 2, 1795.
Robert Maxwell-Sally Shackleford. Apr. 29, 1795.
Thomas Malone-Elizabeth Cummings. Dec. 3, 1795.
Greenbury Majors-Sarah Wolfe. Sept. 23, 1795.
George McKinney-Anne Ruby. July 27, 1795.
Wm. Miller-Winney Helm. May 24, 1796.
John Murphy-Polly Yarbourgh. July 14, 1796.
Thomas Murrell-Rachel Holt. May 14, 1796.
Daniel McIlvoy-Sally Ford. Nov. 1, 1796.
Joshua Moore-Ann Burton. Sept. 20, 1796.
James Montgomery-Elizabeth Marshal. Oct. 10, 1796.
James Mitchel-Mattie Proctor. June 17, 1796.
Adam Mounce-Eleanor McWhorter. June 27, 1796.
Smith Morine-Rachel Montgomery. Mar. 31, 1796.
John Mannean-Nancy Noel. Mar. 10, 1796.
David Myers-Dotea Hughes. Jan. 18, 1796.
George McRoberts-Sallie Embre. ———, 1796,
John McDaniel-Margaret Trueman. Nov. 30, 1796.
Robert Montgomery-Polly Bucknall. May 17, 1797.
Rane McKinney-Sabra Vardeman. Jan. 13, 1797.
Archabald Mills-Nancy Hargrave. Jan. 29, 1797.
Robert Modrel-Jenny McClure. Mar. 25, 1797.
James Miller-Betsey Josling. Feb. 6, 1797.
Thomas McRoberts-Julia Embry. Sept. 4, 1797.
James Menefee-Nancy Hutch. Dec. 25, 1797.
James Moore-Sarah Isbell. Oct. 4, 1797.
Frederick Monser-Betsey Donar. June 25, 1797.
Ebenezer McKinney-Susanna Rutherford. Sept. 25, 1797.
Francis McCowan-Nancy Swinney. Feb. 15, 1798.
Joseph Morgan-Ann Bryan. May 1, 1798.
James McKinney-Levisa Whitley. July 10, 1798.
John Matthews-Elizabeth Hartridge. Nov. 24, 1798.
James Meek-Susannah Hilton. Aug. 28, 1798.
Asa McKenzie-Janet Roper. Jan. 31, 1799.
Thomas Moore-Elizabeth Anderson. Dec. 5, 1799.
Charles McClure-Elizabeth McDaniel. Mar. 7, 1799.
Stephen Milam-Patsy Nash. Nov. 18, 1799.
Jonathan Miller-Sarah Harris. Dec. 5, 1800.
Christopher Myers-Polly Funk. Mar. 25, 1800.
James McCormack-Sarah Thurmond. Oct. 6, 1800.
Reuben Menefee-Jemima Renfro. Nov. 12, 1800.
Benjamin McDowell-Hanna Daugherty. Nov. 24, 1800.
John May-Nancy Blacklege. May 25, 1800.
Geo. McWhorter-Ann Simpson. Feb. 23, 1800.
Thomas Montgomery-Polly Lee. July 17, 1800.
James Montgomery-Mary Colvin. June 16, 1800.
Wm. Moore-Anne Bryant. Apr. 19, 1800.
Samuel Means-Elizabeth Hughes. Oct. 16, 1800.
Thomas Nokes-Nancy Garrick. Feb. 19, 1794.
John Neel-Mary McIntire. July 1, 1785.
William Nash-Anna Hudgins. Jan. 16, 1787.
William Neal-Rebecca Magraw. Aug. 6, 1789.
George Noaks-Nancy McGraw. Aug. 18, 1789.
Isaac Neeley-Ann Coppage. Oct. 6, 1789.
Ezekiel Newland-Milly Douglass. Nov. 8, 1791.
John Nash-Mary Milner. Nov. 25, 1794.
Henry Nixon-Jennette McDaniel. Mch. 4, 1795.

Abraham Nossir-Elizabeth Downing. Apr. 6 1795.
Joel Noell-Judith Moody. Nov. 2, 1796.
Pleasant New-Sary Ball. Oct. 13, 1796.
Pallis Neal-Sally Moore. May 13, 1796.
Henry Neff-Susannah Sampson. Oct. 18, 1796.
William Norcut-Mary Hill. Mar. 3, 1796.
Marvel Nash-PollyHughes. May 10, 1798.
James Noe-Ann Waters. Mar. 15, 1798.
John Nokes-Francis Jackman. May 29, 1799.
William Owens-Nancy Pounter. Nov. 9, 1785.
William Orear-Ann Cook. Jan. 21, 1786.
Joseph Oatman-Christina Pope. July 10, 1786.
Daniel Owsley-Ann Slade. July 9, 1790.
Thomas Owsley, Jr.-Chlory Owsley. Sept. 6, 1796.
William Oliver-Fanny Warren. ——— —, 1796.
William Owsley-Patsy Davis. Jan. 21, 1796.
Jacob Ortkees-Polly Garshuiler. Mar. 26, 1799.
Nehemiah Poore-Elizabeth Ellis. Mar. 23, 1784.
William Purnell-Susanna Barbee. Dec. 18, 1784.
Samuel Prior-Mary Curd. Sept. 30, 1785.
Thomas Proctor-Polly O'Neil. Aug. 30, 1785.
John Pitman-Dorothy Peyton Robinson. May 10, 1785.
William Pope-Jemimah Vardeman. July 3, 1785.
James Penix-Elizabeth Farris. Jan. 4, 1782.
Thomas Pitman-Rachel Berry. Mch. 13, 1782.
Henry Pope-Margaret Goodnight. June 4, 1782.
Lewis Peyton-Winfred Fowell. Nov. 8, 1786.
Edward Prather-Mary Dennis. June 13, 1786.
Humphrey Pope-Lettice Wilcox. Feb. 19, 1787.
Alexander Pope-Susanna Sutton. Jan. 6, 1787.
John Ping-Elizabeth Bryant. Mch. 28, 1787.
William Powell-Mary Marshall. Oct. 4, 1787.
William Parks-Agnes Collier. Jan. 23, 1788.
James Pollard-Agnes Terry. Nov. 7, 1788.
William Pon-Jerusha Brown, Mch 10, 1789.
Isaiah Parker-Betsey Simpson. Jan. 15, 1790.
Reuben Payne-Elizabeth Pigg. Aug. 23, 1790.
Jonahtan Peters-Mary Ratcliff. June 27, 1790.
Martin Peyton-Rachel Arbuckle. Feb. 11, 1790.
George Phelps-Polly Doss. Jan. 20, 1791.
Francis Pelham-Nancy Galloway. Sept. 15, 1791.
Wm. Peters-Margaret Lowe. Aug. 2, 1791.
George Paisley-Elizabeth Harris. Aug. 27, 1791.
Abraham Price-Lettie Ann Smith. Dec. 1, 1791.
Henry Pope-Eva Switzer. Dec. 26, 1793.
Benjamin Pettett-Hannah McNelly. Aug. 27, 1793.
Andrew Pigg-Polly Perry. Apr. 22, 1793.
Stephen Pimberton-Sally Rutherford. Dec. 15, 1794.
Humphrey Pope-Elizabeth Duncan. Feb. 19, 1794.
Edwin Paine-Polly Hill. June 2, 1795.
Wiliam Perrin-Ruth Clark. Aug. 5, 1795.
Laban Paine-Polly Gray. ———, 1795.
David Perknis-Nancy Cotterell. ———, 1795.
William Preston-Annie Dove. June 7, 1792.
John Pope-Polly Vance. Mch. 10, 1795.
Samuel Porter-Martha Gilmore. Dec. 30, 1795.
William Pearl-Elizabeth Aikman. Mch. 9, 1796.
Thomas Poynter-Iby Deaman. Aug. 23, 1796.
William Powell-Patsy Blanks. Sept. 25, 1796.
John Preston-Phoebe Adams. Sept. 11, 1797.
William Pong-Polly Bullock. June 28, 1797.

Ichabod Parker-Mary Noble. Feb. 10, 1797.
John Preston-Patsy Mackness. June 12, 1797.
Wm. Patterson-Elizabeth Hardgrove. Sept. 22, 1798.
Wm. Phillips-Fanny Joslen. Jan. 1, 1798.
Moses Preston-Sarah Poynter. Nov. 21, 1798.
James Price-Margaret Westerman. June 25, 1798.
Lindsay Powell-Margaret Carpenter. Feb. 24, 1798.
Jessee Peter-Milley Sminey. Nov. 1, 1798.
Wm. Phillips-Fanny Rice. Sept. 2, 1799.
Dennis Pennnigton-Elizabeth English. Sept. 4, 1800.
Pearl Henry-Mary Owsley. Sept. 22, 1800.
Wm. Pigg-Polly Wood. Feb. 13, 1800.
—— Ryker-Mary Vancleve. June 9, 1784.
James Rains-Nancy Owens. July 4, 1784.
Nathan Roberts-Elizabeth Taylor. Aug. 2, 1785.
Amos Ragan-Amy Rennick. Sept. 20, 1785.
Wm. Roberson-Ann Wickliff. Aug. 29, 1785.
Lewis Roberts-Rachel Donaldson. Mar. 1, 1785.
James Robison-Ann Thompson. Dec. 20, 1783.
James Ray-Millie Yocum. July 5, 1781.
John Royal-Betty Jones. July 17, 1786.
Hugh Ross-Mary Kennedy. Feb. 21, 1786.
Daniel Ross-Elizabeth Burke. June 29, 1786.
Barent Renerson-Anny Banta. June 6, 1786.
Charles Rice-Sarah Bryant. July 11, 1786.
John Rudeford-Mary Simpson. Aug. 29, 1786.
Ambrose Ross-Elizabeth Gordin. Apr. 3, 1786.
James Ramsey-Elizabeth Semon. May 10, 1786.
Jacob Ruknell-Ann Spillman. Jan. 2, 1786.
Moses Riddell-Catherine Hazel. July 18, 1787.
Robert Robinson-Jenny Stevenson. Jan. 12, 1787.
James Rock-Mary Sword. Nov. 12, 1787.
Amos Reagan-Esther Black. Jan. 8, 1888.
Alexander Roberts-Lucy Shackleford. July 14, 1788.
Hozea Roberson-Druscilla Neville. Feb. 4, 1788.
John Rowe-McCain ————. Dec. 11, 1789.
Seth Ramsey-Lucy Hiatt. Feb. 5, 1790.
Larkin Rutherford-Peggy Hamilton. July 6, 1790.
John Rutherford-Jansey Bailey. July 12, 1790.
James Roberson-Sarah Murfit. Sept. 23, 1791.
Wm. Rogers-Elizabeth Low. Jan. 12, 1791.
Jonathan Ridgeway-Elizabeth Menefee. Jan. 17, 1792.
John Rice-Patsy Johnson. Jan. 24, 1793.
Peter Romine-Catherine Cater. Dec. 9, 1793.
Henry Renicks-Prudence Hall. Sept. 15, 1794.
William Russell-Francis Cravens. Nov. 24, 1794.
Luke Robinson-Susanna Hansborough. Nov. 4, 1795.
Samuel Routen-Elizabeth Walker. Aug. 22, 1795.
John Ragland-Sarah Akins. Oct. 12, 1795.
Wm. Robinson-Sidney Smith. Oct. 20, 1795.
William Reed-Peggy Smith. July 6, 1796.
Samuel Rennick-Ruth Hale. Apr. 1, 1796.
Jonathan Richardson-Jane Morrison. Dec. 19, 1796.
Matthew Roach-Margaret Dodds. June 3, 1797.
John Richie-Tabitha Spencer. Apr. 18, 1797.
Amos Richardson-Sally Morrison. Apr. 11, 1798.
Benjamin Rice-Delilah Alcorn. June 17, 1799.
Andrew Russell-Hannah Hargrove. June 28, 1799
Jacob Reed-Bess Elmore. Oct. 11, 1799.
James Reaves-Peggy Drake. Nov. 2, 1799.
Joseph Rutledge-Winnie Josling. Oct. 13, 1800.

Richard Surrett-May Cates. Sept. 20, 1784.
Jacob Stephens-Annie Warren. Apr. 5, 1784.
Thomas Simpson-Sarah Phillips. Feb. 9, 1884.
Abraham Stevens-Susanna Burnon. Mar. 15, 1784.
Joseph Sidebottom-Agatha Stepp. Aug. 14, 1784.
Adam Shepherd-Rachel Drake. Apr. 20, 1784.
John South-Elizabeth Hoy. Apr. 20, 1784.
John Smith-May English. May 9, 1785.
John Smith-Eleanor D. Green. July 25, 1785.
George Spears-Mary Nely. Feb. 19, 1785.
William Smith-Hannah Davis. Jan. 19, 1785.
George Smith-Polly Gorden. Jan. 27, 1785.
Obediah Short-Mary Jackson. Oct. 10, 1785.
John Summers-Ann McMurtry. Nov. 21, 1785.
John Sample-Ansley Hinton. July 20, 1785.
Hugh Shannon-Fanny Bright. Jan. 19, 1785.
John Summet-Margaret Snap. Dec. 24, 1785.
John Stevens-Sarah Yocum. Sept. 8, 1783.
William Slack-Mary Vinvolkather. Mar. 20, 1782.
Henry Shively-Mary Bonta. Mar. 15, 1783.
James Stevens-Susanah Haydon. July 9, 1783.
Wm. Stafford-Leah Westerfield. July 3, 1783.
Jacob Spears-Elizabeth Nealy. June 3, 1781.
Thomas Stephens-Elizabeth Calk. June 28, 1785.
Jacob Stephens-Rachel English. Nov. 6, 1786.
James Smith-Margaret Irvin. Aug. 5, 1786.
Simeledge Stringer-Jenny Bly. Dec. 18, 1786.
John Shepherd-Elizabeth Arnold. Dec. 19, 1786.
James Scott-Jean Fullerton. Apr. 1, 1786.
John Sconce-Margaret Hamilton. Jan. 16, 1787.
Richard Shackleford-Tabitha Baldrock. Nov. 12, 1788.
John Sandusky-Nancy Brunts. Apr. 26, 1788.
Golson Step-Richard Nelson. July 17, 1789.
James Sutton-Jane Flacke. Nov. 14, 1789.
Thomas Stephenson-Hannah McHolly. Jan. 7, 1789.
George Smith-Nancy Wash. March 3, 1789.
Stephen Stammons-Sally Vanwinkle. Mar. 26, 1790.
Alexander Sloan-Agnes Dobson. June 6, 1790.
Jacob Swope-Margaret Pope. Aug. 23, 1790.
John Scott-Elizabeth Baldridge. Sept. 6, 1790.
Joseph Sellers-Rachel Summers. Jan. 10, 1790.
John Smith-Jane McCarty. Apr. 9, 1790.
Thomas Smiddy-Sarah Simpson. July 1, 1790.
Robert Simpson-Hannah Powel. Apr. 6, 1791.
Jacob Short-Elizabeth Foreman. Nov. 27, 1791.
James Sellers-Mary Crawford. Dec. 19, 1791.
Nathaniel Street-Rosana Cox. Apr. 19, 1791.
Joseph Skidmore-Hannah McKinney. Aug. 20, 1791.
David Stephenson-Betty Logan. Apr. 9, 1791.
John Skidmore-Sarah McClure. Apr. 11, 1791.
Mils Stephenson-Jennie Kilpatrick. Oct. 20, 1791.
Gotlep Schmerick-Polly Alspaw. Aug. 9, 1791.
Jacob Spears-Abigal Huston. Dec. 1, 1791.
Jesse Shumaker-Franky Smith. Apr. 23, 1792.
David Swope-Polly Montgomery. July 25, 1792.
Patrick Sheets-Maryann Worthington. July 18, 1792.
Henry Stemmons-Margaret Wiley. Apr. 18, 1792.
John Smiley-Nancy Joslon. Feb. 18, 1793.
Robert Stephenson-Elizabeth Whitley. May 28, 1793.
John Singleton-Mary White. April 1, 1793.
Thomas Smith-Elizabeth Peters. Aug. 28, 1793.

Charles Sweeney-Frances Shackleford. Dec. 14, 1793.
James Smith———— McLain. Dec. 17, 1793.
Christopher Smith-Nancy Brown. Dec. 20, 1793.
Benjamin Sampson-Margaret Warren. Dec. 9, 1793.
James Sutton-Polly Walker. Aug. 7, 1793.
Moses Short-Sarah Bright. Aug. 21, 1793.
Jesse Smith-Nancy Byas. Apr. 1, 1793.
Andrew Spratt-Polly Tipton. Feb. 17, 1794.
Jesse Smith-Sarah Wash. Mar. 12, 1794.
John Smith-Catherine Rutherford. Aug. 7, 1794.
Phillip Spoonamore-Elizabeth Henry. Dec. 17, 1794.
Frederick Spoonamore-Nancy Harvie. Dec. 22, 1795.
Jackman Smith-Nancy Smith. Jan. 15, 1796.
John Stotts-Lucy Stone. Feb. 17, 1796.
Henry Sword-Elizabeth Cummins. Sept. 6, 1796.
Andrew Shuck-Polly Young. May 7, 1796.
Wm. Seller-Sarah Crawford. Feb. 2, 1796.
David Sanders-Elizabeth Lacefield. Dec. 23, 1796.
Phillips Sublett-Isabel Whitley. Nov. 21, 1797.
George Shelby-Betsy Lee. Dec. 27, 1797.
Thomas Storms-Tempy Crafton. Sept. 4, 1797.
David Sparks-Minty Cox. Dec. 30, 1797.
Shepherd Sweeney-Susy Thomas. Jan. 5, 1797.
Nicholas Smith-Jenny Adams. Jan. 20, 1797.
Wm. Sampson-Winnie Masterson. Jan. 25, 1797.
Abraham Shaw-Catherine Ellshort. Aug. 21, 1797.
Wm. Stennett-Jenny Ratcliff. April 17, 1797.
Thomas Smith-Nancy Holton. Jan. 23, 1797.
John Smith-China Hart. Oct. 17, 1797.
Edmond Sweeney-Polly Johnson. May 20, 1797.
Job Sweeney-Sarah Allen. June 27, 1798.
Jeptha Spencer-Leah Johnson. June 20, 1798.
James Sedgerwood-Jennie McFadgen. Feb. 27, 1798.
Wm. Smith-Chloe Johnson. Mar. 6, 1798.
Absolom Shannon-Jemima Miller. Apr. 9, 1798.
Hugh Swan-Elizabeth Feland. Nov. 29, 1798.
Elmbeck Stringer-Jennie Reed. Jan. 2, 1798.
Wm. Spears-Mary Jasper. Oct. 1, 1798.
Wm. Smith-Elizabeth Singleton. Aug. 20, 1798.
Benjamin Stacy-Barbara Coombs. Dec. 29, 1798.
Samuel Shackleford-Sucky Withers. Jan. 7, 1798.
Wm. J. Sipon-Winfred Roberts. May 14, 1799.
Reuben Sharley-Sophia Johnson. Jan. 27, 1799.
John Shackleford-Polly Lawrence. Dec. 16, 1799.
Peter Sowden-Sallie Lacefield. Oct. 13, 1799.
Joseph Slatter-Martha Allen. June 10, 1799.
Daniel Sweeney-Elizabeth Jones. Dec. 15, 1800.
Corder Stone-Polly Mason. Aug. 19, 1800.
Henry Spoonamore-Eliphen Hammonds. May 19, 1800.
John Sallee-Edith Stephenson. Oct. 9, 1800.
Limeledge Stringer-Betsey Scott. June 18, 1800.
William Talley-Eleanor Potts. Mar. 1, 1783.
James Thompson-Ruth Peyton. Sept. 10, 1784.
John Thomas-Elizabeth Poage. June 18, 1784.
Edward Taylor-Elizabeth Brown. Apr. 28, 1782.
Archibald Thompson-Margaret McClure. Aug. 6, 1784.
Joseph Thomas-Catherine Jones. Apr. 27, 1786.
Richard Taliaferro-Sarah Jones. Feb. 20, 1786.
Jabez Townson-Mary Bailey. Sept. 11, 1786.
George Tinsley-Polly Gaines. June 29, 1786.
John Taylor-Sarah Murphy. July 26, 1786.

John M. Taylor-Mary Powell. Feb. 12, 1788.
Geo. Trumbo-Susannah Coffman. Aug. 3, 1789.
James Talbot-Unity Dewitt. Sept. 17, 1789.
George Tinkle-Sarah Proctor. Jan. 15, 1790.
John Tuley-Abediah Davis. Jan. 10, 1790.
Edward Tomlinson-Sally Maxey. Aug. 12, 1790.
John Trousdale-Milly Allen. May 7, 1792.
David Thurmond-Margaret Middleton. Aug. 21, 1792.
Stephen Tate-Betsey Bailey. ——— ———, 1793.
James Tinsley-Mary Graham. July 13, 1794.
——————— Turnball-Margaret Clark. Oct. 15, 1784.
Hemlin Tomlinson-Elizabeth Burton. Mar. 24, 1794.
Martin Tanner-Jennie Canab. Jan. 29, 1795.
Isaac Trowbridge-Nancy Campbell. Dec. 20, 1796.
Wm. Tubbs-Jennie Innis. Apr. 7, 1796.
Phillip Tucker-Elizabeth Collier. Feb. 19, 1796.
Geo. Tubbs-Mrs. Martha McNess. Apr. 10, 1796.
Dennis L. Turgot-Sallie Scott. Mar. 18, 1797.
Cabb Turner-Ann L. Wilson. Apr. 17, 1797.
Jeremiah Tungale-Magdaline Sally. Apr. 21, 1797.
Wm. Tinsley-Mrs. Agnes Logan. Feb. 9, 1798.
James Thomas-Mary English. Nov. 25, 1799.
Jonathan Trowbridge-Sally Lampton. June 12, 1799.
Joseph Turner-Lucy Parks. May 20, 1799.
Wm. Threlkeld-Rebecca Helm. Mar. 4, 1800.
John Thomas-Polly Johnson. Feb. 11, 1800.
Jacob Underwood-Hannah Roberson. Dec. 7, 1793.
John Vardeman-Mary Spalding. Sept. 7, 1785.
Isaac Vanmeter-Martha Hogland. July 29, 1783.
James Vaughan-Bedey Farris. Jan. 27, 1789.
Amanach Vardeman-Nancy Wright. Mar. 7, 1791.
Morgan Vardeman-Mary Trousdale. Jan. 17, 1792.
James Vaughan-Susanna Stotts.; Mar. 10, 1792.
John Votan-Ulsey Scott. May 13, 1792.
William Vaughan-Anna Payne. July 20, 1795.
David Vanwinkle-Vianna Sallee. July 5, 1796.
Francis Velugot-Anne Sartin. Aug. 29, 1797.
Ashberry Vandiveer-Rachel Mason. Oct. 29, 1798.
Jeremiah Vardeman-Elizabeth James. Feb. 12, 1799.
John Welton-Patience Coleman. Sept. 7, 1783.
John Wyatt-Susanna Summitt. Dec .2, 1784.
John Wilson-Mary Plunkett. Oct. 5, 1784.
Thomas Wilson-Mary Adams. Mar. 24, 1784.
Henry Wise-Eliza Young. Oct. 25, 1784.
John Willis-Lucy Rice. June 13, 1785.
Wm. Williams-Elizabeth Duncan. Dec. 16, 1785.
Peter Walker-Barbara Ferguson. Nov. 25, 1785.
Peter Watts-Margaret Fisher. Nov. 11, 1785.
Henry Wilson-Franky Faulkner. Sept. 12, 1782.
Thos. Wilson-Mary Adams. Apr. 5, 1783.
Ozias Welch-Hannah Lynn. Feb. 7, 1783.
George Watts-Prudence Blan. Mar. 20, 1786.
Christian Wyman-Ann Tyburn. Mar. 10, 1786.
Wm. Wright-Margaret Galloway. Jan. 9, 1786.
Jacob Withmore-Caty Smith. Mar. 4, 1786.
George Wilson-Polly Mitchell. July 29, 1786.
John Woodruff-Mary Ownby. Mar. 21, 1786.
Jesse Wright-Dorothy Peyton. Apr. 7, 1786.
John Wyatt-Mary Pearl. Oct. 6, 1785.
Alexander Walker-Jane McClure. Mar. 28, 1785.
James Woodson-Anny Jackson. Sept. 7, 1785.

Thomas Ward-Mary Beard. July 27, 1789.
Andrew Williams-Mapey McQuerry. Sept. 29, 1789.
John Waggoner-Peggy Zacharias. Nov. 11, 1789.
John Wyatt-Elizabeth Gibbs. Mar. 20, 1790.
Aquilla Wyley-Hannah Warren. Jan. 25, 1790.
James Warren-Catherine Falin. Mar. 1, 1790.
Reuben Warren-Betsey Preston. Aug. 31, 1790.
Walter Williams-Elley Owsley. ———— —, 1790.
David Warren-Sally Feland. July 8, 1791.
Benjamin Wyley-Elizabeth Warren. Aug. 29, 1792.
James Welch-Nancy Wilson. Sept. 9, 1792.
John Ward-Jenny Levea. Nov. 19, 1793.
John Williams-Mary Rutherford. Feb. 28, 1793.
Wm. Wyatt-Rebecca Pearl. Apr. 8, 1793.
John Woods-Peggy Martin. June 25, 1793.
Joseph West-Gemima Peyton. Oct. 22, 1793.
Malachi Ware-Jane Salven (?). Jan. 27, 1794.
Robert Wathen-Sally Montgomery. Dec. 15, 1794.
Henry Winfred-Sally Thomas. Nov. 28, 1794.
Sampson Wilhite-Hannah Jackman. Dec. 22 ,1794.
James Warren-Margaret Dunbar. Feb. 25, 1795.
Barry Ward-Susanna Zachree. May 11, 1795.
John Wilson-Peggy Stephenson. Feb. 5, 1795.
Elijah Whitton-Elizabeth Lowe. May 21, 1796.
John Wright-Patsey Moore. Jan. 2, 1796.
James White-Jemima Downing. May 16, 1796.
Wm. Woodburn-Patsy Jackson. Apr. 27, 1796.
John Welch-Sarah Withers. Aug. 29, 1796.
Charles Warren-Caty Floyd. Feb. 1, 1796.
David Wood-Elizabeth Carrier. Nov. 20, 1797.
James Williams-Mrs. Sallie Oliver. Dec. 13, 1797.
Joseph Waters-Celah Swiney. Nov. 27, 1798.
John Winfrey-Hannah Benedict. Mar. 13, 1798.
Rafe Williams-Patsy Owsley. Aug. 11, 1798.
John Withers Jr.-Sally Morgan. Sept. 28, 1798.
Absolom Woods-Ruth Thomas. July 12, 1798.
John Wilson-Richard Richardson. Jan. 7, 1799.
Robert Williams-Betsey Hanks. June 1, 1799.
Geo. Weatherford-Milly Spraggins. Sept. 28, 1799.
James Wright-Frances Spraggins. Dec. 29, 1800.
James L. Worthington-Margaret Slade. Dec. 1, 1800.
Mathias Yocum-Levina Coleman Wright. Apr. 12, 1784.
Abraham Yager-Mary Wiley. Jan. 9, 1786.
Charles Yeats-Prudence Poynter. Nov. 10, 1787.
Edward Younge-Kiziah Rennecks. Nov. 2, 1789.
James Younge-Sally Breeding. Oct. 8, 1789.
Isham Younce-Leach Masterson. June 2, 1790.
James Young-Betsy Noaks. May 10, 1791.
Peter Young-Elizabeth Zachara. June 29, 1793.
Thomas Young-Elizabeth Hughes. May 18, 1796.

MADISON COUNTY MARRIAGES

(Donated by Mrs. Joseph Beard)

Caleb Buchanon-Sarah Wood. Jan. 19 ,1836.
Barbee Collins-Hannah Wood. May 27, 1823.
Thomas Miller-Anney Woods. July 29, 1806. By Peter Woods.
William Mullins-Nancy Woods. June 18, 1801.
John Taylor-Judah Woods. Mch. 11, 1802.
Talton Taylor-Elizabeth Woods (of Michael Woods). Feb. 4, 1802.

Milton White-Ann Wood. Aug. 15, 1835. By Thomas Bellou.
Abraham Wood-Eddy Yates. Nov. 29, 1806.
Adam Wood-Poly Kerley. Mch. 24, 1807.
Adam Wood-Batsy Crigler. Aug. 26, 1817.
Adam Woods, son of Michael Woods-Nancy Hancock. Mch. 18, 1802.
Anderson W. Wood-Lucy Sullivan. Oct. 30, 1836.
Andrew Jackson Wood-Anna Bently. Nov. 7, 1844.
Archibald Woods-Elizabeth Shackelford. Oct. 9, 1810.
Archibald Woods-Polly Wallace. Oct. 4, 1814.
Archibad Woods-Fannie Hill. June 5, 1806. By Peter Woods.
Elliott Wood-Sucky Purkins. Feb. 6, 1812.
Frances Woods-Nancy Austin. Dec. 11, 1815.
Green V. Woods-Mrs. America White. May 18, 1854. By Roswell Brown.
Jarvis William-Susannah Woods. Apr. 30, 1801.
James Wood-Pheobe Hardin. Dec. 31, 1833.
James Woods-Sally Candle. Nov. 18, 1832.
James Woods-Betsy Embry. Aug. 24, 1809.
James Woods-Sophia Oldham. June 17, 1830.
John Woods-Pheby Skinner. Feb. 6, 1821.
John Woods-Elizabeth Duncan. Dec. 28, 1809.
John Woods (son of Michael and Hannah)-Mary H. Thomas. July 2, 1812.
John S. Woods-Polly Mitchell. July 10, 1817.
Patrick Woods-Rachel Cooper. July 19, 1792.
Patrick Woods-Fanny Delaney. Feb. 6, 1813.
William Woods-Susannah Clark. Aug. 13, 1801.
William Woods-Nancy Harris. Nov. 25, 1802.
William Woods-Ruth Kinkead. Aug. 1, 1792. (Wm. son of Michael and Hannah).
William Woods-Polly Harris. Jan. 15, 1802.
William Wood-Elizabeth Nolan. Jan. 10, 1808.
William S. Woods-Nancy Boon Gentry. Oct. 9, 1843. By G. Kelly.
Tarlton Woodson-Sally Woods. Mch. 20, 1814.

MARRIAGES

(Donated by Miss Margaret Steele)

Marriage bond. John Steele and Jane Cunningham. Dated Apr. 22, 1807. Signed John Steele and Wm. Drake. Teste, J. Stonestreet, D. C. Rev. John Steele and Jane Cunningham, were married by Rev. A. Craig. John Steele, born Dec. 17, 1772. Jane Cunningham, born Staunton, Va., Feb. 19, 1784.

Marriage licence. William Drake and Agnes Cunningham, solemnized by Rev. Ger. S. Smith. Mch. 21, 1799.

MERCER COUNTY, KENTUCKY

MARRIAGE RECORDS FROM 1800 TO 1870

(Copied by Miss Marie Menaugh, Harrodsburg, Ky.)

Marriage Register No. 1

William Roberts-Betsy Nichols. Jany. 11, 1800. Page 78.
Joseph Chalfan-Judith Malone. Jany. 7, 1800. Page 78.
Gorhail (?) Smock-May French. Jany. 9, 1800. Page 78.
Abraham Carmale-Ely Rynerson. Jany. 30, 1800. Page 78.
John Montgomery-Betsy Drake. April 3, 1800. Page 78.

William Hungate-Sally Coffman. July 8, 1800. Page 78.
Archibald Woods-Mary Thixton. March 1, 1800. Page 80.
Wm. McKee-Jane Davis. Feby. 20, 1801. Page 80.
Newman Miskel-Elizabeth Trayor. March 15, 1800. Page 80.
James Adams-Peggy Woods. March 14, 1800. Page 80.
Samuel Adams-Jenny Woods. April 21, 1800. Page 80.
Willis Hawkins-Polly Barnes. Jany. 23, 1801. Page 80.
John Springate-Sarah Egbert. Aug. 27, 1801. Page 80.
James Westerfield-Catharine Sortoe Dec. 13, 1801. Page 80.
John Stuck-Susan Lipsey. Feby. 19, 1801. Page 80.
Samuel Robertson-Janey Fulkers. Feby. 19, 1801. Page 80.
John Dean-Jane McFatridge. March 23, 1801. Page 80.
John Gallagher-Barbara Jones. Apr. 23, 1801. Page 80.
William Thomas-Lydia Bruner. Aug. 20, 1801. Page 80.
Samuel Kelsoe-Sally Hungate. Oct. 4, 1801. Page 80.
Daniel Lillard-Sally Gates. Nov. 22, 1801. Page 82.
Goodrich Lackey-Sarah Coburn. Jany. 18, 1802. Page 82.
Sam'. W. Carr-Polly Delaney. Apr. 27, 1801. Page 82.
Henry Comingore-Peggy Terhune. May 10, 1802. Page 82.
William Grimes-Nelly Thompson. May 10, 1802. Page 82.
John Fauntleroy-Margaret Harrod. May 2, 1802. Page 82.
Peter Legrange-Lane Covert. Jany. ———, 1802. Page 82.
Peter Bonta-Rachel Bonta. Jany. ———, 1802. Page 82.
James Reed-Mary Evans. Sept. 19, 1802. Page 82.
Sam'l Debond-Polly Devine. Mch. 13, 1800. Page 82.
Dan'l F. Kinney-Margaret Arbuckle. Mch. 20, 1800. Page 82.
John Hunt-Alery Jones. Apr. 12, 1800. Page 82.
Thomas Clarkston-Elizabeth Whitehouse. Apr. 17, 1800. Page 82
George Brown-Hannah McKinney. Apr. 17, 1800. Page 82.
John Davenport-Joanna Crutchfield. Apr. 19, 1800. Page 84.
Sam'l Kennedy-Lucy Prewitt. Apr. 29, 1800. Page 84.
James Kerr-Phebe Bonham. July 24, 1800. Page 84.
Jacob Morner (Morgan)-Nancy Jones. July 29, 1800. Page 84.
Cornelius Rynerson-Peggy Johnson. July 31, 1800. Page 84.
Frederick Arnold-Susanna Shouse. Aug. 12, 1800. Page 84.
William Locke-Susanna Alspau. Aug. 14, 1800. Page 84.
Samuel Cole-Alley McKinney. Sept. 18, 1800. Page 84.
Joseph Cashwiler-Betsey Watts. Sept. 18, 1800. Page 84.
Walter Harlow-Elizabeth Ortkin. Oct. 16, 1800. Page 84.
James Halloway-Celia McKinney. Oct. 30, 1800. Page 84.
Peter Sparrow-Milley Edwards. Nov. 25, 1800. Page 84.
John Eccles-Nancy Shepherd. Dec. 11, 1800. Page 84.
John Brewer-Nelly Smock. Nov. 18, 1800. Page 84.
James Ryley-Catharine Jamieson. Dec. 2, 1800. Page 86.
Abraham Comingore-Jenney Vanarsdall. Jany. 9, 1803. Page 86.
John Cooney-Ann Currey. Jany. 28, 1802. Page 86.
Lanty Armstrong-Jenney Darland. March 4, 1802. Page 86.
James Vanice-Katey Demaree. March 25, 1802. Page 86.
William Robertson-Ann Adams. May 25, 1802. Page 86.
Thomas Cunningham-Ann Lucas. July 6, 1802. Page 86.
William Hogue-Betsey Dunn. Dec. 2, 1802. Page 86.
John McGill-Nancy Henderson. Sept. 7, 1802. Page 86.
Thos. King-Ann McAfee. Dec. 14, 1802. Page 86.
John Maxwell-Sarah Dunn. Feby. 4, 1802. Page 86.
James Warren-Phebe Briscoe. Feby. 25, 1802. Page 86.
Sam'l. Latimore-Polly Daugherty. Feby. 4, 1802. Page 86.
John Ripperdan-Polly Shepherd. May 20, 1802. Page 86.
George Crecy-Lecey Camron. Nav. 4, 1802. Page 88.
Peter Shaver-Sally Watts. Dec. 2, 1802. Page 88.
Thos. McKinney-Sally Lawrence. Jan. 11, 1803. Page 88.
Ansel Hall-Nancy Whitley. Jan. 13, 1803. Page 88.

John M. Williams-Polly Hall. Jan. 18, 1803. Page 88.
Uriah Humble-Elizabeth Roney. Jany. 18, 1803. Page 88.
Jesse McGinnis-Agnes Hix. Aug. 19, 1801. Page 88.
Enoch Swier-Ann Hix. Oct. 7, 1801. Page 88.
George Grisham-Mary Pennington. Oct. 14, 1801. Page 88.
John McCowan-Nancy Johnson. Oct. 28, 1801. Page 88.
Richardson Brown-Betsey Wicker. Dec. 9, 1801. Page 88.
James Marten-Betsey Gill. Dec. 11, 1801. Page 88.
Lewis Powell-Milley Bottom. Jany. 6, 1802. Page 88.
James Wyatte-Betsey Wright. Mch. 28, 1802. Page 90.
Moses McCown-Rachael McGee. Mch. 25, 1802. Page 90.
Whitfield White-Judith Boston. Oct. 21, 1802. Page 90.
Joseph Burcham-Melvina Bucks. Dec. 21, 1802. Page 90.
John Burks-Margaret Lyon. Jan. 10, 1803. Page 90.
James Phillips-Agnes Pherrigo. July 21, 1803. Page 90.
James Dunn-Jane Davis. Oct. 21, 1800. Page 90.
Thomas Hanlan (Harlan)-Susanna Lamb. Apr. 24, 1802. Page 90.
Richard Davis-Jane Fulkerson. Aug. 26, 1802. Page 90.
Abraham Fitsworth-Margaret Bonta. Feb. 14, 1802. Page 90.
Phillip Monroe-Mary Woods. Feb. ——, 1803. Page 90.
John Harris-Rody Huff. Feb. ——, 1803. Page 90.
John Hale-Elizabeth Hungate. Aug. 30, 1801. Page 90.
Stewart White-Amelia Flournoy. Sept. 3, 1801. Page 90.
Jacob Moore-Rebecca Paddox. Sept. 27, 1801. Page 92.
Mark Coulter-Ruthey Scott. Oct. 1, 1801. Page 92.
Sam'l. Lyon-Margaret Sailas. Nov. 1, 1801. Page 92.
Sam'l. Hedger-Lucy Sales. Nov. 4, 1801. Page 92.
Bernard Noel-Nancy Goard. Jany. 2, 1802. Page 92.
Richard Fallis-Nancy White. May 21, 1802. Page 92.
Richard Kinney-Sally Wilson. June 22, 1802. Page 92.
Thomas Hale-Elizabeth Devine. June 12, 1803. Page 92.
Richard Colbert-Nancy Hopewell. Mch. 31, 1803. Page 92.
Reed McGraw-Polly Fulkerson. May 5, 1803. Page 92.
John Brants-Barsheba Bennett. June 24, 1803. Page 92.
Moses Lambert-Nancy McGraw. Oct. 2, 1803. Page 92.
Presley Brown-Elizabeth Lawrence. Dec. 8, 1803. Page 92.
Alexander Mahan-Margaret Hampton. Dec. 29, 1803. Page 92.
Joseph Scott-Rhoda Hale. Oct. 2, 1803. Page 94.
William Gritton-Jenney Lipsey. Jany. 27, 1804. Page 94.
Dennis Sparrow-Susannah Daviess. Feb. 14, 1804. Page 94.
John Bilbo-Nancy Bromfield. Mch. 1, 1804. Page 94.
George Hice-Nancy Bellas. Mch. 15, 1804. Page 94.
Moses McCowan-Rachel McGee. Mch. 25, 1802. Page 94.
Joseph Krouchenaur-Nancy Newtown. Nov. 10, 1803. Page 94.
Cornelius Vanarsdall-Catherine Huff. Nov. 10, 1803. Page 94.
James Tolly-Nancy Silvertooth. Feb. 7, 1804. Page 94.
Garret Brewer-Mary Verbryke. Feb. 5, 1804. Page 94.
John Bosley-Sarah Trapnall. Mch. 12, 1804. Page 94.
Peter Tellsworth-Betsey Hale. Mch. 11, 1804. Page 94.
Abraham Huff-Patsey Coovert. Mch. 13, 1804. Page 94.
John Coovert-Caty Vebryke. Mch. 14, 1804. Page 96.
Thomas McClure-Easter Cahoon. Mch. 18, 1804. Page 96.
Joseph Burcham-Malinda Birks. Dec. 22, 1802. Page 96.
John Burks-Margaret Lyons. Jan. 10, 1803. Page 96.
John Tadlock-Ann Harrod. Sept. 21, 1803. Page 96.
Elijah Barret. Judith Noris. Jan. 18, 1804. Page 96.
Francis Cole-Mary Harrison (Hanner). Aug. 24, 1802. Page 96.
Edmund Day (Davy)-Ann Hanner (Hanna). Oct. 14, 1802.
Page 96.
Thomas Noble-Polly Brynton. Nov. 18, 1802. Page 96.
Robt. Brumfield-Elizabeth Bilboe. Nov. 26, 1802. Page 96.

Benj. Durham-Peggy Robertson. Dec. 11, 1802. Page 96.
Lewis Pitman-Nancy Johnston. Dec. 25 ,1802. Page 96.
Jesse Smith-Eliz. Glasebrook. Jany. 27, 1803. Page 96.
William Whoberry-Ann Day. Feb. 11, 1803. Page 96.
James Durnham-Peggy Whoberry. Mch. 22, 1803. Page 98.
Jas. Simpson-Lucy Webb. Aug. 28, 1803. Page 98.
Mark Noble-Rachel Gee. Oct. 3, 1803. Page 98.
John Lewelling-Nancy Bottom. Mch. 25, 1804. Page 98.
Samuel Yocum-Mary McClure. May 5, 1804. Page 98.
Noah Hadon (Haydon)-Elizabeth Gilpin. June 11, 1804. Page 98.
Robert Telsort-Jane Miles. June 16, 1804. Page 98.
John Hunter-Jerusha Smith. Sept. 10, 1804. Page 98.
Peter Smock-Judith Clarke. Sept. 10, 1804. Page 98.
William Shepherd-Nancy Sturman. April 26, 1804. Page 98.
Phillip Board-Mary Melchlor (Mechlor). May 24, 1804. Page 98.
George French-Elizabeth Sturman. June 14, 1804. Page 98.
James Warren-Elizabeth Shaw. July 19, 1804. Page 98.
Richard League-Ellen Roberts. Aug. 7, 1804. Page 98.
Christopher Ludwick-Elizabeth Collier. Aug. 16, 1804. Page 100.
Joseph Collier-Sophia Ludwick. Sept. 2, 1804. Page 100.
John Ludwick-Susannah French. Oct. 5, 1804. Page 100.
Cornelius Vanarsdall-Suda (?) Vandivier. Oct. 21, 1804. Page 100.
Henry Taylor Lightfoot-Nancy Webster. Nov. 18, 1804. Page 100.
John L. Bridges-Nancy Adair. Mch. 7, 1803. Page 100.
Jacob Rugle-Margaret Thompson. July ——, 1803. Page 100.
Joseph Woods-Ann Buchanan. Oct. 5, 1803. Page 100.
William Grisholm-Rebecca Pipes. Feb. 11, 1804. Page 100.
Thomas Carr-Peggy Buchanan. Mch. 21, 1804. Page 100.
Peter Stuck-Mary George. Sept. 15, 1804. Page 100.
Samuel Russell-Rebecca Litman. Oct. 2, 1804. Page 100.
John Gaunt-Jane Darland. Oct. 11, 1804. Page 100.
Abraham Vanhice-Sally James. Oct. 11, 1804. Page 100.
Jeremiah Bunnel-Rebecca Hardin. Nov. 27, 1804. Page 102.
Robert McAfee-Priscilla Armstrong. Nov. 29, 1804. Page 102.
Daniel Lamb-Eleanor Johnson. Nov. 30, 1803. Page 102.
Patrick Preston-Rosanna Russell. April 5, 1804. Page 102.
Thomas Prather-Marian Lawrence. Mch. 25, 1804. Page 102.
Benjamin Chatham-Nancy Gates. Jan. 10, 1805. Page 102.
Vincent Morgan-Hanna Hungate. Apr. 5, 1804. Page 102.
Samuel Haydon-Rhody Hungate. Apr. 5, 1804. Page 102.
John Bolds-Polly Stinnett. Jan. 10, 1805. Page 102.
George Whittinghill-Betsy Robertson. Feb. 7, 1805. Page 102.
Cornelius Cozine-Polly Vanarsdall. Nov. 9, 1804. Page 102.
Edmond Byers-Nancy Fisher. Jany. 24, 1805. Page 102.
Thomas Fisher-Charlotte Stone. April 11, 1805. Page 102.
John Mays-Nancy Hale. April 11, 1805. Page 104.
William Tolly-Easter Ayers. July 30, 1805. Page 104.
James Downey-Mary Riley. July 31, 1805. Page 104.
Wm. Kilpatrick-Sally Voorhies. Aug. 1, 1805. Page 104.
William Wales-Caty Voris. Aug. 22, 1805. Page 104.
Thomas Shepherd-Betsey Cowan. 1805. Page 104.
John Ransdell-Betsey Connville. 1805. Page 104.
Robert Brown-Sarah Temmons (Timmons). 1805. Page 104.
Moses McClure-Peggy Dennis. 1805. Page 104.
Thomas Andover-Ann Ashby. 1805. Page 104.
William Ferrigo-Ann Talbott. 1805. Page 104.
James Campbell-Nancy Haydon. 1805. Page 104.
Thos. Doke-Fanny Smith. Jan. 3, 1805. Page 104.
James Venable-Elizabeth Cowan. Feb. 5, 1805. Page 106.
James Fields-Sarah Ripperdon. Dec. 10, 1805. Page 106.
Uriah Childs-Charity Preston. Dec. 27, 1805. Page 106.

Thomas B. Reed-Polly C. Richardson. June 30, 1805. Page 106.
James Hughes-Milders Ross. Jany. 4, 1806. Page 106.
John Farris-Mary Shelton. Oct. 31, 1805. Page 106.
Robert Cahoon-Ruth Chamberlain. Feb. 14, 1805. Page 106.
Simon Vanarsdall-Sally Brown. Feb. 28, 1805. Page 106.
James McCampbell-Jennett Buchanan. Mch. 28, 1805. Page 106.
James Board-Martha Adams. May 21, 1805. Page 106.
William Sterling-Polly McDowell. June 13, 1805. Page 106.
Henry Eccles-Polly Gaunt. Aug. 15, 1805. Page 106.
Joseph McGee-Ann Dyon. Sept. 5, 1805. Page 106.
Samuel McClure-Ann Curry. Sept. 12, 1805. Page 106.
Dan'l. Brown-Nancy Smith. Oct. 10, 1805. Page 108.
John Pherigo-Polsey Adams. Nov. 28, 1805. Page 108.
Thomas Stevenson-Betsy Cowan. 1805. Page 108.
John Yocum-Sarah Sportsman. Dec. 4, 1805. Page 110.
David Clayback-Catharine Vooris. Dec. 24, 1805. Page 110.
Thomas Logan-Sally Denton. Jan. 2, 1806. Page 110.
Benjamin Head-Patsy Bohon. Jan. 16, 1806. Page 110.
Simon Hendrickson-Kezziah Paddox. Mch. 25, 1805. Page 110.
James Hall-Sarah Paddox. May 7, 1805. Page 110.
Jacob Bottom-Polly Bridges. May 15, 1805. Page 110.
Hall Peirson-Elizabeth Bridges. Aug. 15 ,1805. Page 110.
William Cannon-Anny May. Oct. 10, 1805. Page 112.
William Givings (Givins)-Elizabeth Prather. Dec. 1, 1804
Page 112.
Jeremiah Mathers-Caty Mizner. Nov. 13, 1804. Page 112.
John Tadlock-Mrs. Rochester. July 19, 1805. Page 112.
John Logan-Armititia Rochester. July 19, 1805. Page 112.
Benjamin Abbott-Elizabeth Decker. Nov. 21, 1805. Page 112.
John Austin-Polly Bohon. Mch. 26, 1806. Page 112.
Sam'l. McNutt-Susannah Jeffries. Nov. 24, 1806. Page 112.
Thomas Fry-Elizabeth J. Smith. July 11, 1805. Page 112.
Thos. Doxy-Anna Wilson. Aug. 18, 1805. Page 112.
William Fenn-Sarah Bennett. Sept. 19, 1805. Page 112.
Henry Gimble-Sally Hunter. Oct. 1, 1805. Page 112.
Matthew Nelson-Mary Hicks. Oct. 8, 1805. Page 112.
Isaac French-Nancy Stone. Oct. 13, 1805. Page 112.
John Gritton-Rebecca McKinney. Apr. 24, 1806. Page 114.
Coleman Minor-Ruth Harberson. July 24, 1805. Page 114.
Joel Compton-Polly Taylor. Feb. 14, 1805. Page 114.
Greenberry McGinnis-Sally Laws. Feb. 28, 1805. Page 114.
Jacob Whoberry-Mary Harbeson. March 5, 1805. Page 114.
Hance McClelend-Elizabeth Cooley. June 20, 1805. Page 114.
George Davis-Elizabeth Sparrow. July 2, 1805. Page 114.
Jeremiah Laws-Susannah Bailey. Aug. 27, 1805. Page 114.
Henry Blackerton-Olive Lockeman. May 29, 1806. Page 114.
Hezekiah White-Susannah Jackman. May 31, 1806. Page 114.
George Neff-Sally Cole. Aug. 14, 1806. Page 114.
James Vanhice-Tyne Bice. Oct. 1st, 1806. Page114.
John Terhune-Ann Comingo. March ——, 1806. Page 114.
James Smock-Charity Brewer. May 3, 1806. Page 114.
Philip Trapnall-Nancy Casey. July 29th, 1806. Page 116.
David Nichols-Elenor Griffin. Sept. 11, 1806. Page 116.
Mark Hardin-Mary Adair. Oct. 14, 1806. Page 116.
John Adams-Polly Evans. Dec. 19, 1805. Page 116.
Daniel Plough-Phebe Satterly. March 9, 1806. Page 116.
Lewis Hammond-Polly Selch. Oct. 8, 1806. Page 116.
Jacob Kurtman-Leah James. Oct. 8, 1806. Page 116.
Thomas Chatham-Rebecca Nichols. Oct. 28, 1806. Page 116.
William Terhune-Rachel Lowe. Nov. 27, 1806. Page 116.
John Comingore-Sally Cozine. Jan. 22, 1807. Page 116.

Stephen Sally-Polly Lockhard. Sept. 18, 1806. Page 116.
Caleb Goff-Mary Sullivan. Jany. 8, 1807. Page 116.
Wm. Bottom-Betsey Williams. Jany. 8, 1807. Page 116.
John Shrum-Nelly Campbell. April 8, 1806. Page 116.
Joseph Hall-Betsey Sinnett. April 13, 1806. Page 118.
John Wilson-Polly Carmicle. April 13, 1806. Page 118.
Jacob Claunch-Polly Gray. June 26, 1806. Page 118.
Sam'l. Huff-Polly Hungate. June 29, 1806. Page 118.
Sam'l. M. Lion-Rebecca Wilson. July 21, 1806. Page 118.
John Robard-Nancy Sandifer. Sept. 18, 1806. Page 118.
Job. Johnson-Margaret Robertson. Oct. 24, 1805. Page 118.
John Laverty-Mary Freeman. Dec. 5, 1805. Page 118.
James Curry-Polly Cooney. Dec. 28, 1805. Page 118.
Jacob Voris-Jaley Coombs. Dec. 29, 1805. Page 118.
Joseph Denton-Betsey Key. Mch. 9, 1806. Page 118.
John Powell-Amy Bunch. Mch. 12, 1806. Page 118.
Micajah Mosby-Fanny Hughes. Feb. 26, 1806. Page 118.
John Burford-Frances Brown. April 17, 1806. Page 118.
John Jones-Polly Sutterfield. June 1, 1806. Page 120.
Martin Duncan-Polly Ray. Sept. 16, 1806. Page 120.
Thomas Fielding-Elizabeth Slaughter. Sept. 22, 1806. Page 120.
Jiles Mitchell-Polly Moore. Oct. 23, 1806. Page 120.
Cornelius Vanarsdall-Polly Burton. Nov. 25, 1806. Page 120.
John Reed-Martha Slaughter. Dec. 16, 1806. Page 120.
Samuel Mosby-Nancy Hughes. Dec. 25, 1806. Page 120.
William Brown-Sarah Roach. Dec. 25, 1806. Page 120.
Benjamin Mayhall-Ellen Flannegan. Dec. 10, 1806. Page 120.
S. R. Demaree-Nancy McCormack. Mch. 21, 1806. Page 120.
James C. Barnett-Elizabeth Graham. Apr. 17, 1806. Page 120.
William S. Demmitt-Ally Vanarsdall. Apr. 23, 1806. Page 120.
William Bohon-Nancy Lanford. June 5, 1806. Page 120.
John Brewer-Polly Salter. Nov. 27, 1806. Page 122.
George Green-Polly Smith. Feb. 6, 1806. Page 122.
Samuel Grundy-Elizabeth Caldwell. Apr. 22, 1806. Page 122.
Martin Hardin-Rosanna Fisher. July 1, 1806. Page 122.
George Simpson-Peggy Smith. Mch. 22, 1807. Page 122.
Robert Scott-Jane Bady. Apr. 25, 1807. Page 122.
Levi Hammond-Janie Hardy. Aug. 11, 1806. Page 122.
Drury Clarkson-Jemima Whooberry. Aug. 28, 1806. Page 122.
Joseph Ryan-Rachel Anderson. Oct. 5, 1806. Page 122.
Joshua Wiley-Mary Ashley. Oct. 29, 1806. Page 122.
Thomas Whitehouse-Elizabeth Wigham. Mch. 8, 1807. Page 122.
William Steele (Street)-Elizabeth Brown. April 16, 1807. Page 122.
Pleasant Watkins-Kerenhoppock Bingham. June 18, 1807. Page
122.
Steven Montgomery-Polly Harrod. Apr. 7, 1807. Page 122.
Daniel Damaree-Lythe Vandivier. Apr. 9, 1807. Page 124.
Nathan Stein-Sally Hale. Apr. 16, 1807. Page 124.
Daniel Coovert-Nelly Vanarsdall. Sept. 21, 1807. Page 124.
John Bohon-Patsy Lightfoot. Dec. 22, 1807. Page 124.
John Britt-Nancy Miller. Oct. 22, 1807. Page 124.
William Gordon-Avella Darnaby. June 12, 1808. Page 124.
John Bingham-Jane McGee. Mch. 19, 1807. Page 124.
John Lyon——————— Voorhies. 1807. Page 124.
Joseph Blackwood-Sarah Neald. June 3, 1807. Page 124.
Peter Murphy-Sally Nation. June 3, 1807. Page 124.
Archibald Woods-Ammy Adams. Octo. 1, 1807. Page 124.
Robert B. McAfee-Peggy Caldwell. Octo. 5, 1807. Page 124.
David Adams-Peggy Dixon. Dec. 17, 1807. Page 124.
Samuel Woodson-Nancy Allin. Dec. 23, 1807. Page 124.
Goldson Prewitt-Fanny Leachman. Dec. 24, 1807. Page 126.

Joseph Gilmore-Betsey Wells. Dec. 29, 1807. Page 126.
John Stagg-Rachel McGohon. Dec. 3, 1807. Page 126.
Simon Vanarsdall-Nancy Eccles. Jany. 5, 1808. Page 126.
Green Nichols-Polly McGinnis. Dec. 20, 1807. Page 126.
Nelson Tully-Sally Graves. Dec. 24, 1807. Page 126.
Nathaniel Harris-Fanny Brewer. Dec. ——, 1807. Page 126.
Isaac Sutton-Elizabeth Jeffries. Octo. 30th, 1807. Page 126.
William Sturman-Sally Willis. Nov. 17, 1807. Page 126.
John Burton-Sally Lewis. June 29, 1807. Page 126.
John F. Carlton-Mary Watson. Octo. 5, 1807. Page 126.
James Raney-Ruthey Freeman. Aug. 18, 1807. Page 126.
Joseph Allen-Betsey Wright. June 28, 1807. Page 126.
James Burton-Betsey N. Bealler. June 25, 1807. Page 126.
John B. Thompson-Nancy P. Robards. Nov. 10, 1807. Page 128.
Elias Thomkins-Anna Roach. Sept. 22, 1807. Page 128.
John Curry-Lain (?) Demaree. June 15, 1807. Page 128.
John Haley-Ann Coghill. Feby. 17, 1807. Page 128.
William Harris-Polly Bruner. Jany. 22, 1807. Page 128.
John Gordon-Sally MackIntire. Octo. 19, 1807. Page 128.
Joseph Hungate-Sally Hall. March 26, 1807. Page 128.
Charles Hungate-Peggy Bottom. Jan. 17, 1807. Page 128.
Thomas Bottom-Polly Whitter. Dec. 17, 1807. Page 128.
Edmond Goodnight-Sarah Dye. Dec. 24, 1807. Pag e128.
James Matthews-Kezziah Linnett. Dec. 30, 1807. Page 128.
Martin Bottom-Nancy Hackney. Dec. 30, 1807. Page 128.
John Duncan-Elizabeth Neff. July 30, 1807. Page 128.
John Gee-Patsey Colter. Aug. 6, 1807. Page 128.
Obediah Brumfield-Nancy Crowe. Feby. 11, 1807. Page 130.
Robert Compton-Jennie Taylor. Feby. 18, 1808. Page 130.
George Pipes-Polly Jackman. Mch. 10, 1808. Page 130.
Garrett Vandivier-Sarah Chatham. Nov. 5, 1807. Page 130.
Isaac Sanders-Ann Vanarsdallen. Jan. 7, 1808. Page 130.
Isaac Voorhies-Laney Davis. Feby. 21, 1808. Page 130.
Samuel Peters-Sally Lowler. July 25, 1808. Page 130.
Henry Smock-Ann Westerfield. Mch. 12, 1808. Page 130.
Nathean Stein-Ann Coffman. Mch. 13, 1808. Page 130.
Nathan H. Hall-Ann Crawford. July 16, 1807. Page 130.
James Gilkerson-Eliza Crawford. Mch. 23, 1808. Page 130.
John Satterly-Polly Bowman. Mch. 23, 1808. Page 130.
John Mattocks-Sophia Wales. Mch. 4, 1807. Page 130.
Joel Downey-Sally T. Colonier. Dec. 24, 1807. Page 130.
John Thompson———————— McKnight. July 8, 1808. Page 132.
Benjamin Armstrong-Rebecca McConnell. Aug. 24, 1804. Page 132.
James Jones-Francis Gillispie. Jan. 27, 1805. Page 132.
Nathaniel Brown-Nancy Blacketer. Aug. 4, 1807. Page 132.
Basil Hoskinson-Diana Bosley. Dec. 17, 1807. Page 132.
Michael Whoberry-Lucy Durham. Jany. 1, 1808. Page 132.
Masten Maill-Anna Durham. May 12, 1808. Page 132.
Norman Blacketer-Patsey Whoberry. Aug. 11, 1808. Page 132.
Aaron Crouch-Polly Cassiday. Aug. 11, 1808. Page 132.
Elias Fisher-Sally Cosby. Aug. 18, 1808. Page 132.
Sam'l Irvine-Casanna Briscoe. Aug. 3, 1808. Page 132.
James Phillips-Mary Minor. July 28, 1808. Page 132.
John Grant-Sarah Briscoe. July 26, 1808. Page 132.
Richard Glazebrook-Nancy Ashberry. Sept. 15, 1808. Page 132.
John Foley-Rachel Stevens. Octo. 24, 1808. Page 134.
Isaac Smock-Rachel Demaree. Octo. 22, 1808. Page 134.
Garrett Bonta——————— Bantee. Nov. 12, 1808. Page 134.
John Speed-Lucy G. Fry. Nov. 15, 1808. Page 134.
Simon Vanarsdall-Nancy Eccles. Jany. 5, 1808. Page 134.
Daniel Utley-Jane Clelland. Mch. 3, 1808. Page 134.

Thomas Gilkerson-Nancy Buchanan. April 14, 1808. Page 134.
John Daugherty-Dorcas Evans. May 13, 1808. Page 134.
Cornelius Demaree-Polly Vanardsdall. Sept. 24, 1808. Page 134.
James Alexander-Rebecca Bohon. Nov. 10, 1808. Page 134.
John McAmy (McKamey)-Margaret Adams. Nov. 29, 1808. Page 134.

John Green-Leah Dunn. Dec. 28, 1808. Page 134.
Peter Cozine-Sarah Hall. Dec. 20, 1808. Page 134.
Foushee T. Taylor-Polly C. Warren. Aug. 22, 1808. Page 134.
Dennis Brashear-Lucindia McDowell. Apr. 14, 1808. Page 136.
Daniel Neal (Nual)-Rebecca Pancake. Jany. 1, 1809. Page 136.
Lambert Banta-Ida Vanarsdell. Feby. 18, 1809. Page 136.
William Jones-Betsey Sutherland. Feby. 23, 1809.
John Westerfield-Hannah Hale. Feby. 25, 1809. Page 136.
Ralph Canine-Peggy Warman. Feby. 26, 1809. Page 136.
Peter Vandivier-Sallie Gashwiler. Mch. 2, 1809. Page 136.
James Smith-Peggy Fisher. Mch. 6, 1809. Page 136.
William Springate-Dorcas Gritton. Mch. 16, 1809. Page 136.
Barna Verbryke-Catharine Low. Apr. 8, 1809. Page 136.
William Hamner-Barbara Day. June 23, 1808. Page 136.
James Tabee-Nancy Craih. June 16, 1807. Page 136.
John Shannon-Betsey Duncan. Aug. 30, 1808. Page 136.
Charles McKinney-Mary A. Russell. June 7, 1809. Page 136.
Henry Willis-Maria Tadlock. July 31, 1809. Page 138.
Matthew Burks-Elizabeth Hawkins. May 18, 1809. Page 138.
Benjamin Whitehouse-Polly Sparrow. July 9, 1809. Page 138.
Zachariah Barnett-Nancy Jackman. Aug. 4, 1808. Page 138.
Noah Caton-Jemima Caton. Oct. 20, 1808. Page 138.
John Fife-Nancy McGinnis. Nov. 17, 1808. Page 138.
George Davis-Sally Bilbo. Jan. 13, 1809. Page 138.
William Bryant-Nancy Shelton. March 19, 1809. Page 138.
John Speed-Betsey Hutchins. April 20, 1809. Page 138.
William Caton-Nancy Ridgway. June 8, 1809. Page 138.
Valentine Day-Elizabeth Adams. July 31, ———. Page 138.
John Roach-Elizabeth Baker. March 10, 1808. Page 138.
William Axton-Peggy Murphy. Aug. 6, 1808. Page 138.
Henry Hanbolt-Lelia Halloway. Oct. 13, 1808. Page 138.
John Murphy-Ana Colson. Sept. 27, 1808. Page 138.
John Cochrel-Frances Brown. Feb. 15, 1808. Page 140.
Thomas L. Smart-Nancy Brown. Nov. 27, 1808. Page 140.
William McMurtrie-Priscilla Sharpe. Dec. 1, 1808, Page 140.
Jonathan Watkins-Janny Hughes. June 21, 1808. Page 140.
Jesse Corn-Janny Vanarsdall. March 24, 1808. Page 140.
William Cilley-Polly Doty. Feby. 28, 1808. Page 140.
Thompson Thomas-Mariah Haley. Feby. 28, 1808. Page 140.
Jacob Silvertooth-Barbara Yankee. Apr. 30, 1809. Page 140.
Bailey Harbart-Amy Galloway. July 17, 1809. Page 140.
John Carey-Polly Hungate. Aug. 19, 1809. Page 140.
John Hale-Sarah Barnett. Dec. 8, 1809. Page 140.
John Bottom-Betsey White. Dec. 10, 1809. Page 140.
Henry Blagrave-Sarah Blevins. Nov. 15, 1809. Page 140.
Isaac Rynerson-Polly Orkeys. July 13, 1809. Page 142.
Cornelius Covert-Sally Smock. Oct. 3, 1809. Page 142.
Cornelius Canine-Dorothy Vance (Vannice). Oct. 17, 1809. Page 142.

John Condor-Elizabeth Manelly. Nov. 2, 1809. Page 142.
Lewis Thomas-Sally Alexander. 1809. Page 142.
Jesse Long-Mary Rolleland. 1809. Page 142.
Stephen Davis-Betsey Moore. Nov. 1, 1809. Page 142.
Benjamin Hodges-Jenny McCoombs. Feby. 14, 1809. Page 142.
John Brown-Jemima Myers. Dec. 28, 1809. Page 142.

William Patterson-Elizabeth Newton. Jan. 24, 1809. Page 142.
Ambrose Burton-Janey Jones. Nov. 23, 1809. Page 142.
John Gales-Polly Barber. May 5, 1809. Page 142.
Gamaliel Dodge-Margaret McCoy. Oct. 1, 1809. Page 142.
William Clarke-Sarah Childs. May 2, 1809. Page 142.
Samuel Street-Sally Wood. May 27, 1809. Page 144.
Jesse Davis-Polly Hays. Sept. 4, 1809. Page 144.
Davis Ryon (Ryan)-Patsey Burford. Dec. 21, 1809. Page 144.
William Fench-Sally Barber. May 4, 1809. Page 144.
Michael Nifong (Nisong)-Mary Curd. Oct. 18, 1809. Page 144.
Henry Willis-Maria Tadlock. Aug. 1, 1809. Page 144.
Micajah McKinney-Lackey Overstreet. July 2, 1809. Page 144.
Elias Wingate-Esther Ripperdan. Mch. 31, 1809. Page 144.
Thomas McGinnis-Anne Moseby. June 15, 1809. Page 144.
Richard Reed-Polly Prather. June 18, 1809. Page 144.
Aaron Gritton-Elizabeth House. Oct. 4, 1809. Page 144.
James Burton-Frances Burton. Jan. 3, 1809. Page 144.
James Samuel-Sally Munday. Feb. 19, 1801. Page 144.
Alexander Adams-Janie Wilson. Feb. 23, 1801. Page 144.
Meredith Wilkerson-Sally Kinney. May 16, 1807. Page 146.
James Hall-Poaley Lowden. Aug. 9, 1808. Page 146.
Jesse Kinney-Peggy Salter. Dec. 19, 1803. Page 146.
Joseph Haines-Pooley Roach. 1804. Page 146.
Alexander Adams-Jane Wilson. Jan. 23, 1801. Page 146.
James Cummins-Lucy Morvell. July 16, 1804. Page 146.
Cornelius Bonta-Elizabeth Thomas. Aug. 20, 1804. Page 146.
Joseph Durr-Rachael Kinney. Dec. 22, 1807. Page 146.
Alexander Wilson-Nancy Fowles (Towles). Jan. 25, 1808. Page 146.

George Cochran-Margaret Fowles. Oct. 20, 1808. Page 146.
John Shields-Rody (Rhody) Bowman.. Mch. 7, 1808. Page 146.
Charles Bunch-Fanny Lyons. Feb. 3, 1808. ` Page 146.
Peter Tomey-Margaret Rigway. Feb. 25, 1809. Page 148.
Abraham Rynearson-Letty Demaree. Nov. 11, 1809. Page 148.
George Debond-Priscilla Robson. Oct. 29, 1809. Page 148.
John Harrod-Polly Moore. Oct. 29, 1809. Page 148.
George C. Thompson-Mary McDowell. Aug. ——, 1809. Page 148.
William Powell-Mary Taylor. Aug. ——, 1809. Page 148.
John A. McDowell-Lucy T. Starling. Nov. 8, 1809. Page 148.
John Adkin-Betsy Silvey. Mch. 27, 1810. Page 148.
William Harlin-Mary Harlin. July 28, 1809. Page 148.
James Clarke-Dorothy Woodson. July 3, 1809. Page 148.
Josiah Mann-Elizabeth Schooling. Feb. 9, 1809. Page 148.
William Jennings-Polly Thompson. Jany. 31, 1809. Page 148.
Robert McKamey-Susanna McAfee. Feby. 21, 1809. Page 148.
George Corn-Ann Cooney. March 2, 1809. Page 150.
Wm. Rice-Polly Vanarsdale. April 13, 1809. Page 150.
Joshua Cummins-Nancy Noel. Apr. 20, 1809. Page 150.
John Cardwell, Jr.-Jane McCown. Apr. 20, 1809. Page 150.
Joseph Poal (Pool)-Sabrey Padget. May 4, 1809. Page 150.
John Smock-Ann Gray. June 1, 1809. Page 150.
Isaac Mitchell-Peggy Vandyke. June 22, 1809. Page 150.
Fielden Ransdell-Peggy Bohon. July ——, 1809. Page 150.
John Wallace-Frouchey Taylor. July 13, 1809. Page 150.
Peter Vanarsdall-Charity Demaree. Sept. 16, 1809. Page 150.
William McGee-Jane Bigham. Oct. 12, 1809. Page 150.
———————————— Twalt ?-Anne Pherigo. Nov. 16, 1809. Page 150.
John Green-Sally A. Fry. Sep. 26, 1810. Page 150.
Samuel Daviess-Hannah McAfee. Sep. 27, 1810. Page 150.
Joshua Sappell (Saffell)-Betsey Middleton. 1810. Page 152.
May Burton-Nancy Woodfork. 1810. Page 152.

Jonathan Patterson-Rebecca Lipaun. 1810. Page 152.
John Bowman-Sally Driskell. 1810. Page 152.
Henry Barnes-Elizabeth Huff (Hupp). 1810. Page 152.
Robert Montgomery-Virginia Miller. 1810. Page 152.
Thomas Buntain-Jerusha Plough. 1810. Page 152.
David Maxwell-Polly Dunn. Sept. 21, 1809. Page 152.
Jacob Yeast-Elizabeth Phillips. Feb. 22, 1809. Page 152.
Andrew Dine-Susanna Vincent. Feb. 22, 1809. Page 152.
Abraham Miller-Kezziah Kelly (Kelley). June 12, 1809. Page 152.
Gabriel Alexander-Sally Coleman. June 14, 1809. Page 152.
William Simpson-Polly Davis. July 15, 1809. Page 152.
James Wills-Polly Nance. July 28, 1809. Page 152.
Robert Godfrey-Nelly Dean. Oct. 10, 1810. Page 152.
Sam'l. Hogue-Polly McMurtry. Oct. 24, 1810. Page 154.
William Sharpe-Sally McMurtry. Oct. 24, 1810. Page 154.
Isaac Brocaw-Polly Brewer. Dec. 24, 1810. Page 154.
John James Marshall-Nancy Reed Birney. Sep. 15, 1809. Page 154.
John Byers-Anne Scomp. Sep. 23, 1810. Page 154.
Joseph Wilson-Cynthia Sneed. Nov. 29, 1810. Page 154.
Abraham Ripperdan-Nancy Pritchard. Aug. 1, 1811. Page 154.
Alexander Murray-Fanny Watts. Nov. 15, 1810. Page 154.
Elisha Denny-Mary Hedger. Nov. 8, 1810. Page 154.
Ellis Stone-Peggy Denny. Aug. 2, 1810. Page 154.
William Bradshaw-Poley Ford. Apr. 28, 1810. Page 154.
Matthias Bowers-Peggy Rock. Nov. 6, 1810. Page 154.
Enoch Stone-Polly Denny. Sept. 21, 1810. Page 154.
John Lowry-Elizabeth Bigham. Sept. 25, 1810. Page 154.
Richard M. Sutfield-Polly Thomas. Sept. 25, 1810. Page 156.
William Daniel-Susanna Burton (Bunton). Sept. 20, 1810. Page
156.
Abzoniel King-Edith Burks. Aug. 15, 1810. Page 156.
Amos Davis-Disey Evans. Apr. 3, 1810. Page 156.
Robert Hambleton-Polly Graham. Apr. 3, 1810. Page 156.
Thomas Overstreet-Mary McKinney. Sept. 5, 1810. Page 1565.
Eli Allin-Betsey McDaniel. Feby. 1, 1810. Page 1556.
William Barber-Jane E. Walker. May 10, 1810. Page 156.
John Scomp-Docea Timmons. Feby. 1, 1810. Page 156.
Burnett May-Nancy Gibson. Apr. 3, 1810. Page 156.
John Gibson-Dicey May. Mch. 2, 1810. Page 156.
John West-Elizabeth A. Curd. Feby. 4, 1810. Page 156.
Benja. Watson-Kitty Ford. May 10, 1810. Page 156.
Henry Smart-Fenton Daniel. Aug. 22, 1810. Page 156.
John Briscoe-Margaret Harrison. May 10, 1810. Page 158.
Joseph Neff-Sally Cochran. 1810. Page 158.
Strother Gaines-Anne Fisher. Jany. 9, 1810. Page 158.
Josiah Jones-Nancy Finley. Feby. 5, 1811. Page 158.
Joel Noel-Tabitha Dickens. Mch. 28, 1811. Page 158.
Daniel Wickersham-Susanner Martin. June 4, 1810. Page 158.
Daniel Cooney-Betsey Hale. Aug. 16, 1810. Page 158.
Christopher Vanarsdall-Elizabeth Tolley. Sept. 3, 1810. Page 158.
John Kirkland-Barbara Walker. Nov. 15, 1810. Page 158.
Thomas Bottom-Jane Thompson. Oct. 22, 1810. Page 158.
David Leonard-Mary Thompson. Nov. 29, 1810. Page 158.
George Silvertooth-Hannah Colyer. Dec. 13, 1810. Page 158.
William Colyer-Nancy Kirkland. July 13, 1810. Page 158.
Wm. Gentry-Mary Whitenhill. Feb. 10, 1810. Page 158.
Silas Edinton-Fanny Latheram. Apr. 2, 1810. Page 160.
Chesly Lawson-Alsa Lambert. May 7, 1810. Page 160.
David Crain-Polly Pipe. March 13, 1810. Page 160.
Henry Harper-Pamelia Husbands. Oct. 8, 1810. Page 160.
James Pipes-Sally Pipes. Dec. 11, 1810. Page 160.

John Margrove-Lucy Crain. Apr. 11, 1811. Page 160.
William Milfry-Jane Biles. Oct. 11, 1811. Page 160.
Pristle White-Lucy Hawkins. Nov. 30, 1808. Page 160.
James Overstreet-Susanna Campbell. Sept. 12, 1809. Page 160.
Alexander Ridgeley-Jenney Whitehouse. Dec. 21, 1810. Page 160.
James Gray-Betsey Gray. Jan. 31, 1810. Page 160.
James Campbell-Charlotte Whitehouse. July 5, 1810. Page 160.
James Crow-Rhoda Stemmons. Oct. 25, 1810. Page 160.
Isaac Christison-Lucy Reins. Mch. 7, 1811. Page 160.
John Richardson-Polly Neff. Feb. 26, 1811. Page 162.
Henry Snider-Polly Latimore. May 28, 1811. Page 162.
Henry Minor-Lydia McGinnis. July 23, 1811. Page 162.
Berryman Combs-Sally Cole. Sept. 21, 1811. Page 162.
Christopher Hutchins-Rachel Pitman. Sept. 25, 1811. Page 162.
William Spratt-Peggy Simpson. Oct. 25, 1811. Page 162.
William Mitchell-Polly Basey. Apr. 30, 1810. Page 162.
Joel Lawson-Susanna Lambert. May 29, 1810. Page 162.
Daniel Jusks-Lydia McGohon. May 29, 1810. Page 162.
Abra. Nichols-Polly Bohon. Oct. 9, 1810. Page 162.
Cornelius Demaree-Polly Waddle. Nov. 14, 1810. Page 162.
Simeon House-Nancy Philips. Nov. 20, 1811. Page 162.
Adam Herseperger-Edith Gash. Feby. 19, 1811. Page 162.
William Huff——————— Hale. Apr. 15, 1811. Page 162.
Jacob Sortor-Rachel Hardenbrook. Sep. 12, 1811. Page 164.
William Pennington-Chancy Dallenhill. Oct. 13, 1811. Page 164.
Philip Barnes-Catharine Gabhart. Oct. 1, 1811. Page 164.
Josiah Wilson-Polly Comingore. Oct. ——, 1811. Page 164.
William Moseby-Susanna McFatridge. Oct. 31, 1811. Page 164.
Martin Green-Mahala Wood. Jan. 23, 1812. Page 164.
George W. Farris-Nancy Shelton. Jan. 1, 1811. Page 164.
Elisha Edward-Lucy Richardson. Jan. 3, 1811. Page 164.
Brockman Adkins-Polly Silvey. Feby. 21, 1811. Page 164.
James Gillispie-Eliza L. McDowell. May 14, 1811. Page 164.
John Driskell-Nancy Thomas. Aug. 15, 1811. Page 164.
Thomas Harrison-Polly Sneed. Dec. 11, 1811. Page 164.
Tumey Harold-Delphia Hughes. Dec. 24, 1811. Page 164.
William Huff-Lucy Gates. Mch. 4, 1811. Page 164.
Robert Curry-Polly Skinner. Apr. 9, 1811. Page 166.
John Nicholas-Sally Coleskein. June 13, 1811. Page 166.
Henry Fields-Susanna Ripperdan. Sept. 20, 1811. Page 166.
Allen Ranes-Martha Terhune. Oct. 19, 1811. Page 166.
Dan'l. Comingore-Rachel House. Jan. 30, 1812. Page 166.
Jesse Dilider-Isbel Gibson. June 11, 1811. Page 166.
Jacob Bishop——————— Keller. Dec. 11, 1811. Page 166.
George Mitchell-Dorthy ———————. Jan. 18, 1811. Page 166.
George Stenshon-Margaret ———————. Aprl. 16, 1811. Page 166.
William Boman-Faneney Jones. Sept. 9, 1811. Page 166.
George Worley-Ann Moore. Feby. 1, 1811. Page 166.
Joseph Hughes-Polly Dickey. Oct. 5, 1810. Page 166.
Andrew MacCombs-Hannah Homes. Feb. 12, 1811. Page 166.
Christian Gore-Chatham Hains. Nov. 11, 1811. Page 166.
Benjamine Alderson-Leah Lucas. May 13, 1811. Page 168.
William Stevenson-Nancy Lyon. Mch. 25, 1812. Page 168.
James Thompson-Caty Bottom. May 30, 1811. Page 168.
William Martin-Rebecca Pryor. Sep. 24, 1811. Page 168.
Robert McClary-Nancy Dickey. Dec. 17, 1811. Page 168.
Jacob Miller-Polly Borders. Dec. 26, 1811. Page 168.
John Moore-Cassey Martin. Feb. 27, 1812. Page 168.
Thomas Crain-Polly Potts. Apr. 21, 1812. Page 168.
William McElroy-Catherine Crawford. Feb. 7, 1811. Page 168.
Edward Butler-Polly Wright. May 23, 1811. Page 168.

Robertson Johnston-Anne Butler. Apr. 9, 1812. Page 168.
Sylvanus May-Elizabeth Hite. June 23, 1812. Page 168.
Benj. D. Armstrong-Elizabeth Scott. June 30, 1812. Page 168.
William Minor-Polly Rains. Apr. 29, 1812. Page 168.
Samuel Sally-Betsey Stokes. Apr. 5, 1812. Page 170.
Kneeley Bennett-Lucy Bradshaw. July 3, 1812. Page 170.
Michael Goodnight-Comfort McCormack. Dec. 31, 1812. Page 170.
Nelson Harris-Polly Corn. March 4, 1812. Page 170.
Wm. Adams-Lucy Odel. Dec. 31, 1812. Page 170.
James Springer-Phebe Burton. Sep. 29, 1812. Page 170.
Daniel Crump-Elizabeth Fisher. Apr. 20, 1812. Page 170.
Stephen Sale-Melinda Hedger. Oct. 22, 1812. Page 170.
Henry Winlock-Margaret Miller. Oct. 24, 1812. Page 170.
Wm. R. Bohon-Betsey Stein (Steen). Feb. 4, 1812. Page 170.
Walter Hicks-Susan Pullam. June 16, 1812. Page 170.
James Cooney-Polly Booth. Apr. 2, 1812. Page 170.
Samuel Curry-Susanna Devine. Mch. 12, 1812. Page 170.
Luke Ellis-Susan Bohon. Apr. 7, 1812. Page 170.
William Plough-Debby Bowles. May 24, 1812. Page 172.
Levi Dunn-Nancy Graham. July 5, 1812. Page 172.
William Graves-Polly Graham. July 11, 1812. Page 172.
Reuben Hawkins-Betsey Quigley. Aug. 27, 1812. Page 172.
Lucas Voris-Fanny Fitzpatrick. June 14, 1812. Page 172.
George Phillips-Agnes Pryor. Aug. 5, 1812. Page 172.
Thomas B. Mourse-Eliza Adair. Nov. 3, 1812. Page 172.
Jonathan Royalty-Ann Thomas. Nov. 8, 1812. Page 172.
Isham Pearson-Sally Ford. Oct. 16, 1812. Page 172.
Elijah Bohon-Lucy Lightfoot. Nov. 24, 1812. Page 172.
Enoch Thomas-Fanny Sanford. Dec. 22, 1812. Page 172.
David Comingore-Peggy Smith. July 23, 1812. Page 172.
William Minor-Polly Rains. Apr. 29, 1812. Page 172.
George Davis-Polly Moody. Nov. 5, 1812. Page 172.
Ezekiel Gaines-Susanna Fisher. Dec. 31, 1812. Page 174.
Cornelius Lyster-Elizabeth Utley. Mch. 19, 1813. Page 174.
Temple Tewmey-Sally Lyster. Mch. 16, 1813. Page 174.
Sam'l. Wilson-Mary Templeton. Apr. 8, ———. Page 174.
William Nourse-Rebecca Kyle. May 2, 1813. Page 174.
Fallen Crain-Polly Rugles. Aug. 5, 1812. Page 174.
Turner Bottom-Nancy Bridges. Aug. 6, 1812. Page 176.
Nathan Nicholas-Cassey Matherly. Jany. 25, 1813. Page 176.
Pleasant Martin-Sally Bottom. Jany. 5, 1813. Page 176.
William Sinnett-Barsheba Barnett. Mch. 21, 1813. Page 176.
James Thompson-Betsey May. Apr. 7, 1813. Page 176.
Loyd Hitch-Harriet Greenwood. May 11, 1813. Page 176.
George Burton——— Lathram. June 15, 1813. Page 176.
Shippy Allen Dye-Elizabeth Goodnight. June 22, 1813. Page 176.
Claiborn Franklin-Elizabeth Sparrow. July 22, 1813. Page 176.
Davies Hart-Erman Atkins. July 8, 1813. Page 176.
Michael Harmon-Patsey Holland. July 22, 1813. Page 176.
William Sage-Sarah Harbison (Harberson). July 22, 1813. Page
176.
Harry Tolman-Martha Johnston. Nov. 21, 1812. Page 176.
Andrew McCormack-Mary Denny. Dec. 23, 1812. Page 176.
James Wilson-Nancy Minor. Nov. 4, 1812. Page 178.
Thos. Little-Nancy Hope. Dec. 23, 1812. Page 178.
Cornelius Lyster-Elizabeth Utley. May 4, 1813. Page 178.
Robt. Sandifer-Sally Wilson. Nov. 3, 1813. Page 178.
David Evans-Elizabeth McAlister. Feb. 5, 1814. Page 178.
Jacob Combs-Margaret Alexander. 1814. Page 178.
Nicholas Booher (Booker)-Patsey Adams. 1814. Page 178.
John Little-Polly Holmes. 1814. Page 178.

Robert McMichael-Rachel Biles. 1814. Page 178.
Robert Johnson-Elizabeth Barnes. 1814. Page 178.
Daniel Shaw-Patsey Pipes. Feb. 23, 1814. Page 178.
William Douglass-Mary Days. Feb. 23, 1814. Page 178.
Patrick Galligher-Nancy Ridgeway. Feb. 8, 1813. Page 178.
John Comingore-Charity Green. Feb. 25, 1813. Page 178.
Christopher Miller-Elizabeth Adams. May 31, 1813. Page 180.
William Dickey-Sally Gabhart. July 29, 1813. Page 180.
William Burks-Charity Riggs. Sept. 2, 1813. Page 180.
James Armstrong-Mary D. Richardson. Oct. 9, 1813. Page 180.
James Wood-Elizabeth Harris. Dec. 23, 1813. Page 180.
Wm. M. Owings-Ann Moore. Dec. 28, 1813. Page 180.
Levi Grithe-Anna Myers. Dec. 28, 1813. Page 180.
Garret Terhune-Nancy Davis. Aug. 15, 1814. Page 180.
William Wigor-Polly Shackelford. June 4, 1814. Page 180.
Davies Dunlays-Elizabeth Gilman. June 5, 1814. Page 180.
John Hubbard-Elizabeth Wilson. May 9, 1814. Page 180.
David Todd-Sally Smith. June 3, 1814. Page 180.
John Mahan-Nancy Woodson. June 8, 1814. Page 180.
James Smith-Sally Taylor. Jany. 10, 1814. Page 180.
Abraham Brewer-Anna Cozine. Jany. 13, 1814. Page 182.
Garret Terhune-Rachael Rynerson. Jany. 16, 1814. Page 182.
Michael Horn-Polly Gabhart. Jany. 20, 1814. Page 182.
Abish Matherly-Susan Sullivan. Jany. 25, 1814. Page 182.
George Thurman-Nancy Musgrove. Feby. 28, 1814. Page 182.
Elias Davidson-Jane Starling. Oct. 13, 1812. Page 182.
Dr. Joseph McMurtrie-Sally Haggin. Apr. 8, 1813. Page 182.
Leonard Parker-Elizabeth Holeman. Apr. 9, 1813. Page 182.
George May-Peggy Walker. Aug. 5, 1813. Page 182.
John Laughlin-Rebekah Walkup. Aug. 5, 1813. Page 182.
Davis Kindly-Rachel Harbeson. Sept. 9, 1813. Page 182.
John Lewis-Elizabeth Reed. Oct. 23, 1813. Page 182.
Stephen Lyon-Polly Stephenson. Oct. 9, 1813. Page 182.
Alexander Dale-Nelly Silvers. Oct. 30, 1813. Page 182.
John M. Foster-Catharine P. Adair. Feb. 22, 1814. Page 184.
Abraham Hawkins-Mary Hawkins. Mch. 9, 1814. Page 184.
Joseph Woods-Elizabeth Wilson. Mch. 17, 1814. Page 184.
Robert Smithey-Nancy Cardwell. Mch. 31, 1814. Page 184.
John Wycoff-Elizabeth McGohon. Apr. 1, 1814. Page 184.
John Ares-Betsey Cole. Sep. 28, 1813. Page 184.
John Smith-Hesther Snodgrass. June 12, 1814. Page 184.
Charles Snodgrass-Judy Brewer. Aug. 11, 1814. Page 184.
Robert Mosby-Harriet Smith. July 12, 1814. Page 184.
Tho. Allin, Jr.-Mary B. Thompson. Sep. 15, 1814. Page 184.
John Leonard-Deborah Thompson. Nov. 24, 1813. Page 184.
John Horn-Peggy Bottom. Oct. 14, 1814. Page 184.
Jeremiah Donovan-Martha Cooney. Feb. 3, 1814. Page 184.
William Gabbard-Betsey Nicholds. Feb. 27, 1814. Page 186.
Wm. Moore-Jemima Hendrickson. Feb. 7, 1814. Page 186.
Carey Crane-Betsey Hall. Aug. 4, 1814. Page 186.
Samuel Crawford-Catharine Ewing. Nov. 3, 1814. Page 186.
Stephen Lyster-Mary Vandivien. Mch. 17, 1814. Page 186.
Isaac Coovert-Rebecc Brocaw. Mch. 19, 1814. Page 186.
Henry Scomp-Flora Vannice. May 26, 1814. Page 186.
Samuel Baxter-Elizabeth Gritton. May 29, 1814. Page 186.
Solomon Phillips-Judy Cooney. Jan. 3, 1815. Page 186.
Barnett Hall-Betsey Cooney. May 22, 1815. Page 186.
Stephen Lyon-Nancy Bell. Apr. 22, 1814. Page 186.
John Keller-Jane Bunton. May 12, 1814. Page 186.
John R. Mooreland-Rachel Stagg. June 4, 1814. Page 186.
Samuel Silvey-Betsey Biass. June 15, 1814. Page 186.

Elijah Voorhies-Hetty Voorhies. July 28, 1814. Page 188.
Leroy Short-Polly Yewell. July 28, 1814. Page 188.
Daniel McDaniel-Catey Vanniss. Aug. 18, 1814. Page 188.
William Currens-Catharine Armstrong. Sept. 27, 1814. Page 188.
William P. Anderson-Margaret L. Adair. Sept. 29, 1814. Page 188.
Wm. Cunningham-Lucinda Boston Simmons. Dec. 8, 1814. Page 188.
Wm. Davis-Lucy Ann Roach. Dec. 8, 1814. Page 188.
John Adams-Peggy Dur. Jan. 5, 1815. Page 188.
Solomon Phillips-Judy Cooney. Jan. 5, 1815. Page 188.
Joseph Woods-Dorcas Buchanan. June 29, 1815. Page 188.
John McGinnis-Sally Riley. July 13, 1815. Page 188.
Austin Moore-Patsey Goolman. July 20, 1815. Page 188.
Charles Bosley-Ann Craddock. Aug. 23, 1815. Page 188.
John May-Nancy Hitt (Hite). June 21, 1815. Page 188.
Garret Johnson-Sarah Hite. June 21, 1815. Page 190.
Benjamin Gore-Lydia Harbison. Aug. 3, 1815. Page 190.
Alexander K. Thompson-Martha C. Napier. Nov. 25, 1815. Page 190.
John Britton-Nancy Napier. Nov. 25, 1815. Page 190.
Jesse Shy-Mary Jones. Nov. 25, 1815. Page 190.
Moses Freeman-Patsey Huff. Nov. 25, 1815. Page 190.
George Crawford-Elizabeth Embry. Mch. 16, 1815. Page 190.
Basil Corn-Hannah Bohon. Mch. 15, 1814. Page 190.
Wilson Worman (Warman)-Rebecca Doty (Dotey). Mch. 15, 1814. Page 190.
John Smith-Elizabeth Lewis. May 26, 1814. Page 190.
David M. Coyle-Catharine Stagg. May 26, 1814. Page 190.
Elias Passmore-Elizabeth Chinewith. May 17, 1814. Page 190.
Philip Kennedy-Sally Bright. Sep. 8, 1814. Page 190.
John McIntire-Rebecca Hale. July 12, 1814. Page 190.
William Davis-Patsey Covert. Apr. 29, 1813. Page 192.
Wm. Shy-Patsey Jones. Apr. 5, 1815. Page 192.
Thomas Edmonson-Sally Bohon. Nov. 23, 1815. Page 192.
Jacob Border-Sarah Doata. Sep. 1, 1815. Page 192.
Levi Lockhard-Elizabeth Hungate. Aug. 10, 1815. Page 192.
Joseph Case-Sarah Phillips. Nov. 18, 1815. Page 192.
Richard Lockhart-Isabel Hale. Dec. 22, 1815. Page 192.
Ebenezer Carey-Pamelia Hadon. May 3, 1815. Page 192.
Elias Roman-Mary Armstrong. Mch. 16, 1815. Page 192.
John McKinney-Nancy Prior. Sep. 16, 1815. Page 192.
David Devine-Casandra Hale. Jan. 19, 1815. Page 192.
Henry Comingore-Elizabeth Smock. Jan. 26, 1815. Page 192.
John Smock-Jane Brewer. Sep. 13, 1814. Page 192.
David Wattersford-Rhoda Lyon. Sep. 8, 1814. Page 192.
John Donald-Sarah Hunter. Oct. 14, 1814. Page 194.
John Phillips-Mary Severe. Oct. 12, 1814. Page 194.
Robert Nield-Jane Passmore. Aug. 23, 1815. Page 194.
John Ray-Sarah Hickley. Sep. 12, 1815. Page 194.
Sam'l. Hart-Sarah Hickey. Sep. 12, 1815. Page 194.
Thomas Hartgrove-Palina Bullock. Sep. 28, 1815. Page 194.
Don C. Dixon-Mary J. Allin. Nov. 1, 1815. Page 194.
John J. Allin-Sally A. Hopkins. Nov. 15, 1815. Page 194.
Lewis Garr-Nancy Threlkeld. Oct. 19, 1815. Page 194.
Elijah Webster-Jane Raines. Sep. 7, 1815. Page 194.
Davies Sparrow-Sally Whitehouse. Nov. 5, 1816. Page 194.
Joseph A. Woodson-Annie (?) Sutfield. Nov. 29, 1816. Page 194.
John McKay-Jane Boston. Nov. 28, 1816. Page 194.
Thomas Moore-Jane P. Moore. Apr. 1, 1815. Page 194.
Jacob Bowman-Barsheba Barnett. Aug. 19, 1813. Page 196.

John Prewitt-Elizabeth Harrison. June 4, 1811. Page 196.
James P. Mitchell-Sarah Hamner. Mch. 8, 1815. Page 196.
Joshua Alexander-Barsheba Roland. Nov. 10, 1814. Page 196.
James Marshall-Eliza Watts. Dec. 8, 1815. Page 196.
James Chatham-Mary (May) Owings. Dec. 19, 1815. Page 196.
John Shy-Margaret McGuffie. Jan. 4, 1816. Page 196.
Davis Wood-Mary Moore. Feb. 22, 1816. Page 196.
John Davis-Polly Hall. Feb. 29, 1816. Page 196.
Mason Vamoy-Fanny Shy. Feb. 29, 1816. Page 196.
Ezekiel Montgomery-Margaret McCormick. Mch. 12, 1816. Page
196.
Abraham Smith-Nancy (Nanny) H. Smith. Jan. 25, 1816. Page
196.
Ezra Williams-Polly Fisher. Feb. 13, 1816. Page 196.
John Roe-Anny Shackelford. May 11, 1815. Page 196.
Reuben Shackelford-Sophia Worley. May 16, 1815. Page 198.
Patrick Preston-Harriet Rankin. May 13, 1816. Page 198.
Richard Phillips-Ann Ewing. Dec. 19, 1816. Page 198.
Thomas J. Crawford-Margaret Crawford. Mch. 7, 1816. Page 198.
Thomas Crawford-Ketera (?) Ewing. May 9, 1816. Page 198.
Joel Noel-Betsey Shackelford. June 21, 1815. Page 198.
———— Driskel-Luse Dean. Aug. 15, 1815. Page 198.
Horace Noel-Polly Asher. Nov. 16, 1815. Page 198.
Alexander Cummings-Susanna Adams. Jan. 10, 1816. Page 198.
Benjamin Dunlanand-Jane Duncan. Mch. 9, 1818. Page 198.
Samuel Ward-Rachsel Bennett. Sep. 7, 1815. Page 198.
Franklin Best-Susanna Brooks. Aug. 11, 1815. Page 198.
James Pherigo-Anny Bigham. Aug. 4, 1815. Page 198.
Sam'l. Eccles-Jane Grant (Gaunt). Nov. 6, 1815. Page 198.
Horatio Cleland-Sally Irvin. Nov. 10, 1815. Page 200.
George Talbott-Catharine Coleman. Jan. 11, 1816. Page 200.
William Powell-Katy King. Jan. 22, 1816. Page 200.
Ambrose Lambert-Anny Adams. Jan. 23, 1816. Page 200.
Roger Thompson-Patsey K. Tilford. Feb. 21, 1816. Page 200.
William Orr-Polly H. Smith. Feb. 2, 1816. Page 200.
Wm. F. McCalla-Mary Higgins. Feb. 22, 1816. Page 200.
John McGee-Jane Curry. Feb. 29, 1816. Page 200.
John McAfee-Dicey Curry. Mch. 12, 1816. Page 200.
Jacob G. Denton-Rachel Lychlyter. Mch. 14, 1816. Page 200.
Jacob Cunningham-Nancy Kelley. Mch. 29, 1816. Page 200.
William Evans-Elizabeth Hawkins. May 8, 1816. Page 200.
Joseph McCoun-Esther Eccles. June 18, 1816. Page 200.
Joseph Viles-Patsey Martin. Dec. 8, 1814. Page 200.
Thomas Bottom-Nancy Thompson. Dec. 8, 1814. Page 202.
Elijah Moore-Lydia Hendrickson. May 23, 1815. Page 202.
Aaron Hendrickson-Polly Moore. June 23, 1815. Page 202.
Berryman Harold-Polly Parr. July 4, 1815. Page 202.
Austin Moore-Patsey Goldman. July 20, 1815. Page 202.
John Sennet-Ellender May. Sep. 1, 1815. Page 202.
David Casey-Elizabeth Whoberry. Oct. 12, 1815. Page 202.
Benjamin Walter-Matilda Burford. Feb. 15, 1816. Page 202.
George Boswell-Anna Rynearson. Oct. 9, 1816. Page 202.
John Lamb-Betsey McGinnis. Jan. 23, 1816. Page 202.
John B. Lockman-Hetty Blacketer. Jan. 25, 2816. Page 202.
Thomas Moore-Jane Pitman. Apr. 3, 1816. Page 202.
Daniel Broyles-Milly Broyles. July 9, 1816. Page 202.
Jeremiah Owens-Margaret Pitman. Oct. 5, 1816. Page 202.
Robert H. Nantz-Mary Ann Demmit. July 12, 1816. Page 204.
James Montgomery-Delphin McCormack. Aug. 7, 1816. Page 204
Jesse Jones-Elizabeth Dean. Sep. 3, 1816. Page 204.
John Donal———— McGlackland. Nov. 4, 1816. Page 204.

James Donghy-Lucy Moss. Nov. 5, 1816. Page 204.
John Hungate-Annie Lepaw. Feb. 1, 1816. Page 204.
John Kirkland-Rachel Barnett. Aug. 20, 1816. Page 204.
John Gabbart-Polly Kirkland. Sep. 24, 1816. Page 204.
John Thompson-Susan Yankee. Oct. 29, 1816. Page 204.
Pardon Tabor-Deborah May. Dec. 12, 1816. Page 204.
Christian Glass—Peggy Rogers. Apr. 30, 1817. Page 204.
John Black-Polly Harris. Apr. 30, 1817. Page 204.
Seaton Beadles-Elizabeth Gashweiler. Apr. 30, 1817. Page 204.
John Faulkner-Selia (?) Cozine. May 15, 1817. Page 204.
John Davis-Anna Thomas. Jan. 16, 1815. Page 206.
Joab Green-Patsey Adkins. Jan. 22, 1815. Page 206.
James Sanders-Susan Odel. Mch. 8, 1815. Page 206.
Stephen Odel-Sally Veatch. Mch. 18, 1815. Page 206.
Daniel Dunklin-Emily Haley. Apr. 28, 1815. Page 206.
Francis Cook-Sally Mosby. July 3, 1815. Page 206.
James Sportsman-Anna Halligan. Aug. 8, 1815. Page 206.
John Halligan-Fanny Godfrey. Nov. 29, 1815. Page 206.
Wildy Newton-Milly Cousin. Nov. 21, 1815. Page 206.
Isaac Pritchett-Matilda Rogers. Dec. 7, 1815. Page 206.
Ezekiel Fisher-Ann Watts. Dec. 12, 1815. Page 206.
George B. Thompson-Lucy T. Timberlake. Mch. 17, 1816. Page
206.
Lewis Moore-Betsey Grayham. Mch. 24, 1816. Page 206.
Charles Hungate-Catharine Odel. Aug. 6, 1816. Page 204.
William Haley-Eliza Roachwell. Aug. 29, 1816. Page 208.
John Lennear-Sally Lyon. Sep. 23, 1816. Page 208.
Benjamin Elkin-Nancy Gordon. Sep. 25, 1816. Page 208.
Amos Gritton-Betsey Holt. Oct. 14, 1816. Page 208.
William Rose-Polly Everly. Oct. 9, 1816. Page 208.
Isaac Massey-Sally Darnaby. Dec. 28, 1816. Page 208.
John Delell (Odell)-Frakey Page. Dec. 26, 1816. Page 208.
Robert Robards-Nancy Piper. Dec. 12, 1816. Page 208.
George Coombs-Susan Eperly. Dec. 17, 1816. Page 208.
Moses Brown-Polly Sortor. Jan. 16, 1816. Page 208.
William Corn-Delilah Gritton. Mch. 13, 1816. Page 208.
Jacob Wickersham-Elizabeth Hadon. Apr. 13, 1816. Page 208.
Coleman Short-Peggy Watts. May 19, 1816. Page 208.
William Agin-Polly McDonald. June 12, 1816. Page 208.
John Phillips-Betsey Cunningham. July 19, 1816. Page 210.
William McClure-Elizabeth Vandivier. Aug. 27, 1816. Page 210.
James Givens-Mickey Clemons. Sept. 10, 1816. Page 210.
Henry Gabbart-Elizabeth Whittinghill. Oct. 5, 1816. Page 210.
Thomas Wilham-Polly Radford. Oct. 17, 1816. Page 210.
Abraham D. Whiteneck-Peggy Delam. Nov. 13, 1816. Page 210.
John Devine-Nancy Bottom. Dec. 7, 1816. Page 210.
William McClain-Sally Wilson. Dec. 31, 1816. Page 210.
John Ward-Peggy A. Latimer. Nov. 7, 1816. Page 210.
David Chambers-Polly Prewitt. Apr. 8, 1817. Page 210.
T. T. Moss-Judith C. Bullock. June 25, 1817. Page 210.
George Phillips-Anna Wells. Apr. 15, 1815. Page 210.
John Doty-Susanna Elder. Mch. 7, 1815. Page 210.
Barnett Hall-Betsey Cooney. May 25, 1815. Page 210.
James Devine-Lucy Carey. June 30, 1815. Page 212.
William Long-Betsey Hale. Aug. 2, 1815. Page 212.
James Thompson-Anna Cannon. Aug. 12, 1815. Page 212.
James Pearson-Nancy Quigley. Sep. 18, 1815. Page 212.
Thomas Viles-Barsheba Phillips. Oct. 24, 1815. Page 212.
George Monroe-Polly Barnett. Oct. 24, 1815. Page 212.
Daniel Thompson-Lucy Fisher. Sep. 10, 1815. Page 212.
James Sanford-Anny Wilson. June 27, 1815. Page 212.

John Brady-Fenly Austin. July 17, 1815. Page 212.
David Parent-Polly Austin. Sept. 13, 1815. Page 212.
Simon Smock-Catharine Demott. Oct. 23, 1815. Page 212.
Edward Spencer-Elizabeth McGinnis. Oct. 23, 1815. Page 212.
John Haynes-Betsey Harlan. Sept. 19, 1815. Page 212.
John Patterson-Polly Matherly. Nov. 23, 1815. Page 212.
Benjamin Irvin-Polly Billis (Belles). Mch. 4, 1815. Page 214.
Bryson Irvin-Patsey B. Davis. Nov. 25, 1815. Page 214.
Sam'l. Adams-Catharine McClain. Aug. 17, 1816. Page 214.
William Holeman-Phebe Gray. Oct. 24, 1816. Page 214.
Daniel Demott-Mary Brown. Oct. 31, 1816. Page 214.
Clarkson E. Randolph-Phebe Demaree. Dec. 17, 1816. Page 214.
George Hill-Polly McGee. Feb. 14, 1817. Page 214.
Benjamin Pleasants-Isabella Adair. Mch. 4, 1817. Page 214.
Simon Coovert-Polly Voorhies. Mch. 27, 1817. Page 214.
Sam'l. L. Irvin-Elizabeth Adams. Mch. 8, 1817. Page 214.
Thos. B. Hooe-Ann G. Thompson. June 21, 1817. Page 214.
John Spencer-Polly Gallagher. July 10, 1817. Page 214.
John Techiner-Leah Comingore. Aug. 28, 1817. Page 214.
John Harvey-Elizabeth Walkup. Sep. 9, 1817. Page 214.
Samuel Nevins-Polly McClain. Oct. 16, 1817. Page 216.
George Bohon-Ann Woods. Dec. 4, 1817. Page 216.
Braxton Mitchell-Paulina Paush. Dec. 30, 1817. Page 216.
John Walter-Margaret McGinnis. Mch. 20, 1817. Page 216.
Joel Mellon-Elizabeth Walters. Mch. 20, 1817. Page 216.
Peter Cozine-Phebe Vanarsdall. Mch. 8, 1817. Page 216.
Jesse Hamner-Tabitha Bilbo. July 10, 1817. Page 216.
William C. Logan-Sarah B. Bell. Dec. 16, 1817. Page 216.
John W. Kyle-Mary Sargent. Feb. 19, 1818. Page 216.
Samuel Huff-Elizabeth Vanarsdall. Mch. 19, 1817. Page 216.
Joseph Kirkland-Ruth Wickersham. Apr. 8, 1817. Page 216.
William Patterson-Sally Nicholds. May 24, 1817. Page 216.
William Bottoms-Polly Sanders. Apr. 8, 1817. Page 216.
Separate Hendrickson-Susanna Patterson. Dec. 11, 1817. Page
216.
John Preston-Hannah Kombs (Lambs). Apr. 28, 1817. Page 218.
Austin Moore-Nancy Steels. Jan. 29, 1818. Page 218.
John W. Lewis-Elizabeth Remington. July 8, 1817. Page 218.
Stephen Stone-Sally Faulkner. Dec. 10, 1816. Page 218.
Joseph McCoy-Fanny Vandike. Dec. 22, 1816. Page 218.
James Lyon-Polly Brinton. Dec. 21, 1816. Page 218.
Daniel Ellis-Keziah Moore. Feb. 24, 1817. Page 218.
Greenberry Bishop-Elizabeth Hays. Mch. 19, 1817. Page 218.
Abraham Kirkland-Betsey McGee. Oct. 2, 1817. Page 218.
James Cockran-Fanny Slaughter. Mch. 2, 1818. Page 218.
Eli Warman-Rachel Lacefield. Feby. 25, 1818. Page 218.
Sam'l. Downing-Priscilla Moore. Dec. 21, 1815. Page 218.
Isaac Hays-Fanny Turney. Dec. 28, 1815. Page 218.
Valentine Bishop-Eve Horine. Dec. 24, 1815. Page 218.
John McMickle-Catharine Whelan. Oct. 6, 1813. Page 220.
John Caldwell-Mary Knox. Dec. 9, 1813. Page 220.
Robert Russell-Susan Wheeler. Feb. ——, 1813. Page 220.
William Alexander-Martha L. Dunn. Jan. 18, 1814. Page 220.
William Right-Elizabeth Patterson. Mch. ——, 1814. Page 220.
John Gill-Mary Watts. Jany. ——, 1814. Page 220.
Abraham Fulkerson-Sally Briscoe. Dec. ——, 1814. Page 220.
John Brown-Hannah Rochester. Oct. ——, 1814. Page 220.
John Hanna-Nancy Moore. Feb. 2, 1814. Page 220.
George H. Briscoe-E. R. Ewing. Jan. 12, 1814. Page 220.
Isaac Terhune-Betsey Shepherd. Mch. 18, 1815. Page 220.
Moses Parks-Sally Henderson. Jan. 12, 1815. Page 220.

Christopher A. Reed-Ann B. Palmer. Dec. 10, 1816. Page 220.
Abraham Prtichard-Ann Henderson. Jan. 12, 1815. Page 220.
John Fendley-Louisa Strong. Sep. 20, 1816. Page 222.
William Butler-Sarah P. Adair. Sep. 20, 1816. Page 222.
John Beedles (?)-Elizabeth F. Richardson. Apr. 4, 1816. Page
222.
Meeshak Williams-Sarah Johnston. Feb. 9, 1816. Page 222.
George Yeiger-Margaret Jameson. Jan. 30, 1817. Page 222.
Joseph Venable-Mary Cowan. Mch. 31, 1817. Page 222.
Robert Russell-Malinda Parish. Apr. 28, 1817. Page 222.
John Thompson-Mary Brown. July 24, 1817. Page 222.
John McIntosh-Sally Cowley. June 10, 1817. Page 222.
John Hughes-Jane Dunn. Oct. 30, 1817. Page 222.
James Short-Abegail Boyd. Sept. 29, 1817. Page 222.
Benjamin H. Perkins-Isabella Caldwell. June 18, 1817. Page 222.
Howson H. Duncan-Hanna Southern. Dec. 16, 1817. Page 222.
John L. Ewing-Betsey May. Nov. 4, 1817. Page 222.
David Wilson-Meriah Knox. Nov. 18, 1817. Page 224.
John Hight-Elizabeth Bilbo. Dec. 23, 1817. Page 224.
Henry Amcut-Polly McGinnis.. Jany. 8, 1818. Page 224.
Joseph Baker-Judy Lynch. Jany. 8, 1818. Page 224.
John Minor-Mary Owens. Feby. 5, 1818. Page 224.
John Blacketer-Elizabeth Hamilton. Mch. 24, 1818. Page 224.
Peter Selch-Susan Richardson. Apr. 8, 1818. Page 224.
Severs (?) Tadlock-Melinda Berry. Feb. 12, 1818. Page 224.
Priestley White-Lucy Hawkins. Nov. 30, 1818. Page 224.
James S. Lowry-Nancy Huff. May 16, 1818. Page 224.
Thomas Smithfield-Lydia Smith. Apr. 30, 1818. Page 224.
John S. McElwood-Ann Beasey. June 5, 1818. Page 224.
James Ellexander-Polly Cardwell. No date given. Page 224.
John Jordan-Margaret Jordan. No date given. Page 224.
James Nevins-Betsey Deen (Dean). No date given. Page 226.
John Penny, Jr.-Nancy Burross. No date given. Page 226.
William Montgomery-Nancy Downing. No date given. Page 226.
Zachariah Barnes-Mary Hawkins. No date given. Page 226.
William Baskett-Susan Phillips. No date given. Page 226.
Henry Seviers-Sally Currens. No date given. Page 226.
John Waters-Lucy Ellexander. No date given. Page 226.
John Adams-Susana Nevins. (No date given.) Page 226.
Wm. Robertson-Jane Ronalds. Page 226.
Wm. Raines-Peggy Dampson. No date given. Page 226.
Richard Phillips-Sarah Egbert. Nov. 12, 1817. Page 226.
Robert Miller-Jemima McCallister. May ——, 1817. Page 226.
Mason Vannoy-Jane Ward. May 22, 1818. Page 226.
Nathaniel Crain-Sally Lynch. May 22, 1818. Page 226.
Abraham Many-Nancy B. Bell. Sep. 10, 1818. Page 228.
James Noel-Fanny Prewitt. Oct. 8, 1818. Page 228.
John H. Dunn-Patsey Sortor. Oct. 4, 1818. Page 228.
Richard Nicholds-Rachel Goodnight. Dec. 23, 1817. Page 228.
Samuel Noel-Anna Carol. July 18, 1818. Page 228.
Moses Overstreet-Rebecca Bilbo. Dec. 25, 1817. Page 228.
Garrett W. Ellis-Patsey Crain. Mch. 5, 1818. Page 228.
John Wiett-Polly Boles. Nov. 28, 1818. Page 228.
George Shante-Nancy Chambers. Dec. 15, 1818. Page 228.
David McGee-Sally A. Duncan. Jan. 8, 1818. Page 228.
Lewis Hamilton-Susan Riley. Jan. 22, 1818. Page 228.
Henry Whiteneck-Sarah Vanarsdall. Jan. 29, 1818. Page 228.
Thomas Lewis-Margaret Bailey. Feb. 5, 1818. Page 228.
John Dean-Harriet Anderson. Mar. 19, 1818. Page 228.
William Johnson-Patsey Parish. Apr. 1, 1818. Page 230.
William Cowan-Polly McMordie. May 12, 1818. Page 230.

William Brumfield-Catharine Robards. June 13, 1818. Page 230.
Isaac Kirkland-Malinda Mann. June 25, 1818. Page 230.
Edward Atkins-Nancy Atkins. July 2, 1818. Page 230.
Ivans Brown-Sally Clark. July 16, 1818. Page 230.
William Saunders (Sanders)-Polly Rainey. Aug. 3, 1818. Page 230.
David Adams-Nancy Lambert. Sept. 1, 1818. Page 230.
Hugh Lambert-Nancy McClain. Sept. 3, 1818. Page 230.
Aaron James-Rebecca Eccleo (Eccles). Sept. 3, 1818. Page 230.
James H. Stagg-Polly Rynearson. Oct. 1, 1818. Page 230.
William Markspile-Ann H. Hawkins. Oct. 22, 1818. Page 230.
James Woods-Polly Starnes. Nov. 12, 1818. Page 230.
William Nourse-Polly Eccles. Nov. 24, 1818. Page 230.
James Kennedy-Nancy Lyon. Nov. 26, 1818. Page 230.
David Bright-Nancy Bailey. Nov. 26, 1818. Page 232.
Elijah Law-Catharine Vorhies. Nov. 26, 1818. Page 232.
Charles McKinney-Elizabeth Crews. Dec. 31, 1818. Page 232.
Michael Kanary-Elizabeth Gashweiler. May 10, 1818. Page 232.
Philip Bringer-Susan Neff. May 14, 1818. Page 232.
David H. McCullock-Polly Green. July 30, 1818. Page 232.
William Broiles-Polly Claunch. Sept. 8, 1818. Page 232.
Benjamin Martin-Mary Martin. Sept. 10, 1818. Page 232.
William McGinnis-Patsey McGinnis. Dec. 3, 1818. Page 232.
Mason Vannoy-Jane Ward. Aug. 11, 1818. Page 232.
Jane Yeager-Nancy Yeager. May 5, 1818. Page 232.
John Kincaid-Mary C. Waggoner. June 28, 1818. Page 232.
Joseph Devine-Elizabeth Wingate. Jany. 15, 1818. Page 232.
Joseph Peavler-Mary Ridge. Feb. 5, 1818. Page 234.
William Hale-Sally Borders. Mch. 3, 1818. Page 234.
William Nicholds-Rhoda Martin. June 8, 1818. Page 234.
Archibald Prewett-Tempy Bryant. July 21, 1818. Page 234.
Allen Bryant-Mary Silvey. July 28, 1818. Page 234.
Vincent Duggan-Nancy Darnall. July 28, 1818. Page 234.
George Tewmey-Nelly Houst. Sept. 28, 1818. Page 234.
Richard Smith-Nancy Carr. Oct. 3, 1818. Page 234.
John Smith-Esther Dennis. Oct. 8, 1818. Page 234.
George Cozine-Charity Banta. Oct. 13, 1818. Page 234.
James R. Burrus-Catharine Whiteneck. Nov. 4, 1818. Page 234.
Harrison Anderson-Sarah Vannest. Nov. 24, 1818. Page 234.
Martin Williams-Sally Petty. Feb. 11, 1817. Page 234.
Robert Griffin-Sarah Hewer (Hower). Mch. 15, 1817. Page 234.
John Potter-Mary Threlkeld. Apr. 12, 1817. Page 236.
Jacob Wickersham-Elizabeth Hadden. Apr. 13, 1817. Page 236.
Samuel Bunton-Charlotte Young. Apr. 16, 1817. Page 236.
Joshua Gill-Nancy Haynes. May 8, 1817. Page 236.
James Sussell-Susanna White. May 12, 1817. Page 236.
Moses Carey-Betsey Devine. May 12, 1817. Page 236.
Abrm. Brewer-Mary Wells. June 6, 1817. Page 236.
Jacob Horn-Polly Gabbert. June 12, 1817. Page 236.
James Nicholds-Catharine Gabbert. June 21, 1817. Page 236.
William Saton-Julian Bowman. July 24, 1817. Page 236.
Chaney McCarty-Ann Hall. July 27, 1817. Page 236.
William Barnett-Sarah Stone. Aug. 14, 1817. Page 236.
David Lambert-Alley Dennis. Sep. 28, 1817. Page 236.
William Freeman-Margaret Casey. Oct. 5, 1817. Page 236.
James Sample-Mary Sinnett. Nov. 13, 1817. Page 238.
Nathaniel Burrus-Agnes Whiteneck. Dec. 18, 1817. Page 238.
John Asher-Anne Johnson. Mch. 31, 1818. Page 238.
Isaiah L. Lewis-Polly Parsley. Mch. 31, 1818. Page 238.
Robert James-Polly Sael. Apr. 26, 1818. Page 238 .
Jesse Carter-Sally Rice. Feb. 28, 1819. Page 238.
Benjamin Edgerton-Susanna Stone. June 18, 1818. Page 238.

Henry Stopher-Ela S. Ryan. Mch. 8, 1819. Page 238.
Austin Parish-Fanny N. Dismukes. Feb. 9, 1819. Page 238.
George Ward-Polly Lister. Feb. 10, 1819. Page 238.
Joseph Wigham-Mary Riperdan. Apr. 6, 1819. Page 238.
Jonathan Sandifer-Polly Owing. Dec. 9, 1818. Page 238.
Joseph Wheat-Mary Searcey. Jan. 17, 1819. Page 238.
Sterling Colter-Polly Guthrie. Mch. 18, 1819. Page 238.
William Brumfield-Susanna McGinnis. Dec. 10, 1818. Page 240.
Robert Jones-Patsey Gash. June 8, 1819. Page 240.
James Walkup-Nelly Skelton. June 10, 1819. Page 240.
Zachariah Hartgrove-Nancy Williams. May 9, 1819. Page 240.
Michael Phillips-Jane Sally. Oct. 24, 1819. Page 240.
John Williams-Polly Stimmons. July 15, 1819. Page 240.
William Hancock-Fanny Brown. Feb. 18, 1819. Page 240.
Joshua Jones-Nancy Saunders. Jany. 9, 1819. Page 240.
John Martin-Mary Meredith. Feby. 25, 1819. Page 240.
William Utley-Martha H. Richards. Nov. 16, 1817. Page 240.
John Ireland-Eliza Stirman. Nov. 16, 1817. Page 240.
James Bradshaw-Barsheba Bradshaw. June 18, 1819. Page 240.
Elijah Thomas-Margaret Godfrey. Feb. 14, 1819. Page 240.
Gideon Woods-Mary Bice. Jany. 19, 1819. Page 240.
Joseph Sanson (Sansan)-Nancy Mitchell. Mch. 22, 1819. Page 242.
Hiram Chambers-Hannah Thompson. March 30, 1819. Page 242.
Lawrence Demott-Phebe Banta. Nov. 17, 1819. Page 242.
Jacob Smock-Mary Demott. Dec. 23, 1819. Page 242.
Hiram T. Duese-Kitty Duese. Aug. 1, 1818. Page 242.
James Cochran-Fanny Slaughter. Mch. 2, 1818. Page 242.
Barton Harris-Elizabeth Rice. Mch. 18, 1818. Page 242.
John H. Tomlinson-Eliza M. Thompson. July 2, 1818. Page 242.
William Earbee-Betsey Bice. July 5, 1818. Page 242.
Thomas Taylor-Nancy Greenwood. Aug. 9, 1818. Page 242.
John Bohon-Mary Crawford. Oct. 8, 1818. Page 242.
William Rogers-Temperance Willis. Oct. 22, 1818. Page 242.
Joseph Rutherford-Sarah Graham. Nov. 1, 1818. Page 242.
Edward Dean (or Edmond)-Nancy Wilson. Nov. 2, 1818. Page
242.
William Cox-Judy Hambleton. June 2, 1819. Page 244.
James Coburn-Jane Steele. July 1, 1819. Page 244.
Samuel Davenport-Martha Rogers. July 1, 1819. Page 244.
Isham Prewitt-Agnes Green. July 27, 1819. Page 244.
Samuel Guthrie-Betsey Hope. Aug. 2, 1819. Page 244.
Isaac Gray-Polly Bohon. June 14, 1819. Page 244.
Dan'l. Galloway-Saly Jones. Feb. 25, 1819. Page 244.
Isaac Vanarsdall-Rebekah Huff. Mch. 11, 1819. Page 244.
Wm. McGee-Sally Voorhies. Mch. 4, 1819. Page 244.
Jeremiah Harbee-Nancy Bohon. May 20, 1819. Page 244.
Squire Bunton-Nancy Keller. May 27, 1819. Page 244.
Richard Holeman-Jane Vanarsdall. July 22, 1819. Page 244.
John Hardin-Sarah Boyce. Aug. 5, 1819. Page 244.
John Steele-Jane B. McMordie. Sept. 13, 1819. Page 224.
Edmund Quinn-Nancy Parish. Sept. 14, 1819. Page 246.
William Wilson-Eleanor Crawford. Sept. 16, 1819. Page 246.
Ephriam Smith-Jane Campbell. Sept. 16, 1819. Page 246.
James McCoy-Nancy Tompkins. Sept. 30, 1819. Page 246.
Terah T. Haggin-Adeline S. Benali. Oct. 7, 1819. Page 246.
Thomas Mann-Elizabeth Butler. Oct. 28, 1819. Page 246.
Jesse Gritton-Annie Demott. Nov. 4, 1819. Page 246.
Thomas Moore-Nancy Butler. Nov. 11, 1819. Page 246.
Samuel Craig-Mary Sharpe. Nov. 18, 1819. Page 246.
Austin Sea-Susanna Leckteter (?). Nov. 23, 1819. Page 246.
Constantine Brown-Elizabeth Jones. Nov. 25, 1819. Page 246.

Isaac Vandivier-Mary Vanarsdall. Dec. 23, 1819. Page 246.
Joseph Burton-Sally Armstrong. Dec. 23, 1819. Page 246.
Wagland (Wayland) James-Francis Burrus. Jany. 6, 1820. Page 246.

Lewis L. Slaughter-Sally Slaughter. Jany. 6, 1820. Page 248.
Hosea Sutherland-Betsey McCallister. Jany. 6, 1820. Page 248.
William B. Slaughter-Elizabeth Bell. Jany. 6, 1820. Page 248.
William Powell-Lucinda Smock. Jany. 6, 1820. Page 248.
Abraham Barbond-Rebecca Carter. Jany. 6, 1820. Page 248.
Cyrus Edwards-Nancy H. Reed. Apr. 21, 1818. Page 248.
George Plough-Sarah Rains. June 5, 1819. Page 248.
Anthony Cox-Palsey Murphy. June 5, 1819. Page 248.
John G. Cardwell-Ann Cardwell. June 5, 1819. Page 248.
Henry Saunders-Mildred Jones. June 5, 1619. Page 248.
John Turner-Sarah Robinson. June 5, 1819. Page 248.
William Barnes-Shaddy Gill. June 5, 1819. Page 248.
Robert Miller-Jemima McCallister. June 5, 1819. Page 248.
Samuel Hawkins-Elizabeth Barnes. June 5, 1819. Page 248.
Isaac Darland-Alsey Runnalds. June 5, 1819. Page 250.
Joseph Barnes-Tabitha Frazier. June 5, 1819. Page 250.
Jeremiah Riley-Manellros Phillips. June 5, 1819. Page 250.
Elijah Gudgell-Lidda Bell. June 5, 1819. Page 250.
James Starks-Dorotha Gordon. Feb. 4, 1819. Page 250.
William Chizor-Elizabeth Ward. Feb. 26, 1819. Page 250.
William Hungate-Nancy White. Mch. 26, 1819. Page 250.
Samuel Comingore-Polly Gill. Apr. 11, 1819. Page 250.
Andrew Nicholds-Sally Martin. Apr. 15, 1819. Page 250.
Linkhorn (Sinkhorn)Henry-Mary Rose. Apr. 15, 1819. Page 250
Abraham Debond-Elleanor Lister. May 8, 1819. Page 250.
Henry H. Smith-Polly Cabbage. July 8, 1819. Page 250.
Garland Sims-Nancy Mason. July 9, 1819. Page 250.
William Green-Judy McKinney. Aug. 9, 1819. Page 250.
Thomas Green-Peggy Davis. Oct. 3, 1819. Page 252.
Jacob Hall-Nancy Thomas. Oct. 12, 1819. Page 252.
Abraham Voris-Polly Davis. Nov. 9, 1819. Page 252.
Bluford Poulter-Polly Yates. Dec. 6, 1819. Page 252.
Lawrence Demott-Mary Davis. Jany. 4, 1820. Page 252.
William Sargeant-Jane Davis Kyle. July 12, 1820. Page 252.
Micajah Hamilton-Elizabeth Lyster. Feb. 17, 1820. Page 252.
Hardin McKinney-Eleanor Cole. Apr. 6, 1820. Page 252.
Wm. McGohon-Polly McCormack. Nov. 23, 1819. Page 252.
Chaffin Brown-Jane Linch (Lynch). Jan. 2, 1820. Page 252.
Thomas Leckman-Polly Skelon. Feb. 7, 1820. Page 252.
William Bilbo-Lucinda Durham. June 5, 1820. Page 252.
James Rogers-Sarah Marshall. Nov. 23, 1820. Page 252.
George W. Masden-Rachel Benn. Feby. 24, 1820. Page 252.
William Blacketer-Betsey Claunch. Jany. 27, 1820. Page 254.
John Sally-Nancy Claunch. Apr. 20, 1820. Page 254.
Thomas Rowland-Elizabeth Alexander. May 9, 1820. Page 254.
Thomas Davis-Polly Henderson. May 23, 1820. Page 254.
John Briles-Elizabeth McGinnis. Sept. 19, 1820. Page 254.
James Blacketer-Susanna Hamilton. Nov. 18, 1820. Page 254.
Matthew Gilkerson-Polly Coleman. Jan. 4, 1820. Page 254.
Francis Kirby-Mary Curry. Jan. 6, 1820. Page 254.
John Jones-Milly Bryant. Jan. 13, 1820. Page 254.
Francis Cochran-Sally Bogart. Jany. 27, 1820. Page 254.
Peter B. Huff-Jerusa Vanarsdall. Feby. 17, 1820. Page 254.
John Jordan-Murillis Breckenridge. March 2, 1820. Page 254.
Jacob List-Elizabeth Wycoff. March 7, 1820. Page 254.
William H. Butler-Lucinda Harmon. June 29, 1820. Page 254.
John Johnson-Charity Rynearson. July 27, 1820. Page 256.

William Milligan-Jane Rynearson. July 27, 1820. Page 256.
Henry Shackelford-Barbhena Lyon. Aug. 24, 1820. Page 256.
Abraham Sharpe-Sally Brewer. Aug. 29, 1820. Page 256.
Peter Dunn-Mary Buchanon. Sept. 19, 1820. Page 256.
Jacob Sharpe-Ann Edwards. Oct. 3, 1820. Page 256.
Joseph M. Michael-Jane McCoun. Oct. 26, 1820. Page 256.
William Harrison-Ann Jane Magoffin. Nov. 8, 1820. Page 256.
Daniel Coovert-Rachel Voorhies. Nov. 16, 1820. Page 256.
Edward S. Slaughter-Susan Armstrong. Dec. 21, 1820. Page 256.
Dyner Downing-Harriet B. Elgin. Dec. 28, 1820. Page 256.
Duff Green-Lucy Creasey. March 3, 1820. Page 256.
John Kent-Betsey Phillips. July 14, 1820. Page 256.
Samuel McCoun-Prechey Jones. Feb. 2, 1820. Page 256.
Nicholas Simms (Sims)-Nicey Jones. May 14, 1820. Page 258.
Joseph Wells-Ann Bull. June 1, 1820. Page 258.
Fleming Bradshaw-Catharine Whitenack. June 15, 1820. Page 258.
George Sinnett-Susan Daviss. June 15, 1820. Page 258.
Henry Ortkies, Jr.-Ruth Ann C. Gill. July 19, 1820. Page 258.
William McCool-Mary Pierce. July 20, 1820. Page 258.
Willis Lee-Sally Cox. Sept. 13, 1820. Page 258.
Alexander McClure-Betsey Lister. Oct. 24, 1820. Page 258.
James Powell-Eleary Wheeler. Oct. 24, 1820. Page 258.
Phillip Gill-Letitia Roy (Ray). Oct. 30, 1820. Page 258.
James Stinnet-Elizabeth Snider. Nov. 18, 1820. Page 258.
Hutchin Williams-Elizabeth Franklin. July 18, 1820. Page 258.
Samuel McGinnis-Polly Nicholds. Aug. 7, 1820. Page 258.
William Pipes-Nancy Gray. Feby. 26, 1820. Page 258.
James Dawson-Lucy Harmond. Oct. 19, 1820. Page 260.
James Rogers-Nancy Flournay. Sept. 14, 1820. Page 260.
Georger Neel-Elizabeth French. Aug. 8, 1820. Page 260.
Thomas Cowley-Elizabeth Moore. April 25, 1820. Page 260.
William Pauling-Elizabeth Cleland. Jany. 20, 1820. Page 260.
Thomas L. Prewitt-Dorka Brown. Jany. 25, 1821. Page 260.
Absolem Quinn-Elizabeth Yager. Jany. 28, 1821. Page 260.
Isaac Vannice-Eleaner Varbrike. Mch. 8, 1821. Page 260.
Turner Hanks-Nancy Holeman. July, 1821. Page 260.
Garret Darland-Edney (?) Daniel. July, 1821. Page 260.
Robert Lyons-Elizabeth Burrus. July, 1821. Page 260.
William Baskett-Lucy Phillips. July, 1821. Page 260.
Eli Penny-Mary Burris. July, 1821. Page 260.
Jonathan Downey-Betsey Hendrickson. July, 1821. Page 260.
William Bunch-Martha Ellis. July, 1821. Page 262.
Robert Locke-Polly Holeman. July, 1821. Page 262.
William Rynolds (Reynolds)-Margaret Abbitt. July, 1821. Page 262.
Henry Vaughter-Jane Jones. July, 1821. Page 262.
Thomas A. Hawkins-Jane Darland. July, 1821. Page 262.
James Leathers-Nancy Yest. July, 1821. Page 262.
Robert Lawrence-Mary Broxdale. Sept. 12, 1821. Page 262.
Joseph Frost-Rachel Butler. Sept. 19, 1821. Page 262.
John Brown-Fanny Barnett. Sept. 20, 1821. Page 262.
Michael Bright-Mariah Thompson. Apr. 18, 1821. Page 262.
John Starky-Rabecca Jones. Apr. 26, 1821. Page 262.
William Carter-Phebe Vanderipe. Sept. 5, 1821. Page 262.
John Semonis-Martha Claunch. Feb. 27, 1821. Page 262.
James Daugherty-Mariah Meaux. Mch. 8, 1821. Page 262.
Mason Owing-Phebe Durham. Mch. 21, 1821. Page 264.
Jonathan H. Royce-Harriet Warren. Apr. 15, 1821. Page 264.
John Gashweiler-Jennetta Gashweiler. Apr. 27, 1821. Page 264.
Robert Hugins-Fanny Gibson. May 8, 1821. Page 264.
George Bessix-Sophia Hitch. May 9, 1821. Page 264.

Sam'l Scott-Betsey Neff. May 1, 1821. **Page 264.**
Amos Kibler-Sally Finch. May 31, 1821. Page 264.
George Bast-Emily H. Kirtner (Curtner). July 2, 1821. Page 264.
William Clemons-July Christison. Sept. 20, 1821. Page 264.
David Kellough-Margaret Bilbo. Sept. 25, 1821. Page 264.
Benj. Speak-Polly Neff. Oct. 9, 1821. Page 264.
Abraham Stagg-Sally Banta. Oct. 11, 1821. Page 264.
William S. Muller-Polly Daugherty. Nov. 12, 1821. Page 264.
John Walker-Tabitha Taylor. Dec. 11, 1821. Page 264.
James Jackson-Catharine Vanderipe. Dec. 24, 1821. Page 266.
Thomas Walker-Nancy Hutchens. Oct. 27, 1821. Page 266.
Jacob Derr-Mary Robertson. Jany. 9, 1821. Page 266.
John Neeley-Emily Gash. Jany. 9, 1821. Page 266.
Charles Ficklin-Jane Rose. Feby. 8, 1821. Page 266.
Clabourne Kinney-Hannah Allen. Mch. 15, 1821. Page 266.
Abraham Vanarsdall-Margaret Davis. Apr. 26, 1821. Page 266.
Cornelius Canine-Sarah Wicoff. May 17, 1821. Page 266.
Sam'l. Dixon-Eliza Smith. July 9, 1821. Page 266.
James Thompson-Nancy McKinney. Aug. 23, 1821. Page 266.
William Mitchell-Rachel Thompson. Sept. 6, 1821. Page 266.
Allen Rains-Rosanna Parker. Sept. 6, 1821. Page 266.
James Mitchell-Elizabeth Hall. Sept. 6, 1821. Page 266.
John C. Stagg-Jane Vanarsdall. Sept. 20, 1821. Page 266.
Abraham Comingore-Lydia Young. Sept. 27, 1821. Page 268.
Simon Vanarsdall-Catharine Whiteneck. Oct. 4, 1821. Page 268.
Samuel McGinnis-Margaret McGinnis. Oct. 4, 1821. Page 268.
Wiley Shaw-Sally Reland. Dec. 6, 1821. Page 268.
Jonah Marshall Abraham-Jane Simens. Dec. 18, 1821. Page 268.
John Russell-Polly J. Daugherty. Dec. 30, 1821. Page 268.
Uel Sanford-Fanny Threlkeld. Jan. 3, 1822. Page 268.
William Withrow-Nancy Little. Feb. 5, 1822. Page 268.
Cornelius Vermillion-Elizabeth Sanford. Mch. 20, 1821. Page 268.
Josiah Simpson-Polly Gashweiler. Nov. 6, 1821. Page 268.
Frederick R. Shaw-Nelly Coovert. Jan. 1, 1821. Page 268.
Thos. Henderson-Mary Demott. Jany. 2, 1821. Page 268.
Peter Cozatt-Nancy Tewmey. Jany. 1, 1821. Page 268.
David Board-Mary Low (Law). Feby. 1, 1821. Page 268.
Abraham Smith-Milly Ray. Feby. 22, 1821. Page 270.
William Terhune-Ann Sortor (Sorter). Apr. 2, 1821. Page 270.
John Hale-Louisanna Badger. Apr. 2, 1821. Page 270.
Nathaniel Randolph-Rachel Banta (Bonta). Apr. 12, 1821. Page
270.
James Robertson-Dianna Sorter. May 29, 1821. Page 270.
John Powell-Mary Thompson. June 24, 1821. Page 270.
Absolem Kelly-Margaret Ryan. June 21, 1821. Page 270.
Warren Davis-Nancy Page. July 19, 1821. Page 270.
Samuel Hemphill-Mary McCaslin. Jan. 5, 1821. Page 270.
Alexander Gilmon-Jane Vandivere. Sept. 19, 1821. Page 270.
Jefferson D. Jones-Elender Tracy. Sept. 20, 1821. Page 270.
David Young-Mary Coffman. Sept. 27, 1821. Page 270.
Thomas Moore-Anne Sorter. Oct. 25, 1821. Page 270.
William Richardson-Elizabeth Moore. Oct. 21, 1821. Page 270.
John Quigley-Polly Thickston. Nov. 27, 1821. Page 272.
Samuel Rinearson-Catharine Bice. 1822. Page 272.
Samuel Thurman-Elizabeth Richardson. Jany. 17, 1822. Page 272.
Thomas Snider-Nelly Lyster. June 13, 1822. Page 272.
Robert Gordon-Priscille Henderson. Aug. 15, 1822. Page 272.
John Wilson-Mary Roland. Sep. 5, 1822. Page 272.
Andrew Devine-Margaret Downey. Oct. 10, 1822. Page 272.
Starling Carver-Jane Durham. Jan. 17, 1822. Page 272.
Wilson Tharpe-Levicey Bolling. Jan. 30, 1822. **Page 272.**

Henry Sparrow-Ailsey Smith. Feb. 19, 1822. Page 272.
Eli Hart-Casandra J. C. Flournoy. Nov. 30, 1821. Page 272.
Richard D. Bradshaw-Susan Ellis. Feb. 7, 1822. Page 272.
John Woods-Eliza Starns. Feb. 27, 1822. Page 272.
William Ransdell-Hanna Vanarsdell. Feb. 27, 1822. Page 272.
James Cochran-Elizabeth Lyon. Mch. 12, 1822. Page 274.
Aaron Alexander-Nancy McMurtrie. Mch. 27, 1822. Page 274.
James Curry-Catharine Coile. Mch. 28, 1822. Page 274.
John M. C. Irvin-Martha Nourse. Apr. 2, 1822. Page 274.
Joseph Bybee-Elizabeth Rone. Apr. 4, 1822. Page 274.
Wesley Trower-Elizabeth Jones. May 14, 1822. Page 274.
William Crawford-Jane Vandike. July 25, 1822. Page 274.
Isaac Vorhies-Polly Parker. Aug. 22, 1822. Page 274.
James McMichael-Nancy Boston. Sept. 12, 1822. Page 274.
John J. Allin-Cynthia McAfee. Oct. 16, 1822. Page 274.
John Curry-Liney Smock. Oct. 17, 1822. Page 274.
William McKitrick-Betsey McCoun. Oct. 24, 1822. Page 274.
John Vandivier-Catharine Vanarsdall. Nov. 21, 1822. Page 274.
Jacob Rickenbaugh-Nancy McKamey. Dec. 4, 1822. Page 274.
James Turner-Rebecca B. Dean. Oct. 5, 1822. Page 276.
Samuel McAfee-Martha A. Curry. Oct. 5, 1822. Page 276.
Tapley H. Dye-Mary Ann Sanders. Dec. 27, 1822. Page 276.
William Keys-Rebecca Noel. Feb. 21, 1822. Page 276.
George Bailey-Elizabeth Beadles. May 18, 1822. Page 276.
Stephen Fields-Lucy Knuckles. Apr. 16, 1822. Page 276.
James Jones-Judy Cox. May 27, 1822. Page 276.
George Moore-Rebecca Sanders. Sept. 12, 1822. Page 276.
Liberty Noel-Ann Hamner. Nov. 19, 1822. Page 276.
Cornelius Vannoy-Jane Greenwood. Dec. 14, 1822. Page 276.
John Bottom, Jr.-Mahala Sanders. Jan. 2, 1823. Page 276.
Yelvington Atkins-Elizabeth Maxe. Dec. 18, 1821. Page 276.
John Rutherford-Judy Riley. Dec. 22, 1821. Page 276.
Daniel McGumrick-Dircas Burks. Jan. 8, 1822. Page 276.
William Goodlet-Câtharine Clarke. Mch. 21, 1822. Page 278.
Allen Davenport-Drucilla Burks. Mch. 28, 1822. Page 278.
Frederick Brown-Eady Riley. Aug. 8, 1822. Page 278.
James Curry-Nelly Boats. Dec. 5, 1822. Page 278.
Henry Rodes-Elizabeth Springate. Dec. 12, 1822. Page 278.
James Green-Elizabeth Durham. Feb. 28, 1822. Page 278.
Francis Mahan-Nancy Clark. Mch. 6, 1822. Page 278.
John Knox-Martha Durham. Mch. 21, 1822. Page 278.
John Harlan-Clarissa Black. Mch. 26, 1822. Page 278.
Washington Latimore-Jane Walker. May 28, 1822. Page 278.
William Sarvent-Leah Hope. June 18, 1822. Page 278.
John Jolly-Kitty Blackstone. June 27, 1822. Page 278.
Anthony Johnston-Priscilla May. Sept. 10, 1822. Page 278.
Robert Knox-Elizabeth Durham. Nov. 21, 1822. Page 278.
Alexander Sinkhorn-Nancy Taylor. Mch. 21, 1822. Page 280.
Cleaton Taylor-Martha Sinkhorn. Feb. 26, 1822. Page 280.
Robert Low-Jerusha Brewer. Mch. 18, 1822. Page 280.
James Terhune-Barthena Pancake. Jany. 11, 1823. Page 280.
William Young-Elizabeth Hall. May 18, 1820. Page 280.
Jacob Cox-Rachel Hawkins. May 16, 1820. Page 280.
John L. D. Smedley-Patsey Letcher. Apr. 21, 1820. Page 280.
John Wadle-Nancy Stagden. Apr. 6, 1820. Page 280.
Benjamin Ransdell-Sally Higgin. Jan. 20, 1820. Page 280.
Robert Right-Sally Dean. Aug. 31, 1820. Page 280.
John A. Grabbs-Nancy Moore. June 15, 1820. Page 280.
Segistmund (?) Scott-Nancy Thompson. Oct. 23, 1820. Page 280.
Christopher Graham-Theresa Sutton. Oct. 8, 1820. Page 280.
Elijah Thompson-Diana Dean. Nov. 23, 1820. Page 280.

Allin Richards-Rachel Mainard. Nov. 26, 1820. Page 282.
Patterson Elder-Frances Elder. Dec. 4, 1820. Page 282.
Lendon (Nowel)-Lucy Miller. Feb. 8, 1821. Page 282.
George Boyd-Theresa Starke. Apr. 18, 1821. Page 282.
John L. D. Vanarsdall-Lancy Bonta. Apr. 19, 1821. Page 282.
Levi Herndon-Lelinda Passmore. Aug. 9, 1821. Page 282.
Solomon Ryan-Elizabeth Stap. Jan. 17, 1822. Page 282.
Larkin Casey-Elizabeth Gill. May 29, 1822. Page 282.
Hiram Smith-Drucilla Moore. June 27, 1822. Page 282.
Lewis Shepherd-Nancy Price. Nov. 10, 1822. Page 282.
Brice Bradshaw-Elizabeth West. Nov. 12, 1822. Page 282.
Asher Laberton-Elizabeth Denny. Nov. 19, 1822. Page 282.
Noah Hayden-Unity Patterson. Dec. 12, 1822. Page 282.
William Shearley-Rhoda Evans. Dec. 31, 1822. Page 282.
John Bogart-Polly Gritton. Oct. 25, 1822. Page 284.
Charles C. Gray-Marther Cammack. Dec. 7, 1819. Page 284.
Asher Laberton-Barsheba Brocaw. Dec. 30, 1819. Page 284.
Uriah Ashby-Sally Spounomer. Nov. 25, 1822. Page 284.
James S. Currens-Elizabeth Lickester. May 16, 1822. Page 284.
John Abbott-Mary Ann Runnels. May 8, 1822. Page 284.
William Abbott-Nancy Sutherland. July 11, 1822. Page 284.
David P. Nelson-Eliza Slaughter. Aug. 12, 1822. Page 284.
Elias D. Lawrence-Mary Ann P. Frey. Aug. 14, 1822. Page 284.
John Cecil-Lucinda Jones. July 5, 1822. Page 284.
Joseph Alexander-Nancy Steele. June 22, 1823. Page 284.
Wm. C. Clark-Mary J. Bradshaw. July 17, 1823. Page 284.
John W. Hayden-Mary Ann Cary. Oct. 9, 1823. Page 284.
Thos. W. Conder-Nancy Whittinghill. Oct. 30, 1823. Page 284.
John Taylor-Louisa Mason. Nov. 27, 1823. Page 286.
Edmund Ellexander-Eliza Phillips. July, 1823. Page 286.
James Griffin-Moran Phillips. July, 1823. Page 286.
Wm. Jones-Elizabeth B. Lillard. July, 1823. Page 286.
Jacob Kennedy-Isabella Coombs. July, 1823. Page 286.
Edward Baber-Sally Dority. Jany. 27, 1823. Page 286.
John Beard-Elizabeth Neff. Jany. 16, 1823. Page 286.
James Butler-An Jackman. Mch. 6, 1823. Page 286.
Troy Daviess-Nancy Prewitt. Mch. 18, 1823. Page 286.
Ephraim Stout-Jacey Buckley. Mch. 18, 1823. Page 286.
Bennett Bull-Louisa Harper. Apr. 17, 1823. Page 286.
Adam Coulter-Sally Jones. May 20, 1823. Page 286.
Wm. Bennington-Tabitha Whooberry. Aug. 21, 1823. Page 286.
Joel Yates-Harriet Owings. Oct. 15, 1823. Page 286.
Baker T. Ewing-Sarah M. Durham. Nov. 13, 1823. Page 288.
George Brown-Sarah Cole. Nov. 27, 1823. Page 288.
Thomas Pitman-Eliza Hanes. Dec. 21, 1823. Page 288.
Peter T. Conover-Jemima ————. Jan. 8, 1823. Page 288.
John Adams-Elizabeth Sharpe. Jan. 30, 1823. Page 288.
Bales Freeman-Mary Freeman. Feb. 4, 1823. Page 288.
Harrison Ransdell-Mary Vanarsdall. Feb. 6, 1823. Page 288.
William Wicoff-Sally Smock. Feb. 6, 1823. Page 288.
Robt. Forsythe-Kezziah Cardwell. Feb. 20, 1823. Page 288.
Allen Raines-Margaret Whiteneck. Mch. 6, 1823. Page 288.
Henry Miller-Margaret Sharpe. Apr. 10, 1823. Page 288.
Joseph Vorhies-Jane Covart. Apr. 15, 1823. Page 288.
Landy Briner-Polly Phonys. June 2, 1823. Page 288.
Abraham McMordie-Jane H. Armstrong. June 17, 1823. Page 288.
John R. Carver-Jemimah W. Horine. Aug. 5, 1823. Page 290.
Squire Carr-Betsey Johnson. Aug. 2, 1823. Page 290.
Luster T. Brown-Nancy Overstreet. Aug. 19, 1823. Page 290.
Armstead Miller-Polly Breckenridge. Aug. 26, 1823. Page 290.
Daniel Vanarsdall-Leah Stagg. Sept. 18, 1823. Page 290.

Peter Vandivier-Elizabeth Traney. Oct. 1, 1823. Page 290.
Anthony Cardwell-Patsey Sanford. Oct. 1, 1823. Page 290.
William Smithey-Martha Cardwell. Oct. 1, 1823. Page 290.
William Terhune-Charlotte Tewmey. Nov. 6, 1823. Page 290.
Cornelius Smock-Elizabeth Adams. Nov. 6, 1823. Page 290.
William Scott-Betsey Livingston. Dec. 18, 1823. Page 290.
Isaac Wilham-Catharine Threlkeld. Dec. 18, 1823. Page 290.
Andrew Mann-Sally Smock. Dec. 18, 1823. Page 290.
Samuel Reed-Betsey Riglett. Dec. 25, 1823. Page 290.
Presley Rogers-Elizabeth Foley. July 6, 1823. Page 292.
Joseph Green-Christiana Ryan. Oct. 21, 1823. Page 292.
John Robertson-Fanny Prewitt. Jany. 30, 1823. Page 292.
Hiram Kenley-Patsey Gray. April 4, 1823. Page 292.
Aaron Overstreet-Susan Brumfield. May 29, 1823. Page 292.
William T. Shelton-Elizabeth Jones. Oct. 7, 1823. Page 292.
William Webster-Lucy Gray. Nov. 27, 1823. Page 292.
William Thomas-Elizabeth Christison. Dec. 4, 1823. Page 292.
Willson Green————— Hutchings. Dec. 23, 1823. Page 292.
John C. Walls-Malinda Fields. Sep. 14, 1823. Page 292.
William Wilson-Sarah McGinnis. Nov. 27, 1823. Page 292.
Burkley Overstreet-Nancy Brumfield. Oct. 25, 1823. Page 292.
William S. Minor-Elizabeth Hammond. Nov. 20, 1823. Page 292.
Hollington B. Hebb-Lucia Dawson. Jany. 24, 1823. Page 292.
Thomas Collins-Harriet Alsop. Jan. 26, 1824. Page 294.
Charles Caldwell-Elizabeth Clemons. Aug. 28, 1823. Page 294.
Charles Barnett-Betsey Maddox. Dec. 28, 1823. Page 294.
William Bowman-Elizabeth Scomerhorn. Mch. 10, 1824. Page 294.
James Crews-Magdelen Jordan. Mch. 28, 1824. Page 294.
James Freeman-Sally Carr. June 8, 1823. Page 294.
Josiah Meredith-Sarah Slake. Aug. 12, 1823. Page 294.
David Outs-Eliza Johnson. July 28, 1823. Page 294.
John Leayree-Margaret Garrs. July 28, 1823. Page 294.
Jesse Simpson-Jane Culton. Nov. 9, 1823. Page 294.
Moses Beel-Susan Beel. July 11, 1823. Page 294.
John Barnes-Elsira Gill. Mch. 21, 1823. Page 294.
Wesley Craig-Nancy Wheat. May 31, 1823. Page 294.
James Barnes-Susan Miskel. April 3, 1823. Page 294.
John Hiatte-Sally McCarster. Sept. 15, 1823. Page 296.
Joel Nowland-Nancy Moore. Oct. 5, 1823. Page 296.
Job Sharp-Elizabeth Graham. Dec. 2, 1823. Page 296.
Martin Nichols-Susan Thompson. Jany. 1, 1824. Page 296.
Frederick R. Braxdell-Susanna B. Prewitt. Dec. 9, 1823. Page 296.
Frederick Law-Rebecca Demott. Feb. 5, 1824. Page 296.
Joseph Lyster-Susanna Lyster. Mch. 15, 1824. Page 296.
Milton Jameson-Nancy Ann Lecht. Aug. 26, 1824. Page 296.
Davis Petty-Sarah Douglass. Dec. 4, 1823. Page 296.
Daniel Moore-Hannah Kinsay. Oct. 14, 1823. Page 296.
Alexander Broys-Charlotte Gibson. Dec. 23, 1823. Page 296.
Joseph Yonce-Anne Davenporte. Dec. 23, 1823. Page 296.
John B. Fouchee-Sarah Broyles. Dec. 24, 1823. Page 296.
Roberson Seamon-Rebecca Brown. Jany. 15. Page 296.
Elijah Peck-Elizabeth Prewitt. Jany. 25, 1824. Page 298.
William Gates-Betsey Vermillion. Apr. 6, 1824. Page 298.
Charles Hale-Margaret Buchannan. May 29, 1824. Page 298.
John Watts-Lydia Boathe. June 20, 1824. Page 298.
Argales Pancake-Palsey May. June 23, 1824. Page 298.
Isaac VanLeet-Elizabeth Miller. June 17, 1824. Page 298.
William Compton-Sarah Broxdel. June 24, 1824. Page 298.
Elias Hale-Polly Plue. July 15, 1824. Page 298.
Albert Banta-Polly Wigham. July 22, 1824. Page 298.
Josiah Bass-Elizabeth Moore. Aug. 21, 1824. Page 298.

Daniel Cassall-Elizabeth Tewmey. May 23, 1824. Page 298.
Simon Hamilton-Anny Huff. Aug. 21, 1824. Page 298.
James P. Allin-Jane Glazebrook. Sept. 28, 1824. Page 298.
Benjamin Bradshaw-Nancy Bailey. Oct. 6, 1824. Page 300.
Jeremiah Wade-Nancy Compton. Feby. 10, 1824. Page 300.
Benjamin Viles-Sarah Powell. Feb. 19, 1824. Page 300.
William Bottom-Rebecca Latimer. Aug. 5, 1824. Page 300.
Charles Gray-Nancy Caton. Aug. 5, 1824. Page 390.
James Caldwell-Phebe Henderson. July 22, 1824. Page 300.
Richard Crump-Elizabeth Gutherie. May 27, 1824. Page 300.
James F. Harberson-Martha C. Hall. Jan. 29, 1824. Page 300.
John Webster-Charlotte Rains. Mch. 9, 1824. Page 300.
James Blacketer-Phebe Romine. Jan. 3, 1824. Page 300.
Nelson Prewitt-Lourinda S. Caton. Feby. 3, 1824. Page 300.
Henry Forehead(hand)-Harriett Helms. Aug. 27, 1824. Page 300.
John Allgood-Martha Davis. Dec. 9, 1824. Page 300.
Edmond Holland-Drucilla Martin (Morton). Aug. 19, 1824. Page 300.

Solomon Kays-Nancy Noel. Mch. 3, 1824. Page 302.
Reuben Peter-Lydia Turner. July 15, 1824. Page 302.
James Ellison-Eleanor Poulter. Jan. 1, 1824. Page 302.
Madison S. Worthington-Mary T. A. Worthington. Jan. 13, 1824. Page 302.
William Demott-Mary Vanhice. Feby. 18, 1824. Page 302.
Walter Bohon-Martha Jones. Feby. 19, 1824. Page 302.
Alexander Wilson-Catharine Allison. Mch. 18, 1824. Page 302.
Thomas Crawford-Sarah Sharpe. July 13, 1824. Page 302.
Samuel Brewer-Eleanor Smock. Aug. 24, 1824. Page 302.
William Lewis-Milly Wright (Right). Aug. 26, 1824. Page 302.
James H. Davis-Caroline C. Haggin. Sept. 7, 1824. Page 302.
William Pawling-Catharine M. Bridges. Oct. 5, 1824. Page 302.
John Smithey-Margaret Woods. Oct. 7, 1824. Page 302.
Abram B. Voorhies-Polly Voorhies. Nov. 4, 1824. Page 302.
William Stagg-Sally Keller. Nov. 25, 1824. Page 304.
Cornelius Vanhice-Ann Adams. Dec. 16, 1824. Page 304.
Robert Scott-Isabella Craig. Jan. 8, 1825. Page 304.
Thomas Prewitt-Catharine Buckle. Aug. 12, 1825. Page 304.
Ruliff Terhune-Polly Vermillion. Aug. 26, 1824. Page 304.
Thomas Utley-Sally Vanarsdall. Aug. 26, 1824. Page 304.
James Ison-Nancy Keen. Sept. 2, 1824. Page 304.
James May-Polly Vanarsdall. Sept. 25, 1824. Page 304.
Jefferson McGinnis-Elizabeth B. May. Sept. 26, 1824. Page 304.
Noel Arnold-America Noel. Oct. 21, 1824. Page 304.
William Vannoy-Celia Peck. Oct. 28, 1824. Page 304.
Custas Bowman-Rebecca Sparrow. July 30, 1824. Page 304.
John Sparrow-Peggy Davis. May 30, 1824. Page 304.
Sam'l Davis-Mary Ann Niping. Jany. 6, 1825. Page 304.
Micajah Pendleton-Emily Flourney. Jany. 8, 1824. Page 306.
Benjamin Crowe-Eliza Rogers. Nov. 24, 1824. Page 306.
Nathan Lawson-Peggy Divine. Feby. 28, 1824. Page 306.
Elijah Gabbert-Malinda Divine. Nov. 18, 1824. Page 306.
Thomas Bunton-Elizabeth McCarty. Feby. 13, 1824. Page 306.
John Downey-Nancy Wingate. Dec. 22, 1824. Page 306.
Robert Knuckles-Rachael Martin. Feby 26, 1824. Page 306.
John C. Martin-Ann Drues. May 15, 1825. Page 306.
Matthew O'Brien-Elizabeth Cochran. Feby. 11, 1825. Page 306.
John Boice-Elizabeth Light. March 8, 1825. Page 306.
Thomas S. Daniels-Martha Robinson. May 29, 1825. Page 306.
Francis Clark-Nancy Walker. Sept. 2, 1824. Page 306.
James Settles-Elizabeth Riley. July 1, 1824. Page 306.
William Cunningham-Nancy Dawson. Apr. 20, 1824. Page 306.

Thomas F. Crutchfield-F. M. Lampton. Oct. 17, 1824. Page 308.
Archibald Moss-Lucy Boston. Nov. 11, 1824. Page 308.
Thomas Williams-Mary Williams. Nov. 25, 1824. Page 308.
Nathan Hawkins-Margaret Burns. Dec. 7, 1824. Page 308.
William Patterson-Martha Bell. March 10, 1825. Page 308.
Isaac Westerfield-Elizabeth Mahan. Feby. 6, 1825. Page 308.
William Higgins-Lucinda Gibson. Feby. 3, 1825. Page 308.
Jermiah Hamilton-Ammy Lister. June 2, 1825. Page 308.
Joseph Rice-Nancy McGraw. Jan. 2, 1824. Page 308.
Hawkins Pophan-Sarah Curry. June 27, 1824. Page 308.
Cornel Dernott-Barbra Holt. Oct. 14, 1824. Page 308.
John Black-Christina Harlow. Dec. 21, 1824. Page 308.
Tho. Richardson-Mary Clark. Apr. 24, 1825. Page 308.
Isaac Vanarsdall-Elizabeth Casady. March 17, 1825. Page 308.
Ashby Lillard-Rebecca Lay. Sept. 21, 1825. Page 310.
William Trimble-Mary Green. Nov. 1, 1825. Page 310.
William Mosby-Lucinda Parks. Feby. 10, 1825. Page 310.
Stephen May-Malinda Harper. Apr. 7, 1825. Page 310.
Jacob Whooberry-Mary Claunch. June 20, 1825. Page 310.
Sam'l Cox-Ellen Brown. Oct. 25, 1825. Page 310.
Foster L. Webb-Martha Bilbo. Jany. 27, 1825. Page 310.
Frederick Algood-Jane Wigham. Mch. 13, 1825. Page 310.
Jacob Spears-Martha B. Mitchell. Nov. 30, 1825. Page 310.
Morris Pipes-Sally Montgomery. Mch. 31, 1825. Page 310.
Edmond Murry-Dianah Hoskins (Hopkins). Mch. 21, 1825. Page 310.
Washington Willard-Margaret Mullins. May 22, 1825. Page 310.
William Laws-Elizabeth Whooberry. Dec. 22, 1825. Page 310.
Rabsdell Poulter-Elizabeth Gritton. Nov. 13, 1825. Page 312.
James Vandivier-Barbara Cannary. Feby. 12, 1825. Page 312.
Charles Gallager-Martha Brown. Feby. 19, 1824. Page 312.
William McIntire-Sarah Gabhart. Mch. 25, 1824. Page 312.
John Smith-Sally Morton. May 19, 1824. Page 312.
George Hays-Casandra Horine. Dec. 9, 1824. Page 312.
Richard Brown-Martha Bingham. Jan. 2, 1824. Page 312.
Henry King-Levina Spencer. Aug. 12, 1824. Page 312.
Isaac Silcox-Margaret Vanfleet. Sept. 9, 1824. Page 312.
Phillip Gabhert-Polly Bowman. Oct. 7, 1824. Page 312.
Isaac Vanarsdall-Nancy Smock. Oct. 14, 1824. Page 312.
Michael Gabhart-Elizabeth Cannon. Dec. 1, 1824. Page 312.
Jacob Bice-Jane Vanarsdall. Dec. 14, 1824. Page 312.
Peter Vanarsdall-Ann Vanarsdall. Dec. 30, 1824. Page 312.
Nicholas Wycoff-Anna Comingore. Jany. 13, 1825. Page 312.
Marshall Gibson-Phoebe Clemmons. Feb. 9, 1825. Page 314.
Christopher Jones-Lucy May. Feby. 22, 1825. Page 314.
Peter Higgins-Margaret Dean. Mch. 8, 1825. Page 314.
Lewis Hamilton-Malinda Haden. Mch. 24, 1825. Page 314.
James Haden-Ellen Wright. Mch. 24, 1825. Page 314.
Peter Vanarsdall-Mariah Cunningham. Mch. 31, 1825. Page 314.
William Patterson-Elizabeth Devine. Apr. 5, 1825. Page 314.
Charles Sallee-Nancy Thickston. Apr. 13, 1825. Page 314.
James Lyon-Malinda Sorter. May 12, 1825. Page 314.
William Gray-Elizabeth Stewart. Aug. 7, 1825. Page 314.
John Chancellor-Polly Thomas. Sept. 22, 1825. Page 314.
Phillip Keller-Betsey Ryan. Nov. 1st, 1825. Page 314.
Peter Patterson-Caltha Evans. Dec. 21, 1825. Page 314.
Jeremiah Raines-Frances Guthrie. Jan. 6, 1825. Page 316.
James Knox-Casanora Walker. Jan. 13, 1825. Page 316.
John Potts-Catharine Baker. Feb. 1, 1825. Page 316.
Phillip Walker-Patsey Henry. Feb. 3, 1825. Page 316.
James M. Carty-Nancy Bennington. Apr. 21, 1825. Page 316.
Edmond Kindoll-Dorothy Pittman. Feb. 8, 1825. Page 316.

Enoch Harley-Millie Corby. Apr. 28, 1825. Page 316.
John C. Vanarsdall-Mary Westerfield. May 5, 1825. Page 316.
John Lyster———— Cannon. July 7, 1825. Page 316.
Frederick B. Powell-Betsey Clarkson. Aug. 14, 1825. Page 316.
Hansen Rush-Margaret Lout. Oct. 14, 1825. Page 316.
Frederick Braxdell-Elizabeth Slaughter. Oct. 11, 1825. Page 316.
Rodney Combs-Elizabeth Burton. Oct. 21, 1825. Page 316.
John Neff-Elizabeth Kenton. Nov. 10, 1825. Page 316.
Soloman Green-Mary Ann Randolph. Nov. 24, 1825. Page 314.
Thos. Bottom-Elizabeth Drew. Oct. 21, 1825. Page 318.
William Jones-Nancy Alexander. Nov. 5, 1825. Page 318.
Francis Wayland-Janie Black. Apr. 7, 1825. Page 318.
Phillip Penny-Margaret Burrus. Jan. 2, 1825. Page 318.
George Alexander-Kitty Phillips. Sept. 20, 1825. Page 318.
Luke Lillard-Elizabeth Hawkins. July 27, 1825. Page 318.
James Caldwell-Margaret Yowell. Sept. 28, 1825. Page 318.
John B. Bell-Phoebe Durr. Dec. 8th, 1825. Page 318.
John Robertson-Nancy Gray. Dec. 20, 1825. Page 318.
William H. Phillips-Elizabeth Jordon. Dec. 27, 1825. Page 318.
John Nevins-Margaret Reynolds. Jan. 1st, 1826. Page 318.
Isaac Cunninghan-Hester H. Right. Jan. 8th, 1826. Page 318.
David Outs-Nancy Downey. Apr. 5th, 1826. Page 318.
Thos. D. Ball-Levina Debaun. Jan. 20, 1826. Page 318.
George W. Sanford-Tilly Bohon. Feb. 10, 1825. Page 320.
John Sullivan-May Hite. Apr. 28, 1825. Page 320.
James Westerfield-Ludisha Shields. June 16, 1825. Page 320.
Isaac Voris-Rachel Whitenack. July 21, 1825. Page 320.
Ephrian J. Wilson-Mary Bright. Aug. 10, 1825. Page 320.
Lewis Rose-Flora Vouhice. Aug. 11, 1825. Page 320.
Henry Smock-Mary McKarney. Aug. 10, 1825. Page 320.
Henry C. Whitenack-Mary Dunn. Aug. 30, 1825. Page 320.
Francis R. Richardson-Sarah McGuffin. Sept. 22, 1825. Page 320.
Elijah H. Burford-Mary McMurtree. Nov. 3, 1825. Page 320.
John McGee-Mary D. Smith. Dec. 15, 1825. Page 320.
David Plough-Dianna Kinsey. Apr. 3, 1826. Page 320.
Beverly Curry-Nancy Cunninghan. Aug. 7, 1825. Page 320.
James Brown-Catharine Cunninghan. Feby. 16, 1826. Page 320.
Cornelius Donavan-Martha Watts. Apr. 13, 1825. Page 320.
Pitman Claudus-Joice Nelson. May 18, 1826. Page 320.
Walker Door-Susan B. Fisher. Mch. 30th, 1826. Page 320.
John Russell-Polly Speaks. Jan. 9, 1826. Page 320.
Sam'l Hale-Eliza Rice. Feby. 9, 1826. Page 320.
John L. Lillard-Nancy Armstrong. Jan. 3, 1826. Page 322.
Isaac Voris-Jane Vanarsdall. Feb. 9, 1826. Page 322.
Kirkham Fallis-Mary Anderson. Feb. 9, 1826. Page 322.
Randal Davis-Peggy Armstrong. Feb. 16, 1826. Page 322.
Lawrence Egbert-Catharine Storm. Feb. 16, 1826. Page 322.
William McCormack-May Parish. Mch. 23, 1826. Page 322.
Thomas J. Brecken-Mary Ann Johnson. May 11, 1826. Page 322.
Cornelius Riker-Ann Davis. May 17, 1826. Page 322.
Lanty Holeman-Jane Brewer. May 10, 1826. Page 322.
Gabriel Ellis-Nancy Jane Logan. June 25, 1826. Page 324.
Weekley Dale-Eliza G. McCoun. Aug. 10, 1826. Page 324.
William C. Parish-Sally Bishop. Sept. 13, 1826. Page 324.
Peter Lagrange-Patsey Ransdell. Sept. 14, 1826. Page 324.
Wm. L. Rowan-Eliza Boyce. Sept. 14, 1826. Page 324.
James Gibson-Polly Allison. Sep. 17, 1826. Page 324.
Lambert Brewer-Sally McAfee. Sep. 26, 1826. Page 324.
William Bogart-Sarah Smithey. Nov. 16, 1826. Page 324.
William L. Cozel-Sarah Brewer. Dec. —, 1826. Page 324.
Samuel Bottom-Mariah Bottom. Jan. 26, 1826. Page 324.

Samuel Lyon-Sally Smith. Jan. 29, 1826. Page 324.
Lee Tucker-Miranda Durham. Feb. 4, 1826. Page 324.
Peter Vandiver-Ann Vanfleet. Feby. 16, 1826. Page 324.
Benjamin Freeman-Polly Watts. Feb. 29, 1826. Page 324.
John Hale-Catharine Dorothy Rice. May 18, 1826. Page 326.
Adam Sharp-Mary Ewing. June 1, 1826. Page 326.
Wm. Servant-Jane Guthery. June 22, 1826. Page 326.
Tho. Sparrow-Sally Smith. Aug. 2, 1826. Page 326.
Jacob Neff-Gabnella Skinner. Aug. 5, 1826. Page 326.
Robert Lowe-Cynthia Jones. Aug. 3, 1826. Page 326.
William Bottom-Elizabeth Odle. Aug. 7, 1826. Page 326.
James W. Jones-Sarah Wingate. Aug. 8, 1826. Page 326.
Michael Robertson-Caty Norton. Sept. 7, 1826. Page 326.
Thomas Hale-Elizabeth Coleman. Sept. 27, 1826. Page 326.
John Thurman-Sarah Whitenack. Nov. 16, 1826. Page 326.
Vardman Smith-Sarah Dismuke. Nov. 16, 1826. Page 326.
Isaac Tewmey-Esther Dotson. Dec. 19, 1826. Page 326.
John J. Sweeney-Mariah Board. Dec. 26, 1826. Page 326.
Banister Taylor-Elizabeth Guthrie. Jan. 27, 1826. Page 328.
Tho. Gash-Eliza Wilson. Nov. 20, 1826. Page 328.
William Owens-Diana Nation. Oct. 15, 1826. Page 328.
James Phillips-Ann Kirkland. Aug. 3, 1826. Page 328.
James C. Minor-Elizabeth Guthrie. Sept. 10, 1826. Page 328.
David Powell-Lucinda Shewmaker. Oct. 24, 1826. Page 328.
Jonathan Stonner-Catharine Yager. Oct. 12, 1826. Page 328.
Atterson Walden-Elizabeth McGinnis. July 5th, 1826. Page 328.
William Duncan-Nancy Goodnight. Oct. 8th, 1826. Page 328.
Enoch Coffman-Sarah Whooberry. March 8th, 1826. Page 328.
Henry Bonta-Dorothy Demott. March 25, 1826. Page 328.
Solomon Trower-Polly Burks. Nov. 9th, 1826. Page 328.
John Woods, Jr.-Sarah Haynes. Nov. 25, 1826. Page 328.
Harvey Lane-Phoebe Pendleton. June 26, 1826. Page 330.
David Young-Mary Ann Eccles. June 16th, 1826. Page 330.
Wm. Hayes-Mary Turner. June 9th, 1826. Page 330.
James Thompson-Abigail Dean. Sept. 14th, 1826. Page 330.
David Divine-Susan H. McDowell. Nov. 15, 1826. Page 330.
Nathaniel Russell-Sarah Cheatham. Sept. 16, 1826. Page 330.
Peter G. Hall-Rebecca Patterson. Jan. 7th, 1826. Page 330.
Alex'r. Shannon-Clarissa Curtrier. Apr. 18, 1827. Page 330.
Michael Sullivan-Sarah McDowell. June 26, 1827. Page 330.
John A. Pitts-Sarah R. McDowell. Sept. 26, 1827. Page 330.
John Meuldlow-Rhoda Wade. Feb. 28, 1827. Page 330.
James Westerfield-Deliah Bennington. June 28, 1827. Page 330.
Robt. Compton-Sarah Little. Feb. 5th, 1827. Page 330.
John Drew-Nancy Jones. Aug. 10, 1827. Page 330.
John A. Jacob-Susan W. E. Powell. Aug. 31, 1827. Page 332.
Roney L. Sallee-Sally Kittinger. Nov. 29, 1827. Page 332.
Nelson Bowles-Elizabeth Anderson. Mch. 10, 1827. Page 332.
James C. Hackney-Elizabeth Neff. Mch. 29, 1826. Page 332.
Covert Vanarsdall-Elizabeth Thompson. July 10, 1826. Page 332.
Archiland Ferril-Nancy Riley. Aug. 29, 1826. Page 332.
Lawrence Egbert-Susanna Slaughter. Nov. 25, 1826. Page 332.
Frederick W. Phillips-Caroline Singleton. Dec. 29, 1826. Page 332.
Rich'd J. Dugan-Catharine Bick. Nov. 21, 1826. Page 332.
Thomas Board-Martha Hart. Feb. 13, 1827. Page 332.
James Meredith-Rosanna Wilhite. July 12, 1827. Page 332.
John Powell-Polly Martin. May 26, 1826. Page 332.
William Ford-Mahala Kelly. May 4, 1826. Page 332.
Charles Lambert-Pheby Westerfield. Nov. 5, 1828. Page 332.
Jacob Cox-Rachel Hawkins. May 16, 1826. Page 334.
Raphael Terhune-Elizabeth Green. Oct. 5, 1826. Page 334.

152

Uriah Hawkins-Nancy Dean. Aug. 14, 1826. Page 334.
James Cunningham-Hulda Lizenby. Aug. 15, 1826. Page 334.
Hiram Able-Patsey Harlow. Sept. 21, 1826. Page 334.
Samuel Stagg-Margaret Goodknight. Oct. 16, 1827. Page 334.
Augustus Dorn-Ruth Hawkins. Oct. 29, 1827. Page 334.
Isaac Vanarsdall-Lucinda Brown. July 27, 1827. Page 334.
Hiram Gwinn-Polly Pearson. June 9, 1827. Page 334.
William Sutton-Elizabeth Burks. Aug. 16, 1827. Page 334.
Aaron Vandivier-Elizabeth Vanfleet. Apr. 19, 1827. Page 334.
Hiram Collier-Elizabeth Huffman. Sep. 1, 1827. Page 334.
Isaac Brickey-Mariah Rulw. Apr. 28, 1827. Page 334.
William Guthrie-Billy Brown. June 27, 1827. Page 334.
Daniel Sleet-Sarah Dermott. June 27, 1827. Page 336.
Alexander Tilford-Agness Green. Feby. 22, 1827. Page 336.
Martin Bottom-Levice Goodknight. Apr. 5, 1827. Page 336.
Samuel Royalty-Lucinda Hedges. Nov. 22, 1827. Page 336.
William Godfrey-Rosanna Dean. May 1, 1827. Page 336.
Archibald Bonnell-Sally Bonnell. Oct. 9, 1827. Page 336.
Benjamin T. Head-Elizabeth Bohon. Oct. 10, 1827. Page 336.
Michael Yankee-Lyseney Graves. June 4, 1827. Page 336.
William Wigham-Mary May. June 11, 1827. Page 336.
Garland Petty-Sally Cayton. Feby. 1, 1827. Page 336.
Thomas Martin-Mary Powell. Feby. 8, 1827. Page 336.
William Powell-Catharine Sanders. June 29, 1827. Page 336.
John Edmondson-Catharine Lyster. Dec. 4, 1827. Page 336.
Alexander Kirkland-Charity Debaun. Dec. 20, 1827. Page 336.
Joseph Parkinson-Sophia Mitchell. Dec. 25, 1827. Page 338.
Sydney Prewitt-Elizabeth Brown. Dec. 24, 1827. Page 338.
Samuel Berryman-Eleanor H. Ellis. Jany. 18, 1827. Page 338.
William Carr-Anna Cox. Jany. 22, 1827. Page 338.
Davies Mann-Martisha May. Feb. 27, 1827. Page 338.
Adell Ross-Catharine Wilson. June 14, 1827. Page 338.
Cornelius Vanarsdall-Ida Faris. June 19, 1827. Page 338.
James C. Ransdell-Mary Cozine. Aug. 16, 1827. Page 338.
William Mitchell-Mary C. Adams. Oct. 18, 1827. Page 338.
John Brewer-Laura Curry. Nov. 1, 1827. Page 338.
William Buchannan-Phebe A. C. McCoun. Nov. 27, 1827. Page 338.
James Adams-Rebecca Rose. Dec. 4, 1827. Page 338.
William Mardis-Mary Hughes. Nov. 11, 1827. Page 338.
William Wade-Eliza Gilkerson. Dec. 11, 1827. Page 338.
Henry Speirs-Rhoda Johnson. Aug. 3, 1827. Page 340.
James Palmer-Nancy Jefferson. Oct. 31, 1828. Page 340.
David Gabhart-Nancy Niell. Jany. 22, 1828. Page 340.
George Horine-Belloney Murphy. June 20, 1828. Page 340.
Henry Casatt-Susan Gritton. Feby. 28, 1828. Page 340.
James Beasley-Judith Jefferson. Oct. 31, 1828. Page 340.
William B. Buchannan-Mahala Green. Sep. 10, 1828. Page 340.
Solomon Petty-Amelia Mitchell. June 2, 1828. Page 340.
John Brown-Clorinda Cleland. Oct. 7, 1828. Page 340.
Dr. James N. Cocke-Lucy Fry. Sep. 11, 1828. Page 340.
Anslem Minor-Elizabeth Brumfield. July 10, 1828. Page 340.
Jediah Gill-Frances Threkeld. Oct. 23, 1828. Page 340.
William Badget-Janie Hover. Oct. 11, 1828. Page 340.
James Drown-Nancy M. Culton. Sept. 11, 1828. Page 342.
John Conway-Fanny Coffman. Sept. 25, 1828. Page 342.
Jacob Vanarsdall-Emily Rains. May 29, 1828. Page 342.
Joseph Cloyd-Nancy Wilham. Oct. 1, 1828. Page 342.
William Deshazer-Rebecca Cloyd. Oct. 2, 1828. Page 342.
Adam Riley-Avalina Bass. Oct. 30, 1828. Page 342.
Samuel Stevens-Milly Dean. Nov. 18, 1828. Page 342.
James Tolly-Polly Blackgraves. Mar. 11, 1828. Page 342.

Dickson Robins-Ellen Vanarsdall. Sep. 11, 1827. Page 342.
Abram Vanarsdall-Rebecca Bice. Feb. 7, 1827. Page 342.
Eli Crumbough-Eleanor Brumfield. Mar. 4, 1827. Page 342.
Peter C. Venice-Sara Ann Smith. Feb. 14, 1827. Page 342.
Joseph W. Davis-Casanora Hardesty. Apr. 22, 1828. Page 342.
Isham Prewett-Eliza Fletcher. June 22, 1828. Page 342.
Jesse Berryman-Mildred Burks. Jan. 26, 1827. Page 344.
James H. Cleland-Susan Ramsey. June 28, 1827. Page 344.
Thomas Yowell-Millie Barnes. Dec. 26, 1827. Page 344.
Henry Hunt-Delila Minor. Jan. 17, 1828. Page 344.
Gobiel Slaughter-Sarah Burrus. Jan. 23, 1828. Page 344.
George Phillips-Maria Deaman. Mar. 15, 1828. Page 344.
Samuel Lyons-Elizabeth Cunningham. July 31, 1828. Page 344.
Samuel Heirogous-Sarah White. Oct. 7, 1828. Page 344.
Robert Wilson-Catharine Lillyers. July 1, 1828. Page 344.
Stephen Armstrong-Polly Matherford. Aug. 21, 1828. Page 344.
William Sharpe-Elizabeth Mathews. Dec. 4, 1828. Page 344.
Frederick Jones-Elizabeth Chance. Dec. 18, 1828. Page 344.
Robert Armstrong-Martha Watherford. Dec. 23, 1828. Page 344.
James Haines-Nancy McKinney. Apr. 5, 1828. Page 344.
Aaron Rynerson-Elizabeth Lewallin. July 14, 1828. Page 346.
William Wigham-Mary Green. June 26, 1828. Page 346.
Barnabas Withers-Tempy Harlow. Feb. 28, 1828. Page 346.
John Vanfleet-Elizabeth Vanardsall. Oct. 9, 1828. Page 346.
Wm. Jackson-Ann Perry. Oct. 13, 1828. Page 346.
Wm. Monly-Elizabeth Sevier. Oct. 14, 1828. Page 346.
Matthew Slaughter-Catharine Slaughter. Dec. 16, 1828. Page 346.
James Sutherland-Judeth Townsend. Dec. 31, 1828. Page 346.
Isaac Bishop-Rossy Burks. Mar. 23, 1828. Page 346.
Peter Green-Nancy Bristol. Sep. 3, 1827. Page 346.
John B. Frost-Lucinda Ray. Oct. 30, 1827. Page 346.
Tho. Board-Martha Hart. Feb. 13, 1827. Page 346.
Abr. Ripperdon-Margaret Tackman. Aug. 30, 1827. Page 346.
Selets Smith-Elizabeth Brice. Dec. 24, 1828. Page 346.
Uriah P. Randolph-Catharine Sutton. Apr. 2, 1828. Page 348.
William Jackson-Sally Guff. Apr. 3, 1828. Page 348.
John Sallee-May Peavler. July 10, 1828. Page 348.
William Vorbrike-Sarah Holt. Jan. 28, 1828. Page 348.
Philip Kelly-Charity Johnson. Aug. 11, 1828. Page 348.
John Duncan-Mary Cornish. Aug. 13, 1828. Page 348.
George Davis-Elizabeth Parker. Jan. 24, 1828. Page 348.
Malachia Randolph-Sarah Randolph. Mar. 7, 1828. Page 348.
James Walker-Eretta Huffman. July 7, 1828. Page 348.
Berry Gettings-Eleanor Harley. March 5, 1829. Page 348.
John M. Gamble-Margaret Wheeler. June 25, 1829. Page 348.
A. W. Knox-Mary Davis. Apr. 19, 1829. Page 348.
Berry Carter-Margaret Ranes. Sep. 24, 1829. Page 348.
George W. Hurst-Emily Hawkins. Oct. 8, 1829. Page 348.
Abr'm Vanarsdall-Narcissa Blackwood. Oct. 14, 1829. Page 350.
Isaac Terhune-Sarah Vanarsdall. Oct. 15, 1829. Page 350.
Tho. C. Moore-Sarah H. Lillard. Nov. 5, 1829. Page 350.
Charles Green-Elizabeth Stone. Feby. 4, 1829. Page 350.
Berry Wright-Martha Thomas. Feb. 19, 1829. Page 350.
John Stuck-Francis Wigham. Aug. 6, 1829. Page 350.
James Ollaman-Mary Ann Tecengor. June 17, 1829. Page 350.
Michael S. Shuck-Priscilla Irvin. Feby. 12, 1828. Page 350.
George Byers-Mary Miscy. March 14, 1828. Page 350.
Luther Luckett-Ann Jane Harrison. May 22, 1828. Page 350.
Robert C. McKamey-Lucinda Blackwood. May 8, 1828. Page 350.
Abraham D. Irvin-Mary P. Irvin. May 15, 1828. Page 350.
Thomas Dean-Margaret F. Bohon. June 5, 1828. Page 350.

Simon French-Mary Smock. Aug. 12, 1828. Page 350.
Frederick A. Olds-Sarah C. McAfee. Sept. 4, 1828. Page 352.
Jas. Taylor-George Ann Timberlake. Nov. 20, 1828. Page 352.
Peter Whiteneck-Elerina Jane Harris. Nov. 27, 1828. Page 352.
Benj. Robertson-Ann R. Prather. Aug. 20, 1829. Page 352.
George Campbell-Lucy Farris Martin. July 23, 1829. Page 352.
Stith T. Mays-Elizabeth Debaun. Oct. 13, 1829. Page 352.
David Brewer-Rachel Sally. Oct. 2, 1829. Page 352.
Cred T. Wilson-Ann Eliza Marshall. Feby. 8, 1829. Page 352.
Warren Wallace-Mariam M. Lapsley. Feby. 17, 1829. Page 352.
Cornelius Huff-Mary McChord. Apr. 3, 1829. Page 352.
Isaac Brown-Nancy Taylor. Jany. 28, 1829. Page 352.
Francis Wilson-Elizabeth Tyson. Feby. 2, 1829. Page 352.
Fauntleroy D. Greenwood-Martha Suttle. May 17, 1829. Page 352.
Rual (?) Hite-Lucinda Rogers. June 11, 1829. Page 352.
Labon Jones-Rachel A. Walker. May 26, 1829. Page 354.
Banister C. Hankla-Mary Collier. Jany. 29, 1828. Page 354.
Abel Lyons-Elizabeth Carteel. Feby. 3, 1828. Page 354.
Spencer Algood-Nancy Blaketer. Feby. 8, 1828. Page 354.
William W. Warren-Maria S. Speed. Mch. 26, 1828. Page 354.
William Taylor-Virinda Broils. Mch. 14, 1828. Page 354.
William Bull-Rachel Hope. June 19, 1828. Page 354.
Charles Powell-Susan May. Aug. 1, 1828. Page 354.
Robert Sandifer-Harriett Flint. Aug. 19, 1828. Page 354.
Charles Murphy-Susan Coulter. Sept. 11, 1828. Page 354.
John Stull-Mary Jane Davenport. Sept. 16, 1828. Page 354.
Richard Martin-Sarah Davenport. Sept. 18, 1828. Page 354.
William Bottom-Elizabeth Jane Cornwell. Sep. 23, 1828. Page 354.
David Scott-Eleanor Bass. Sep. 28, 1828. Page 354.
Enoch Sevier-Eliza McGinnis. Oct. 16, 1828. Page 356.
John Annis-Lebina Potts. Nov. 25, 1828. Page 356.
Samuel Hocker-Francis Haines. ov. 25, 1828. Page 356.
Thomas Claunch-Lucinda Claunch. Jan. 1, 1829. Page 356.
Alford Wortham-Charlotte Swindler. Jany. 15, 1829. Page 356.
Robert McCoun-Isabella J. Eccles. Jany. 29, 1829. Page 356.
John Wiggs-Nancy Prather. Feb. 26, 1829. Page 356.
Melvin Wheat-Mary Ransdell. May 14, 1829. Page 356.
William Lea-Elizabeth Sharpe. July 14, 1829. Page 356.
William Jenkins-Mary Craig. Oct. 20, 1829. Page 356.
Paul Mullens-Elizabeth Asher. Nov. 10, 1829. Page 356.
Moses Foley-Nancy Brown. Mch. 5, 1829. Page 356.
Washington McGinnis-Lucy Cox. Mch. 9, 1829. Page 356.
Lewis Elliott-Hannah Petty. Sep. 24, 1829. Page 356.
John Neff-Nancy Skinner. Oct. 4, 1829. Page 356.
Jacob Legacer-Sally Pile. Mch. 1, 1830. Page 358.
Felix G. Matheney-Mary E. McCoun. Jany. 13, 1829. Page 358.
Joel Beadles-Thelia B. McGee. Feb. 26, 1829. Page 358.
Thomas J. Thomas-Lucinda Threlkeld. Mch. 25, 1829. Page 358.
Charles R. Rose-Barthena Mitchell. Sep. 6, 1829. Page 358.
Robert L. McAfee-Jane R. Moore. Nov. 3, 1829. Page 358.
James B. Irvin-Lucretia Starnes (Stames). Nov. 5, 1829. Page 358.
John T. Bohon-Polly Threlkeld. Nov. 12, 1829. Page 358.
Joshua Armstrong-Ida Elizabeth Vanarsdall. Nov. 18, 1829. Page 358.

William P. Springate-Amelia Davenport. Dec. 15, 1829. Page 358.
Thomas McClannahan-Maria J. Nourse. Dec. 17, 1829. Page 358.
Joseph Dawson-Adeline Eccles. Dec. 22, 1829. Page 358.
John Vanarsdall-Catharine Terhune. Dec. 3, 1829. Page 358.
William Scott-Patsey Short. Mch. 20, 1829. Page 360.
Isaac Coovert-Lucinda McKinney. Aug. 20, 1829. Page 360.
Isaac Dean-Ruth Lineback. Oct. 13, 1829. Page 360.

Vachel Phillips-Eleaner K. Horine. Dec. 23, 1829. Page 360.
Eyer Askew-Louisa Trower. Oct. 21, 1829. Page 360.
Williamson Mosby-Elizabeth Speed. April 20, 1830. Page 360.
Wm. G. Grisholm-Kitty Ann Pile. Mch. 19, 1830. Page 360.
Alex. McKinzie-Catharine Yeiger. Apr. 20, 1830. Page 360.
Moses Ray-Mary Anderson. Sept. 18, 1828. Page 360.
Henry Banta-Eliza Hungate. July 31, 1828. Page 360.
Jacob Long-Elizabeth Ficklin. Oct. 1st, 1829. Page 360.
Osburn Pendergrass-Lucinda Montgomery. Oct. 1, 1829. Page 360.
Peterson Gibbs-Elizabeth Speak. July 23, 1829. Page 360.
James Bolling-C. M. Hardesty. Nov. 19, 1829. Page 360.
John H. Pitman-Sarah Brumfield. Dec. 31, 1829. Page 362.
Alfred Clubb-Mary Taylor. Apr. 30, 1830. Page 362.
Gabriel S. Caldwell-Lucinda S. Moss. Feb. 4, 1830. Page 362.
John Parr-Elizabeth Compton. Apr. 22, 1830. Page 362.
Thos. Gaunt-Mary Davis. Oct. 1, 1830. Page 362.
Granville Alfred-Martha Ray. Oct. 14, 1830. Page 362.
Harvey Cozine-Mary Ann C. Snider. Mch. 14, 1830. Page 362.
Wm. A. Tyler-Cinderella Holt. Apr. 29, 1830. Page 362.
Robert J. Wilson-Elizabeth Fraiks. June 11, 1830. Page 362.
Wm. Kelley, Jr.-Sally Adkisson. Aug. 12, 1830. Page 362.
Lorenzo D. Farr-Mary Allin. Oct. 24, 1830. Page 362.
Hiram G. Procise-Mary Barnes. Mch. 11, 1830. Page 362.
Thos. Brown-Sally Riley. Nov. 24, 1830. Page 362.
Wm. Reed-Jane Riley. Nov. 24, 1830. Page 362.
Wm. Richardson-Mary Gray. June 2, 1830. Page 364.
Wm. Rains-Elizabeth H. Holt. Aug. 12, 1830. Page 364.
John Neff-Elizabeth Ludwick. Jany. 13, 1831. Page 364.
Wm. Lemon-Averill Bull. Jan. 6, 1831. Page 364.
William Martin-Nancy Neff. Feb. 3, 1831. Page 364.
Shelton Ransdell-Elizabeth Cozine. Jany. 14, 1830. Page 364.
William Chambers-Elizabeth Nourse. Jany. 27, 1830. Page 364.
Wm. McMurtrie-Sarah Maria Vemangan. Feb. 24, 1830. Page 364.
Rice McAfee-Ann Maria Armstrong. Feb. 24, 1830. Page 364.
John C. Cozine-Martha Light. Feb. 25, 1830. Page 364.
Jacob Crow-Mary Crawford. Mch. 1, 1830. Page 364.
William Woods-Jane O. Caldwell. Mch. 11, 1830. Page 364.
James Woods-Priscilla Armstrong. Mch. 25, 1830. Page 364.
Buckner Miller-Comfort D. Worthington. Apr. 13, 1830. Page 364.
Thos. Reed-Elizabeth Parish. Apr. 20, 1830. Page 366.
Stephen Jones-Mary Ann Barclay. Apr. 29, 1830. Page 366.
John Kirkpatrick-Ann Smithey. May 14, 1830. Page 366.
Aaron James-Mary Starnes. June 23, 1830. Page 366.
Jesse Hale-Mary Stagg. July 22, 1830. Page 366.
Jos. Chamberlain-Cynthia B. Roberts. Aug. 5, 1830. Page 366.
John Kemper-Francis A. Daggett. Aug. 11, 1830. Page 366.
John Cardwell-Margaret Ransdell. Sept. 2, 1830. Page 366.
Harvey T. Ray-Eliza A. W. Cozine. Sept. 21, 1830. Page 366.
C. W. Cunningham-Hannah McGoffin. Sept. 21, 1830. Page 366.
Wm. H. Adair-Elizabeth Cromwell. Sept. 28, 1830. Page 366.
Willis Burford-Julia Forsythe. Oct. 21, 1830. Page 366.
Jos.(Jas.) McAfee-Priscilla Ann Armstrong. Oct. 26, 1830. Page 366.
Andrew Forsythe-Narcissa W. McAfee. Oct. 27, 1830. Page 366.
Harvey Cunningham-Rebecca Cardwell. Dec. 2, 1830. Page 368.
Saml. Kennedy-Susan Jordan. Dec. 16, 1830. Page 368.
Greenberry D. Murphey-Susan Boyce. Dec. 16, 1830. Page 368.
Samuel Davis-Elizabeth Banta. Nov. 1, 1830. Page 368.
John T. Fleming-Sally Turner. Feb. 25, 1830. Page 368.
Thomas Moreman- ———— McGinnis. Sept. 9, 1830. Page 368.
James C. Hutton-Jane Badget. Dec. 24, 1829. Page 368.
Eli Peters-Dorothy Demott. Jany. 14, 1830. Page 368.

Lewis C. Raily-Susan Mary Hardin. Aug. 26, 1830. Page 368.
Harvey Adair-Phebe Curry. Aug. 21, 1830. Page 368.
Tho. Bishop-Priscilla Cummins. Nov. —, 1839. Page 368.
Julius Jenkins-Matilda Demaree. Feb. 24, 1830. Page 368.
Saml. Lewis-Nancy Gallagher. July 15, 1830. Page 368.
Obediah Taylor-Nancy Brown. June 8, 1830. Page 368.
George Stewart-Harriet Fletcher. Jany. 3, 1829. Page 370.
Michael Young-Lucinda Goodknight. Oct. 3, 1829. Page 370.
Robt. C. Compton-Agnes Parr. Aug. 29, 1829. Page 370.
John Vandivier-Mary Vanfleet. Dec. 31, 1829. Page 370.
Charles Wright-Catharine Wilham. May 6, 1830. Page 370.
William Dean-Elizabeth Lawson. Nov. 20, 1830. Page 370.
Thos. Patterson-Dorothy Vanfleet. Nov. 11, 1830. Page 370.
William Kelley-Mary Violet. Nov. 14, 1830. Page 370.
Daniel Milburn-Charity Vandivier. Feb. 7, 1830. Page 370.
Wesley Bishop-Lucretia Higgins. Jany. 7, 1830. Page 370.
John Coulter-Lucinda Steel. Jany. 1, 1830. Page 370.
William Cochran-Louisa Lamb. Apr. 8, 1830. Page 370.
Sam Hogue-Pamelia Trower. Mch. 24, 1830. Page 370.
Isaac Pearson-Susan Bush. Mch. 17, 1830. Page 370.
Elisha Low (Lew)-Elizabeth Gallagher. Apr. 8, 1830. Page 372.
John B. Coye-Martha Higgins. Mch. 25, 1830. Page 372.
Elisha Cummins-Mary Ann Bishop. June 16, 1830. Page 372.
Levi Burks-Anny White. July 1, 1830. Page 372.
William Corn-Catharine Talbott. Dec. 2, 1830. Page 372.
Thos. Vaughn-Francis Rains. Nov. 26, 1830. Page 372.
Jordon M. Pope-Jane Romley. June 15, 1830. Page 372.
Lewis Powell-Doshia Herrington. Dec. 8, 1829. Page 372.
John J. Tucker-Jane McCubbin. July 15, 1830.
Henry Blacketer-Dicey Franklin. July 15, 1830. Page 372.
Joshua Eccles-Nancy Smith. Aug. 14, 1830. Page 372.
John Shields-Martha Denny. Dec. 20, 1830. Page 372.
Benj. Cummins-Mildred Asher. Sept. 26, 1830. Page 372.
Saml. E. Burks-Martha E. Magee. Sept. 9, 1830. Page 372.

COPY OF NEWSPAPER ARTICLE, PRINTED IN "SENTINEL-DEMOCRAT," MT. STERLING, KY., MCH. 14, 1929.

Permission given by Mrs. Rezin G. Owings, Ex-State Consulting Registrar Kentucky D. A. R.

"We are publishing below, through the courtesy of Mrs. Rezin Owings and Mrs. W. P. Oldham, a sketch of the life of Rev. John (Raccoon) Smith and the marriages he solemnized in Montgomery and adjoining counties during the years from 1816 to 1852. These records were destroyed when the court house burned in Mt. Sterling and this is the only record now in existence. * * * Rev. John Smith, was born in Sullivan county, Tenn., Oct. 15, 1784. * * * He married Miss Anna Townsend, of Monticello, and after her death in 1814 he came to the Blue Grass. * * * In 1816 he was married to Miss Nancy Hurt, of Wayne county. He was the first pastor of the Spencer, Lulbegrud, North Middletown and Grassy Lick churches for several years. He also helped to organize the Somerset, Sharpsburg and Owingsville churches and was at one time pastor of the Mt. Sterling Christian church. In 1834 he became an evangelist and his services covered nearly every county in Kentucky and parts of Tennessee and Alabama * * * After the death of his wife he spent the remainder of his life with his daughters, Mrs. J. A. J. Lee, in Owingsville, and Mrs. Ringo, in Mexico, Missouri, where he died."

MARRIAGES IN MONTGOMERY COUNTY, KY.

1817—Wm. Clark and Hannah Jones, Nov. 13.; Henry Coons and Nancy Evans, Dec. 4.; James Clark and Susanah Jones, Dec. 18.

1818—James Moreland and Ann Bramill, Jan. 29.; Alexander Kelly and Nancy Rafferty, Feb. 12.; Joseph Smith and Polly Rice, Feb. 19.; John Roberts and Ann Dobbins, Feb. 26.; Henry Woodard and Louisa Heflin, March 12.. Phillip McDaniel and Polly Tapp, March 15.; Nathan Davis and Nancy Kidd, March 19.; David Rice and Polly Cave, March 31.; John Hampton and Sally May, March 31.; Henry Brothers and Patsey Sallee, May 31.; Landy Richardson and Nancy Williams, July 28.; Andrew Crase and Nancy Rogers, Aug. 27.; Hiram Bartlett and Nancy Priest, Sept. 8.; Jonathan McFerrin and Rebecca Harper, Oct. 12.; Robert Allen and Polly Ellison, Oct. 15.; George Thompson and Rachel Crabtree, Oct. 17.; Wm. Bradshaw and Elizabeth Campbell, Oct. 25.; Wm. F. Lucket and Harriett Simson, Oct. 29.; Stephen Eubank and Nancy Burkley, Nov. 4.; Peter Wills and Rebecca Fowler, Nov. 26.; Dillingham Ward and Susan McFerrin, Nov. 26.; Robert Heggins and Fannie Wise, Dec. 3.; Robert Ringo and Sarah Hodge, Sept. 24.; Alexander McDaniel and Priscilla Carington, Dec. 24.

1819—James M. Miller and Polly Wayne, Jan. 1.; John Ficklin and Polly Anderson, Jan. 27.; James Dale and Ann Wills, Feb. 2.; John Moseley and Judith Moseley, Feb. 18.; Glover Smart and Louisiana Mosley, Feb. 18.; Rezin M. Bran and Elizabeth McDaniel, Feb. 25.; John W. Rodgers and Bethsheba Howel, March 7.; Thomas Reids and Margaret Boxley, March 11.; Elias Tolin and Elizabeth Perks, March 21.; Nicholas Harper and Lucy Jameson, daughter of John Jameson, March 30.; John Pritchett and Hannah Pritchett, Apr. 18.; Jesse Kelly and Elizabeth Stringer, Apr. 25.; Isaac Fowler and Caroline Green, Aug. 1.; Wm. Gaitskill and Polly Green, Aug. 5.; Peter Cox and Mary B. Grinstead, Apr. 4.; Henry C. Woolf and Susanah Barnett, Aug. 12.; Benjamin Ayles and Jane Spiller, Aug. 12.; John Trimble and Margaret Turley, Sept. 9.; Benjamin Johnson and Polly Shults, Sept. 12.; Brannoch Phillips and Eliza Wells, Sept. 30.; Wm. Garrett and Polly Reid, Oct. 6.; Wm. Taylor and Lucy Nichols, Dec. 12.; James Scearce and Maria Cluke, Dec. 22.; Elkanah Smith and Frences Botts, Dec. 24.; Wm. Barrow and Goodwin Marshall, daughter of John Marshall, Dec. 25.

1820—Reece Rabourn and Nancy Ridon, Jan. 6.; Harvey Wilson and Betsy Smith, Jan. 20.; John McDonnald and Elizabeth Kemper, Jan. 20.; Westley Arnold and Nancy P. Wool, March 30.; Wm. Vestal and Easter Moore, Apr. 9.; Cuthbert B. Baker and Sally McCarty, Apr. 13.; John Monroe and Matilda Shouse, Apr. 22.; John Kelly and Delia Hays, May 6.; David Casady and Polly Clements, May 18.; Joseph Beaty and Nancy Conley, May 30.; Ruben Redmon and Margaret Ringo, June 1.; Paul Durrett and Gabriella L. Banks, June 1.; Joseph Nelson and Polly Thompson, Sept. 10.; Jesse Yeats and Polly Badger, Sept. 14.; John Nichols and Fannie Moise, Sept. 21.; John F. Mitchell and Enfield Rails, 21.; Thomas Slavens and Lucy Perks, Sept. 26.; Wm. A. Butler and Sally Ringo, Oct. 1.; John Cave and Polly Reely, Oct. 11.; Samuel G. Herndon and Louisa Rankins, Oct. 12.; David Pugh and Sally Castledine, Oct. 19.; Wm. Williams and Polly Blackwell, Oct. 31.; Wm. Davis and Ann Smith, Nov. 2.; Samuel Shortridge and Sarah Yeats, Nov. 5.; Wm. Garrison and Rhoda Linyoir, Nov. 12.; Pentecost Taul and Sally Riggs, Nov. 16.; Wm. Nelson and Sally Smith, Nov. 16.; Gideon Feathering and Elizabeth Sampson, Nov. 16.; Wm. Curl and Dolly Haddon, Nov. 23.; Charles Harrah and Sarah Harrah, Dec. 19.; Henry Rabourn and Lucy Garrett, Dec. 21.; Ellison A. Daniel and Frances Ringo, Dec. 21.

1821—Thomas White and Polly Jones, Jan. 11.; Jepthah Kemper and Nancy Pettet, Jan. 25.; John Anderson and Susannah Darnal, Feb. 8.; Absolom Rice and Eleanor Covington Hensley, Feb. 15.; Lewis Dalton and Matilda Rabourn, Feb. 20.; Robert Stevens and Sarah Ellington, Feb. 25.; Lewis Priest and Fannie Badger, March 8.; George Piercy and Sally Case, March 22.; George Hymore and Ann Smith, March 22.; Joseph Donahew and Rachel McClain, Apr. 12.; John H. Dabney and Eliza Anderson, Apr. 19.; Nathaniel Hanline and Anny Whitset, Apr. 22.; Kinchen Johnson and Jane Harris, Apr. 29.; Andrew Helms and Malinda Wyett, May 3.; Elijah Birch and Marrieta Griffin, May 17.; Anderson Pasley and Jane Scott, July 3.; Isaac Lewis and Nancy Brooks, June 10.; Marcus Hughes and Permelia Fortune, July 24.; Samuel H. Taul and Phebe Frankes, Aug. 23.; Isaac Smith and Malinda White, Sept. 9.; Wm. Darnall and Amelia Darnall, Sept. 16.; Israel Rose and Polly Dixon, Oct. 4.; Charles Nicholas and Rutha Dixon, Oct. 11.; Moore Johnson and Margaret Ringo, Nov. 15.; John Varval and Margaret Phillips, Nov. 22.; James Marrow and Nancy T. Crawford, Dec. 20.; Robert Conley and Mary Ann Campbell, Dec. 27.

1822—Phillip Hathaway and Sarah Williams, Jan. 1.; John Crooks and Peggy Hughart, Jan. 1.; Zachariah Johnson and Delilah Evans, Jan. 3.; Wm. Cave and Martha Martin, Jan. 10.; Oliver Caldwell and Ann Smart, Jan. 10.; John Thompson and Mary Warner, Feb. 7.; Tapley Wilson and Hannah Motley, Feb. 7.; Payton Hall and Betsy Orear, Feb. 28.; Turpin Darnal and Louisa Yeats, March 14.; James Coliver and Nancy Yeats, March 24.; Wm. Perks and Betsy Burk, March 27.; John Cooper and Sarah Motley, Apr. 25.; John William and Nancy Jamison, Apr. 25.; John A. Fortune and America Higgins, May 3.; Henry Jenkins and Rachel Walker, May 30.; Henry Cooper and Matilda Walker, June 6.; John R. Carter and Nancy Jeans, June 13.; Robert Dale and Polly Johnson, July 11.; Joshua Yeats and Nancy Jones, Aug. 22.; Enoch Thompson and Lucinda Gardner, Aug. 29.; Timothy Pagut and Mary Drummons, Sept. 4.; James Jones and Agnes McDaniel, Sept. 5.; Willoughby N. Lane and Betsy Barker, Sept. 5.; Samuel Reese and Elizabeth Strange, Oct. 3.; James McKee and Sally Wilkerson, Oct. 18.; Hayden Wyatt and Polly Kirk, Nov. 21.; Tobias James and Elizabeth Adams, Nov. 28.; Levi Whitsitt and Sally Strange, Dec. 5.; James McClain and Nancy Oakley, Dec. 22.; Robert Sanders and Elizabeth Gilkey, Dec. 22.; Benjamin Davis and Nancy Harper, Dec. 22.

1823—Wm. Downs and Levina Ballard, Jan. 9.; Wm. Coons and Polly Ragan, Jan. 16.; Brice Miller and Betsy Glover, Feb. 16.; Shadrach Runnels and Lucy Riden, Feb. 27.; Elswich Rish and Polly Kitchen, March 6.; Hiram Wilkerson and Elizabeth Hawley, March 9.; Lewis Fortune and Hannah Nickels, Apr. 20.; Joel While and Sallie Evans, June 19.; Isaac Simpson and Poly Howard, June 26.; Ptolemy Wilson and Patsey Roberts, July 10.; Wm. Chiles and Margaret Prather, July 31.; Wm. Fortune and Sally Pickleheimer, Sept. 23.; Wm. Payne and Margaret Wiley, Sept. 25.; Wm. Glover and Nancy Anderson, Oct. 2.; John Schoby and Nancy Dawley, Oct. 14.; Fielding Priest and Nancy Badger, Oct. 23.; Joseph Coliver and Hannah Brothers, Oct. 30.; John Pritchett and Rebecca Myers, Oct. 30.; John Ringo and Elizabeth Rice, Oct. 30.; Robert Wills and Elizabeth Jones, Nov. 4.; Wm. O. Wylie and Jean M .Brother, Nov. 20.; John McDonald and Mrs. Lydia Barnard, Nov. 27.; John Brown and Mary Williams, Dec. 11.; Henry Kente and Mahala Bagby, Dec. 18.; Jesse Orear and Fannie Orear, Dec., 21.; Jacob Maritt and Barbary Cooper, Dec. 28.

1824—Dudley Wells and Ruth Woodard, Jan. 4.; James Hampton and Sidney Clark, Jan. 21.; Morton Davis and Patsy Smart, Jan. 22, Thomas Fletcher and Eliza Ann Thomas, Jan. 29.; John Pritchett and Hannah Myers, Feb. 17.; David Thompson and Lucinda M. Creason, Feb. 17.; Peyton Utterback and Rachel Caldwell, Feb. 26.; Willis West and Nelly Dixon, Feb. 26.; Thomas Ragan and Lucy Jones, March 18.; Benjamin Davis and Polly Martin, March 18.; James Warner and Manervia Thompson, March 25.; Hawley Wilkerson and Patsey McClure, March 28.; John Ford and Mariah McDonald, Apr. 11.; John Means and

Polly Smith, April 20.; Lemuel Francis and Elizabeth Nickle, Apr. 24.; Samuel Chism and Sally Clark, Apr. 24.; Joshua Hart and Betsey Pebworth, June 24.; Richard H. Sandford and Mariah Oden, Aug. 5.; Wm. M. Davis and Sally Howard, Aug. 1.; Zedikiah Davis and Virginia Martin, Sept. 28.; Thomas Snell and Emily Yates, Sept. 30.; Aaron Masterson and Matilda Higgins, Oct. 7.; Richard Clark and Hannah Colliver, Nov. 25.; James Ewing and Jane McCrosky, Dec. 16.; Thomas W. Miller and Frances N. Brother, Dec. 30.

1825—David Riggs and Priscilla Williams, Jan. 13.; David Stuart and Margaret Jameson, Jan. 20.; John Warren and Malinda Chisholm, Jan. 20.; Charles Bivins and Sarah Bittington, Feb. 3.; Walter Ellis and and Cynthia Wells, Feb. 6.; John McIntire and Jane Jones, March 8.; Fielding Fletcher and Elizabeth Sharp, March 15.; Marcus Hughs and Rebecca Hathaway, Apr. 3.; Robert P. B. Caldwell and Eliza Simpson, Apr. 14.; James Simpson and Emma Hathaway, Apr. 28.; Nimrod A. Wilkerson and Mariah Wells, May 29.; John H. Wilson and Nancy Ringo, June 30.; Mathew Jones and Isabella McMillen, July 21.; John White and Asenith Thompson, Sept. 8.; Wm. Ralston and Frances Massee, Sept. 13.; John King and Malinda Tolin, Oct. 19.; Johnson Barnard and Fanny Coliver, Oct. 20.; Wm. Tatman and Lucinda Hunt, Nov. 10.; John McDanold and Elizabeth Kemper, Nov. 22.; Joseph Thomas and Sarah Oden, Dec. 1.; Jesse Fletcher and Nancy Taylor, Dec. 15.

1826—Newton Reed and Evaline Lane, Jan. 26.; Hugh A. Young and Rebecka W. Gillispie, Feb. 15.; Septimess T. Whitman and Lucinda Warner, Feb. 5.; James Butt and Sally Allison, Feb. 16.; Robert A. Gilmore and Nelly Garrett, March 1.; John Young and Amanda Randolph, March 14.; James M. Johnson and Elizabeth Hathaway, March 22.; Jesse M. Shannon and Caroline Hays, Apr. 25; David McKee and Elizabeth Thompson, May 8.; John J. Jewett and Phebe McDannold, May 9.; Wm. A. Carter and Sidney Chisolm, June 29.; Micah Taul and Mary Oden, July 2.; Wm. N. Williams and Judith B. Jameson, Aug. 10.; Moore Johnson and Eliza Marshall, Sept. 28.; Levi Y. Millspaugh and Polly Crawford, Oct. 19.; Asashel Atherton and Rebecca Rice, Oct. 4.; Samuel Pettitt and Susan Coons, Oct. 31.; James D. Fisher and Ann Eliza Rodoker, Dec. 7.; John Leach and Nancy Dale, Dec. 24.

1827—David Cheatam and Polly Garrett, Feb. 1.; Henry Smith and Eliza Hall, March 1.; Samuel Wilson and Nancy Frazer, March 8.; Charles R. Harris and Nancy Moore, March 15.; Thomas Jefferson Ellis and Cassa Wells, March 28.; David A. Thompson and Mary Ann Taul, Apr. 5.; John C. McMeniway and Eliza Phillips, Apr. 26.; Bryan Maher and Juliett Thomas, May 15.; Francis Aldridge and Polly Harper, May 24.; James D. Ballard and Lucinda Ringo, May 24.; James H. Lane and Sally Jameson, June 3.; Johnston Darnal and Martha Ann Yeates, June 14.; John Miller and Delilah Hathaway, June 15.; Alexander Williams and Mariah D. Fawkner, July 22.; Benjamin Hedger and Matilda Loid, Sept. 5.; James Smith and Elizabeth Smith, Sept. 27.; Garrison Thompson and Sarah Dale, Oct. 18.; James Long and Jennella Porter, Oct. 25.; Linvill Dooley and Louisa Biggers, Nov. 8.; Lewis Utterbach and Amanda Ramey, Nov. 8.; Wm. Crim and Frances Duncan, Nov. 13.; Elijah Garrett and Patsy Ann Glover, Nov. 22.; Wm. B. McClure and Elizabeth McClure, Nov. 22.; Thomas Smart and Harriett Thompson, Nov. 22.

1828—Charles Howard and Malinda Burke, Jan. 13.; Mason Morris and Acenith Ringo, Jan. 31.; Robert Dickey and Palina Anderson, Feb. 3.; Andrew Alexander and Mary G. Glover, Feb. 28.; Zacariah Darnel and Patsy Ann Jones, March 10.; John McBride and Nancy Pedworth, Apr. 10.; Jesse Davis and Nancy Fletcher, May 1.; David Scott and Catherine Rinus, May 8.; Obadiah A. Melon and Emily Scruggs, May 8.; Thomas J. Sallee and Ophelia Cooper, May 8.; Willis Hampton and Winifred Clark, May 30.; James Leach and Mahalla Montjoy, June 12.; Absolem S. Wells and Polly Kemper, Aug. 14.; Benjamin Botts and Frances Graves, Aug. 19.; Thomas Foster and Rebecca Young, Aug. 28.; Elijah Hanly and Rebeca Bryant, Sept. 3.; David Riggs and Olivia Reed, Sept. 25.; George R. Rogers and Louisiana Hathaway, Oct. 1.; Sandford Jameson and Martha Ann Sallee, Oct. 16.; Thomas Helms and Polly Hawley, Nov. 6.; Caleb W. Anderson and Sarah Hulse, Nov. 10.; George A. Smith and Polly Ann Scott, Nov. 13.; Robert Evans and Susan Ringo, Nov. 27.; James Roberts and Sally Foster, Dec. 18.

1829—Milton Jameson and Sarah Badger, Jan. 18.; Daniel Harrow and Polly Moore, Jan. 29.; Wm. Lockridge and Louisa Ramey, Jan. 29.; Sandford Smith and Adeline Campbell, Feb. 26.; George W. Gillispie and Malinda Allen, March 5.; Cyrus Thompson and Eliza Oakerson, March 11.; George W. McDannold and Eliza Hayes, March 31.; Thomas Simpson and Caroline Badger, July 28.; David Hathaway and Elizabeth Williams, Aug. 11.; Samuel Wheeler and Caroline Mason, Oct. 1.; John Thompson and Debora T. Wood, Nov. 8.; John Phelps and Amanda Wood, Dec. 10.; Coleman R. Ringo and Ann Harden Scruggs, Dec. 3.; George Goodloe and Betsy Lane, Dec. 3.; Wm. Baldridge and Elizabeth R. Rogers, Dec. 17.

1830—John Brown and Judith William, Feb. 11.; Hiram Duncan and Matilda Alle, March 11.; Christopher C. Acuff and Mildred Rogers, March 18.; Walker Carter and Lucinda Combs, March 21.; Aaron McFerrin and Elizabeth Mountgomery, Apr. 13.; James Scott and Susan Jones, Apr. 19.; Curtis S. Brown and Mary Foster, Apr. 25.; John Coons and Elizabeth Wells, Aug. 19.; Thomas Swearingen and Judith Mosley, Aug. 26.; John Trimble and Rachel Price, Sept. 9.; Joseph Howe and Elizabeth Coons, Sept. 30.; Harvey Wilson and Narcissa Hansborough, Sept. 30.; Joseph Smith and Eliza Hunt, Oct. 7.; Wm. Ragan and Elizabeth Roberts, Oct. 28.; Samuel Smith and Manerva Randall, Dec. 19.

1831—Milton Bridges and Polly Foster, Feb. 3.; Lewis C. Tomlinson and Elizabeth Smith, Feb. 17.; David B. Davis and Rebecca C. Hour, March 1.; John Z. Price and Lucy S. Williams, March 9.; James Gilmore and Adeline Yeates, March 17.; James Howard, Sr. and Rhoda Debord, Apr. 5.; Seth Botts and Emily Campbell, June 14.; James Coons and Mary Cheatam, June 22.; Benjamin Masterson and Lucilla Green, July 27.; Riley Perdue and Rebecca Garrett, Aug. 31.; Wm. Bradson and Nancy Martin, Oct. 18.; Tobias James and Polly Adams, Nov. 23.; Jesse Tharp and Sally Waller, Dec. 8.; James Gardner and Malinda Parks, Dec. 20.

1832—Jackson Warder and Catherine Roberts, Jan. 17.; Wm. M. Ragland and Gillean Cheatam, July 26.; Achilles McGinnis and Olivia Morgan, Oct. 16.; Edmund G. Smart and Matilda Gore, Nov. 6.; Wm. R. Moffett and Elenor Ringo, Oct. 11.

1833—Reuben Cluke and Elizabeth Ann Crawford, Feb. 14.; Tarlton Taylor and Elizabeth Wood, Feb. 20.; Alvin Ringo and Emily R. Masterson, Apr. 10.; James F. Mason and Lidia Ann Smith, June 6.; Hugh Thompson and Sally Markham, July 11.; James Thompson and Dulcinea Black, Aug. 22.; Enoch White and Winningford Jones, Aug. 29.; Roland Moore and Eliza Ann Hammonds, Sept. 19.; James Phipps and Mahala Spiller, Oct. 1.; Wilson W. Yeates and Dulcina Badger, Oct. 3.; Martin Sidner and Nancy Stofer, Oct. 31.; Augusta Taylor and Amilda Allen, Dec. 24.; Harry S. Lane and Pamelia Jameson, Dec. 24.

1834—James Edward and Sally Coons, June 24.; John Grabt and Maria Louise Wilson, Jan. 19.; Ambrose Knox and Polly Read, Jan. 12.; John McClure and Mahala Stofer, Feb. 12.; Ambrose D. Kemper and Louisa Shafer, March 19.; Benjamin Robinson and Emily Richardson, July 8.; Henry West Crooks and Elizabeth McGhee, May 12.; Henry Lockhart and Sarah Richardson, July 8.

1835—Benjamin Hurt and Mary V. Reid, Jan. 8.; John Allen and Eliza Taylor, Feb. 22.; Jones Taylor and Adeline Pew, Feb. 26.; Bedford Wade and Elizabeth Mason, March 5.; Harrison Alexander and

Nancy Moxley, March 12.; Joseph Woodard and Chastena Tharp, March 12.; Levi Yocum and Lucy Garden, March 24.; Jeremiah Vardeman Kemper and Mary Ramey, June 11.; Daniel C. Conner and Luranda Thompson, June 20.

1836—Alfred Ragan and Lucinda Stevens, Feb. 25.; Wm. K. Wall and Clementina Machir, March 8.; Mark H. Woodford and Sarah A. Haden, Apr. 6.; Oliver H. P. Thompson and Matilda Virginia Glover, May 12.; Nathaniel Morrison and Elizabeth Cox, Nov. 3.; John Hanley and Margaret A. Hoffman, Nov. 15.; Martin B. Moseley and Emily Bridges, Dec. 8.

1837—Hezekiah Coons and Pamelia Wade, Apr. 20.; Samuel Willis and Dulcinea Thompson, June 20.; Higgins Lane and Angeline L. Thompson, Aug. 17.; Michael Judge and Elizabeth Ramey, Sept. 28.; Benjamin F. Hays and Mary Ann Hanley, Nov. 9.; Isaac Walden and America Jameson, May 18.

1838—Henry P. Reed and Elizabeth Davis, Jan. 4.; Jesse Grant and Amanda M. Crawford, May 18.; Joseph Frakes and Nancy Armstrong, July 12.; Jeremiah V. Judy and Lucella Allen, Aug. 16.; George J. Stockton and Gusta Ann Somersall, Oct. 2.; James Bean and Mary Smith, Oct. 25.; Achilles J. Gatewood and Frances Gatewood, Nov. 15.

1839—Marcus Gill and Sarah Ann Bruton, Jan. 23.; Henry Bramblett and Ann Eliza Gillispie, Feb. 29.; Wm. L. Sudduth and Ann M. Howard, Apr. 9.; James W. Harris and Lucy Ann Jones, Aug. 13.; John A. Hannah and Mary P. Simpson, Oct. 3.; Levi Butler and Julia Ringo, Nov. 7.

1840—Meredith Wright and Harriett Hopwood, Aug. 6.; Sandford Foster and Mary Jane Bruton, Sept. 2.; Daniel McDonold and Louisa Northcutt, Sept. 3.

1841—Chilton Allen and Mary Ann Taylor, Jan. 17.; Charles T. Thornton and Catherine M. Hathaway, Aug. 4.; Philip Hathaway and Martha J. Marsh, Aug. 5.

1842—Andrew Fesler and Mary Grubbs, Jan. 4.; Wm. J. Bryan and Dulcinea Myers, Jan. 16.; Hezekiah C. Allis and Elizabeth Smith, Jan. 19.; Wm. Jackson and Amanda Jackson, June 28.; John Anderson and Margaret A. Mitchell, Aug. 5.; Benjamin M. Smith and Frances M. Stoner, Dec. 20.; Henry P. Reed and Mary Davis, Dec. 25.

1844—Richard M. Stith and Harriett C. Ferguson, Feb. 18.; Samuel E. Tipton and Louisa T. Wilkerson, Feb. 25.; Enoch White and Dulcinea Willis, June 23.; Absalom Robinson and Sallie Ann Bruton, July 28.; Moses Smith and Elizabeth Ferguson, Dec. 31.

1845—Charles S. Gatewood and Maria Louisa Grant, Jan. 9.; Paul W. Reed and Frances A. Wilson, Jan. 16.; Joseph W. Irwin and Frances D. Johnson, Jan. 16.; John E. Stevenson and Mary Ann Wallen, Feb. 27.; James F. Means and Nancy McClure, March 26.; Willis Jones and Emily Thompson, Apr. 3.; James B. Jarman and Zelinda J. Hays, Aug. 9.; Alexander M. Barnes and Elizabeth H. Thomas, Aug. 19.; Alvin Ringo and Mary Jane Masterson, Aug. 26.; Areve Gunsalley and Mary Ann Wilson, Dec. 23.; James A. Powell and Susan Ferguson, Dec. 30.

1846—Thomas Ellis and Manerva White, Jan. 22.; Wm. Ragan and Jane Elizabeth Chism, Aug. 20.; James S. Roberts and Susan Stofer, Aug. 27.; Algernon Smith and Amanda F. Thomas, Oct. 1.; Wm. T. French and Louisa C. Thomas, Oct. 15.

1847—Abraham Phipps and Nancy Kemper, Feb. 28.; Wm. D. Reed and Catherine Thompson, Oct. 5.; Wm. S. Young and Elizabeth H. Thompson, Oct. 5.; Joel H. Grubbs and Mary Green, Oct. 21.; S. W. Atkinson and Maria S. Gatewood, Oct. 27.; John B. Wilgus and Lucy L. Cox, Nov. 23.; Lafayette Tates and Susan G. Bruton, Dec. 7.

1848—John A. Williams and Mary S. Hathaway, Feb. 15.; James M. Cutright and Louisa Campbell, Feb. 24.; Samuel N. Gatewood and Nancy W. Bruton, March 7.; James H. Anderson and Lucy A. Young, May 18.; E. M. Taylor and Mary J. Miles, Oct. 10.; James H. Holliday and Mary R. Winston, Nov. 14.; Wm. J. Freeland and Nancy S. J. Evans, Nov. 23.; David Ramsey and Rachel A. Moxley, Dec. 10.

1849—James M. Winston and Arolena Harris, Apr. 3.; Samuel M. Stevenson and Edith A. Bruton, June 19.; Lindorf A. Glover and Elizabeth Young, June 19.; George W. Proctor and Nancy N. Hayden, Aug. 1.; Joseph G. Nelson and Eliza A. Clark, Aug. 30.; Peter G. Flood and Sarah B. Everett, Sept. 13.; James D. Anderson and Emily J. Hanks, Oct. 4.; George W. Bolls and Juliet C. Parmer, Oct. 4.; George J. Dooley and Mary Scobee, Dec. 27.; Wm. P. Hurt and Catherine Bruton, June 19.

1850—Dr. G. N. Herst and Frances Greene, Jan. 10.; Mitchell Grimes and Elizabeth F. Smith, Jan. 22.; James H. Davis and Lucinda White, Aug. 13.; Simon Shears and Eliza H. Woodard, Oct. 3.; Henry W. Dooly and Ann Davis, Oct. 10.; Radford M. Robinson and Mary Jane Barnes, Oct. 15.; James R. Johns and Elizabeth Donohew, Oct. 17.; James E. Hart and Julia Hazelrigg, Dec. 4.

1851—Aaron B. McMonigle and Sarah J. Allison, Jan. 23.; Milton Allison and Mary A. Fergeson, March 2.; Samuel Carrington and Margaret Lacy, Apr. 2.; Thomas C. Stoner and Nannie J. Hathaway, Sept. 3.

BATH COUNTY

1819—Richard Ringo and Nancy Jones, Sept. 19.

1820—John D. Breckenridge and Jane Peebles, Sept. 28.; Samuel Young and Marget Higgins, Dec. 14.; George Secrest and Sophia Sanders, Dec. 26.

1821—John Hanna and Polly Jones, Jan. 25.; Joseph Donohew and Rachel McClain, Apr. 12.; John H. Dabney and Eliza Anderson, Apr. 19.; Thomas Jones and Patsy Tally, June 14.; Andrew Davis and Kesiah Munns, June 21.; Elwen Henderson and Letty Fanning, Oct. 9.; Hugh Dugan and Mary Williams, Dec. 20.

1822—John Cartmell and Rebecca Hendricks, Feb. 21.; Wm. E. Wing and Susan Ficklin, Apr. 14.; Wm. Lane and Polly Wade, June 23.; Robert N. Badger and Eliza Wheeler, Aug. 20.; Reuben Moore and Emily Thompson, Oct. 3.; John E. McDonald and Elizabeth Iles, Oct. 8.; Presly Moore and Rodha English, Dec. 12.

1823—Drury B. Boyd and Lydia Jones, Apr. 24.; Joseph H. Lockridge and Patsy Cassity, May 1.; John Farmington and Polly Myers, July 8.

1824—Ren Edmunson and Elizabeth English, Apr. 22.; James Barclay and Polly Muns, May 13.; Wm. McIlvain and Elizabeth Mackbee, Sept. 1.

1825—James Smart and Elizabeth Hughes, Jan. 27.; Sanders P. Day and Leah Ann Catlett, Aug. 11.; Reuben Young and Nancy Warner, Aug. 30.; David B. Carter and Virginia McKenney, Sept. 8.; Anderson Caret and Nancy Randolph, Nov. 24.

1826—Jonathan L. Camplin and Louisa Moore, Feb. 16.; Absolam Goodman and Nancy Young, March 1.; Clark Priest and Grizella Edwards, March 5.; Elijah H. Lockridge and Lavina Cassity, May 18.; John Ficklin and Judith Goodlow, July 13.; Ebenezer Scroggs and Rachel Owings, Nov. 5.; Mm. Crain and Rebecca Moffett, Dec. 21.

1829—Walker Bourn and Clarrissa M. Payne, March 24.; James Slavens and Polly Davis, May 10.; Albert Randolph and Eliza Switzer, Oct. 1.; David Martin and Polly Ragland, Dec. 2.

1830—Wm. Smith and Sharlett Goodlow, Dec. 30.

1831—Levi Chastine and Louisa Martin, Feb. 3.; Josephus Hewett and Lucilla H. Payne, May 5.; John Williams and L. C. Morrow, Aug. 30.

1832—Andrew Francisco and Leah Anderson, Sept. 17.

1834—Archer S. Paxton and Eliza Ann Young, Sept. 2.; Samuel H. Tally and Susan M. Brother, Dec. 18.

1835—Joshua Ewing and Elizabeth Conner, Oct. 18.

1836—George W. Tollin and Harriett Gills, Jan. 14.; Charles Whitington and Susan Tindell, Apr. 21.; Robert H. Gatewood and Mary Ann

Stoner, Apr. 12.; Andrew C. Vint and Nancy Farris, Apr. 18.; Francis W. Allen and Maria Herndon, May 19.; Nelson T. Rice and Frances A. Richards, May 29.; John Stanfield and Nancy Read, Aug. 4.; Wm. L. Freeman and Susan R. Ralls, Oct. 27.; Alvin Stevens and Mildred Hughes, Dec. 20.

1837—Randle Yarbrough and Ann Griffin, March 16.; John Becraft and Dulcena Gore, Oct. 8.; Barton W. Hall and Malinda Ann Ryan, Oct. 12.; Frank Hopkins and Frances Roe, Nov. 15.; Jackson Kindel and Elizabeth Jackson, Nov. 20.; George Toy and Melvina Newman, Dec. 10.

1838—James H. Richards and Eliza Shroutt, Feb. 28.; John W. Wells and Caroline Tindle, May 17.; Jonathan Williams and Almira Poor, May 24.; Churchel Allen and Mary Anderson, Aug. 10.; Benjamin Snelling and Polly Doggett, Aug. 23.; Andrew Jackson Safely and Elizabeth Croak, Aug. 14.; Alexander Scott and Ellen Roe, Oct. 11.; Aaron Goodwin and Nancy F. Hendrix, Dec. 6.

1839—Wm. Castigan and Lidian Davis, Oct. 24.

1840—Henry DeWitt and Polly Ferguson, Aug. 4.; Robert Pringle and Martha N. Chetham, Feb. 11.

1842—Wm. Robinson and Mary W. Glover, May 4.; Edward K. Owsley and Frances Tribble, June 8.; Wm. Turner and Lucy Ham, June 21.; Creed Smith and Eliza Barnes, Nov. 22.

1843—Wm. Campbell and Dolly Reed, Jan. 1.; Thompson B. Oldham and Nancy B. Phelps, Feb. 23.; Wm. Clayton and Virginia Smith, June 6.; Hugh Lane and Sally Montjoy, Aug. 10.

1844—Wm. Fenwick and Elizabeth Porter, Feb. 22.; Thomas Beckner and Emaline N. Smathers, March 7.; James Hornback and Eliza Lee, May 16.; James H. Lacey and Nancy Willson, Sept. 1.; Peter S. Stoner and Mary F. Phelps, Oct. 10.

1846—Edwin D. Payne and Maria C. Ryan, Jan. 27.; James Downing and Cynthian McCormick, Feb. 11.; Wm. A. Lane and Elizabeth Lane, Aug. 19.

1847—Wm. Phelps and L. A. Sanderson, Nov. 11.; Sylvester L. James and Mary Tomlinson, Dec. 19.

1848—John H. Hedges and Sarah Smathers, Jan. 18.; John T. Stevenson and Eliza B. Coleman, May 16.; Preston Ham and Elizabeth Berry, Dec. 28.

1849—T. M. Hart and Mary M. Bogee, Feb. 11.

BOURBON COUNTY

1818—Thomas Wilson and Rhoda Booth, Aug. 6.; James Workman and Christena Fitzpatrick, Sept. 3.; Jeremiah Cravens and Nancy Booth, Sept. 3.; Joseph Allen and Catherine Skillman, Nov. 12.; Wm. Lander and Sally Whaley, Nov. 19.; Stuart Slaven and Betsy Elsbury, Aug. 25.

1819—Wm. Thomas and Elizabeth Thomas, Aug. 18.

1921—James Clements and Nancy Bramlett, Sept. 20.; Gustavis Clements and Milly Bramlett, Sept. 20.

1828—Charles B. Higgins and Judith Stone, Nov. 18.

1833—George Moore and Catherine Arnold, Feb. 28.; Hamilton Shouse and Sarah Smallwood, Sept. 19.; Benjamin F. Smith and Polly Ann Wilson, Nov. 28.

1839—Hinson Davis and Cathrin Laughlin, Sept. 16.

1846—Benjamin W. Jamison and Matilda D. Adams, Apr. 22.

1849—Wm. M. Adams and Mary J. Brown, Aug. 26.

1851—Henry C. Howard and Betty P. Lewis, Feb. 11.; George W. Stoner, Jr. and Ann Grimes, June 18.

1852—James C. Adams and Mary E. Shirley, Jan. 1.

CLARK COUNTY

1817—Martin Judy, Jr. and Nancy Burroughs, Nov. 27.

1818—Samuel Copher and Ann Thompson, Feb. 12.; Wm. Neely and Ann B. Irwin, June 30.; John G. Stuart and Sally Gaitskill, Nov.

20.; Aaron Forman and Sally H. Walker. Dec. 20.; Simon Davis and Polly Dooly, Dec. 8.

1824—Ely Bigger and Kitty Thomson, Jan. 15.

1826—Parker Otwell and Sarah H. Taul, July 27.; Jacob Gasset and Nelly Hill, Sept. 24.

1827—James Allen and Peggy Bratton, Apr. 22.

1829—Preston Pendleton and Rebecca Hurt, July 23.

1830—Asa T. Pettett and Sally Ann John, June 24.

1833—Garrett Fletcher and Caroline Barrow, Oct. 16.

1842—Franklin Bridges and Elizabeth Hill, Dec. 1.

1843—Richard L. Williams and Sally P. Gay, Apr. 6.; James F. Wiloughby and Amanda J. Kemper, Aug. 31.

1846—Benjamin B. Groom and Elizabeth C. Thompson, Nov. 5.; James P. Combs and Polly Jane Howard, Sept. 6.

1847—Edmund Wade and Sally Ann Morris, Oct. 19.; Benjamin Gore and Evaline Wade, Oct. 20.

1849—Wm. H. Smith and Ann E. Duerson, Sept. 6.

FAYETTE COUNTY

1820—Augustine F. Eastin and Judith Darnaby, Jan. 27.

1827—Alfred Hurt and Harriett Grinstead, Jan. 11.

1841—Berryman Hurt and Sarah Jane True, Feb. 18.

FLEMING COUNTY

1832—Phillip Smith and Eliza Shockey, Sept. 13.

1847—Samuel F. Gault and Sarah A. Taylor, Jan. 21.

SCOTT COUNTY

1852—A. B. Theabold and Elizabeth Pendleton, Aug. 24.; Harvey J. Smith and Mary C. Steadham, Dec. 15.

1853—Orville O. West and Mary Loreesce Ray, Apr. 5.; A. B. Ringo and Emily F. Smith, Dec. 21.

WOODFORD COUNTY

1834—Peter Hull and Eliza Long, June 12.

WAYNE COUNTY

1815—James Betram and Gilly Heaton, Dec. 28.; Charles Overstreet and Fanny Miller, Dec. 28.

1816—John Chrisman and Sally Stone, Feb. 27.

1817—Jacob Eades and Adah Norman, March 27.; Silas Young and Elizabeth Conalson, Apr. 1.; John Williams and Lavina Butram, March 20.; Joseph Hurt and Polly Eades, Feb. 27.; Joshua Buster and Julia Haden, Oct. 9.

1818—Silas Shepherd and Polly Stone, Oct. 1.

CHURCH RECORDS

CHURCH OF THE ADVENT

Cynthiana, Harrison County, Kentucky

Among the first services of the Episcopal Church at Cynthiana, was the work of Mr. N. Cowgill, who carried on a flourishing school, about 1838. In 1839, Rev. Mr. Crow, a Deacon from Ireland, opened a School and carried on the Church Services which Mr. Cowgill had started. He also held Services at the neighboring Station of Leesburg, Bishop Smith, Rev. Edward Berkley, from Lexington, and Rev. G. G. Moore, from Paris, held occasional Services to help the work in Cynthiana. The Services were held in the Presbyterian, Methodist and Campbellite churches and in the Court House.

Dr. George H. Perrin, a prominent Physician became interested, and he with his wife, were baptised, by the Rev. G. G. Moore, in Dec., 1846. In 1847, the Parish was duly organized and admitted. Dr. Perrin and Mr. William Hearne being the delegates. The cornerstone of the Episcopal Church was laid on the 5th. day of May, 1855, Rev. Carter Page, at that time having taken charge and at the same time teaching School. Mr. Wm. Thompson at this time came into the Church and took much interest in it, (note: tradition says he gave all the stone for the building) also Mr. Edwd. Coleman. The work on the Church was pushed rapidly, almost the entire expense, however, being defrayed by Dr. Perrin. Mr. Thompson also gave $1000. In the Spring of 1860 the tower was completed, enabling the Church to be Consecrated, as was done on Sat., May 19th, 1860, the Rev. B. B. Smith, officiating, assisted by Rev. Carter Page. The name "Church of the Advent" was chosen because the parish was organized on or near the Advent Season. The Church Ediface, is the first one of stone erected in the Diocese and cost about $7000.

Clergymen in Charge

1847: Rev. G. G. Moore. 1849: Rev. H. H. Reid. 1850: Rev. Carter Page, after Mr. Page's departure, which occurred during the Civil War, for several years the Church was left without regular ministration. 1866: Rev. Charles Stewart served one year. Rev. Dr. Silas Totten, from Lexington. did able and wise Service during the next 2 yrs. 1869: Rev. Walter Hearne, served two years. 1871: Rev. Dr. Silas Totten, again took charge. 1875: Rev. Charles T. Kellogg residing in Covington, officiated one year. 1876: Rev. J. S. Johnston, took charge in the Spring of 1876, for 3 years. 1880: Rev. G. A. Weeks, took charge. Rev. Edward S. Cross, took charge June 4th, as Rev. Mr. Weeks, being obliged on account of ill health, to confine his efforts to his charge at Paris, Ky., resigning his charge. The Rev. John S. Spivey, removed to Cynthiana from Iowa, Jan. 1885, took charge of the parish. Was advanced to the Priesthood at Louisville May 1883, died while Rector of the Parish, Mch. 27, 1884. His remains were taken and interred in his native place, North Carolina (?). Rev. G. A. Weeks, again took charge and served with great fidelity up to his death. The Rev. L. C. Pindar, took charge in 1892, for 5 years. The Rev. Franklin A. Redout, of Virginia, came Jan. 8, 1898, and served on alternate Sundays at Cynthiana (where he resided) and Richmond, giving his whole attention to Cynthiana during 1899. He resigned Nov. 1, 1899, and removed to Virginia. The Rev. Estin Spears, was ordained to the Priesthood and became Rector of the Parrish Mch. 4, 1901, resigned Apr. 1901, and removed to Southern Ohio. The Rev. H. H. Sneed, rec. of Holy Trinity Church, at Georgetown, Ky., took charge, giving Cynthiana, the 2nd. and 4th. Sundays each month, until Mch. 1st, 1902, when he was called to the Pastorate.

FAMILIES

Cook, Mrs. Catherine, Laura Cook, Lillie Lee Cook (Ashbrook), Hattie May Cook.

Grinnan, Daniel Montcure, Mrs. Sarah   Grinnan, James Grinnan, Thomas Grinnan, Ethel Grinnan.

Grinnan, Miss Lizzie.

Grinnan, John, Nancy Grinnan.

Musser, Laura (Cook), Mrs. Carl Musser, Catherine Musser, Lizzie Musser, Joseph Musser.

Peck, John W., Mrs. Nancy Jane Jeck, Lucy W. Peck.

Nebel, Henry Christian, Amelia Nebel, Mary Nebel, Amelia (Lalla) Mrs. Lalla, Mrs. Amelia (Nebel), Nebel Lalla, Henry Lalla.

McNees, Mrs. Sarah, Amy Sands McNees, Lucy Finley McNees.

Wolford, Mrs. Josephine (Cook), Mary Lydia Wolford (Megibben), Louis Carl Wolford, Josephine Alberta Wolford.

Megibben, James William, Mary Lydia (Wolford) Megibben and James Wolford Megibben.

Handy, William T., Mrs. Mary (Welch) Handy, Nancy Brownson Handy, Priscilla Welch Handy, Rebecca Handy.

Gibson, Miss Sarah R.

Ashbrook, Aaron Samuel, Mrs. Lillie Lee (Cook) Ashbrook, Samuel J. Ashbrook, Catherine Elizabeth Ashbrook, Cyrus Beecher Ashbrook.

Hedges, James T., George Perrin Hedges, Gertrude Hedges, Arabella Hedges, Wm. Trimble Hedges, James Thacker Hedges, Robert Hedges.

Ashbrook, Felix Grundy.

Norris, Martha Matilda (Cook), and son, Frank W. Norris, (wife) Mattie (Swonger) Norris.

Victor, Kate (Webster), Gertie Victor, Webster Victor.

Wilson, Charles T., Mary Hannah Wilson.

Webster, Mrs. Anna (Newport, Ky.)

Thompson, W. H. (of Falmouth), Fanny (Quarrier) Thompson, Phillip R. Thompson, W. G. Thompson, H. T. Thompson, F. C. Thompson.

Quarrier, Mollie, of (Falmouth, Ky.)

Sallie Clark, (of Falmouth, Ky.)

Wright, Edward, Isabella (Armstrong) Wright, Charles Frederick Wright, Emma Elizabeth Wright, Edward W. Wright.

Wright, William (Lair, Harrison Co., Ky.)

Rieckel, Charles, Mattie (Foster) Rieckel, Carrie Rieckel and Christina Rieckel, Lillie Rieckel.

Dickey, George M., Lucy R. (Brewington) Dickey, and Florence Dickey.

Brewington, Mollie.

Adair, A. Percy, Kittie Adair, George Holworthy Adair, Samuel Ewalt Adair, Sallie Elizabeth Adair, (Bourbon Co., Ky.)

1 8 9 8

Anderson, Mary, Martha Porter Anderson, Georgie Estelle Anderson, David Anderson, Robert Anderson.

Addams, Mrs. William, Elizabeth Addams, Ruth Addams.

Gertrude Victor Oxley, Jeff Oxley.

Robinson, Mrs.

Parks, Miss Minnie.

Phillips, Miss Julia, (married Ed Smizer), Miss Lucy Phillips.

Boyd, Samuel, Mrs. Boyd.

Martin, Margaret.

Shawhan, Mrs.

Keller, Lizzie.

Jewett, Daisy, Mary Jewett, Nina Jewett.

Neeble, Mr. and Mrs., Sally Neeble, Emilie Neeble.

Ewing, Mary Neebl.

Frazer, Mrs. W. D.

Thompson, Mrs. Loyd, Violette Thompson.

Ashbrook, Aaron, (of Aaron and Lilly Cook Ashbrook).

Lammons, Mr. and Mrs.

Reynolds, Mrs. Wm., Marie Louise Powell.

Foster, George, Mrs Mattie Reikle Foster.

BAPTISMS

Dec. 1, 1846. George Perrin. Born Lincoln Co. Ky. Nov. 9, 1794 (of Josephus and Elizabeth Perrin).

Dec. 1, 1846. Arabelle Perrin. B: Bourbon Co., Ky. Dec. 9, 1799 (of John and Mary).

Apr. 12, 1847. Eliza Trimble, adult.

Apr. 12, 1847. Arabella Trimble, infant.

1850. Robert Wm. Thompson. B: Cynthiana, Ky. June 1, 1850 (of Marculla and Sarah L.)

Henry Page, Lillie Page, Newton Page (of Carter Page).

1857. Nancy Jane Peck.
1859. June 8. Lida Welthy Peck (of John W. and Nancy J. Peck).
Mary Kilbourn Peck (of John W. and Nancy J. Peck).
Lucy Wilson Peck (of John W. and Nancy J. Peck).
1859. James Page.
1860. Ephraim B. January, Caseyville, Ky. (born) Sept. 21, 1858 of Eph. B. and Mary J. January.
1869. Oct. 10. Jessie Lewis Peckover. B: Nicholasville, Ky. Apr 20, 1861. Of Edmund J. and Jane E. Peckover.
1867. Fannie Louise Dilling. B: Cynthiana, Ky., Nov. 22, 1865. Of C. T. and L. A. Dilling.
1870. Apr. 12. Frederick Wilmore Peckover. B: Nicholasville, Ky. Apr. 7, 1865. Of Edmund J. and Jane E. Peckover.

MARRIAGES

Nov. 7, 1848. Marcalla Thompson-Sarah L. Jones. (Son of Wm. and Sarah Thompson).
Dec. 6, 1855. Hugh M. Keller-Philadelphia Thompson.
1865. Apr. 11. Nicholas Davis-Lucy Jane Trigg.
1869. Nov. 2. John Deboll-Clendina Younger.
1870. Aug. 2. George W. Turrell-Aletha S. Dunn.
1870. Sept. 6. William O. Young-Anna P. Hayes.
1872. Oct. 15. Hiram H. Peck-Mary K. Peck.
1876. Oct. 5. T. Lloyd Thompson-Lura C. Violet.
1879. Apr. 10. William Boyle-Sallie E. Ludwig.
1852. Carter Page-Sarah B. Miller.
1880. Nov. 30. Henry Warfield-Louise Nebel.
1881. Sept. 19. Gano May-Nannie B. Barkley. Scott Co., Ky.
1881. Dec. 30 Joseph Igo-Sarah Hill.
1884. May 28. Achilles Perrin-Mrs. S. Eliza Jones.
1883. Oct. 31. Aaron S. Ashbrook-Lillie Lee Cook.
1885. Nov. 18. George R. Foster-Mattie Rieckel. (G. Foster of Carlisle, Ky.)
1886. Sept. 2. Frank W. Norris-Mattie C. Swonger.
1887. Mch. 9. George M. Dickey-Lucy R. Brenington.
1883. Jan. 16. Evans D. Veach-Georgia A. Smith. (Mar. in Paris, Ky).
1888. Jan. 11. James W. Megibben-Mary Lydia Wolford.
1888. Apr. 25. John Thomas Martin-Margaret Givens Vanhook (in Paris, Ky.)
1888. June 28. James M. Hedges-Arabella E. Smith.
1889. Feb. 27. John E. Garnett-Elizabeth M. Frazer.
1890. Nov. 5. William R. Curle-Fannie Gibson McShane.
1892. May 15. John W. Lake-Lena R. Mulberry. (Sadieville, Ky.)
1893. Feb. Samuel Martin-Bettie Johnson. (Harrison Co.)
1894. Apr. 19. Joseph Boyd-Hattie May Cook.
1894. July 1. Andrew Jackson Ritchey-Sarah Barton.
1895. Nov. 4. Albert Feeback-Lizzie B. Williams. (Carlisle, Ky.)
1896. Feb. 11. Enoch Williams-Mrs. Hallie Williams. (Harrison Co., Ky.)
1896. Apr. 15. Peregine H. Phillips-Clara Belle Taylor. (Harrison Co., Ky.)
1896. Oct. 14. Henry Williams Oxley-Gertrude Webster Victor. (Son of Jefferson and Laura Oxley. Dau. of Jas. Wm. and Susanna Kate Webster Victor).
1899. June 7. H. D. Frisbee, Jr.-Elizabeth Addams.
1899. Oct. 17. Sterling B. Smith-Martha E. Waits. (Harrison Co., Ky.)
1901. Apr. 30. D. Bradley Shawhan-Louise Smiser.
1902. Nov. 19. James T. Hedges-Miss Amy S. McNeese.
1902. Nov. 25. Christopher F. Fink-Miss Violette Thompson. (Dau.

of T. L. and Lura Thompson.

1903. July 23. (In Cynthiana Church). Hal C. Bangs (of Evanston, Chicago, Ill.)-Martha P. Anderson. (Dau. of T. W. and Mary E. Anderson).

BURIALS

1858. Sarah Thompson.
1859. June 10. Lida W. Peck. Age 4 yrs.
1862. Nov. 6. Wm. Henry January.
1863. Nov. 22. Robert W. Thompson. Age 13 yrs. Covington, Ky.
1868. Aug. 25. Mary Louisa Ridgley.
1864. Oct. 28. Mary Jane January. Age 37 yrs.
1870. Feb. 17. Rosa Debolt. Age 16 yrs.
1870. Feb. 20. Levia Stevens. Age 86 yrs.
1870. Dec. Mrs. Banks, wife of John Banks.
1870. Dec. Elizabeth Johnson. Age 75 yrs.
1871. Feb. 19. William Thompson. Age 83 yrs.
1873. Apr. 19. Broadwell C. Dills. Age 4 and a half yrs.
1877. May Robert H. Peck. Age 4 yrs.
1879. Sept. Cornelia J. Peck. Age 14 months.
1880. Nov. 18. Cyrus B. Cook.
1881. July 29. Mrs. Mary Ford.
1881. Dec. 11. Mrs. Louise Warfield. Age 23 yrs.
1882. May 6. Thomas Otwell Williams. Age 2 yrs.
1883. Mch. 4. Cecil Vanhook Perry. Age 1 yr.
1883. July 21. Mrs. James Hedges. Age 33 yrs.
1883. July 22. Robert Hedges. Age 5 days.
1884. Oct. 18. Arabella Perrin. Age 84 yrs., 10 months.
1883. Feb. 14. James E. Cattle. Age 32 yrs.
1885. Feb. 14. M. Theresa Grinnan.
1885. June 21. Sarah Eliza Perrin.
1886. Sept. 2. William W. Trimble. Age 65 yrs. Covington, Ky.
1888. Jan. 6. Mary E. Hedges.
1888. Apr. 9 Lawren.ce B. Trimble. Age 32 yrs. Covington, Ky.
1888. Sept. 23. Harriet Ware. Covington, Ky.
1889 July 27. James W. Victor. Age 33 yrs.
1890. Dec. 15. Lillie Lee (Cook) Ashbrook. Aged 28 yrs, 8 months, 29 days.
1891. Mch. 7. Hattie (Lowry) Williams. Age 37 yrs. Res. Bowling Green, Mo.
1891. July 17. George H. Perrin, M. D. Age 96 yrs., 8 months, 10 days.
1892. June 20. Robert Jones. Age 89 yrs.
1896. May 15. Willie Dillard.
1895. Mch. 19. Joseph Musser.
1896. Oct. 21. Laura Cook Musser.
1898. Mch. 18. William Fison. Age 19 yrs. Res. Berea, Ohio.
1899. Jan. 11. William Garnett. Age 7 yrs.
1899. Aug. 17. Emma M. Frazer. Age 45 yrs. Res. Winchester, Ky.
1899. Dec. 8. William D. Frazer. Age 40 yrs.
1900. Apr. 11. James Garrett Wall. Age 61 yrs.
1900. Oct. 17. Dorcas Elizabeth Garnett. Age 10 months.
1900. Nov. 18. David L. Evans. Age 36 yrs.
1901. Feb. 15. William Trimble Hedges. Age 26 yrs.
1901. July 4 Mattie M. (Cook) (Norris) Hedges. Age 57 yrs.
1902. Feb. 28. Mary Towles Sasseen.
1902. Mch. 22. Otis Bodine Scott. Age 34 yrs.
1902. July 5. Zerelda Lair Sammons Age 29 yrs. Res. Dayton, Ohio.
1902. Sept. 29. John W. Peck. Age 83 yrs.

1903. Mch. 17. James Garnett. Age 13 yrs.
1904. Feb. 4. Louise Smiser Shawhan.
1905. Apr. 5. Martha Grinnan. Age 86 yrs.
1905. Apr. 20. Samuel Rogers Boyd.
1904. May 12. Georgia Estelle Anderson.
1905. June 14. Catherine Cook. Age 77 yrs.
1905. Sept. 11. Catherine Musser. Age 31 yrs.
1907. Mch. 20. Jacob A. Wolford. Res. New York City.
1907. Sept. 14. Nancy Jane Peck. Age 82 and one-third yrs.
1908. Oct. 27. Hattie Cook Boyd. Age 41 yrs, 3 months.
1908. Apr. 9. Amelia Nebel. Age 83 yrs.

BETHEL CHURCH, PRESBYTERIAN
(Copied by Mrs. H. K. McAdams)

Bethel Church is in Fayette County, Ky., about 7 and one-half miles from Lexington, off the Leestown pike. Session book dated 1823, begins:

"About the month of Dec. 1818, the Rev. Robert M. Cunningham, declined preaching at Bethel. In June following, Mr. Marshall was invited * * * He proposed to preach one-half his time at Bethel for one year, and whatever sum could be raised for his preaching, to be appropriated towards building a Meeting house, at the same time he opened a subscription for building the house. About this time a subscription was opened for his salary, not as he proposed for one year, but annually. This plan continued for nearly five years, and the house was in a considerable degree completed. No Session records of former proceedings could be found, and until the house was built, it was problematical whether a congregation could exist, as the people had remained so long in this situation. He drew up, in the Fall of 1822, the following statement, as tho' it were a new organization; * * * Therefore we, whose names are hereunto annexed, being members of Bethel Congregation in full communion, do hereby again associate anew, and join ourselves together with our families, to be known as heretofore by the name of Bethel Congregation, and we promise subjection in the Lord to the regular officers, that are, or may be appointed and ordained over us; to study the peace, purity and harmony of the Church. * * * (Extracts from first two pages of Session book.) The following names are a list of members in full communion.

Robert Marshall.
William Irwin, Ruling Elder.
Catherine C. Irwin.
Robert Stephenson (since deceased) and wife.
James Officer. Died.
Jane Officer. Died.
Samuel Laird, Elder and wife, since deceased.
Mary Stephenson.
James Daugherty and wife.
John Irwin, Elder, and wife.
Elizabeth Marshall.
James L. Marshall.
Mrs. Linn.
Martha Morris.
Delinda Logan.
Mary Logan.
Jane Logan.
Mrs. Presly Self.
Callin Duncan.
Kitty Duncan.
Martha Beauford.

James Vanee, since died.
Margaret Vanee.
Robert Long.
Ann Rusk.
Thomas Kenny.
Martha Kenny.
James McConnel.
Sarah McConnel.
Widow Scroggin.
Roland Chambers. (Died), and wife.
Mrs. Wm. Stephenson.
Sarah Lyle.
Thomas Dinwiddie, Elder.
John Lackland, and wife, since removed to Indiana.
Widow Logan. Removed to Missouri.
Sally White. Removed.
James Stephenson, Sr., Elder. Died, and wife, Jane Stephenson. Died
Rebecca Averil.
Henry C. Offutt and his wife.
Mary Offutt. Removed.
Mrs. Charles Beauford.
Nancy Bird. Removed.
Fanny Irwin.
Jane W. Night.
Rachel Chambers.
Eliza Emmons.
Catherine Laird.
Wm. Chambers, Sr.
Sarah Glass.
Ann Kelly.
Hanah Morris.
David Morris, (member of 1st. church at Lexington).

DEATHS AND BAPTISMS

James Stephenson, departed this life Oct. 12, 1823.
James Vance, departed this life May 21, 1824. Aged 49 years.
Robert Stephenson, departed this life July 20, 1824.
Alexander and Montgomery Vance, children of James Vance (deceased) and Mrs. Vance, were baptized Nov. 1824.
Mary Eliza and William Edward Chambers, children of Thomas Chambers, and his wife, Rachel, were baptized Nov. 1824.
1825. In the preceeding year John Bell Offutt and Alex and William Offutt, children of Offutt, were baptized.
Henry Lawson Offutt, baptized June 26, 1825.
Martha Jane Irwin, baptized July 10, 1825.
Maria Louisa Averill, baptized Oct. 16, 1825.
Robert Nourse Irwin, son of Jno. Irwin, baptized Sept. 24, 1826.
In the preceeding year Thomas Dinwiddie, ruling Elder, departed this life. Aged 74 years.
Robert John McIllroy, infant son of ——— McIllroy, baptized Oct. 1, 1826.
James W. Connel, departed this life Mch. 4, 1827. Aged about 70 years.
Mrs. Ann Rush and her 4 youngest children baptized, Sarah Margaret, John Henry, Martha and Susan Rush. May 27, 1827.
Pauline Glass, baptized, Dec. 23, 1827.
Catherine Chambers, baptized, Feb. 2, 1828.
Moses Randolph, baptized, Feb. 2, 1828.
Eliza Ann Glass, baptized, Feb. 2, 1828.
Catherine Sanderson Glass, baptized, Feb. 4, 1828.
Eliza Jane Campbell, baptized, Feb. 4, 1828.

171

William Irwin, a ruling Elder, departed this life Mch. 20, 1828. Aged 76 yrs.

Charles Nourse Irwin, son of M. C. Irwin, baptized Apr. 4, 1828.

Eliza Alexander, Mary Alexander, and Melinda Ware Alexander, baptized, May 11, 1828.

William Schench Reader, son of Mrs. M. Reader, (from Cincinnati), baptized June 1, 1828.

Eliza Jane Kelly, infant dau. of James and Ann Kelly, baptized, June 1, 1828.

Ann Vance, baptized, Aug. 2, 1828.

Baptized the following children, Aug. 9, 1828. Septimus Clark and George Granville, sons of Wm. C. Stephenson. Sally Ann and Augustus, children of James Stephenson.

Eliza Margaret and Jno. Wm., children of Elliott Stephenson.

Franklin Smith, son of Polly Marshall, widow.

James Duncan, Benj. Cox, Wm. Mathewson, Jno. Duglas, Saml. Troup, and Mary Jane, children of Henry Stephenson, Bapt. Aug. 8, 1828.

Aug. 26, 1828. Baptized for Sarah Glass, her 5 youngest children; viz: Margaret Jane, James Davis, Wm. Robert, John Thompson and Davidella Marshall.

Baptized for Benj. Windsor and his wife, Margaret, their children: Jos. Mastin, Jane Ann, Mary Eliza, George Logan, and James Scudder.

Mrs. Mary Stinson, wife of James Stinson, departed this life June 20, 1829.

Mrs. Martha Irwin, departed this life Aug. 28, 1829.

George Ebenezer, infant son of Jno. M. C. Irwin, baptized, Aug. 29, 1829.

Mrs. Jane Officer, wife of James Officer, Sen. departed this life Oct. 27, 1829. Aged 72 and one-half yrs.

Mrs. Martha Chambers, consort of Roland Chambers, departed this life, Apr. 12 ,1830. Aged 62 years.

Sept. 19, 1830. Mrs. Henrietta Beauford, wife of Charles Beauford, had her children baptized, Henry, Patsy and Nancy.

July 7, 1831. Baptized Robert Glass infant son of Mary S. Glass, wife of Dr. S. Glass.

Aug. or Sept. Nancy Bledsoe, departed this life.

Nov. 7, 1831. Mrs. Wm. Vance had 3 children baptized, viz: Samuel, Elisa Jane, and Margaret Ann.

Nov. 12, 1831. Mrs. Ann Rush had her child baptized, viz: Amanda Dougherty.

Nov. 27, 1831. Mr. H. Bell and wife had their youngest child, Joseph Wm., baptized.

1832. Jan. 9. Departed this life, Mary H. Vandergraff, wife of John Vandergraff. Aged about 25 years.

1832. Apr. 29. Mrs. Ann Vance, departed this life. (Wife of Wm. Vance).

1832. May 25. Colin Duncan, departed this life Aged about 81 years.

June 15. Departed this life * * the Rev. Robert Marshall. Aged 71 years and 42nd of his Ministry, and for many years the venerable Pastor of this Church.

1833. Jan. 5. Eleanor C. Chambers had her children, Catherine and Rowland baptized.

1833. Apr. 6. James Dougherty, departed this life in 72 years of his age.

1833. June 19. Martha Ann Marshall, departed this life. Aged about 22 yrs.

1833. July 3. Mary Robertson, departed this life.

July 10. Thomas Kenney, departed this life, aged 80 yrs.

1833. Aug. 21. Mrs. Kitty Duncan, widow of Colin Duncan, departed this life in about the 80th. year of her age.

1833. Sept. 14. Baptized, Edmund Drake.

1833. Nov. 3. Baptized, Elizabeth Marshall Irwin, infant daughter of John M. C. Irwin and Elizabeth G. Irwin, also Emily Jane Bell, infant dau. of John H. and Elizabeth Ann Bell, and also Ezra Albert Offutt, son of Wm. C. and Malissa Offutt.

1833. Dec. 8. Baptized Wm. Maddox.

1834. Feb. 4. Mrs. Mary Daugherty, widow of James Daugherty, dec'd., departed this life.

1834. Apr. 6. Miss Amanda Logan, departed this life.

1834. May 5. Mrs. Martha Morris, widow of Robert Morris, dec'd., departed this life.

1834. June 14. Mrs. Sarah M. Maddox, Consort of Wm. Maddox, departed this life.

1834. Aug. 3. Baptized, Sarah Agness Glass, infant dau. of Sarah and David Glass.

1835. June 21. Baptized, Elizabeth Ann Stevenson, and Sarah Stevenson, children of Henry Stevenson.

1835. Aug. 2. Baptized, Nancy McClay Chambers, infant dau. of Ellen and George Chambers.

1835. Oct. 29. Miss Jane Logan, departed this life.

1835. Nov. 14. Baptized, James Venable Logan, infant son of James H. and Mary V. Logan.

1835. Nov. 18. Baptized, Mary M. Robinson, Julia Ann Morris, Jane Holland.

1835. Baptized, Mrs. Catherine Daugherty and Westley Moore Morris.

1835. Dec. 31. Baptized Elizabeth McRoberts.

1836. Jan. 3. Baptized, Jane Smede, Abagail Robinson Logan, Lillah Frazer Logan, Robert Alexander Morris.

1836. Mch. 5. Baptized, Miss Cornelia Vandgraff and Fanny Blackburn.

1836. Nov. 10. Rowland Chambers, Sen. departed this life.

1836. Dec. 11. Baptized, Mary Francis, James Henry, John Thomas and Alexander Moses Daugherty, children of Wm. and Catherine Daugherty.

1837. Mch. 12. Baptized, Susan Ellen and Sarah Catherine Irwin, infant chidlren of Wm. and Eliza Ann Irwin.

1837. Mch. 23. Departed this life, James Officer, Sen. in the 79th. year of his age.

1837. Mch. 25. Baptized, John Irwin Chambers, infant son of George and Ellen Chambers.

1837. Apr. 7. Baptized, Nancy Margaret and James Vanie (?) Glass, infants of Mary S. Glass.

1837. Apr. —. Departed this life, John Risk.

1837. Aug. 19. Departed this life, Catherine M. Irwin, in the 78th. year of her age.

1837. Dec. 30. Baptized, Robert Marshall Irwin, infant son of J. M. C. and Elizabeth Irwin.

1838. Feb. —. Dr. John P. Elbin, departed this life.

1838. June 3. Baptized, Sarah Allen Bell, infant dau. of Elizabeth Ann Bell, and Mary Washington Marshall, infant dau. of Glass and Mary Ann Marshall.

1838. Sept. 15. Baptized, Margaret Elizabeth Daugherty, infant dau. of Wm. and Catherine Daugherty.

1838. Nov. 11. Baptized, Mrs. Jane Vandegraff, also Mary Hughes Vandegraff, infant dau. of John Vandegraff, dec'd., presented by her step-mother, Mrs. Eliza Vandegraff. Also John Steele Vandegraff, infant son of John Vandegraff, dec'd. and Eliza Vandegraff.

1839. May 19. Baptized, Wm. Halbert, Thomas and Alexander R. McClure, infant children of Jane and John McClure.

1839. Sept. 22. Baptized, Nancy Jane Stevenson, infant dau. of James D. and Catherine R. Stevenson.

1839. Sept. 29. Baptized, Mary Frances Logan, infant dau. of James H. and Mary V. Logan. And also Joseph Stiles Herriott, infant son of Zebulon Pike and Mary Ann Herriott, members of North Middletown Church.

1839. Dec. 14. Samuel Robinson, departed this life, in the 86th. year of his age.

1840. Jan. 27. Baptized, Mary Patric Robinson, Catherine Glass Robinson, and Paulina Robinson, infant dau's. of Mary M. and Alexander Robinson.

1840. Feb. 9. Mary M. Robinson, wife of Alexander Robinson, died.

1840. June 14. Baptized, McClay Irwin, infant son of J. M. C. and Elizabeth G. Irwin.

1841. June 4. Baptized, Robert and Elizabeth Glass Marshall, infant children of Mary Ann and Glass Marshall.

1841. June 25. John Herriott, sen., died.

1841. Sept. Baptized, Martha Venable Logan, infant dau. of James H. and Mary V. Logan.

1841. Oct. 23. Baptized, Isabella Frances Crooks, infant daughter of Wm. H. and Matilda Crooks. Also Martha Jane McClure, infant dau. of Jane McClure.

1841. Oct. 24. Baptized, Elizabeth Washington, Hetty Logan, Margaret R. Logan and Wm. Riske.

1841. Oct. 27. Baptized, Robert Daugherty, Harriett Ann Daugherty, Otis Patten, Eliza Patten, Mariah Combs, Sarah Walker, George Carter and Thomas Jones.

1841. Oct. 31. Baptized, Lewis Alfred, Rosanna McElheny, Marshall and Joseph Williamson Washington, children of Ed. T. and Ann E. Washington.

1842. Jan. 13. Alexnader Robinson, departed this life.

1842. Jan. 23. Baptized, Frances Wingate, Hetty Ann Riske.

1842. Apr. 24. Baptized, Martha Ann Marshall, infant dau. of Glass and Mary Ann Marshall.

1842. June 11. Baptized, Emaline Taylor Daugherty and Jane Ann Daugherty, infant children of Robert and Harriett Ann Daugherty. Also Rosanna Belinda Herriott, infant dau. of Zebulon Pike and Mary Ann Herriott.

1842. July 24. Baptized, Catherine Eleanor Herriott, infant dau. of John and Isabella Herriott.

1842. Sept. 9. Verlinda Ann Washington, wife of Joseph H. Washington, departed this life.

1842. Sept. 25. Baptized, Samuel Morrow and his daughter, Ann Morrow.

1843. May 7. Baptized, Elizabeth Marshall Polk, infant child of Sarah B. and Ed. T. Polk.

1843. July 2. Baptized, Samuel Wilson, infant son of Glass and Mary Ann Marshall.

1843. July 18. Francis Downy, died, in connection with this church, but no minute was made of the fact.

1843. Aug. 26. Baptized, Sarah Ann Logan, infant dau. of James H. and Mary V. Logan.

1843. Oct. 30. Mrs. Susan Long, consort of Wm. Long, of Shelby Co. died at her Mother's in Woodford Co. aged 18 years.

1843. Nov. 26. Baptized, Ann Eliza and Wm. Harrison, chidlren of Gilead and Margaret Polk.

1844. Feb. 25. Mrs. Isabella C. Herriott, wife of John Herriott, departed this life.

1844. Apr. 21. Baptized, Julia Isophenia Daugherty, infant dau. of Robert and Harriett Ann Daugherty.

1844. Sept. 26. Mrs. Elizabeth G. Irwin, wife of J. M. C. Irwin, departed this life.

1845. Mch. 30. Baptized, Joseph Glass Marshall, infant son of Glass and Mary Ann Marshall.

1845. Apr. 14. Mrs. Ann Risk, departed this life.

1845. June 14. Baptized, Margaret Agnes Logan, infant child of James H. and Mary V. Logan.

1845. June 15. Baptized, Robert Bernard Moore, infant son of Mrs. Sarah Moore.

1845. July 20. Baptized, Mary Elizabeth Glass Polk, infant child of Mrs. Sarah B. Polk.

1845. Aug. 31. Baptized, James Harvy Risk, infant son of John Harvy and Hetty Ann Risk.

1845. Sept. 7. Baptized, Thomas Edward Daugherty, infant son of Robert and Harriet Ann Daugherty.

1845. Nov. 23. Baptized, Edward Sanford Washington, and Alfred Offutt Washington, children of Edward S. and Ann Elizabeth Washington.

1846. May 31. Baptized, Dr. Ed. T. Polk, Elizabeth Ann Wingate, James B. Moore, James Truea (?) and Esther Carter.

1846. Baptized, Cannon Wingate and Patric Dolan.

1847. May 16. Baptized, Edith Ann Moore, infant dau. of James B. and Sarah Moore.

1847. Aug. 29. Baptized, Luvina Alice Herriott, infant dau. of John and Ursula Emarine Herriott, and also Mary Hannah Herriott, infant dau. of Z. Pike and Mary Ann Herriott.

1848. Jan. 29. Nathaniel McClure, departed this life.

1848. Mch. 26. Baptized, Alfred Washington Marshall, infant son of Glass and Mary Ann Marshall.

1848. Apr. 9. Baptized, Wm. Lawson Crooks, infant son of W. H. and Matilda Crooks, and also James Wm. Daugherty, infant son of Robert and Harriet Ann Crooks.

1848. Aug. 12. Baptized, Joseph Alexander Logan, infant son of James H. and Mary V. Logan.

1848. Sept. 19. Mrs. Margaret McClure, departed this life.

1848. Sept. 24. Baptized, Robert Alexander Risk, infant son of John H. and Hetty Ann Risk.

1848. Oct. 13. Mrs. Mary Anna Washington Herriott, wife of Mr. Z. P. Herriott departed this life.

1848. Nov. Baptized, Miss Mary Nuckols, Miss Margaret Smee. Miss Elizabeth Morris, Mrs. Paulina Lewis, Miss Catherine Lewis.

1848. Nov. 12. Mrs. Elizabeth Marshall, relict of the late Rev. Robert Marshall, departed this life. Aged 78 years.

1849. Jan. 20. Cannon Wingate, departed this life.

1849. July 17. Miss Jane Herriott, departed this life.

1850. Jan. 22. Mrs. Elizabeth Catherine Offutt, departed this life.

1850. Mrs Margaret Vance, long a respected and exemplary member of Bethel Church, departed this life

1850. June 2. Baptized Wm. Dougherty Risk, infant son of John H. and Hetty Ann Risk.

1850. June 4. Mrs. Jane Vance, widow of David Vance, dec'd., departed this life.

1850. Nov. 2. Mrs. Hannah Morris, died.

1851. Mch. 15. Baptized Mrs. Ivey Herriott and Miss Emaline Smee.

1851. Apr. 27. Baptized, Margaret E., infant dau. of Wm. Cross, and also Henrietta Hays Daugherty, infant dau. of Robert Daugherty.

1851. Sept. 8. Baptized, John Robert Marshall, son of Edward and Sarah Polk. Also, Henry Beatty, infant son of James and Jane Moore.

1852. June 14. Baptized, Elizabeth Elanor Herriott, infant dau. of E. A. and E. S. Herriott. June 20. Anna Catherine, infant of John and Hester Risk.

1852. Aug. 14. Died, J. T. Glass.

1853. Sept. 10. Baptized, Mary Lutecia Herriott, infant dau. of L. A. and Virginia C. Herriott.

1853. Sept. 20. Baptized Theadora Jane, infant child of Mary L. Christian.

1854. May 6. Baptized, John W., infant son of E. A. and Elizabeth Herriott.

1854. Aug. 26. Baptized, Frances T., infant of John and Hetty A. Risk.

1855. July 14. Baptized, Benjamin F., Martha S., and Mary F. Herriott, children of Z. P. and Ivy Herriott.

1855. Dec. 2. Baptized, James Smee and George Smee, chidlren of James and Margaret Smee.

1858. Mrs. Jane Matilda Crooks, widow of Wm. H. Crooks, departed this life. Aged 49 years, 9 months and 8 days.

1858. Aug. 28. Baptized, Georgia Guthrie, infant son of Z. P. and Ivy Herriott. Also Henrietta Josephine, infant dau. of John and Emarine Herriott. Also James Warren Herriott, infant son of E. A. and Elizabeth Herriott. Also Thomas Davuss, Joseph Wm., and Marcus Browning, children of James B. and Sarah B. Moore.

1860. July 13. Mrs. Mary J. Brown, died, aged 52 years.

1861. Jan. 22. Mrs. Hannah Herriott, relict of John Herriott, Sen., dec'd., departed this life in her 82nd. year.

1861. Mch. 16. Baptized, Charles C. Graham, infant son of Wm. H .and Mary C. Crooks. Also David Burton Smee, infant son of James and Margaret J. Smee.

A loose sheet in this Bethel book, is a "Resolution of Respect" on the death of Glass Marshall, died Apr. 26, 1899. Served as Deacon and Elder 57 years.

Another loose sheet: "Sacred to the Memory of Joseph G. Lyle. Born Apr. 23, 1797. Died July 25, 1842."

Another loose sheet: "Robert Marshall, died Oct. 11, 1864." "Henry Stevenson died at Georgetown, Ky., Feb. 17, 1879." "Ephriam Herriott died Apr. 1, 1855." Robert Marshall, Sr. and Jinny Vance were married Aug. 2, 1792." "Jinny Marshall died Feb. 21, 1798, aged 30 yrs. 16 days. Children of R. and Jinny Marshall: Rachel Vanie, died Jan. 28, 1812, aged 18 yrs. James L., born Jan. 28, 1796, died at Guyandotte, Va. on his way to Gen'l. Assembly, as a Delegate, May 11, 1834. Samuel Vanee, born Feb. 1798. Died Nov. 30, 1860, at Madison, Ia."

Robert Marshall, Sr. and Betsy Glass were married Dec. 27, 1796. Their Children: Joseph Glass Marshall, died Apr. 8, 1855. Betsy Glass Marshall, died Sept. 26, 1844. Robert Marshall, died Oct. 11, 1864. Sarah Bare (?) Marshall, died in Louisville, Apr. 8, 1869.

BEREA CHURCH.
4-235, Aug. 23, 1828.

James Cord to John Runyon, John Graves, Adam Kemple and Thomas Cord, Trustees of Berea Church, in Fayette Co. * * * conveys land on the waters of Cane Run.

BETHEL BAPTIST.
Co. Ct., B-365, 29th January, 1807.

William Patrick, attorney in fact for John Patrick of Fayette Co., to William McClure, Anthony Logan and Thomas Ramsey, Trustees of Bethel Congregation of the county aforesaid * * * conveys land on the waters of the town fork of Elkhorn containing two acres and eleven poles.

176

BAPTIST CHURCH OF JESUS CHRIST.
4-365, 9th April, 1828.

Lydia Ford of Fayette County to Will Z. Thomson, Azariah S. Higgins, Michajah Stone, Starke Taylor and Philemon Stout. Cons. $25.00 conveys land to said parties (as Trustees for the Baptist Church of Jesus Christ on Cane Run) one-half acre of land on waters of Cane Run.

In presence of Roger Quarles, William Ford, Reuben Houghton.

CLEAR CREEK WOODFORD CO. BAP. SOCIETY.
F-450, Sept. 10, 1815.

Peyton Short to Dudley Mitchum, J. Woolfolk, Lewis Sullivan, John Graves and Henry Shouse, Trustees of the Baptist Society at Clear Creek in the County of Woodford.

DAVID'S FORK BAPTIST CHURCH.

This Church is in Fayette County, Ky., about 9 miles from Lexington. The copy of the list of members and notes from the minutes of the meetings was made by Mrs. H. K. McAdams, through the kindness of Miss Susie S. Darnaby, Winchester Pike. The first few pages of the book are missing and the names are repeated and numbers omitted without explanation. The first date is: "Meeting held at the house of Brother James Welch, Dec. 15, 1802, and signed B. Robinson, Moderator, and Richard Hulet, Clerk." Feb., 1803, Ambrose Dudley was appointed Moderator. Names not found on list, but in the minutes of the meetings: Nelson Smith, dismissed Feb., 1803. John Cusanbary, received Sept., 1803. Johnathan Thompkins, received Jan., 1804. James Randolph and wife, dismissed 1804. Isaac Hendrickson, dismissed Dec., 1803. Henry Coons and wife, dismissed Apr., 1804. John True, Joseph Kelly, John Gausney, Thomas Constant and James Franklin, dismissed June, 1804. Levi Bobins, received 1805. Wm. George, received Aug., 1805. Betty Franklin and daughter, Polly, dismissed Nov., 1805. Patty Tompkins, dismissed Dec., 1805. George Allen, dismissed Mch., 1806. James Patterson, received July, 1806. Reuben Adams and Wm. Gausney, dismissed Feb., 1807. Sally Farguson, dismissed May, 1807. Vinson and Daniel Cusanbary, brothers, dismissed Sept., 1809. James Pittman, received Mch., 1809, and dismissed with wife, June, 1811. Fanny Sage (once Crim), dismissed 1810. John Bridges and wife, dismissed Oct., 1810. Priscilla Lamme, dismissed Feb., 1811. Johnathan Parrish, dismissed Mch., 1812.

Clement Estes, dismissed Nov., 1813. James Welch, received May, 1814, and dismissed Oct., 1815. Lucy Stewart, dismissed June, 1814. Barbara Jones McGill, dismissed Sept., 1815. Sally Noe, received June, 1816. Elizabeth Scott and Jude Goodloe, received May, 1817. Strother Jones, dismissed Mch., 1820. Ellender McGill, dismissed Aug., 1822. Benjamin Robinson, Sr., received Oct., 1822. Edwin Berry, received Sept., 1823. Agnes Macinsey, dismissed 1824. Betsy Hudson, dismissed Feb., 1825. Middleton Estes and wife, dismissed Oct., 1825. Nancy Allen and Betsy Prather, dismissed Dec., 1825. Absalom Adams and wife, dismissed Sept., 1826. Julian and Dulcemia Vardeman, received Dec., 1827. Francis Long and wife, dismissed Nov., 1827. Jeremiah Vardeman, Jr., and Julian Tyre, received Jan., 1828. Mary Bourn, dismissed Mch., 1828. Hayes Gilbert, dismissed June, 1828. Sally Collins, dismissed Oct., 1828. Elizabeth Welch, dismissed Sept., 1828. Malinda Hedrington, dismissed 1830. Spire Abraham, dismissed Sept., 1831. Mary M. L. Ellis and Elizabeth Franklin, dismissed Jan., 1830. Sally Gaugh, dismissed Sept., 1829, and received Elizabeth Johnson, and dismissed Nancy Jones. Received, Ann Crim, Polly Coons; dismissed, Cynthia Ann Owens, Aug., 1831. Elizabeth Hunt and Polly Handbach, dismissed Dec., 1831. B(?) Mitchell and wife, Eliza Jane and Ann Mitchell, dismissed Jan., 1837. Elizabeth

Harthman, dismissed Sept., 1833. Oct., 1836, dismissed, Polly Jones, and received, Nancy Robinson. George Terrell, dismissed Aug., 1837. Z. Briant and Elizabeth Briant, received Oct., 1837. Addaline Early, dismissed Apr., 1838. Harriett Whitesides and Nancy Hulett, dismissed Nov., 1838. Lucy Wilson, Lydia Miller, Agnes Scott, dismissed Sept., 1839. Edwin White, received Aug., 1840. James A. Bryant, dismissed Oct., 1843. Elizabeth Buchannon, dismissed Dec., 1845. Armstrong Dawson, received Sept., 1846. John Robinson and L. Koyd, received Nov., 1846. Abner Wilson, dismissed Mch., 1848. James Mitchell and wife, dismissed Feb., 1849. Lucy Ann McCann, received, and Francis Daniel, dismisesd June, 1850.

List of Male Members.

George Boswell, 117—Received Jan., 1808; died. (Note: Will probated
    Fayette Co., Apr., 1817.)
Robert Prewitt, 118—Received Jan., 1808; dismissed, with wife, Patty,
    May, 1816.
Joseph Allen, 119—Received, with wife, Sarah, Jan., 1808; died, 1825.
Robert R. Hunt (Rev.), 1920—Received, with wife, Polly, Feb., 1808;
    died, 18—.
John Coons, 121—Died, 1821.
William Boon, 122—Dismissed, with wife, Sept., 1814.
James Pittman, 123—Dismissed, June, 1811.
J——Vardeman, 124—Dismissed, Sept., 1811.
Martin Moore, 125—Dismissed, with wife, Feb., 1818.
Martin Coons, 126.
Ezikiah Peak, 127—Dismissed, Jan., 1827.
Frank Long, 128—Dismissed, 1827.
Ambrose Mallory, 129—Dismissed, Mch., 1828.
William Wilson, 130—Dismissed, June, 1833.
Claiborn Mitchell, 131—Died, 1829.
Walter Herrick, 132—Dismissed, with wife, Ruth, July, 1813.
Samuel Coons, 133—Dismissed, Mch., 1811.
Dudley Robinson, 134—Dismissed, with wife, Betsy, Dec., 1814.
Wyatt Hulet, 135—Dismissed, with wife, Peggy, Nov., 1813; received,
    Mch., 1817.
James Stevens, 136—Dismissed, with wife, Mch., 1807.
Robinson Hulet, 137.
John Goodlow, 138—Dismissed, Oct., 1819.
Alexander Woods, 139—Dismissed, with wife, Caty, May, 1812.
Asa Foster, 140—Dismissed July, 1822.
Thomas Price, 141—Dismissed, 1813.
James Mitchell, 142—Dismissed, June, 1818.
Hillory Wright, 143—Dismissed, Mch., 1818.
Edmond Chapman, 144—Dismissed, Mch, 1818.
Pen Price, Jr., 145—Dismissed, July, 1813.
George Swan, 147—Dismissed, with wife, Polly, and his sister, Jane
    Swan, June, 1812.
William Boyce, 148.
Bernard Simpson, 149—Dismissed, Oct., 1810.
Jesse Bryan, 150.
Elias Crim, 151—Died, 1833.
James Welch, Jr., 152—Dismissed, 1812.
Henry Pope, 153.
George Boon, 154—Dismissed, with wife, Mary, Sept., 1814.
Rowling Bush, 155.
Reason Ridgway, 156—Dismissed, Dec., 1810.
Four names torn away.
—nsby W. Allen, 161—Dismissed, 1814.
Henry Pebboth, 162—Dismissed, with wife, Rachel, Aug., 1817.
Phillip Poole, 163—Dismissed, Mch., 1811.
Robert Greenens, 164—Dismissed, with wife, Apr., 1835; died.

Reuben Croswit, 165.
John Hughs, 166.
Reuben Rankins, 167—Died, Oct., 1811.
John Holloway, 168—Received, Sept., 1810; died, 1823.
Peter Eddleman, 169—Received, Sept., 1810; dismissed, 1824.
Henry Enlowes, 170—Dismissed, Mch., 1820.
Harvy Prewit, 171—Dismissed, Apr., 1816.
James Dawson, 172.
Stephen Hulet, 173—Dismissed, 1830.
William Hayes, 174—Died, 1828.
Mason Owen, 175—Dismissed, Mch., 1811.
Abraham Estes, 176.
Henry White, 177—Dismissed, Jan., 1816.
James Noe, 178—Dismissed, with wife, Sally, 1819.
George Mitchell, 179.
William Cochrial, 180—Received, Apr., 1811; died, June, 1812.
Levi Poston, 181—Dismissed, Oct., 1816.
William Mansfield, 182—Dismissed, June, 1813.
Enoch Bryant, 183—Dismissed, 1813.
Uriel Chambers, 184—Dismissed, Jan., 1817.
James Harris, 185.
Frederick Adams, 186—Died, Feb., 1813.
Wm. Duerson, 187—Dismissed, with wife, Elizabeth, 1819; received, 1821; dismissed, 1840.
John Dawson, 188—Dismissed, 1819; received, 1821; dismissed, with wife, 1824.
Thomas Ellis, 189.
Enoch Hunt, 190—Dismissed, Nov., 1822.
George Todd, 191—Dismissed, Mch., 1814.
Wm. Allen, 192—Dismissed, with wife, Nancy, Dec., 1816.
Jacob Burrass, 193—Dismissed, with wife, Nancy, Feb., 1813.
Presley Talbert, 194—Dismissed, with wife, Mch., 1815.
Samuel J. Dawson, 195—Received, Feb., 1813.
David Chivis, 196—Dismissed, June, 1818.
Coleman Ross, 197.
Thomas Dawson, 198—Dismissed, with wife, Sally, May, 1821.
James Haney, 198—Received, with wife, Dolly, Apr., 1818; dismissed, Oct. 8, 1827.
Richard Hulet, 200.
Richard Jones, 201.
Henry Lighter, 202—Dismissed, Sept., 1820.
Joseph Hulet, 203—Dismissed, with wife, Mch., 1825.
Silas Hunt, 204—Received, with wife, Mary, Mch., 1819; dismissed, Apr., 1821.
Thomas Poindexter, 205—Received, with wife, Mary, Mch., 1819; dismissed, Apr., 1821.
Wm. Scott, 206.
James Mars, 207—Received July, 1821; dismissed, Oct., 1825.
Ambrose Buford, 208—Dismissed, Aug., 1827.
William Ellis, 209—Received, with wife, July, 1822; dismissed, Dec. 1830.
Jesse Hulet, 210.
Josiah Bounds, 211—Received, Feb., 1824.
Nimrod Hutchcraft, 212—Received, Aug., 1825.
John Dawson, 213—Died, 1825.
Benjamin Hulet, 214—Died.
A. Dudley Vardamen, 215—Died, 1829.
Benjamin Hulet, 216.
Thomas M. Hart, 217.
James Shoot, 218—Dismissed, with wife and daughter, Apr., 1829.
Dudley Shipp, 219.

Wm. Hooper, 220.

Abner Wilson, 221—Dismissed, 1848.

Barnet Geter, 222—Received, Dec., 1827.

John B. Gaines, 223—Dismissed, Jan., 1828.

Moses Wilson, 224.

Rev. Jeremiah Vardaman, 225—Received, with wife, Elizabeth, Apr., 1810; dismissed, Sept., 1830.

Gilson Berryman, 226—Died.

Wm. Darnaby, 227.

Samuel Coleman, 228.

Matison Thomas, 229—Received, 1828.

Jefferson Weathers, 230—Received, Jan., 1828.

Rowland Proctor, 231—Received, Jan., 1828.

Sidney True, 232—Received, Jan., 1828.

Wm. Haley and Judith Haley, 233—Dismissed, Oct., 1838.

James Wilson, 234—Dismissed, with wife, Sept., 1831.

Benjamin Haley, 235—Received, Jan., 1828; dismissed, 1833.

Johnson Mitchell, 236—Dismissed, with wife, Dec., 1828.

James Dunn, 237—Received, Jan., 1828.

Alexander Stewart, 238—Received, Jan., 1828.

John Clay, 239.

John C. H. Albertie, 238.

Thomas M. Wilson, 239.

James McGill, 240—Dismissed, Aug., 1829.

Anthony Foster, 241.

Thomas Rules, 242—Received, Jan., 1828; dismissed, Nov., 1830.

James Collins, 243—Received, Jan., 1828; dismissed, Sept., 1829.

Merit White, 245.

Reuben R. Hunt, 246.

Wm. True, 247.

John Grimes, 248—Died.

Anthony Pool, 249—Dismissed, with wife, 1831.

Enoch Bryant, 250.

Jephthah Hulett, 251.

Jesse Barker, 252.

Winslow L. Robinson, 253—Received, July, 1828.

Alexander Gibbs, 254—Dismissed, with wife, Margaret, June, 1828.

William McCann, 255.

James Beach, 256—Dismissed, Aug., 1835.

Thomas G. Fisher, 257—Dismissed, Jan., 1830.

John Shoot, 258.

Frances Preston, 259—Received, Oct., 1841; dismissed, Feb., 1845.

John Duvall, 260—Dismissed, with wife, Aug., 1831.

John Estes, 261—Received, Nov., 1832; dismissed, May, 1841.

Benjamin Crim, 262—Received, Aug., 1831.

Hugh B. Todd, 263.

George Mitchell, 264—Dismissed, 1845.

Lewis Crim, 265.

Jeremiah White, 266—Dismissed, with wife, Aug., 1843.

James Rogers, 267—Died Feb., 1813 (?).

Samuel Ewins, 268.

John J. Miller, 269—Dismissed, 1839.

Roger Robinson, 270—Received, Oct., 1837.

Peter Ellis, 271—Received, Oct., 1837.

William Clark, 272—Received, Oct., 1837.

George Darnaby, 273—Received, Oct., 1837.

Abner Yates, 274—Received, Oct., 1837.

John Crim, 275—Received, Oct., 1837.

Wm., John and James Briant and Ann Bryan, 276, 277, 278—Received, Oct., 1837.

Fielding Crim, 279—Received, Oct., 1837.

John Darnaby, 280—Received, Oct., 1837.
Wm. Buckner, 281—Received, Oct., 1837.
James Weathers, 282—Received, Oct., 1837.
Wm. Weathers, 283—Received, Oct., 1837; died, June, 1849
Albert Weathers, 284—Received, Oct., 1837.
Benjamin Wilson, 285—Received, Oct., 1837.
James Mitchell, 286—Received, Oct., 1837; dismissed, 1849.
Austin White, 287—Received, Oct., 1837.
George Briant, 288—Died. 1841.
John H. Darnaby, 290.
Milton White, 291—Died.
Turner Haydon, 292—Dismissed, with mother, Ann Hayden, 1838
Champion Hutsil, 293.
Addison Mitchell, 294.
Joseph Robinson, 295.
Patrick Stevens, 296.
Noah Low, 297.
Luther Darnaby, 298.
Wm. Hall, 299—Died, 1845.
Benjamin Hardesty, 300.
Solomon Law, 301.
Pige Thompson, 203—Dismissed, Sept., 1841; also Montgomery P.
    Thompson.
John M. Thompson, 303—Dismissed, Nov., 1843.
Wm. E. Thompson, 304—Dismissed, Oct., 1842.
M. Darnaby, 305.
Thomas Clark, 306—Dismissed, Sept., 1839.
Daniel Duvall, 307—Received, Dec., 1837.
Edwin Ship, 308—Received, Oct., 1837.
Joseph Coons, 309—Dismissed, Nov., 1839.
Richard Shipp and Mary Shipp, 310—Dismissed, Oct., 1838.
Achilles A. Sayre, 311—Dismissed, Dec., 1840.
Benjamin D. Kemper, 312—Dismissed, Sept., 1839.
Augustine F. Eastin, 313—Received, Aug. 29, 1840.
Ambrose Barnett, 314—Received, Aug., 1840.
Edwin White, 315—Died, Dec., 1846.
Hezekiah Ellis, Jr., 316.
Wm. D. Haley and Lucinda Haley, 317—Received, Oct., 1841.
James A. Darnaby and Emerine Darnbay, 318—Received, Oct., 1841.
Thomas E. Eastin, 319—Received, Oct., 1841.
Wm. Hamilton, 320—Received, Oct., 1841; died Jan., 1847.
Caswell Weathers, 321—Received, Oct., 1841.
Lunceford Carter, 322—Received, 1841.
Jesse Hutsell, 323—Received, Oct., 1841.
David Southerland, 324—Received, Aug., 1842.
Joseph Crim, 325—Received, Aug., 1842.
Thomas Bryant, 326—Received, Sept., 1942; died, May, 1846.
James Crim, 327—Received, Sept., 1842; died, 1849.
John Alberti, 328—Received, Sept., 1842.
Ambrose Haley, 329—Received, Sept., 1842; died, 1849.
Richard Jones, 330—Received, May, 1844; dismissed, Feb., 1845.
Garrett Watts, 331—Received, July, 1844.
N. B. Johnson, 332—Received, July, 1844.
Thomas Lyon, 333—Received, Nov., 1846.
Harvey Weldon, 334—Received, Nov., 1846.
John M. Robinson, 335—Dismissed, with wife, Feb., 1828.
Hawkins Weathers, 336—Received, Nov., 1846.
John Darnaby, Jr., 337—Received, Nov., 1846.
Radford M. Robinson, 338—Received, Nov., 1846.
John Parrish, 339—By letter, May, 1849.
Joseph Rogers, 340—Received, Aug., 1849.

James Coons, 341—Received, Aug., 1849.
Martin Coons, 342—Received, July, 1849.
Abner Wilson, Jr., 343—Received, Aug., 1849.
Claibourn E. Crim, 344—Received, Aug., 1849.
Joseph Mitchell, 345—Received, Aug., 1849.
Samuel R. Holt, 346—Received, Aug., 1849.
Nathaniel Lackey, 347—Received, Aug., 1849.
Charlton Low, 348—Received, Aug., 1849.
Noah Ferguson, 349—Received, Aug., 1849.
George E. Darnaby, 350—Received, Aug., 1849.
Thomas Jones, 351—Received, Aug., 1849.
Lucian Darnaby, 352—Received, Aug., 1849.
John Boyls, 353—Received, Aug., 1849.
Clifton Crim, 354—Received, Aug., 1849.
Joseph Cushion, 355—Received, Aug., 1849.
Jeremiah Kizzee, 356—Received, Aug., 1849.
Andrew Cole, 357—Received, Aug., 1849.
Elijah True, 358—Received, Aug., 1849.
George Hunt, 359—Received, Aug., 1849.
Robinson White, 360—Received, Aug., 1849.
Wm. Ferguson, 361—Received, Aug., 1849.
George Goodwin, 362—Received, Aug., 1849.
Richard Hulett, 363—Received, Aug., 1849.
George Mitchell, Jr., 364—Received, Aug., 1849.
Robert Lackey, 365—Dismissed, Nov., 1849.
Cicero Coleman, 366—Received, Aug., 1849.
James E. Weathers, 367—Received, Aug., 1849.
George Carter, 368—Received, Aug., 1849.
Marquis Coleman, 369—Received, Nov., 1849.
Andrew J. Staples, 370—Dismissed, June, 1850.
Albert G. Dudley, 371—Received, Sept., 1849.
David Tingle, 372—Received, Oct., 1849.
Barnard Bryan, 373—Dismissed, Sept., 1849.

Female Members.

Mary Parish, 1—Died, 1824.
Nancy Mallory, 2.
Mary Northcutt, 3—Dismissed, with husband, Jeremiah, Apr., 1803.
Milly Davis, 4—Dismissed, July, 1803.
Tabitha Ratcliff, 5—Dismissed, Oct., 1803.
Eliza Franklin, 6—Dismissed, 1830.
Polly Franklin, 7—Moved away; dismissed, 1830.
Nancy Shropshire, 8—Dismissed, Nov., 1803.
Eliza Ellis, 9—Died, 1834.
Francis Crim, 10—Dismissed, Jan., 1810.
Eliza Rash, 11—Dismissed, with husband, William, and also John Rash,
    June, 1804.
Fanny Estis, 12—Dismissed, with husband, Wm., and daughter, Sally,
    Apr., 1805.
Sally Estis, 13—Dismissed, Apr., 1805.
Nancy Welch, 14—Died.
Milly Robinson, 15—Died, May 1, 1811.
Mary Robinson, 16—Dismissed, with husband, Joseph, Mch., 1805.
Susanna Robinson, 17.
Susanna Parish, 18—Died, Nov., 1807.
Ann Thomas, 19—Dismissed, Oct., 1807.
Eliza Graves, 20—Died Mch., 1808.
Polly Hinson, 21—Dismissed, 1830.
Nancy Ellis, 22—Died.
Sally Duval, 23—Died, Apr., 1806.
Margaret Schooler, 24.
Polly Schooler, 25.

Eliz Berry, 26—Dismissed, with husband, John Berry, Sept., 1807.
Patsey Berry, 27—Dismissed, Apr., 1815.
Eliza Berry, 28.
Mary Adams, 29—Died.
Betsy Adams, 30—Dismissed, Oct., 1825; died.
Sally Adams, 31—Dismissed, 1804.
Agnes Ellis, 32—Died, Mch., 1807.
Nancy Hulet, 33—Dismissed, June, 1838.
Mary Shropshire, 34—Died, 1828.
Mary Coons, 35—Dismissed, Apr., 1804.
Susanna Coons, now Rogers, 36—Dismissed, Apr., 1814.
Sarah Lary, 37—Died.
Nancy Mitchell, 38—Dismissed (with husband, Richard), Mch., 1805;
    died, Mch., 1814.
Rebeccah Jones, 39—Dismissed, July, 1803.
Betsy Jones, 40—Died.
Polly Cusanbary, 41—Dismissed, Oct., 1808.
Milly Chinn, 42—Dismissed, with husband, John Chinn, Dec., 1804.
Gemima Laywell, 43—Died, June, 1849.
Mary Graves, 44—Dismissed, Oct., 1802.
Ann Northcutt, 45—Dismissed, with husband, Wm., Jan., 1810.
Dorothy Goodlow, 46—Dismissed, Oct., 1819.
Mary Smith, 47—Died.
Lettice Whiten, 48—Dismissed, Nov., 1802.
Nancy Goodlow, 49.
Francis Shamlin, 50—Dismissed, with husband, George, Apr., 1803.
Eliz Estes, 51—Dismissed, Dec., 1807.
Sally Berry, 52—Dismissed, Feb., 1828.
Fanny Berry, 53—Dismissed, Nov., 1826.
Susanna Collins, 54—Dismissed, with husband, Robert, and son, James,
    Sept., 1829.
Sally Mallory (Now Wood), 55—Dismissed, Oct., 1812.
Mary Coons, 56—Died, Feb., 1806.
Lucy ——ns——, 57—Dismissed, Mch., 1807.
Eli— ————, 58—Dismissed.
Lucy Duval, 59—Received, Nov., 1807, with husband, Wm. Dismissed.
Nancy Scott, 60—Dismissed, May, 1825.
Sally Scott (Now Farguson), 61—Dismissed, Oct. 1816.
Gemima Hayback, 62—Dismissed, Aug., 1831.
Ann and Rachel Cusanbary, 63—Dismissed, Aug., 1809.
Betsy Weathers, 65—Died, 1821.
Eliz Foster, 66—Died, May, 1819.
M. Foster, 67—Died, Feb., 1813.
Phebe Bernard, 68—Dismissed, Oct., 1810.
Jane White, 69—Died, Aug. 26, 1802.
Patsy White, 70—Died.
Sally White, 71—Dismissed, Sept., 1829.
Lucy Ellis, 72—Received, Oct., 1837; died.
Polly Brittenham, 73—Moved; died.
Peggy White, 74—Died, Sept. 8, 1816.
Agnes Haley, 75—Died, 1829.
Nancy Estes, 76—Removed; dismissed, Mch., 1808.
Nancy Estes, 77—Dismissed, with husband, Middleton Estes, Feb., 1809.
Rachel Cutright, 78—Died, 1817.
Milly Darnaby, 79—Died.
Agnes Berry, 80—Dismissed, with husband, Lewis Berry, Feb., 1816.
Betsy McCann, 81—Received, 1846; died, May, 1847.
Jane Proctor, 82—Dismissed, Feb., 1836.
Polly and Sally Cusanbary, 83—Dismissed.
Patsy Schooler, 84—Dismissed, Nov., 1819.
Susanna Callaway, 85—Dismissed, Nov., 1813.

Sally Blanton, 86—Died.
Nancy Burbage, 87—Dismissed, with L. Burbage, Sept., 1814.
Sally Davis, 88—Dismissed, Apr., 1827.
Sally Harris, 90—Dismissed, Mch., 1816.
Nancy Wilson, 91—Dismissed, July, 1804.
Caty Jones, 92—Died, July, 1827.
Nancy Jones, 93—Dismissed, June, 1811.
Betsy Jones, 94—Dismissed, Jan., 1826.
Molly Hulet, 95—Died, 1821.
Betsy Hulet, 96—Received, Aug., 1817.
Polly Robinson, 97—Died, 1822.
Nancy True, 98—Died, 1826.
Catherine, Eliz and Nancy Gausney, 99, 100, 101—Dismissed, June, 1804.
Orinda Bush, 102—Dismissed, June, 1803.
Sally Chapman, 103—Dismissed, Oct., 1802.
Phebe True, 104—Died, May, 1811 (?).
Eliz. Brasfield, 105—Died.
Lucy Robinson, 106.
Fanny Leach, 107—Dismissed, June, 1825.
Patty Lampton, 108—Dismissed, Apr., 1804; received, Aug., 1806.
Sary True, 109—Died, Apr., 1808.
Sally McCann,, 110—Died.
Delilah Crim, 111—Died, 1847.
Sally Grimes, 112.
Patsy Duvall, 113—Removed.
Caty Whitesides, 114—Died.
Franky Cusanbary, 115—Dismissed, Apr., 1811.
Mary Duvál, 116—Died, Apr., 1812.
Sally Wilson, 117.
Betsy Kelly ,118—Dismissed, June, 1804.
Linny M. Daniel, 119.—Absent.
Obedience Barnet, 120—Dismissed, with sister, Phebe, Mch., 1807.
Polly Gray, 121—Dismissed, Nov., 1805.
Elizabeth Ellis, 122—Dismissed, Oct., 1810; received, Sept., 1822.
Patty Tompkins, 123—Dismissed, Dec., 1805.
Susanna Randolph, 124—Dismissed, Mch., 1804.
Sally Coons, 125—Dismissed July, 1802.
Sytha Payne, 126—Dismissed, Sept., 1804.
Rhoda Franklin, 127—Dismissed, June, 1804.
Nancy Bridges, 128—Dismissed, Oct., 1810.
Barbara Jones (Now McGill), 129—Received, Apr., 1803; dismissed, Sept., 1815.
Mary Hunt, 130—Received, Sept., 1803; dismissed, Sept., 1830.
Sally Montague, 131—Received, 1805; dismissed, 1810.
Elizabeth Barnard, 132—Received, 1805; dismissed, Nov., 1808.
Nancy Mitchell, 133—Died, Mch., 1814.
Patty Lampton, 134—Absent.
Lucy Duval, 135—Dismissed, Oct., 1814.
Eliz Noe, 136—Received, Jan., 1808; dismissed, July, 1813.
Sarah Allen, 137—Received (with husband, Joseph Jean), 1808; died.
Polly Hunt, 138—Received, Feb., 1808; dismissed, 1811; returned, July, 1812.
Polly Hulet, 139—Received, Oct., 1808; died, Mch., 1814.
Lucy Stewart, 140—Received, Oct., 1808; dismissed, 1814; died, 1827.
Keziah Boon, 141—Received, Oct., 1808; died, Sept., 1814.
Elizabeth Vardeman, 142—Died.
Polly Coons, 143—Dismissed, Oct., 1831.
Jane Sharp, 144—Dismissed, with daughter, Betsy, July, 1811.
Lucy Dudley, 145—Received, June, 1810; dismissed, Aug., 1816.
Peggy Shropshire, 146.

Susanna White, 147—Dismissed, 1828.
Polley White, 148—Died, 1832.
Peggy Moore, 149—Dismissed, with husband, Martin, Feb., 1818.
Anne Pitman, 150—Dismissed, June, 1811.
Salley Long, 151—Dismissed, 1827.
Polley Duval, 152—Dismissed, with husband, Thompson Duval, Feb., 1818.
Betsy Rash, 153—Dismissed.
Fanny Goodlow, 154—Dismissed.
Judith Waller, 155—Dismissed, Apr., 1818; received, July, 1822.
Polly Crim, 156—Died.
Polly Ellis, 157.
Betsy Franklin, 158—Dismissed, Nov., 1824.
Nancy Stewart, 159—Dismissed, May, 1813.
Betsy Robinson, 160—Dismissed, 1814; received, July, 1819.
Becky Blackwell, 161—Dismissed, June, 1812.
Jane Blackwell, 162—Dismissed, with 2 daughters, Becky and Nancy, June, 1812.
Betsy Stevens, 163—Dismissed, 1823.
Mary Grimes, 164—Dismissed, Oct., 1810.
Betsy Holdsclaw, 165—Dismissed, Dec., 1810.
Sally Holdsclaw, 166—Dismissed, Dec., 1810.
Nancy Wilson, Sr., and Jr., 167—Received, Jan., 1828.
Polly Robinson, 168—Dismissed, Mch., 1817.
Susanna Tommas, 169—Dismissed, Oct., 1810.
Ellender Boon, 170—Dismissed, Sept., 1814.
Sally Jones, 171.
Rhoda Pickett, 172—Dismissed, June, 1817.
Polly Foster, 173—Dismissed, with husband, Asa, July, 1822.
Letetia Price, 174—Died, Sept., 1813.
Betsy White, 175—Died, June, 1815.
Betsy Sharp, 176—Died, 1819.
Sally White, 177—Dismissed, Oct., 1828.
Polly Wright, 178—Dismissed, Mch., 1815.
Fanny Davis, 179—Dismissed, June, 1813.
Tabitha Brasfield, 180—Dismissed, Oct., 1811.
Caty Woods, 181—Dismissed, with husband, Alexander Woods, May, 1812.
Biddy McCann, 182—Died, Apr., 1812.
Sally Mallory, 183—Dismissed, Oct., 1812.
Nancy Holloway, 184—Dismissed, Jan., 1828.
Aggy Mallory, 185—Dismissed, Feb., 1823.
Nancy Guess, 186—Dismissed, Sept., 1811.
Gemima True, 187.
Ebby Berry, 188—Dismissed, Feb., 1812.
Mary Boon, 189—Dismissed, with husband, George, Sept., 1814.
Betsy Terrell (Now Poole), 190—Dismissed, Jan., 1819.
Nancy Lad, 191—Dismissed, 1823.
Betsy Weldon, 192—Dismissed, Dec., 1810.
Fanny Weldon, 193—Dismissed, Dec., 1810.
Harriot Young, 194.
Priscilla Samuel, 195—Dismissed, Feb., 1811.
Polly Leforce, 196—Died, Feb., 1811.
Nancy Blackwell, 197—Dismissed, June, 1812.
Betsy Bartlet, 198—Dismissed, Feb., 1812.
Polly Swan, 199—Dismissed, June, 1812.
Fanny Lusk, 200.
Jane Swan, 201—Dismissed, June, 1812.
Polly Berry, 202—Dismissed, Sept., 1814.
Nelly White, 203.
Rachel Pebboth, 204—Dismissed, with husband, Henry, Aug., 1817.

Polly Sagasar, 205—Removed.
Betsy Dixon, 206.
Mary Troutman, 207—Died.
Silome Enlow, 208—Dismissed, Mch., 1820.
Milly Ennis, 209—Dismissed, Feb., 1822.
Patty Greenens, 210.
Nancy Dawson, 211—Died, Apr., 1819.
Rachel Eddleman, 212—Received, Sept., 1810; dismissed, Nov., 1824.
Margaret Eddleman, 213—Dismissed, Jan. 7, 1819.
Elizabeth Holloway, 214—Dismissed, Jan., 1828.
Ruth Herrick, 216—Received, Sept., 1810; dismissed, July, 1813.
Lucy Hayes, 216.
Anne Mansfield, 217—Dismissed, July, 1843.
Christian Poole, 218—Died, Sept., 1813.
Betsy Gallop, 219—Dismissed, 1824.
Betsy Griffith, 220—Dismissed, with husband, Todd Griffith, Mch., 1814.
Caty Hedges, 221—Died, Mch., 1814.
Leparah Thatcher, 222—Dismissed, July, 1822.
Nancy Coons, 223—Dismissed, Mch., 1811.
Polly Ellis, 224.
Sally Payne, 225—Dismissed, Apr., 1812.
Susanna Young, 226—Dismissed, Nov., 1811.
Polly Mitchell, 227.
Betsy Welch, 228—Dismissed, Feb., 1814.
Judith Hunt, 229—Dismissed, with husband, Enoch, Nov., 1822.
Franky Adams, 230.
Henritty Haley, 231—Died, May, 1814.
Mary Matthews, 232—Died, Sept., 1813.
Jane Bryant, 233—Dismissed, with husband, Enoch, July, 1817.
Susanna Grennen, 234.
Patty Prewet, 235—Dismissed, May, 1816.
Peggy Hulet, 236—Dismissed, Nov., 1813.
Betsy Grennen, 237—Removed.
Nancy Harris, 238—Dismissed, Nov., 1815.
Mocha Boon, 239—Absent.
Betsy Bryant, 240—Dismissed, Apr., 1818.
Jane Williams, 241—Dismissed, Mch., 1812.
Nancy Dawson, 242—Dismissed, May, 1819.
Fanny Scott, 243—Dismissed, Oct., 1891; died.
Polly Peak, 244—Dismissed, Mch., 1819.
Aggy Reese, 245—Dismissed, Aug., 1830.
Betsy Shryock, 246—Dismissed, Nov., 1815.
Nancy Naile, 247—Dismissed, Sept., 1815.
Anne Hughs, 248—Removed.
Agnes Robinson, 249—Died.
Mary Talbert, 250—Dismissed, Mch., 1815.
Mary Jones, 251—Dismissed, Dec., 1813.
Nancy Allen, 252—Dismissed, with husband, William, Dec., 1816.
Eliz. Duerson, 253—Dismissed, June, 1819.
Nancy Burrass, 254—Dismissed, Feb., 1813.
Sally Spickard, 255—Received, Aug., 1812.
Fanny Talbert, 256.
Wealthy Goodlow, 257—Dismissed, with husband, John, and also Dolly
    Goodloe, Oct., 1819.
Penellope Dawson, 258—Received, July, 1813; dismissed, Sept., 1824.
Anna Chapman, 259—Died, June, 1816.
Peggy Stevenson, 260—Died.
Lydia Wheeler, 261.
Eliz Marshall, 262.
Kitty Grimes, 263.
Nancy Noe, 264—Absent.

Polly Ross. 265—Dismissed, Aug., 1821.
Nancy Welch, 266—Dismissed, Aug., 1818.
Nancy Mitchell, 267—Received, with husband, Richard, May, 1806.
Sally Dawson, 268—Dismissed, Aug., 1821.
Patty Jones, 269—Dismissed, Oct., 1825.
Lucy Brown, 270—Dismissed, Apr., 1817.
Fanny Goodlow, 271—Dismissed, Oct., 1819.
Docia White, 272—Dismissed, Sept., 1833.
Bettsy Hulet, 273—Dismissed, Apr., 1830.
Polly Mallory, 274—Removed.
Sally Hinson, 275—Dismissed, May, 1822.
Livine Moore, 276—Dismissed, Sept., 1819.
Molly Shoot, 277—Died, June, 1827.
Dorothy Haney, 278—Dismissed, Oct., 1827.
Agnes Montague, 279—Dismissed, Apr., 1818; died, 1824.
Elizabeth Moody, 280—Received, June, 1818; died, July, 1819.
Mary Buford, 281—Received, June, 1818; dismissed, Sept., 1819.
Rachel Grimes, 282—Died.
Kitty Welch, 283.
Penellope Calbert, 284—Dismissed, Oct., 1822.
Susanna McHinsey, 285—Dismissed, Mch., 1822.
Fanny Hulet, 286.
Mary Lighter, 287—Dismissed, with husband, Henry, Sept., 1820.
Sally Crow, 288—Dismissed, Aug., 1821.
Polly Crow, 289.
Polly Hulet, 290—Received, Mch., 1821; dismissed, Apr., 1828.
Lucinda McCann, 291—Dismissed, Apr., 1827.
Delia Davis, 292—Dismissed, May, 1819.
Eleanor Hulet, 293—Dismissed, Mch., 1825.
Mariah White, 294.
Betsy Shoot, 295—Dismissed, Apr., 1829.
Polly Jones, 296—Dismissed.
Mary Ann Shamlin, 297—Died, 1824.
Eleanor Jones, 299—Dismissed, July, 1822.
Elizabeth Pinkard, 300—Received, Dec., 1819; dismissed, Apr., 1823.
Polly Hulet, 301—Died, 1829.
Polly Coons, 302—Died.
Nancy Allen, 303—Received, Aug., 1821; dismissed, 1825.
Polly and Peggy Graves, 304, 305—Received, Nov., 1821.
Nancy Buford, 306—Dismissed, Aug., 1827.
Elizabeth Pool, 307—Dismissed, Aug., 1837.
Malinda Hutchcraft, 308.
Elizabeth Ellis, 309.
Elizabeth Huston, 310—Dismissed, Sept., 1824.
Elizabeth Pitman, 311—Received, Oct., 1822; dismissed, 1823.
Rebecca Hulet, 312—Dismissed, Apr., 1830.
Rachel Bounds, 313—Received, Mch., 1824; dismissed, Apr., 1830.
Ann Hulet, 314.
Delphy Clark, 315—Died, 1834.
Elizabeth Hughes, 316—Died, Oct., 1827.
Lucy Vardaman, 317—Dismissed, Sept., 1830.
Elizabeth Guess, 318—Died.
Theodocia Hamilton, 319—Dismissed, Nov., 1828.
America Dunn, 320.
Eliza Buckner, 321.
Nancy Hooper, 322.
Eliza Weathers 323—Received, Dec., 1827.
Mildred Mitchell, 324—Received, Dec., 1827; dismissed, Oct., 1836.
Julian Vardaman, 325—Dismissed, Sept., 1830.
Dulcenia Vardaman, 326—Dismissed, Sept., 1830.
Polly Ellis, 327—Received, Dec., 1827.

Susan White, 328—Received, Dec., 1827.
Malinda Norton, 329—Received, Jan., 1828; dismissed, Dec., 1837.
Mildred Mitchell, 329—Died, Mch. 20, 1849.
Julian True, 340.
Perlina Coons, 341—Received, Jan., 1828; died.
Malinda Grimes, 342—Received, Jan., 1828; dismissed, Sept., 1844.
Ann Berryman, 343.
Elizabeth Higgins, 344—Dismissed, Aug., 1830.
Elizabeth Haley, 345—Dismissed, with husband, Benjamin, Sept., 1833.
Isabella S. Q. Hunt, 336.
Sarah Berryman, 346.
Elizabeth Coleman, 347.
Nancy Wilson, 348.
Alonza McCall, 349—Received, Jan., 1828. (Man member).
Malinda Lawell, 350—Received, Jan., 1828; dismissed, Jan., 1830.
Eliza Clay, 351—Received, Jan., 1828; died, 1833.
Susanna Hart, 352—Received, Jan., 1828.
Nancy Wilson, Sr. and Jr., 353—Received, Jan., 1828.
Sophia True, 345—Received, Jan., 1828.
Mary Wilson, 346—Received, Jan., 1828; died.
Agnes Darnaby, 347—Received, Jan., 1828; died.
Emily Herick, 348—Received, Jan., 1828; died.
Polly Anderson, 349—Received, Jan., 1828; dismissed, Sept., 1832.
Polly Handback, 350—Dismissed, Aug., 1831.
Patsy Gowes, 351—Dismissed, Apr., 1829.
Mary Winn, 352.
Mildred Carter, 353—Died, Aug. 1, 1842.
Sophia Grig, 354.
Jemima Handback, 355—Dismissed, Aug., 1831.
Susanna Hall, 356—Dismissed, June, 1832.
Cinthy Ann Anderson, 357.
Susan Shoot, 358—Dismissed, Apr., 1829.
Lucy Welch (Now Boon), 359—Dismissed, Feb., 1829.
Nancy Albertie, 360.
Amy Pool, Sr., 361—Dismissed, 1830.
Nancy Jones, 362—Died.
Lucinda Wilson, 363—Dismissed, 1829.
Barbary Welch, 364.
Martha Ann Prewitt, 365—Dismissed.
Judy Eastin, 366—Died, May 13, 1839.
Mary Shoot, 367.
Elizabeth Gaines, 368—Dismissed, Apr., 1829.
Nancy Crawford, 369—Died.
List skips to No. 390.
Susan Mitchell, 390—Dismissed, Dec., 1828.
Elizabeth C .Hunt, 391—Dismissed, Nov., 1831.
Permelia Hinson, 393—Dismissed, Aug., 1830.
Lucy Cockeral, 394.
Eliza Haley, 395—Dismissed, Sept., 1833.
Sarah Featherstone, 396—Dismissed, Mch., 1830.
Elizabeth Hamilton, 397—Died, 1837.
Jane Bryant, 398—By letter.
Elizabeth Handback, 399—Dismissed, with husband, William, Aug., 1831.
Lucy Darnaby, 400.
Nancy Darnaby, 401—Dismissed, June, 1838.
Sally Ann Ellis, 402.
Charlotte, Warren, 403—Dismissed, Sept., 1835.
Sally Bryant, 404.
Permelia Bryant, 405.
Katherine L. Robinson, 406.

Jemima Hulett, 407.
Polly Ellis, 408—Dismissed, Jan., 1830.
Mourning Coons, 409.
Louisa Bush, 410.
Polly Ann Payne, 411.
Margaret Gibbs, 412—Dismissed, Oct., 1830.
Elizabeth Cross, 413.
Jane McCann, 414—Died.
Elizabeth Johnson, 415—Dismissed, June, 1838.
Elizabeth Preston, 416—Dismissed, Feb., 1845.
Nancy Preston, 417—Dismissed, Aug., 1843.
Lucy Lanigore, 418—Dismissed, July, 1840.
Ann Crim, 419.
Polly Coons, 420—Died.
Rebeckah Hedgwedgs, 421—By letter.
Lucinda Crim, 422—Died.
Susanna Crim, 423.
Nancy Jones, 424—Died, 1837.
Sarah Ann Thomas, 425—Dismissed, Mch., 1836.
Lucinda Dawson, 426—By examination.
Polly McCann, 427.
Addaline Rogers, 428—Received, Nov., 1834.
Nancy Stephens, 429—Received, July, 1836.
Lucy Yates, 430.
Ann Hayden, 431—Dismissed, Nov., 1838.
Lucy Furgerson, 432—Received, Sept., 1837; dismissed, Nov., 1841.
Elizabeth Bryant, 433—Dismissed, Apr., 1818; died, Jan., 1844.
Elizabeth Wilson, 434—Dismissed, Feb., 1849.
Elizabeth Shipp, 435—Dismissed, 1845.
Lucy Chiles, 436.
Elizabeth Crim, 437—Received, Oct., 1837; died.
Susanna Clark, 438—Received, Oct., 1837; died, Aug., 1847.
Elizabeth Darnaby, 439—Received, Oct., 1837.
Susannah Alexander, 440—Received, Oct., 1837; died, July, 1842.
Ann M. Ellis, 441—Dismissed, Sept., 1841.
Polly Haly, 443—Received, Oct., 1837.
Emily Haly, 444—Received, Oct., 1837; died, 1st Sat. in Apr., 1846.
Mildred Eastin, 445—Received, Oct., 1837.
Lucy Leforce, 446—Received, Oct., 1837; died.
Mary Eastin, 447—Received, Oct., 1837; died.
Judith Ann Rogers, 448—Received, Oct., 1837.
Agnes Wilson, 449—Received, Oct., 1837; dismissed, Sept., 1839.
Liddy Wilson, 451—Received, Oct., 1837; dismissed, Sept.; received, 1847.
Lucy Carter, 452—Received, Oct., 1837.
Polly White, 453—Received, Oct., 1837; died.
Elizabeth Wilson, 454—Received, Oct., 1837.
Elizabeth Bush, 455.
Sarah Hutsel, 456—Dismissed, Nov., 1847.
Docia Carver, 457—Dismissed, Sept., 1838.
Martha Crim, 458.
Mary Ellis, 459—Dismissed, Oct., 1838.
Lucy White, 460.
Nancy Hardesty, 461—Died, Aug., 1847.
Frances Duvall, 462.
Sally, Susan and Elizabeth Coons, 463, 464, 465—Received, Oct., 1837.
Malinda Darnaby, 466—By letter.
Delia Rosdale, 467—Died.
Rebeckah Low, 468.
Frances Shryock, 466.
Artilla Shryock, 467.

L. Luiza Ship, 468.

Lucy Robinson, 469—By letter.

Martha Johnson, 470—Died.

Polly Martin, 471—Received, June, 1838.

Nancy Berry, 472.

Betsy Clark, 473—Received, July, 1838.

Rachel Grimes, 474.

Ann E. Darnaby, 475—Received, Oct., 1837.

Katherine Rogers, 476.

Emily Crim, 479.

Patsy Carver, 480—Dismissed, Sept., 1838.

Eliz Bryant, 481.

Lucy Waller, 482—Received, Oct., 1837; died, Dec., 1844.

Mary Ann Coons, 484.

Judith Haley, 481—Received, Aug., 1822; dismissed, Oct., 1838.

Ann Sayer, 486—Dismissed, with husband, D. A. Sayer, Dec., 1840.

Lucinda Hardesty, 487—Received, Nov., 1840; dismissed, Oct., 1842.

Frances Preston, 488—Dismissed, June, 1850.

Emarine Darnaby, 489—Received, Oct., 1841.

Susannah D. Haley, 490.

Agnes Mitchell, 491—Received, Oct., 1841.

Lucinda Haley, 492.

Nancy Hardesty, 493.

Matilda J. Wilson, 494—Received, Sept., 1841.

Mary E. Carter, 495—Received, Sept., 1841.

Lutitia Parrish, 497—Received, Sept., 1841.

Lucinda Darnaby, 497—Received, Sept., 1841.

Mary E. Robinson, 498—Received, Sept., 1841.

Mrs. Polly Smith, 499—Received, Jan., 1842.

Polly Barbee, 500—Received, Sept., 1842; died, May, 1848.

Betsy Dodd, 501—Received, Aug., 1842; dismissed, Dec., 1845.

Dorinda and Mary Eliza Crim, 502, 503—Received, Aug., 1842.

Elizabeth True, 504—Received, Sept., 1842.

Nancy Eastin, 505—Received, Aug., 1842.

Lucy Alexander, 506—Received, Sept., 1842.

Elizabeth Harwood, 507—Received, 1845.

Mary E. Darnaby, 508—Received, Nov., 1846.

Margaret and Martha Coons, 510—Received, Nov., 1846.

Mary and Amanda Weathers, 510, 511—Received, Nov., 1846.

Elizabeth Coons, 512.

Martha Coons, 513.

Susan Hardesty, 514.

Sarah Hardesty, 515.

Lucy J. Ellis, 516—Received, Nov., 1846.

Susan Crim, 517—Received, Nov., 1846.

Febe True, 518—Received, Nov., 1846.

Mary Haley, 519—Received, Nov., 1846.

Louisa Mitchell, 620—Received, Nov., 1846.

Mary J. Bryant, 521—Received, Nov., 1846; dismissed, Nov., 1849.

Mary Downing, 522; Frances Mitchell, 523; Zerelda McDonald, 524;
Margaret Martin, 525; Hannah Downing, 526; Mildred Darnaby,
527; Lucy Ellen Robinson, 528—All received, Nov., 1846.

Lucy Dudley, 529; Frances Mary Crim, 530; Sarah Low, 531; Mildred
McCann, 532; Sarah Mitchell, 533; Mildred Lyon, 534; Mary Lucy
Garnett, 535; Frances Mary Stevens, 536; Sarah Wilson, 537; Sarah
Darnaby, 538; Eliza Cole, 539; Jane Scott, 540; Sarah Kizee, 541;
Mary E. True, 542; Permelia Wilson, 543; Ann Elizabth Clark,
544; Sarah Dawson, 545—All received, Aug., 1849.

FIRST BAPTIST CHURCH, LEXINGTON.
R-250, Date 29th September, 1789.

Trustees of Lexington to Reverend John Gano, Edward Payne, Thomas Lewis, William Payne, William Stone, Jr., and Elisha Winters in trust and for the sole use of the Baptist Church holding the doctrines and maintaining the discipline set forth in the Baptist confession of faith, accepted by a number of Churches in London and the country adjacent in the year 1643, and by the Baptist Association met in Philadelphia September the 25th, 1742, and in 1785 by the ministers and messengers of the several churches in the District of Kentucky.

R-252, March 19, 1806.

James Beatty appointed in room of Rev. John Gano, deceased; Henry Payne in the room of Elder William Payne, who has removed to Mason County, and Lewis E. Turner in the room of Elisha Winter, who has removed out of this State.

Witnesses—Edward Payne, Thomas Lewis, William Stone.

April 11, 1818.

We, the Trutees for a lot of ground in Lexington for the Baptist Society, do hereby appoint Richard Gray in the place of Edward Payne, deceased, and James Fishback in the place of Thomas Lewis, deceased. Trustees

Trustees—Brice Steele, Abm. S. Drake.

Witnesses—William Stone, Henry Payne, James Beatty, Lewis E. Turner.

1ST BAPTIST CH., LEX.
U-237, 5th May, 1818.

Thomas January and Mary, his wife; Daniel Bradford and Eliza, his wife; John Fowler and Millicent, his wife, to Benjamin Stout, Mathew Elder, Samuel Ayres and Abraham S. Drake, a committee appointed by the First Baptist Church of Lexington to purchase a lot and erect a meeting house thereon.

DEEDS, OLD CHURCHES, HARRISON COUNTY, KY.

PRESBYTERIAN—Deed Book 6, page 532. Aug. 21, 1820. Indenture between Richard Henderson and Fanny, his wife, of Harrison Co., Ky., of first part and Benjamin Robinson, Alexander Downing and Isaac Miller, Trustees of Cynthiana Congregation of Presbyterians, of the second part. Out lot No. 1, in that part of town called Hinkstons' Addition. Witnesses: Henry Edger, Joseph Ward, Justices of the Peace. On page 533. Aug. 21, 1820. Indenture between Isaac Miller and Elizabeth, his wife, of Harrison Co., of first part, and Benjamin Robinson, Alexander Downing and Isaac Miller, Trustees of Cynthiana Congregation of Presbyterians, of second part. (Note: Adjoining lot described above.)

OLD SCHOOL PRESBYTERIAN—Deed book 39, page 161. May 3, 1877. Identure between William and Joseph Hearne of Fayette Co., of the first part, and Wm. A. Walker, Wm. Moore, Thomas Shields, Alexander Paul, all of Harrison Co., Trustees of Old School Presbyterian Church, in U. S. A. * * * lot of ground in Town of Leesburgh, Harrison Co. * * * The lot heretofore occupied by Episcopal Church. Tste: Burton Hearne and Paschal Kirtley.

MT. ZION M. E. CHURCH—Deed book 6, page 148. Apr. 12, 1819. Identure between Andrew Baird, of Harrison Co., and Sarah Baird, his wife, of the first part, and John Barnes, David Woodruff, Benjamin Sallee, Abraham W. Rutledge and Neugen H.

Matthews, of the second part * * * and their successors forever * * * tract of land.

BAPTIST CHURCH—Deed book 6, page 407. Sept. 25, 1819. Indenture between Alexander McNees of Harrison Co., Ky., of the first part, and Abraham McN'ees, Wm. Adams, James Swinford and Absalom Adams, Trustees of the Baptist Church at the mouth of Raven Creek * * * lying in Harrison Co. Teste: W. Moore, C. H. C.

METHODIST CHURCH—Deed book 6, page 22. Oct. 9, 1818. Indenture between Richard Henderson and Fanny, his wife, of Harrison Co., of the first part, and Leroy Cole, Peter Barret, John Frazier, Joshua Jones, James Finley, James Chambers and Carter Anderson, Trustees, of the second part * * * lot No. 2 * * * in town of Cynthiana.

INDIAN CREEK CHURCH—Deed book 7, page 347. Feb. 17, 1820. Indenture between Robert Stevenson of Christian Co., Ky., of one part, and Trustees of Indian Creek congregation of the other part * * * parcel of land lying in Harrison Co. * * * adjoining the land of Paul Smith and Cave Carrol.

MT. GARRISON—Timberlake heirs. Deed book 9, page 111. Indenture between James Finley, George B. Baylor, Betsy O. Baylor, Rebecca Finley, Mary Timberlake, all heirs of Richard Timberlake, deceased, of Bourbon and Harrison Counties, 3-4 acres of land on Paddys Run (between Richard Timberlake and Samuel Broadwell) * * * now fenced in on east side reserved for a private burying ground, for use of Richard Timberlake and his heirs forever, of first part, and John Lair, Samuel Broadwell, Abraham Dills, Samuel Rankin, Hugh Larimore and Peter Barrett, Trustees of Methodist Episcopal Church at Mt. Garrison.

MT. PLEASANT—Deed book 11, page 67. Indenture between Andrew F. McMillin and James Coleman, Executors of Samuel McMillin, deceased, of Harrison and Fayette Counties, and John Patterson, Thomas Threilkill and Martha, his wife, late Martha Patterson, of Harrison Co., James Martin and Sarah, his wife, late Sarah Patterson, of Bourbon Co., Eliza Patterson and Mathew E. (?) Patterson, of Scott Co., heirs of Mathew Patterson, deceased, of one part, and John Ward and Francis Gray, Deacons of Mt. Pleasant Church, Grays Run, South fork of Licking River, and being part of tract of land patented to Mathew Patterson and Samuel McMillin. Recorded Oct. 27, 1827.

CHRISTIAN CHURCH—Cynthiana, Ky. Deed book 11, page 458. Indenture between John C. Hamilton and Sally, his wife, of one part, and Enoch Worthem, Thomas Smith and John Hendricks, Trustees of the Christian Church in Cynthiana, of the other part. Recorded Dec. 5, 1829.

REPUBLICAN CHURCH—Deed book 12, page 376. Indenture between Robert Morrow of Harrison Co., of the first part, and John M. Raymon, Robert Smith and Wm. Marshall, Trustees of the Republican Meeting-house on Beaver Creek, one-half acre of land. * * * Recorded Nov. 14, 1831.

HOPEWELL PRESBYTERIAN CHURCH, BOURBON CO., KY.
Organized 1789.
"See also records of West Lexington Presbytery, Vol. 1, Page 7, date Oct. 1, 1799."

Deaths

Dr. John H. Brooks, Apr. 1862.
Mrs. Elizabeth Bryant, formally Elizabeth Kenney, Sept. 11, 1850.
Margaret Clark, wife of William Clark, 1811.
Thomas L. Cunningham, a Ruling Elder of this Church, Apr. 1, 1862.
Jacob Fry, "died several years since," entry in book 1810.
William Graham, "died summer of 1824."
Mary Graham, wife of Wm. Graham, Apr., 1923.
Mrs. Sally Hardesty, Jan. 1, 1858. For 16 years a member of this
church.
Mrs. Huffman, wife of Michael Huffman, Feb. 10, 1857.
Samuel Henderson, a Deacon of this Church, Oct. 3, 1844.
Miss Sarah Henderson, Sept. 4, 1843.
Miss Sally Howard, 1819.
Thomas Hughes, Mch. 20, 1862, in the 74th year of his age.
Mrs. Mary Jackson, a widow, died Sept. 15, 1843.
Mrs. Sally Kenney, wife of Robert P. Kenney, May 15, 1856.
Mr. I. Kerr, July, 1855.
Rev. W. C. Kniffin, our beloved Pastor, May 31, 1857.
George Wythe Lewis, July 19, 1865, in the 51st year of his age.
Henry Liter, Dec. 31, 1863, at an advanced age.
James Logan, Apr. 24, 1857, an Elder since Jan. 11, 1824.
Mrs. Logan, wife of Wm. R. Logan, Aug. 10, 1857.
Mrs. Margaret Moreland, Oct. 20, 1850.
Miss Margaret Moreland, Aug., 1855.
Mrs. Rebecca McConnel, May 1, 1860, in the 81st year of her age.
Mrs. Mary McMeekin, widow of Robert McMeekin, Oct. 23, 1859, in
the 75th year of her age. A native of Scotland, and member of
this church 23 years.
Robert McMeekin, Sept. 24, 1858.
Mrs. Elizabeth Payne, 1819.
Miss Mary Ann Scott, died Sept. 8, 1843.
Miss Mary Scott, died Nov. 28, 1843.
Andrew Scott, Oct., 1850, a ruling elder for the last 20 years.
Thomas J. Scott, Dec. 7, 1866.

PISGAH CHURCH

Pisgah Church, is in Woodford County, Ky., eight miles due West
of Lexington and five miles from Versailles, on the waters of Shannon
Run, within a short distance of the line separating the counties of
Woodford and Fayette. For further history of the church see book,
"The Pisgah Book, by W. O. Shewmaker, printed 1909."

"A Session Book or Register, of the Church of Pisgah, commenc-
ing from the beginning of the Year of Our Lord 1808." Extracts,
copied by Mrs. H. K. McAdams:

This Church at the period above mentioned consisted of the following Members in communion, to wit, first Church Session, as follows:

James Blythe, Pastor.   James Wardlow, Sr.
Francis Allen.   Hugh Ferguson.
James Martin.   Isaac Stevenson.

SECONDLY, all other persons in communion as follows, to wit,

Moses McIlvain,   William McPheeters,
Margaret, his wife.   Agnes, his wife.
William McIllvain.   Hugh Muldrew.
John Armstrong.   Jane, his wife.
James Ritchey,   Samuel Stevenson,
Jane, his wife.   Jane, his wife.
Phebe Ferguson.   Mary Stevenson.

193

George Campbell,
Nancy, his wife.
Nancy Kirkham.
James Rennick,
Mary, his wife,
Lydia Rennick.
Margaret Rennick.
John Elliott,
Ellender, his wife.
Rebecca Allen.
James White.
Elizabeth, his wife.
John McMahan,
Polly, his wife.
Benjamin Stevenson.
Mary, his wife.
Arthur Campbell,
Elizabeth Campbell.
Joseph Robb.
Eleanor Robb.
Alexander Black,
Agnes, his wife.

Agnes Steel.
Polly Steel.
Mary Long, wife of
John Long, Jun.
Joanna Campbell.
Peggy Stevenson, wife of
James Stevenson.
Mary Stevenson, wife of
James Stevenson.
Betsy Elliott, wife of William.
James Stevenson, Sen.
----------, his wife.
Joshua Whittington.
Mary Stevenson.
Sarah Dunlap.
Archibald Kinkead.
William Stevenson,
Susanna, his wife.
Martha Martin.
Susanna Aking.
Sarah Gay.
Salley Gay.

Jan. 1st, 1808. Here follows a list of all of the above named Communicants who are heads of Families with their children, at this time under their charge:

James Wardlow, Sen.—John Wardlow, James Wardlow.

Frances Allen, Rebecca, his wife—John W. Allen, James Allen, Polly Allen, William Allen, Hugh M. Allen, Jane Allen, Franklin Allen.

Nathaniel Ferguson, and Phebe, his wife—Alexander Ferguson, Joseph M. Ferguson, Elizabeth C. Ferguson, Thomas J. Ferguson, Bryant Ferguson, George Ferguson, Susan A. Ferguson.

James Martin and Martha, his wife—William Martin, Mary E. Martin, Robert Martin, James Martin, Elijah Martin.

Isaac Stevenson and Mary, his wife—(Children all baptized) William Stevenson, Mileah Stevenson, Priscilla C. Stevenson, Benjamin Stevenson, Jane Stevenson, Samuel Stevenson.

Moses McIlvain, and Margaret, his wife—Andrew McIlvain, Elizabeth McIlvain.

James Ritchey, and Jane, his wife.

Arthur Campbell and Elizabeth, his wife—Mary Anne Campbell, Elizabeth, Robert, Sarah, Isabella.

Joseph Robb, and Eleanor, his wife—Samuel Robb, James Robb, Robert F. Robb, Elizabeth Y. Robb, John H. Robb, Sarah Robb, Maryanne Rob.

Alexander Black and Agnes, his wife.

Agnes Steel—Samuel Steel, Mary Steel, John Steel, Jeanet Steel.

William McPheters, Agnes, his wife—Addison McPheters, Margaret C. McPheters, Martha McPheters, John C. McPheters, William G. McPheters, Charles McPheters.

Hugh Muldrew, and Jane, his wife—John Muldrew, Sarah Muldrew, George Muldrew, Jane Muldrew, Ann Muldrew.

Samuel Stevenson and Jane, his wife—Mary Stevenson, Robert Stevenson, Jane Stevenson, William Stevenson, Alexander Stevenson.

George Campbell and Nancy, his wife—Samuel Campbell.

James Rennick and Mary, his wife—Lydia Rennick, Margaret Rennick.

John Elliott and Elander, his wife—John Elliott, Rebecca Elliott, Andrew Elliott, Isaac Elliott.

James White and Elizabeth, his wife—Robert White, Andrew

White, Patsey White, John White, Cary White, Claybourn White, Sally White.

John McMahan, and Polly, his wife.

Benjamin Stevenson, and Mary, his wife—Benjamin Stevenson, John Stevenson, William Stevenson, Henry Stevenson, Sarah Stevenson.

Mary Lang, wife of John Lang—James Lang.

Joanna Campbell—Robert Campbell, Sarah Campbell.

Peggy Stevenson, wife of James Stevenson—Campbell Stevenson, Cox Stevenson.

Mary Stevenson, wife of James Stevenson.

Betsy Elliott, wife of William Elliott—James Elliott, John Elliott, Elizabeth Elliott.

James Stevenson, Sen., and ————, his wife, and formerly the Widow Walker—Agnes Walker, Mancy Walker, Peggy Walker, James Walker.

Joshua Whittington—Thomas Whittington, Betsy Whittington, Mary Whittington, Isaac Whittington, Jane Whittington.

Archibald Kinkead—Mary Kinkead, Abalina Kinkead, Pelina Kinkead, Elizabeth Kinkead.

William Stevenson, Sen., and Susanna, his wife—Mary Stevenson, William Stevenson, Elizabeth Stevenson, Jane Stevenson.

Susanna Aking.

John Armstrong—James Armstrong, Sally Armstrong.

Thus far with respect to the situation and standing of the aforenamed CHURCH of Pisgah, at the said beginning of the Year 1808.

Next follows in order, the preceedings, of said Church, Births, Baptisms, Marriages, Deaths, Removals.

James and Sally Armstrong, Children of John Armstrong, baptised, Aug., 1808.

William Stevenson, Sen., departed this life, July 12th. day, 1808.

Oct. —— day, 1808. Nancy Kirkham, widow, received in Communion.

Martha Stevenson, daughter of Samuel Stevenson, departed this life Mch. 21st, 1809.

John and Polly McMahan, Children of John McMahan, and Polly his wife, baptised May 8, 1809.

Elijah Martin, son of James Martin, baptised 30th. April, 1809.

Isaac W. Stevenson, son of Isaac Stevenson and Mary, his wife, baptised, June 10th. day, 1809.

James Stevenson, Sen., departed this life July 10th. day, 1809.

William McIlvain and Sarah Gay, married, by the Rev. James Blythe, May, 1809.

Charles W. McPheters, son of William McPheters and Agnes, his wife, baptized Sept. 24th, 1809.

October 7th. day, 1809. Agnes Marshall, received the Communion.

Thomas, Charles, Alexander and John C. Marshall, Baptised, Jan. 14th, 1810.

William McIlvain had a son born Mch. 27th, 1810.

Robert McIlvain, son of William and Sarah McIlvain, baptised Apr. 28th, 1810.

Mary Blythe, daughter of James and Peggy Blythe, baptised Apr. 28th, 1810.

James and Prudence Elliott had a son born Sept. 10, 1810.

The Rev. James Blythe, annual Salary amounts to————$130.00
Money received,

By James Wardlow	$28.00
By Nathaniel Ferguson	20.33
By Isaac Stevenson	16.00

By James Martin_____ 26.00
_____

Amount rec'd_____$90.33
Balance due_____$39.67

John M. McIllvain, son of William and Sarah McIllvain, baptised, Apr. 14th, 1811.

Jane Muldrow, departed this life, Mch. 1st, 1811.

Agnes Marshall, wife of Lewis Marshall, had a son born—1810.

James and Martha Martin, had a son born Oct. 19th, 1811.

Nathaniel and Phebe Ferguson had a son born Nov. 3rd, 1811.

John and Elizabeth Andrews had a son born Dec. —, 1811.

Isaac Stevenson, removed Dec., 1811.

Agnes Marshall, wife of Lewis Marshall, had a son born, Mch. —, 1812.

Sarah Dunlap, married by the Rev'd. John Andrews, Oct., 1811, and removed.

Alexander P. Andrews, son of John and Elizabeth Andrews, baptised, Mch. 29th, 1812.

James White, removed Mch. 15th, 1812.

Walter C. Ferguson, son of Nath'l and Phebe Ferguson, baptised Apr. 5, 1812.

John Martin, son of James and Martha Martin, baptised Apr. 5th, 1812.

James Elliott, removed Mch. 15th, 1812. Joshua Whittington, removed, 1812. Susanna Akin, removed.

Jacob B. McPheters, son of Wm. and Agnes McPheters, baptised Aug. 30th, 1812.

James Rennick, departed this life, Aug. 10th. day, 1812.

William and John Elliott, sons of James and Prudence Elliott, baptised Apr. —, 1813.

Nathaniel and Phebe Ferguson, had a son born Oct. the 26th, 1813.

Mrs. Agnes Steele, departed this life, the 6th..day of March, 1814.

William and Sally McIllvain had a son born Mch. 27th, 1814.

William Ferguson, son of Nath'l. and Phebe Ferguson, baptised May the 15th, 1814.

William Harvey McIllvain, son of Wm. and Sally McIllvain, baptised May the 25th, 1814.

Sat., May 25th, 1814. Mrs. Mary Lacklin admitted to Communion. Also Mrs. Jane Carr, formally of the Methodist Society.

William and Agnes McPheters had a son born, June 12th, 1814.

James and Martha Martin had a daughter born June 22nd, 1814.

Martha Martin, dau. of James Martin and his wife, was baptised Sept. 14, 1814.

Julyann, Ashbel Green and Sandford Payne Martin, children of Henry Martin and Priscilla, his wife, were baptised Sept. 18, 1814.

William McIlvain, departed this life, Sept. 28th, 1814.

Lewis Marshall and Agathy, his wife had a daughter born Oct. 16th, 1814.

Apr. 23, 1815. Thomas Sthreshley, a member of the Methodist Society, admitted to occasional Communion.

Henry Martin and Priscilla, his wife, had a son born May 20, 1815.

John A. Crow, son of John Crow and his wife, was baptised July 9, 1815.

Mary Marshall, dau. of Lewis Marshall and Agatha, his wife, was baptized Aug. 20th, 1815.

Joseph Martin, son of Henry Martin and Priscilla, his wife, was baptized Aug. 20th, 1815 .

Moses McIlvain, departed this life Jan. 12th, 1816.

James Wardlow, Sen., departed this life Mch. 2nd, 1816.

Margaret, Elizabeth, Rebecca, Caleb, Martha Ann, and Eliza Jane

196

Worley, children of Caleb Worley and Mary, his wife, were baptized Mch. 23, 1816.

Sept. 14th, 1816. Mrs. Mary Smith and Colonel Tunstal Quarles, admitted to Communion.

Sabbath morning Sept. 15th, 1816. Mrs. Mary Smith, an adult was Baptized.

Alexander, Benjamin, Elizabeth, Joanna, Margaret and Polly Stevenson, children of James Stevenson and Margaret, his wife, were Baptized Oct. 15th, 1816.

James Martin and Martha, his wife, had a daughter born Dec. 22, 1816.

Jane Martin, dau. of James Martin and Martha, his wife, was Baptized May 5, 1817.

Sat., May 17th, 1817. Mrs. Mary Gordon, Jane Allen and Rebecker Gay, admitted to Communion.

John and Samuel Short, children of Mary Short, were Baptized Aug. 16, 1817.

Sam'l, Milley and William Hoolman, children of Cornelious Hoolman, and Elizabeth, his wife, were Baptized Dec. 10, 1817.

Colo. Tunstal Quarles departed this life Feb. 18th, 1818.

Sabbath Morning, 15th. Mch., 1818. Cornelious Hoolman, Jane Carr and Mrs. Campbell, admitted to Communion.

Joseph H. McPheters, son of Wm. McPheters and Agnes, his wife, was Baptized.

Mch. 17, 1818. William McPheters removed.

Sat., June 27th, 1818. Mrs. Polly McCullough, Mrs. Kitty Milton and Mrs. Fanny Armstrong, were admitted to Communion. Mary Martin, dau. of Henry Martin and Priscilla, his wife, was Baptized.

Sabbath Morning, June 28, 1818. Mrs. Fanny Armstrong, an adult was Baptized.

George M. Campbell, son of Samuel Campbell and Phebe, his wife, was Baptized Aug. 2nd, 1818.

Mrs. Nancy Black, departed this life Aug. 29th, 1818.

Mrs. Mary Short, departed this life Sept. 25th, 1818.

Sat., Oct. 10, 1818. Mrs. Nancy Quarles and Livy Bohannon, admitted to Communion and also George Burgen and Rebecca, his wife.

Apr. 10, 1819. Edward Hoolman, son of Cornelious Hoolman and Elizabeth, his wife, was Baptized.

Livy Bohannon, departed this life June 23rd, 1819.

Sat., July 31st, 1819. Mrs. Margaret Cumpton was admitted to Communion.

Mrs. Menzies departed this life Aug. 7th, 1819.

Sat., Nov. 13th, 1819. Wm. R. Thompson and Wm. Breckinridge, admitted to Communion.

James Cumpton, son of Margaret Cumpton, was Baptized Mch. 11th, 1820.

Sat., Mch. 11, 1820. William Green, Mirah Maddison, Charles Marshall, John McClung, Wm. Marshall, James Boardman, Lewis Green, Thomas Taylor, admitted to Communion.

Sabbath Morning, Mch. 12, 1820. America Mattox, admitted to Communion. Before service, Willis Green, John MrClung were Baptized.

Willia Green departed this life May 3rd, 1820.

Lewis Green and John McClung removed at this time. Susanna Martin, dau. of Henry Martin and Priscilla, his wife, was Baptized, May 7th, 1820.

Thomas Taylor departed this life June 8th, 1820.

Wm. Breckinridge, removed at this time.

Sat., June 17th, 1820. Mrs. Rachel Muldrow, was admitted to Communion.

Charles Hoolman, son of Cornelius Hoolman and Elizabeth, M. wife was Baptized, July 2nd, 1820.

Sat., Sept. 23rd. Mrs. Mary Allen was admitted to Communion.

Elly Ann Allen, dau. of Wm. Allen and Mary, his wife, was Baptized Sept. 23, 1820. Also Mrs. Matilda Berryman and Mrs. Jane Harris, admitted to Communion.

Sabbath Morning, 24th, Sept., 1820. Saml. Menzies was admitted to Communion.

Sept. 24. Baptized, George Maddison, son of George Maddison, dec'd.

William R. Thompson, removed about this time.

Sept. 3rd, 1820. Thomas Little was baptized.

George I. Biergen and Rebeccah, his wife, removed Mch. 10th, 1821.

June 30, 1821. Mrs. Mary Martin and James Stevenson, Jun. were admitted to Communion.

Wm. R. Thompson, who removed last Fall, has returned and taken his seat at the Communion table.

Louis Marshall and Agatha, his wife, had a son born Aug. 10, 1821.

Mrs. Margaret McIlvain, departed this life Sept. 16th, 1821.

James Boardman, son of James Boardman, and Mary, his wife, was Baptized Sept. 16, 1821.

Oct. 14, 1821. Mrs. Martha Hamilton, admitted to Communion.

Henry Thornton, an orphan child, under the care of John Lockland, was Baptized Oct. 21, 1821.

John K. Lee, an adult was Baptized Mch. 3rd, 1822.

Apr. 6th, 1822. Mrs. Nancy Watson, John K. Lee and Eliza Raleigh, were admitted to Communion. * * Eliza Raleigh, an adult, was Baptized.

Robert P. Allen, son of Wm. Allen and Mary, his wife, was Baptized July 14th, 1822.

Levina Boston, an orphan child, bound to John Shaw, was Baptized Sept. 22nd, 1822.

Nancy Martin, dau. of Henry Martin and Priscilla, his wife, was Baptized Sept. 22, 1822.

James Ritchie, departed this life Sept. 23rd, 1822.

Oct. 13, 1822. Robert Elliott, admitted to Communion.

Nov. 1, 1822. John Lackland and his wife removed.

May 10, 1823. Sarah Williams and Mrs. Isabella Scott, admitted to Communion.

May 11th, 1823. Sarah Williams, an adult was Baptized, and also William Scott, son of Mrs. Isabella Scott.

Mrs. Mary Stevenson, departed this life June——1823.

Aug. 9, 1823. James Elliott was admitted to Communion.

Feb. 22, 1824. Mrs. Sarah McClure was admitted to Communion, also Archibald Kinkead was again admitted to Communion.

Feb. 25, 1824. Henry Martin removed.

Aug. 25, 1824. Cornelious Hoolman, applied for a certificate of dismission to join elsewhere.

Mrs. Mary Worley, departed this life July 11th, 1825.

Aug. 6, 1825. Wm. Shaw, admitted to Communion, America Mattox applied for a certificate of dismission to join elsewhere.

Aug. 7, 1825. Mary E. Shaw, dau. of Wm. Shaw was Baptized.

Mrs. Polly Stevenson, widow of Isaac Stevenson, who removed from this Congregation some years past, has lately been married to Mr. James Cox, and returned and settled amongst us, about the first of Sept., 1825.

Susanna Stevenson, departed this life, Dec. 16, 1825.

Samuel Stevenson, Sen., departed this life, Dec. 18, 1825.

June 4, 1826. Eliza Jane Stevenson and Samuel Shaw Ware, admitted to Communion for the first time.

Sept. 16, 1826. Mrs. Sarah Elliott, wife of James Elliott, admitted to Communion for the first time.

Sept. 17, 1826. Mrs. Elizabeth Cotton, Mrs. Frances Bohannon, and Mrs. Isabella Scott, applied for certificates of dismission to join elsewhere.

Aug. 26, 1827. Salley Armstrong admitted to Communion.

Alexander Black, departed this life Apr. 18, 1827.

Joanna Campbell, departed this life, June 22, 1827.

Dec. 1, 1827. Mrs. Susan Hart, Mrs. Margaret Thompson, Samuel Thompson, Samuel Stevenson, Kinkead Gay, Robert E. Scrogin, admitted to Communion.

Dec. 2, 1827. Mrs. Jane Worley, Mrs. Jane Gay, Mrs. Eliza Jane Stevenson, Harriot Scrogan, Ann Scrogan, Nancy Young, admitted to Communion. Col. Hugh Muldrow, and Wm. Scrogin, admitted again to Communion. * * * Robert E. Scrogin, Mrs. Eliza Jane Stevenson, and Nancey Young, all being adults, were Baptized.

Dec. 6, 1827. Elijah Milton, Frederick Waltz, Wm. Allen, John Milton, Louisa Milton, Catherine Taylor, Wm. Stevenson, Jane Stevenson, Isaac Stevenson, Bushrod Milton, George Lingenfelter, Jane Martin, Hannah W. Blair, admitted to Communion.

Dec. 25, 1827. Daniel Orr, admitted to Communion.

Jan. 13, 1828. Lancelot Clark. Betsy Ann Stevenson, Mrs. Sally Elliott, and John W. McIlvain, admitted to Communion.

Feb. 3rd, 1828. Irena Hensley, Elijah Martin, Jane Eliza Orr, Martha Martin, admitted to Communion.

Feb. 24, 1828. Samuel Akin, Mrs. Elizabeth Clark, Mrs. Sally Bohannan, admitted to Communion.

Mrs. Ann Akin, an adult, was Baptized Mch. 21, 1828.

James, Wm., Martha Ann, Samuel, John and Mary, children of Samuel Akin and Ann, his wife, were Baptized Mch. 21, 1828.

Sarah Ann Gay, dau. of Kinkead Gay and Jane, his wife, was Baptized Mch. 21, 1828.

Mch. 21, 1828. Sophia Frazier, Mary Frazier, James Gay, Mrs. Kitty Gay, Mrs. Ann Akin, Jane Young, Elizabeth Waltz, and Lucinda Young admitted to Communion.

Mrs. Kitty Gay and Lucinda Young, two adults, were Baptized Mch. 22nd, 1828.

Edward C., Jefferson M., Maria L., John P., and Thomas W. Broughton, children of Edward Broughton and his wife, were Baptized Mch. 22nd, 1828.

Mary, Robert P., Wm., John A. and James W., children of Daniel Orr, and Mary, his wife, were Baptized Mch. 22nd, 1828.

Mch. 23rd, 1828. Minerva Scrogin, admitted to Communion.

Apr. 6th, 1828. John Buford, Emily Stevenson, Wm. Rankin and Mrs. Margaret Rankin, were admitted to Communion.

Apr. 13, 1828. Angeline Rankin, and Betsy Ann Rankin, children of Wm. Rankin, and Margaret, his wife, were Baptized.

May 30, 1828. Mrs. Sarah Williams and Jane Allen were admitted to Communion.

June 1, 1828. Mrs. Italy Martin, Mrs. Mary Burnum, Andrew Z. Sowin were admitted to Communion. And Italy Martin, Mary Burnum, Andrew Z. Sowin, John Steele, Wm. Wallace, were Baptized.

The following persons were admitted to Communion at Versailles, but wished to have their names registered at Pisgah: John Martin, Jane Simonton, Margaret Hommons, and James Williams.

July 6, 1828. Sarah L. Frazier and Harvey Wasson, admitted to Communion.

Mrs. Kitty Milton, departed this life July 29, 1928.

Harriott M. Elliott, dau. of Robert Elliott and Sally, his wife, was Baptised, Aug. 29, 1828.

Aug. 30, 1828. Wm. H. Bennum, Margaret S. Stevenson, Emaline

I. Broughton, and John Martin, Jr., were admitted to Communion.

Aug. 31, 1828. Luther Scrogin, Milley Davis, Elizabeth Scrogin, admitted to Communion.

Aug. 31, 1828. Baptized: Wm. H. Brennum, and Robert H. Wasson, adults.

Sept. 1, 1828. Robert Elliott and his wife, about to remove to the State of Missouri, apply for a certificate of dismission, which was granted.

Sept. 21, 1828. Mary I. Ritchey, was admitted to Communion.

John W. Burnum, son of of Wm. Burnum and Elizabeth, his wife, was Baptized Apr. 26, 1829.

Franklin, Ellinor, Margaret and Martha Ann Martin, children of Robert Martin and Italy, his wife, were Baptized Apr. 26, 1829.

Mrs. Sarah Gay, departed this life, May 14, 1829.

Wm. H. Stevenson, son of Wm. Stevenson and Jane, his wife, was Baptized Aug. 9th, 1829.

Sarah C. Elliott, dau. of James Elliott and Sarah, his wife, was Baptized Aug. 8, 1829.

Aug. 9, 1829. Mrs. Sally Ann Young was admitted to Communion, and was Baptized.

Aug. 25, 1829. Mary C. Taylor, a member of the Church, was married to Henry Berry, not a member.

Mrs. Margaret Rankin, departed this life Sept. 4th, 1829.

Oct. 10, 1829. Lancelot Clark, and Elizabeth, his wife, about to remove to the State of Illinois, applied for a Certificate of dismission, granted.

Mch. 3rd, 1830. George Lingenfelter, about to remove to Shelby County, applied for a Certificate of dismission, granted.

Elizabeth A. Stevenson, a member of the Church, was married to William Cooper, not a member, by Rev. Doct. James Blythe, Mch. 11th, 1830.

Sarah E. Akin, dau. of Samuel Akin, and Ann, his wife, was Baptized Mch. 20, 1830.

Rebecca Allen, dau. of Wm. Allen and Mary, his wife, was Baptized, May 2, 1830.

Mary Elizabeth Stewart, dau. of Charles Stewart, and Mary, his wife, was Baptized, July 25, 1830.

Horace B. and Thornton A. Boardman, children of James Boardman and Mary, his wife, were Baptized July 30, 1830.

Robert Martin, son of Robert Martin and Italy, his wife, was Baptized, July 30, 1830.

July 30, 1830. Mrs. Elizabeth Waltz, admitted to Communion.

July 31, 1830. Frederick Bush, admitted to Communion.

William Bennum, son of William Bennum and Mary, his wife, was Baptized, Aug. 15, 1830.

William Milton, son of John Milton, and Louisa, his wife, was Baptized, Aug. 29th, 1830.

Virginia Berry, dau. of Henry Berry and Mary C. Berry, his wife, was Baptized, July 29th, 1830.

Sept. 5, 1830. Hannah W. Blair, removed.

Robert Martin removed to Missouri, Oct. 10, 1830.

Mrs. Mary Stewart, removed, Oct. 30, 1830.

Oct. 6, 1830. Kinkead Gay and Jane, his wife, removed to Illinois.

Nov. 18, 1830. Polly I. Ritchey, married to John Pearson.

Jan. 30, 1831. James Martin, Jun. and Margaret, his wife, removed.

George B. Stevenson, son of Wm. Stevenson and Jane, his wife, was Baptized, Mch. 13, 1831.

Samuel Akin and his wife removed, Mch. 13, 1831.

William Allen and Mary, his wife, had a daughter born Mch. 15, 1831.

Apr. 20, 1831. Mrs. Nancy Winkfield, departed this life.

Mary Ann Allen, dau. of William Allen and Mary, his wife, was baptized, Aug. 28, 1831.

Sept. 30, 1831. Wm. H. Bennum and Mary, his wife, removed, also Mrs. Jane M. Williams and Salley Williams, removed.

Lydia Rennick, departed this life, Oct. 4, 1831.

Mrs. Jane Ritchey, departed this life, Nov. 22, 1831.

Lucinda Young, married to ————— McMillen, Nov. 24, 1831.

Mch. 11, 1832. Mrs. Mary Stevenson, Mrs. Elizabeth Stevenson, and Martha McClure, were admitted to Communion. * * * all were then Baptized.

Robert E. Scrogin, departed this life, Aug. 15, 1832.

Sept. 21, 1832. Mrs. Emily Milton was admitted to Communion.

Sept. 23, 1832. Sarah Cligget, admitted to Communion and Baptized.

Sept. 24, 1832. Sophia Jane, dau. of Charles and Mary Stewart, Baptized.

Sept. 30, 1832. Elijah Bushrod Taylor, Martha Catherine, Caroline Louisa, John, Sarah Elizabeth, and Addison, and Mary Ann, children of Ebin and Emily B. Milton were baptized. Ann Eliza, dau. of John and Louisa Ann Milton, Benjamin Taylor, son of Henry K. and Mary Catherine Berry, baptized.

Benjamin Stevenson, Sr., departed this life Oct. 1832.

Oct. 21, 1832. William B. Rankin, son of William Rankin, was baptized.

Mariah E., Harvey W. and Joshua L. Worley, children of Joshua Worley and Jane, his wife, were Baptized Oct. 28, 1832.

Samuel Akin and Ann, his wife, who were dismissed from this Church Feb. 27, 1831, have returned, and settled again, received as members.

Mrs. Elizabeth Cunningham, from Concord Church, Ala., received as a member.

Salley Frazier, a member of Pisgah Church, married to David Logan, a member of Horeb Church, Jan.; 1833.

Apr. 27, 1833, Mrs. Mary Claggat, and Mrs. Sally Elliott, received as members, from Woodford and Greers Creek Churches. Also Ann Elliott and Mrs. Elizabeth Bush, on examination.

May 13, 1833. Mrs. Jane Berry was Baptized.

Mrs. Susan Hart, departed this life, June 21, 1833.

Mrs. Sally Elliott, departed this life, Aug. 17, 1833.

Aug. 24, 1833. Thomas Wasson, admitted to Communion.

Aug. 25, 1833. Mrs. Jane Ritchey and Mary Ann Carlisle admitted to Communion.

Mary Ann Carlisle, was dismissed to Woodford Church.

Aug. 26, 1833. Walter C. Ferguson and Ferabanite Hensley, admitted.

Aug. 25, 1833. Rev. Joseph C. Cunningham resigned as Preacher at Pisgah Church.

Aug. 26, 1833. Charles A. Stevenson, son of Wm. Stevenson and Jane, his wife, and Rebeckah Jane Worley, dau. of Joshua Worley and Jane, his wife, were Baptized.

The Rev. Joseph P. Cunningham, pastor of Pisgah Church, departed this life, Sept. 29, 1833.

Elijah Milton, departed this life Oct. 15, 1833.

Nov. 22, 1833. Elected Rev. Jacob F. Price as Pastor.

Nov. 23. Elizabeth Stevenson, and Mrs. Juliet U. Jackson, admitted to Communion.

Mrs. Susanna Quarles, departed this life, May 19, 1834.

Mrs. Nancy Buford (formerly Mrs. Watson), departed this life, June 26, 1834.

Col. Hugh Muldrow, departed this life Aug. 21, 1834.

William Rankin, departed this life, Oct. 29, 1834.

Sophia M. Frazier, departed this life, Feb. 4, 1835.

Feb. 22, 1835. Members added to the Church, Mrs. Mary Ann Milton and Mrs. Elizabeth Milton.

Luther C. Scrogin, about to remove to Missouri, dismission granted, Feb. 28, 1835.

Mrs. Elizabeth Waltz, departed this life, May 14, 1835.

Charles W. Price, son of Jacob F. Price and Maria, his wife, was Baptized, May 23, 1835. John W. Allen, son of Wm. Allen and Mary, his wife, and William Bush, son of Frederick Bush were baptized.

May 24, 1835. Jane Morgan, admitted to the Church and Baptized.

Mrs. Polly Cox, departed this life, July 10, 1835.

Mrs. Mary Stewart, departed this life, June, 1835.

Aug. 22, 1835. Mrs. Jane Sandusky, Mary F. Akin and Martha Ann McCrosky, admitted to Communion. And John Milton and Louisa, his wife, dismission granted.

Aug. 23, 1835. Mrs. Jane Sandusky and Martha Ann McCrosky, two adult persons, Baptized.

Oct. 11, 1835. Mrs. Sophia Smedley and James Martin, admitted to Communion.

Feb. 27, 1836. America Gaines, Samuel Scrogin, and John W. Stevenson, admitted to Communion.

Feb. 28, 1836. M. L. Robinson, admitted to Communion, and America Gaines, John W. Stevenson, Baptized.

May 8, 1836. M. L. Robinson, dismission granted.

July 10, 1836. Charles Wm. Cassleman, admitted to the Church, formerly a member of the Regular Baptist Church.

John W. Edger, son of Sirus Edger and Jane, his wife, was Baptized, July 10, 1836.

Martha Jane Martin, dau. of James Martin and Jane, his wife, Baptized July 17, 1836.

James E. Martin, son of Elijah Martin and his wife, Baptized July 17, 1836.

Dec. 11, 1836. Martha Payten, infant dau. of Charles Castleman; and ,Sarah and Tedbald, children of Emily Milton, Baptized.

Feb. 25, 1837. Ralph C. Smith and Catherine Hunter, received in membership.

Apr. 30, 1837. Dr. Lewis Marshall and Agatha, his wife, received as members, from Versailles Church.

May 28, 1837. Infants Baptized, Sarah Ann, of Frederick and Elizabeth Bush. Jas. Abraham, Abner C., Catherine C., and Mary Bell, children of Mrs. Hunter.

James Martin, Sen. Elder, died Aug., 1837.

Aug. 27, 1837. George Parsons, received from New Providence Church. Mrs. Collins, dismission, granted.

Sept. 27, 1837. Miss Sarah Clicket, dismission granted.

Nov. 26, 1837. Miss Eliza Alexander, received into membership.

May 27, 1838. Rebecca McIlvain, and George C. Spencer and Amelia Spencer, received into membership. Cloe Isabella, inft. of Rev. J. F. Price, and Joseph F., inft. of June Hedges were Baptized.

June 29, 1838. Mrs. Jane Sandusky's chidlren Baptized, Frances Ann, Hugh Allen and William, Eliza Jane and Malison Sandusky.

Aug. 29, 1838. Baptized * * Mary E. and Alexander D. Wasen, infant children of H. Wasen and Margaret, his wife, also Mary Elizabeth, inft. of James and Jane Martin.

Sept. 24, 1838. Session met * * * Mrs. Margaret Thompson, dismissed to join the Church, in Lexington.

Nov. 4, 1839. W. P. Cravens and Louisa Bohannon, received into Membership.

May 26, 1839. Mary Ann Phillips and Miss Nancy McClure, received into Membership, from Bethel Church. Eliza Ann and Seth Stevens, infants of Gamwell Aiken, and wife, were Baptized. Mana

Louise, infant dau. of J. F. Price and Maria R., his wife, were baptised.
The 4th. Sabbath in Aug., 1839. Lucretia ,infant dau. of William and Mary Bissell, was baptised.
On 4th. Sabbath of Nov., 1839. Agatha Marshall and Cyrus Hedges, received into the Church.
Dec., 1839. The Second Sabbath and the Semi Centinary Celebration was observed.
Nov. 14, 1840. Alexander Dinsmore, from Presby. Church, at Washington, Pa., Mrs. Mary Bissell, from the 1st. Presby. Church, Ochio City, and Mr. Will C. Bissell, from _____, Ohio, all received as members.
Feb. 28, 1841. Mrs. Matilda Cox, received as member.
On Sat. before the 4th. Sabbath in Aug., 1841. Infants baptised: Joseph Stiles and Phoebe Crocket, children of Thomas and Sarah Ann Young; Bushrod and Milton Young, children of Charles and E. Castleman; Lucy, Eliza, Laura, and Anderson, children of Henry and Catherine Berry; Jeanette Margaret, adopted child of James and Jane Martin, having been adopted the 3rd. Sabbath of June.
Camp Meeting, held in the Grove near Pisgah, Sept. 23-Oct. 4, 1841. 21 tents. Assisting at different times, Rev. Robert J. Breckenridge, W. Y. Allen, N. L. Rice, N. H. Hale, J. G. Gemeial (?), J. H. Logan, Wm. R. Preston, Wm. L Breckenridge, John F Coons, J. J. Bullock, R. Davidson, D. D., J. D. Mathews, J. Lyle, G. W. McElroy, C. Stewart, J. C. Hanson, J. K. Burch.
Persons received, Sept. 26, Eben Milton, Hugh Allen, Augustus Bailey, and James Wardlow, Mrs. Ann L. McGee. The first 3 were Baptised. Also Dr. Reuben Berry, Eliza Bushrod Milton, Alexander Stevenson, Thos. Paxton Allen, Polly Allen, Malinda Rennick, Wm. Colmeny, Elizabeth Kent Alexander, Ann Smedley, Louisa Carolina Milton, Martha Ann Aiken, Samuel Aiken, Jr., Harlow Spencer, Susan Risk, Martha Jane Irvine, Thomas Young, Archimedes Elliott, John Milton, Jr., Stephen G. Tutt, Amanda O. Risk, Elizabeth Milton, John J. Reid, Margaret C. Reid, Robb Allen, Jas. Abraham Hunter, John P. Aiken, Samuel Ritchie, Mary Williams, Elliott Glass Marshall, Mary Patterson Thompson, all of whom had previously been baptised. Received and baptised, Gillead Polk, Bushrod Castleman, Garret Young, Eliza Ann Sullivan, Eliza McCrosky, Catherine Burrier, William Burrier, Rebecca Burrier, Wm. E. Milton, Henry Berry, Hannah E. Castleman, John R. Stogdol, Nancy Stogdal, Martha Allen, Hulda Ann Elliott, Zerelda Sanders, Will H. Martin, John Neet, Columbia Offit, Alice Ann Allen, Elizabeth Lucy Hunter, making 56 in all. J. J. Reid, Margaret C. Reid, Columbia Offit, Stephen G. Tutt, and Gillead Polk, dismissed to join Woodford Church, and Glass Marshall, Martha Jane Irvine, Susan Risk, Amanda D. Risk, to Bethel Church.
Nov. 4, 1841. Dismissed Mary P. Thompson, to join some Church in the South.
Nov. 26, 1841. Baptised Elizabeth, James Trimble, Louisa Jane and William Allen, children of Robert Allen, and Patsy, his wife.
Feb. 6, 1842. Wm. C. Bissel and Mary C., his wife, removed.
May 4, 1842. Joseph Frazier, received from the 1st. Church at Lexington.
Aug. 25, 1842. Robert Wilkerson, Addison Milton, and Elizabeth Florida Miles, received .
Sept. 5, 1842. Mrs. Sarah Elizabeth Castleman, received from Baptist Church. Ann Mary, infant dau. of Jacob F. and Maria R. Price, baptised.
Sept. 13, 1842. Mr. M. Scott, Friend Perrin and John Jackson, were received into the Church.
Dec. 2, 1842. Robt. H. Wason and wife, and Rebecca McIlvain, were dismissed, at their request.
Jan. 1, 1843. James Stevenson requested dismissal, and also Polly

Stevenson, of Boon Co., Ky., granted.

Jan. 15, 1843. Friend Perrin requested dismission, to Church in Ohio.

Apr. 1, 1843. Wm. Coleman, dismission to Church in New Albany, Indiana.

July 15, 1843. Robert Wilkerson, dismissed to Church in Illinois.

Oct. 1, 1843. Garret Young, about to remove to Missouri, dismission granted.

Nov. 4, 1843. Baptized, Ebin, Benjamin Taylor and James Berryman, children of Ebin Milton, and Emily, his wife.

Dec. 25, 1843. John Neet, infant son of Frederick Bush and Elizabeth, his wife, baptized. Mary Ann Phillips, dismission granted.

1844. The 4th. Sabbath of Feb. John Valentine, received and baptized.

The 1st. Sabbath of March. Frederick and Elizabeth Bush, Ann Elliott, Augustus Barkley and Mary William Poage, (?), Mary W. Elliott, were dismissed to other Churches.

June 1. Baptized Mary Louisa, infant dau. of Charles W. Castleman and Elizabeth, his wife. Also baptized Charlotte Ellen, infant dau. of Jacob F. and Maria R. Price.

Sept. 26, 1844. A. Elliott, dismissed to Church in Missouri.

2nd. Sabbath in June. Agatha Marshall, infant dau. of Caleb Logan and Agatha, his wife, baptized.

4th. Sabbath. Benjamin, son of Dr. R. Berry and wife, baptized, also Mary Ellen, inft. dau. of Cyrus Hedges and Jane, his wife.

Nov. 22, 1845. Infants baptized: Margaret Elizabeth, dau. of Archimedes and Hulda Elliott; Elizabeth Waltz, inft. of John Young, and Eliza Ann, his wife.

Nov. 23. Clark McDermont, presented letter from 1st. Presbyterian Church at Dayton, O. and Mrs. M. G. Martin from New Providence Church, both accepted.

Feb. 22, 1846. The following persons were received: R. M. (?) Stevenson, Robert L. Stevenson, (baptized). Mrs. Mary Jane Neet, and Margaret E. McKing.

4th. Sabbath in May, 1846. Mary Ann Allen, Louisa Allen, Rebecca Allen and Alexander K. Cox, were baptized.

June 20, 1846. Dismission granted, John Stogdal and Nancy, his wife, to join the Harmony Church.

3rd. Sabbath of July, 1846. Baptized, Nancy Margaret and Elizabeth Sarah, infant children of James and Patsey Level (or Serel).

Aug. 4th. Sabbath. Mary Jane Sullivan, received.

4th. Sabbath of Sept. William Milton, dismissed to McCord Church.

4th. Sabbath of Nov. John Knox Price, infant son of Rev. J. F. Price, and Maria R., his wife baptized.

June 3rd 1847. Our beloved pastor, Rev. Jacob Fishback Price, departed this life, very suddenly in the Stage, near Brownsville, Pa., on his return from the General Assembly of the Preby. Church, which sat at Richmond, Va. Was interred at Pisgah June 6.

Aug. 20, 1847. The following received into the church: Virginia Berry, Elizabeth Stevens, Davidella H. Neet, Elizabeth S. Berry, Robert L. Haney, Davis S. F. McPheters, Sarah C. Stevenson (Mrs). Mrs. Isabella Parsons, Lucy Berry, Wm. H. Stevenson, Charles W. Price, George Bushrod Stevenson, James R. Gay, Tarlton C. Miles, Mary Waltz, Virginia Louisa Neet, Clarinda E. Stevenson, Lucy Ann Stevenson, Nicholas Walden, Sarah R. Milton, Mary Milton, Mary Elizabeth Wason, Margaret Gay, Martha Peyton Castleman, Walter Ferguson, Mrs. Henrietta C. Bohannon, James H. Henderson, Cloe Isabella Price.

Nov. 14, 1847. Received into the Church, Miss Elizabeth Johnson, from Cedar Creek Church. David Riley and Martha, his wife, from Harrodsburg Church.

Dec. 5, 1847. In the Versailles Church, baptized, Charles Montgomery, infant of David and Martha Riley.

Feb. 24, 1848. Service to Ordaining of Rev. S. M. Bayless, Pastor.

Feb. 27, 1848. Received into the Church: Guy Hamilton, and Marcia P. Hamilton, from Woodford Church. David Smith, from Northfield Church, Ohio.

Aug. 7, 1848. Baptized Charles, infant of Cyrus and Jane Hedges.

Aug. 25. Baptized Mary Caroline, infant dau. of Robert and Martha Allen.

Sept. 3, 1848. Baptized, Griffin Taylor, infant of Eben and Emily B. Milton.

Sept. 17. Tarlton C. Miles, dismissed to Church at Charleston, Ill., and James H. Henderson, to Bethel Church.

Oct. 15. Mrs. Catherine Hunter, dismissed to Church at Versailles. Mrs. Alice Ann Settle (late Alice Ann Allen) at her request, was dismissed. Agatha Logan, dismissed to 1st. Pres. Church at Louisville. David Smith, dismissed, at his own request.

Feb. 9, 1849. Guy Hamilton and Marcia P., his wife, were dismissed at their request.

May 26, 1849. Baptized, Josephine, infant dau. of John and Mary Jane Neet, and May 27 to Ann Eckhart, infant dau. of A. S. and Huldah Ann Elliott, and to Anna Margaret, infant dau. of Dr. R. H. Wason. Agnes Gay, received.

Aug. 25. Baptized Ann Edmonia, infant of John and Catherine Valentine; Emily, infant dau. of Saml. Akin, Jr., and Charles William, Inft. of Harlow and Martha Spencer.

Aug. 26. Robert Garrett, received.

Sept. 23, 1849. Joseph Madison, dismissed to the Marion Church, Muhlenberg, Presbytery.

Oct. 7, 1849. Mrs. Alice Ann Little returned to the bounds of Pisgah, and returned her letter.

Mch. 5, 1850. David Riley and Martha, his wife, dismissed to Church at Versailles, and Joseph Frazer, to the 1st. Church at Lexington.

Apr. 2, 1850. Miss Mary Allen, dismissed to Church at Covington.

May 26. Miss Mary Stevenson, dismissed to Church in Versailles.

Aug. 26, 1850. Baptized: Jas. Elliott, infant son of John ana Mary Neet; Marietta, infant dau. of John and M. T. Martin; Sally Elliott, infant of I. R. and S. C. Stevenson.

Jan. 8, 1851. Dr. R. B. Berry and his daughter, Mary Berry dismissed to Church in Memphis, Tenn., and his daughter, Elizabeth Wood, to the Church at Baton Rouge, La.

Feb. 23 ,1851. Saml. Akin, Jr., dismissed to Church in Missouri.

July 26, 1851. Addison Milton, dismissed to the 2nd. Church, Lex.

May 7, 1851. Miss Jane Young, dismissed to join Church in Missouri.

Aug. 27, 1851. "Conjointly, to the memory of Robert Stevenson, (who died 26th. of July last) and his Father and Mother, Samuel and Jane Stevenson, "who were removed by death, some years since," "out of regard for the upright and Christian character of Robert Stevenson * * his great kindness "in donating 30 acres of land, for a Parsonage." Also out of respect for the character of Saml. and Jane Stevenson, and of their donating for the use of the Church many years ago, the land on which the Church now stands." A collection was taken to erect a monument in their honor.

Oct. 1, 1851. Mrs. Maria R. Price, Cloe Isabella Price and Charles W. Price, dismissed to Church in Frankfort. Mrs. Harriett, received as member, from church at Midway.

Nov. 9, 1851. Baptized Rebecca Wright, infant dau, of Dr. R. H. and Margaret Wason.

Jan. 8, 1852. Baptized Ann Virginia and Jacob Price, children of Charles W. and Sarah Elizabeth Castleman.

Jan. 10, 1852. Addison Milton, returned to bounds of Pisgah Church from 2nd. Church, Lex.

Aug. 23, 1852. Elder I. S. Berryman and Matilda Berryman, his wife, dismissed to the 1st. Pres. Church of Lex.

————, 1853. Samuel Akin and wife, John P. Akin, A. L. (S ?) Elliott and wife and Malinda Rennick, dismissed to join other churches.

4th. Sabbath, Nov., 1853. Mrs. Juliet W. Jackson, dismissed to join Church at Hopkinsville, Ky.

Feb. 6, 1853. Mrs. Virginia Moore (late Virginia Neet) dismissed to church at Harrodsburg. Mrs. F. I. Patrick, was received from Harrods Creek Church.

Sept. 18, 1853. Addison McPheters and Davis McPheters, dismissed, at their request.

Nov. 19, 1853. Tidball Milton, received, and Harlow Spencer, from Parksville Pres. Church, Missouri.

Nov. 27, 1853. Rev. Robert W. Allen, elected Pastor of Pisgah Church, Rev. Samuel M. Bayless, having resigned on Mch. 28, 1852.

Jan. 7, 1854. Service to Install Rev. Robert W. Allen, as Pastor. James Allen and Elizabeth, his wife, from Frankfort Church, Indiana, accepted as members, also Margaret Ann M. Allen, wife of Rev. Robert W. Allen, from same church.

May 27, 1854. Received, Mrs. Sarah Stevenson.

May 28, 1854. John Dudley, infant son of John and Mary Jane Neet, also John William, infant son of John and Catherine Valentine, Baptized.

Sept. 2, 1854. Bennet Price and Mary Louisa, children of T. I. Settle and Alice Ann, his wife, baptized.

Sept. 3. Joseph Hale, received as member.

Sept. 10, 1854. Miss Lucinda Haney, received into the church and Baptized.

Nov. 26, 1854. The Pastor was assisted by his brother, Rev. A. C. Allen, of Franklin, Ind.

Feb. 24, 1855. James R. Gay, dismissed to Church at Harrodsburg, and Jane Morgan, dismissed at her request.

Feb. 25, 1855. Dr. W. Douglas Gay, admitted to the church and baptized.

May 27, 1855. Mrs. Martha Frazer, wife of Joseph G. Frazer, dismissed to 1st. Pres. Church at Lex.

Aug. 1, 1855. Jas. R. Gay, received, by return of letter granted in Feb. last, also Kate Gay, wife of Jas. R. Gay, from Church at Midway.

Aug. 8, 1855. Mrs. Ann Wheeler, received into the Church.

Aug. 13, 1855. Mr. Samuel Ritchie, departed this life.

Aug. 26. Mrs. Anna Wheeler, baptized.

Sept. 4, 1855. Mrs. Jane Ritchey, departed this life.

Nov. 25, 1855. Received as members: Misses Jennie Worley, Jennie Walker, Rebecca W. Gay, Messrs. C. T. Cox, Hugh Hedger, Wm. Dunn, James B. Milton, Harvey Doggins, Wm. T. Smith, Ebin Taylor, James S. Wason, John Scarce. Were baptised: Jennie Worley, Jennie Walker, Rebecca W. Gay, C. T. Cox, Wm. Dunn, Harvey Doggins, Wm. T. Smith, John Scarce.

Dec. 9. Bushrod Castleman and Ebin Milton, Jr., received.

Dec. 16, 1855. Miss Isabella Alexander, received into the Church.

Dec. 21, 1855. Miss I. Alexander, died.

Feb. 17, 1856. Mrs. Sarah Stevenson, dismissed at her request.

May 4, 1856. Carrie Logan, infant dau. of Rev. R. W. Allen, Baptised.

May 25, 1856. Mrs. Theodosia S. Hall, received from Mt. Sterling Church.

Aug. 17. Baptised, Eva Sackett, inft. dau. of Rev. S. B. and

Theodosia Hall.

Aug. 23. Laura Augusta, infant dau. of John and Mary I. Neet.

Sept. 20, 1856. John Valentine and Catherine, his wife, dismissed to join Pres. Church in Decatur, Ills. Miss Maria Sackett, received as member. Also Mrs. Rebecca Scott (Rebecca Allen), dismissed to join Church at Covington.

Dec. 7, 1856. Mrs. Theodosia Hall and Miss Maria Sackett, dismissed to join Church at Pine Ridge, Miss.

March 14, 1857. Watson Gay, member of this church, died.

Mch. 29, 1857. Mrs. Mary Jane Spencer, received into church, and baptised.

Apr. 4, 1857. Rev. R. W. Allen, resigned as Pastor.

Apr. 9, 1857. Baptized: Kate Claggett, inft. dau. of Dr. R. H. and Margaret Wason

July 22. Mr. Ebin Milton and Emily, his wife, also Miss Caroline, Mollie, Sallie and James Milton, dismissed to the Church at Jeffersonville, Ind.

Sept. * * * Addison, Tidball, and Ebin Milton, dismissed at their request.

Oct. 20. Mrs. Bettie Bayless, dismissed to 1st. Pres. Church at Lex.

Jan. 1, 1858. Americus Gains, departed this life.

Jan. 6, 1858. Mrs. Ann Wheeler, departed this life.

Mch. 10. Mr. John Martin and Susan, his wife, dismissed to join the O. S. Pres. Church at Versailles.

Apr. 22. Rev. R. Douglas, Ordained Pastor, installed.

May 10, 1858. Departed this life, Capt. John Neet, a ruling Elder in this Church.

Mr. Joseph Hale dismissed at his own request.

4th. Sabbath, Oct., 1858. Robert Hedges and Wm. T. Wason, received into the Church, and John C. Young Douglass, infant son of the Pastor and Carrie Douglass, his wife, baptized.

4th. Sabbath of Feb., 1859. Mrs. M. A. M. Allen dismissed to Church at Jacksonville, Ills.

Feb. 11, 1859. Mrs. Isabella Parsons, departed this life.

Apr. 23. Carrie Douglass, inft. dau. of Dr. R. H. and Margaret Wason, baptized.

4th. Sabbath in Apr. Sarah Bettie Gay, received as member, and baptized.

1st. Sabbath of May. Received, Mrs. Mary Bosworth, as member.

May 12. Mrs. Mary Bosworth, dismissed to join Methodist Church in Lexington.

June 22. Mrs. William Martin, received into the Church.

June 29. Miss Ann D. Martin, was received into the Church.

July 3. Wm. Martin and Ann D. Martin, baptized.

Oct. 15. Mattie Allen and Annie Jefferson, infant daughters of Thos. and Alice Ann Little, baptized.

Nov. 9. William Allen, baptized.

1860. Apr. 11. Miss Martha A. McCrosky, dismissed to Mount Pleasant Church, (Baptist) Jessamine Co., Ky., and Mrs. Caroline Douglass from 2nd. Pres. Church at Danville, received as member, and Mary Louisa Castleman.

July 2, 1860. Mrs. Mary Jane Spencer, wife of Harlow Spencer, died.

July 21, 1860. Mr. Cyrus Hedges, died.

Aug. 26. Cornelia Crittenden Rout, infant of Gelon H. and Mary Rout, was baptized. (G. H. and M. Rout, members of the Pres. Church of Danville, Ky.) Also John G. Young Craft, infant son of Mrs. Frances Craft, member of Pres. Church at Holly Spring, Miss.

Oct. 21. George Latimer Douglass, infant son of Rev. Rutherford and Carrie Y. Douglass, baptized.

1861. 4th. Sabbath of Oct. Received, Mrs. N. M. Douglass, from

Pres. Ch. of St. Charles. Missouri, also Mrs. Elizabeth Coffman from Nicholasville Church, Jessamine Co., Ky.

1861. Miss Mary Ellen Hedger, received from Versailles Church, and Anna M. Wason on profession of Faith, on Apr. 24.

July 26, 1861. Miss Lucy Stevenson, departed this life.

Aug. 14, 1861. Baptized, Maggie Cheeney, infant dau. of Rev. Mr. Cheeney, also Hervey,. infant son of R. H. and Margaret Wason.

1862. Apr. 22. Mrs. Jane S. and Miss Jennie Worley, dismissed to 2nd. Pres. Lexington.

1863. 4th. Sabbath of May. Miss Mary Caroline Allen, received as member, Mrs. Nannie M. James, received from the Burlington Ch. Ebenezer Presby.

June 12, 1864. Robert Allen, infant son of Thomas and Alice Little, baptized.

Nov. 12, 1864. George Waltz and Mary, his wife, received as members.

Apr. 19, 1865. Baptized: John Thornwell Wason, infant son of Dr. R. H. and Margaret Wason.

May 10, 1865. James Cox, infant son of C. T. Cox and Mary Cox, baptized.

Sept. 6, 1865. Mrs. Agnes Ardinger (formerly Gay) was dismissed to Old School Pres. Church at Lexington, Missouri.

Dec. 12, 1865. Received, Benjamin Stevenson and on Dec. 24. Charles Hedger as members.

Jan. 26, 1866. Received Mrs. Kate Garrett, from the Church at Harrodsburg.

Jan. 30, 1866. Received into the Church; Walter F. Bohon, Miss Josie Neet, Samuel Holloway. On 31st., Wm. A. Hall, and Saml. Hall, Miss Bettie Allen, Miss Rebecca W. Wason, William Wright, James Stevenson, I. Smith Taylor, Hugh Allen. Feb. 3, Miss Sallie E. Stevenson, Jas. E. Neet.

Apr. 1, 1866. James Garret, received.

July 22. Robert Coleman, infant son of Capt. John G. and Nannie James, was baptized.

July 28, 1866. Received, Mrs. Lucinda Capell, from the Pres. Church of Independence, Missouri, and Jacob Sandusky, from the Methodist Church of Nashville.

2nd. Sabbath, Sept.. 1866. Mrs. Mary McNeely (formerly Castleman), dismissed to the Pres. Ch. at Newport, Ky.

Oct., 1866. Received by letter: Col. Oliver Anderson, from the Pres. Ch. at Lexington, Missouri, and Mrs. Louisa Anderson and Mrs. Kate Akers, same Church. Lelia Anderson, infant of T. P. and Kate Akers, baptized.

Nov. 7 ,1866. Mrs. Mary Jane Neet, departed this life.

Nov. 23, 1866. Elder Wm. L. Allen, departed this life.

Mch. 1, 1867. Wm. Wright, dismissed to the Pres. Ch. at Mattoon, Ills.

June 9, 1867. Mat Gay, infant of Thomas and Bettie Jepee, was baptized.

Nov. 24, 1867. Received, John Stockdale and wife, having removed to Missouri several years ago, * * their house burned with all contents * * * have returned to Pisgah * * received into the Church. J. F. Hedger, at his request, dismissed.

May 17, 1868. Received into the Church, John W. Evans.

Sept. 20, 1868. Baptized the following: Infants, Mary Elizabeth, dau. of H. W. and Bettie Worley. Watson McIlvain, son of Thos. and Bettie Jepee, Mary Lowry, dau. of Zelah and Martha Peyter Boyer, Clarence Zelah, son of C. C. and Mary McNeeley, and on the 27th, Elizabeth Allen, dau. of Jacob and Caroline Sandusky. Received into the Church, A Spencer and Jane M., his wife, from the Pres. Ch. at Talladega, Alabama.

July 23, 1869. Baptized, Rutherford, infant son of Rev. Rutherford and Caroline Douglass, also on the 24th. Jane Elizabeth, infant of Joshua and Sallie Falconer. Mrs. Sallie Falconer was received from Cheraw Church, S. C.

Sept. 29, 1869. Col. O. Anderson, dismissed to join Pres. Ch. at Nicholasville, Ky.

Oct. 24, 1869. Baptized, Henry Humphreys Jepee, infant son of John T. and Sarah E. Jepee.

Dec. 24, 1869. Mrs. Jane McEachin, received from Providence Church, Montgomery, Ala.

Apr. 27, 1870. Anna Margaret, infant dau. of W. H. and Mary E. Worley, was baptized.

Mch. 2, 1870. Elizabeth, infant dau. of John and Florence Williams (formerly Bohon), was baptized.

3rd. Sabbath, Oct. 1870. I. W. McIlvain and Mary, his wife, received from the Pres. Ch. at Versailles, Ky.

5th. Sabbath in Jan. 29, 1871. Received, George L. Douglass, Wm. A. Cox, Mary Rebecca Wright, Maggie Gay, and James L. Gay.

Mch. 15, 1871. Baptized, Mary Worley, infant dau. of I. C. and Anna Margaret Anderson.

Mch. 22, 1871. Thomas H. Wallace, formerly of Midway Pres. Ch. and also ruling Elder, was received into the Church.

4th. Sabbath, Apr., 1871. Miss Sallie McEachin, received into the Church.

July 9, 1871. James E. Neet, dismissed to the Pres. Ch. at Versailles. F. Bohon, returned letter, of dismission having changed his intention of removing to Missouri.

Aug. 30, 1871. Mrs. F. I. Patrick was dismissed to Pres. Ch. at Bethel, and Francis Breckinridge, infant son of Rutherford and Catherine Douglass, was baptized.

Sept. 10, 1871. Was baptized, Catherine Bunting, infant dau. of Joshua and Sarah Falconer.

Sept. 23. Was Baptized, Henry Stevenson, infant son of John and Sarah Jepee, and Thomas, infant son of Thos. and Bettie Jepee, and Peter G., infant son of P. G. and Henrietta Powell.

Jan. 22, 1872. Kate C. Wason, received into the Church.

Mch. 31, 1872. Mr. Benj. Stevenson, dismissed to the Pres. Ch. at Versailles.

Apr. 19, 1872. Mrs. Lou E. Rennick, Henry Mehring, Miss Maggie Cheeney, received into the Church, and on Apr. 20, Miss Carrie D. Wason, and Apr. 23, Charles Heber. On Apr. 23, Miss Annie Spencer.

July 10, 1872. Mrs. Josie Smith (formerly Neet), was dismissed to the Pres. Church at Bonham, Texas.

July 31. John Lafon, was received into the Church, and was baptized.

Oct. 19, 1872. Watson Gay, was received into the Church, and baptized.

Mch. 5, 1873. Dr. Wm. Brother, and C. E. Brother, his wife, received into the Church from Pres. Ch. at Lancaster.

Apr. 13, 1873. Mary Cox, was received into the Church.

1874. 4th. Sabbath in Jan. Added to the Church were, Mary McEachin, Bettie Powell, and Willie Gay. Feb. 1, Thomas Shelby, and Charles Wallace, and Ella Wallace and I. A. Falconer, and on Feb. 8, Mrs. Jane Holloway, from the Baptist Ch. at Versailles.

May 27, 1874. Baptized, Joshua, infant son of H. W. and Mary Worley.

July 19, 1874. Dismissed, C. W. Castleman and S. E., his wife, Martha P. Boyer, Thomas M. Wallace, Charles and Ellen Wallace, to 1st. Pres. Ch. at Lexington.

Aug. 5th. Sabbath, 1874. Allena, infant dau. of Dr. Wm. and Kate Brother.

Dec. 23, 1874. Thomas Shelby, dismissed to the 1st. Ch. at Lexington.

1875. Jan. 17. Derrell Hart and Mrs. Louisa Hart, his wife, received from the Providence Pres. Ch. of Alabama.

Mch. 3, 1875. Dr. R. S. Hart, received, from the Providence Pres. Ch. of Alabama.

3rd. Sabbath, May 1875. The Pastor, being called to Danville to the funeral of Mr. George Young.

Aug. 11. Baptized, Elizabeth Nell, infant dau. of A. and Jane Spencer, and infant son of Wm. and Lou E. Rennick.

Sept. 12, 1875. Mrs. Eliza Stanhope, received into the Church.

Nov. 7, 1875. Miss Mattie A. Settle and I. Wilmore Garrett, received into the Church.

A. Spencer and Jane, his wife, and their dau., Annie Spencer, were dismissed to the Pres. Ch. at Columbus, Ga.

Jan. 1, 1876. Miss Lucy A. Armistead, received from the Providence Church, Ala. Jan. 3rd, Maggie Burrier, Nancy Arnsparger, Sarah Frances Arnsparger and John Arnspager, and on Jan. 5, Mary T. Dillard, Jan. 6, Mary Heber. Jan. 7, Charles A. Stevenson, and John T. Wason, Jr. Jan. 9, Mrs. C. A. Stevenson, were received into the Church. Baptized, John, Nancy and Sarah Frances Arnsparger, Mrs. Burrier, Mary Heben, Mrs. Sue Ann Gittner, Miss Kate Hall, Miss Stella Knode and James Gay.

Mch. 22, 1876. Mrs. Bettie Gay, received from Pres. Church at Winchester.

May 6, 1876. Was Baptized, John Rutherford, infant son of Joshua A. and Sallie M. Falconer.

July 5, 1876. Was Baptized, Robert Wason, infant son of I. C. and Anna M. Anderson, of Idaho, Tex. On 9th, Nancy, Caroline, Laura, Mary and Sallie Arnsparger, children of John and Nancy Arnsparger.

Nov. 19, 1876. W. A. Slaymaker and his wife, Mrs. H. C., received from 1st. Pres. Church of Louisville, Ky. On Nov. 26. Received Hunter Brother, Jacob Sandusky, and Caroline, his wife, (last two) from Pres. Ch. at Millersburg, Ky.

Mch. 29, 1877. Baptized, Majean Rebecca Burrier.

May 27. Received, Richard Kerby Stanhope, into the Church, and Baptized.

May 30. Baptized Paul Brother, infant son of Wm. and Kate Brother, Blackburn Monroe, Joseph Carter and Catherine Taylor, infant children of Richard and Eliza Stanhope. And June 3, 1877. Marion Thomas, infant dau. of H. W. and Jennie Worley.

June 6, 1877. W. A. Slaymaker and H. C., his wife, dismissed at their request.

Aug. 26, 1877. Pastor being absent in Europe, at their own request, Derrel Hart and Louisa, his wife, were dismissed to the Pres. Ch. in Weatherford, Texas, and Miss Mary Dillard to Pres. Ch. (Providence) of Alabama.

Oct. 21, 1877. Received from Columbus Church, Georgia, A. Spencer, and Jane, his wife, and daughter, Miss Annie Spencer.

Feb. 9, 1878. Mrs. Lettie Sandusky, received into the Church.

July 14. Misses Laura Bohon and Kitty Sandusky, received into the Church.

July 15. Baptized, William, infant son of Wm. and Maggie Burrier.

Mch. 9, 1879. Received into the Church, Miss Allene Brother, Lewis M. VanMeter, and Mary E. Worley. Baptized, Rutherford Douglass, infant son of John and Nancy Arnsparger.

Aug. 16, 1879. Samuel Holloway and Jane, his wife, were dismissed to Pres. Church of Versailles.

Dec. 7, 1879. Mrs. Bettie Jepee, dismissed to Pres. Ch., Versailles.

Jan. 4, 1880. Mrs. Maggie Bird (formerly Maggie Gay), dismissed to Church at Versailles, Ky.

Jan. 11, 1880. Mrs. Kate Goodwin, dismissed to Pres. Ch. at Salem, Clarke Co., Ky., and Jan. 25 * * * James Cox, received, and Jan. 24, Mary Lee Gay, who was Baptized. Michael Powell, Robert James, Joseph Garrett, and Allie Spencer, and on the 26th, Anna M. Worely, received into the Church.

Mch. 28, 1880. Mrs. Lou E. Rennick, dismissed, to the 1st, Pres. Church at Lexington, Ky.

May 12, 1880. Eveline Elizabeth, infant dau. of Wood and Sallie Powell was Baptized.

Nov., 1880. Mrs. Sallie Gay, presented a letter from Pres. Church at Paris, and was received as member.

May 4, 1881. Miss Laura Bohon, was dismissed to the Harrods-burg Pres. Church, Cass Co., Missouri.

Aug. 28, 1881. Roberta Allen, infant dau. of Jacob Sandusky, was Baptized.

Dec. 8, 1881. Mrs. Susie L. Sandusky, received from Courtland Pres. Church, of Alabama.

Jan. 4, 1882. Miss Martha Cox, received into the Church. Jan. 29, 1882, Jacob Sandusky, dismissed to join 1st. Pres. Church at Lexington, Ky.

June 3, 1881. Baptized, Benjamine Robert, infant son of Dr. R. S. and Rebecca W. Hart, Pauline Stevenson, dau. of C. A. Stevenson and Lenia Stevenson, his wife.

June 25, 1882. Mrs. Samuel Hall and Miss Bettie Hall, dismissed to Pres. Church, Independance, Missouri.

Nov. 24, 1882. Miss Carrie Rutherford Gay, received and Baptized.

Apr. 1, 1883. H. W. Worley, received into the Church.

Apr. 21, 1883. Received into the Church, Miss Bettie Falconer, Miss Bessie Sandusky. Apr. 22, Miss Kate Falconer and I. E. Boatright. Miss Belle Hall, dismissed to Independance Church, Missouri.

June 8, 1884. Henrietta Falconer, infant dau. of I. W. and Bettie Rhodes, was Baptized.

July 6, 1884. Jesse Hart, infant son of Wm. and Maggie Burrier, was Baptized.

July 4, 1884. Additions to the Church, Miss Mary L. Gay. July 6, Julia Sandusky. July 7, Miss Drusilla Douglass and Laura Arnsparger. July 7, Mrs. Ruth E. Heiber and Mrs. Hattie Letrell. July 8, Horace Gay, Mrs. Mary Heiber, Charles Heiber, Kirby Grimes. July 9, Miss Molly Dole, Richard Heiber. July 10, B. R. Marshall. July 11, John Reese. July 13, Baptism followed.

July 16, 1884. Miss Mollie Dole, dismissed to Pres. Church, at Mattoon, Ill.

Dec. 3, 1884. Mrs. T. Stevenson and Miss Cleodia Stevenson, dismissed, to Versailles Church.

Apr. 1, 1885. Eddie Boterite, dismissed * * * removed.

May 5, 1885. Baptized, Margaret Wason, inft. of I. Wilmore and Carrie D. Garnett.

May 23, 1885. Baptized Margaret Rebecca, inft. of Dr. R. S. Hart and wife,

Apr. 7, 1886. Mrs. Bettie Rhodes, dismissed to join the First Presbyterian Church, Lexington.

May 16, 1886. Mrs. and William Laurie, late from Scotland, received into Pisgah Church, from the Parrish of Crossmichael, Kirkandburghshire.

Oct. 20, 1886. Isabella, infant dau. of above Wm. Laurie and wife, baptized.

Oct. 27. Miss Lou Armstead, dismissed, to Weatherford, Texas.

Dec. 26, 1886. Mrs. Mary Lee Mitchell, (formerly Mary Lee Gay) and Mollie R. Robertson, (Miss Mollie R. Wright), dismissed to Church at Paris.

DEATHS, 1890-MARCH, 1916

Rev. Rutherford Douglass, died after a brief illness, at his home, Travilla, in Fayette Co., Ky., Apr. 9, 1890. He was born June 30, 1828.

Robert H. Wason, M. D., died Oct. 30, 1891, aged 80 yrs. and 7 months. Was born Mch. 11, 1811.

Mr. Charles Heiber, died Apr. ____, 1894.

Mrs. Mary Heiber, died Apr. ____, 1894.

Carrie Douglass Garrett, wife of J. W. Garrett, died Feb. 14, 1895.

Charles C. Heiber, died _____, 1895.

Charles T. Cox, died Mch. 17, 1897, was born June 7, 1829.

Mrs. M. Wason, died Feb. 9, 1897.

Mrs. H. A. Cox, wife of Wm. A. Cox, died Aug. 31, 1897.

Alma Brooks Wason, wife of J. T. Wason, died Nov. 17, 1900.

Katherine Coleman Smedley, died Apr. ____, 1901.

Mr. James Garrett, died Apr. 6, 1902.

Mr. Elijah Watkins, died Feb. 22, 1903.

Charles T. Cox, Jr., died May 30, 1903.

John W. McIlvain, the oldest member of this Church, died Oct. 20, 1903.

Miss Mollie Daugherty, died Oct. ____, 1903.

Miss Kate Gay, Jan. 9, 1906.

Mrs. Mary Agnes Powell, wife of Mr. P. G. Powell, Jr., died Dec. 12, 1905.

Mary Worley Hart, daughter of Dr. R. S. Hart and his wife, Rebecca, died Aug. 29, 1906.

Mr. James R. Gay, died Sept. ____, 1906.

Mrs. Sarah Bunting Falconer, wife of Mr. J. A. Falconer, died Nov. 16, 1908.

Mrs. Mary Allen Cox, wife of Mr. Charles T. Cox, died Feb. 23, 1909, in her 78th year.

Mr. George W. Smedley, died June 25, 1909.

Sarah Falconer Kendall, died Feb. 9, 1911.

Mrs. Caroline Young Douglass, wife of Rev. Rutherford Douglass, died June, 1911.

Miss Katherine Bunting Falconer, died Nov. 1, 1911.

Mrs. Bettie Boyle Gay, died Feb. 1, 1912.

Mrs. Mary Wardle, died at the home of her daughter, Mrs. Ed. Preston, of Fayette Co., Ky., July, 1913.

Dr. Robert Singleton Hart, born Jan. 9, 1843, died Mch. 21, 1916.

PASTORS OF PISGAH CHURCH

(Copied from "Pisgah Book" by Shearer)

Beginning with:

Rev. Adam Rankin, summer of 1784-1792; deposed.

Rev. James Blythe, D. D., from 1791 to 1832. He was the first D. D. West of the Appalachian Range of Mountains. Resigned.

Rev. Joseph P. Cunningham, 1832-1833. Died in office.

Rev. Jacob Fishback Price, 1834 to 1847. Died suddenly in Stage Coach, (on June 3rd, 1847).

Rev. Samuel M. Bayless, Feb. 24, 1848-Mch. 28, 1852. Resigned.

Rev. W. C. McPheeters. Stated Supply, only. 1852-1853.

Rev. Robt. W. Allen, Jan. 7, 1853-Apr. 4, 1857. Resigned.

Rev. Rutherford Douglass, D. D., Apr. 22, 1857-Apr. 8, 1890. Died in office.

Rev. E. E. Erwin, Nov. 17, 1890. Resigned in 1897.

Rev. Coleman O. Groves, June 12, 1897-Mch. 8, 1903. Resigned.

Rev. W. O. Shewmaker, Sept. 27, 1903-Oct. 1, 1912. Resigned.

Rev. I. C. Hunt, May 4, 1913-Dec., 1914.

Rev. George M. Telford, Oct. 10, 1915-.

SEMINARY.
Dist. Ct., A-346, 10th Sept., 1797.

Hugh McIlvain and Polly, his wife, of Lexington, to Adam Rankin, John McChord and David Logan for and in behalf of themselves and others for the express purpose of a seminary, Trustees of the Lexington Seminary of Education and other religious purposes, and for the benefit of the societies in this State under the inspection of the Associate Reformed Synod, of which are at present members John Mason of New York, Robt. Amman of Philadelphia and Adam Rankin of Lexington, adhering to the Westminister confession of faith, Catechism —longer and shorter—directory for public worship and the form of the Presbyterian Church government. Consideration, 36 pounds, conveys in Lexington a parcel of ground fronting on Walnut Street, being part of lot 21. * * *

SOUTH ELKHORN CHURCH.
Dt. Ct. D-60, 26th Dec., 1801.

Abraham Bowman and Sarah, his wife, to John Keller and Samuel Ayres, Deacons of South Elkhorn Church, in consideration of five pounds conveys to John Keller and Samuel Ayres, Deacons and officers of South Elkhorn Baptist Church, on the waters of Elkhorn containing one acre.

Including a brick meeting house nearby in the cemetery.
Signed—Abraham Bowman, Sarah Bowman.
Witnesses—David Bryan, Jno. Parker, Will Gist, Jno. Higbee.

SOUTH ELKHORN BAPTIST CHURCH.
35-378, 14-N, Nov., 1859.

Nicholas Warfield and Susan E. Warfield, his wife, to John H. Williams, Benjamin Bosworth and B. L. Watt, Trustees of South Elkhorn Baptist Church * * * in the vicinity of Slickaway on the Versailles Road and Lexington Pike.

TOWN FORK BAPTIST CHURCH.
Dt. Ct., C-148, 29th January, 1800.

Henry Payne and Anna, his wife, to William Hous, Nathaniel Ashby, Peter Couchover, Thomas Lewis, Edward Payne and Jedica Stout, Trutees for the regular Baptists, now known by the name of the Town Fork Baptist Church, in consideration of the respect and good will to the aforsesaid Baptist Church for the use of the said Baptist Church.

For the particular use of containing a house for public worship and for no other * * * so long as the aforesaid church or people practice the same fair, and order and no longer. * * *
Witnesses—Benj. Stout, John Wilson, Levi Calvert, Jonathan Chinn.

ADDITIONAL HISTORY OF DAVID'S FORK BAPTIST CHURCH BOOK
(Abstract donated by C. R. Staples)
See Pages 177 to 189

Minute Book of the Bryan't Station Book now on file in Kentucky Historical Society at Frankfort, Ky. (Labeled "The Particular Baptist Church.")

"At a church meeting held at Bro. Ambrose Dudley's on the 3rd Saturday in January, 1799—Bro. Leonard Young and John Mason are appointed to attend to the executing of deeds for the lots on which our meeting houses stand at Bryan't and David's Fork and the deeds to be made to Bro. Ambrose Dudley in behalf of the Church." "At a meeting held at Bro. Joseph Rogers on the 3rd Saturday in March, 1799— Motion made, agreed that our deacons pay Bro. Richard Mitchell five dollars for his services in keeping the meeting house at David's Fork the last year. Bro. Richard Hulett has agreed to take charge of the meeting house at David's Fork for the present year. Then dismist.

"Ambrose Dudley, moderator; John Mason, Clerk."

"At a meeting held in meeting house at Bryan't Station on the 3rd Saturday, February, 1806. Agreed that we appoint seven of our brethren commissioners to let the building of a brick meeting house at Bryan't, fifty feet long, forty feet wide, out to out, and twenty feet high; said committee—Leonard Young, Asa Tompson, William Dudley, John Darnaby, John E. Richardson, Hezekiah Harrison and John Mason, to sell old meeting house on six months' credit." "At a meeting held at the place where the new meeting house is to be built, near Jeremiah White's, first Sunday in July 1789. No business."

Page 29. "At a church meeting held at the meeting house at David's Fork the first Saturday, September, 1789." (No business.)

CEMETERIES AND FAMILY BURYING GROUNDS

BURIALS IN BATTLE GROVE CEMETERY, AT CYNTHIANA, KY., FROM 1869 TO 1881.

(Copied by Mrs. H. K. McAdams from Office Book in Cemetery.)
*Indicates "Reinterred from Old Cemetery or Private Cemetery.

George W. Coats, from Cynthiana, aged 35 years.
Apr. 21, 1869—Mrs. B. C. Day, from city.
Apr. 21, 1869—Emma Kennard, from city; age 35.
Apr. 21, 1869—Sallie E. Kennard, from city; age 28.
Apr. 23, 1869—James I. Victor, county.
Apr. 24, 1869—Thomas B. Woodyard, city.
Apr. 25, 1869—Susan Woodyard, city.
Apr. 25, 1869—Henry C. Moore, city.
Apr. 25, 1869—James Moore, city.
Apr. 25, 1869—Thomas W. Moore, city.
Apr. 25, 1869—Andrew Moore, city.
Apr. 25, 1869—Mrs. M. C. Tebbs, city.
Apr. 25, 1869—Mary A. Boswell, city.
Apr. 25, 1869—Lucy Moore, city.
Apr. 25, 1869—William Moore, city.
Apr. 30, 1869—John M. Kimbrough, county.
Apr. 30, 1869—Samuel Kimbrough, county.
Apr. 30, 1869—Henry Kimbrough, county.
Apr. 30, 1869—Moses Kimbrough, county.
May 1, 1869—William Magee, county.
May 1, 1869—W. H. Forsythe, county.
May 1, 1869—Mrs. Forsythe, county.
May 1, 1869—Lafayette Wilson, county.
May 1, 1869—Mrs. Cora Dills, county.
May 1, 1869—John M. Anderson, county.
May 1, 1869—Henry Nichols, city.
May 1, 1869—Mrs. Catherine Nichols, city.
May 1, 1869—J. Brown Nichols, city.
May 1, 1869—Bessie Cromwell, county.
May 13, 1869—Nanie B. Munday, city.
May 13, 1869—Mrs. Mary M. Barrett, city.
May 18, 1869—Jos. Patterson, county.
May 18, 1869—Susan Patterson, county.
May 18, 1869—Jos. M. Patterson, county.
May 18, 1869—Jos. M. Patterson, Jr., county.
May 18, 1869—Hannah Smith, county.

May 19, 1869—Sarah Jane Garnett, county.
May 19, 1869—A. A. Garnett, city.
May 18, 1869—Jno. L. Shawhan, county.
May 21, 1869—A. Keller, county.
May 21, 1869—Sarah Thompson, city.
May 21, 1869—Alice P. Keller, city.
June 2, 1869—John Lair, county.
June 2, 1869—Sarah Lair, county.
June 2, 1869—Mattie Lair, county.
June 2, 1869—George Smiser, county; age 83 yrs., 4 months, 22 days.
    (Born 1786.)
June 2, 1869—Martha Smiser, county; age 76 yrs., 9 months, 9 days.
June 4, 1869—James Frazer, county; age 59 yrs., 8 months, 7 days.
    (Born 1810.)
June 4, 1869—J. M. Lair, county.
June 27, 1869—James Burkfield, county; age 22 yrs.
Aug. 16, 1869—William Tuttle, county.
Aug. 16, 1869—W. H. Shawhan, city; age 29 yrs.
Aug. 23, 1869—Rev. Samuel Kelley, city; 45 yrs., 5 months, 18 days.
Aug. 25, 1869—Matt D. Fisher, county.
Sept. 1, 1869—George W. Nichols, county.
Sept. 13, 1869—William Alexander, city; age 40 yrs.
Nov. 5, 1869—Dr. S. E. Broadwell, city; age 40 yrs.
Nov. 5, 1869—J. A. Broadwell, city; age 24 yrs, 8 months.
Nov. 5, 1869—Asbury Broadwell, city; age 52 yrs, 7 months, 17 days.
    (Born 1817.)
Nov. 9, 1869—Jeremiah Megibben, county; age 27 yrs., 7 months.
Dec. 3, 1869—John R. Lail, county; age 34 yrs.
Dec. 24, 1869—M. E. Perrin, city; age 50 yrs.
Feb. 17, 1870—Rosa Debold, city; age 16 yrs., 10 months, 16 days.
Mch. 18, 1870—*Moses Moore, county; died Sept. 3, 1822; age 57 yrs.
Mch. 18, 1870—*Moses Moore, Jr., county; died Oct. 7, 1844; age
    22 yrs.
Mch. 18, 1870—*Julia Ann Desha, county; died Dec., 1839; age 26 yrs.
Mch. 19, 1870—*Jo. Desha Dills.
Mch. 19, 1870—*Maude Dills.
Mch. 23, 1870—*Mary N. Talbott, county; age 66 yrs.
Mch. 24, 1870—*Isaac Miller, city.
Mch. 24, 1870—*Mrs. E. Miller, city.
Mch. 24, 1870—*A. H. Miller.
Mch. 24, 1870—*Mrs. E. Hodges, city.
Mch. 24, 1870—*Mary C. Miller, city.
Mch. 25, 1870—Thomas Ware, city; age 61 yrs., 1 month.
Mch. 25, 1870—*Mrs. H. Ware, city; age 64 yrs., 3 months, 13 days.
Mch. 25, 1870—*J. F. Ware, city; age 40 yrs., 2 months, 11 days.
Mch. 25, 1870—*Henry Warfield, city.
Mch. 26, 1870—*Mrs. E. Ware, city; age 39 yrs., 20 days.
Apr. 12, 1870—*Eliza J. Nelson, county; age 33 yrs., 9 months.
Apr. 14, 1870—Mrs. Belle Patterson, county.
Apr. 15, 1870—John Jameson, county.
Apr. 25, 1870—Lewis Vanhook, city; age 26 yrs.
May 4, 1870—*Samuel Williams, city; age 70 yrs.
May 4, 1870—*Nancy Williams, city; age 70 yrs., 5 months.
May 4, 1870—*Hiram Williams, city; age 53 yrs., 7 months.
May 4, 1870—*Eliza Williams, city; age 51 yrs., 2 months.
May 4, 1870—*David Williams, city; age 59 yrs., 3 months.
May 17, 1870—*Mary Bryan, city; age 56 yrs., 2 months.
May 17, 1870—*Mary Lilly Lockridge, county; age 14 yrs.
May 25, 1870—*Mrs. Sarah Shawhan, county.
May 25, 1870—*Joseph Shawhan, county.
June 9, 1870—*Miles Sweeney, county; age 63 yrs.

June 30, 1870—I. T. Martin, city; age 46 yrs.
July 5, 1870—M. L. Broadwell, Sr., city.
Aug. 7, 1870—Sarah W. Shawhan, county; age 24 yrs.
Aug. 20, 1870—Mrs. Mary Sweeney, county; age 78 yrs.
Sept. 26, 1870—Lydia McKee (Mrs.), county; age 35 yrs.
Oct. 6, 1870—*Mrs. Nannie G. McClintock, county; age 22 yrs.
Oct. 14, 1870—Henry Jackson, county.
Jan. 1, 1871—Andrew Garnet, county; age 50 yrs.
Feb. 20, 1871—William Thompson, city; age 85 yrs.
Mch. 8, 1871—Mary Rachel Day, city; age 37 yrs., 7 months.
Mch. 22, 1871—Mrs. Elly Nevil, county.
May 22, 1871—Mary Gray, county.
June 14, 1871—Miss Molly Hutchinson; age 20 yrs.
July 3, 1871—David E. Worst.
Sept. 17, 1871—Joseph Shawhan, of Bourbon Co.
Oct. 20, 1871—Mrs. J. Lair, city.
Jan. 26, 1872—Miss Hattie Miller, county.
Apr. 5, 1872—Mrs. Nancy Frazer, city.
Apr. 5, 1872—*Dr. Joel C. Frazer, city.
Apr. 5, 1872—*Dr. H. W. Frazer, city.
Apr. 14, 1872—H. Barintzer, city; age 18 yrs.
Apr. 15, 1872—Mrs. C. Turtoy, city; age 18 yrs.
Apr. 22, 1872—Miss Anna Musburg, city; removed from vault.
Apr. 25, 1872—Mrs. C. L. Ford, county; age 28 yrs.
May 1, 1872—*N. D. Berry, county.
—————————D. H. Wherritt, from Shreveport, La.
May 4, 1872—Joseph Howard, county.
May 4, 1872—*Geo. M. Howard, county.
May 4, 1872—*Samuel Howard, county.
May 6, 1872—Sheridan Magee, city; from Virginia.
May 13, 1872—Mrs. Mary McShane, county.
Aug. 26, 1872—Nannie F. Patterson, county; age 16 yrs.
Nov. 18, 1872—Miss Molly Ziler, county; age 14 yrs.
Dec. 10, 1872—Paulina Scott.
Mch. 8, 1873—Nannie Shawhan, city.
Mch. 10, 1873—Moses J. Kimbrough, from Missouri.
Mch. 11, 1873—*Sarah T. Williams, Sr., county.
Mch. 11, 1873—*Mary Williams, county.
Mch. 11, 1873—*Hubbard M. Williams, county.
Mch. 11, 1873—*Sarah Williams, Jr., county.
Mch. 11, 1873—*Susan Redmon, county.
Mch. 11, 1873—*John Redmon, county.
Mch. 11, 1873—*Archer Webber, county.
Mch. 11, 1873—*Mrs. Archer Webber, county.
Mch. 11, 1873—*John Williams, Sr., county.
Mch. 19, 1873—*Andrew Scott.
Mch. 19,1873—*Mary Forman.
Apr. 26, 1873—Miss Hattie F. Webb, city.
Apr. 30, 1873—*Willie Rowland, city.
Apr. 30, 1873—*W. G. Hedges, city.
Apr. 30, 1873—*Mrs. W. G. Hedges, city.
May 1, 1873—Broadwell C. Dills, county.
May 6, 1873—Sarah Shawhan, county; from vault.
May 6, 1873—*W. B. Shawhan, county.
May 6, 1873—*Daniel Shawhan, county.
May 6, 1873—*George Lail, county.
May 6, 1873—*Mrs. George Lail, county.
May 7, 1873—*Captain John Shawhan.
May 7, 1873—*Mrs. Captain John Shawhan.
May 7, 1873—*Joseph Shawhan, county.
June 3, 1873—Mary Jameson; age 18 yrs.

Aug. 27, 1873—Mrs. Foreman, city; removed to Danville, Ky.
June 25, 1873—James A. Cook, city; died June 23, 1873.
Oct. 14, 1873—*Joseph H. Blair, county; age 67 yrs., 8 months, 12 days.
Nov. 15, 1873—*William Whitehead, county.
Nov. 15, 1873—*John Whitehead, county.
Nov. 15, 1873—*Elizabeth Whitehead, county.
Nov. 15, 1873—*Margaret Whitehead, county.
Nov. 15, 1873—*Laben S. Whitehead, county.
Nov. 15, 1873—*Hannah A. Whitehead, county.
Nov. 15, 1873—*Elizabeth C. Whitehead, county.
Nov. 15, 1873—Sally Ann Whitehead, county.
Nov. 15, 1873—*Inft. of N. R. Whitehead, county.
Nov. 15, 1873—*Mary E. Curran, county.
Nov. 15, 1873—*A. J. Harding, county.
Nov. 15, 1873—*A. H. Innis, county.
Nov. 15, 1873—*Sallie A. Innis, county.
Nov. 15, 1873—*John Innis, county.
Nov. 15, 1873—*Inft. of A. H. and S. A. Innis.
Nov. 15, 1873—*Robert Garner.
Nov. 15, 1873—*Margaret Garner.
Nov. 15, 1873—*Elizabeth Haviland.
Nov. 15, 1873—*Mary F. Haviland.
Dec. 15, 1873—*Ferdinand Fearber, Jr., city.
Dec. 15, 1873—Mrs. Hannah Berkley, city.
Dec. 16, 1873—F. Fearber, city.
Feb. 28, 1874—John T. McClintock, city.
Feb. 28, 1874—Mrs. G. W. Scott.
Mch. 12, 1874—Stephen B. Cook, city; age 77 yrs.
Mch. 14, 1874—Mrs. Jane Lair, Covington, Ky.; age 85 yrs.
Mch. 25, 1874—Margaret Kendell, Covington, Ky.
Mch. 25, 1874—Nute Kendell, Covington, Ky.
Apr. 7, 1874—*Mathias C. Lair, county.
Apr. 7, 1874—*Mary Pope, county.
Mch. 12, 1874—Emma Frazer, city.
Apr. 20, 1874—Dr. Rutherford, city.
May 19, 1874—Dr. Samuel W. Davis, county; age 25 yrs.
May 19, 1874—*M. Frankey Davis, county; age 16 yrs., 4 months,
    22 days.
June 12, 1874—Mrs. Caleb Walton, city (Broadwell lot).
July 4, 1874—Wm. McDavis, county.
Aug. 21, 1874—J. Mannen Victor, county.
Sept. 14, 1874—Mrs. Orleans Perry, city.
Sept. 17, 1874—Mrs. Grey Larrimore, city.
Sept. 19, 1874—Larkin Garnett, Sr., county.
Sept. 20, 1874—James J. Garnett, county.
Oct. 1, 1874—T. B. Ashbrook, city.
Oct. 13, 1874—McCauley Martin, county.
Oct. 13, 1874—Inft. of E. M. Auston, county.
Nov. 4, 1874—J. H. Meade Smith, city.
Dec. 1, 1874—Miss Margery Stirman, city.
Dec. 2, 1874—*Lewis P. Cook, city; age 24 yrs., 5 months, 6 days.
Dec. 2, 1874—*Jimmie Albert Cook, city; died Sept. 9, 1865.
Nov. 5, 1874—James Robinson, county.
Nov. 5, 1874—John O. Day, city.
Nov. 14, 1874—Mrs. Josie M. Warnock, Kansas City, Mo.
Nov. 27, 1874—Emily Murphy, county.
Jan. 4, 1875—Mrs. Mary Perrin, city.
Jan. 23, 1875—Miss Celia Smiser, city.
Jan. 23, 1875—Caleb Walton, city.
Feb. 12, 1875—Winston Roberts, county.

Mch. 18, 1875—Mary E. Brannock, county.
Apr. 5, 1875—Lizzie Grinnan, city.
Apr. 6, 1875—Mrs. Hattie L. McKee, county.
Apr. 15, 1875—John Stump, county.
Apr. 16, 1875—Mary Curran, county.
Apr. 20, 1875—Mrs. Ruth G. Redmon, city.
May 21, 1875—Case Desha, county; age 26 yrs., 1 month, 9 days.
June 6, 1875—S. G. Stearman, city.
July 31, 1875—Dr. E. J. Peckover, city.
Aug. 9, 1875—Miss Sarah C. Smith, city.
Aug. 21, 1875—Mrs. A. N. Jett, county.
Aug. 21, 1875—Richard N. Jett, county.
Oct. 6, 1875—Tobias Yeager, county.
Oct. 10, 1875—Mrs. Maria W. Williams, county.
Dec. 2, 1875—Johnnie Pullum, city.
Jan. 2, 1876—W. Vanhook, county.
Jan. 7, 1876—Mrs. Eliza Bell, city; age about 70; from vault.
Jan. 13, 1876—Bettie Stirman, county.
Feb. 2, 1876—Miss Annie R. Shawhan, county.
Feb. 15, 1876—Mrs. Murphy, city; from vault.
Mch. 6, 1876—W. W. Broadwell, Cincinnati, O.
Mch. 9, 1876—Minor H. Simms, county; from vault.
Apr. 11, 1876—James Patterson, Jr., county.
Apr. 23, 1876—Mrs. Len J. Rouse, city.
Apr. 27, 1876—Nancy James, city.
May 6, 1876—Miss Ida Rouse, city.
May 8, 1876—Mrs. Cassey Veatch, city.
June 16, 1876—Elizabeth Ellen Cason, county; age 43 yrs.
June 30, 1876—Mrs. Adalixa Broadwell Murphy, Covington, Ky.
July 22, 1876—Jno. R. Warnock, Jr., county.
Aug. 5, 1876—Mrs. Nat Smith, county.
Aug. 7, 1876—Lou Dickey, city.
Oct. 6, 1876—Mrs. Ellen D. Winston, county.
Oct. 8, 1876—*James Tomlinson, city.
Oct. 8, 1876—Susan Tomlinson, city.
Dec. 3, 1876—I. N. Miller, city.
Dec. 16, 1876—I. N. Webb, city.
Jan. 7, 1876—*James Bell, city.
June 30, 1876—*Martha Virginia Fenley, city; age 75 yrs.
June 30, 1876—*Joelett Fenley, city.
Feb. 4, 1877—Mrs. Sally C. Ford, county.
Feb. 5, 1877—Mrs. Harriet Weesburg, city.
Feb. 13, 1877—Miss Lethia James, city.
Mch. 15, 1877—Miss Nannie B. Ammerman, county.
Apr. 12, 1877—Wiliam Nesbitt, county.
Apr. 13, 1877—*Jonnie Hutchison, county.
Apr. 13, 1877—*Elizabeth Hutchison, county.
Apr. 18, 1877—*Lydia Talbert, county.
Apr. 18, 1877—*Chas. M. Bailey, county.
Apr. 30, 1877—F. Grater, Sr., city.
May 4, 1877—*Mrs. Nesbitt, county.
June 30, 1877—B. F. Dills, county.
July 13, 1877—Mona Renaker, city.
July 14, 1877—Mrs. Zarelda Wherritt, city.
July 27, 1877—Louis Crook, city.
July 30, 1877—Hub, son of L. H. Williams, city.
Dec. 15, 1877—*David Dills, county.
Dec. 15, 1877—*Mrs. Lydia Dills, county.
Feb. 15, 1878—Jas. H. Grey, county.
Mch. 13, 1878—Warren G. Ammerman, county (from vault).
Mch. 13, 1878—Miss Belle Kimbrough, city.

Mch. 21, 1878—S. H. Williams, city (from vault).
Mch. 25, 1878—E. N. Martin, county.
Mch. 26, 1878—Mrs. A. R. Magee, city.
Mch. 29, 1878—Abraham Keller, Jr., city; age 28 yrs.
Apr. 4, 1878—Pugh Miller, county (from vault).
Apr. 4, 1878—*Henry Miller, county.
Apr. 4, 1878—*Joseph Miller, county.
Apr. 4, 1878—*James Miller, county.
Apr. 13, 1878—Mrs. Shuff, city.
Apr. 13, 1878—Emily Lair, county (from vault); age 29 yrs.
Apr. 13, 1878—Newton B, Lair, from Lair Vault; age 21 yrs.
Apr. 13, 1878—James K. Megibben, from Lair Vault.
Apr. 13, 1878—Thomas Hinkston, from vault.
Apr. 13, 1878—Bennie Hinkston.
Apr. 20, 1878—Miss Annie Keller, city (from vault).
May 26, 1878—Mrs. Mary Renaker, county.
June 24, 1878—Geo. L. Magin, city.
Aug. 13, 1878—Mrs. Laura Warfield, city.
Sept. 30, 1878—Mrs. Alexander McClintock, county.
Oct. 22, 1878—Chas. A. Webster, city.
Nov. 7, 1878—John S. Lail, city.
Nov. 9, 1878—*Bonnie M. Parks, county.
Nov. 9, 1878—*Alex L. Parks, county.
Nov. 14, 1878—Frank Slade, city; age 6 yrs.
Dec. 7, 1878—Mattie Long, city.
Jan. 1, 1879—Mrs. Althea W. Webb, city.
Feb. 4, 1879—Willie Smith, city.
Feb. 5, 1879—Miss Mary Roberts, county (from vault).
Feb. 25, 1879—Mrs. Sallie Shawhan, county.
Apr. 4, 1879—Mrs. John M. Lair, county.
Apr. 9, 1879—Miss Sarah M. Burns, county.
Apr. 24, 1879—Lewis Merdiar, county.
Apr. 26, 1879—Mrs. Jane T. McKee, county (from vault).
Apr. 29, 1879—Henry Crenshaw, county.
Apr. 30, 1879—Major Kimbrough, county (from vault).
May 2, 1879—Jessie H. Dugan, county.
May 8, 1879—*N. B. Coleman, county.
May 10, 1879—Louisa Grater, city; age 16 yrs.
May 1, 1879—Mrs. R. H. Ridgley, city (from vault).
May 27, 1879—Mrse. Betty Dills, county.
June 19, 1879—Sarah E. Smith, county.
July 5, 1879—Jas. H. Martin, Jr.; age 22 yrs.
July 17, 1879—Thomas Turner, city.
Aug. 28, 1879—Sallie G. Peck, county.
Oct. 1, 1879—Mrs. Hattie Thompson, city.
Oct. 10, 1879—*McCalla Thompson, city.
Oct. 10, 1879—*William Thompson, city.
Oct. 11, 1879—Clifton Lucas, county (on G. Desha lot).
Jan. 7, 1880—Laurence Swartz, county.
Feb. 26, 1880—Jas. Polk Hutchison, county.
Apr. 1, 1880—Thos. L. Garrard, county (from vault).
Apr. 8, 1880—Mrs. Sallie A. Conrad (from valut).
Apr. 10, 1880—Mary A. Cleveland, city (from vault).
Apr. 10, 1880—R. W. Lair, county.
Apr. 10, 1880—Lucy L. Addams, city (from vault).
Apr. 14, 1880—Abbie Barnhard, city (from vault).
Apr. 21, 1880—P. C. Pixley, county.
Apr. 24, 1880—D. Fightmaster, county.
Apr. 24, 1880—Maggie A. Martin, county (from vault).
May 11, 1880—Miss Lena Winston, county (from vault).
May 19, 1880—Emily Hardin, city.

June 14, 1880—May Frazer, Mt. Sterling; age 6 months.
June 22, 1880—Rebecca Snell, county.
July 10, 1880—Harry Rignell, S. G. killed on railroad.
July 10, 1880—Mrs. Warfield, city.
July 14, 1880—Jas. H. Martin, county.
Aug. 11, 1880—H. J. Cleveland, city.
Sept. 1, 1880—Judge Curry, city.
Sept. 2, 1880—J. J. Parrish, city.
Sept. 20, 1880—Child of Levite Leeds, county.
Oct. 2, 1880—Louis Garrard, county.
Nov. 8, 1880—Mrs. John W. Ibrain, Bourbon Co., Ky.
Nov. 18, 1880—C. B. Cook, city.

LOTS IN BATTLE GROVE CEMETERY.

Beale-Renaker Lot—Ammerman-Howk Lot.

Cornelius A. Renaker—Born 1850; died 1926.
Beale Renaker—Son of C. A. and Julia Renaker; born 1878; died 1881.
Andrew Jackson Beale—Born 1831; died 1909.
Mary Anne Tucker Beale—Born 1829; died 1901.
Margaret Beale—Mother of A. J. Beale; born 1806; died 1885.
John William Elliott—Born 1851; died 1886.
Harmon Tucker Beale—Born 1868; died 1869.
Chas. Bronough Beale—Born 1871; died 1877.
William D. Renaker—Son of C. A. Renaker; born 1853; died 1885.
Sarah Margaret Beale Ridgley—Born 1857; died 1879.
Richard H. Ridgley—Born 1854; died 1886.
Little Maggie, Daughter of R. H .Ridgley—Born 1879; died 1879.
Newby Renaker Hayes—Born 1889; died 1919.
J. J. Haley—Born 1851; died 1924.
Wesley Ammerman—Born 1825; died 1877.
Louisa Ammerman—Wife of Wesley; born 1827; died 1916.
J. Roger Ammerman, Sr.—Born 1859; died 1888.
Lena Lydick Ammerman Haley—Born 1859; died 1927.
Ella Clay Ammerman—Born 1857; died 1864.
Henrietta Ammerman—Born 1850; died 1869.
Walter H. Ammerman—Born 1865; died 1874.
E. Clifton Ammerman—Son of Lena and J. Roger; born 1884; died 1918.
W. Bassett Ammerman—Son of Lena and J. Roger; born 1888.
George Howk—Born Jan., 1822; died Oct., 1881.
Mary Howk—Wife of George; no date on marker.
Charlie Howk—Son of George; no date on marker.
Myrtie Whaley Howk—Wife of Wm.; no date on marker.
 Dr. Abram Addams and 2nd wife buried in Battle Grove Cemetery.
 (First wife and children buried in Old Graveyard, Cynthiana, Ky.)
Dr. Abram Addams—Born 1800; died 1875.
Mary Taylor Wall—His 2nd wife; born 1817; died 1883.
Priscilla E. Addams—Daughter of Dr. A. and M. T. W. Addams, and wife of A. S. Welch; born 1838; died 1908.
Ashbel Stanard Welch—Of A. S. and P .E. A. Welch; born 1833; died 1907.
W. W. Longmoor—Born June 21, 1840; died Mch. 20, 1894.
Lula B. Addams—Daughter of Dr. A. and M. T. W. Addams, and wife of W. W. Longmoor (No date.)
 (Note: John Addams, brother of Dr. Addams, died in Colorado.)
Aaron A, Son of L. and J. H. Garnett, born Nov. 17, 1867; died Feb. 16, 1867.
Dorcas V. Hawkins—Born Dec. 8, 1801; died Apr. 20, 1864.
Mrs. Sarah G. Totten—Born 1821; died 1895.

NEWSPAPER LISTS OF DEATHS

Jan. 26, 1900.
Albert K. Lail, city.

Jan. 6, 1900
Miss Mary Anderson, Lexington, Ky.
Michael Maloney, age 65 yrs.
Addison Ashcraft.
Mrs. Sarah Woolery.
Thomas Current, age 88.

Jan. 30, 1900
Mrs. George Martin.
Mrs. J. W. McDaniel, city.

Feb. 2, 1900.
Mrs. Lewis R. Martin.

Feb. 6, 1900
Dr. J. M. Boyers.
Mrs. Minnie Lancaster.
William J. Collier, age 66.
Mrs. Addie M. Berry, age 32.
Milt Ross.
Aldred Barlow, age 84.
Ed Carter, age 32.
Alexander Williamson.
Mrs. John Petty.
Thomas Bell.

Feb. 27, 1900
Mrs. Simon Magee, ctiy, age 40.

Feb. 15, 1900
Mrs. Ida M. Simmons, county, age 28.
Mrs. Ann Stewart, city ,age 74.
Mrs. Mary Kelly, Paris, Ky., age 73.

March, 1900.
Mrs. Ann Logan.
Ben F. Atkinson.
Jo Huggins.
Mrs. Eva Ashcraft.
Jenny Gregg.
Mrs. Lem Ryles.
Robert Lilly, age 86.
W. L. Northcutt, age 70.
Frank McClure.
Mrs. Lena Darosett, Bourbon Co., Age 27.
Miss Ida Heten.
Mrs. Martha Kayse, city, age 70.
Thomas Furnish, county, age 88.

April, 1900.
Mrs. Wm. E. Slade (Vashte Slade), city.
Mrs. I. T. Martin, city.
Mrs. Martha Breeze.
Richard Fight, age 78.
J. J. Good of Harrodsburg.
Mrs. Sue Conner, age 53.
John Nagle, age 81.
Mrs. Polly Ann Florence.
Mrs. Lucinda Beckett.

Mrs. Ann C. Cleary.
Mrs. J. T. Stewart, Los Angeles, Calif., age 68.
N. C. Day.
Lucinda Webber, county, reinterred.
Jas. H. Webber.
Miss A. Conner, Connersville, Ky.
George Conrad, county.
Mrs. Richard Blackburn.
Mrs. George Gardner.
Nelson Conner, age 84.
Lucien Hedger, age 35.

May, 1900.
James Baldwin, age 80.
John D. Cummins, age 56.
Mrs. Annie Ward Clay.
Daniel McShane, county, age 68.
Mrs. Nia Rankin, county, age 61.
Lewis D. Terry, Bellemont, Ky.
Mrs. Josephine Lake, Poindexter, Ky.
Bryant King.
Jesse Roper.
Frank Juett, age 88.
Mrs. James Light.
Marion Fightmaster, age 28.

June, 1900.
U. S. Asbury, age 83.
G. Wash Turner, age 71.
J. Russell Brown, Los Angeles, age 24.
Mrs. Sarah Hendricks, age 72.
Vertner S. Asbury, age 83.
Mrs. J. Quincy Ward, Jr., age 25.
Mrs. Thomas Hiten, age 42.
James Wolfe.
Cass Woolery.
William Veach, age 80.
John Reber, Sr., age 76.

July, 1900.
Mrs. Eliza Ewing.
Thomas Morgan.
Lewis Day (or Dale).
James Ashbrook.
Mrs. Catherine Chinn.
Link Dale.
Annie Humphrey.
Van H. Pate, age 59.
Russell Blount.
Mrs. Lucinda Conrad.
Edmond Hayes.
Mrs. (Henry) Lucy Williams, age 74.
Henry S. Belhards, age 68.
Jo. Ann Taylor, age 38.
Trim Hedges, who died in Phillipine Islands.

August, 1900.
Samuel January, age 91.

Marion Simms McDowell.
George Phillips.
Smith Whalin.
Harry Webster.
Kathleen Lafferty.
Mrs. H. Clay Allen.

September, 1900.

Julia Sullivan, age 27.
H. E. Eals, age 82.
Mrs. John F. Parker, age 40.
Miss Mary Seitz.
Mrs. J. W. Perkins, age 35.
Pat Hill.
Mrs. Jas. M. Terry.
Dos Ritchie.
Mrs. Harvey White.

October, 1900.

Thomas Dills, age 77.
Mrs. Mary Whalin.
John W. Lang, age 65.
Miss Elizabeth Megibben.
James Craig, county, age 62.
Mrs. Sudie Wyatt.
Edgar Nichols.
Mrs. Ellen Wigglesworth.
Mrs. Willis Boston, Bourbon Co., Ky.
Lee Ray Pennell, city.

November, 1900.

Mrs. Ed Fredericks.
John B. Casey, age 39.
Fletcher M. Cosby.
Miss Nellie Kehoe.
John W. Fisher, age 70.
E. Hamilton, age 84.
David L. Evans.
Mrs. (Jesse) A. Lee Calhoun, age 30.
Cash Maguire.
Mrs. (Mary) Chris Hehr, Broadwell, Ky.
Andy S. Anderson.
Dr. Thomas H. Hood.
Charles Bishop.
R. Fields, age 49.
M. C. Hiatt, age 50.
Anna L. Fisher, county.

December, 1900.

Mary E. Dickey.
Cass Garnett.
Robt. Kendall.
Richard Hoffman.
Frank Collins, age 19.
Willie Williams, age 20.
John W. Carter, age 80.
Thomas J. Jones.
Barrett Howk.
Mrs. F. G. Craig, age 52.

ORIGINAL LOT OWNERS. OLD GRAVEYARD ON MAIN ST., CYNTHIANA, KY.

(Copied by Mrs. H. K. McAdams.)

3. E. Amend.
4. Methodist Clergy.
5. C. A. Webster.
6. John Wilson.
7. Wm. H. Adair.
8. Jno. A. Kirkpatrick.
9. Wm. M. Miller.
10. T. R. Rankin.
11. John Spohn.
12. F. G. Veatch.
13. G. Remington.
14. J. B. McKinley.
15. John D. Ward.
16. Mrs. L. A. Delling.
17. C. T. Delling.
18. Harrison Magee.
19. Wm. H. Righter.
20. Wm. Shumate.
21. Will A. Calhoun.
22. Chas. B. Curl.
23. M. L. Lair.
29. J. A. Cook.
30. Henry Vanhook.
31. John Shawhan.
32. Henry Shawhan.
33. Thomas A. Frazer.
34. Joel F. Love.
35. Larkin Garnet.
37. L. Oxley.
38. Wm. Magee.
44. Mary W. Talbott.
45. Jon. S. Smith.
46. John Bruce.
47. Mrs. Mary Palmer.
48. John N. Crenshaw.
49. Walter Hawkins.
50. Saml. Rogers.
53. John Flad.
54. Thomas English.
55. John A. Kellar.
56. Thomas V. Dills.
57. John W. Peck.
58. Robert Jones.
59. Caleb Walton.
61. Lucius Desha.
62. Lucius Desha.
63. John Harman Dills.
67. Jno. L. Shawhan.
68. Jno. Shawhan.
69. Henry C. Eales.
70. Saml. C. Frazier.
71. David Boggs.
72. J. S. Withers.
73. S. F. January.

75. R. M. Calhoon.
78. Tho. P. Lair.
79 Wm. H. Forsythe.
80. Wm. A. Stewart.
81. John Stump.
82. John H. Frazier.
84. Benson Roberts.
85. Jas. R. Curry.
86. Wm. Roper.
87. Ben C. Day.
88. Henry Cox.
89. J. J. Parish.
90. J. B. McClintock.
95. Jonathan Bassett.
106. Dr. J. P. Madison.
107. Thomas Hogg.
108. Abm. Keller.
110. Aaron Karrick.
111. W. W. Trimble.
112. R. I. Cummins.
113. W. L. Northcutt.
114. Jas. T. Nichols.
115. Leon Cuson.

118. G. W. Berry.
119. Mary Hoffman.
120. N. D. Moore.
121. W. H. Throckmorton.
122. T. V. Ashbrook.
123. Wm. G. Hedges.
124. Benson Roberts.
125. Wm. B. Glave.
126. Jos. C. Ballou.
127. A. H .Ward.
128. C. G. Land.
129. John McKee.
131. Catherine Houston.
136. J. R. Lail.
138. H. Nichols.
140. J. W. Lair.
141. J. D. George.
147. T. W. Anderson.
151. F. Robitzer.
152. I. N. Walker.
153. Wm. L. Young.
154. J. C. Hardy.

Record of graves still to be seen in "Old Graveyard" at Cynthiana, Harrison County, Ky. (Records copied from tombstone by Mrs. H. K. McAdams and John Cromwell, Sept., 1928.)

John Flad—Born Jan. 1, 1812; died Aug. 27, 1861.
George M. Redmon—Died Oct. 8, 1858; aged 24 yrs.
John K. Redmon—Son of G. M. and J. Redmon; born Aug. 25, 1858; died Apr. 3, 1860.
Richard Tisdal—Born 1774; died Jan. 27, 1816. (Body removed to Lexington.)
Catherine, Wife of Robert Houston—Born Mch. 19, 1786; died Sept. 21, 1861.
Inft. son of Thomas and Annie Dills. (No date.)
Minnie, Daughter of C. E. and Susanah Clifford—Born July 16, 1882; died Jan. 17, 1891.
William G. Hedges—Born Oct. 12, 1817; died Nov. 25, 1859.
Mary Josephine—Daughter of J. C. and N. E. W. Bellew; born Dec. 5, 1858; aged 1 year., 2 months, 27 days. On same stone, but no name, ——, died Apr. 24, 1858; age 23 years., 1 month, 9 days.
George L. Cox—Aged 32 years; died Apr. 13, 1859. Masonic Emblem.
William Higgins—Born Oct. 22, 1787; died May 2, 1854.
Hester Ann, Wife of Rev. I. J. ——rry—Died Sept., 1858. In the 24th years of her age. (Stone broken off.)
Mrs. S. W. Dunlap—Died May 31, 1836; aged 35 yrs.
Matilda F., Wife of W. R. Houston—Died Mch. 23, 1848; aged 20 yrs., 4 month and 1 day.
Robert Houston—Died Jan. 16, 1838; aged 74 yrs.
Julius, Son of William K. and Elizabeth Reed—Born Aug. 17, 1850; died July 12, 1851.
Junius, Son of Wm. and Elizabeth Reed—Born Aug. 17, 1850; died July 15, 1851.
David Snodgrass—Born Apr., 1787; died Oct. 26, 1857; aged 70 yrs., 6 months and 20 days. Masonic Emblem.
Mary, Wife of Judge David Snodgrass—Died Mch. 6, 1859; aged 69 yrs.
Marcus D., Son of G. A. and E. A. Boyd—Born Mch. 29, 1852; died July 18, 1855; aged 3 yrs., 3 months, 19 days.
Dr. D. L. Ormsby—Born in Mercer Co., Pa., April 22, 1822; died

Mch. 11, 1853, and "Little Emma" (on same stone); also Emma, daughter of D. L. and L. A. Ormsby, born July 29, 1849; died May 28, 1854.

Mary Jane, Consort of L. Oxley—Died in the 29 yr. of her age. Also on her bosom rests her inft. daughter, Josephine, in the 4 month of her age.

Mary J., Wife of John A. Keller—Born July 27, 1817; died June 12, 1855; aged 37 yrs., 11 months, 15 days.

Thomas Rankin—Born Apr. 11, 1784; died Dec. 18, 1851. Masonic Emblem.

Andrew F. Rankin—Born Jan. 10, 1825; died Nov. 12, 1853; aged 28 yrs., 10 month and 2 days.

Rosanah, Mother of L. Oxley—Born Dec. 5, 1779; died Sept. 20, 1851.

Daughter of George K. and Mary E. Dills—Born Mch. 21, 1853; died infant.

Son of Geo. K. and Mary E. Dills—Born Mch. 10, 1852; died infant.

Thomas E. Trimmell—Born Oct. 15, 1817; died Sept. 15, 1851.

Mary, Daughter of T. E. and M. A. Trimmell—Born July 31, 1849; died Mch. 27, 1854.

Ann H., Daughter of T. E. and M. A. Trimmell—Born Feb. 28, 1851; died Mch. 6, 1852.

Jerome, Son of Abraham and Debora Lighter—Born Apr. 18, 1838; died Mch. 28, 1841.

Eliza G., Consort of Wm. W. Trimble—Died Sept. 7, 1850; aged 27 yrs.

Elizabeth D. Trimble—Consort of John Trimble; died Mch. 16, 1843; age 39.

Eliza, Daughter of Jesse and Nancy Henry—Died Aug. 31, 1834; age 14.

Charity E. Lowry—Born Aug. 6, 1829; died Oct. 4, 1886.

Virginia Belle, Wife of E. F. Payne—Born Jan. 5, 1844; died Apr. 5, 1886.

Elizabeth Bassett—Born Dec. 15, 1803; died Sept. 11, 1884.

Jonathan Bassett—Born Jan. 13, 1801; died Jan. 30, 1862.

A. A. Bassett—Born Nov. 27, 1839; Jan. 8, 1869.

Rev. Joseph G. Veach—Died June 5 ,1849; age 55 yrs., 2 month, 15 days.

Joseph, Son of R. and B. Leach—Born Feb. 6, 1853; died May 2, 1861; age 8 yrs., 4 months and 18 days.

Reuben Leach—Died Aug. 30, 1860; age 53 yrs.

Little George Edward, Son of J. R. and M. A. Barbee—Born Dec. 3, 1852; died Sept. 21, 1854.

Fannie E., Daughter of J. R. and M. A. Barbee—Born Mch. 8, 1862; died Sept. 13, 1875.

Mrs. Evelina Wiglesworth—Born Aug. 10, 1801; died Apr. 14, 1861.

Aurelius Constantine Wiglesworth—Aged 5 years, and Eveline Wiglesworth Cox, aged 21 months.

James Thomas January—Son of Samuel F. and Martha D. January; born July 4, 1845; died Feb. 17, 1861.

Martha D. January—Daughter of Thomas and Elizabeth Hall; died May 9, 1846, in the 28th year of her age.

Elizabeth T. Hall—Died Feb. 28, 1845, in the 25th year of her age.

John D. Ward—Born May 8, 1808; died Apr. 13, 1857.

S. T. Hamilton—Born June 5, 1805; died Oct. 16, 1892.

Olivia H. Pomeroy—Born Nov. 15, 1805; died Sept. 14, 1833.

James Pomeroy—Born Oct. 10, 1790; died May 21, 1850.

Olivia H. Pomeroy—Died Nov. 28, 1847; aged 16 years, 2 months, 26 days.

Mary M., Wife of Rev. Thos. E. Birch—Born July 28, 1782; died Jan. 17, 1845.

James Tomlin—Died July 26, 1838; age 40 years.

Sarah, Wife of Robert Bruce, and Daughter of Dr. D. and S. Woodruff—Born March 15, 1819; died March 4, 1856.

Thomas S. Murphy—Born Dec. 30, 1821; died May 16, 1849.

James T. West—Son of A. J. and C. W. West; died July 21, 1846; aged 3 months and 10 days.

Sarah, Wife of G. Remington—Born Dec. 15, 1800; died Jan. 10, 1833; age 32 years and 26 days.

Dr. H. T. Vanhook—Born Oct. 9, 1840; died Jan. 12, 1892.

Sallie, Wife of W. H. Vanhook—Born 1821; died Nov. 13, 1858.

Sudie, Daughter of J. B. and S. J. Curl—Died Sept. 12, 1863; age 1 yr., 7 months and 15 days.

Mahala, Wife of Wm. Schumate—Born July 2, 1797; died March 29, 1882.

Wm. S. Schumate—Born Mch. 1, 1801; died July 30, 1873.

Wm. L. Shumate—Son of Wm. and Mahala; died Nov. 26, 1855; age 27 yrs., 3 days.

Richard Kimbrough—Born June 22, 1793; died Oct. 26, 1863.

Nancy, Wife of R. Kimbrough—Born July 3, 1800; died July 11, 1857.

"To George Kirkpatrick and Margaret, his wife, by their grateful children." "Their grandchild sleeps near them." (On small stone) "Little Jonny."

"Aunt Mary," Mary H. Kimbrough—Born Apr. 12, 1804; died Mch. 5, 1883.

Eliza Jones—Died Apr., 1832; aged 17 years.

Joshua Jones—Died July 8, 1833; age 57 years.

Elizabeth Carr Finnell—Wife of J. W. Finnell and daughter of W. K. and P. M. Wall; born Apr. 26, 1822; died Feb. 23, 1842.

Mary C. January—Died May 31, 1834; age 31 years.

Priscilla M. Wall—Late consort of W. K. Wall, Esq.; died June 14, 1833; age 36 years. Died of cholera.

Mary Brocken—Wife of Alex. Downing; died Sept. 24, 1824; aged 33 years (on same stone), and James Curry, their son; died Jan. 12, 1837; age 18 yrs.

"Here lies the innocent, but persecuted, Margaret Goudy—Born May, 1792; died Oct. 6, 1814.

Wesley Broadwell—Died June 22, 1833 A. D.; age 38. "With an attack of cholera.

James Coleman—Born Nov. 29, 1773; died Oct. 13, 1828.

Martha W. Odor—Wife of Thomas Oor; born Jan. 5, 1798; died Feb. 9, 1846.

James C. and John E. C. Adams (Brothers)—Children of Dr. A. and Mary A. Addams. Jas. C. died in his 3rd year, July 17, 1833, and John G. died in his 1st year and 2 days before his brother.

Mrs. Mary Ann Addams—Late consort of Dr. A. Addams; died Oct. 9, 1834, in 31st year of her life. In her arms rests her new born babe (a daughter), and by her side lie her two sons.

(Note: Dr. A. Addams and 2nd wife, and children, are buried in the "Battle Grove Cemetery."

Jeremiah Ingraham—A native of Attleborough, Mass.; died Apr. 23, 1823, in the 77th year of his age.

Elizabth, Wife of A. C. Bryan—Born Apr. 7, 1829; died Mch. 28, 1852.

Hon. Jno. Trimble—Born December 4, 1783; died June 17, 1852.

Eliza D., Wife of Hon. Jon. Trimble—Born July 2, 1804; died March 16, 183—.

Sally G. Trimble—Born Nov. 2, 1831; died Apr. 3, 1852.

Jas. A. Trimble—Born May 13, 1830; died Sept. 15, 1830.

Jas. Trimble—Born Nov. 22, 1833; died Aug. 11, 1836.

Georgie T., daughter of G. T. and Mary J. Scroggins—Born Feb. 7, 1861; died Sept. 2, 1875.

Maggie, Daughter of J. T. and S. Nichols—Died Feb. 21, 1861; age 1 month and 9 days.

Inft. Son of J. T. and S. Nichols—Died Feb. 9, 1862.

Jonnie, Son of J. T. and S. Nichols—Died Mch. 30, 1867; age 8 months and 4 days (twin stone).

Garry, Son of J. T. and S. Nichols—Died July 20, 1870; age 8 months.
George W., Son of Roland and Martha Cutter—Born Boston, Mass., Dec. 7, 1833; died Mch. 9, 1864.
Mary F. Stephens—Born July 7, 1805; died May 6, 1863.
Lucy Stephens—Born June 10, 1850; died Mch. 7, 1850.
Joseph L. Stephens—Born Apr. 22, 1761; died Feb. 11, 1815.
Mar. Stephens—Born July 14, 1801; died June 22, 1821.
Josephine B., Wife of S. F. January—Born Jan. 28, 1811; died Dec. 2, 1880.
Samuel F. January—Born Mch. 26, 1809 (no date). Note: First Mayor of Cynthiana, Ky.)
Inft. Son of S. F. January—No date.
Mattie Keady, Daughter of J. F. and S. S. Reed—Born July 12, 1889; died Mch. 13, 1890.
Samuel C. Frazier—Born June 17, 1819; died Feb. 5, 1859.
Mary L., Daughter og H. G. and A. E. Earls—Born July 26, 1853; died Dec. 24, 1860.
Nannie M., Daughter of H. G. and A. E. Eals—Born Aug. 26, 1856; died Jan. 16, 1861.
Mattie D., infant of H. G. and A. E. Eals—Born Dec. 3, 1858; died Jan., 1861.
James H., Son of H. G. and A. E. Eals—Born July 15, 1850; died July 1, 1854.
Paul Champayne—Died Dec. 4, 1867; age 47 years. (A native Frenchman.)
Lucinda, Daughter of W. T. and M. E. Magee—Born July 5, 1857; died Mch. 15, 1860.
Edwin T. Ellis—Died Mch. 1, 1846; age 30 years. Erected by Mrs. Mary Palmer.
George Palmer—Born July 16, 1777; died Oct. 4, 1843.
Georgie A., Daughter of G. and M. Palmer—Born Sept. 16, 1831; died Jan. 1, 1833.
Amanda J., Wife of R. H. Forrester—Born Mch. 4, 1820; died Oct. 6 ,1858.
Mary A., Daughter of R. H. Forrester—Born Apr. 6, 1856; died Mch. 7, 1859.
Lucy A., Wife of E. B. Hawkins—Born Sept. 22, 1828; died Mch. 10, 1863.
Mary Seargeant—Born May 29, 1805; died Sept. 2, 1871; age 69 yrs., 3 months and 3 days.
Walter Hawkins—Born Sept. 6, 1846; died Sept. 10, 1872.
Capt. W. S. Rogers—"Was a brave Confederate soldier and a Christian gentleman, he fell in the Battle of August (Ky.) Sept. 27, 1862.
Mary A. Masterson—Died May 20, 1866.
"S. R." Samuel R. Rogers—Pioneer preacher.
William Yord—Born June 6, 1812; died Oct. 22, 1850.
(Note: Two stones were lying face down and could not be moved. Also two were sealed over, so no one can know who they are, but all others graves still left in the Old Cemetery are given above.)
Unmarked graves, names given to me by lot owners:
Martin Luther Lair—Son of Charles and Sallie (Anderson) Lair; was born Sept. 6, 1811; died Sept. 20, 1857.
Nancy (Williams) Lair—Wife of Luther Lair. Also 5 grandchildren of above, children of Nannie Lair and John Baltzelle.

BULLOCK-HUNT FAMILY GRAVEYARD

On farm, first owned by James Bullock and wife, Ann Waller Bullock. Now owned by J. W. Denton, on Richmond and DeLong Pikes, near Lexington, Ky. Copied by Mrs. J. W. Denton and Mrs. H. K. McAdams.

"This monument was erected by a fond father, in memory of a most amiable affectionate and dutiful child." Mary Elizabeth Rodes, only daughter of William and Sarah W. Rodes. Born July 8, 1815; died July 7, 1833. Aged eighteen years, lacking 1 day.

P. Gordon Hunt—(Note: Father of Judge J. D. and Rev. George Hunt.) Born Aug. 23, 1852.

Maria Overton—Wife of Waller Bullock. Born Oct. 25, 1788; died Aug. 4, 1831. Note: Maria Overton Burch was 1st wife of Waller Bullock.)

Susan Mary—Infant of P. G. and J. A. Hunt. Born May 20 ——; died 1831.

Samuel Redd Bullock—Born Aug. 1, 1817; died July 12, 1849. (Note: He was grandfather of Dr. Waller Overton Bullock.)

John M. Bullock—Born Nov. 29, 1825; died Oct. 12, 1826.

Eliza Bullock—Born Oct. 17, 1821; died Aug. 29, 1824.

Frances B. and Sarah G.—Infants of Rev. J. J. Bullock and Caroline Breckinridge.

James Bullock—Born February 23, 1735; died June 29, 1813. (Note: Father of Waller Bullock and grandfather of Joseph J. Bullock.)

Anna Waller—2nd wife of James Bullock: Born Nov. 23, 1742; died Feb. 3, 1828. (Note: 1st wife was Miss Wingfield.)

Samuel B. Simrall—Born June 19, 1845; died Jan. 6, 1846.

Mrs. Dorothy Redd—Died Oct. 3, 1811, in the 28th year of her age; also her inft. daughter, Dorothy Lucy, who departed this life Nov. 19, 1811. Aged 2 months and 2 days.

BEARD GRAVEYARD.

Inscriptions taken from "Old Joseph Beard burying ground, on Stone Road, leading off Clays Mill. Place belongs to Wm. Wilson, descendant of Joseph Beard, near Lexington, Ky.

Joseph Beard, Sr.—Born Dec. 21, 1765, in Strabane, Co. of Tyrone, Kingdom of Ireland; died Nov. 11, 1839. His wife, Ann Beard, born 1765, died July 15, 1824; aged 59 yrs.

Col. Henry Beard—Born July 3, 1788; died Mch. 18, 1838. Son of Joseph Sr., and Ann Beard.

Charles McClear—Born May 4, 1785, in County of Tyrone, Province of Ulster, Ireland; died Dec. 2, 1827.

Isabella Beard McClear—Born May 27, 1797; wife of Chas. McClear; died Feb. 5, 1879.

Ann E., Wife of A. W. Cromwell—Born Apr. 19, 1823; died Dec. 1, 1849. dau. of Charles and Isabella McClear.

Francis M., Son of A. W. and Ann E. Cromwell—Born Mch. 3, 1846; died Jan. 11, 1848.

LAIR FAMILY VAULT, LAIR STATION, HARRISON CO., KY.
Donated by Miss Eliza Lair.

Mathias Lair—Son of Mathias and Cathrina Lehrer; born Feb. 16, 1752; died Oct. 16, 1795.

Ann Elizabeth (Rush) Lair—Consort of Mathias Lair; died April 8, 1806; aged 53 years.

Caty (Lair) Smiser—1st wife of George Smiser; born March 30, 1778; died June 27, 1800.

Mary (Lair) Smiser—2nd wife of George Smiser; born Aug. 6, 1780; died July 2, 1802.

Betsy Lair—Dau. of Mathias and Ann Elizabeth Lair; died May 19, 1803; aged 18 years.

Sally (Lair) Allon—Wife of John Allon; died July 6, 1809; aged 20 years.

Charles Lair—Son of Mathias and Ann Elizabeth Lair; born 1774;

died Aug. 4, 1860.

Sarah (Anderson) Lair—Wife of Charles Lair; born 1781; died Apr. 9, 1860.

Joseph Lair—Son of Charles and Sarah Lair; born June 10, 1818; died July 11, 1861.

William, Son of Charles and Sarah Lair—Born Jan. 28, 1816; died Jan. 15, 1860.

Mary Lair—Wife of William Lair; born June 16, 1827; died Mch. 18, 1865.

Emma Alice Lair—Dau. of Wm. and Mary Lair; born Apr. 26, 1854; died Mch. 19, 1877.

Sarah Eliza Lair—Dau. of Wm. and Mary Lair; born Jan. 31, 1852; died Apr. 30, 1859.

George Cosby—Son of Joseph and Charles Ann Cosby; born May 8, 1861; died Aug. 25, 1861.

Mathias Lair, Jr.—Son of Mathias and Ann Elizabeth Lair; born Jan. 4, 1795; died March 10, 1841.

Rachel Sidle Lair—Wife of Mathias Lair, Jr.; born Dec. 9, 1805; died May 13, 1838.

Cynthia Redmon—Dau. of George and Eliza Lair Redmon; born June 11, 1847; died Dec. 19, 1859.

Jennie Lair—Dau. of Mathias and Roenna Lair; born 1851; died 1863.

Andrew Lair—Son of Mathias and Roenna Lair; born 1836; died 1854.

These bodies were placed on concrete, on Feb. 28, 1909, in the Charles Lair Family Vault, built in 1845, blown out of solid rock, with iron door, and marble slab over door, with inscription: "Please do not disturb the remains of the sleeping dead, A. D., 1845." Located on Charles Lair's farm on Licking river, in Harrison County, Ky., about one and a half miles from Lair Station.

Two marble slabs are placed in front of the concrete giving the names and dates above. There are also two bodies, daughters of Charles and Sarah (Anderson) Lair, in stone coffins, in the front part of the valut. One has the following inscription: "Within this coffin rests the mortal remains of Eliza Redmon, wife of George Redmon, and dau. of Charles and Sally Lair, who departed this life June 11, A .D. 1847, in the 27th year of her life." The other: "Cinthy, wife of John Redmon, died July 22, 1845; aged 22 years.

SOME EARLY GRAVES IN LEXINGTON, KY.

Lizzie M. Payne—Born Jan. 7, 1837; died Jan. 2, 1864.

James Parker—Died Dec. 12, 1797; age 81 yrs.

Mary Parker—His wife; died Aug. 28, 1789.

Robert Parker—Born Oct. 12, 1760; died Mch. 4, 1800.

Elizabeth R. Parker—Born Sept. 27, 1769; died (stone covered). (See Todd-Parker Bible record.)

Prudence Jones—Died May 17, 1862; age 84 years.

Ann Bell—Born Apr. 17, 1800; died May, 1857.

Daniel W. Bell—Born in Salisbury, Md., Feb. 27, 1831; died in St. Louis, Mo., Sept. 4, 1877.

Josephine Mansfield—1852.

Mary Lutz—1846. (2 slabs close together.)

Richard P. Diamond—Born Mch. 11, 1832; died Aug. 23, 1862.

Mary B. Diamond—Born July 2, 1840; died July 8, 1890.

Frances Estes—Wife of John Estes; born Aug. 15, 1810; died July 25, 1853.

Robert A. Kersey—Born Apr. 21, 1822; died Mch. 23, 1857.

Robert, Son of R. A. and N. Kersey—Died Aug. 29, 1854.

Garland B. Hale—Born Feb. 11, 1809; died Nov. 14, 1893.

His Wife, Emily McCracken—Born Feb. 14, 1817; died Aug. 3, 1893.

Leonard Taylor—Born Jan. 4, 1794; died Nov. 29, 1865; age 71 yrs.,

10 months, 25 days.

Ann Taylor—(Same stone); born July 30, 1800; died Dec. 19, 1879; age 79 yrs., 4 month and 20 days.

Sarah A. Schoonmaker—Born Aug. 17, 1825; died Feb. 12, 1910.

Samuel Schoonmaker—Born in New York City, Sept. 17, 1816; died in Lexington, Ky., Apr. 11, 1873.

John L. Barkley—Died Apr. 20, 1860.

Lucy Morgan, Wife of John L. Barkley—Died Oct. 23, 1860.

James M. Barkley—Died Mch. 5, 1863.

Hetty Mary Bowmar—Wife of J. M. Barkley; born Oct. 30, 1831; died Dec. 20, 1858.

H. Bowmar Barkley—Born Aug. 13, 1840; died May 26, 1879.

Alexander Brand Barkley—Born Sept. 27, 1861; died Nov. 14, 1884.

Annie C. Brand Barkley—Born Oct. 18, 1839; died Oct. 21, 1912. (All 3 one one stone.)

Mary Brainard Brown—Born May 4, 1836; died Sept., 5, 1851.

Mary J. Brown—Wife of James Brown; born Sept. 18, 1810; died July 13, 1860.

James Brown—Born Jan. 2, 1809; died Feb. 25, 1869.

Elen J. Hall—Born Sept. 21, 1833; died 1852.

S. L. Helm, D. D.—For 50 years a Baptist Minister in Ky.; born May 16, 1816; died Oct. 26, 1885.

Lewis Faulconer—Born Oct. 29, 1776; died Feb. 26, 1856.

Susan, His Wife—Born Oct. 26, 1777; died July, 1828.

Sarah W. Stephens—Born Nov. 23, 1802; died July 31, 1887.

Septimus Wardle—Born in Manchester, England, Mch. 2, 1777; died Jan. 16, 1850.

Elizabeth Wardle—Born Apr. 18, 1787; died Dec. 5 ,1859.

Mary W. Crittenden—Born Oct. 7, 1782; died Feb. 15, 1869.

Mary C. Hall—Wife of John G. Hall; born May 18, 1812; died Feb. 9, 1886.

William Stanhope—Born May 21, 1786; died Nov. 6, 1844.

Amelia, Wife of Wm. Stanhope—Born Oct. 13, 1788; died Aug. 12, 1849.

William F. Stanhope—Born Apr. 3, 1814; died Sept. 26, 1881.

Nancy C. Bowman, Wife of Wm. F. Stanhope—Born May 25, 1826; died Aug. 22, 1889.

Fannie H. Stannhope—Born Feb. 1, 1857; died June 11, 1886.

Vincent M. Stanhope—Born 1854; died 1896.

Harry H. Stanhope—Born 1865; died 1916.

Belfield Stanhope—Born 1861; died 1926.

Sarah G., Wife of W. F. Stanhope—Born Jan. 17, 1828; died May 23, 1847.

A. W. Stanhope—Born Dec. 6, 1812; died Mch. 8, 1842.

Richard Stanhope—Born May 14, 1811; died Nov. 5, 1840.

On "Stanhope" monument (next 2 names):

Edward Carter—Born Aug. 1, 1796; died Aug. 11, 1851.

Eliza Stanhope—Wife of Edward Carter; born 1809; died 1888.

Capt. W. S. Carter—Born 1833; died 1863. ("C. S. A.")

Amelia H. Carter—Born 1837; died 1849.

Bettie G. Middleton—Born 1840; died 1925.

Lucy Carter—Born 1842; died 1926.

James Lee Carter—Born 1835; died 1909.

Joseph Bowman—Born Sept. 30, 1793; died Aug. 25, 1859.

Elizabeth, Wife of Joseph Bowman—Born Aug. 16, 1798; died June 12, 1835.

Catherine D. Downing—Born 1830; died 1901.

Richard Downing—Born 1825; died 1901.

Hiram Batterton Searcy—Born Dec. 28, 1828; died Nov. 4, 1906.

Mary Jane, 1st Wife of H. B .Searcy—Born Nov. 21, 1828; died Mch. 27, 1854.

Sarah, 2nd Wife of H. B. Searcy—Born Aug. 9, 1829; died Feb. 5, 1868.

John Utley—Born Sept. 9, 1798; died June 10, 1851.
Nancy, Wife of John Utley—Born Sept. 10, 1803; died Dec. 10, 1862.
J. H. Sallee—Born May 14, 1839; died Nov. 26, 1911.
Z. E., Wife of J. H. Salle—Born Aug. 5, 1820; died Jan. 7 ,1884; age 64 yrs., 5 months and 2 days.
Annie, Wife of William White—Born Sept. 19, 1790; died Jan. 24, 1833.
Corrilla J. Thornton—Born Oct. 18, 1832; died Sept. 1, 1876.
Eliza A .Shattuck—Born Feb. 27, 1811; died Oct. 15, 1876.
Dr. B. C. Snedaker—Born Sept. 9, 1820; died Sept. 8, 1880.
Mrs. Sally Snedaker (no date).
Mrs. M. A. Snedaker—Born Feb. 10, 1827; died Oct. 22, 1918.
(On one stone: 3 names, one date):
> Dr. Preston B. Snedaker (no date), Flora L., Frank D., and Mattie B. Snedaker—Born Mch. 30, 1875; died Jan. 14, 1862. "Our children."
Mrs. Sallie Downing—Died Mch. 14, 1875; age 75 yrs.
Henrietta Downing, Wife of John Davis—Born 1830; died 1916.
John Davis—Born June 11, 1830; died Nov. 18, 1891.
Daniel Bryan, Sr.—Nephew of Daniel Boone and son of 1st settler of Bryan Station; born Feb. 10, 1758; died Feb. 28, 1845.
Elizabeth, Wife of D. B. Bryan, Sr.—Born Nov. 13, 1761; died Jan. 29, 1833.
Daniel Bryan, Jr.—Born June 15, 1794; died July 12, 1822.
Elizabeth Vardeman, Twin Sister of D. B., Jr.—Died Sept. 27, 1822.
Joseph Bryan, Sr.—Born Oct. 30, 1797; died Aug. 6, 1887.
Margaret G., Wife of Joseph Bryan, Sr.—Born Feb. 9, 1804; died Sept. 29, 1874.
Mary Boone Kay—Born Mch. 29, 1806; died July, 20, 1852.
"Mother," Lucy K. Bryan—Born Nov. 7, 1830; died Apr. 14, 1881.
"Father," Elijah C. Bryan—Born Dec. 5, 1823; died June 30, 1890.
Elijah Cartmell—Born Feb. 25, 1763; died Aug. 26, 1831.
Mary, Wife of Elijah Cartmell—Died Aug. 8, 1832; age 67 yrs.
Asa Cartmell—Born Jan. 6 ,1802; died June 6, 1839.
John Cartmell—Born Oct. 30, 1806; died Nov. 29, 1839.
Elizabeth, Wife of George W. Brown—Born Apr. 28, 1797; died Aug. 14, 1832.
Eliza T., Wife of Isaac Barkley—Born Dec. 23, 1811; died Nov. 25, 1835.
Mary Ann, Wife of John R. Cleary—Died Aug. 28, 1872; age 58 yrs.
Walter Connell—Died Mch. 25, 1825.
Catherine Connell—"His wife"; died Mch. 2, 1858. (Parents of Mary Ann Cleary.)
Carl T. Reinhardt—Born Roedelkeim, Germany, Mch. 24, 1836; died Lexington, Ky., Dec. 27, 1862.
Jonas Sugden—Born July 13, 1832; died June 21, 1900.
Hannah, Wife of Jonas Sugden—Born in Yorkshire, England, Feb. 29, 1832; died July 28, 1883.
George Y. Johnston—Died Feb. 27, 1900; age 84 years.
John Fisher—Born May 5, 1794; died Mch. 18, 1880. (Masonic lot.)
Elisha H. Cravens—Born Dec. 12, 1826; died Nov. 10, 1868. (Masonic lot.)
George Cleveland—Born Nov. 29, 1804; died Feb. 24, 1867.
Hugh A. Emison—Born Dec. 16, 1810; died Oct. 28, 1874.
Jane, Wife of H. A. Emison—Born Dec. 8, 1812; died Feb. 9, 1873.
Casimir Pieri—Born Aug. 19, 1831; died Apr. 10, 1872.
Pollie, Wife of Harvey Moore—Born Sept. 24, 1804; died June 28, 1875.
Harvey Moore—Born 1797; died Aug. 20, 1864.
Frances Moore—Daughter of H. and P. Moore; born Oct. 25, 1838; died Dec. 16, 1859.
Nancy, Wife of A. Rucker—Born 1780; died May 23, 1860.
Mrs. Margaret Hill—Died Mch. 1, 1846; age 74 yrs.

Mrs. Dorthea Coons—Consort of H. C. Coons; died June 4, 1836, in 34th year of her age.

Louisa J. Smith—Consort of Dr. C. J. Smith—Died May 15, 1858, in 29th years of her age.

(These 2 above were removed from some other cem. in Oct., 1854.)

Mary Springle—Born Jan. 10, 1798; died Jan. 11, 1887; of Woodford Co.; aged 88.

John Springle—Died Jan. 14, 1813; age 42 yrs. (Removal.)

Elizabeth, Wife of John Springle—Died Feb. 9, 1846. (Removal.)

Catherine Webb—Buried Aug. 19, 1871.

Thomas Webb—Buried Mch. 26, 1835. (Removal.)

John and Milly Smith—Parents of Sarah A. E. Roach.

John A .Roach—Died Oct. 22, 1845.

Sarah A. E. Roach—Wife of John; born Mch. 20, 1806; died Jan. 31, 1891.

John Smith Roach—Their son; born Oct. 20, 1827; died Mch. 26, 1864.

Nancy S. Robb, sister of Sarah A. E. Roach—Born Dec. 30, 1823; died Sept., 1833.

Polly L. Ficklin—A native of Va.; died Aug. 17, 1849; age 67 yrs.

John Bruce, Esq., a native of Morpeth, Northumberland Shire, Eng— Born 1786; died Feb. 9, 1836.

John T. Bruce, Sr.; Margaret R. Bruce.

John Thompson Bruce—Born July 16, 1816; died Oct. 23, 1853.

William W. Bruce—Born May 9, 1821; died Nov. 15, 1896.

Elizabeth T. Colesberry, wife of Wm. W. Bruce—Born Dec. 4, 1821 in Wilmington, Del.; died Mch. 20, 1911, Lexington, Ky.

Rebecca B. Morgan—Born June 18, 1830; died July 21, 1861.

Infant son of J. H. and R. B. Morgan—Died Sept., 1853.

John T. Bruce—Born May 8, 1852; died Mch. 15, 1889.

Dr. J. M. Bruce—Born Sept., 1822; died Jan. 31, 1881.

Elizabeth Bruce—Born Apr. 23, 1824; died Mch. 6, 1892.

Sanders D. Bruce—Born Aug. 16, 1825; died Jan. 31, 1902.

(Same stone) Mary H. Bruce—Born Aug. 17, 1833; died July 30, 1912.

Margareta, wife of J. J. Hunter—Born Oct. 25, 1818; died June 21, 1870.

Frank T. Bruce—Born Jan. 16, 1851; died Dec. 2, 1886.

William H. Brand—Born May 28, 1826; died Oct. 14, 1866.

Horace H. Brand—Born Apr. 4, 1832; died Mch. 13, 1863.

William Moses Brand—Born Nov. 29, 1803; died Nov. 22, 1843.

"Our Parents," Alexander H. Brand—Born Lexington, Ky., Mch. 21, 1818; died May 10, 1881.

His wife, Mary Chew Brand—Born Fayette Co., Ky., 1821; died Apr. 26, 1856.

Mary E. Brand Avery, dau. of Alex H. and Mary Chew Brand—Born July 19, 1851; died July 7, 1907.

Betsey Anderson—Born in Perth, Scotland; died in Lexington, Ky., Sept. 7, 1877.

John Brand—Born Montrose, Scotland, Nov. 26, 1785; died Sept. 9, 1849.

Elizabeth Hay Brand—Born in Cullen, Scotland, Oct. 19, 1782; died Dec. 5, 1849.

Three on one stone—George W. Brand—Born Dec. 10, 1812; died Jan. 9, 1883.

Fannie M. Brand—Died Sept. 27, 1883; age 57 yrs.

Nannie A. Brand, wife of George W. Brand, and dau. of John T. Griffith—Born Natchez, Miss., Nov. 7, 1819; died Lexington, Ky., Sept. 5, 1849.

Harriet Abercrombie, dau. of Geo. W. and Nancy Brand—Born May 23, 1845; died Oct. 19, 1864.

Edward Macalester—Born Sept. 17, 1805; died Oct. 2, 1866.

Eliza Macalester Woodward—Born Oct. 13, 1811; died May 9, 1897.

Orpha J. Blair, wife of H. B. Preston—Born Sept. 15, 1815; married

July 1, 1840; died Jan. 6, 1881.
Captain John Postlewaite—Died 1833.   Moved from Episcopal Ch. Cem.
James Postlewaite, Infant—Died 1833.   Moved from Episcopal Ch. Cem.
Mary B. Postlewaite—Died 1844; age 2 months.   Moved from Episcopal Church Cem.
Frances Postlewaite—Died 1843; age 3 years.   Moved from Episcopal Church Cem.
Mrs. Sarah M. Postlewaite—Died Feb. 20, 1879.   Moved from Episcopal Church Cem.
Gabriel Lewis Postlewaite—Died Dec. 18, 1874.   Moved from Episcopal Church Cem.
Miss Sarah D. Postlewaite—Died Dec. 8, 1910; age 67 yrs.
Mrs. Sarah F. Todd—Died Oct., 1926; age 90 yrs.
Dr. L. B. Todd—Died May 15, 1902.
Miss Massie Todd—Died May 16, 1896.
Maria Blair Todd, wife of James C., died Mch, 1834; age 30.
Samuel B. McDowell—Died Apr. 18, 1903.
Jas. C. Todd—Born 1802; died Dec. 8, 1849.
General Levi Todd—Born Oct., 1756; died Sept., 1807.
Ann Todd—Born Aug., 1758; died 1828; wife of Gen. Robt. Todd.
Hannah Owen Todd—Born June, 1729; died May, 1805; wife of David Todd.
David Todd—Born Feb., 1785; died April, 1823.
Sarah Burch Rodes and Mary Burch.   Joseph Burch.
Lieut. Alex. H. Todd—Died June 30, 1892.
Robert S. Todd—Died Dec., 1849, aged 59 years.
Elizabeth Slaughter, Clifton Rodes, Jane Holmes Todd, General Robert Todd.
Jane Briggs, wife of Gen. Levi Todd—Born June, 1761; died July, 1800.
Jane Holmes, 2nd Wife of Gen. Levi Todd—Born Aug., 1770; died Mch., 1856.
Mary H. Rodes—Born 1842; died Oct. 6, 1901.
Levi Todd Rodes—Born 1831; died Aug. 10, 1890.
Mrs. Margaret B. Rodes—Born June, 1799; died Oct. 29, 1863.
Col. Wm. Rodes—Born 1793; died July 22, 1856.
Miss Mattie Kellogg—Died Nov. 11, 1924.
Eliza P. Todd—Died July 25, in her 30th year.   Wife of Robert S. Todd.
Elizabeth Todd—Died 1874.
Joseph Burch—Born June, 1763; died Dec., 1843.
Martha Todd, daughter of Robert and Elizabeth L. (and wife of C. B. White of Selma, Ala.)—Born June, 1833; died July, 1868.
Margaret Kellogg (Todd), daughter of Robt. and Elizabeth L. (wife of Charles H. Kellogg)—Born Dec, 1828; died 1904.
Gen. Robert Todd—Born Apr., 1754; died Mch., 1814.
Kitty Todd, daughter of R. S. and L. E. Todd, and wife of W. W. Herr —Born Oct., 1841; died Apr., 1875.
Samuel B. Todd—Born Mch., 1830; killed in Battle of Shiloh, Apr., 1862.
Capt. Alexander H. Todd—Born Feb., 1839; killed at Baton Rouge, Aug., 1862.
Maria Logan, daughter of Gen. Levi Todd, and wife of Waller Bullock—Born Oct., 1788; died Nov., 1861.
Mary A. Witherspoon, daughter of R. and A. Todd—Born Mch., 1796; died Aug., 1812.
Dr. Lyman B. Todd—Born 1832; died 1902.
Robert Stuart, D. D.—Born Aug., 1772; died Aug., 1856.
Hannah Todd Stuart—Born Feb., 1781; died Mch., 1834.
Thomas Carr, Sr.—Born March, 1779; died May, 1836.
John D. Young—Born, 1783; died June, 1856.
Elisha Winter—Born July, 1781; died June, 1849.
Virginia Carr, wife of Thomas Carr—Born, 1785; died, 1828.
John L. Winter—Aged 65 years.

Mary E. Winter—Born 1818; died Sept., 1838.

Charlotte, wife of W. H. Parker, and daughter of Capt. John and C. Ashby, of Va.—Born Feb., 1785; died Aug., 1851.

Wilson H. Parker—Died Dec. 1, 1863; aged 73 years.

Lucy J. Parker, wife of Dr. H. N. Gragg—Born Feb., 1857; died Mch., 1895.

Moved from Hill St. Lutheran Church and Re-interred Oct. 30, 1907 in Lexington Cemetery

George Shindlebower—Died 1827.

Annie Shindlebower—Died 1833.

Mrs. Sarah Brisby—Died 1836.

George Brisby; age 15 years.

Samuel Smedley—Died 1830.

Mrs. Margaret Brisby—Died 1856.

Frazer Family, moved from county, 4 miles on Versailles Pike March 11, 1908

Dr. Charles C. Frazer.

Anna E. Frazer—Died Dec. 12, 1822.

John F. Frazer—Died Aug. 6, 1824.

John Calvin Frazer—Died May 8, 1831.

Margaret S. Frazer—Died June 30, 1831.

S. S. Frazer—Died 1824.

On Major Flournoy's Monument: "He served his Country faithfully, both in Counsel and in the Field."

Major Mathew Flournoy—Born July 14, 1776; died June 15, 1852; married Emily W. Smith, Aug. 15, 1799.

Emily, wife of Maj. Mathew Flournoy—Born Apr. 26, 1783; died July 11, 1833.

Alpheus B. Johnson—Born Feb. 5, 1820; married Virginia Harring, on Sept. 2, 1851. He died Mch. 25, 1855.

Sallie A. Johnson—Died June 9, 1874; aged 52 yrs.

Miss Laura A. Johnson—Died July 31, 1920.

Mrs. Sophia Johnson Campbell, wife of W. R. Campbell—Born Aug. 17, 1844; died Feb. 3, 1902.

Wm. R. Campbell—Born Sept. 25, 1841; died Apr. 20, 1878.

Martha Flournoy—Buried Sept. 7, 1855.

Patsy Matilda Flournoy, dau. of Maj. Mathew and Emily Flournoy—Born Nov. 25, 1805; died July 28, 1818.

Rev. Charles P. Williamson—Born in Carolina Co., Va., 1848-1903.

Charlie Coleman Williamson, son of C. P. and B. J. Williamson.

Mrs. Mary V. Gallaway—Died Mch. 13, 1927.

Laura G. Gallaway—Born Nov. 12, 1885; died Feb. 22, 1901.

Louis G. Gallaway—Died Apr. 13, 1917.

Charles Williamson Campbell—Born Aug. 18, 1877; died Nov. 12, 1895.

Victor M. F. Johnson—Born Jan. 31, 1836; died July 20, 1885.

Elizabeth J. Flournoy, wife of V. M.—Died Jan. 22, 1875; age 62 yrs.

Victor M. Flournoy—Born Jan. 16, 1808; died Jan. 22, 1866.

Remus Payne—Born 1881; died 1908.

Elder John T. Johnson—Died Dec. 18, 1856; age 69 yrs.

Sophia Johnson, wife of Elder J. T.—Born Oct. 13, 1796; married Oct. 18, 1811; died Aug. 23, 1849.

Elder J. T. Johnson was noted minister of Christian Church. Inscription on stone: "After 25 yrs. devoted services to his Savior's cause. His whole life was truly a labor of love, and his works do follow him. Long will he live in the hearts of those for whom he labored. Thanks be to God, who giveth us Victory through our Lord Jesus Christ."

Elder John (Raccoon) Smith—Born Oct. 15, 1784; died Feb. 29, 1865; was a noted preacher and writer of songs.

Nancy Smith, second wife of Elder John Smith—Born Nov. 15, 1792; died Nov. 4, 1861.

Harvey J. Smith—Died Feb. 22, 1859; age 36 yrs.
Mrs. Mary S. Smith—Buried Dec. 4, 1861.
Mrs. Mary A. Weigan—Born 1827; died Nov. 11, 1918.
Miss Emma V. Smith—Died Apr. 14, 1922; age 68 yrs.
    (Thompson lot, graves moved from farm of Phil Chinn.)
Diana, wife of Asa Thompson—Born June 8, 1761; died Oct. 31, 1844.
Clifton Thompson—Born Oct. 15, 1761; died Jan. 23, 1833.
Mary (Ragland), wife of Clifton Thompson—Born Feb. 3, 1768; died
    Oct. 28, 1809.
Second wife, Eliza (Ford) Thompson—Born June 22, 1777; died
    Apr. 25, 1844.
Clifton R. Thompson, son of Clifton and Mary Thompson—Born Nov.
    16, 1803; died Mch. 5, 1845.
Susan T. Thompson, second wife of J. K. Thompson—Born Sept. 29,
    1819; died Aug. 2, 1849.
Filmore Thompson, son of J. K. and M. A. Thompson—Born Oct. 19,
    1853; died Dec. 27, 1853.
John J. Thompson—Born May 11, 1823; died Oct. 8, 1852.
Foot stones without dates—S. T. Thompson, J. K. Thompson, Dr. W.
    G. Offutt and wife, E. T. Offutt.
Jeremiah Featherstone—Born Nov. 7, 1776; died July 11, 1854.
Elizabeth, wife of Jeremiah Featherstone—Born Mch. 7, 1771; died
    Mch. 30, 1864.
Elizabeth E. Elmore—Born Apr. 23, 1801; died Aug. 8, 1882.
Robert Featherstone—Born Mch. 30, 1803; died Mch. 24, 1899.
Elizabeth Featherstone—Born Nov. 13, 1807; died Jan. 18, 1891.
Franklin W., son of Robert and Elizabeth Featherstone—Born Aug. 3,
    1836; died Jan. 17, 1858.
Dr. J. M. Rice—Born Dec. 5, 1827; died Dec. 27, 1891.
Lizzie Featherston, wife of Dr. J. M. Rice—Born Sept. 6, 1838; died
    June 18, 1887.
John A. McClure—Born Aug. 13, 1804; died Nov. 19, 1854.
Elizabeth, Wife of John A. McClure—Born Feb. 25, 1802; died Apr.
    13, 1890.
Susan McClure Williams—Born Sept. 18, 1828; died Mch. 24, 1907.
D. J. Williams, Jr.—Born July 10, 1821; died Oct. 6, 1881.
Sarah Elizabeth, Wife of John O. Rogers—Born Oct. 11, 1861; died
    June 11, 1893.
Elzy Harney—Born Apr. 5, 1804; died Sept. 10, 1849.
Mary Ann, second wife of Elzy Harney—Born Aug. 15, 1821; died
    Sept. 13, 1849.
Eliza, first wife of E. Harney—Born Mch. 11, 1804; died Oct. 31, 1845.
Margaret, Wife of Adam Keiser—Born July 25, 1777; died Jan. 30,
    1839.
James T. Pierson—Born Nov. 20, 1819; died Aug. 16, 1882.
Priscilla G., Wife of James T. Pierson—Born Dec. 3, 1827; died Feb.
    25, 1901.

Removed From Athens to Lex. Cem., Sec. P, Lot 69.

Wm. Prewitt Spurr—Born July 4, 1834; died May 27, 1838; age 4 yrs.
Margaret Montgomery Spurr—Born June 27, 1832; died Aug., 1840;
    age 8 yrs.
Lydia Spurr—Born July, 1838; died Aug., 1840; age 2 yrs.
Richard Spurr—Born Mch. 21, 1809; died Feb. 8, 1851; age 42 yrs.
Martha Ann Prewitt, Wife of Richard Spurr—Born Nov. 11, 1813;
    died Dec. 8, 1902.
Henry Clay Spurr—Born Feb. 8, 1846; died Feb. 8, 1851; age 5 yrs.
Edmonston Spurr—Born Mch. 28, 1842; died May, 1834; age 2 yrs.
Lillie Marion Spurr—Age 2 yrs.
Martha Sweeney Spurr—Age 2 yrs.
Bettie Spurr Taylor—Born 1850; died 1926.
George Bruce Taylor—Born 1845; died 1924.

Richard Spurr Miller—Born Feb. 4, 1917; died May 19, 1923.

Roy Hearne Taylor—Son of G. B. and B. R. Taylor—Born Apr. 27, ——; died Oct. 27, 1880.

Mrs. Margaret Cook—Born May 31, 1796; died Aug. 25, 1868.

William Cook—Aug. 1, 1803.

John Bowman—Born Oct., 1807; died May 7, 1866.

Parmelia, Wife of John Bowman—Born Feb. 8, 1808; died Sept. 16, 1883.

George H., Son of John and Parmelia Bowman; born Oct. 25, 1850; died Feb. 8, 1852.

Elizabeth E. Harrison—Born June 10, 1796; died Apr. 22, 1856.

William E. Harrison—Born Feb. 13, 1825; died Mch. 3, 1857.

John H. Harrison—Born Aug. 26 ,1827; died Dec. 12, 1855.

Hannah B. Harrison—Born Aug. 11, 1829; died May 2, 1838.

Mary A. E. Harrison—Born Nov. 9, 1815; died June 21, 1870.

J. Alex. Edger—Born Feb. 17, 1814; died Mch. 30, 1871. (Confederate soldier.)

James McCoy—Born Apr., 1789; died Oct. 4 ,1868.

Jesse, Wife of Jos. Turner—Born July 16, 1844; died Oct. 3, 1872.

Mary Ann, Wife of Isaac Turner—Born in Yorkshire, England, Dec. 25, 1804; died Dec. 10, 1889.

Isaac Turner—Born 1811; died 1871.

Mary Ann, Daughter of Isaac Turner—Born Jan. 3, 1848; died Jan. 2, 1866.

Abraham Turner—Born Oct. 1, 1838; died Aug. 20, 1862.

Jos. W., Inft. Son of W. and S. E. Landers—Born Mch. 22, 1860; died Dec. 16, 1862.

Charlton, Inft. Son of W. M. and S. E. Landers—Born Aug. 1, 1865; died Jan. 1, 1867.

Margaret Parker—Born July 24, 1797; died Mch. 6, 1865.

Margaret Ann, Wife of W. A. Gilbert—Born Mch. 4, 1840; died Oct. 16, 1876.

James B. Parker—Born May 20, 1830; died Nov. 14, 1896.

Nancy E., Wife of Madison Gaines—Born Oct. 4, 1816; died Oct. 21, 1876.

Madison Gaines—Born Mch. 20, 1814; died Apr .10, 1881.

Wm. Christie—Born in Wigtown, Scotland, Dec. 23, 1799; died in Lexington, Ky., June 27, 1827. "A trusted official of the Northern Bank for half a century."

Elizabeth H. Parker—Born Apr. 5, 1802; died Nov. 27, 1862.

Oswald Parker—Born Jan. 30, 1806; died Apr. 4, 1865.

Henry A. Saxton—Born 1846; died 1915.

William Jackson—Died Nov. 23, 1850; aged 66 yrs.

Elizabeth Jackson—Died May 16, 1862; age 65 yrs.

Sabina Rice, consort of Caleb Rice—Born Apr., 5, 1781; died Aug. 14, 1861.

Louisa Jane, Wife of William Rice—Born Dec. 23, 1813; died Oct. 4, 1864.

William Rice—Born Jan. 31, 1806; died June 3, 1868.

Ann Rice—Born Nov. 30, 1802; died Mch. 16, 1888; age 85 yrs., 4 months.

Marcia Duval Ashby—Formerly Marcia D. Wells; born Jan. 15, 1807; died Nov. 14, 1893.

John Wells—Born Sept. 8, 1799; died Dec. 25, 1835.

Gen. Gordon Granger—Born Wayne Co., New York, Nov. 6, 1821; died Sante Fe, N. M., Jan. 10, 1876; in command of Dist. of New Mexico. Brevet Maj. Gen. Gordon Granger was twice brevetted during Mexican War, and 5 times breveted for gallantry in Battles of Wilson Creek, Mo.; Chattanooga, Tenn.; Mobile, and Forts Gaines and Morgan, Ala.

Martha H. Letcher, Wife of Brevet Maj. Gen. Gordon Granger, and

Child, Ellen Gordon—Age 10 months. (No date.)

W. C. Letcher, M. D.—Died Mch. 3, 1859; age 26 yrs.

Margaret J. H., Wife of Dr. W. C. Letcher—Born Aug. 19, 1831; died July 2, 1853.

Dr. Joseph P. Letcher—Born June 6, 1807; died Jan. 6, 1894.

Florida, Wife of Dr. Jos. P. Letcher—Born Sept. 14, 1827; died Nov. 1, 1881.

Maybelle Price—Died Apr. 21, 1875.

Florrie M., Daughter of J. P. and F. M. Letcher—Died July 17, 1866; age 9 months and 21 days.

Mathew T. Woods—Born 1777; died July 16, 1849; age 72 yrs.

Mary. T. Woods—Born 1800; died Mch. 31, 1875; age 75 yrs. and 9 months.

James Bourne—Father of Walker Bourne; died June, 1847; age over 90 yrs.

Walker Bourne—Born in Culpepper Co., Va., May 5 ,1790; died in Montgomery Co., Ky., Feb. 6, 1873.

Willey B., Wife of Walker Bourne—Born in Montgomery Co., Ky., Jan. 6, 1816; died Oct. 26, 1893.

Edward C. P., Son of Walker and Clarrisa Payne Bourne; born 1830; died 1843.

Butler, Son of Walker and Willey B. Bourne; born 1844; died in Greene Co., Ala. He was a gallant Confederate soldier and his death resulted from long confinement in Camp Douglas.

On Stone of Walker Bourne—"Walker Bourne came to Ky. when 12 yrs. old. His father was a soldier of the Revolution, and he if 1812. He was a man of strong will, clear intellect, extended information, courteous manners, temperate habits, affectionate disposition, decided political and religious views and honorable in all his dealings. He served his county faithfully as a Magistrate and Sheriff and was for many years a teacher of high reputation. His words of wisdom, deeds of charity, sure friendship and Christian walk through life, are the enduring monuments he erected to his memory, more lasting than marble."

James M. Bourne—Born in Montgomery Co., Ky., Apr. 21, 1838; died in Louisville, Ky., Nov. 16, 1906. Civil engineer and Confederate soldier, in Orphan Brigade.

McGOWAN-HULL BURYING GROUND.
(Copied by Mrs. Jos. B. Beard, Lexington, Ky.)

On farm of Mrs. C. W. Burt, one mile south of Lexington, Ky., on Nicholas Pike.

Jacob Hull, Jr.—Died July 4th, 1840, in 30th year; born 1810.

Mrs. Marthy Hull—Died Feb. 17th, 1845; 51 years old; born 1794.

Jacob Hull, Sr.—Died Jan. 13th, 1835; 46 years old; born 1783. (Note: Jacob, Sr., and Marthy, mar. about 1809.)

Charles McGowan—Died Jan. 17th, 1842.

Elizabeth McGowan—June 13th, 1833, died; 68 years of age. Consort of Charles McGowan.

John Kay—Died June 12, 1833; 48 years old; born 1785. Note: Mar. Nancy McGowan.)

Elizabeth Jane Hull—Wife of Jacob Hull, Jr.; died July 2nd, 1842; 21 yrs. old; born 1821.

STEELE GRAVEYARD.
(Copied by Miss Margaret Steele.)

At Steele's Ford, near Millersburg, Ky.

Mary Gault—Spouse of William Steele: Died May 20, 1812; aged 73 years, 8 months.

William Steele, Sen.—Died May 13, 1827; aged 87 years.
William Steele—Died June 20, 1848, in the 80th year of his age.
Joseph Steele—Son of Wm. and Mary Steele: Died Aug. 27, 1793; age 22 yrs., 10 mo.
Walter, Son of Rev. J. and J. C. Steele—Born in Xenia, O., Feb. 1, 1823; died June 7, 1844. Aged 21 yrs. and 4 months.
John Steele—Who departed this life, on the 29th day of July, 1831. Aged 2 years, 5 months and 27 days.
Joanna Steele—No date.
    (Note: William Steele, Private in Capt. Charles McClay's Co. 1st Battalion, Cumberland Co. Milita 1778. Vol. six, Page 40. Pa. Archives, 5th. Series.)
    (Note: Authority, Cunningham History, Mrs. Anna Steele Brice, Due West, South Carolina: Capt. Walter Cunningham and wife, Jean, children; Mary Cunningham, mar. Lowry; Sarah Cunningham, mar. Lamine; Agnes (Nancy) Cunningham, mar. Wm. Drake; Jane Cunningham, mar. Rev. John Steele; Isabella Cunningham, mar. Bailey, and John Cunningham, mar. Lucy Wilson.)
    Old Graveyard, at Millersburg, Ky. Copied by Miss Margaret Steele.
John Woods—Died Apr. 23rd, 1853, in the 90th year of his age.
John Miller—Born Sept. 21st, 1753; died Seyt. 5th, 1815. "The deceased was born in Carlisle, Penn., emigated to Ky., in 1775, located the land upon which Millersburg is situated, soon after he returned to Cumberland Co., Pa., married Ann McClintock, returned with his wife to Ky. Beneath this monument repose the remains of both."
Mary, Wife of Henry Thompson, Sr.—Born in Pa., in 1742; died 1827.
Henry Thompson, Sr.—Who was a ruling Elder in Associate Reform Church, 24 years: Born 1740, in Pa.; died 1827.

PART OF OLD UNION CEMETERY, RUSSELL CAVE PIKE.
Donated by J. R. Cooper, Lexington, Ky.

Abram M. Andrews, 1792-1875.
Sarah, wife of Abram M. Andrews, 1797-1884.
Mary, wife of Caleb Andrews, 1829-1870.
Letha Jane, wife of James Atcherson, 1830-1854.
Lindsey Childers, 1791-1856.
Jacob G. Childers, 1819-1853.
William Cox, 1784-1857.
Lucy Hopkinson Cox, 1794-1835 (wife of Wm. Cox).
William Conner, 1766-1841.
Mary, wife of Wm. Conner, 1774-1841.
Elizabeth A., wife of Reuben Cavender, 1823-1853.
Elizabeth Vance, wife of Hiram Etherington, 1789-1886; age 97 years.
William Gaines, 1801-1868.
Conrad Harp, 1789-1849.
Catherine Harp (wife of Conrad, 1784-1849.
Julia, wife of George Harp, 1812-1862.
Matilda C., wife of John Harp, 1818-1859.
Bethiah, wife of Boston Harp, 1813-1900.
Henry Huffman, 1771-1862.
Joanna Huffman, 1787-1886.
John Calvin Frakes, 1807-1871.
Eliza J., wife of John Calvin Frakes, 1827-1882.
William A. Hardwick, 1815-1857.
Grandville Hulett, 1818-1859.
Paul Huls, 1802-1868.
Koron Holtzclaw, 1823-1842.
Mary A., wife of Wm. Hufford, 1817-1851.

Nancy Ann, wife of Henry Wood, 1782-1851.
J. A. Watson, 1819-1890.
Ellen Lancaster, wife of J. A. Watson, 1819-1897.
L. Fannie Lydick, wife of H. C. Funk, 1840-1863.
Sarah Hurst, 1822-1872.
William W. Ivey, Col. 13th Ky. Inft., 1833-1906.
Charles W. Lincoln, 1798-1868.
Jacob Lydig, 1769-1814.
Martin Lydick, 1808-1876.
Emily A. Lydick, 1826-1863.
Jacob Lydick, 1805-1895.
Mary S. Lydick, 1807-1882.
John Markham, 1806-1860.
Daniel McIntyre, 1802-1880.
Elizabeth Ann, wife of H. G. Moore, 1822-1852.
Spence Menifee, 1821-1859.
William Ross, 1778-1854.
Conrad Sidener, 1756-1824.
Jacob Sidener, 1788-1884.
Mary, wife of Jacob, and dau. of J. and B. Lydick, 1788-1861.
Jane Sidener, 1776-1866.
Rachel Sidener, 1789-1827.
Henry Sidener, 1763-1857.
Elizabeth Sidener, 1805-1832.
Verlinda D., wife of Jacob Sidener, Jr., and dau. of Joseph and Sallie
    Risk, 1832-1858.
David Smith, 1781-1850.
Lucy, wife of David Smith, 1781-1859.
Elizabeth H. Taylor, 1797-1839.
Susan, wife of Joseph Tinsley, 1818-1853.
James Harvey Vance, 1823-1909.
George Ann, wife of James Harvey Vance, 1821-1866.
Ann, wife of B. B. Wood, 1817-1848.
B. B. Wood, 1814-1861.
Margaret B. Wood, 1810-1868.

WALNUT HILL CEMETERY, IN FAYETTE COUNTY, KY.
Donated by J. R. Cooper, Lexington, Ky.

Israel A. Bodger, 1737-1814.
Ansel A. Brockway, 1807-1849.
Elizabeth, wife of Joseph C. Calloway, and daughter of Rev. James
    Crawford, 1789-1845.
Joseph Calloway, 1782-1842.
Rebecca F. Calloway, 1821-1845.
Alexander Crawford, 1782-1845.
Rev. James Crawford, A. M., 1752-1803.
Rebecca, wife of Rev. J. Crawford, 1755-1830.
Bebecca Crawford, 1803-1833.
Sarah Crawford, ——1841.
Charles McPheeters, 1764-1836.
Martha, wife of Charles McPheeters, 1775-July 29, 1831, aged 56 yrs.
Isabella Rogers, died Mch. 22, 1844, age 77 yrs.
Elizabeth Todhunter, died Mch. 11, 1833, aged 51 yrs.
Elizabeth, wife of John Wallace, 1784-1848.
Martha J. Wallace, daughter of John and Elizabeth Wallace, born
    Apr. 20, 1820; died Dec. 26, 1850.
John Wallace, 1785-1865.
John Wallace, died Feb. 25, 1812, age 65 yrs.
James F. Wallace, died Feb. 1, 1816, age 25 yrs.
Joseph Wallace, died Mch. 31, 1791, age 67 yrs.

CEMETERY RECORD OF MUDDY CREEK CHURCH
Near Adamstown, Pa.
(Donated by James J. Colder, Denver, Pa.)
(Found in search for Beecher Family, but not related to John Beecher.)

Johannes Bicher—Born 1791; died 1847. Catherine, wife of Johannes Bicher—Born 1794; died 1852. Jacob Bicher—Born Nov. 24, 1818; died Sept. 6, 1878. Sarah, wife of Jacob Bicher—Born Mar. 23, 1824; died Nov. 17, 1887. Anna Bicher, wife of Benjamin Bicher— Born July 22, 1803; died Feb. 22, 1826. Isaac Bicher—Born Feb. 1, 1827; died Oct. 8, 1855. Sarah, daughter of Isaac Bicher—Born Sept. 30, 1847; died Mch. 28, 1852.

A tombstone on the site of McConnell's Station grave yard where McConnell's cabin stood, the first house on the site of Lexington, Ky., and was built in 1776: Joseph McAdams—Born in Warrentown, Ohio, A. D., Aug. 12, 1799; died June 28, 1843.

BIBLE RECORDS

BIBLE OF JAMES ARNETT AND SARAH WOODGATE.
Now Owned by Mrs. Eva Arnett Sutton, Lexington, Ky.
(Donated by Mrs. Lon McCarty.)

James Beadel was born Feb. 27, 1755.
Jane Daniels, his wife, was born Dec. 18, 1759.
Zachariah Arnett was born Oct. 10, 1777.
Nancy Beadel was born Aug. 23, 1779. Children:
James Arnett was born July 8, 1801.
Jefferson Arnett was born June 13, 1803.
Richard and Robert Arnett (twins) were born Feb. 13, 1805.
William Arnett was born Sept. 5, 1807.
Lizzie Ann Arnett was born Apr. 22, 1811.
Louisa Ann Arnett was born Sept. 22, 1819.
Zachariah Arnett and Nancy Beadel were married Sept., 1800.
James Arnett and Sarah Woodgate were married Dec. 26, 1822.
Thomas B. Arnett and Susan E. McDaniel were married Apr. 12, 1849.
R. F. Arnett and E. A. Bond were married July 30, 1861.
Elizajane, dau. of James and Sarah Arnett, was born Sept. 12, 1823.
Thomas Billinsley, son of Jas. and Sarah Arnett. was born Nov. 9, 1825.
Nancy Ann, dau. of James and Sarah Arnett, was born Jan. 27, 1828.
James Harvey, son of James and Sarah Arnett, was born Mch. 12, 1830.
John Fletcher Arnett, son of J. and S. Arnett, was born Aug. 15 ,1832.
Robert Franklin Arnett, son of J. and S. Arnett, was born Oct. 26, 1834.
Mandy Eveline Arnett, dau. of J. and S. Arnett, was born Apr. 23, 1837.
Mary Frances Arnett, dau. of J. and S. Arnett, was born Jan. 5, 1840.
Children of James and Sarah Arnett:
Nancy Ann Arnett died Aug. 31, 1831, in the 4th yr. of her age.
James Harvey Arnett died Sept. 23, 1831, in the 2nd yr. of his age.
Eliza Jane Arnett died July 30, 1843, in the 20th yr. of her age.
John Fletcher Arnett died Feb. 26, 1848, in the 16th yr. of his age.
Robert Franklin Arnett died Tuesday, Aug. 6, 1912, A. D., in the 78th yr. of his age.
Children of Zachariah and Nancy Arnett:
Richard Arnett died; William Arnett died.
James Arnett died Sept. 18 ,1845.
Sarah Arnett, wife of James Arnett, died Sunday, May 24, 1885.
Elizabeth A. Arnett, wife of Robert Franklin Arnett, died May 13, 1918.

BIBLE OF MR. AND MRS. F. A. ATKINS
F. A. Atkins married Roberta Ryland, both of Lexington, Ky.; married by Rev. Robert Ryland, father of the bride; Dec. 11, 1873.

F. A. Atkins died Apr. 29, 1929.

Antoinette Thornton Atkins died June 2, 1897.

Ethel Bondar Atkins, wife of Presley Thornton Atkins, died in Richmond, Va., Mch. 10, 1919.

Winn Gunn Harrison, husband of Roberta Atkins Harrison, died Feb. 1, 1919.

Funeral Notices Lying in Atkins Bible—Extracts

Funeral of Miss Lucy B. Atkins, from residence of Mr. John Estis, Dec. 16, 1851.

Funeral of Mr. James M. Atkins, Mch. 27, 1855.

Funeral of Mr. Lewis Atkins, from residence of David Shepherd, Sept. 16, 1854.

Funeral of Mrs. Frances Estes, wife of John Estes, July 26, 1853.

BATTERTON BIBLE

Now owned by Mrs. Stanfield; donated by her daughter, Mrs. Carl Plank, Lexington, Ky.

Presby Batterton—Born Dec. 16, 1848.

Benjamin Batterton—Born March 28, 1851.

William Batterton—Born May 14, 1855; died Sept. 4, 1864.

Oliver Batterton—Born Dec. 16, 1856; died Sept. 4, 1864.

Massa Batterton—Born June 8, 1860.

Henry Batterton, Jr.—Born Dec. 5, 1863; died Apr. 15, 1865.

BELLES BIBLE RECORD.

(From an Old Record Owned by Miss Sallie V. Ashbrook, Cynthiana.)

John Belles was born Oct. 26, 1781; died June 5, 1839.

Artemisia Tarlton Belles was born Oct. 9, 1788; died Aug 14, 1826.

Children of John Belles and 1st wife, Artemisia Tarlton Belles:

 John James Belles—Born Sept. 6, 1807.

 Henry T. Belles—Born Dec. 2, 1809.

 Caleb Belles—Born July 29, 1811.

 Mary Ann Belles.

 William Harrison Belles.

 Richard Johnson Belles—Born Feb. 6, 1818.

 Nancy Bean Belles—Born Jan. 20, 1820.

 Catherine Belles.

 Joshua Belles—Born Jan. 4, 1826.

Dorcas Sanders Belles—Born Dec. 8, 1801; died Apr. 20, 1864.

Child of John Belles and 2nd wife, Dorcas Sanders Belles:

 Artemisia Tarlton Belles—Born Feb. 10, 1832.

Mary Belles Tyner died Feb. 4, 1838.

William Harrison Belles died Sept. 28, 1854.

Catherine Belles Johnson died.

John James Belles died Sept. 28, 1857.

 Additional Information: John Belles (1781-1839) was the son of Henry and Mary Belles. The will of Henry Belles is recorded in Scott County, Kentucky, Will Book B, page 35, dated July, 1807., probated Dec., 1809. The will of Mary Bellas (or Bellows), widow of Henry Belles, is recorded in Fayette County, Kentucky, Will Book L, page 459, dated June 13, 1833, probated Sept., 1834. Dorcas Sanders, 2nd wife of John Belles, was the daughter of John Sanders (born Jan. 22, 1756; died Feb. 5, 1809, son of James and Sara Tully Sanders) and Sara Grant Sanders (born Jan. 25, 1759; died Mch. 29, 1814; daughter of William and Elizabeth Boone Grant). Dorcas Sanders married (1) John Snell, (2) John Belles, (3) Thomas Hawkins. Artemisia Tarlton Belles (born Feb. 10, 1832; died Oct. 7, 1904), daughter of John Belles and his 2nd wife, Dorcas Sanders Belles, married, Harrison County, Kentucky, Sept. 3, 1857, Thomas Veach Ashbrook (born Aug. 22, 1828; died Sept. 30, 1874), son of Aaron Ashbrook and Sara Steward Veach Ashbrook. Sanders is sometimes spelled Saunders. Belles is sometimes spelled Bellows and Bellis. For further information see Sanders Bible records, also "The Boone Family" by Hazel Atterbury Spraker.

BIBLE OF REBECKAH BOONE.
(Wife of Roger Jones and Niece of Daniel Boone)
Now Owned by Susan Barker Lyon, Chilesburg and Walnut Hill Pike, Near Lexington, Ky.
(Copied by Mrs. H. K. McAdams and Mrs. J. W. Dentou.)

Roger Jones and Rebeckah Boone were married the 6th day of Feb., 1787.

Joseph Barker and Nancy Smith Burton were married on the 10th day of Dec., 1845.

Thomas F. Barker and Penelope J. McDonald were married on the 4th day of Sept., 1849.

Joseph R. Barker and Susan W. Hays were married on the 30th day of Sept., 1862.

Sarah Barker was born Dec. 15, 1806.

John William Barker was born Jan. 18, 1864.

Robert Lee Barker was born Feb. 15 ,1865.

Joseph Thomas Barker was born the 8th day of May, 1866.

Roger Jones was born Apr. 19, 1763.

Rebeckah Boone was born the 30th day of Apr., on the 7th day of the week, 1768.

Nancy Jones, daughter of Roger Jones and Rebeckah, his wife, was born the 20th day of Jan., 1788.

James H. Barker was born Jan. 2, 1809.

Hannah Jones was born Jan. 13, 1790.

Joseph Barker was born Jan. 22, 1785.

Helena Barker was born Mch. 17, 1812.

Elizabeth Barker was born Mch. 20, 1814.

Rebeckah Barker was born Nov. 10, 1816.

Nancy Barker was born Nov. 24, 1819.

William Jones Barker was born July 24, 1822.

Hannah B. Barker was born Dec. 4, 1824.

Thomas F. Barker was born Apr. 15, 1828.

Joseph Robert Barker was born May 7, 1830.

Fayette Merrica's first boy was born Nov. 24, 1827.

Matison was born the 7th day of Mch., in the year of our Lord, 1831.

Mary Jane was born Oct. 4, 1817.

Sidney, their son, was born on the 27th day of Oct. in the year of Our Lord, 1839.

Roger Jones departed this life Jan. 9, 1836, in the 72nd yr. of his age.

Rebeckah Jones departed this life Mch. 20, 1842, in the 74th yr. of her age.

William Jones Barker died June 6, 1825.

Nancy Barker died June 18, 1825.

Sarah Barker died Sept. 3, 1828.

Hannah Burton died Jan. 17, 1847.

Elizabeth Donnihue died the 13th of Sept., 1847.

Nancy Barker died May 28, 1859, in the 77th yr. of her age.

(Note by Mrs. Susan Lyon: Susan Barker married Thomas Bascom Lyon. Her father was Joseph R. Barker, her mother Susan Hays. Jos. R. Barker was the son of Joseph Barker and Nancy Jones. Nancy Jones was the daughter of Roger Jones and Rebeckah Boone. She (Mrs. Susan Lyon) owns the quilt, made by Nancy Barker, of the dresses of her mother, Rebeckah Boone, after Rebeckah died. Susan was a great-great-granddaughter of Samuel Boone.)

BIBLE OF THOMAS S. BRONSTON, SR.
(Copied by Katherine Marshall Collins, Wife of Jacob Smith Collins, and Granddaughter of Thomas Springer Bronston, Sr.)

Thomas S. Bronston and Lucy A. Clarke were married Oct. 10, 1814.
Eliza Jane Bronston and Samuel Black were married Apr. 4, 1833.
Mary A. Bronston and William S. Collins were married Oct., 1839.
Samira M. Bronston and Dr. J. E. Baker were married Mch., 1849.
Sally A. Bronston and Thomas Bronston were married June 24, 1846.
Lucy C. Bronston and David K. Best were married Feb. 5, 1846.
Emma Bronston and L. E. Francis were married.
Ettie Bronston and R. C. Chenault were married July 22, 1856.
Thomas Springer Bronston was born Dec. 27, 1791.
Lucy Bronston, his wife, was born Sept. 9, 1792.
Eliza Jane Bronston was born Oct. 9, 1815.
Mariann Bronston was born the 30, 1817.
Pelyna Bronston was born Jan. 18, 1819.
Semyra Bronston was born Apr. 9, 1822.
Salyan Bronston was born Feb. 14, 1823.
Thomas Clarke Bronston was born Jan. 15, 1825.
Lucy Bronston was born Feb. 23, 1827.
Elizabeth Carline Bronston was born Apr. 12, 1829.
Emily Frances Bronston was born Dec. 23, 1833.
Henrietta Bronston was born Oct. 4, 1835.
Jacob Dudley Bronston was born July 12, 1838.
Pelyna Bronston departed this life July 23, 1820.
Elizabeth Carline Bronston departed this life Sept. 24, 1834.
Lucy J. Bronston departed this life Sept. 19, 1846.
Sally Ann Bronston, wife of Thomas S. Bronston, departed this life
    Aug. 6, 1849.
Samiria departed this life Apr. 24, 1856.
Thomas S. Bronston departed this life Jan. 5, 1869.
Emma Bronston, wife of L. E. Frances, died Oct. 8, 1871.
Eliza Jane Bronston, wife of A. N. Dale, died Apr. 4, 1882.
Mary Ann Bronston, wife of W. Smith Collins, died Apr. 23, 1884.
Thomas Bronston died Aug. 24, 1906.

BIBLE OF THOMAS SPRINGER BRONSTON
(Copied by Daughter, Alice Bronston Oldham (Mrs. William
Dowell Oldham.)

Thos. S. Bronston and Sally Ann (Bronston) were married June 1, 1846.
Thos. S. Bronston and Elizabeth H. Ballard were married Dec. 24, 1850.
Thos. Bronston and Henrietta Aurelia Baker were married in South
    Carolina Dec. 14, 1850.
Thos. S. Bronston was born Feb. 14, 1817.
Sally Ann Bronston was born Feb. 14, 1823.
Charles Jacob Bronston was born June 20, 1848.
Elizabeth H. Bronston was born June 20, 1830.
Thomas Ballard Bronston was born Feb. 14, 1852.
Henrietta Aurelia Bronston was born Aug. 8, 1832.
Joseph Springer Bronston was born Mch. 15, 1854.
John Baker Bronston was born Apr. 12, 1856.
Mattie Lany Bronston was born Aug. 28, 1857.
Henrietta Aurelia Bronston was born Feb. 28, 1859.
Bettie Baker Bronston was born Sept. 27, 1860.
Nannie Tighlman Bronston was born Mch. 21, 1862.
Loulie Carty Bronston was born Apr. 15, 1864.
Alice Julia Bronston was born Mch. 12, 1866.
James Baker Bronston was born Mch. 19, 1869.
Walter Scott Bronston was born Feb. 27, 1871.
    (Notes by Family in Thomas Springer Bronston Bible.)
Charles Jacob Bronston and Susie Cromell Hughes, 1876.
Charles Jacob Bronston and Belle Frances Wisdom, 1898.
T. Ballard Bronston and Annie Stivers, 188—.
Bettie Baker Bronston and David Anderson Chenault, 1833.

Alice J. Bronston and William Dowell Oldham, 1887.
Lulie Carty Bronston and George Gay Prewitt, 1890.
Mattie McCreary Bronston and Major John Gayle Davis, 1890.
Henrietta Aurelia Bronston and Jeptha Sherman Dudley, 1896.
Joseph Springer Bronston and Katie B. Douglas, 1884.
James Baker Bronston and Lizzie Laughlin, 1901.
Grandchildren of Thomas Springer Bronston, children of Charles J.
    Bronston: Sallie Aurelia; Thomas Hughes, who married Edith Alex-
    ander; Nettie, Louise, Henry, who died in infancy; Katherine Mc-
    Creary, who married Guy Warren; Charles Jacob, Jr., who married
    Edna Land; William Hughes, who married Nadine Snyder.
John B.., son of T. Ballard Bronston.
Sallie Ann Bronston died Aug. 6, 1849.
Elizabeth H. Bronston died Feb. 26, 1852.
John Baker Bronston died Apr. 18, 1856.
Nannie Tighlman Bronston died June 22, 1875.
Thomas S. Bronston died Dec. 18, 1890.
David A. Chenault died Jan. 21, 1903, at his home near Pine Grove,
    Clark Co., Ky.
Walter S. Bronston died May 4, 1903. Buried in Lexington Cemetery.
Jacob Bronston died in Garnett, Kan., Mch. 15, 1903. Brother of
    Thomas S. Bronston.
Joseph S. Bronston died July 17, 1892.
T. Ballard Bronston died Sept. 1, 1890.

(Note by Family.)

Mattie Bronston Davies died at her home in Orlando, Fla., Mch. 24,
    1928. Buried in Arlington Cemetery by the side of her husband,
    Major John Gayle Davis.
Bettie Bronston Chenault, wife of David Anderson Chenault, died in
    Hendersonville, N. C., Sept., 1906. Buried in Lexington, Ky.
Henrietta Aurelia Baker Bronston, wife of Thomas Springer Bronston,
    died Dec. 8, 1906. Buried in Richmond, Ky., Cemetery.
Children of Bettie Bronston and David Anderson Chenault:
    Henriette Bronston Chenault, who married Henry Berry.
    Walter Scott Chenault, who married Dorothy Weisinger.
Children of Alice Bronston and William Dowell Oldham:
    Edwin Bronston Oldham, who married Nina Otis.
    William Dowell Oldham, Jr., who married Frances Deering McClure.
Children of Lulie Bronston and George Gay Prewitt:
    1. Ben T. Prewitt, who married Elizabeth Hodgkins; 2. Bonnie
    Eager.
Daughters of Mattie Bronston and Major John Gayle Davis:
    Dorothy Davis, who died in infancy.
    Gayle Davis, who married Henry Fordham.
Son of Henriette Aurelia Bronston and J. Sherman Dudley died in
    infancy.

Great Grandchildren of Thomas Springer Bronston.

Sons of W. Dowell Oldham, Jr., and Frances Deering McClure:
    William Dowell Oldham III., and John Allen Oldham.
Children of William Hughes Bronston and Nadine Snyder Bronston:
    William Hughes Bronston, Jr., and Bettie Taylor Bronston.
Children of Ben T. Prewitt and Bonnie Eager Prewitt:
    Ben T. Prewitt, Jr., Edythe Eager Prewitt, and Louella Prewitt,
    who died Oct. 25, 1927.
Son of Walter Scott Chenault and Dorothy Weisinger Chenault:
    David Anderson Chenault.

BIBLE OF JOSEPH CABELL BRECKINRIDGE AND HIS WIFE, MARY CLAY SMITH.

Bible Now Owned by Cabell Breckinridge Bullock of Lexington.

Joseph Cabell Breckinridge and Mary Clay Smith were married by the
Rev. Samuel Stanhope Smith (who was president of Princeton
University) on May 11, 1811: Children:
1. Frances Ann Breckinridge—Born in Fayette Co., Ky., Feb. 24,
   1812.
2. Caroline Laurens Smith Breckinridge—Born in Fayette Co.,
   Ky., Oct. 12, 1813.
3. Mary Cabell Breckinridge—Born Lexington, Ky., Jan. 7, 1815.
4. John Cabell Breckinridge—Born Lexington, Ky., Jan. 16, 1821.
5. Leatitia Porter Breckinridge—Born at Frankfort, Ky., Oct.
   26, 1822.
6. Joseph Cabell Breckinridge—Born at Frankfort, Ky., Sept.
   1, 1823.
7. Ann Cabell Breckinridge—Born the following Feb., 1824, and
   died July 25, 1826; aged 2 yrs. and 4 months.

BIBLE RECORD OF BURGESS FAMILY.
(Bible Owned by E. T. Burgess at Tilton, Fleming Co., Ky.)

Births of G. W. Burgess Thomas Family.
G. W. Burgess was born Mch. 5, 1803.
Lucinda Pearce was born Nov. 1, 1813.
Isaac F. Burgess was born Feb. 25, 1833.
Amanda J. Burgess was born Nov. 21, 1835.
Wm. T. Burgess was born Sept. 12, 1837.
Mary Burgess was born July 9, 1838.
Henry Burgess was born Nov. 25, 1840.
Martha M. Burgess was born Nov. 13, 1842.
Rebecca Burgess was born Feb. 10, 1845.
Elizabeth Burgess was born Mch. 23, 1847.
Lucinda B. Burgess was born Sept. 1, 1849.
John P. Burgess was born Nov. 15, 1851.

Marriages.
G. W. Burgess and Lucinda Peace, Sept. 13, 1830.
Isaac F. Burgess and Mary L. Thomas, Sept .13, 1860.
Alvin R. Burgess and Lutie Perkins, Oct. 18, 1888.
James F. Hinton and Permelia T. Burgess, Nov. 28, 1889.
Jesse T. Hinton and Eliza B. Burgess, Dec. 30, 1891.
Elijah T. Burgess and Minnie Zoellar, Oct. 5, 1897.
Harry T. Burgess and Emma E. Kerns, Nov. 28, 1901.
Elijah Thomas and Permelia H. Smith, Feb. 23, 1833.
I. F. Burgess and Mary L. Thomas, Sept. 13, 1860.
Wm. S. Thomas and A. Eliza Baltzelle, Oct. 22, 1861.
James M. Thomas and Mattie Foxworthy, Mch. 26, 1889.
Kay B. Hinton and Jeanette Brewer.
Anita M. Hinton and Henry W. Gentry.
Jesse B. Hinton and Nell Paris.

; Births of Elijah Thomas Family.
Elijah Thomas was born Dec., 1810.
Permelia Hamlet Smith, his wife, was born 1813.
Wm. S. Thomas, was born Apr. 18, 1836.
Eliza Ann Thomas was born Dec. 13, 1833.
Marcus A. Thomas was born Feb. 8, 1838.
James M. Thomas—Born Oct. 21, 1839.
Mary L. Thomas was born July 9, 1841.

Deaths of Elijah Thomas Family
Eliza Ann Thomas died July 5, 1835.
Elijah Thomas was drowned Dec. 9, 1873.
Permelia H. Thomas died Apr. 26, 1887.
James M. Thomas died Sept. 10, 1889.
Mary L. Burgess died Feb., 1923.

Deaths of G. W. Bugress Family.
Lucinda Pearce Burgess (wife) died Dec. 1, 1851.
Elizabeth Burgess died Mch. 10, 1858.
Martha Burgess Magowan.
Lucinda Burgess Hysong died May 10, 1889.
G. W. Burgess died Feb. 1, 1893.
Alvin R. Burgess, son of I. F. Burgess, died Sept. 12, 1906.
Isaac F. Burgess died May 4, 1912.
Arthur T. Burgess died Apr., 1923.
Mary B. Hinton died Sept. 17, 1890.
Rena Hinton died Jan. 17, 1894.

Births of I. F. Burgess Family
Isaac F. Burgess was born Feb. 25, 1833.
Mary L. Thomas, his wife, was born July 9, 1841.
Permelia T. Burgess was born Dec. 4, 1861.
Alvin R. Burgess was born Mch. 26, 1864.
Eliza B. Burgess was born May 23, 1869.
Elijah T. Burgess was born Nov. 11, 1872.
Harry T. Burgess was born Nov. 27, 1877.
Arthur T. Burgess, son of Alvin, was born Feb. 30, 1890.
Mary B. Hinton was born Sept. 9, 1890.
Kay B. Hinton was born Feb. 17, 1892.
Rena Hinton was born Mch. 28, 1893.
Jesse B. Hinton was born Sept. 1, 1897.
Frances Hinton was born Mch. 5. '
Anita M. Hinton was born May 29, 1899.
Children of James F. Hinton and Permelia Burgess:
    F. Frayser Hinton, who was born Dec. 7, 1892.
    Mary Louise Hinton, who was born Oct. 5, 1897.
Children of Jesse T. Hinton and Lida Burgess:
    Mary Ellis and Katherine Burgess (twins), who were born Mch.
    23, 1899.
    Mary Ellis died Aug. 16, 1899.

BURGIN FAMILY RECORD.
From a Burgin Family Bible Owned by Mrs. Harry Kerslake, Paris, Ky.

Tacitus Burgin was born Feb. 7, 1829.
Mary Helen Hinds was born Mch. 3, 1830.
Perry Burgin was born Aug. 22, 1852.
Sithey Hedges Gaitskill was born Aug. 17, 1854.
Mary Kate Burgin was born May 15, 1879.
Henry Tacitus Burgin was born Oct. 9, 1882.
Frederick Allen Burgin was born Feb. 28, 1890.
Tacitus Burgin and Mary H. Hines were married Sept .16, 1851.
Perry Burgin and Sithey Gaitskill were married Jan. 18, 1876.
Harry Kerslake and Mary K. Burgin were married Feb. 6, 1907.
Dr. Perry Burgin died Apr. 7, 1919.
Sithey Burgin died Aug. 26, 1926.

WILLIAM CLARK BIBLE
(Owned by John Darnaby)
Donated Record by Mrs. John Wesley Marr, Lexington, Ky.

William Clark was born Nov. 1, 1790.
Betsy Clark was born June 1, 1799, and was married by Rev. Jeremiah
    Vardeman on the 13th day of Nov., 1823.
James Sandford Clark was born Nov. 9, 1824.
John Wm. Clark was born Mch. 31, 1827.
Thomas George Clark was born July 17, 1832.
Ann Elizabeth Clark was born June 12, 1834.
John Wm. Clark departed this life Aug. 7, 1857.

William Clark died July 26, 1870.
Thomas George Clark departed this life Jan. 5, 1875.
Betsy Clark died Oct. 30, 1879.
James Sandford Clark died May 2, 1906.
Thomas C. Wood and Ann Elizabeth Clark were married Feb. 10, 1858.
Nannie Clark Wood was born July 15, 1864.
Robert Lee Wood was born July 15, 1864. (Note by Mrs. J. W. Marr:
   Betty Lee Wood, changed "Betty" to "Robert" in the Bible.)
William Hewitt Wood was born Aug. 6, 1877.
   (Note: Betsy Clark was Betsy Darnaby.)

OLD BIBLE OWNED BY SAMUEL CLARK OF COVINGTON, KY.
Now Owned by Mrs. Robert Alexander of Lexington. Ky.
James Clark and Susan Ellis were married the 28th of Sept., 1785.
   (Susan Ellis, daughter of Wm. Ellis and Agnes Brooks Carr.)
James Clark, Sen., was born Apr. 30, 1759.
Susan Ellis Clark was born Oct. 11, 1766.   Their children:
   1. John Clark was born Jan. 4, 1787.
   2. Lucy Clark was born Feb. 25, 1788.
   3. Edmond Clark was born Mch. 23, 1789.
   4. William Clark was born Nov. 1, 1790.
   5. James Clark was born Feb. 17, 1792.
   6. Hipkins Clark was born Dec. 25, 1792.
   7. Delphia Clark was born Aug. 31, 1794.
   8. James Clark was born July 1, 1796.
   9. Hipkins Clark was born Mch. 29, 1798.
  10. Thomas Clark was born Jan. 10, 1800.
  11. Peter Clark was born Oct. 15 ,1801.
  12. Samuel Clark was born Aug. 10, 1803.
  13. Sidney Clark was born May 7, 1805.
  14. Betsy Clark was born Nov. 16, 1806.
  15. Susan Clark was born Aug. 19, 1809.
James Clark, Sen., died June 6, 1810.
James Clark, Jr., died Mch. 2, 1792.
Hipkins Clark died July 1, 1794.
Delphia Clark died Nov. 23, 1833.
Hipkins Clark died Apr. 22, 1821.
Thomas Clark died Mch. 4, 1843.
Betsy Clark died Nov. 16, 1810.
   (Note by a Descendant: William Carr was a son of Thomas Carr.
Agnes B. Carr was a daughter of William Carr and Susan Brooks, 2nd
wife of Wm. Carr. Wm. Ellis and wife were from Virginia. James
Clark and Susan Ellis were married in Stamford, Ky.)

COPY OF " CYRUS BEECHER COOK" BIBLE
   (Owned by his daughter, Cora Virginia Cook Adams, Cynthiana,
Ky.   Copied by Mrs. H. K. McAdams.)
   Cyrus Beecher Cook (son of Stephen B. Cook and Lydia Beecher)
—Born Forge Springs, Lancaster County, Pa., on March 31, 1823; died
Nov. 14, 1880, at Cynthiana, Ky. He married Permelia Catherine
Knight, of Hagerstown, Maryland (daughter of Sam and Catherine
Crist Knight), on the 19th of Nov., 1844. Permelia Catherine Knight
was born in Washington Co., Md., Dec. 9, 1828; died June, 1905, at
Cynthiana, Ky.   Children of Cyrus B. and Permelia C. Cook:
Laura Permelia Cook—Born Aug. 1, 1847, in Clark Co., Va.; died
   Oct., 1892, at Cynthiana, Ky.
Lidia Catherine Cook—Born Feb. 12, 1849, in Clark Co., Va.; died June
   1, 1849.
Cora Virginia Cook—Born Apr. 17, 1855, in London Co., Va.
Ida Irene Cook—Born Sept. 3, 1857, in Stanton, Augustus Co., Va.;
   died Jan. 13, 1862.

Cyrus Knight Cook—Born Feb. 19, 1863, in Madison Co., Ky.; died Mch 9, 1899.

Lilly Lee Cook—Born Mch. 14, 1863, at Milford Mills, Harrison Co., Ky.; died Dec. 13, 1890, Cynthiana, Ky.

Hattie May Cook—Born Aug. 21, 1867, in Cynthiana, Ky.; died 1908.

Cora Virginia Cook, daughter of Cyrus B. and Permelia Knight Cook, married William Addams, Oct., 1872. Their children:

1. Urilla Addams—Born Oct. 25, 1873; married June 3, 1896, Perry Megibben, Cynthiana.
2. Elizabeth—Born Nov. 3, 1875; married Harry Frisbee, Jr.
3. Cora—Born Aug. 17, 1878.
4. Cyrus—Born Aug. 11, 1881.
5. Ruth—Born Sept. 21, 1883.
6. Annie May—Born Oct. 20, 1886.
7. Lucy Logan—Born Dec. 10, 1889.
8. William—Born Aug. 5, 1895.

Cyrus Addams (4th child) married Gladys Milner (of A. F. and Delia Hamon Milner, of Scott Co., Ky.) Feb. 3, 1910. Children: (1) William Milner Addams; (2) Eugene Bayne Addams; (3) Cyrus Cook Addams.

Ruth Addams (5th child) married Thomas King (of Wm. King and Mary Griffin).

Annie May Addams (6th child) married (2nd wife) Tom E. Moore (of Capt. T. E. Moore, Pendleton Co., and Sarah J. Shawhan, Harrison Co). One child, Ann Moore.

William Addams, Jr. (8th child) married Margaret Elizabeth Shropshire (of Wm. Clay Shropshire) June 15, 1925.

Cyrus Knight Cook (of C. B. and P. C. Cook) married Meddie Lydick (of Andrew Lydick and Ella Houston), children: (1) Ella Cook; (2) Catherine Cook; (3) Cyrus Beecher Cook; (4) Lena Cook.

Laura Permelia Cook married Caleb Musser Oct. 3, 1866; children: (1) Joe Musser—Born Aug. 22, 1867; died Mch. 19, 1895; (2) Carl Musser—Born Nov. 12, 1871; (3) Catherine Musser—Born Sept., 1874; died Sept. 9, 1905; (4) Elizabeth married Albert Griffee. Carl Musser married Minnie Parks; 1 child, Martha Franklin Musser.

Lilly Lee Cook married Aaron Ashbrook (of Sam.); children: (1) Samuel Ashbrook; (2) Catherine Elizabeth Ashbrook; (3) Cyrus Beecher Ashbrook; (4) Felix Ashbrook.

Hattie May Cook married Dr. Joe Boyd, April 19, 1894.

Ella Cook (of C. Knight Cook and M. Lydick) married J. Ernest Thorne. Children: (1) Ernestine—Born July, 1916; (2) Jessie McKee Thorne—Born Feb. 4, 1823.

Catherine Cook (of C. Knight Cook and M. Lydick) married Louis Conrad July 28, 1904.

Cyrus Beecher Cook (of C. Knight Cook and M. Lydick) married (first) Blanche Dunn (of Jeptha Dunn and Nanna L. Beagle) Mch. 28, 1907; Blanche died Aug. 9, 1913; children: (1) Cyrus Beecher Cook, Jr.—Born Oct. 12, 1908; (2) Charles Jeptha Cook—Born Sept. 11, 1911. Cyrus Beecher Cook married (second) Sarah Will Haley, of Berry Station, Ky. (of Ollie and Burt Haley), children: (1) Billy.

BIBLE OF ELIZABETH COOPER.
Now Owned by Miss Sally Bronston

(Records Donated by Mrs. William Bronston, Lexington, Ky.)

Joseph Cooper and Elizabeth Houghton were married Mch. 15, 1808.

Sallie K. Cooper was married to William Hughes Oct. 4, 1853.

Mary E. Cooper was married to William Cromwell Feb. 26, 1856.

John H. Cooper and Susan Wallace were married May 10, 1832.

John H. Cooper and Judah Carroll were married July 29, 1836.

John Cooper was married to Margaret Haggin the 12th of Oct., 1853.

Joseph Cooper was born Feb. 21, 1782.
Elizabeth Cooper was born Sept. 13, 1786.
Samuel H. Cooper was born Sept. 24, 1854.
Jane P. Cooper was born Mch. 18, 1857.
Sarah Kirkpatrick Cooper was born Dec. 23, 1808.
John Houghton Cooper was born May 1, 1810.
Washington Cooper was born July 8, 1812.
(?)Gerry Cooper was born June 9, 1814.
Joseph Cooper was born May 19, 1816.
Sallie Kirkpatrick Cooper was born Feb. 15, 1833.
Susan Cooper was born Oct. 10, 1808.
Mary Elizabeth Cooper was born Nov. 29, 1837.
Judah Cooper was born June 3, 1819.
Susan Frances Cooper was born Dec. 12, 1839.
Joseph Cooper died May 7, 1816.
Sarah Kirkpatrick Cooper died Oct. 22, 1824.
(?)Gerry Cooper died May 13, 1815.
Washington Cooper died Mch. 22, 1829.
Joseph Cooper died Aug. 8, 1829.
Susan Cooper died May 27, 1833.
Judah Cooper departed this life on the 10th day of July, 1842, in the
    24th year of her age.
Elizabeth Cooper departed this life on the 23rd day of July, 1850, in
    the 64th year of her age.
Susan Frances Cooper departed this life on the 1st day of Jan., 1856,
    in the 17th year of her age.
Our father, John H. Cooper, died Mch. 5th, 1878, in the 68th year of
    his age.

BIBLE OF MRS. SARAH HAINES COOPER, DATED 1812
Kindness of Mrs. Jos. B. Beard.

(Copied by Mrs. Mary G. Webb)

Simeon Haynes was born Dec. 17, 1777.
Jane Haynes was born Feb. 5, 1794.
Thomas Haynes was born May 31, 1806.
Sally Ann Haynes was born Sept. 16, 1812.
Mary Haynes was born Aug. 15, 1814.
Sarah Jane Haynes was born Oct. 16, 1816.
Ann Elizabeth Haynes was born Dec. 22, 1818.
John Haynes was born Nov. 25, 1820.
Simeon Haynes was born Feb. 23, 1823.
Margaret D. Haynes was born Oct. 19, 1824.
Susan M. Haynes was born Jan. 30, 1827.
Catherine L. Haynes was born Jan. 30, 1829.
Samuel S. Haynes was born July 31, 1831.
Charity C. Haynes was born July 31, 1834.
Elizabeth Haynes died Oct., 1808.
Sally Ann Haynes died Aug., 1813.
John Haynes died Oct. 11, 1823.
Simeon Haynes died Dec. 16, 1823.
Simeon Haynes, Sr., died Dec. 30, 1862.
Jane Haynes died May 6, 1878.
Sarah J. Haynes died Apr. 6, 1889.
Mary A. Haynes died Nov. 29, 1889.
Catherine Laird Record died Jan. 22, 1889.
Susan M. Conyer died Apr. 12, 1898.
Samuel S. Haynes died Mch. 14, 1896.
Ann Elizabeth Haynes died Aug. 3, 1900.
Margaret D. Webb died Sept. 22, 1903.

T. B. COLLINS BIBLE.

(Copied by his Niece, Mary Collins Arbuckle.)

William Smith Collins was born Sept. 27, 1810.
Mary Ann Bronston was born Mch. 30, 1817.
Joseph Collins was born Aug. 2, 1840.
Thomas Bronston Collins was born Oct. 4, 1842.
Lucy Ann Collins was born Feb. 21, 1846.
William Joel Collins was born June 20, 1848.
Jacob Smith Collins was born May 18, 1857.
William Smith Collins and Mary Ann Bronston were married Oct. 3, 1839.
Lucy Ann Collins died May 20, 1863.
Thomas B. Collins died Apr. 12, 1869, in Paris, France.
Mary Ann Collins died Apr. 23, 1884.
William Smith Collins died Oct. 28, 1885.
(Notations by Kate Marshall Collins, Wife of Jacob Smith Collins.)
Jacob Smith Collins, son of William Smith Collins, and Mary Ann Bronston Collins, was born May 15, 1857.
Jacob Smith Collins married Kate Marshall Dec. 8, 1885 (born Sept. 4, 1867). Children:
Marshall Collins born Sept. 19, 1886.
Lucie McCord Collins born Aug. 26, 1888.
Mary Ann Collins born Apr. 23, 1891.
William Joel Collins born Mch. 24, 1894.

Children of Jacob Smith Collins and Kate Marshall Collins.

Marshall Collins married Katherine Temple Abbey, Sept. 4, 1915; their child, Cutler Goodrich Collins—Born Boston, Mass., May 15, 1917.
Lucie McCord Collins married Robert E. Burke Jan. 19, 1904.
Mary Ann Collins married James Oliver Armstrong Oct. 10 ,1923.
William Joel Collins married Mary Allen Deatherage July 27, 1920.
Children, Rose Katherine Collins, born Apr. 23, 1922, and Elizabeth Ann Collins, born Apr. 10, 1925.
William Smith Collins was born June 20, 1848; died April 6, 1905; married Aug. 3, 1869.
Elviree Phelps was born June 2, 1848; died Dec. 18, 1820.
Peter Phelps Collins was born Dec. 3, 1872; married Etta Kurtz; son, Peter Phelps Collins, was born May 12, 1902.
William Smith Collins was born Apr. 4, 1874; died Feb. 11, 1900.
Charles Bronston Collins was born Nov. 29, 1878; died young.
M. A. Collins was born June 29; married Mary Fraices Hisler June 12, 1914.
William Joe Collins was born May 20, 1915.
Mary Anne Collins was born Oct., 1917.
Robert Smith Collins was born May 5, 1922.

COLMESNIL FAMILY BIBLE

Bible owned by John D. Colmesnil and wife, Sarah Courtney Taylor Colmesnil, in 1816. Now owned by Mrs. M. Simmons, granddaughter of John D. Colmesnil.
John D. Colmesnil—Born in France, July 31st, 1787.
Sarah Courtney Taylor—Born in Kentucky, Feb. 22nd, 1809; married 1825. Their children:
Edmund Taylor Colmesnil—Born 1827.
William G. Colmesnil—Born Feb., 1829.
Lodoiska Colmesnil—Born Sept., 1830.
Emma Elizabeth Colmesnil—Born 1833.
Courtney C. Colmesnil—Born June 1st, 1835.
James Guthrie Colmesnil—Born Feb., 1837.
Carroll C. Colmesnil—Born Jan., 1841.
William Taylor Colmesnil—Born Jan. 1874.
William H. Murphy, Bardstown, Ky., married Courtney C. Colmesnil,

Dec. 6, 1853. Their children:
Courtney Taylor Murphy—Born Feb. 1st, 1855.
Felix G. Murphy—Born Sept. 18, 1857.
Mary May Murphy—Born Oct. 18, 1861.
Lodoiska Josephine Murphy—Born Feb., 1864.
William Murphy—Born Oct. 18, 1871.
Ida B. Murphy—Born June 10, 1873.
Fannie Burbank Murphy—Born 1875.
Nannie Tarascon Murphy—Born July 10, 1877.
Charles Thurston Murphy—Born July, 1879.

Notes taken from authentic records: "John D. Colmesnil was born in San Domingo, which island belonged to France. His father and mother, of noble birth, had gone on a visit to his coffee plantations, while there John D. Colmesnil was born. There was an insurrection of the slaves, so they escaped and came to the United States. My grandfather grew up in the U. S. and became a naturalized citizen, was interpreter at the Battle of New Orleans, 1815. Sarah Courtney Taylor, his wife, was the daughter of Major Edmund Taylor, U. S. A., War of 1812, and a granddaughter of Capt. Edmund Taylor, of Revolutionary fame."

Names and dates on tombstones, in the old grave yard at the former home of Joseph G. and May M. Simmons, five miles west of Bardstown, Ky., known as Hayes or Simmons farm:

Micheal Rench—Born 1772; died (erased).
Mary, wife of Micheal Rench—Born 1774; died 1864.
Greenberry Simmons—Born 1801; died 1851.
George M. Hayes—Born 1795; died 1871. (Mexican War veteran.)

Greenberry Simmons was the grandfather of J. G. Simmons, and his wife was Elizabeth Rench.

Record signed by (Mrs.) May M. Simmons, 2834 Virginia Ave., Louisville, Ky.

BIBLE OF JAMES CROW.
Present Owner Chas. Lewis Crow, Danville, Ky.
(Copied by Mrs. J. A. Mitchell, Bowling Green, Ky.)

Andrew Lewis Crow married to Margaret Montgomery on the 21st day of Feb., 1799.
James Crow, son of Andrew L. Crow, married to Permelia T. Carter on the 12th day of Jan., 1826.
John Crow, son of Andrew L. Crow, Sen., married to Permelia Mayfield on the 8th day of Sept., 1829.
Andrew Lewis Crow, Jr., son of Andrew L. Crow, Sen., married to Elvira Hahn on the 25th of Feb., 1830.
Elizabeth Crow, daughter of Andrew L. Crow, Sen., married to James Robinson on the 15th day of Oct., 1829.
Charles Lewis Crow, son of Andrew L. Crow, married to Rebecca Goodlett on the 21st day of Dec., 1831.
Margaret Crow, daughter of Andrew L. Crow, married to Thomas B. Dodds on the 28th day of June, 1832.
James Crow (2nd mar.) married to Amanda T. Alcorn, Aug. 14, 1855.
Children of Andrew Lewis Crow, Sen.:
William Crow, who was born the 21st day of Feb., 1800.
James Crow, who was born the 24th day of Apr., 1801.
John Crow, who was born the 25th day of Oct., 1802.
Andrew Lewis Crow, Jr., who was born the 30th day of May, 1804.
Elizabeth Crow, who was born the 13th day of Dec., 1805.
Charles Lewis Crow, who was born the 11th day of Oct., 1807.
Margaret Crow, who was born the 20th day of May, 1814; died Apr. 1, 1862.
Children of James Crow and Permelia Carter Crow:
1. Elizabeth T. Crow, who was born May 7, 1827.

2. Parmelia Carter Crow, who was born Mch. 6, 1829.
3. James Collin Crow, who was born Apr. 10, 1831.
4. Parmelia Jane Crow, who was born Apr. 30, 1833.
5. Joseph Andrew Crow, who was born May 22, 1835.
6. Oliver Jackson Crow, who was born June 26, 1837; died the 29th of June, 1907.
7. William Porter Crow, who was born Feb. 29, 1840.
8. Carroll Kendrick Crow, who was born the 23rd day of Aug., 1843; died at Atlanta, Ga., July 27, 1904.
9. Talbott Logan Crow was born the 31st day of Mch., 1845.
10. Robert Holliday Crow, who was born the 14th of Jan., 1848.
11. Mathew David Crow, who was born the 3rd of Aug., 1850.
12. and 13. Margaret Montgomery Crow and Fanny Dorcas Crow, twin daughters, who were born Apr. 14, 1857.
14. Charles Lewis Crow, who was born Oct. 3, 1862.

Newspaper clipping, Bowling Green, Ky., June 29, 1929—The will of John Crow, the founder of Danville, Ky., is on record in the Stanford Court House. He located in Danville in 1774 and died in 1801. His will, witnessed by Dr. Ephraim McDowell and Joshua Barbee, was made in 1797. * * * *

He consigned all his worldly goods to his wife and children. He had been twice married. His last wife was a widow and, among other things, he wills to her a farm in Garrard County, which she inherited from her first husband. * * * In the deed to Walker Daniel, Crow sold 76 acres of the town's land of Danville. * * * William Crow, who owned what is now the Guy Jones farm, was a son of John Crow and died in 1821. His will is also of record in the Stanford Court House. Wm. Crow was a very rich man * * * among his last acts was to free some of his slaves and make provision that they must never become charges upon the county. John Crow mentions the following children: Abraham and William Crow, Mrs. Elizabeth Messick, Mrs. Mattie Jamesson, Mrs. Mary Flack, Miss Sarah Crow and Miss Ann Crow. While looking through the records, a deed from George Caldwell to Rev. Francis Clark on the banks of Salt River was found, dated Nov., 1784.

CROMWELL BIBLE.
(Donated by John Cromwell, Cynthiana, Ky.)

Vincent Cromwell—Born 1752; died 1819 in Fayette Co., Ky.

Joseph Cromwell—Born 1784; died 1866 in Missouri.

Henry Fry Cromwell—Born 1811; died Jan. 10, 1898 in Cynthiana, Ky.

Elizabeth Miller Cromwell—Born 1819; died Sept. 22, 1905, in Cynthiana, Ky.

Mary Miller Cromwell—Married Ben Desha; born 1838; died 1909.

Jas. W. Cromwell—Born Aug. 31, 1840; died Jan. 14, 1917.

Margaret A. Cromwell—Born Sept. 19, 1844. Living in Cynthiana, Ky.

Ella Cromwell—Born July 8, 1847; married D. C. Lauderdale; died Arkansas, 1914.

Bettie M. Cromwell—Born Aug., 1856. Living in Cynthiana, Ky.

Jas. M. Desha—Born May 1, 1858.

Marcus R. Desha—Born Aug. 28, 1861.

John M. Cromwell—Son of Jas. W. Cromwell; born Feb. 25, 1862. Living in Cynthiana, Ky.

Lillie Lee Cromwell—Daughter of Jas. W. Cromwell; born Jan. 29, 1863. Living in Long Beach, Calif.

Sallie Christine Cromwell, daughter of Jas. W. Cromwell—Born Aug. 11, 1870. Living in Cynthiana, Ky.

Joe Desha—Born in 1870.

Bessie C. Desha—Born 1868. Living in Cynthiana, Ky.

Christina Fry Cromwell—Wife of Joseph Cromwell; died in Missouri, Apr. 27, 1864.

Henry Frye Cromwell—Son of John M .Cromwell and Eva G. Berry; born Jan. 21, 1894; died May 10, 1923.

Eva Berry Cromwell—Wife of John M. Cromwell; born Sept. 7, 1865. Died 1929.

Henry Fry Cromwell—1st; died Mch. 21, 1898.

Elizabeth Miller, his wife, died Apr. 11, 1905.

Mary Miller Cromwell, wife of Ben Desha, died Jan. 6, 1909.

NICHOLS FAMILY BIBLE.
Date of Bible 1856.
(Donated by John Cromwell, Cynthiana, Ky.)

Henry Nichols and Sarah Fenton Smith were married July 1, 1834.

Thomas Nichols, 1st, aged 65 years, died Oct. 15, 1824.

Cassandra Nichols, wife of Thos., aged about 100 years, died Mch. 18, 1866.

Henry Nichols—Born Sept. 28, 1803; died Mch. 5, 1866.

Sarah F. Nichols—Born Nov. 1, 1810; died July 20, 1888.

Thomas A. Nichols II.—Born July 26, 1836, in Mo.; died Jan. 11, 1906.

Mary B. Nichols—Born Feb. 8, 1843; married Jas. W. Cromwell; died Nov. 25, 1927.

Jas. B. Nichols—Born Sept. 18, 1838; died Nov. 29, 1868.

Dennis Nichols—Born Oct. 12, 1840, in Mo.; died June 19, 1908.

Nancy Nichols—Born Sept. 21, 1846, in Mo.; died Dec. 5, 1909.

Geo. T. Nichols—Born July 11, 1849, in Mo.; died July 15, 1918.

Sarah M. Nichols—Born Sept. 11, 1851. Living in Missouri.

BIBLE OF ELIZA ANN DRAKE.
(Copied by Mrs. H. K. McAdams.)

Edmund Drake was born Oct. 3, 1736.

Fanny Williamson was born Mch. 16, 1722; married Oct. 31, 1807.

Children:
Charles Drake, who was born Aug. 18, 1808.
John Bound Drake, who was born Sept. 1 ,1810.
Eliza Ann Drake, who was born Mch. 6, 1813.

Charles Drake and Lucinda Carter were married Nov. 8, 1832.

John Drake, son of Charles Drake, died Apr. 26, 1836.

Eliza J. Drake was born Sept. 12, 1833.

John Drake was born Oct. 5, 1835.

John Drake died Apr. 26, 1836. (Last 3 names on loose leaf.)

Funeral notice lying in same bible: Funeral of Mrs. Elizabeth Beatty, from the residence of her daughter, Mrs. Barbara Spurr, this evening, at 3 o'clock, Sat., Aug. 14, 1841.

DOWNING BIBLE RECORD.
Copied From Old Records of Mrs. Wm. Sandifer of Lexington, Ky.

Joseph Downing was born Nov. 4, 1795; died 1874; married, 1818, Sarah Taylor, daughter of William Taylor and Hannah Guilliam, was born 1800; died 1875. Their children:

Martha Downing, who married William Darnaby.

William Downing, who married Sarah Keiser.

Margaret Downing, who married 1st William Stipp and 2nd John Woodford Taylor of Winchester, Ky.

Hannah Downing, who married John Davis.

Elizabeth Downing, who married A. J. Rose.

Joseph Downing, who married Lucy Wilson.

Stark Taylor Downing, who married Ann Parker.

Samuel Downing, who married Ann Muir.

Jerry Vardeman Downing, who married Ann Crutcher.

Simeon Downing, who died young.

Mary Downing, who was born June 2, 1822; died July 12, 1910; married Feb. 2, 1851, John Hundley (son of Zacharia Hundley and Prudence Metcalf, who were married Mch. 4, 1815).

John Hundley, born 1824, and died Nov. 18, 1899, and Mary Downing Hudley. Their children:
William Hundley, who died single.
John H. Hundley, who married 1st Addie Johnson and 2nd Ellen Chapman of La.
Sarah Ellen Hundley, who married Edward Cobb of S. C.
Charleston Clay Hundley, who married Amanda Moore.
Nancy Margaret Hundley, who was born Apr. 4, 1854; died Aug. 11, 1922; married Dec. 1, 1870.

William Jefferson Hogan was born July 8, 1839; died May 16, 1878; married Dec. 1, 1870.

Children of Nancy Margaret Hundley and William Jefferson Hogan:
Mollie Belle Hogan, who married John Morgan Gentry; born Oct. Oct. 22, 1871; married Aug. 7, 1889.
Maggie May Hogan, who was born Apr. 30, 1874; married Oct. 5, 1899, Vertna Blackford.
William Preston Dillard Hogan, who was born July 6, 1877; died May 25, 1878.

Nancy Margaret Hundley Hogan married 2nd Fountain Robert Holman, who was born May 9, 1860; died Dec., 192—; married Mch. 3, 1881. Their children:
Allie Elliott Holman, who was born Dec. 3, 1881; died Jan. 4, 1929.
Addie Keene Holman, who was born May 20, 1884; married Percy Stackhouse, son of Rev. T. C. Stackhouse.
John Robert Holman, who was born Oct. 29, 1886; died 1886.
Daniel Thornton Holman, who was born Sept. 29, 1889; married Carrie Polsgrove. World War soldier.

Children of John Morgan Gentry and Mollie Belle Hogan:
Charles Moore Gentry, who married Mary Alice Bunston; born Dec. 29, 1891; married Aug. 16, 1916.

Children of Charles Moore Gentry and Mary Alice Gentry:
Charles Morgan Gentry, who was born Jan. 22, 1919.
Mary Margaret Gentry, who was born Nov. 24, 1920.

DOWNING BIBLE
(Donated by Mrs. M. B. Herring, Georgetown, Ky.)

John Downing—Born April 12th, 1776.
Francis Downing—Born Jan. 6th, 1778.
Neuesha Downing—Born Feb. ——, 1780.
Sarah Downing—Born April ——, 1782.
Mary Downing—Born ———, 1784. (Grandmother of Mrs. M. B. Herring.) Married John Adams; left Hartford County, Maryland, Oct. 23, 1791, landed at Limestone (now Maysville), Dec. 1, 1791.
Wm. Downing married Nov. 21, 1793.
Wm. Downing, Jr.—Born Sept. 5th, 1794.
Joseph Downing—Born Nov. 4th, 1795.
Ruth Downing—Born Oct. 9th, 1797.
Richard Downing—Born May 9th, 1799.
Samuel Downing—Born Aug. 27th, 1804.
Mariah Downing—Born June ——, 1802.
Eliza Downing—Born Aug. ——, 1803.
Elizabeth Downing—Born Oct. 15th, 1805.
Morgan Downing—Born ———, 1807.
Priscilla Downing—Born Nov. 29th, 1808.
Wm. Downing, Jr., married Charlotte Wymore Nov. 2nd, 1920; she was born Aug. 17, 1798; died Sept. 23rd, 1868. Wm. Downing Jr., died April, 1871. Their children:

Willis Downing—Born Oct. 4th, 1821; died Oct. 4th, 1888.
Samuel Downing—Born June 4th, 1823.
Jas. E. Downing—Born April 18th, 1827; died Feb. 4th, 1905.
(Note: See Collins History for Christopher Gist, who married Edith Downing, a sister of Wm. Downing.)

REV. JOHN RICHARD DEERING BIBLE

Now owned, and copied, by his daughter, Rowena Deering Shearer, Lexington, Ky.

"My father, Rev. Richard Deering, was born in Greenup Co., Ky., on August 15th, 1811. Died August 15, 1892, while in Chattanooga.

"My mother, Mrs. Amanda Deering, was born in Shelbyville, Ky., Nov. 1st, 1813. Died in Louisville, Ky., May 8th, 1892, almost 79 years.

John R. Deering was born in Lexington, Ky., July 2, 1842. Baptized in infancy by Bishop Waugh, M. E. C.

"Fannie Covin was born in Troup Co., Ga., Dec. 31st, 1844. Baptized when about 12 years old by Rev. Baggerly.

"On the evening of Oct. 4th, 1864, at the home of D. T. Covin, in Troup Co., Ga., C. S. A., by Rev. John McGehee, Rev. John R. Deering was married to Miss Fannie Covin.

"David T. Covin died Feb. 7, 1895. Was born Oct. 4, 1813.

"Mrs. Caroline Covin died July 6, 1896; was born Mch. 22, 1819.

"McGaughey Bible, inscribed 'Mrs. Rachel McGaughey, Jan. 17, 1856. Now owned, and copied by Mrs. Anne Deering McClure, Lexington. (Note by Mrs. McClure—Mrs. Rachel McGaughey was grandmother of Rev. John R. Deering.)

"John McGaughey died June 17, 1846.

"Rachel McGaughey died Feb. 11, 1873."

DENTON FAMILY BIBLE

Owned by J. T. Denton, Sr.; copied by Mrs. H. K. McAdams.

Family record of James Thompson Denton and Wife, Josephine C. Harris.

James Thompson Denton—Born Apr. 6, 1865, Garrard Co., Ky.

Josephine C. H. Denton—Born Mch. 4, 1818, Garrard Co., Ky.; died Jan. 7, 1875.

Russell Rhodes Denton—Born June 18, 1842, Garrard Co., Ky.

Nancy Thomas Denton—Born Feb. 29, 1844, Garrard Co., Ky.; died 1927.

Mary Elizabeth Denton—Born Feb. 18, 1845, Garrard Co., Ky.; died Sept. 22, 1844.

Pauline Roberts Denton—Born Aug. 28, 1846, Garrard Co., Ky.

John Tyree Denton—Born Dec. 25, 1848, in Russell Co., Ky.

Martha Rachel Denton—Born Aug. 18, 1852, Russell Co., Ky.; died Feb., 1825.

Samantha Ann Denton—Born Oct. 13, 1854, Garrard Co., Ky.; died Jan. 26, 1926.

James Oberton Denton—Born June 17, 1856, Russell Co., Ky.; died Sept. 13, 1857.

William Henry Denton—Born Aug. 16, 1858, Russell Co., Ky.

Emma Josephine Denton(dau. of J. T. and America Jane Jones Denton)—Born Oct. 17, 1876, Fayette Co., Ky.

Thomas Jones Denton (son of J. T. and America Jane Jones Denton)—Born May 1, 1880, Fayette Co., Ky.; died Oct. 1, 1924, in Carolina.

John Willie Denton (son of J. T. and A. J. J. Denton)—Born Nov. 25, 1884, Fayette Co., Ky.

America Jane Jones Denton—Born Feb. 18, 1854; died Oct. 24, 1892; aged 38 yrs.

Annie Mary Grimes Denton—Born May 18, 1857.

John Tyree Denton married (first) America Jone Jones, Jessamine Co., Ky., on Oct. 12, 1875.

John Tyree Denton married (second) Annie Mary Grimes, in Lexington, Ky., May 24, 1894.

Emma Josephine Denton married John Hughes Young, Oct. 12, 1892, Lexington, Ky.

John W. Denton married Matilda Leer, Apr. 29, 1908, Lexington, Ky.

JAMES ELKIN, SR. BIBLE (of Clark Co., Ky)

Now owned by Richard King, Rutledge, Mo. Copied and donated by Mrs. Joseph Beard, Lexington, Ky.

James Elkin, Sr. was born (in what is now Henry Co., Va.) April 16, 1755.

Martha Jackson was born February 6, 1765.

James Elkin, Sr. and Martha Jackson were married in Washington Co., Va., Sept. 23rd, 1782. Their children:

Katherine Elkin was born June 2, 1784.

Mary Elkin was born ————, 1786.

Dorcas Elkin was born July 20, 1788.

Martha Elkin was born August the 9th, 1791.

Jane Elkin was born Jan. 15th, 1793.

Rhoda Elkin was born March the 7th, 1796.

Nancy Elkin was born Feb. the 20th, 1799.

James Elkin was born May 19th, 1800.

Zachariah Elkin was born Oct. 12, 1803.

William Elkin was born Dec. 30, 1805; died Nov. 6, 1807.

Sibbe Elkin was born Aug. 11, 1808.

Elizabeth Elkin was born April the 17th, 1811.

Marriages of James Elkin, Sr.'s Children

Katherine Elkin and Frances White were married Ang. 24, 1801(or '2).

Mary (Polly) Elkin and William Richason were married Dec. 15, 1808.

Dorcas Elkin and ———————— married Sept. 13, 1810.

Martha (Patsy) Elkin married Bradley Richason, Feb. 8, 1810.

Jane Elkin and William Barnes married Sept. 10, 1818.

Rhoda Elkin and John Crow married June 17, 1819.

Nancy Elkin and William Crow married March 2, 1824.

James Elkin and Lucinda Osborne married Dec. 12, 1822.

Zachariah Elkin and Ann Stokely married Dec. 5, 1822.

James Elkin, Jr., was born May 19, 1800; was married Dec. 12, 1822.

James Elkin died Aug 5, 1878.

Lucinda Elkin died June 1, 1884, in the 80th year. Born 1804 (this date was taken from her grave stone, James Elkin's grave yard, in Clark Co., Ky., farm on Lulbegrud Creek and Red River) Children:

William P. Elkin, son of James Elkin and Lucinda, his wife, was born Jan. 31, 1824; died June, 1888.

James M. Elkin was born Jan. 17, 1826; died Jan. 17, 1892.

Luvicy Bowen Elkin was born Jan. 7, 1828.

Thomas Boon Elkin was born Oct. 31, 1830 (or 1831).

Martha K. Elkin was born Sept. 11, 1833; died Mch. 10, 1887.

Benjamin Chilton Elkin was born July 11, 1835.

Zachariah Fielding Elkin was born Aug. 31, 1837; died Apr., 1907.

John D. Elkin was born Sept. 4, 1839; died May 16, 1863.

Solomon C. Elkin was born Dec. 30, 1841; died Feb. 20, 1885.

Silas A. Elkin was born Oct. 27, 1843.

Josephine Cinderella Elkin was born Feb. 4, 1846.

Joseph Richason, son of Bradley Richason and Martha, his wife, was born Mch. 20, 1811.

William Richason, son of aforesaid, was born Sept. 10, 1813.

James Richason, son of aforesaid, was born Feb. 29, 1816.

John Richason, son of aforesaid, was born Apr. 17, 1818.

Absalom Richason, son of aforesaid, was born May 26, 1821.

Patsy Mima Richason, daughter of aforesaid, was born Mch. 8, 1824.

Bradley Richason, son of the aforesaid, was born June 7, 1826.
Zachariah Richason, son of the aforesaid, was born Dec. 7, 1828.
Elizabeth Richason, daughter of the aforesaid, was born Jan. 19, 1831.
Bradley Richason, father of the aforesaid family, was born Mch. 10, 1781.
William P. Elkin, son of James and Lucinda Elkin, was born Mch. 31, 1824, and Miranda Elkin (late Miranda Fisher, daughter of John and Sarah Fisher), was born Dec. 7, 1827; united in matrimony Feb. 22, 1846, by John Niblick. Children:
   James S. Elkin was born May 11, 1847. Died.
   John W. Elkin was born Dec. 27, 1848.
   Sarah A. Elkin was born Sept. 7, 1850. Died.
   James T. Elkin was born Jan. 28, 1852.
   Sarah Lucinda Elkin was born Nov. 20, 1853.
   Susan J. Elkin was born May (torn paper), 1856.
   Elizabeth Elkin was born May 17, 1858. Died.
   Benjamin C. Elkin was born May 26, 1859.
   Martha E. Elkin was born July (torn paper) 2, 1861.
   Solomon H. Elkin was born Sept. 9, 1863.
   Miranda C. Elkin was born Sept. 5, 1865.
   Ulysus G. Elkin was born Apr. 30, 1867.
   Fielding R. Elkin was born Oct. 25, 1869.
S. C. Elkin died Feb. 20, 1865.
Miranda C. Elkin died Feb. 24, 1866.
Martha E. Elkin died June 4, 1881.
William P. Elkin died June 2, 1888.
Miranda Elkin died Dec. 16, 1893.

Z. F. ELKIN BIBLE.
(Copied by Mrs. Jos. B. Beard.)

Zachariah Felding Elkin and Minerva Ann Wood were married Feb. 25, 1858.
George E. Chapman and Elizabeth Ann Elkin were mar. Dec. 23, 1879.
John O'Brien and Lucinda Elkin were married Jan. 6, 1881.
George O. Poole and Laura Elkin were married Oct., 1883.
James W. Elkin and Lucy Ann Martin were married Aug. 13, 1885.
Z. F. Elkin and Mrs. Bettie Adams were married Thursday, Jan. 22, 1885. (2nd marriage of Z. F. Elkin.)
Zachariah Fielding Elkin was born Aug. 31, 1837.
Minerva Ann Elkin, his wife, was born Feb. 25, 1841. Their children:
   1. Elizabeth Ann Elkin—Born Dec. 14, 1858.
   2. Lucinda Elkin—Born Dec. 5, 1860.
   3. James William Elkin—Born Aug. 11, 1862.
   4. Marinda Ellen Elkin—Born July 1, 1864.
   5. Laura Elkin—Born Apr. 18, 1866.
   6. John Columbus Elkin—Born Aug. 20, 1867.
   7. Minerva Rella Elkin—Born Oct. 13, 1869.
   8. Fielding Clay Elkin—Born Sept. 26, 1871.
   9. Mattie Frances Elkin—Born Apr. 20, 1873.
   10. Woodie Bowen Elkin—Born Aug. 10, 1875.
Child of John Hall Weeks and Mattie Frances Elkin:
   Marjorie Weeks—Born Sept. 8, 1901.
Children of Mattie F. Elkin and James Redfern:
   Almira Elizabeth Redfern—Born Dec. 3, 1906.
   James Clay Redfern—Born Mch. 8, 1909; died Feb. 27, 1912.
   Jerome J. Redfern—Born May 19, 1911.
Z. F. Elkin and M. A. Elkin's children:
   Marinda Ellen Elkin—Died June, 20, 1865.
   John Columbus Elkin—Died Aug. 13, 1868.
Minerva Elkin, wife of Z. F. Elkin, died July 21, 1881.
Fielding Clay Elkin died Aug. 15, 1905.

Zachariah Fielding Elkin died Apr. 9, 1907, aged 69 yrs., 7 months and 11 days.
Elizabeth Ann Chapman died Aug. 3, 1907.
James W. Elkin died July 10, 1912.

BEARD-ELKIN BIBLE

Joseph B. Beard and Minnie R. Elkin, both of Lexington, Ky., were married Apr. 16, 1890, by Rev. William Rupard of Clark Co., Ky.
Joseph Breckinridge Beard, Jr., and Eugenia Mildred Le Compte were married Oct. 11, 1919, in Asheville, N. C. ,by Rev. W. F. Powell.
Elkin Wood Beard and Vera Eubank were married Oct. 28, 1925, and 2nd married Bertha Stafford Aug. 31, 1929.
Ruth Beard and T. Vernon Forman were married July 2, 1927.
Joseph Breckinridge Beard Sr., was born July 4, 1857.
Minnie R. Elkin was born Oct. 13, 1869.   Their children:
Joseph B. Beard, Jr., was born Feb. 20, 1891.
Ruth Beard was born Jan. 14, 1893.
Nannie Myers Beard was born Aug. 4, 1895.
Clay Elkin Wood Beard was born Aug. 25, 1903.
Julian Boswell Beard was born Oct. 21, 1905.
Eugenia M. Le Compte, wife of J. B. Beard, Jr., was born Aug. 17, 1892.
Children of J. B. Beard, Jr., and Eugenia Le Compte Beard:
1. Joseph Breckinridge Beard III. was born Oct. 22, 1920.
2. Charles Le Compte Beard was born Dec. 12, 1924.
3. Jean Campbell Beard was born Sept. 24, 1926.
Judith Boswell Forman, daughter of T. Vernon and Ruth Beard Forman, was born Oct. 24, 1929.
Nannie M. Beard, infant daughter of J. B. Beard, Sr., and Minnie Elkin Beard, died July 22, 1896.
Joseph B. Beard, Sr., died Feb. 26, 1929; aged 71 yrs., 7 months and 22 days.

THOMAS ALEXANDER FRAZER BIBLE.

(Donated and Copied by Owner, Miss Nellie Frazer, Cynthiana, Harrison Co., Ky.)

John Frazer, son of George and Mary Frazer, was born Mch. 17, 1770.
Sarah Veatch, daughter of John and Sarah Veatch, was born Feb. 17, 1777.
Wilson Frazer, son of John and Sarah V. Frazer, was born Aug. 27, 1796
Joel Cartwright Frazer, son of John and Sarah V. Frazer, was born Dec. 8, 1797.
Nancy Frazer, dau. of John and Sarah V. Frazer, was born July 3, 1800.
Sallie Stewart Frazer, dau. of John and Sarah V. Frazer, was born Aug. 7, 1803.
John Wesley Frazer, son of John and Sarah V. Frazer, was born 1805.
Eliza Frazer ,dau. of John and Sarah V. Frazer, was born 1808.
Harriett Frazer, dau. of John and Sarah V. Frazer, was born Nov. 8, 1811.
Mary Louisa Frazer, dau. of John and Sarah V. Frazer, was born Mch. 5, 1814.
William H. Frazer, son of John and Sarah V. Frazer, was born Mch. 17, 1816.
Erasmus D. Frazer, son of John and Sarah V. Frazer, was born Jan. 4, 1820.
Sarah Mountjoy Monroe, John Frazer's 2nd wife, was born Mch. 17, 1789.
Thomas Alexander Frazer, son of John and Sarah M. Frazer, was born Apr. 16, 1827.
James Newton Frazer, son of John and Sarah M. Frazer, was born July 1, 1831.

Emily Frazer, dau. of John and Sarah M. Frazer, was born 18—.

James Willett Frazer, son of Thomas A. and Ellen E. Frazer, was born July 21, 1853.

Bettie Kimbrough Frazer, dau. of Thomas A. and Ellen E. Frazer, was born July 28, 1856.

John Harmon Frazer, son of Thomas A. and Ellen E. Frazer, was born Aug. 12, 1858.

Nellie Frazer, dau. of Thomas A. and Ellen E. Frazer, was born Jan. 26, 1861.

Virginia Lee Frazer, dau. of Thomas A. and Ellen E. Frazer, was born Dec. 13, 1863.

Thomas Alexander Frazer, Jr., son of Thomas A. and Ellen E. Frazer, was born May 4, 1867.

Otwell Frazer, son of Thomas A. and Ellen E. Frazer, was born May 9, 1870.

Hubbard Shawhan Frazer, son of Thomas A. and Ellen E. Frazer, was born June 27, 1873.

Edith Mountjoy Frazer, dau. of Thomas A. and Ellen E. Frazer, was born June 4, 1876.

Charles Royall Frazer, son of James Willett and Mary Cook Frazer, was born Oct. 17, 1877.

May Frazer, dau. of James Willett and Mary Cook Frazer, was born Dec. 19, 1879.

Jay C. Frazer, son of James Willett and Mary Cook Frazer, was born Aug. 10, 1883.

James Royall Frazer, son of Charles Royall and Pauline S. Frazer, was born Dec. 1, 1915.

John Alexander Mountjoy Frazer, son of Charles Royall and Pauline S. Frazer, was born Mch. 16, 1918.

John Frazer and Sarah Veatch were married Oct. 15, 1795.

John Frazer and Sarah Mountjoy Monroe, 2nd wife, were married 182—.

Thomas Alexander Frazer and Ellen Elizabeth Willett were married Apr. 6, 1852.

James Willett Frazer and Mary Cook were married Oct. 10, 1876.

Charles Royall Frazer and Pauline Gertrude Somers were married Dec. 8, 1910.

Sarah Veatch Frazer, wife of John Frazer, departed this life Apr. 10, 1820.

John Frazer departed this life 1836.

Sarah Montjouy Frazer (2nd wife) departed this life Nov., 1838.

John Harmon Frazer departed this life Jan. 13, 1864.

May Frazer departed this life June 12, 1880.

Jay C. Frazer departed this life Jan. 26, 1884.

Ellen Elizabeth Willett Frazer, wife of Thomas Alexander Frazer, departed this life Sept. 21, 1892.

Edith Mountjoy Frazer departed this life June 8, 1894.

Thomas Alexander Frazer, Jr., departed this life Dec. 30, 1895.

James Willett Frazer departed this life Sept. 20, 1905.

BIBLE OF ROBERT GIBSON, SR.
(In His Own Handwriting.)
Now in Possession of Miss Dazey Gibson, Crestwood, Ky.
(Donated by Mrs. Joseph Beard, Jr.)

Robert Gibson came to America July 8, 1773, and married Mary Stewart April 15, 1783. Their children:

Jennie Gibson—Born Feb. 13, 1784.

William Gibson—Born Mch. 17, 1786.

Polly Gibson—Born Apr. 5, 1788.

John Gibson—Born Jan. 6, 1791.

Joseph Gibson—Born May 21, 1793.

James Gibson—Born Dec. 29, 1795.

Robert Gibson—Born Aug. 21, 1798.
Samuel Gibson—Born Feb. 28, 1801.
A child born, died (no date).
Betsy Gibson—Born Feb. 14, 1806.
Mary Stewart Gibson deceased this life Feb. 14, 1806. Betsy was born in the morning and her mother died after night. We were married about 22 years and 10 months.
Betsy Gibson died July 10, 1806.
Jenny Gibson married Robert Wead Sept. 30, 1806. She died Nov. 7, 1811.
Polly Gibson and Robert Wead were married Nov. 25, 1813. I heard William died in Natchez.
In another handwriting:
John Gibson and Mary M. Roberts were married Dec. 14, 1815.
Their children:
Frances Gibson—Born Sept. 23, 1817.
Mary Gibson—Born June 20, 1819.
Elizabeth Walker Gibson—Born Apr. 22, 1821.
Joseph Roberts Gibson—Born June 1, 1823.
Robert Wead Gibson—Born Apr. 1, 1825.
Angelina Gibson—Born July 20, 1827.
Corella Gibson—Born May 15, 1829.
Lucy Ann Gibson—Born Feb. 1, 1831.
John Triplett—Born Apr. 9, 1833.
William Stewart—Born Feb. 15, 1835.
Samuel R. Gibson—Born Oct. 23, 1836.
Mildred Hannah Gibson—Born Dec. 28, 1838.
George Washington Gibson—Born Dec. 25, 1840.
Corella Gibson died Aug. 27 ,1844.
Joseph Roberts Gibson died in California Oct., 1850.
John Gibson, Sr., died June 24, 1860.
Samuel R. Gibson died in Georgia Sept. 8, 1865.
Mary M. Gibson died Apr. 6, 1871.
Marian E., wife of George Washington Gibson, died July 11, 1861.
Lydia Ann, wife of Robert W. Gibson, died July 9, 1868.
Angelina Riner died Feb .21, 1871.
Dr. John P. Campbell died Dec. 18, 1869, in Shelby Co., Ky.
John S. Clark died Dec., 1876, in Henry Co., Ky.
Mildred Ann, wife of W. S. Gibson, died Dec. 25, 1869, in Shelby Co., Ky.
John T. Gibson died July 23, 1895, at old home in Shelby Co., Ky.
Angelina Riner died in Boone Co., Ind., Feb. 21, 1871.
Elizabeth Clark died in Cincinnati, O., July 15, 1898.
Frances Gill died July 24, 1906, in Maryland.
George Washington Gibson died Aug. 13, 1906, in Florida.
Mary J. Bergen died June 10, 1888.
Mildred H. Campbell died July 20, 1890.
Robert Wead Gibson died July 18, 1850.
Lucy Ann Powell died Nov. 26, 1908.
Samuel Roberts Gibson died at end of the war, 1865.
Joseph Gibson died in California about 1850.
W. S. Gibson died Jan. 14, 1916, in Louisville, Ky., aged 80 yrs., 10 months.

The Data Below Was Written by W. S. Gibson.
(Copied by Mrs. Joseph Beard, Jr.)
"My Mother's Family":
Joseph Roberts married Fanny Triplett. Their children:
1. Betsy Roberts. 2. Dr. Huston Roberts. 3. William Roberts.
4. Cassey Roberts. 5. Ben Roberts. 6. Harry Roberts, married
——Bellow. 7. Tom Roberts. 8. Hanna Roberts married Chap Clifton.
9. Mary Magdalene Roberts, born Dec. 23, ——; married John Gibson Dec. 14, 1815. 10. Fanny Roberts. 11. George Roberts.

12. Mildred Roberts, married Wermence O'Bannon. 13. Corella Roberts, married Dan Bohon. 14. Joseph Roberts, married Mary Porter. 15. Philip Roberts, married Sarah Porter.

GRIFFIN KELLY BIBLE.
Record Cont. by Mr. Isaac Le Compte of Fulton, Mo.
(Copied by Mrs. Jos. Beard, Jr.)

Griffin Kelly, Sen., was born Feb. 16, 1770, and departed this life the 17th of Mch., 1855.

Sarah, his wife, was born Sept. 11, 1773, and departed this life the 4th of Feb., 1859.

Griffin Kelly was married to Sarah Sutton, his wife, the 26th of Dec. 1793.

James F. Kelly was born June 27, 1800.

Mellissa McConnell, his wife, was born Aug. 14 ,1807.

James Kelly married Mellissa McConnell Jan. 24, 1826.

Frances Kelly, 2nd wife of Jas. Kelly, was born Dec. 1, 1817.

Sally M. Kelly, daughter of James and Melissa Kelly, was born Feb 22, 1827.

Cassandra was born July 3, 1833.

Lucinda Jane was born Nov. 28, 1838.

James Ovid Kelly was born Sept. 27, 1844.

Melissa, wife of James Kelly, departed this life Mch. 16, 1845, in the 38th year of her age.

Casandra departed this life Mch. 4, 1843, aged 9 yrs., and 8 months.

Lucinda Jane departed this life Apr. 2, 1851, in the 13th yr. of her age.

James O. Kelly departed this life the 26th of Jan., 1865, aged 20 yrs., 3 months and 29 days.

Frances Kelly, 2nd wife of Jas. Kelly, died Jan. 2, 1902.

OLD GUTHRIE BIBLE.
(Copied by Roberta B. Lary.)

Julius Gibbs Guthrie was born Oct. 12, 1812.

Sarah White Guthrie, his wife, was born July 2, 1818. They were married 24th day of Sept., 1835.

(Note: Grandfather and grandmother of Roberta B. Lary.)

BIBLE OF ELIJAH HAYDEN.
Record Donated by His Grandson, W. J. Rees, Lexington, Ky.
(Copied by Mrs. H. K. McAdams.)

Sarah Evans was born Oct. 7, 1756.

Mary Evans was born Mch. 10, 1758.

Charles Evans was born Dec. 30, 1759.

Job Evans was born Apr. 3, 1762.

Amos Evans was born July 15, 1764.

John Evans was born May 11, 1766.

Robert Evans was born Aug. 1, 1768.

Elizabeth Evans was born July 2, 1770.   (Married Elijah Hayden.)

Daniel Evans was born July 9, 17— (torn paper).

Signed by John Evans, his hand and pen.

Elijah Hayden was born Jan. the 8th day, the year of Our Lord, 1763.

(Note: His parents of Scottish descent.)

Elizabeth Evans Hayden, his wife, was born July the 2nd, 1770.

Mary Evans Hayden, their daughter, was born the 25th of Dec. in the year 1813 (or 1811).   Children:

John W. Rees was born June 7, 1835.

Elizabeth M. Rees was born Feb. 17, 1836.

Elijah T. Rees was born May 20, 1839.

Evoline L. Rees was born Jan. 1, 1843.

Daniel J. Rees was born May 25, 1845.

Minerva E. Rees was born Mch. 28, 1847.

William J. Rees was born June 20, 1850.

HAYNES-HINDE BIBLE.
Copied From Old Bible, Dated 1791, Owned by Miss Frances Haynes, Greendale, Ky. By Mrs. Mary G. Webb, Oct. 1, 1921.
(Given by Mrs. Jos. B. Beard.)
William Merrill was born Nov. 13, 1773.
William Merrill and Ruth Stout were married Nov. 30, 1800.
Nancy Merrill, dau. of Wm. and Ruth Merrill, was born Apr. 10, 1804.
David Stout Merrill was born Sept. 9, 1806.
Elizabeth Merrill was born June 10, 1809.
Simeon Haynes was born July 10, 1829.
Copied From Family Bible Owned by Mrs. Ann E. Callahan, and After Her Death by Mrs. Wm. Y. Frisbee of Manilla, P. I.
John P. Callahan and Ann E. Hinde were married Sept. 2, 1847.
John Boyd and Sarah Elizabeth Callahan were married Sept. 9, 1873.
John Paul Callahan was born Apr. 22 ,1814.
Ann Elizabeth Callahan was born Mch. 22, 1829. Children:
1. Sarah Elizabeth Callahan—Born Jan. 15, 1849.
2. John Dillard Callahan—Born Jan. 26, 1852.
3. Edward P. Callahan—Born Sept., 1853.
4. Mary Samuel Callahan—Born May 25, 1855.
Thomas and Mary Hinde were married Sept. 24, 1767. Children:
1. Elizabeth Clifford Hinde—Born June 11, 1768.
2. Susannah Brooks Hinde—Born Dec. 15, 1770.
3. John W. Hinde—Born Mch. 31, 1774.
4. Hannah Hubbard Hinde—Born Mch. 6, 1777.
5. Mary Todd Hinde—Born Jan. 27, 1780.
6. Mary Winston Hinde—Born Dec. 12, 1783.
7. Thomas Spotswood Hinde—Born Apr. 19, 1785.
8. Martha Harrison Hinde—Born May 21, 1787.
John W. Hinde and Elizabeth, his wife, were married ―― 16, 1797.
Children:
1. Clarissa Minor Hinde—Born Jan. 31, 1798.
2. Mary Sydnor Hinde—Born Apr. 19, 1799.
3. Peter Mark Hinde—Born June 16, 1800.
4. Thomas Hubbard Hinde—Born Sept. 2, 1801.
5. Susan Cole Hinde—Born Jan. 17, 1805.
6. John McKindue Hinde—Born June 15, 1806.
7. Martha Ann Hinde.
8. Sophia Hinde.
9. James (Ooton) Hinde—Born Sept. 22, 1809.
10. and 11. Rodney and Edward—Born June 11, 1811.
12. Elizabeth Ann Hinde—Born Jan. 17, 1814.
13. John Wood Hinde was born Sept. 15, 1817.
Elizabeth Sydnor Hinde, wife of John W. Hinde, died Feb. 10, 1850.
John W. Hinde died Apr., 1856.
Edward P. Callahan, son of John P. Callahan and Ann E. Callahan, died Apr. 6, 1854.
John P. Callahan died June 27, 1855.

HENDRICSON-RUMMONS BIBLE
(Donated by Mrs. Clarence Ellroy Rummons)
William D. Hendricson and Mary Rowland married June 12th, 1828.
William D. Hendricson (son of Daniel and Sarah Hendricson) was born Nov. 5th, A. D., 1801.
Mary Hendricson (daughter of James and Dorcas Rowland) was born Jan. 31st, 1807.
Robert Hendricson was born Oct. 3rd, 1824.
James Hendricson (son of William and Mary Hendricson) was born May 14th, 1829.

John Hendricson was born February 5th, 1831.

William R. Hendricson was born May 1st, 1833.

Sarah D. Hendricson was born August 5th, A. D., 1835.

Daniel Hendricson was born June 7th, A. D., 1837.

George Hendricson was born July the 25th, A. D., 1839.

Mary E. Hendricson was born Jan. the 6th, A. D., 1842.

Ann Eliza Hendricson was born July 6th, A. D., 1844.

Susan E. Hendricson was born Oct. 11th, A. D., 1846.

William D. Hendricson died May 29, 1847; aged 45 years, 6 months and 24 days.

John Hendricson died September 28, 1848; aged 17 years, seven months and 22 days.

Susan E. Hendricson died Oct. 24, 1853; aged 7 years and 13 days.

Sarah D. Hendricson died February 27, 1864; aged 28 years, six months and 22 days.

George Hendricson died December 17th, 1867; aged 28 years, 4 months and 19 days.

James Hendricson died April 29, 1877; aged 47 years, 11 months and 15 days.

Mary Hendricson, wife of William D. Hendricson, died October 31, 1883; aged 76 years and 9 months.

Extract from obituary notice pinned in the Bible:

"W. R. Hendricson, whose death was mentioned in last week's issue of the Vanceburg Sun, was born at Popular Flat, Ky., 76 years ago. Mr. Hendricson's first wife was a daughter of Mose Ruggles, by this wife he has four living children, Laban T., of Ripley, O.; Thomas, of Piqua, O.; Edward, of East Bank, W. Va., and one daughter in the west. Mr. W. R. Hendricson lived in Vanceburg, moved in 1870 to Portsmouth, O., for about 20 years. About 12 years ago he was living in Ripley, O. As per request he was laid to rest in Salem churchyard, at Poplar Flat, Ky."

Clarence E. Rummans and Mary D. Rash married Oct. 1, 1885.

William Delass Rummans (son of C. E. and Mary D.) and Mabel Laverna Wright married February, 1912.

Clarence Ellroy Rummans was born April 15, 1863, son of William H. and Mary E. Rummans.

Mary Davis Rash was born October 1st, 1863, daughter of William F. and Margaret Rash.

An infant son of C. E. and M. D. Rummins was born May 5, 1887; died May 8, 1887.

William Delass Rummans was born May 19th, 1889, son of Clarence E. and Mary D. Rummans.

Mabel Laverna Wright—No date.

William Henry Rummans died December 25, 1903, son of Alexander and Elizabeth Rummans.

Mary Elizabeth Rummans died July 4, 1907, daughter of William D. and Mary Hendricson.

Note:

Mary Laverna Rummans, daughter of Will and Mabel L. Rummans—Born March 18th, 1913.

William Deloss Rummans, Jr., son of Will and Mabel L. Rummans—Born March 12th, 1914.

Albert Ellroy Rummans, son of Will D. and Mabel L. Rummans—Born December 4th, 1920.

Extracts from newspaper pinner in Bible:

"Wm. H. Rummans, son of A. M. and Elizabeth B. Rummans, was born May 15, 1842, near Tolesboro, Ky."

"Mrs. Mary Rummans * * * most of her life was spent at Tolesboro, in Lewis County, Ky. * * * She leaves one sister, Mrs. Eliza May, of West Virginia, and one brother, Wm. Hendricson, of Vanceburg, Ky."

HINTON BIBLE

Bible of Thomas Jefferson Hinton. Now owned by Mrs. Jesse T. Hinton, Memphis, Tenn. Donated by Mrs.Jas.H.Hinton, Lexington, Ky.

Thomas Jefferson Hinton, born March 7, 1829.
Sarah Ann Hinton, born July 2, 1836.
Edwin Leander Hinton, born Aug. 9, 1855
Kate Ellis Hinton, born March 10, 1858.
James Fitch Hinton, born May 11, 1860.
Jesse Thomas Hinton, born March 24, 1865.
Rosa Nettie Hinton, born Oct. 28, 1867.
Laura Belle Hopper born May 7, 1854.
James William Shouse, born Aug., 1853.
Lida Burgess Hinton born May 23, 1869.
Frank Frayser Hinton, born May 7, 1892.
Mary Louise Hinton, born Oct. 5, 1897.
Thomas Jefferson Hinton and Sarah Ann Fitch, married May 23, 1854.
Edwin Leander Hinton and Laura Belle Hopper, married Jan. 21, 1875.
James William Shouse and Kate Ellis Hinton, married Sept. 9, 1875.
James William Shouse, died Aug. 13, 1886.
Kate Ellis Shouse, died Jan. 1, 1904.
Anna Otie Shouse, died Nov. 11, 1905.
Jesse Thomas Hinton, died May 15, 1922.
Mary Louise Hinton, died Mar. 10, 1825.

HIGGINS-MOORE BIBLE
Bible of Mary Elizabeth Coons of Fayette Co., Ky.
(Donated by Miss Anna Gertrude Carter.)

William Higgins and Lydia Smith were married Jan. 7, 1808.
Thomas L. Moore and Mary Ann Amanda Higgins were married Jan. 27, 1829.
Aaron D. Higgins and Elizabeth Shy were married July 11, 1841.
William Higgins was born May 29, 1786.
Lydia Smith was born May 22, 1790.
Aaron Durrette Higgins was born Oct. 17, 1808.
Mary Ann Amanda Higgins was born Jan. 5, 1811.
Francis Smith Higgins was born May 31, 1813.
Malinda Cathernie Higgins was born June 8, 1815.
William Franklin Higgins was born July 17, 1817.
Eliza Jane Higgins was born Dec. 26, 1819.
Drusilla Winn Higgins was born Dec. 25, 1822.
Charles Thomas Higgins was born Feb. 27, 1832.
Franklin Blackwell Moore was born Feb. 1, 1830.
William Francis Moore was born Nov. 7, 1837.
Eliza Jane Moore was born Apr. 29, 1839.
Thomas Winn Moore was born May 16, 1841.
John Moore was born Mch. 28, 1843.
Lydia Minerva Higgins was born Aug. 7, 1843.
Amelia Barthenia Winn Higgins was born Apr. 29, 1846.
Simeon Shy Higgins was born Feb. 10, 1850.
William F. Higgins died June 27 ,1824.
Mary Ann A Moore died Feb. 28, 1835.
William H Moore died Sept. 12, 1836.
Eliza Jane Higgins died Mch. 6, 1839.
Lydia Higgins died Mch. 13, 1841.
Francis S. Higgins died Oct. 25, 1841.
Malinda C. Moore died Apr. 29, 1843.
Drusilla W. Moore died Mch. 17, 1846.
William Higgins, Sr., died Oct. 26, 1847.
Sarah Ann Elizabeth Higgins died June 18, 1852.
Aaron D. Higgins died Mch. 20, 1853.
Charles Thomas Higgins died Jan. 21, 1856.

OLD BIBLE OF M. H. AND E. A. HISLE.

Now Owned by Mrs. Oscar Lyne, Lexington.

Hamilton Hisle was born June 20, 1800.
Margaret G. Hisle was born Apr. 27, 1794.
Hamilton Hisle and Margaret G. Foster were married Mch. 2, 1824.
Their children:
Evaline R. Hisle—Born Jan. 28, 1825.
Wm. A. Hisle—Born July 19, 1826.
George W. Hisle—Born May 10, 1828.
Wickliff Hisle—Born Oct. 5, 1830, and died Mch. 13, 1836.
Jonas G. Hisle—Born Feb. 11, 1833, and died Mch. 27, 1836.
Minor H. Hisle—Born Dec. 21, 1835.
Hamilton G. Hisle—Born Nov. 3, 1837.
M. H. Hisle and Elizabeth A. Strode were married Dec. 2, 1857.
Nelson Strode married (first) Elvina H. Rash, May 26, 1836.
James N. Hisle and Roxie A. Sphar were married May 24, 1882.
G. Hamilton Hisle and Lucie Sphar were married Mch. 24, 1897.
Anna May Hisle and Oscar L. Lyne were married Oct. 27, 1909.
Vernon Strode Hisle and Illa Quisenberry Stewart were married Apr. 27, 1910.
Otho Graves Hisle and Marguerite Angeline Mathews were married Feb. 4, 1920.
Minnie Ruth Hisle and Wm. Edwin Arnold were married Aug. 16, 1922.
Nelson Strode was born Oct. 18, 1813.
Elvina H. Rash, his wife, was born Feb. 5, 1819. They were married May 26, 1836. She died Nov. 12, 1844, aged 25 yrs., 9 months and 7 days.
Wm. D. Strode was born July 23, 1837.
John T. Strode was born Dec. 8, 1838.
Elizabeth A. Strode was born Sept. 28, 1840.
James R. Strode was born Nov. 14, 1842.
Edward R. N. Strode, son of Nelson and Susan B. Strode, was born Sept. 24, 1849.
Children of Minor H. and E. A. Hisle:
James N. Hisle—Born Oct. 17, 1859.
George H. Hisle—Born Mch. 4, 1866.
Girl baby born dead Oct. 25, 1878.
Roxie A. Hisle—Born Aug. 12 ,1859.
Vernon Strode Hisle, son of J. N. and Roxie Hisle, was born May 1, 1883.
Anna May Hisle, dau. of J. N. and Roxie Hisle, was born July 24, 1885.
Otho Graves Hisle, son of J. N. and Roxie Hisle, was born Feb. 4, 1888.
Elgin Sphar Hisle, son of G. H. and Lucile Hisle, was born Feb. 23, 1899.
Minnie Ruth Hisle, daughter of G. H. and Lucile Hisle, was born Sept. 12, 1900.
Anna Belle Strode Hisle, daughter of G. H. and Lucile Hisle, was born June 19, 1906.
Minor Hart Hisle, Jr., son of Vernon Strode and Illa Hisle, was born Dec. 26, 1911.
Hamilton Hisle died Oct. 8, 1842.
Elvina H. Strode died Nov. 12, 1844.
Evaline R. Ramey died Oct. 12, 1864.
Wickliff Hisle died Mch. 13, 1836.
Jonas G. Hisle died Mch. 27, 1836.
Leonard Foster died May 10, 1877.
Nelson Strode, Sr., died July 30, 1895.
George W. Hisle died Feb. 25 (no year).
Hamilton G. Hisle died June 13, 1924.
Miner H. Hisle died Jan. 30, 1913; aged 77 yrs., 1 month, 8 days.
Vernon Strode Hisle died Dec. 21, 1919; age 36 yrs., 7 months, 21 days.

Elizabeth S. Hisle, wife of M. H. Hisle, died Jan. 5 (no year given); age 87 years, 3 months, 8 days.

HOGAN BIBLE RECORD.
Bible Owned by Mrs. Martha Parrish, Daughter of John M. Hogan, of Fayette Co., Ky.
(Copied by Mrs. Mollie Hogan Gentry.)

(Note by Mrs. Gentry: John M. Hogan (born July 16, 1788) fought in the War of 1812, was wounded in Battle of the River Raisin. his brother, William Hogan, was captain of his company in Civil War and was killed in action.)

John M. Hogan was born July 16, 1788, in Goochland Co., Va.; married 1830; died July 20, 1865.

Margaret Ann Baker was born Feb. 4, 1811, formerly of Culpepper Co., Va.; died Jan. 23, 1885. Children:

Isham Talbot Hogan was born Mch. 7, 1832; died Apr. 25, 1896.

John Henry Hogan was born Sept. 12, 1834; married Mary Baker Feb. 7, 1877; died Mch. 7, 1909.

Lucy Ann Hogan was born Mch. 24, 1837; married James Stipp July 3, 1862; died Apr. 21, 1896.

Samuel Preston Hogan was born June 29, 1841; died Feb. 2, 1871; married Belle Montgomery of Frankfort, Ky., Aug .25, 1870. He was a Baptist Minister.

James Hamilton Hogan was born Mch. 28, 1844; died Aug. 24, 1856.

Margaret Jane Hogan was born Sept. 26, 1846; died Mch. 3, 1917; married Joseph Stipp Jan. 5, 1871.

Martha Hane Hogan was born July 1, 1850; married Joseph Parish Dec. 29, 1869.

Nannie Olivia Hogan was born July 18, 1860.

William Jefferson Hogan was born July 8, 1839; married Nancy Margaret Hundley, daughter of John Hundley and Mary Downing, on Dec. 1, 1870.

William J. Hogan died May 16, 1878. (He was a Baptist preacher.)

Margaret Hogan died Aug. 11, 1922; born Apr. 4, 1854.

Children of William J. Hogan and Margaret Hundley:

Mollie Belle Hogan—Born Oct. 22, 1871; married John Morgan Gentry Aug. 7, 1889.

Maggie May Hogan—Born Apr. 30, 1874; married Vertna Blackford Oct. 5, 1899.

William Preston Dillard Hogan—Born July 6, 1877; died May 25, 1878.

Children of John Morgan Gentry and Mollie Hogan Gentry:

Charles Moore Gentry married Mary Alice Bunton Aug. 16, 1916, Their children:

Charles Morgan Gentry—Born Jan. 22, 1919.

Mary Margaret Gentry—Born Nov. 24, 1920.

Henry Watterson Gentry—Born Feb. 3, 1893; married Anita Hinton. (Soldier of World War.)

BIBLE OF JOHN HUNTER.

(Donated and Copied by Miss Jennie Bissicks, Owner of Bible, Lexington, Ky.)

Margaret Bruce Hunter was born Aug. 12.

Mary Dewees Hunter and John Bruce Hunter, twins, were born Jan. 12, 1840.

Julia Hunter and twin sister were born May 29, 1844.

Kate Hunter was born Feb. 29, 1848.

John Morgan Hunter was born July 10, 1852.

James Hunter was born May 21, 1855.

Margaret Bruce Hunter died July 3, 1840.

Mary Dewees Hunter died Sept. 9, 1840.
John Bruce Hunter, twin of Mary Dewees Hunter, died Dec. 19, 1842.
Julia Hunter died June 5, 1911. Twin sister died at birth.
John Morgan Hunter died Sept. 10, 1892.

HUTCHCRAFT FAMILY BIBLE
Owned by Miss Helen Hutchcraft, Paris, Ky.

Richard Hutchcraft was born Oct. 5, 1789.
John Hutchcraft was born Sept. 22, 1791.
Reuben Hutchcraft was born Jan. 22, 1794.
Eliza Hutchcraft was born Oct. 5, 1796.
James Hutchcraft was born Feb. 16, 1799.
Nimrod Hutchcraft was born Oct. 2, 1801.
Elizabeth Hutchcraft was born Oct. 10, 1809 (or 1819).
Reuben Hutchcraft was married to Fannie Hedges Feb. 24, 1824.
John Hutchcraft was married to Margaret McIlvaine Dec. 9, 1824.
James Hutchcraft was married to Eliza Ann Williams Jan. 6, 1829.
Sons and Daughters of Reuben and Fannie Hutchcraft:

> John Hutchcraft, who was born Dec. 10, 1824.
> Thomas A. Hutchcraft, who was born July 10, 1827.
> Lucinda Hutchcraft, who was born June 27, 1829.
> Silas Hutchcraft, who was born Mch. 15, 1832.
> Mary Eliza Hutchcraft, who was born May 23, 1834.
> William Hutchcraft, who was born May 10, 1836.
> Henry Clay Hutchcraft, who was born Sept. 1, 1838.
> Reuben Brent Hutchcraft, who was born Jan. 1, 1841.
> Ella A. Hutchcraft, who was born Nov. 17, 1844.
> Nannie Hutchcraft, who was born Jan. 12, 1850.

Lucinda Hutchcraft was married to Washington Fithian, M. D., Sept. 18, 1850.
John Hutchcraft was married to Mollie H. Jones Sept. 4, 1856.
Thomas A. Hutchcraft was married to Liza Hildredth Oct. 28, 1852.
Mollie E. Hutchcraft was married to John D. Ray, M. D., June 2, 1853.
H. Clay Hutchcraft was married to Mary E. Cunningham Jan. 9, 1862.
Notes: (1) These are known to be the children of Thomas Hutchcraft (born 1759; died 1825), who served for 7 years in the Revolutionary War, and Nellie Harrison Apperson, daughter of Francis Apperson. Thomas Hutchcraft and Nellie Harrison Apperson were married in Culpepper County, Virginia, Nov. 28, 1788. Under the name of Reuben Hutchcraft is written the name of his wife, Fannie Hedges, and her birth date, Oct. 28, 1805.

(2) The marriages of the children included in the list of births but not given in the list of marriages are known to be as follows: Eliza Hutchcraft married William P. Hume; Nimrod Htuchcraft married Malinda Cunningham; Elizabeth Hutchcraft married Edward L. McGee; Richard Hutchcraft died unmarried.

(3) The marriages of the children included in the list of births but not given in the list of marriages are known to be as follows: William Hutchcraft marrierd Kate Wells; Reuben Brent Hutchcraft married Dorcas Saunders Ashbrook in Harrison County, Kentucky, May 16, 1882; Ella A. Hutchcraft married R. M. Harris Nov. 7, 1866; Nannie Hutchcraft married Daniel Stuart Apr. 16, 1869. Silas Hutchcraft died unmarried. Thomas A. Hutchcraft married for his 2nd wife Mrs. Mary Hayes, and for his 3rd wife Mary Collins.

JENNINGS BIBLE.
Now Owned by Mrs. H. C. Botts, Lexington, Ky.

Charles M. Jennings and Rachel A .Runyon were married Apr. 16, 1863.
Robert S. Gibbons, Sr., and Elizabeth Ann Mackey were married Nov. 22, 1827.
Joseph Hendrick and Sudie Lee Jennings were married Jan. 2, 1884.

Charles M. Jennings and Elizabeth A. Gibbons were married Dec. 4, 1853.

H. C. Botts and Mollie E. Jennings were married Jan. 25, 1888.

Mollie E. Jennings, daughter of Rachel and Marshall Jennings, was born Feb. 25, 1868.

Sue Jennings, daughter of Rachel and Marshall Jennings, was born Feb. 5, 1864.

Robert Stamp Gibbons, second son of Nehemiah Gibbons and Chloe, his wife, was born Oct. 12, 1791.

Elizabeth Ann Mackey, fourth daughter of James Mackey and Mary, his wife, was born Nov. 19, 1802.

James Nehemiah Gibbons, first son of Robert Stamp Gibbons and Elizabeth Ann Gibbons, was born Nov. 17, 1828.

Mary Agnes Gibbons, first daughter of Robert Stamp Gibbons and Elizabeth Ann Gibbons, was born Aug. 10, 1830.

Robert Stamp Gibbons, second son of Robert Stamp Gibbons and Elizabeth Ann Gibbons, was born Nov. 27, 1832.

Charles M. Jennings, second son of William Jennings and Nancy Marshall Jennings, was born Apr. 6, 1820.

Robert Stamp Gibbons departed this life on the 4th day of July, 1833.

Mary Agnes Gibbons, daughter of Robert Stamp and Elizabeth Ann Gibbons, departed this life Aug. 24, 1830; aged 14 days.

James Nehemiah Gibbons, son of Robert Stamp and Elizabeth Ann Gibbons, departed this life Apr. 21, 1847; aged 18 yrs., 5 months and 4 days.

Robert S. Gibbons, Jr., second son of Robert S .and Elizabeth Ann Gibbons, departed this life Oct. 29, 1847; aged 14 yrs., 11 months and 2 days.

Elizabeth Ann Jennings departed this life Aug. 12, 1860.

C. M. Jennings died Dec. 8, 1872; born Apr. 6, 1820; aged 52 yrs., 8 months and 2 days.

BIBLE OF JOHN S. JOHNSON, PRINTED 1834.
Now Owned by Mrs. Maud South McCarty, Lexington, Ky.

J. S. Johnson was born 1780.

Elizabeth, my wife, was born Dec. 31, 1794.

S. R. Johnson was born Aug. 12, 1815; died Aug. 17, 1837.

T. S. Johnson was born May 2, 1817.

John S. Johnson and Elizabeth, his wife, were married Nov. 16, 1812.

Permelia Johnson was married to Levi Brashear Oct. 28, 1838.

Thomas S. Johnson was married to Maria L. Triplett Feb. 12, 1837.

James Johnson and Sarah Catherine Herndon were mar. Apr. 29, 1845.

Marion Johnson was married to Grandville G. Bond, 1845.

Sallie A. Johnson and William Jones were married Sept. 12, 1848.

Sinclair M. Johnson was married to Nancy A. Threldkeld, 1858.

John S. Johnson was born 1780; died June 14, 1846.

Elizabeth Johnson was born Dec. 31, 1794; died Apr. 12, 1881.

Simeon R. Johnson was born Aug. 12, 1815; died Aug. 17, 1837.

Thomas S. Johnson was born May 2, 1817; died Apr. 29, 1845.

Permelia Johnson was born Oct. 31, 1819.

James Johnson was born Dec .11, 1821.

Marion Johnson was born Mch. 5, 1824.

Louisa Johnson was born June 24, 1825; died Aug., 1834.

Sally Ann Johnson was born Sept. 15, 1827.

William H. V. Johnson was born July 25, 1829; died June 11, 1844.

Sophia H. Johnson was born Dec. 9, 1831; died June 6, 1868.

Sinclair M. Johnson was born June 8, 1836.

Albertus Johnson, May, May 20, 1857.

Nancy M. Johnson, May 19, 1858.

Barry South was born Apr. 24, 1850.

(Note by Mrs. Maude South McCarty: Ann Mary Jones, daughter

of William Jones and Sallie A. Johnson, married W. T. B. South, and her daughter is Maude South McCarty.)

BIBLE OF WILLIAM JONES.

William Jones was born A. D. 1821, Jan. 8.
Sallie Ann (Johnson) Jones was born Sept. 15, 1827.   Children:
Annie Jones was born 24th of Apr., 1850.
James William Jones was born Nov. 10, 1853.
Sarah Elizabeth Jones was born Apr. 4, 1859.

COPIED FROM OLD KENNEY BIBLE.

(By Mrs. Corday Leer Buckley)

Born in the year of Our Lord 1752, Nov. 29, James Kenney, Sr.
Born May 14, 1747, Mary Kenney, wife of James Kenney.
David Kenney was born in the year of Our Lord, Jan. 26, 1772.
Elizabeth Kenney was born Oct. 10, 1773.
John Kenney was born July 8, 1775.
Polly Kenney was born July 4, 1779.
James Kenney, Jr., was born July 24, 1782.
Moses Kenney was born Apr. 4, 1784.
Sallie Kenney was born July 24, 1786.
Nancy Kenney was born Aug. 4, 1788.
Peggy Kenney, 2nd wife of James Kenney, was born the 11th day of
    Jan., 1770.
Marie Kenney was born Mch. 13, 1800.
Abby Kenney was born Oct. 3, 1801.
Helena Kenney was born Jan. 7, 1804.
Joseph B. Kenney was born Jan. 19, 1806.
Napoleon Kenney was born Feb. 12, 1808.
Charlotte Corday Kenney was born Dec. 12, 1809.
Victor Mareau Kenney was born Dec. 14, 1812.
Peggy Kenney was born Dec. 14, 1813.
Mary Ann Kenney was born May 20, 1815.
Marie Kenney married May Joy Robnett July 11, 1816.
Abigail Kenney married James H. Houston Jan. 8, 1824.
Helena Kenney married David Johnson Sept. 15, 1822.
Peggy Kenney married John Johnson Mch. 5, 1836.
Charlotte Corday Kenney married David Leer June 10, 1830.
Joseph B. Kinney mar. Margaret Lander of Flemingsburg, Mch. 8, 1827.
Mary Ann Kenney and Diamal Barnett were married Apr. 18, 1830.
Margaret Kenney departed this life May 16, 1836.
Napoleon Kenney departed this life Oct. 16, 1836.
James H. Houston departed this life May 1, 1849.
Helena Johnson departed this life Aug. 3, 1849.
Marie Robnett departed this life Apr. 26, 1850.
Abigail Houston departed this life July 15, 1856.
Jas. Kenney, Jr., died Jan. 30, 1813, at Fort Defiance.
Mary Kenney, wife of James Kenney, Sr., departed this life Sept. 22,
    1796.
Peggy Kenney, 2nd wife of James Kenney, died May 30, 1829.
James Kenney, Sr., died Mch. 13, 1814.
Joseph B. Kenney died Jan. 1, 1887.
David Leer was born Jan. 16, 1803; died May 14, 1885.
Peggy Johnson died Feb. 14, 1900.
Charlotte Corday Leer died Jan. 14, 1897; aged 87 yrs.
James Monroe Leer was born May 11, 1841; died Dec. 22, 1894.
Charles M. Alberti died Nov. 18, 1897, at Lexington.
Charles Carroll Leer was born Feb. 11, 1835; died June 10, 1922; age 87.

LAMBERT BIBLE RECORD (Carlisle, Nicholas County, Ky.)
Bible Owned by Carlton L. Lambert, 1928.

John L. Lambert and (1st wife) Manerva McLean were married Nov. 3, 1867.

John L. Lambert and (2nd wife) Amanda Ralls were married Oct. 7, 1890.

John L. Lambert was born May 27, 1846.

Manerva McLean, 1st wife of J. L. Lambert, was born June 7, 1845; died Nov. 7, 1887.

Carlton Mostiller Lambert, son of John L. Lambert and Manerva McLean Lambert, was born Mch. 3, 1869.

John Francis Lambert, son of John L. and Manerva McLean Lambert, was born June 9, 1870.

Hallie Clark, daughter of John L. and Manerva McLean Lambert, was born Mch. 9, 1872.

George Price Lambert, son of John L. and Manerva McLean Lambert, was born Oct. 9, 1873.

Nettie Foster Lambert, daughter of John L. and Manerva McLean Lambert, was born June 3, 1876.

John Francis Lambert died Dec. 28, 1898.

BIBLE OF JOEL REID LYLE OF FAYETTE CO., KY.
Now Owned by Charles Nourse Lyle of Lexington, Ky.
(Copied by Mrs. H. K. McAdams.)

Joel Reid Lyle and Agnes M. Kenney were married Sept. 1, 1807.

William C. Lyle and Margaret Ann Caldwell were married on Tues., the 25th of Oct., 1831, by Rev. E. Smith.

William C. Lyle and Sarah Ellen Bell were married 11th of Oct., 1842, by the Rev. John D. Mathews.

John A. Lyle and Laura Chambers were married 22nd of Nov., 1848, by Rev. Jas. S. Kemper.

Joel K. Lyle and Maria Catherine Nourse were married Wed., Dec. 22, 1852, by Rev. R. J. Breckinridge, D. D.

John A. Lyle and Bettie Garrard were married June 7, 1855.

Charles Nourse Lyle and Bettie Breckinridge Richardson were married Wed., June 27, 1917, by Rev. Edwin Muller, D. D., at First Presbyterian Church, Lexington, Ky.

(The above Charles Nourse Lyle was named for his mother's father, Charles Nourse.)

John Lyle, ruling elder in Timberridge Church, Rockbridge Co., Va. (who was the son of John Lyle, Esq., from Ireland, and also a ruling elder in said church), was born in Timberridge, then Augustus Co., July 10, 1746.

Flora (Reid) Lyle, consort of said John Lyle, was born Feb., 1743.

Andrew Lyle, their eld!e!st son, was born Mch., 1758.

Rev. John Lyle was born Oct. 20, 1769.

Martha Lyle (McCutchen) was born Nov., 1770.

Joel Reid Lyle was born Dec. 19, 1774.

William Reid Lyle was born Sept. 19, 1779.

Jane (Finley) Lyle was born May 28, 1782.

(The Joel Reid Lyle in this record was the grandfather of Lizzlie A., Helen and Charles Nourse Lyle. Joel R. Lyle came to Ky. in 1801, being in the 27th year of his age.)

Children of Mathew and Elizabeth Kenney:

Rebecca Kenney (Givens)—Born Sept. 17, 1771.

James Kenney—Born Jan. 5, 1774.

Mathew Kenney—Born Jan. 22, 1776.

Agnes Kenney—Born Mch. 22, 1778.

Elizabeth Kenney (Montgomery)—Born Nov. 12, 1780.

Agnes McCreary (Lyle)—Born Jan. 22, 1783.

Sarah Kenney—Born Jan. 22, 1785.

Robert P. Kenney—Born Jan. 22, 1787.
Alexander Robertson Kenney—Born Jan. 1, 1790; died Dec. 12, 1844, at Millersburg, Ky.
Mary Huston Kenney—Born Sept. 8, 1792.
William McCreary Kenney—Born Aug. 8, 1794.
(Agnes McCreary Kenney Lyle, in this record, is the grandmother of Lizzie A., Helen and Charles Nourse Lyle.)
William Cowler Lyle was born Aug. 16, 1808.
Sarah Lapsley Lyle was born Dec. 28, 1811.
Margaret Reid Lyle was born Feb. 15, 1815.
John Andrew Alexander Lyle was born Mch. 5, 1817.
Joel Kenney Lyle was born July 17, 1824.
Maria Catherine (Nourse), now wife of Joel K. Lyle, was born Aug. 9, 1883.
Children of J. K. and Maria C. Lyle:
    Lizzie Agnes Lyle—Born Oct. 10, 1853, Nicholasville, Ky.
    Flora Reid Lyle—Born June 10, 1857, Lexington, Ky.
    Helen Lyle—Born Nov. 29, 1858, Laird Parsonage, Newton Pike.
    Emma Lyle—Born May 13, 1862, Laird Parsonage, Newton Pike.
    Charles Nourse Lyle—Born Dec. 22, 1865, Lexington, Ky.
John Lyle, father of Joel K. Lyle, died at his res. in Va., Sept., 1815, aged 69 yrs., 2 months and 15 days.
Flora Lyle, his consort, died Jan., 1815, aged 71 yrs. and ab. 11 months.
Andrew Lyle died in Liberty, Va., in 1790 (or Jan., 1791).
Sally Lyle died in early infancy.
Rev. John Lyle died at his res. in Paris, Ky., July 22, 1825.
Joel R. Lyle died at his res, near Paris, Ky., Jan. 18, 1849.
Agnes M. Lyle, his consort, died at res. of her son, William Lyle, Sept. 19, 1849.
Martha Lyle (McCutchen) died in Va., July 16, 1851 near Middlebrook.
William R. Lyle died at Topton, Iowa, 1852.
Sarah Lapsley Lyle, eldest dau. of Joel R and Agnes M. Lyle, died Aug. 22, 1813.
Margaret Reid Lyle, 2nd dau. of Joel R. and Agnes M. Lyle, died Aug. 9, 1815.
Rev. Joel Kenney Lyle died in Lexington, Ky., Apr. 19, 1872.
Maria Catherine Nourse Lyle, widow of Joel Kenney Lyle, died in Lexington, Ky., Aug. 2, 1904.
Lizzie Agnes Lyle, dau. of J. K. and M. C. N. Lyle, died in Lexington, Ky., Jan. 23, 1916.

LARY FAMILY BIBLE.
(Printed and Sold by Collins & Co., of N. Y. in 1814.)
(Copied by Robert Brashear Lary, Winchester, Ky., and Now Owned by Her Husband, J. C. Lary.)
Dennis Lary was born the year of Our Lord, Mch. 18, 1773; died 1824.
Sarah Lary, his wife, was born in the year of Our Lord, Sept. 13, 1777; died in 1839. Their children:
    Rachel Lary—Born Dec., 1795.
    Thomas Lary—Born 1798.
    Elizabeth Larq—Born Feb. 1799; died 1811.
    Dorothy Lary—Born Oct., 1803; died 1826.
    Samuel Lary—Born Jan., 1805; died 1837.
    Buell Lary—Born Oct., 1806.
    Henry Lary—Born Jan., 1808.
    John Curtright Lary—Born July, 1810; died 1815.
    Malinda Lary—Born Oct., 1812; died 1815.
    Washington D. C. Lary—Born July, 1815; died 1831.
    Cornelius Lary—Born Aug. 19, 1816.
    Eliza Lary—Born Oct. 16, 1817.
    Cyrus Lary—Born Sept. 12, 1818; died 1824.

Daniel Lary was married to Sarah P. Thomas June 11, A. D. 1835. She died Dec. 12, 1900.

John C. Lary married Mary Allen Pendleton Oct. 3, 1850.

John Curtis Lary, son of John C. Lary and Mary Allen Pendleton Lary, married Roberta Brashear Lary. They married Sept. 5, 1885. Their sons:

Ben Curtis Lary, Cyrus Allen Lary and Virgil Pendleton Lary. (All three sons were in the World War.)

COPIED FROM THE OLD BIBLE OF DAVID LEER.

(By Mrs. Corday Leer Buckley)

David Leer was born June 11, 1769; married Elizabeth Leer, born Dec. 11, 1770.

Patsy Leer was born Sept. 8, 1795.

Henry Leer was born Mch. 2, 1797.

William Leer was born July 22, 1799.

Daniel Leer was born Mch. 17, 1801.

David Leer was born Jan. 15, 1803.

John Parker Leer was born Jan. 16, 1805.

Samuel Sellers Leer was born Aug. 19, 1806.

David Leer and Elizabeth Leer were married Dec. 2, 1794.

Thos Wright and Patsy Leer were married Sept. 22, 1821.

William Leer and Patsy Champ were married Aug. 3, 1821.

William Leer and Sarah Howard were married Apr. 21, 1822.

A son was born and died the same day, Sept. 8, 1795.

Patsy Wright, daughter of David Leer, died Jan. 27, 1823.

Samuel S. Leer, son of David Leer, died Sept. 25, 1827.

BIBLE OF SAMUEL HIGGINS LEWIS.

Now Owned by Mrs. J. W. Morford, Lexington, Ky.

(Copied by Mrs. H. K. McAdams.)

Abraham Cassell and Sarah Rice were married Dec. 24, 1801.

Samuel H. Lewis and Margaret Cassell were married Nov. 10, 1831.

James A. Farra and Margaret were married Mch. 15, 1855.

William R. Lewis and Margaret Boone were married Sept. 27, 1855.

Joseph Clark and Catherine Lewis were married Feb. 20, 1862.

Samuel Lewis and Maggie Reese were married Feb. 21, 1865.

George H. Kinnear and Annie L. Lewis were married Apr. 17, 1866.

Theodore Lewis and Katie Reese were married Jan. 18, 1870.

Ben F. Roberts and Mary S. Lewis were married Apr. 20, 1871.

William Jackson Young and Carrie Clark Kinnear were married Nov. 12, 1891.

Annie Lewis Kinnear and John Henry Wilson were mar. Nov. 6, 1898.

Helen Kinnear and Joseph Wallingford Morford were mar. Oct. 15, 1902.

Theodore L. Kinnear and Edna M. Woolery married Mch., 1914.

William Kenneth Kinnear and Louise Witt were married in Dallas, Texas, 1911.

Abraham Cassell was born Sept. 10, 1773.

Sarah Rice Cassell was born July 4, 1784. Children:

Mary Cassell was born June 6, 1803.

Joseph Cassell was born Apr. 16, 1805.

Rachel Cassell was born Aug. 11, 1807.

Leonard Cassell was born Mch. 17, 1810.

David Cassell was born Aug. 4, 1812.

Jacob Cassell was born Sept. 29, 1814.

Margaret Cassell was born Sept. 11, 1815.

Nathaniel Cassell was born Nov. 29, 1818.

Sarah Cassell was born Jan. 14, 1820.

Abraham Cassell was born Sept. 3, 1822.

Hulda Cassell was born July 31, 1825.

Elizabeth Cassell was born Oct. 26, 1828.

Samuel Lewis and wife, Miss Whitlet, children:
Jesse Lewis—Born July 20, 1770.
His 2nd wife, Jane Logan, was born Dec. 29, 1783. Children:
Margaret Lewis—Born May 9, 1807.
Samuel H. Lewis—Born Dec. 13, 1808.
Wm. L. Lewis—Born Aug. 18, 1810.
George L. Lewis—Born Feb. 3, 1812.
Children of Samuel H. Lewis and Sarah Jane Lewis, who was born
Oct. 13, 1813:
Elizabeth Lewis—Born Dec. 6, 1833.
Wm. R. Lewis—Born Dec. 13, 1834.
Margaret Lewis—Born Jan. 28, 1837.
Samuel Lewis—Born Feb. 3, 1839.
Margaret Catherine Lewis—Born Dec. 9, 1842.
Annie L. Lewis—Born July 27, 1845.
Theodore Lewis—Born Mch. 16, 1848.
Mary S. Lewis—Born May 1, 1851.
James Kinnear was born Dec. 13, 1792, Dundee, Scotland. Came to
America in 1824, and settled in Paris, Ky. His wife, Elizabeth
Samson, was born Jan. 1, 1795, Dundee, Scotland. Parents of
George H. Kinnear. James had a brother, John, and a sister,
Susan, who married Bands.
George H. Kinnear was born Feb. 9, 1835. His wife, Annie Lewis, was
born July 27, 1845.
Sarah Jane Lewis died Dec. 24, 1835.
Elizabeth Lewis died Feb. 29, 1840.
William R. Lewis died Jan. 4, 1864.
Margaret Lewis died Feb. 4, 1866.   (Wife of Sam. H. Lewis.)
Samuel L. Lewis died Sept. 16, 1868.
Samuel H. Lewis died May 10, 1870.
Kate L. Clark died June 26, 1882.
Margaret L. Farra died June 29, 1885.
Annie L. Kinnear died June 12, 1889.
Mary L. (Roberts) Evans died Jan. 15, 1912.
George Higgins Kinnear died Jan. 2, 1887.
Annie Lewis Kinnear died June 12, 1889.
George H. Kinnear died Dec. 11, 1899.
Theodore L. Kinnear died Aug. 28, 1916.
William Kenneth Kinnear died Apr. 11, 1924.
James Kinnear (born 1792) died Apr. 14, 1852.
Elizabeth Samson Kinnear died Mch. 28, 1875.
Samuel H. Lewis was born Dec. 13, 1809; died May 10, 1870; married
Margaret Cassell, who was born Sept. 11, 1815; died Feb. 4, 1866.
Mary L. Lewis married 1st Ben F. Roberts, and 2nd Rev. C. F .Evans.
Jesse Lewis was born July 20, 1770; died Jan. 11, 1818. His 2nd wife,
Jane Lewis, was born Dec. 29, 1783; died Jan. 15, 1831.

LOGAN BIBLE
Logan record, given by Mrs. John D. Logan, 510 N. Broadway,
Lexington, Ky. (Copied by Mrs. H. K. McAdams.)
Ethelbert Logan and Mary Debell were married Nov. 6th, 1834. Their
children:
Cornelia Logan was born June 1st, 1836.
John Debell Logan was born May 7th, 1839.
James Oruon Logan was born April 10, 1841.
Alice F. Logan was born Sept. 20th, 1845.
Jesse Ethelbert Logan was born Nov. 20th, 1859.
Ethelbert Logan was born Feb. 20th, 1807.
Mary Debell Logan was born Nov. 9th, 1813.
John Debell Logan and Lyde W. Hord were married Dec. 23rd, 1885,
by J. C. Frank, minister Christian church. Their children:

Ethelbert Hord Logan was born Sept. 26th, 1886.
Jesse Ethelbert Logan was born Aug. 22nd, 1888.
Will Irvin Logan was born July 4th, 1890.
John D. Logan was born Aug. 29th, 1894.
Ethelbert Logan departed this life July 8th, 1877.
Mary Debell Logan departed this life March 6th, 1843.
Ruth Smith Logan was born March 10th, 1772.
Mary O'Bannon, mother of Ruth Smith Logan was born Feb. 8th, 1754.
Ruth Smith Logan departed this life June 19th, 1821.
Mary O'Bannon died 2nd day of Oct., 1839.
Four brothers: Logan
Abner Logan—Born Jan. 18, 1802.
Joseph Logan—Born Feb. 28, 1806.
Ethelbert Logan—Born Feb. 20, 1807.
Elijah Logan—Born Jan. 22, 1809.

JOSEPH McADAMS BIBLE
(All children born in Kentucky, near Franklin)
(Donated by F. G. McAdams, Abelene, Kansas)

Joseph McAdams was born in the year of our Lord, 1755. (Note—a Rev. soldier, Va.)
Sarah Bradford McAdams, wife of Joseph McAdams, was born on August the 28tth, in the year of our Lord, 1768.
Samuel McAdams, son of Joseph and Sarah, was born on October 8th, in the year of our Lord, 1782.
John McAdams, son of Joseph and Sarah, was born April the 15th, in the year of our Lord, 1791.
Hannah McAdams, daughter of Joseph and Sarah, was born March the 25th, in the year of our Lord, 1793.
Joseph McAdams, son of Joseph and Sarah, was born November the 7th, in the year of our Lord, 1796.
Mimah McAdams was born March the 1st, in the year of our Lord, 1798.
Thomas McAdams, son of Joseph and Sarah, was born Sept. 5th, in the year of our Lord, 1799.
Sarah Bradford MsAdams, daughter of Joseph and Sarah, was born June 21st, in the year of our Lord, 1800.
Jesse McAdams (of Joseph and Sarah)—Born April the 5th, in the year of our Lord, 1802.
William McAdams, son of Joseph and Sarah, was born Nov. the 10th, in the year of our Lord, 1804.
James McAdams, son of Joseph and Sarah, was born Nov. 14th, in the year of our Lord, 1806.
Robert McAdams, son of Jos. and Sarah, was born July the 7th, in year of our Lord, 1809.
Sloss McAdams, son of Jos. and Sarah, was born April the 5th, in the year of our Lord, 181—.
Margaret Young McAdams, wife of James (of Jos. and S.), was born March 29th, 1818.
Mary McAdams, daughter of James, was born January 5th, 1841.
Samuel McAdams, son of James, was born April 6th, A. D., 1843. (Near Greenville, Ill.)
Henry H. McAdams, son of James, was born Feb. 28th, A. D., 1845. (Near Greenville, Ill.)
Andema McAdams, daughter of James, was born Jan. 12th, A. D., 1849.
Martha Ribin White (daughter of Rev. Thomas White) McAdams, wife of Henry McAdams, was born Feby. 17th, A. D., 1849, in Bond County, Ill.
Fanny Agnes McAdams, daughter of Henry, was born Feby. 13th, 1865, in Newton, Kansas.
James C. McAdams, son of Henry, was born Dec. 10th, A. D., 1867, in Bond County, Ill.
Alice Mary McAdams, daughter of Henry, was born May 8th, A. D.,

1871, in Bond Co., Ill.

Frank G. McAdams, son of Henry McAdams, was born Dec. 25th, A. D., 1876, in Halsted, Kansas.

Carrie Margaret McAdams, daughter of Henry, was born Jan. 17th, ——, A. D., in Newton, Kansas.

Eleanor McAdams, daughter of James C. McAdams, was born Dec. 12th, 1897, near Lawton, Okla.

Thelma McAdams, daughter of James C. McAdams, was born Oct. 25th, 1899, near Lawton, Okla.

Helen McAdams, daughter of James C. McAdams, was born Jan. 17th, 1905.

Frank Mowery, son of Alice McAdams Mowery, was born June 12th, 1898, at Newton, Kansas.

William Chambers, son of Alice McAdams Mowery Chambers, was born April 17th, 1907, at Newkensington, Pa.

Alice Katherine McAdams, daughter of Frank G. and Ella R. McAdams, was born Sept. 8th, 1905.

Priscilla Mae Chambers, daughter of Alice Chambers, was born March 15th, 1911, at New Kensington, Pa.

Gladys C. McAdams, daughter of Frank G. and Ella R. McAdams, was born Sept. 24th, 1908.

Charlotte Martha Wolz, daughter of Fanny Agnes McAdams Wolz, and George Wolz, Jr., was born Feb. 4th, 1908.

Joseph McAdams was married to Sarah Bradford, November, in the year of our Lord, 1789.

James McAdams was married to Margaret Young, at Greenville, Ill., on June 26th, 1838.

P. G. Vawter married Margaret Young McAdams (widow of James McAdams), April 12th, 1849.

Henry H. McAdams and Martha Robin White (daughter of Rev. Thomas White), were married Feb. 21st, 1867, at Greenville, Ill., by Rev. G. W. Wagoner.

James C. McAdams (son of H. H. and M. R.) and Lina Longacre were married at Newton, Kansas; later divorces, no issue.

James C. McAdams (of H. H. and M. R.), and Lillie Carmichael were married at Blackwell, Okla., Dec. 24th, 1896.

Alice McAdams (of H. H. and M. R.), and Mark Mowery were married Apr. 26th, 1896. Divorced. Only one child, Frank Mowery, he died aged 7 years.

Alice McAdams Mowery married W. B. Chambers (of New Kensington, Pa), April, 1905.

Frank G. McAdams (of H. H. and M. R.), and Ella Beckmeyer (nee Krebs) were married Sept. 24th, 1903, in Kay County, Okla.

Fanny Agnes McAdams (of H. H. and M. R.), and George Wolz, Jr. were married 1907, at Newton, Kansas.

Joseph McAdams departed this life Sept. 22, 1840.

Sarah McAdams (wife of Joseph) departed this life Aug. 5th, 1838.

Samuel McAdams departed this life Feb. 2nd, 1849.

John McAdams departed this life April 17th, A. D., 1849.

Hannah McAdams departed this life April 9th, 1845.

Joseph McAdams died Apr. 9, 1845.

Mimah McAdams departed this life Nov. 4th, 1852.

Thos. McAdams departed this life Sept. 10th, A. D., 1869.

Sarah McAdams departed this life March 12th, 1829; age 28 years, 9 months and 21 days.

Jesse McAdams departed this life Sept. 22nd, 1847; age 45 yrs, 7 months.

William McAdams departed this life March 20th, 1852. Age 47 years, 4 months and 10 days.

James McAdams departed this life June 5th, 1848; age 42 yrs, lacked 4 months.

Robert McAdams departed this life. No date given.

Sloss McAdams departed this life May 17th, 1846.

Mary, daughter of James McAdams, departed this life Nov. 26th, 1898, at Los Angeles, Calif. Buried in Rosedale Cemetery.

Samuel, son of James McAdams, killed at the Battle of Stone River, Dec. 31, 1862.

Henry H., son of James, died Feby. 6th, 1920, at Newton, Kansas.

Andema, daughter of James McAdams, died Dec. 10th, 1885. Age 36 years, 10 months and 28 days. (Single.)

Margaret Young, Wife of James McAdams—Born Mch, 1815; died May 4th, 1863.

James C. McAdams, son of Henry H. and M. R., died Sept. 24th, 1906. Buried at Blackwell, Okla.

Thelma McAdams, daughter of James C., died at Newton, Kansas, May 4th, 1922. Without issue.

Frank Mowery, son of Alice McAdams, died Aug. 20th, 1905, at New Kensington, Pa. (Drowned in the Allegheny river.)

Fanny Agnes McAdams, daughter of H. H. and M. R. Adams, died at Newton, Kansas, Jan. 7th, 1918.

Alice Katherine McAdams, daughter of Frank G. and Ella R. McAdams, departed this life Mch. 5th, 1920, at Abilene, Kansas, and was buried at Newton, Kansas.

McDOWELL BIBLE

Taken from Mrs. Sam McDowell's Bible, Jessamine Co., Ky.

Samuel W. McDowell and Georgia Allin were married July 5, 1881.

Garland Allin McDowell was born May 27, 1882.

Samuel M. McDowell was born Aug. 20, 1883.

Farra McDowell, son of Sam, Jr., and Etta Groff, was born Jan. 7, 1907.

Janette Sherer McDowell, son of Allin McDowell and May Taylor, was born Sept. 20, 1907.

Lucien H. McDowell, son of Allin McDowell and May Taylor, was born Jan. 18, 1909.

Bert McDowell, son of Allin McDowell and Mary Taylor, was born Feb. 1st, 1913.

Henrietta Simpson McDowell, daughter of Sam McDowell and Etta Groff, was born June 1st, 1909.

Nancy Groff McDowell, daughter of Sam McDowell and Etta Groff, was born Jan., 1918.

BIBLE RECORD TAZEWELL FRANCIS MARR
(Donated by Mrs. John Wesley Marr)

T. F. Marr was born the 17th day of Oct., 1812.

Eliza B. Rogers was born the 27th day of February, 1804.

T. F. Marr and E. B. Rogers were married the 17th day of Oct., 1833.

T. F. and E. B. Marr's children:

Mary Jane Marr was born the 22nd day of August, 1834.

John Wesley was born the 24th day of July, 1836.

Thomas Jefferson Marr was born the 19th day of February, 1839.

Henry Bascomb Marr was born the 6th day of January, 1842.

William Croutch Marr was born the 5th of June, 1846.

Eliza B. Marr was born the 3rd of February, 1850.

Mary Jane Marr departed this life the 22nd day of July, 1835; aged 11 months.

Mrs. E. B. Marr departed this life June 10th, 1863; aged fifty-eight years, three months and thirteen days.

Mrs. A. E. Marr was born 18th day of December, 1818, and departed this life the 23rd day of April, 1885, being 66 yrs., 4 months and thirteen days old.

T. F. Marr died April 4th, 1887; aged 74 yrs., 6 months and 13 days.

MEGLONE-WALDEN BIBLE RECORD
Donated by Miss Mattie Hutchinson
Montgomery Meglone—Born June 31st, 1808.

Maria Strother Sharp—Born May 15, 1820.

Montgomery Meglone and Maria Sharp were married March 29, 1837, by the Reverend Edward Stevenson.

William Whitney Meglone—Born Dec. 25, 1837.

Mary Morton Meglone—Born Oct. 5, 1839.

Montgomery Meglone died Aug. 17, 1840.

Atterson L. Walden and Maria Sharp Meglone were married in Lexington, Ky., on the 22nd day of September, 1859, by the Reverend T. L. McAdams.

Atterson L. Walden died Aug. 16, 1892.

Maria Sharp Walden died May 8, 1907.

BIBLE OF MAPLES B. MOORE
Bible of Maples B. Moore, Henry Co., Ky., now owned by Mrs. John Moore, 152 N. Birchwood, Louisville, Ky. Copied by Mrs. Gertrude Kirtley.

Maples B. Moore—Born Sept. 22, 1798.

Mariam R. Brite—Born Jan. 7, 1797.

Maples B. Moore and Mariam Brite were married Sept. 1, 1818.

Their children:
> William Henry Moore was born Oct. 30, 1819.
>
> Edmond Bartlert Moore was born Jan. 8, 1821.
>
> Mary Jane Moore was born Mch. 26, 1823.
>
> Cassander Ford Moore was born March 5, 1826.

James Stephens Dawson was born Dec. 1, 1815; married Mary Jane Moore.

Polly Sandford, deceased, Feb. 28, 1822, being thirty-three years of her age.

Daniel Sandford, deceased.

William Henry Moore, son of Maples B. Moore—Born Oct. 30, 1819; and died the 10th day of Dec., 1820.

Sarah McCann Dawson died Jan. 10, 1843.

Mariam Brite Dawson died Mch. 27, 1848.

Lucy Ellen Dawson died Mch. 29, 1848.

Benjamin Maples Dawson died Apr. 4th, 1848.

Henry Moore was born Sept., 1768, and died Feb. 19, 1832.

Nancy Moore was born and died the 15th day of Aug., 1834.

E. B. Moore died June 24, 1897.

Mary Doyle Strode was born Oct. 31, 1793.

Edmond Bartlert Moore was born Jan. 8, 1821.

Martha Ann Moore was born Nov. 6, 1831.

Jerman Baker Moore was born Sept. 10, 1833.

John William Moore was born Aug. 6, 1859.

George Maples Moore was born Dec. 26, 1861.

Theone Belle Moore was born May 26, 1865.

Lizzie Moore, wife of J. Baker Moore, was born Mch., 1862.

Grace Moore, wife of John W. Moore, was born May 25, 1872.

Martha Elizabeth, daughter of Theo. and Ona B., was born and died Apr. 19, 1888.

George Doyle was born Feb. 28, 1798.

Elizabeth Doyle, wife of George Doyle, was born Sept. 14, 1805.

Their children:
> John Alexander Doyle was born Dec. 5, 1832.
>
> Sally Catherine Doyle was born May 29, 1834.
>
> Mary Frances Doyle was born Nov. 23, 1835.
>
> James Strode Doyle was born Aug. 18, 1837.
>
> George Wm. Henry Doyle was born Aug. 26, 1840.
>
> Nelson Constant Doyle was born Feb. 4, 1842.

Ruth Ann Elizabeth Doyle was born Jan. 4, 1844.
Jermana Ellen Doyle was born Sept. 29, 1847.
Edmund Bartlert Moore, son of John W. and Grace Moore, was born Dec. 3, 1891.
Edmund B. Moore and Martha Ann Doyle were married Nov. 4, 1852.
N. C. Moore and Mary Lou Kinkton were married Nov. 28, 1871.
L. W. Sanders and Mary F. Doyle were married Nov. 30, 1871.
George W. Doyle and M. Alice La Master were married Nov. 30, 1871.
Jas. Boyer and Sallie C. Doyle were married Apr. 5, 1877.
J. Baker Moore and Lizzie McGuire were married Dec. 28, 1884.
George W. Doyle, Jr., and Pauline Duvavent were married Oct. 15, 1880.
N. C. Doyle and Mrs. Anna M. Jollie were married Jan. 28, 1886.
Theo. S. Drane and Ona B. Moore were married June 1, 1887. (Theona Belle Moore.)
J. Baker Moore and Sallie McCoy Armstrong were married Apr. 13, 1888.
John W. Moore and Grace Robards were married Nov. 29, 1890.
M. George and Eddie Glady Partlow were married June 24, 1898.
George Doyle, Sr., died Feb. 20, 1861.
Elizabeth Doyle died Dec. 12, 1878.
John A. Doyle died May 24, 1858.
James S. Doyle died May 15, 1861.
Ruth Anne Doyle died May 1, 1848.
Jermana Ellen Doyle died Apr. 18, 1848.
Mary Lou Doyle, wife of Nelson Doyle, died Feb. 8, 1875.
Alice Doyle, wife of George Doyle, Jr., died May 1, 1878.
Lizzie Moore, wife of J. Baker Moore, died July 3, 1885.
Ona B. Moore, wife of T. S. Drane, died Sept. 5, 1889.
J. Baker Moore, son of E. B. and Martha A. Moore, died June 30, 1890.
(Grandchildren of Edmund and Martha Ann Moore):
    Edmund Bartlert Moore—Born Dec. 3, 1891, Smithfield, Ky.
    Ona Mary Moore—Born Oct. 2, 1893, Smithfield, Ky.
    Minnie Ann Moore—Born July 6, 1895, Smithfield, Ky.
    Jack Wilson Moore—Born Sept. 5, 1909, Smithfield, Ky.

BIBLE PRINTED IN LONDON, ENGLAND, IN 1771, FOR THE AUTHOR, REV. SAMUEL NEWTON, D. D., BY T. BREWMAN. SUBSCRIBED FOR BY B. TUCKER.
Now Owned by Mr. E. L. Hutchinson, Lexington, Ky., of the 6th Generation From B. Tucker.

Mary, daughter of Richard and Mary Saltus, was born Mch. 17, 1765.
Archibald, son of Richard and Mary Saltus, was born Sept. 20, 1766.
    (Note by Family: Mary Saltus married B. Tucker.)
Joseph, son of Peter and Elizabeth Pocher, was born Nov. 26, 1784.
Dr. Benjamin L. Perry died 25th of Apr., 1792.
Mathias Hutchinson and Jane Perdnan (1st of 5 wives) were married by the Rev. Offspring Pearce, May 29, 1769.
Jane Hutchinson, wife of Mathias Hutchinson, died July 27, 1775, aged 22 yrs.
Mathias, son of Mathias and Jane, was born Aug. 25 ,1770, and died Oct. 22.
Thomas, son of Mathias and Jane Hutchinson, was born Nov. 14, 1771.
Ester, dau. of Mathias and Jane Hutchinson, was born Oct. 3, 1773.
Mathias Hutchinson and Elizabeth Bradford (2nd wife) were married Dec .19, 1776, by Rev. Offspring Pearce.
Elizabeth, wife of Mathias Hutchinson, died Dec. 8, 1785, aged 40 yrs. and 10 months.
Jane Eliza, daughter of Mathias and Elizabeth Hutchinson, was born Nov. 8, 1785.
Mathias Hutchinson and Louisa Tucker (3rd wife) were married July 27, 1786, by the Rev. Edward Ellington.
Maria, daughter of Mathias and Louisa Hutchinson, was born May 23,

1787, and baptized by Rev. Edward Ellington.

Mary, daughter of Mathias and Louisa Hutchinson, was born Apr. 4, 1790, and baptized by Rev. Edward Ellington.

Hariot Sarah, daughter of Mathias and Louisa Hutchinson, was born Jan. 5, 1792, and baptized by Rev. Edward Ellington.

Edward Louisa, son of Mathias and Louisa Hutchinson, was born Tuesday, Apr. 25, 1797.

Louisa (Tucker) Hutchinson (3rd wife), the amiable consort of Mathias Hutchinson, died Sunday, 14th of May, 1797.

Esther Hutchinson, the dutiful and affectionate daughter of Mathias and Jane Hutchinson, died in Charleston, S. C., Sept. 20, 1798.

Hariot Sarah Hutchinson, the lovely daughter of Mathias and Louisa, died on Thursday, the 30th of Oct., 1798, the fourth day after the decease of her grandmother, Mary Saltus.

Elizabeth Hutchinson (4th wife), formally Mrs. Ioor, consort of Mathias Hutchinson, was born the 1st of May, 1757, and died at Travellers Rest (Plantation House) the 19th of May, 1799, aged 42 years and 19 days. Was married June 5, 1798.

Jane Eliza Hutchinson, daughter of Mathias and Elizabeth Hutchinson, died Apr. 14, 1808.

Thomas Hutchinson, son of Mathias and Jane, died at his home in Georgetown, S. C., Aug. 25, 1808.

Mathias Hutchinson and Ester Roberts (5th wife) were married at Tranquil Dec. 23, 1802.

Ester Hutchinson died Aug. 19th, 1808.

Col. Mathias Hutchinson died on the 15th of June, 1812.

Dr. S. Ffirth was married to Mary Hutchinson on the 2nd day of Feb., 1814, and he died the 4th of July, 1820. Note: Her 2nd husband was Daniel K. Whittaker.)

Hutchinson Dupont Ffirth was born the 27th of Mch., 1817.

Casper Wister Ffirth was born on the 20th of Apr., 1820, and died in Sept. following.

Edward L. Hutchinson was married in New York, by the Rev. Henry Chan, to Elizabeth N. Belden, on Mch. 11, 1830.

24th of Dec., 1830, the daughter of Edward L. and Elizabeth M. Hutchinson was born and died at the residence of their friends, Mr. and Mrs. Joe Hall Waring.

Mathias Edward, son of Edward L. and Elizabeth M. Hutchinson, was born on Mch. 5, 1832, at the residence of their friends, Mr. and Mrs. Joe Hall Waring.

Joseph Hall Waring Hutchinson, son of Edward L. and Elizabeth M. Hutchinson, was born in Smithville on Oct. 17, 1833, and baptized by the Rev. W. Rogers.

Belden, son of Edward L. and Elizabeth M. Hutchinson, was born on the 15th of Nov., 1835.

George Mathews, son of Edward L. and Elizabeth M. Hutchinson, was born the 25th of Jan., 1838, at Travellers Rest, and died Oct. 31, 1838.

Philip, son of Edward L. and Elizabeth M. Hutchinson, was born on Nov. the 4th, 1839. He died Oct. 1, 1910, in the 71st year of his age, in Summerville, S. C.

Mathias Edward Hutchinson and Louisa Ingraham Bonneau were married in Charleston on the 4th of Jan., 1855, by the Rev. Paul Harper Keith.

Charlotte Maryatt, daughter of Mathias Edward and Louisa I. Hutchinson, was born Oct. 8, 1855, and baptized by Rev. Paul Harper Keith.

Major Edward L. Hutchinson died in Summerville on the 17th of Oct., 1855, aged 58 years, 5 months and 22 days.

Edward Louisa, daughter of Mathias Edward and Louisa Ingraham Hutchinson, was born on the 31st of July, 1857. Christened by Rev. Philip Gadsen.

Morton Clement, son of Mathias Edward and Louisa I. Hutchinson, was born in Summerville on the 11th of Feb., 1860. Christened by Rev. Philip Gadsen.

Elizabeth Judd, daughter of Mathias Edward and Louisa I. Hutchinson, was born in Summerville on the 19th of June, 1862. Baptized by Rev. Philip Gadsen.

Joseph Hall Waring Hutchinson and Mary Freer were married on 22nd of Dec., 1850, by Rev. Jno. Douglas on James Island.

Elizabeth McClaskey Hutchinson, daughter of Joseph H. W. and Mary F. Hutchinson, was born Oct. 10th, 1860, and died July,17, 1861.

Philip Henry, son of Joseph H. W. and Mary F. Hutchinson, was born 26th of Dec., 1861, and baptized by Rev. C. S. Veffer.

Symes Bonneau, son of Mathias Edward and Louisa Ingraham Hutchinson, was born on the 4th of July, 1865, and baptized by Rev. Dr. Hanold.

Sarah Caroline, daughter of Joseph H. W. and Mary Hutchinson, was born on the 10th of June, 1863, and baptized by Rev. C. S. Vedder.

Joseph, son of Joseph H. W. and Mary Hutchinson, was born on the 30th of Mch., 1865, and baptized by Rev. C. S. Vedder.

William Moore, son of Joseph H. W. and Mary Hutchinson, was born at Travellers Rest on the 3rd of Dec., 1866. Baptized by Rev. Chas. S. Vedder.

Thomas Grimball, son of Joseph H. W. and Mary Hutchinson, was born Jan. 8, 1870, at Clear Spring. Died Sept. 18, aged 20 months and 10 days.

NEWBOLD-GOINS-HEARNE BIBLES

Records from three bibles, donated by Mrs. Wm. Hearne, Frankfort, Ky.

(Note—Archives of Maryland: Thomas Newbold immigrated to America in 1678, and died 1713; will proved Princess Ann Co., 1713. Commissioned "Lt. of Horse," Somerset Co., 1687. Member of Council 1684-1689. Justice of Peace 1694-1697.)

Note—David Newbold: Born 1775 or 6, came to Kentucky 1803; married Sophia Robinson 1810, and died 1852. Francis Newbold, Sr., was born about 1698; died 1777; will proved Georgetown, Del., Mch. 15, 1777. Francis, Jr., was born 1776; married Sarah Owens; had son, David, born 1775 or 6. Sarah afterwards married James Stafford.)

David Owens Newbold and Julia Moore were married Feb. 2nd, 1843.

A. J. Loecher, of Philadelphia, was married to Nannie Crittenden Newbold, Apr. 24, 1861.

Henry West Boyce, of Illinois, was married to Mary Victoria Newbold, of Kentucky, Oct. 17, 1856.

S. W. Goin, of Frankfort, Ky., was married to Emma Julia Newbold, Jan. 20, 1850.

David Owens Newbold, son of David (son of Francis, Jr.) and Sophia Robinson Newbold, was born Sept. 30, 1814.

Julia Crittenden, daughter of ———— and Nancy Crittenden, was born Oct. 19, 1820.

Nannie Crittenden Newbold, daughter of David O. and Julia, was born Nov. 24, 1843.

Julia Newbold, daughter of David O. and Julia Newbold, was born Nov. 15, 1845.

Thomas Corwin Newbold, son of David O. and Julia Newbold, was born Feb. 4th, 1849.

Emma Julia Newbold, daughter of David and Julia Newbold, was born June 8, 1851.

Mary Victoria Newbold, daughter of David O. and Julia Newbold, was born Feb. 23rd, 1838.

Laura Ann Newbold, daughter of David O. and Julia Newbold, was born Sept. 28th, 1853.

Mary Virginia Newbold, daughter of David O. and Julia Newbold, was born Dec. 3rd, 185—. (Torn paper.

Ella Newbold, daughter of David O. and Julia Newbold, was born Aug. 8th, 1861.

Died—Mrs. Nancy Crittenden, July 10, 1854.

Died—Emily Crittenden, daughter of Mrs. Nancy Crittenden, Apr. 2, 1834.

Died—Julia Newbold, May 26th, 1886.

David Newbold—Died Sept. 29, 1892.

Died Dec. 11th, 1846—Julia Newbold, aged 1 yr., 26 days.

Died of Diphtheria—Laura Ann Newbold, daughter of David O. and Julia Newbold, Sept. 27th, 1860.

Married Mch. 27th, 1836—Sandford Goings to Mary Ann Singleton.

Married —— 16, 1856—Catherine Sneed Goins to Charles Egbert.

Married Dec. 26th, 1866—Mattie J. Buford to Sanford W. Goin.

Married Sept. 3rd, 1867—Phillip H. Goin to Pauline Phillips.

Married June 30th, 1868—Emma W. Goins to John H. Triplett, by Rev. H. A. M. Henderson.

Married in Woodford Co., Ky., Jan. 12, 1869—Sanford W. Goin to Emma J. Newbold, by Rev. H. A. M. Henderson.

Married at Jett, Ky., Oct. 31, 1892—Newbold L. Goin and Mariam Jett, by Rev. J. McGill.

Married at Hill Top, Woodford Co., Ky., Nov. 21, 1894—W. G. Heare and Virgie T. Goin, by Rev. Hugh McClelland.

Married in Cincinnati, O., July 8, 1899—Henry W. Goin and Mrs. Mattie Gaitskill.

Married in Frankfort, Ky., Nov. 29, 1901—Church Jones and Nannie C. Goin, by Rev. George Dorsie.

Married in Lexington, Ky., Oct., 1904—David Goin and Jodie Watts.

Sanford Goings was born Feb. 15th, 1815.

Mary Ann Singleton was born Oct. 7th, 1815.

Catherine Sneed Goings was born Dec. 19th, 1838.

Margaret Roy Goings was born Apr. 20th, 1830.

James Coleman Goings was born Apr. 6th, 1841.

Mandy Powen Goings was born Mch. 7th, 1843.

Sanford Wilson Goings, son of Sanford and Mary Ann Goings, was born Jan. 2nd, 1845.

Emeral Wilidy Goins, daughter of Sanford and Mary Ann Goins, was born Apr. 20th, 1847.

Phillip Henry Goins, son of Sanford and Mary Ann Goins, was born Nov. 31, 1849.

Mary Buford Goin, daughter of Sanford and Mattie Goin, was born Sept. 28, 1867.

Sanford Triplett Goin, son of Phillip and Pauline Goin, was born Jan. 15, 1868.

Mary Lena Triplett, daughter of John and Emma Triplett, was born Mch. 29, 1869.

Children of Charles and Katey Egbert: Emma Wallace Egbert—Born Mch. 16, 1863; Mary Jane Egbert—Born Sept. 12, 1857; Sanford Todd Egbert, Frank Egbert, Sallie Egbert, Charles Egbert, Willie Egbert.

Newbold Loecher Goin, son of Sanford and Emma Goin—Born Nov. 27, 1869.

Henry Goin, son of Sanford and Emma Goin—Born Dec. 18, 1871.

Thomas Goin, son of Sanford and Emma Goin—Born May 22, 1875.

Virginia Goin, daughter of Sanford and Emma Goin—Born Aug. 13, 1877. (Married Wm. G. Hearne, Nov. 21, 1894, Versailles, Ky.)

Phillip Goin, son of Sanford and Emma Goin—Born Dec. 19, 1879.

Nannie Goin, daughter of Sanford and Emma Goin—Born July 19, 1882.

David F. Goin, son of Sanford and Emma Goin—Born Oct. 19, 1884.

Ella Goin, daughter of Sanford and Emma Goin—Born Aug. 13, 1887.

Arthur Goin, son of Sanford and Emma Goin—Born Jan. 25, 1890.
Willoughby Goin, son of Sanford and Emma Goin—Born Feb. 23, 1893.
Margaret Roy Goings departed this life Aug. 2, 1841.
————————— Goin died Aug. 14, 1844.
James C. Goins, died Nov. 13, 1844.
Mary A. Goin, wife of Sanford Goin, died Jan. 2, 1868.
Thomas Goin, son of Sanford and Emma Goin, died Nov. 24, 1877.
Ella Goin, daughter of Sanford and Emma Goin, died Apr. 2, 1890.
S. W. Goin, husband of Emma J. Goin, died Mch. 5, 1904.
Mattie J. Goin died Oct. 10, 1867.
Mattie Bufford Goin, daughter of Sanford and Mattie Goin, died
    July 4, 1868.
Mrs. Emma Newbold Goin died Feb. 9, 1919.
Phillip Goin, died Dec. 13, 1924.
William Graham and Margaret, his wife, were married Jan. 18, 1798.
James M. Graham was married to Polly Keller Dec. 28, 1824.
James M. Graham married (second wife) Naney Sanders June 18, 1829.
Naney Jane Graham was married to Davis Hearne in 17th year of her
    age, Sept. 3, 1829.
Polly Graham was married to Wm. B. Hancock Jan. 13, 1830.
James M. Graham was married the third time to Elizabeth Trotter
    June 21, 1838.
Martha Elizabeth Graham was married to Henry Vandigrift Oct. 8, 1840.
Barthine Graham was born Mch. 22, 1808; died July 22, 1815.
Wm. R. Graham was born Feb. 9, 1817; died Oct. 13, 1817.
Betsy Graham was born Dec. 6, 1805; died July 26, 1818.
Peggy Graham was born Sept. 19, 1814; died Sept. 12, 1831.
Priscilla Graham was born Sept. 15, 1818.
Wm. F. Graham was born Dec. 29, 1820.
Martha Elizabeth Graham was born July 19, 1823.
Rebecca P. Graham was born Dec. 26, 1826.
Nancy's first child, James G. Hearne, was born June 2, 1830.
Nancy's second child, Margaret, was born Sept. 10, 1832.
James H. Hearne, was born Mch. 16, 1853.
Laura B. Hearne was born Oct. 14, 1855.
Thomas P. Hearne was born Aug. 8, 1857.
Mary Lizzie Hearne was born Jan. 25, 1860.
George W. Hearne was born Mch. 20, 1862.
Robert Hearne—Born 1865 (of James G. and Malcina Jane Johnson
    Hearn).
Lettie Hearne (Lamb)—Born Aug. 1, 1869 (of James G. and Malceina
    Jane Johnson Hearn).
Wm. Graham Hearne—Born Jan. 28, 1871 (of James G. and Malcina
    Jane Johnson Hearn).
John Sullinger Hearn—Born Jan. 23, 1874 (of James G. and Malcina
    Jane Johnson Hearn).
Malcina Jane Johnson—Born Feb. 15, 1831; married James G. Hearn
    June 13, 1850. James G. Hearn died Feb. 15, 1912; Mrs. J. G.
    Hearn died Aug. 6, 1922. Mrs. James G. Hearn's mother was
    Mary Elizabeth Payton.
William Graham died Oct. 1, 1845; aged 76 yrs., 10 months, 19 days.
Andrew Hearn died Aug. 13, 1849; aged 73 yrs, 2 months, 1 day.
Mary Montgomery died Apr. 7, 1800.
Thomas H. Graham died Aug. 10, 1825.
William Montgomery died July 15, 1830.

OLDHAM BIBLE
Bible Owned by Will Dowell Oldham, Lexington, Ky.
W. M. Oldham was born in Madison County, Ky., March 31, 1829.
Anna E. Oldham, wife of W. M. Oldham, was born in Urbanna, Mad-
    dison Co., Ohio, June 3, 1835.

Ella Shackelford Oldham, oldest child of W. M. and A. E. Oldham, was born in North Middletown, Bourbon Co., Ky., Jan. 6, 1856.

John Maddison Oldham, second child of W. M. and A. E. Oldham—Born in Collins County, Texas, March 2, 1861.

John Baldwin Oldham, third child of W. M. and A. E. Oldham—Born in Collins County, Texas, March 17, 1862.

William Dowell Oldham, fourth child of W. M. and A. E. Oldham— Born in Collins County, Texas, Oct. 23, 1864.

Mary Roberta Oldham, second daughter of W. M. and A. E. Oldham— Born in Louisville, Ky., Dec. 2, 1869.

William Augustus Daughters, son of J. K. P. and Ella S. Daughters— Born in Louisville, Ky., Feb. 19, 1878; died in Dension, Texas, 1880.

Edwin Bronston Oldham, son of W. D. and Alice Bronston Oldham— Born in Richmond, Ky., on Sunday, Oct. 21, 1888.

William Dowell Oldham, Jr., son of W. D. and Alice B. Oldham—Born at Fort Smith, Arkansas, on Tuesday, July 28, 1891.

John Dowell Wood, son of Wm. M. and Roberta Wood—Born in Denison, Texas, Feb. 20, 1896; died Feb. 21, 1896; buried Fairlawn cemetery, Denison, Texas.

Robert Wood, son of Wm. M. and Mary Roberta Wood—Born in Washington, D. C., Jan. 15, 1907.

Frances Surber McClure, wife of W. Dowell Oldham—Born in Lexington, Ky., Jan. 8, 1896.

Nina Durand Otis, wife of Edwin B. Oldham—Born in Buffalo, Erie Co., N. Y., July 24, 1886.

William Dowell Oldham, Third—Born in Lexington, Ky., Apr. 11, 1918, son of Dowell and Frances S. Oldham.

John Allen Oldham, son of Dowell and Frances S. Oldham—Born in Lexington, Ky., Tuesday, Nov. 9, 1920.

Alice Bronston Oldham, wife of Will D. Oldham—Born in Richmond, Ky., Mch. 12, 1866.

J. C. Robinson and Cornelia A. Baldwin were married by the Rev. Robert C. Hatton, of M. E. church, in Boardman, Trumbull Co., Ohio, on June 28th, 1827.

J. C. Robinson married (second) Mary C. Madison, Jan. 1, 1850; Rev. J. C. Bruce, minister of M. E. church, officiating, near Cynthiana, Harrison Co., Ky.

J. C. Robinson and Ellen Downs were married in Paris, Texas, 1874.

Wm. M. Oldham and Anna E. Robinson were married by the Rev. F. N. Ralston, of the M. E. church, South, in Paris (North Middletown), Bourbon Co., Ky., on Mch. 14, 1855.

J. K. P. Daughters and Ella S. Oldham were married by Rev. R. H. Read, minister of the M. E. church, South, in Lexington, Ky., Oct. 8th, 1874.

Will D. Oldham and Alice J. Bronston were married by Rev. C. P. Williamson, at the Christian church in Richmond, Ky., Dec. 13, 1887.

John Baldwin Oldham and Kate Harrison Pittman were married in Dallas, Texas, Nov. 13, 1889, by Rev. Toofe, of the Christian church.

William M. Wood and Mary Roberta Oldham were married in Denison, Texas, Jan. 28th, 1892, at the First Presbyterian church, by Rev. Lewis J. Adams.

Edwin Bronston Oldham and Nina Durand Otis were married at her grandmother's home, Mrs. Carlisle Durand, in Westfield, New York, on June 3rd, 1913, by Rev. George McClellan, of the Presbyterian church.

William Dowell Oldham, Jr. and Frances Surber McClure were married by Rev. J. T. Daughtery, of the Baptist church, on Sunday, Feb. 4, 1917, in Lexington, Ky., at the home of Edwin B. Oldham.

J. C. Robinson—Born in England, Feb. 26, 1804.

H. A. Baldwin, wife of J. C. Robinson—Born Feb. 17, 1807 in Letchfield Co., Connecticut.

Mary C. Madison, second wife of J. C. Robinson—Born in Harrison Co., Ky., on Feb. 1st, 1815.

Asa B. Robinson—Born Feb. 3rd, 1830; was oldest son of J. C. and C. A. Robinson; baptized by Rev. A. Palmer.

Thos. E. Robinson, second son of J. C. and C. A. Robinson—Born Nov. 24th, 1831.

Ann E. Robinson, oldest daughter of J. C. and C. A. Robinson—Born June 2nd, 1834; baptized by Rev. Wm. H. Roper, of M. E. church.

J. C. Robinson, Jr., third son of J. C. and C. A. Robinson—Born Dec. 25, 1836.

Joseph M. Robinson, fourth son of J. C. and C. A. Robinson—Born Sept. 14, 1840.

Cornelia Robinson, second daughter of J. C. and C. A. Robinson—Born Nov. 1st, 1843.

John Madison Oldham, eldest son of W. M. and A. E. Oldham, died in Collins Co., Texas, May 30th, 1861; aged 2 months and 6 days; buried in Paris, Texas.

John Cook Robinson (grandsire) died in Paris, Texas, May 29, 1876, and is buried there.

Cornelia Baldwin Robinson died in 1849; she is buried in cemetery at Neville, Ohio.

Mary C. Robinson, second wife of John C., died in Paris, Texas, Dec. 7, 1870, and is buried there.

Ellen Downs Robinson, third wife of John Cook Robinson, died in 1911, at Paris, Texas, and is buried there.

William Moberly Oldham died Nov. 11, 1900; buried in Lexington, Ky.

Anna E. Oldham, wife of Wm. M. Oldham, died Sept. 9, 1909; buried in Lexington, Ky.

Ella Oldham Daughters died in Denison, Texas, Feb. 15, 1901.

Roberta Oldham Wood died in New York May 5, 1918, wife of Major W. M. Wood; buried in Lexington, Ky.

Edwin Bronston Oldham—Killed in auto accident near Milwaukee, Wis., Sunday, Aug. 27, 1922; buried in Lexington, Ky., on Aug. 30, 1922.

J .K. Daughters died in Portland, Oregon, Jan. 21, 1925; buried in Denison, Texas.

PAYNE BIBLE

Donated by Mrs. Clifton Thompson, Lexington, Ky.

Note: Sir William Payne married Ann Jennings. His father was Sir John Payne, who emigrated with his brother, William, to America, 1620. Received a special grant of land from James I. near Alexandria, Va.

Ann Payne (who was Ann Jennings), widow of William Payne the elder, was born the 28th day of February, 1740; was married March 1st, 1763, and died May 11th, 1827; aged 87 years.

Gen. John Payne—Born April 8, 1764; died Sept. 9th, 1837.

Betsy Payne—Born April 16, 1772.

John and Betsy (Johnson), his wife, were married June 28, 1787.

Asa Payne, son of John and Betsy, his wife, was born Mch. 19, 1788.

Robert Payne, son of John and Betsy, his wife, was born Dec. 20, 1789; died Aug. 28, 1827

Nancy Payne, daughter of John and Betsy, his wife, was born October 16, 1791.

Salley Payne, daughter of John and Betsy, his wife, was born Nov. 16, 1793; married Charles Thomson 1812; died 1862.

John Payne, son of John and Betsy, his wife, was born Nov. 15, 1795.

Betsy Payne, daughter of John and Betsy, his wife, was born January 22, 1798.

Newton Payne, son of John and Betsy, his wife, was born Jan. 4, 1800.

William Johnson Payne, son of John and Betsy, his wife, was born January 26, 1802; died Jan. 30, 1813.

Thomas J. Payne, son of John and Betsy, his wife, was born Feb. 3, 1804.

Franklin Payne, son of John and Betsy, his wife, was born March 16, 1806; died Sept., 1870.

Richard J. Payne, son of John Payne and Betsy, his wife, was born Feb. 26, 1808; died May 27, 1823.

Emeline Payne, daughter of John and Betsy, his wife, was born Mch. 13, 1810.

Cyrus Payne, son of John and Betsy, his wife, was born Nov. 10, 1812.

Betsy Peak died Sept. 19th, 1832.

CURTIS PENDLETON BIBLE.

Now owned by J. C. Lary. (Copied by Roberta B. Lary.)

Curtis Pendleton was born May 9, 1762.

Nancy Pendleton was born Oct. 18, 1769.

(Note: These are the great-grandfather and great-grandmother of J .C. Lary.)

Gen. Edmund Pendleton was born Oct. 2, 1788. He was the grandfather of J. C. Lary.

PICOT BIBLE

Nathan Picot Bible was presented to him in June, 1854, by James Pitt, of St. Johns, N. F., a first cousin of Nathan Picot, and a son of William Pitt. Wm. Pitt was born in Kent, England, May 28th, 1759, and entered Parliament Jan. 23rd, 1781. Some time later King George III. appointed him Chancellor of the exchequer and first lord of the Treasury. He died Jan. 23rd, 1806. Bible now in possession of H. G. Picot, Louisville, Ky., and was copied by Mrs. H. G. Picot.

John Picot—Born Dec. 9, 1783; married Apr. 5th, 1809; died Mch. 27, 1829.

Rebecca Pitt, wife of John Picot—Born June 27th, 1790. (No record of death.) Their children:

Thomas Picot—Born Nov. 29th, 1810; died Mch. 27th, 1829.

Nathan Picot—Born Apr. 29, 1813; died Apr. 16th, 1893.

Ezra Picot—Born May 21, 1817; died Oct. 31, 1819.

George Picot—Born Sept. 11th, 1819. (No record of death.)

Jemima Picot—Born Sept. 14th, 1822. (No record of death.)

Juliana Picot—Born July 28th, 1824. (No record of death.)

John Elias Picot—Born Nov. 7, 1827; died Mch. 22, 1905.

Elizabeth Jane Picot—Born Sept. 24th, 1829. (No record of death.)

Nathan Picot, son of John and Rebecca—Born Apr. 29th, 1813; married in St. Johns, N. F., Dec. 24th, 1840, Anna Pippy who was born Aug. 10th, 1814; died Sept. 18th, 1900. Their children:

Thomas Picot—Born Jan. 5th, 1844; died Jan. 6th, 1844.

Sophia Picot—Born May 15th, 1845; died Nov., 1846.

Frank Picot—Born Apr. 7th, 1847; died in service of his Country in Civil War, 14th Heavy Artillery of New York.

George Picot—Born May 15th, 1850; died Feb., 1851.

Nathaniel Picot—Born Jan. 15th, 1852; died Apr., 1853.

Julia Elizabeth Picot—Born Nov. 19th. 1854; died May, 1856.

Sarah Jones Picot—Born Jan. 19th, 1856; died Dec. 5th, 1880.

Henry Gilbert Picot—Born June 14th, 1858.

RYLAND BIBLE

Bible of Robert Ryland, owned and copied by Mrs. F. A. Atkins.

Josiah Ryland—Born Mch. 5, 1747.

Katherine Peachey, wife of Josiah Ryland—Born May 10, 1777.

Robert Ryland, son of Josiah and K. P. Ryland—Born Mch. 14, 1805.

Betty Presley Thornton—Born Sept. 24, 1821; married Robert Ryland

June 8, 1848. Children:
William, Josephine, Norvell, Kate, Roberta Ryland Atkins—Born
Feb. 5, 1851 at Richmond, Va.; Antoinette Thornton R. Atkins,
Bessie Ryland Wait.

F. A. Atkins and Roberta married Dec. 11, 1873. Their Children: Mary
L. Atkins, Roberta Atkins (Harrison), F. A. Atkins, Bessie Atkins
(Carpenter), Antoinette Thornton Atkins, Presley Thornton At-
kins, Robert Ryland Atkins, J. Wm. Atkins.

Mary E. Reynolds, wife of Jas. M. Atkins—Born 1820.

SANDERS (or Saunders) BIBLE

(From an old family record owned by Miss Sallie V. Ashbrook,
Cynthiana, Kentucky.)

James Sanders was born December 29th, in the year of our Lord, 1733.

Sarah Sanders, wife of James Sanders and daughter of Thomas Tully,
was born December 18th, in the year of our Lord, 1737.

John Sanders, son of James Sanders and Sarah, his wife, was born
January 22nd, 1756, and died February 5th, 1809, in the 54th
year of his age.

Nancy Sanders, the daughter of James Sanders and Sarah, his wife,
was born January 12th, in the year of our Lord, 1758.

Charity Sanders, the daughter of James Sanders and Sarah, his wife,
was born April the 5th, in the year of our Lord, 1760.

James Sanders, the son of James Sanders and Sarah, his wife, was
born March 18th, in the year of our Lord, 1762.

Sarah Sanders, the daughter of James Sanders and Sarah, his wife, was
born July 7th, in the year of our Lord, 1765.

Polly Sanders, the daughter of James Sanders and Sarah, his wife, was
born March 18th, in the year of our Lord, 1768.

Hardy Sanders, the son of James Sanders and Sarah, his wife, was born
June 22nd, in the year of our Lord, 1770.

Britain Sanders, the son of James Sanders and Sarah, his wife, was
born November 17th, in the year of our Lord, 1773.

Jonathan Sanders, the son of James Sanders and Sarah, his wife, was
born Feb. 26th, in the year of our Lord, 1775.

William Sanders—Born Jan. 23, 1777.

Dorcas Sanders, the daughter of James Sanders and Sarah, his wife, was
born November 21st, (the year is indistinct—1777, 1779.)

John N. Anderson, husband of Sarah Sanders, was born in the year of
our Lord, 1757, July, 15th day.

Betsy Sanders, wife of Hardy Sanders, was born 26th day of September,
in the year of our Lord, 1769.

*Sarah Saunders, daughter of William Grant and Elizabeth, his wife,
was born January 25th, 1759, and died March 29th, 1814. William
Grant, son of William and Margery, was born in Pennsylvania, February, 1726, and died in Fayette County, Ky., June 20th, 1804.
Elizabeth, his wife, sister of Daniel Boone, was born in Pennsylvania, February 5th, 1733, and died in Fayette Co., Ky., February
26th, 1814.

*This Sarah Sanders, daughter of William and Elizabeth Boone
Grant, was the wife of John Sanders, referred to above, and a niece
of Daniel Boone.

John Sanders, son of James Sanders and Sarah, his wife, was born
January 22nd, 1756, and departed this life February 5th, 1809.

Sarah Sanders, daughter of William Grant and Elizabeth, his wife,
was born January the 25th, 1759, and departed this life March
the 29th, 1814.

Elizabeth Sanders, daughter of John Sanders and Sarah, his wife, was
born October 25th, 1776, and was killed by the Indians February
19th, 1787.

Sarah Sanders was born March the 8th, 1779, and departed this life

April 28th, 1779.

William Sanders was born 25th of May, 1780, and departed this life September 15th, 1843.

Sarah Sanders was born 1st of August, 1782, and departed this life 21st of September, 1804.

Nancy Sanders was born 11th of March, 1784.

Mary Sanders was born 16th of September, 1787.

Elilabeth Sanders was born 29th of August, 1789.

John H. Sanders was born May 29th, 1791.

James T. Sanders was born 20th of September, 1793, and was lost in Gen. Winchester's defeat on the Raisen river on 22nd of January, 1813.

Joel B. Sanders was born 2nd of October, 1795, and departed this life Oct. 7th, 1833.

Rebecah G. Sanders was born the 7th of June, 1800, and departed this life July 3rd, 1817. The said Rebecah was married to Mr. Jacob Turner, 1816, and had one daughter.

Dorcas V. Sanders was born December 8th, 1801.

*Artemisia T. Belles was born 10th of February, 1832.

**Daniel Boone—Born 1735; died 1820.

MICHAEL SCHMIESER BIBLE

Now owned by Mrs. George Smiser, Cynthiana, Ky. Copied by Mrs. Harry Frisbee. "Schmieser" changed to Smyser and Smiser.

Michael Schmieser—Born about 1680.

Ann Barber, his wife—Born about 1683 to 1685. Children:

Mathias—Born in Germany, Feb. 17, 1715.

Margareda—Born about 1718 to 1720.

George—Born about 1720 to 1725.

(Mathyas changed their names to Smyser. Note: record above is on separate sheet of paper.)

George Smiser married Katherine Lair (first wife) 29th of Feb., 1798.

George Smiser married Mary Lair (second wife) Dec. 5, 1800. (Mary and Katherine were sisters.

George Smiser married Patsy Lair (third wife) Jan. 11th, 1803. (Patsey was a cousin to Mary and Katherine.)

Darius L. Smiser, son of George and Martha Smiser, married Louisa Smith, May 15th, 1837.

John H. Smiser, son of Darius and Louisa Smiser, married Mary K Ewalt, May 31st, 1870.

Wm. A. Smiser was married the 18th of September, 1844.

George Smiser—Born Dec. 30th, 1772.

Catherine Smiser—Born March 30th, 1778.

Mary Smiser—Born Aug. 6th, 1780.

Patsy Smiser (third wife)—Born Dec. 28th, 1780.

Elizabeth (daughter)—Born Jan. 20th, 1799.

Samuel (son)—Born Oct. 20th, 1804.

John Milton (son)—Born Feb. 10th, 1807.

George—Born 17th of May, 1809.

Katherine—Born Nov. 10th, 1811.

Darius—Born July 4th, 1814.

William—Born Oct. 17th, 1817.

Polly, 2nd—Born Oct. ——, 1820.

Selah An—Born Dec. 24th, 1825.

Grandchildren—

James H. Lair—Born (faded out) in the year of Our Lord 1794.

Mary, daughter of George—Born 13th of Sept., 1831.

George W., Son of George—Born 15th of Feb., 1833.

John Wm.—Born 22nd of Oct., 1835.

Eliza—Born July, 1841.

John A. Lair, III.—Born Aug., 1836; son of ——— Lair.

Helen Lair—Born Sept. 3, 1838.
Arrebeala Lair—Born Mch. 11, 1841.
Mary Leuisy Lair—Born Nov. 4, 1843.
Alfred Newton—Born Nov. 26, 1828.
Wiliam—Born Jan., 1832.
Marthy Cath.—Born Nov., 1834.
Mary Elizabeth—Born Mch., 1837.
John James—Born Apr., 1839.
Hugh Fraizer—Born Oct. 3, 1843.
Polly M. Smiser, George's wife, was born Nov. 27, 1811; died Feb. 26, 1833.
Rebecca Smiser, wife of Sam., was born June, 1805.
Julyan, wife of Milton, was born Apr. 8, 1814.
Arabella, Daughter of Milton—Born Feb. 26, 1835.
John Edward—Born Feb. 14, 1837.
James Samuel—Born July 6, 1839.
William—Died July, 1841.
William—Born 10 ——, 1842.
Thos. Alton—Born Aug. 3, 1845.
Hellena P. Smiser—William's wife, was born Oct. 3, 1826.
Mary—Born Dec. 6, 1839.
Katherine died July 18, 1800.
Mary Died June, 1802. Her 2 infants the same year.
My Mother in the 96th year.
My Father in 1781.
Katherine, wife of J. W. Lair, died ——.
Polly, wife of James Frazer, died Apr. 5, 1891 (?); age 70 yrs., 6 months and 3 days.
James Frazer died ——; ——Smiser died Oct. 22, 1875.
John Milton Smiser died ——.
William A. Smiser died Dec., 1894.
Hellena P. Smiser, wife of W. A. Smiser, died 1900.
George Henry, son of Samuel, died Aug. 1, 1832; age 9 months.
John M., son of George, died Mch. 11, 1833; age 2 yrs. and 6 months.
Deaths of brothers—Henry Smiser died in 72nd year; Phillip died in his 70th year, Jacobin died in his 69th year, John died in his 66th year, Michael died in 1854, age 80; George died Apr. 22, 1856, age 82 yrs., 10 months and 7 days.
Martha Smiser, 3rd wife of George, died Oct. 7, 1857; age 76 yrs., 10 months and 9 days.
George Smiser, Jr., died in Baton Rouge, Louisiana, Oct. 22, 1875.
H. W. Smiser, son of George III., died June 29, 1877.
Mrs. Martha A. Smiser, 3rd wife of George Smiser, died Nov. 13, 1889.
Samuel M. Smiser, son of George I., died Feb. 23, 1870.
Rebecca, his wife, died Jan. 2, 1873.

STONE BIBLE.
Donated by Mrs. B. F. King, Lexington, Ky.
David Stone and Louise Hall were married Sept. 30, 1830.
David Stone and Harriet A. Hampton were married Feb. 22, 1840.
Mary Elizabeth Stone and Joel P. Williams were married Feb. 4, 1851.
Martha Ann Stone and Joel P. Williams were married Nov. 13, 1855.
Laura Stone, daughter of David and Harriet A. Stone, married to George K. Bell Dec. 14, 1880, by Rev. B. F. Clay.
David Stone was born Feb. 14, 1807.
Mary Elizabeth Stone was born Sept. 5, 1831.
Martha Ann Stone was born Mch. 12, 1833.
Maria Louise Stone was born Aug. 27, 1842.
Laura Stone was born Oct. 21, 1854.
Walter Stone Bell, son of G. K. and Laura Bell, was born in Lexington, Ky., Aug. 17, 1882.

Arthur Hampton Bell, son of George K. and Laura Bell, was born in Lexington, Ky., July 10, 1885.
George Scott Bell, son of G. K. and Laura Bell, was born in Lexington, Ky., Nov. 22, 1887.
Louise Stone, consort of David Stone, died Mch. 13, 1836.
Mary Elizabeth Williams, consort of Joel P. Williams, died June 26, 1854.
Harriet H. Stone, consort of David Stone, died June 15, 1855.
David Stone died Nov. 13 (or 19), 1873.
Lou Darnaby, consort of W. G. Darnaby, died June 2, 1867.
Hattie Bell Darnaby, daughter of W. G. and Lou, died Sept. 13, 1868.

STORY BIBLE.
Donated by Mrs. Lola Linney Snyder of Lexington, Ky.
John Story and Parthenie Taylor were married Nov. 26, 1801.
William H. Story and Elenora Adams were married Sept. 15, 1853.
Ben Casey Allin and Jennie L. Taylor were married Jan. 21, 1857.
Samuel W. McDowell and Georgia E. Allin were married July 5, 1881.
Samuel Carlisle McDowell and Etta Farra Groff were married Mch. 26, 1906.
Garland Allin McDowell and Margaret May Taylor were married Nov. 28, 1906.
Harriet Taylor Story was born Aug. 26, 1802.
Polly Story was born June 1, 1804.
Thomas Taylor Story was born Sept. 16, 1805.
Foushee Tebbs Story was born Dec. 12, 1807.
Ruth Ann Story was born Oct. 5, 1809.
John Orville Story was born Feb. 26, 1812.
Ianthia Claremont Story was born Jan. 12, 1814.
William Harrison Story was born Mch. 5, 1816.
Margaret T. Story was born May 22, 1819.
Thomas Harry Story, son of W. H. Story, was born Aug. 22, 1864.
Ianthia C. Story departed this life Oct. 3, 1835.
Ruth Ann Story departed this life July 25, 1837.
Foushee T. Story departed this life Mch 25, 1853.
Parthenia Story departed this life Aug. 11, 1865.
William H. Story departed this life Oct. 1, 1865.
Harriet T. Story departed this life Mch. 4, 1866.
Thomas H. Story, son of William and Elenora Story, departed this life Apr. 16, 1895.
Elenora Story died May 18, 1890.
John Orville Story departed this life May 10, 1827.
John Story departed this life July 23, 1846.
Margaret T. Story departed this life July 1905.

ANTHONY THORNTON BIBLE
Bible of Anthony Thornton, presented by his son, H. F. Thornton, of Petersburg, Va., July 17th, 1862; now owned and copied by Mrs. F. A. Atkins, Lexington, Ky.
James Bankhead Thornton and Mildred Rootes Thornton, mother and father of Anthony Thornton, were united in the holy bonds of matrimony Oct. 23rd, 1794.
Anthony Thornton and Ann Rose were united in the holy bonds of matrimony Oct. 19, 1820.
Robert Ryland and Betty Presly Thornton were united in the holy bonds of matrimony June 8th, 1848, by Rev. J. B. Jeter, at Rovers Rest, Caroline Co., Va.
James Bankhead Thornton and Mary M. DeCamp were united in the holy bonds of matrimony Dec. 22, 1854.
Wm. E. Jones and Rosa Thornton were united in the holy bonds of matrimony Dec. 6, 1855.

H. F. Thornton and Meta G. Chapman were united in the holy bonds of
matrimony Aug. 29, 1867.
Wm. N. Douglas and Mildred R. Thornton, only child of Henry F.
and Meta G. Thornton, were united in the holy bonds of matri-
mony Oct. 15th, 1896.
James Bankhead Thornton was born Apr. 19, 1770.
Mildred Rootes—Born Dec. 18, 1773.
Anthony Thornton—Born Oct. 31, 1798.
Ann Rose Thornton—Born ———, 1802.
Betty Presley Thornton—Born Sept. 24, 1821.
Henry F. Thornton—Born July 24, 1824.
James B. Thornton—Born Apr. 23, 1827.
Mildred Rootes Thornton—Born May 16, 1830.
Rosa Thornton—Born Oct. 1, 1832.
Anthony Thornton—Born Jan. 13, 1835.
Mary E. Thornton—Born May 21, 1837.
Harriett Conway Thornton—Born Mch. 5, 1840.
Roberta, daughter of Robert and Betty Ryland—Born Feb. 5, 1851.
Anthonette T. Thornton—Born Nov. 3, 1854.
William M. Douglas—Born Apr. 5, 1862.
Anthony, son of James B. and Mary Thornton—Born Nov. 4, 1855.
Anthony Thornton Jones, first son of Wm. E. and Rosa Jones—Born
Apr. 3, 1857.
Ann Thornton Jones, first daughter of Wm. E. and Rosa Jones—Born
July 22, 1858.
Mary Jones, second daughter of Wm. E. and Rosa Jones—Born Mch.
19, 1860.
Wm. E. Jones, second son of Wm. E. and Rosa Jones—Born Nov.
4, 1865.
Betty Ryland Jones, third daughter of Wm. E. and Rosa Jones—Born
Dec. 15, 1867.
Martha E. Ryland, third daughter of Robert and Betty Ryland—Born
July 22, 1857.
Milly Rootes Thornton, first daughter of Harry F. and Meta Thorn-
ton—Born July 5, 1868.
Henry Bankhead Jones—Born Nov. 11, 1869.
Henry Thornton Douglas, first son of Wm. M. and Milly Thornton
Douglas—Born Feb. 28, 1900.
Anthony Thornton, third son of Anthony and Ann Rose Thornton—
Died Nov. 18, 1838.
James B. Thornton, father of Anthony Thornton, died Mch. 30, 1843.
Mildred Rootes Thornton, mother of Anthony Thornton, died Apr.
30, 1845.
Mildred Rootes Thornton, second daughter of Anthony and Ann R.
Thornton, died July 16, 1845.
James B. Thornton, second son of Anthony and Ann R. Thornton, died
Nov. 14, 1862.
Ann Rose Thornton, wife of Anthony Thornton, died Nov. 22, 1866.
Anthony Thornton, father of H. F. Thornton, died Mch. 22, 1885, in
the 87th year of his age.
Henry F. Thornton, son of Anthony and Ann R. Thornton, died Dec.
13, 1898.
Meta Chapman Thornton died Aug. 20, 1915.
J. M. Atkins bible, now owned, and copied, by Mrs. F. A. Atkins,
Lexington, Ky.
J. M. Atkins and Mary C. Reynolds were married Jan. 7, 1850.
Francis Allen Atkins was born Oct. 26, 1850.
Lucinda Margaret Atkins was born Dec. 3, 1852, and died Feb. 9, 1854,
aged 14 months and 6 days.
James M. Atkins died Mch. 27, 1855; aged 37 yrs., 4 months and 22 days.
Mrs. Mary Elizabeth Atkins died Dec. 29, 1856.

"BIBLE PURCHASED BY ARGYLE TAYLOR, JUNE 12, 1804."

Records from This Bible Contributed by Mrs. Lola Linney Snyder, Lexington, Ky.

Written on front cover, "At my death this Bible is to be given to Lola Linney Snyder, signed by Anna Barbour."

Mary F. Taylor, daughter of F. T. Taylor, Sen., and Mary, his wife, was born Feb. 7, 1810. Children:

James W. Taylor was born Mch. 27, 1811.

William Taylor was born Apr. 5, 1812.

John G .Taylor was born May 3, 1813.

Ann W. Taylor was born Jan. 22, 1815.

Samuel W. Taylor was born June 14, 1816.

Emily M. Taylor was born Mch. 7, 1818.

Lewis B. Taylor was born Dec. 9, 1819.

Thomas F. Taylor was born June 9, 1821.

Margaret L. Taylor was born Jan. 16, 1823.

George W. Taylor was born July 19, 1824.

Foushee T. Taylor, Jr., was born Jan. 12, 1827.

Mary F. Taylor was married to Samuel C. Givens Feb. 18, 1829.

Ann W. Taylor was married to Felix Hunton Oct. 29, 1833, and departed this life Oct. 12, 1835, in the 21st year of her age.

John F. Warran, son of Wm. Warran, Jr., and Lucresia, his wife, was born the 21st of Apr., 1806.

S. Warran was born the 7th of July, 1807.

Lucretia E. Taylor was married Dec. 6, 1804.

Foushee T. Taylor was married Aug. 23, 1808.

Meredith Furr was married Apr. 8, 1824.

Grayson B. Taylor was married Apr. 7, 1825, to Katherine Rice, and was born Oct. 20, 1804 (or 1809).

Foushee T. Taylor was married to Mary C. Warran Aug. 23, 1808.

Argyle Taylor, son of Lazarus Taylor and Hannah, his wife, was born the 25th day of May, 1750.

Mary Taylor, wife of Argyle Taylor, was born the 30th of May, 1750.

Artemesia Taylor, daughter of Argyle Taylor and Mary, his wife, was born the 17th day of June, 1774.

Catherine Taylor was born the 6th day of Oct., 1778.

Lucresia Taylor was born the 11th day of Sept., 1781.

John F. Taylor, son of Argyle Taylor and Mary, his wife, was born the 6th day of July, 1776.

Meredith F. Taylor was born the 27th day of Feb., 1784.

Foushee T. Taylor was born the 17th day of Sept., 1785.

Willey Taylor was born the 9th day of July, 1788.

James W. Taylor died at Mattanzas, in Cuba, in his 25th year.

John F. Taylor departed this life on the 19th day of Oct., 1802, on Tuesday night about 9 o'clock in his 27th year of his age.

Meredith Fleet Taylor departed this life in Aug., 1793, in the 10th year of his age.

Lazarus Taylor, son of John F. Taylor, deceased, departed this life the 16th day of Mch., 1802.

Harriett Taylor departed this life the 24th day of July, 1804, in the 7th year of her age.

Foushee Tebbs, son of James Tebbs and Mary, his wife, departed this life the 13th, day of Nov., 1807.

Lucretia E. Warren, daughter of Argyle Taylor and Mary, his wife, departed this life the 8th day of Apr., 1815, in her 34th year of her life.

Margaret Tebbs departed this life Apr., 1819, in the 72nd year of her life.

Argyle Taylor, son of Lazarus Taylor, deceased, and Hannah, his wife, departed this life Jan. 8, 1826, in the 76th year of his age.

TAYLOR-SNYDER BIBLE.
(Donated by Mrs. Lola Linney Snyder)

Mary Taylor, consort of Argyle Taylor, departed this life Jan. 4, 1829, in the 79th year of her age.

William B. Taylor, son of Mary and Foushee Taylor, was born Apr. 5, 1812.

Harriott Taylor, daughter of John F. Taylor, deceased, and Ellen, his wife, was born the 1st day of Dec., 1797.

Lazarus Taylor, son of John F. and Ellen, was born the 21st day of Sept., 1799.

Grayson B. Taylor, son of John F. and Ellen, was born the 13th day of Oct., 1801.

Maryann K. Furr was born the 2nd day of Aug., 1806.

Argyle Wesley Furr was born the 18th day of Feb., 1810.

Meridith Furr, son of Stephen Furr and Artemesia (Taylor), his wife, was born the 2nd day of Nov., 1798.

Nancy Furr was born the 4th day of Nov., 1799.

Metilda Furr was born the 10th day of Jan., 1801.

Patsey Furr was born the 9th day of Oct., 1802.

Lucresia Furr was born the 7th day of Mch., 1804.

Woodford T. Furr was born the 3rd day of Dec., 1807.

Warren Emory Linney, son of Betty Davis Taylor Linney, and John H. Linney, died Feb. 7, 1896.

Lola Linney, daughter of Betty Davis Taylor Linney, and John H. Linney, married Claude Freeman Snyder Oct. 15, 1892.

Their children: Nadine Elizabeth Snyder (Bronston), Frances Warren Snyder, Claude F. Snyder, Jr.

Grandchildren of Lola and Claude F. Snyder and children of Nadine and William Bronston: Betty Taylor Bronston, Billy Bronston.

Eight Generations:
1. Betty Taylor and Billy Bronston.
2. Nadine, Frances Warren, Claude F. Snyder, Jr.
3. Lola Linney Snyder and Warren E. Linney.
4. Betty Davis Taylor Linney.
5. Grayson Bradford Taylor and Catherine Rice Taylor.
6. John F. Taylor and Ellen Taylor.
7. Argyle Taylor and Mary Taylor.
8. Lazarus Taylor and Hannah Taylor.

McCALLA THOMPSON BIBLE.
(Donated and Copied by Owner, Mrs. Amy Sands McNees Hedges, Lexington, Ky.)

McCalla Thompson was born Sept. 26, 1823.

Sarah Leonard Thompson, his wife, was born Sept. 21, 1829.

Robert William, son of McCalla and Sarah Leonard Thompson, was born Jan. 11, 1850.

Amy Sands, daughter of William T. and Sarah L. McNees, was born Feb. 3, 1867.

Lucy Finley, daughter of Wm. T. and Sarah L. McNees, was born Apr. 3, 1870.

McCalla Thompson died Nov. 25, 1852.

Robert William Thompson died Nov. 18, 1863.

William T. McNees died Apr. 11, 1901.

Sarah L. McNees died Jan. 4, 1919.

BIBLE OF BENJAMIN W. TALBOTT OF BOURBON CO., KY.
Now Owned by Granddaughter, Sarah Talbott Mastin, Lexintgon, Ky.
(Copied by Mrs. H. K. McAdams.)

Benjamin W. Talott was born Feb. 24, 1809; died Nov. 25, 1890; married Jan. 5, 1832.

Elizabeth Whaley, 1st wife of Benjamin W. Talbott, died Aug. 7, 1854.

Sarah Whaley of Harrison Co., Ky., sister of Elizabeth and 2nd wife of Benjamin Talbott, was born Sept. 27, 1820; died June 11, 1856; married June 11, 1854.

Louisa McConnell of Bourbon Co., 3rd wife of Benjamin W. Talbott, was married Dec. 2, 1856.

Ephrian W. Talbott was born Jan. 25, 1833; died May 3, 1911.

Nannie Jane Talbott, daughter of B. W. and Elizabeth Talbot, was born Jan. 15, 1835; married Nov. 27, 1855, to Richard Cheatam.

James H. Talbott was born Sept. 12, 1837.

COPIED FROM OLD TURNER BIBLE.

Barnett Turner and Nancy Taylor were married Nov. 13, 1814.

Mary Jane Turner was married Oct. 22, 1840.

Marcas A. Turner and Amelia Thistle were married Nov. 12, 1846.

Barnett Turner was born Sept. 30, 1790.

Nancy Turner, his wife, was born Aug. 2, 1798.

Talton T. Turner was born Sept. 15, 1815.

Marcas A. Turner was born Sept. 30, 1817.

Mary Jane Turner was born Sept. 30, 1820.

Curd Turner was born Dec. 30, 1822.

John Turner was born May 14, 1825.

Tabitha Turner was born Oct. 15, 1828.

William V. Turner was born Apr. 27, 1830.

John Turner died May 22, 1827.

Nancy Turner died Mch. 18, 1831.

Talton Turner, son of Barnett Turner, died Sept. 8, 1835.

Barnett Turner died Feb. 12, 1836.

Tabitha Turner died Nov. 10, 1855.

VEATCH OR VEACH.

Jeremiah Veatch died June 5, 1828.

David Veatch died Jan. 28, 1837.

Susan Dills died the 28th day of June, 1840.

Jane Huff, wife of Thomas Veatch, died Oct. 11, 1840.

Children of David Veatch:

Thomas Veatch died Sept. 19, 1842.

Emily was born the 29th of Sept., 1827.

Mary was born the 14th of June, 1829.

Sally was born the 4th day of Jan., 1831.

Charity was born July 9, 1833.

Nancy was born Oct., 8, 1836.

Mahala and John were born Mch. 13, 1843.

From an old Bible owned by Miss Edith Weld Peck, Covington, Ky. The Bible was owned and records kept by Thomas Veatch, born Apr. 19, 1770, and after his death in 1842 by his son, David.

With the exception of Sally Wilson, these are known to be the children of Thomas Veatch and Jane Huff Veatch. Sooky was known also as Susan.

Daniel Veatch was the brother of Thomas Veatch.

J. Veatch was born Mch. 27, 1794, and Cassy Ashbrook, his wife, was born Mch. 20, 1797.

My father, Thomas Veatch, and Jane Huff were married Sept. 30, 1790.

Jane Veach died 23rd of Dec., 1865.

J. Veatch, Jr., died June 11, 1829.

My granddaughter, Harkelena Rankin, died Mch. 29, 1847, in the 5th year of her age.

My daughter, Elizabeth Rankin, died Dec., 1851.

My daughter, Mary Lair, died Oct. 25, 1857; age 22.

Cassy Veatch, consort of Joseph Veatch, died May 7, 1876; age 79 years, 1 month, 15 days.

My father, Joseph Veach, departed this life on Tues., 5th day of June,

1849; aged 55 years.

My grandfather, John Veatch, died the 2nd day of Mch., 1820.
My grandmother, Sarah Veatch, died Sept. 10, 1821.
My brother, Peter Veatch, died Apr. 25, 1819.
My brother, David Veatch, died Jan. 28, 1837.
My sister, Susan Diltz, died June 28, 1840.
My beloved mother, Jane Huff, died Oct. 11, 1840.
My father, Thomas Veatch, died Sept. 19, 1842.
My borther-in-law, Samuel Diltz, died May 5, 1849.
Joseph Veatch and Cassy Ashbrook were married the 13th day of Feb., 1816.
F. G. Veach and America Moffett were married Dec. 27, 1846.
Elizabeth A. Veatch was born 5th day of May, 1818.
J. Veatch was born Feb. 20, 1821.
Felix Grundy Ashbrook Veatch was born 7th day of Oct., 1823.
Jane Veatch was born the 8th day of Oct., 1827.
Mary Brown Smith Veatch was born the 29th day of Oct., 1835.
Erasmus Darwin Veatch, son of Felix G. and A. Veatch, was born May 25, 1848.
My father, Thomas Veatch, was born Apr. 19, 1770.
My beloved mother, Jane Veatch, was born July 8. 1765.
Lewis Veach was born the 23rd day of Nov., 1804. Celebrated his 83rd birthday this 23rd day of Nov., 1887.

From an old Bible owned by Mrs. W. P. Hedges, Cynthiana, Ky.
The Bible was owned and records kept by Joseph Veatch, born Mch. 27, 1794, and after his death, in 1849, by his son.
Samuel Veatch was born June 25, 1791.
David Veatch was born Dec. 9, 1792.
Joseph Veatch was born Mch. 27, 1794.
Sarah Veatch was born Feb. 5, 1796.
Peter Veatch was born Nov. 20, 1797.
Sooky Veatch was born July 20, 1799.
Rebecca Veatch was born Aug. 25, 1801.
Lewis Veatch was born Nov. 23, 1804.
Betsy Hodge Veatch was born Sept. 17, 1806.
Sally Wilson was born Oct. 30, 1788; was maried Feb. 4, 1812.
Births of Daniel Veatch's children:
  Garrett—Aug. 12, 1803.
  Ambrose—Sept. 23, 1804.
  William—May 13, 1806.
  James—Dec. 1, 1807.
  Milton—Sept. 4, 1811.
  John—Jan. 28, 1813.
  Artemisa—Feb. 29, 1814.
  Jeremiah—Apr. 13, 1817.
Thomas Veatch was born Apr. 19, 1770; Jane Huff was born July 8, 1765; they were married Sept. 30, 1790.
Lewis Veatch died Dec. 18, 1891.
Peter Veatch died 25th of Apr., 1819, at New Orleans, aged 21 years, 5 months, 5 days.
My father, John Veatch, died on the 2nd day of Mch., 1820.
Sister Sarah Frazer died on the 10th day of Apr., 1820.
My mother, Sarah Veatch, departed this life on the 10th day of Sept., 1821.
Elizabeth Wilson died Dec. 20, 1854.

BIBLE OF STEPHEN P. WALLER.
Now Owned by Mrs. Laura Mitchell, Lexington, Ky.
(Copied by Mrs. J. W. Marr.)

Stephen P. Waller was born Apr. 17, 1812.

Fannie Barkley Waller, wife of Stephen P. Waller, was born Feb. 24, 1824.
Robert Barkley was born 1848.
Charlie Waller was born Sept. 18, 1856.
Laura Waller was born July 5, 1859.
John L. Waller was born June 28, 1862.
Anna May Waller was born Mch. 17, 1864.
Clarence Waller was born Sept. 8, 1866.
Mally Barkley was born Aug. 13, 1850.
Lizzie Barkley was born Dec. 18, 1852.
Charley Mitchell was born Oct. 17, 1756.

BIBLE OF JAMES WOOD.
Owned by Charles F. Wood of Red House, Madison Co., Ky.
(Copied by Mrs. Jos. Beard, Sr.)

James Wood and Elizabeth Willson were married Jan. 7, 1828, by
William White. Their children:
Amanda Wood—Born Oct. 9, 1829.
John Milton Wood—Born May, 8, 1831.
Elizabeth Wood—Born May 16, 1834.
James William Wood—Born Nov. 8, 1836.
Minerva Ann Wood—Born Feb. 25, 1841.
Marinda Jane Wood—Born Dec. 31, 1843.
Charles Franklin Wood—Born Oct. 17, 1846.
Cassius M. Wood—Born Mch. 22, 1851.
Thomas Dillard Wood—Born May 11, 1854.

WORTHINGTON BIBLE
(Donated by Mrs. Wm. Worthington, Lexington, Ky.)

John Worthington and Ann Sarah Luther (Louther) married Dec.
29, 1823.
Rachel Worthington and J. Allen Wade married Jan. 1, 1851.
Nancy Worthington and Joseph T. Burdett married May 3, 1854.
Finley Worthington and Ellen Savage married Sept. 17, ——.
John Worthington was born June 11, 1801.
Sarah Worthington was born May 7, 1801.
Nancy Worthington was born July 31, 1824.
Rachel Worthington was born July 26, 1826.
James D. Worthington was born May 10, 1828.
David L. Worthington was born Jan. 29, 1830.
William J. Worthington was born Nov. 9, 1832.
Finley Worthington was born Feb. 12, 1834.
Sarah Jane Worthington was born Nov. 3, 1838.
Mary Hannah Worthington was born Nov. 9, 1841.
Charles Worthington was born Sept. 17, 1843.
John Worthington died Nov. 28, 1864 in the 63rd year of his age.
Sarah Jane Worthington died Jan. 1, 1864, in her 26th year.
Ellen Worthington died Aug. 10, 1859.
Mary Hannah Worthington, wife of George Guilkerson, died March
4, 1866; aged 25 years.
Grandmother Sarah Luther died Sept. 2, ——; aged 77 yrs., 4 months.
Grandfather David Luther died Sept. 18, ——; aged 77 yrs., 3 days.

EXTRACTS FROM FUNERAL INVITATIONS

In the Lexington Public Library, there is a large book, pasted full of
Funeral Notices. The inscription in the front of the book reads:
These Funeral Notices were collected by an honest colored man, named
Cyrus Parker Jones who, at his death, bequeathed them to J. M. Duff,

who now donates them to the Lexington Library Company, of Lexington, Ky., this January 1st, 1900. (Note: The object of giving these notices is to show family relationship—therefore I have omitted "You and your family are invited to attend the funeral of————— from his late residence, at 3 o'clock; burial will take place in Lexington cemetery." I only give name and date and the reference to other relatives. All are from Lexington, unless dated otherwise.)

Innes Skillman, infant son of Alex H. and Kate Adams,, from the residence of Mrs. C. A. Innes. July 23, 1868.

Mr. John Abbott, member of The Sons of Temperance * * * Mch. 1, 1849.

William McLean, son of Rev. S. L. and Mary J. Adams. Sept. 2, 1857.

Mrs. Ann Allan. Burial in cemetery at Winchester, Ky. June 18, 1869.

Harrie Bowman Allen, son of John G. and Sarah Emmal Allen, at residence of his grandfather, W. B. Emmal. May 20, 1873.

Mrs. Elenora E. Allen. April 24, 1873.

John P. Allen, Jr., tomorrow at South Elkhorn church. Jan. 12, 1871.

Mrs. Polly Allen. Sept. 27, 1876.

Miss Georgeann Anderson, at residence of her father, Mr. Reuben Anderson, Fayette county. Oct. 11, 1845.

Reuben Anderson. Sept. 26, 1850.

M. R. Armant. July 5, 1866.

Mrs. Mary Ashton. July 3, 1822.

Margaret, infant daughter of William Ashton. Sept. 5, 1842.

Thomas Richard, infant son of Jacob Ashton. Sept. 24, 1825.

Eddy, infant son of W. G. and Annie Bain. Apr. 8, 1868.

Patterson Bain, son of Capt. P. Bain. June 11, 1820.

Mr. Patterson Bain. June 8, 1846.

Mrs. Mary Baker, consort of Mr. Jehu Baker. Apr. 16, 1826.

Edmund Barr. Jan. 29, 1873.

Amelia P. Barr, wife of Samuel Barr. June 7, 1872.

Lewis Reese, infant son of Dr. H. B. Bascom. Jan. 6, 1846.

Archie, infant son of H. C. and Lou Bedford. Oct. 2, 1871.

Mr. David Bell; residence of his son, Dr. D. Bell. Nov. 29, 1848.

Mrs. Judah Bell. Oct. 8, 1849.

Louellen, son of Mr. Henry Bell. May 23, 1849.

A. E. Berry. Nov. 27, 1872.

Mrs. Anna M. Berry, wife of John T. Berry; residence of Col. Lewis A. Berry. March 5, 1868.

Dr. Robert Best. Sept. 29, 1830.

Mr. Joseph Biggs, Jr., July 18, 1849.

Joseph Biggs. March 28, 1868.

Albert R. Biggerstaff; residence of his grandfather, John Holland. Oct. 15, 1874.

Charles H. Biggerstaff; residence of his grandfather, John Holland. Oct. 11, 1872.

Mrs. Nancy Bishop; at the house of Mr. Purnell Bishop. Mch. 31, 1827.

Maggie Hunter Bissicks, daughter of Frank and Julia Bissicks. Feb. 20, 1869.

Mr. Neville Blackemore; from the late residence of Joseph Craig, deceased; Fayette county. Aug. 14, 1848.

A. Edward Blythe, eldest son of Rev. James Blythe. Feb. 26, 1823.

Horace C. Boardman, infant child of H. B. and M. E. Boardman. Dec. 31, 1868.

Mrs. Catherine H. Bodley; residence of her son, Harry I. Bodley. June 25, 1841.

Charles F. Bodley. Oct. 13, 1869.

Mrs. E. L. Bondurant. June 16, 1870.

Joseph Bondurant. May 1, 1868.

Mrs. Ann Mary Boyer; residence of William Van Pelt, Sr. March 6, 1846.

Mr. Benijah Bosworth. Nov. 17, 1849.

Mr. John Boswell; house of Dr. Joseph Boswell. Apr. 19, 1818.

Funeral of Mr. Joseph Bosworth. Apr. 25, 1822.

Mrs. Mary Boswell, consort of Mr. George Boswell, at the residence of R. Keen, Esq. Apr. 22, 1829.

Mrs. Sarah Bosworth; residence of Mr. Benjamin Bosworth. Feb. 23, 1823.

Mr. Robert Boyd; residence of Mrs. Webster. June 17, 1849.

Mrs. Elizabeth Bradford, relict of the late John Bradford, Esq.; residence of her son, Daniel Bradford. Oct. 12, 1833.

Miss Ellen Ross Bradford; residence of her father, Daniel Bradford, Esq. May 31, 1850.

John Bradford. March 22, 1830.

John V. Bradford; residence of his grandfather, John Bradford. Aug. 21, 1824.

Miss Maria Bradford; house of her grandfather, John Bradford. May 1, 1827.

Mr. James L. Bradley. July 2, 1864.

Willie Desha, infant son of J. and Margaret A. Bradley. Oct. 22, 1869.

Mr. William M. Brand. Nov. 23, 1845.

Margaret Brashear, infant daughter of Dr. Walter Brashear. Feb. 7, 1817.

John R. Breckinridge. Apr. 13, 1874.

Robert J., son of Joseph C. and L. D. Breckinridge. Aug. 11, 1871.

Rev. Dr. Robert J. Breckinridge. Dec. 29, 1871.

Mrs. Sarah Brennan; residence of her husband, Mr. John Brennan. July 1, 1828.

Mr. Richard Brent; Masonic Lodge No. 1. Jan. 3, 1850.

Mr. Elisha, Bridges. Dec. 27, 1836. "The Citizens Volunteer Artillery Company."

Mr. Thomas Bridges, eldest son of Mr. John Bridges. Mch. 15, 1824.

Henry S. Briggs. Nov. 7, 1828.

Miss Henrietta Browning; residence of mother, Mrs. Mary Browning. Feb. 21, 1870.

Mrs. Margaret Ross Bruce. July 25, 1868.

Andrew Jackson, infant son of Joseph Bruen. Sept. 9, 1826. (Note: Below written in ink, "Born May 16, 1825.")

Mrs. Kate Bryan, wife of Massie Bryan; residence of her father, A. Headley. Aug. 5, 1868.

Mrs. Mary A. Bryant, daughter of P. B. and Mattie L. Bryant. Oct. 18, 1877.

Robert Callin Bullock. July 14, 1866.

Mr. Samuel R. Bullock. Masonic Fraternity invited. July 13, 1849.

Mrs. Nancy Bunnell, wife of Mr. Jesse Bunnell. Aug. 29, 1825.

Mrs. Mary M. Burrowes. July 5, 1845.

Smith Burton; residence of Mr. Jabez Beach. The I. O. O. F. and Sons of Temperance will attend. July 20, 1849.

Dr. James M. Bush. Feb. 8, 1875.

Mary Charlotte, daughter of Capt. James Butler. Aug. 14, 1868.

Mr. Abraham Cadmus, Jr.; from the residence of Mr. James Hedenberg. Aug. 21, 1828.

Mrs. Jane Caldwell; residence of her husband, Mr. John Caldwell. July 3, 1828.

Mrs. Celeste F. Candy, consort of Mr. John Candy; residence of her mother, Mrs. Jane B. Robert. Jan. 19, 1849.

Mr. William H. Carpenter; residence of his aunt, Mrs. Dunlap. The members of the Lyon Fire Co. to attend. May 22, 1851.

Charles D., infant son of C. D. and M. B. Carr. Aug. 18, 1863.

Mrs. Elizabeth Todd Carr, wife of Mr. Charles Carr. Oct. 31, 1863.

Lunceford Carr; residence of hisfather, D. T. Carr, at Chilesburg. Oct. 5, 1871.

Obadiah Carter; house of Spencer Alsop. July 28, 1820.

William Travis Cave, infant son of R. C. and Fanny D. Cave. Jan. 8, 1873.

Mrs. Edward Ann, wife of Mr. H. W. Chiles. May 14, 1869.

Mrs. Elizabeth Chiles, relict of the late Gen. John G. Chiles. Jan. 19, 1863.

Juretta W. Chinn, wife of Dr. J. G. Chinn. Apr. 5, 1871.

Mrs. Lucy Chinn, wife of A. B. Chinn; residence of E. S. Duncanson. May 27, 1869.

Andrew L. Chisham. July 30, 1849.

Mrs. Elizabeth Christian. Apr. 6, 1871.

N. S. Chiles, from Christ Church. Dec. 21, 1871.

Ezekiel T., infant son of William B. Christie; residence of J. S. Freeman. Sept 10, 1833.

Mr. Edward Church; residence of Mrs. Dunham. Apr. 23, 1845.

Mrs. Fannie T. Clark, wife of John S. Clark. Jan. 25, 1875.

Mrs. Mary Clarke, wife of Mr. Allen H. Clark. Oct. 25, 1851.

Wm. J. Clark; residence of his son, Joseph Clark. Dec. 15, 1868.

John C. J. Clay. Sept. 18, 1872.

Mr. Thomas Clay. Mch. 19, 1871.

Mr. John Hanley Cleary, 2nd son of John R. Cleary. Sept. 28, 1846.

Mrs. Mary E. Cleary; residence of her husband, John R. Cleary. Aug. 81, 1872.

Departed this life on the 2nd inst., Mrs. Sarah Clifford, in the 71st year of her age. Nov. 3, 1820.

Mrs. Sarah Jane Cochran; residence of her father, Mr. James Hamilton. Sept. 28, 1848.

Eleanora, daughter of Mr. Philip Coffman. July 10, 1829.

George S. Coleman, son of D. S. Coleman. June 26, 1873.

Mr. John Adamson Coleman, eldest son of Alexander M. and Eliza Dunn; residence of Mr. Lindsay Coleman. Aug. 13, 1826.

Samuel M. Coleman; residence of John McCauley. Jan. 5, 1870.

Mr. Daniel Comstock, formerly of Providence, R. I.; residence of N. S. Porter. Apr. 7, 1814.

William Conklin; residence of D. A. Sayre, Esq. Dec. 20, 1851.

Mr. Walter Connell. May 15, 1825.

John, infant son of Mr. Isaac Cook. Aug. 10, 1848.

Mrs. Lucinda Cook; residence of Isiah King. Jan. 14, 1870.

Mr. Charles Coolidge. Aug. 6, 1847.

Mr. George Coons, Sr. Mch. 1, 1827.

Hettie R. Corbin, daughter of John and Martha Corbin. June 16, 1871.

Mr. David Cowan; house of Charles Humphreys, Esq. Aug. 13, 1823.

James Cox; residence of his brother, Thornton Cox. Sept. 28, 1850.

Elijah W. Craig, Jr.; residence of his father, James Craig. May 7, 1846.

John A. Craig, Esq. Feb. 20, 1864.

Mrs. Mary Craig. Aug. 30, 1850.

Richard Deering Craig; residence of his father, Mr. Parker Craig. May 11, 1849.

Charles H. Cravens. June 18, 1873.

George Crittendon. Apr. 5, 1875.

Eddie Crockett, infant son of T. G. and Emma Crockett, at residence of Mr. Robert Long. Feb. 18, 1869.

Mrs. Priscilla Cromie. Nov. 9, 1878.

Mrs. Cloe Ann Cromwell, relict of the late Robert Cromwell. Dec. 14, 1847.

Edward Cronly. July 19, 1871.

Sally Madge, infant daughter of Edward and Sarah B. Cronley; residence of Mrs. Wilson. Aug. 31, 1864.

Mr. Christopher Crowe. Oct. 7, 1822.

Mrs. Elenor H. Curd. June 20, 1868.

John Curd, Sr. Feb. 9, 1876.

Mrs. John G. Daby; residence of T. W. White. May 1, 1873.

Mrs. Lou Darnaby. June 7, 1867.

Mr. Thomas Darrach, of Philadelphia, from the house of Mr. Joshua Wilson. Dec. 2, 1808.

Mr. Allen Davis. Nov. 7, 1825.

Lucy J. Davis, infant daughter of Mr. Allen Davis. Sept. 17, 1822.

Lucy, infant daughter of William P. and Elizabeth P. Davis. May 2, 1851.

Martha Ann, infant daughter of Mr. L. T. Davidson. Nov. 15, 1845.

Edward Francis Delph, son of J. E. Delph. Feb. 25, 1871.

Ida May, infant daughter of Rudolph and Jane de Roode. Feb. 23, 1869.

Capt. James Devers. Aug. 26, 1848.

Mrs. Elizabeth Dickinson, wife of Mr. Thomas I. Dickinson. Sept. 13, 1822.

Mrs. Pamelia Dillard; residence of her husband, Rev. Dr. J. T. Dillard. Feb. 24, 1874.

Sophie, infant daughter of Rev. Wm. and Emily A. Dinwiddie. July 8, 1870.

John Johnson; residence of Mr. Thomas B. Megowan. Mch. 20, 1829.

Thomas Dougherty, Esq.; residence of Robert Tilford. Aug. 10, 1822.

Col. A. S. Drake. Sept. 8, 1831.

Miss Hannah Drake; residence of her father, Abr'm S. Drake. Aug. 12, 1871.

Mrs. Hannah Drake. Dec. 15, 1869.

Mrs. Mary A. Drake; residence of Mrs. Chevis. Mch. 13, 1863.

Mrs. Julia Driggs. June 25, 1868.

Mr. David Duck. The Sons of Temperance to attend. Jan. 20, 1849.

Edward W. Dowden; residence of his son, M. S. Dowden. The I. O. O. F. and the Masonic Fraternity to attend. May 7, 1867.

Miss Elizabeth Dowden, age 22 years, daughter of the late Edward W. Dowden. Oct. 24, 1868.

Ernest Clare, age 3 years, 11 months, son of M. S. and Julia A. Dowden. Mch. 7, 1868.

Jeanna, age 7 months, 14 days, infant daughter of Wm. A. and Hullie Dowden. Feb. 27, 1868.

Mrs. Mary Elizabeth Dowden; residence of her husband, E. W. Dowden. Feb. 19, 1850.

Mrs. Mary Dowden, consort of William Dowden. Apr. 22, 1844.

Maj. W. W. Dowden. Members of the I. O. O. F. are invited to attend. (Note: No year date given.)

Major W. S. Downey. Jan. 31, 1868.

John Allen, son of Marcus Downing, Fayette County. Oct. 14, 1851.

Richard Downing, Sr. Feb. 16, 1870.

William Ater Dudley, son of David and (torn paper); residence of Mr. William W. Ater. May 1, 1852.

William Ambrose Dudley. Mch. 21, 1870.

Dr. Benjamin Winslow Dudley. Jan. 30, 1870.

Mrs. Margaret Dudley, wife of Charles Wilkins Dudley; residence of Dr. B. W. Dudley. Aug. 28, 1863.

Mr. J. M. Duff, at Duff Chapel, Campbell-Hagerman College. The Library will be closed on Friday from 1 o'clock to 5 o'clock. Mch. 30, 1911.

Eliza Duncan; residence of her father, H. H. Timberlake. Jan. 9, 1844.

David Dunlop. May 20, 1845.

Mr. Clement R. Dunkin. Feb. 10, 1831.

Robert Eagle. April 19, 1873.

Philip B. Edge. May 27, 1875.

Mr. William W. Edge. Feb. 21, 1865.

Julia, infant daughter of Mr. N. W. Edwards, at the house of Mrs. Parker. Oct. 2, 1836.

Mrs. Margaret Elder, mother of Mathew Elder. Mch. 24, 1814.

Thomas Wood, infant son of H. C. and R. E. Elder. June 9, 1871.

Mrs. Catherine Jane Ellis, at the residence of Mrs. Casey. Feb. 24, 1846.
Wyatt B. Embry, at the residence of Mathias Outten. May 19, 1866.
Alice Dudley; residence of her father, Mr. Wm. D. Emmal. Sept. 6, 1854.
Mrs. Mary Erd, wife of Frank I. Erd. Aug. 25, 1869.
Ellen Ross, infant daughter of John and Frances Estess. Aug. 25, 1846.
Mr. James Estill. July 30, 1849.
Emma Jane Evans; residence of her father, Joseph Evans. June 20, 1850.
Lillie Farra, daughter of B. F. and Sallie Farra. July 19, 1875.
Mrs. Margaret Farar, wife of Samuel Farar. Feb. 18, 1875.
Jennie, daughter of William and Sarah Farley. Nov. 9, 1868.
Mrs. Sarah Farley, wife of William Farley. Oct. 29, 1872.
Mrs. P. L. Ficklin; residence of her husband, Mr. Joseph Ficklin. Aug. 17, 1849.
Mrs. Sarah B. Fisher; residence of John Little. May 1, 1867.
Julia W. Fitch, wife of Fred Fitch. June 9, 1866.
Capt. Samuel Fitch. Lexington Lodge No. 1, Daviess and Nelson Lodge No. 22 will attend. Feb. 27, 1846.
Mr. Robert Fleming. Feb. 16, 1842.
Mrs. Fleming; residence of her husband, Mr. William R. Fleming. Apr. 7, 1863.
Richard Loud, infant son of J. H. and Ida L. Floore, from the residence of the late R. Loud. Sr. July 1, 1871.
Mrs. E. J. Flournoy. Jan. 22, 1875.
Mr. William Flower; house of Mr. Charles Edwards. Nov. 13, 1818.
Mary Gertrude; residence of her father, Mr. Caleb W. Ford. Apr. 1, 1852.
Annie E. Foreman, wife of Thomas Foreman. May 15, 1873.
Eld. Henry Foster. Dec. 11, 1868.
William H. Fox. Members of the Masonic Fraternity will attend. Oct. 20, 1866.
Chris A. Frazer. Mch. 13, 1866.
Joshua Frost. Feb. 23, 1875.
Thomas C. Fry; residence of E. Douglas. Dec. 27, 1869.
Mr. Benjamin Futhey. Jan. 26, 1823.
Capt. Aston Garrett; residence of Capt. John Fowler. Members of Daviess Lodge will attend. Apr. 12, 1834.
Frank George; residence of his father, Mr. Joseph George. May 22, 1866.
Catherine, 2nd daughter of Joseph George. Dec. 16, 1848.
Mr. William Gibbons. July 9, 1825.
Mrs. Mary Gibney; residence of her husband, Mr. Alexander Gibney. Apr. 6, 1850.
Thomas Gibson. Feb. 12, 1872.
James Gilbert. June 17, 1830.
Ellen B. Gillispie, wife of Dr. Benjamin Gillispie, at the residence of her father, Dr. Bell. Aug. 20, 1870.
Mrs. N. A. Gilmore; residence of her husband, Andrew Gilmore. Mch. 11, 1873.
William D. Gilmore. Aug. 8, 1871.
J. Thompson Glass; residence of his father, Mr. David Glass. Aug. 14, 1852.
Belle Sheridan Goodloe, infant daughter of Speed S. and Mary Shreve Goodloe. June 12, 1866.
Mrs. S. A. L. C. Goodloe, wife of D. S. Goodloe. Sept. 28. (No year date given.)
Judge Speed S. Goodloe. May 19, 1877.
Mrs. V. A. Goodloe, wife of W. O. Goodloe, at the residence of her father, Dr. John B Payne. June 16 . (No year date given.)
Judge W. C. Goodloe. Aug. 15, 1870.
Mrs. Mary Grant; from the residence of her sister, Mrs. M'Cullough.

Apr. 2, 1829.

George W. Graves; residence of Dr. John P. Henry. Nov. 1, 1864.

Mr. Richmond Graves. 21st ——, 1852. (Note: Month not given.)

Spencer C. Graves. May 20, 1868.

First Lieut. W. B. Gwynne, from Pheonix Hotel. Feb. 21, 1865.

Mrs. Nancy Hait; residence of Mr. John Estis. May 7 (no year).

Mr. James Hamilton. Feb. 26, 1866.

John W. Hamilton; residence of his brother-in-law, George Stoll, Jr. Sept. 2, 1867.

George Hampton, Jr., infant son of George Hampton. Aug. 16, 1825.

Nannie Mildred, infant daughter of Benj. F. and Mary T. Hardesty. Aug. 13, 1869.

Mr. Joseph Harkins, at the house of Isiah Martin. Jan. 12, 1813.

James A. Harper; residence of C. Y .Bean. Feb. 4, 1878.

Mrs. Ann M. Harrison; residence of her husband, Mr. Thomas J. Harrison. Feb. 14, 1844.

Miss Mary E. Harrison; residence of her brother, S. B. Harrison. June 22, 1870.

Thomas J. Harrison. 27th inst. (no year).

Thomas Hart, Jr.; residence of Mrs. Susan Hart. Sept. 1, 1826.

Mr. E. S. Hastings; residence of his father-in-law, Mr. Thomas B. Megowan. Apr. 12, 1849.

Mary H. Haun, from the residence of Capt. O. P. Beard. The 26th (no year).

Amanda Hawkins; house of her father, Mr. A. F. Hawkins. Aug. 6, 1837.

Mrs. Mary Hawkins and daughter, from the residence of her father. Theo. Tibbaits. Apr. 17, 1823.

Dr. Parry Hawkins, from the residence of his father-in-law, Mr. Thomas Tibbaits. June 7, 1822.

Mrs. Elizabeth Hawks, at the residence of Mr. A. Gaunt. Nov. 11, 1832.

Mr. John W. Hayes, at the residence of his father, T. T. Hayes. Aug. 16, 1862.

Joseph B. Hayes, son of R. A. Hayes. Oct. 18, 1872.

Dr. Robert L. Hayes; residence of his father, Thomas T. Hayes. June 27, 1873.

D. B. Hyman; residence of his brother, J. Q. A. Hayman. Apr. 24, 1869.

Judge Nicholas Headington. Aug. 6, 1870.

Gertrude, infant daughter of A. F. and Sarah E. Heman. Jan. 18, 1871.

Henry C. Hemingway. Oct. 26, 1872.

Mrs. Jane Hemingway; residence of Mr. George Wooley. Apr. 23, 1877.

Thomas Hemingway. June 6, 1872.

James H. Henderson. Jan. 25, 1872.

Mr. James W. Henderson. Nov. 3, 1864.

Thaddeus Henderson. July 22, 1868.

Mrs. Patsey Henly, wife of Mr. Osburn Henley. Aug. 2, 1821.

Capt. James Heran, from house of Mr. Patrick Shields. Aug. 13, 1821.

S. G. Herndon. May 31, 1868.

Mrs. Ann Hewitt. June 5, 1869.

William Hewitt, from the house of his uncle, John M. Hewitt. June 17, 1827.

Rev. John M. Hewitt. Feb. 3, 1851.

Capt. Robert B. Hickman, at Odd Fellows Hall. Jan. 31, 1863.

Mrs. Ellen Higgins, wife of Joel Higgins. May 29, 1875.

Mrs. Laura Higgins, wife of Wilmott R. Higgins. June 15, 1869.

Mrs. P. A. Higgins, at the residence of her husband, W. K. Higgins. June 10, 1869.

Richard Higgins. Oct. 17, 1868.

William M. Higgins; residence of John Allen Higgins. Aug. 12, 1870.

A. P. Hill, youngest daughter of Mrs. Kitty G. Hill. Apr. 4, 1868.

Jerome Morton Hill, infant son of Stephen G. and Jennie B. Sharp. Apr. 7, 1868.

Mrs. Harriet Holmes. Mch. 19, 1851.

Mr. John Holmes. Oct. 21, 1850.

Mrs. Eleanor Hood. Sept. 16, 1872. (Note: Eleanor Davis, married 1st Joseph McAdams; 2nd, Hood.)

Mr. Joseph L. Hopper. June 22, 1849. The members of Transylvania Division Sons of Temperance * * * attend.

John B. Hostetter; residence of his brother, Jacob Hostetter. Mch. 11, 1867.

Susan Frances, infant daughter of Jacob Hostetter. July 14, 1846.

Gibson G. Hough, infant son of Mr. Daniel Hough, from the residence of Mrs. Wigglesworth. Sept. 6, 1822.

W. C. Houghton. Oct. 8, 1866.

Mr. Peter Hull. Members of the Light Infantry * * * attend. July 15, 1827.

Fannie Humbert, consort of Zelime Humbert. Nov. 15, 1826.

Charles Humphreys, Esq. Oct. 3, 1830.

James Humphreys, from the residence of Mrs. Margaret Williams. Sept. 22, 1826.

Mr. Joshua Humphreys. Nov. 24, 1823.

Mrs. S. Humphreys, at the house of Mr. Charles Humphreys. Mch. 24, 1824.

Mr. William Humphreys, from the dwelling of his father, Charles Humphreys, Esq. June 2, 1826.

Dudley Craig, son of Allie G. and Mollie A. Hunt. Jan. 24, 1870.

G. Drummond Hunt, late Adjutant of 3rd Ky. Volunteers. Dec. 25, 1863.

Mr. John Hunt. Aug. 22, 1849.

John W. Hunt, infant son of Charlton Hunt. Aug. 17, 1829.

Mrs. Margaret A. Hunter, from the residence of her husband, J. J. Hunter. June 21, 1870.

Shelton, son of John H. and Augusta Hunter. July 19, 1850.

Thomas Hunter, at W. H. Lusbys'. Feb. 28, 1873.

Mrs. Ann J. Hurst, from the residence of her brother, Mr. C. I. Bodley. Apr. 4, 1853.

Milton, infant son of John Hurst. Aug. 30, 1825.

James B. Houston, from the house of William Houston. Dec. 1, 1817.

Mrs. Jane Houston, from the house of Robert Houston. June 4, 1818.

Joseph Ingels, from the residence of Waller S. Payne. Aug. 11, 1868.

Mr. James Irwin, from his late residence, to the New Cemetery, this Monday evening. June 2, 1851.

Mrs. Elizabeth Jackson. May 18, 1852.

George T. Jackson. Oct. 14, 1870.

Israel Jackson, at the residence of his father, Samuel G. Jackson. Mch. 9, 1852.

Miss Mary January, daughter of Thomas January, Dec'd. Nov. 9, 1825.

Mr. Thomas January. Jan. 27, 1825.

Mr. Henry Jarvis. Apr. 29, 1825.

Darwin W. Johnson, Esq., at the residence of his brother-in-law, Hon. James B. Clay. Oct. 27, 1862.

Mrs. George W. Johnson. Georgetown, Ky. Aug. 9, 1875.

John B. Johnson. Mch. 30, 1875.

Mrs. Sallie A. Johnson. June 10, 1874.

Mrs. Pauline B. Jones, at the residence of her son-in-law, B. T. Watkins. Feb. 7, 1875.

Mrs. Sue W. Joplin, at the residence of her father, G. W. Adams. June 24, 1873.

Mr. Mathew H. Jouett, at the residence of Mrs. Allen. Aug. 11, 1827.

Sue Anna Karsner, from the residence of her father, A. G. Karsner. Dec. 22 (no year).

Miss Ada Eliza Keen, from the residence of her father, G. F. Keen.

Dec. 15, 1849.

Elizabeth M. Keen, daughter of Francis J. and Elizabeth W. Keen, dec'd; from the residence of her grandfather, Mr. A. Legrand. June 15, 1848.

Mrs. Elizabeth W., consort of Francis J. Keen, Esq.; from the residence of Richard Higgins, Esq. Aug. 3, 1846.

Mrs. Sarah Keen, from the house of her husband, Oliver Keen, in Lex. Jan. 23, 1824.

Mrs. Ann Catherine, wife of Mr. Benjamin Keiser. Sept. 25, 1829.

Susan Elizabeth, infant daughter of Mr. Benjamin E. Keiser. June 22, 1826.

Ezekiel Kelly. The members of I. O. O. F. will attend. Mch. 24, 1868.

Harry L. Kemp, son of Mrs. Anna Kemp. Mch. 6, 1866.

S. P. Kenney. June 18, 1878.

Mr. Robert A. Kersey. Mch. 23, 1857.

Augustus Kidd, at the residence of Augustus Clark. May 10, 1871

Forrest, infant son of John W. and Ella Kidd. June 13, 1872.

Henry W. King, son of W. and E. King. Aug. 12, 1864.

Mr. James Madison Kidd. Apr. 24, 1851.

Mr. John Lafon. May 24, 1848.

Mrs. Mary V. Lauckart. Mch. 15, 1876.

Walker Lawless, from the residence of his father, Richard Lawless. Apr. 2, 1851.

John Harry Lee, at the residence of his father, John W. Lee. Jan. 30, 1867.

John W. Lee and his wife, Frances M. Lee. The members of Merrick Lodge No. 31, I. O. O. F., will attend. Feb. 17, 1869.

Mr. Reuben Lee, from the residence of his son, Isaac Lee. Jan. 10, 1853.

Mrs. A. Le Grand, at the residence of her son-in-law, T. H. Gillis. July 29, 1859.

Mr. James Lemon. Apr. 28, 1832.

George R. Letcher. Jan. 22, 1875.

Dr. Samuel Letcher. The Odd Fellows to attend. Feb. 4, 1863.

Mrs. Elvina Lewis, at residence of G. W. Morgan. Oct. 18, 1865.

Dr. Samuel L. Lewis, of Alabama, from the residence of his father, S. Higgins Lewis. Sept. 16, 1868.

Mr. Samuel B. Lewis. The Sons of Temperance to attend. Aug. 31, 1850.

John Adam Link, from the residence of his father, William R. Link. Mch. 17, 1850.

Samuel H. Lisle, at the residence of his father, Rufus Lisle. Feb. 21, 1876.

Mr. James Little, from the Farmers' and Traders' Hotel. Dec. 27, 1845.

Elizabeth, daughter of Henry and Sarah Lockhart. Nov. 19, 1850.

Mrs. Judith Logan, from the residence of her husband, Mr. Joseph Logan. Dec. 7, 1825.

Mr. Samuel Long. July 19, 1851.

William, infant son of Robert Long. June 28, 1845.

Richard Loud. Feb. 24, 1866.

Mr. John W. Lovejoy, from the residence of Charles T. Messick. Apr. 20, 1844.

Mr. William Lovejoy, at the residence of his grandmother. Nov. 12, 1844. The Hickory Artillery will attend the funeral.

Mrs. Mary Lowman, consort of John Lowman. July 8, 1826.

J. L. Lundin. May 24, 1876.

Samuel Lusk. Nicholasville, Ky. Apr. 20, 1873.

Emma Lyle, daughter of Joel K. and Maria C. Lyle. * * * Paris Cemetery at 3 p. m. Apr. 28, 1864.

Caroline, infant daughter of Mr. E. Lynch. July 14, 1826.

Mrs. Catherine Macbean, from the house of Mr. William Macbean. May 24, 1824.

Miss Margaret Macbean. July 29, 1834.
Benjamin F. McCardy, at the residence of his father, J. J. McCardy. May 19, 1874.
Miss Eliza J. McCardy. Jan. 27, 1875.
Miss Pauline McCaw, at the residence of her father, John McCaw. Oct. 9, 1876.
Mrs. Rebecca M'Chesney, consort of Mr. William M'Chesney; from the house of her father, Mr. Richard Ashton. July 14, 1825.
Mrs. Ann McClain, consort of Mr. Joseph McClain; at the house of Mr. James Wilson. Mch. 30, 1816.
Asa McConathy, Sr. Nov. 17, 1872.
David Phillips McConathy, from the residence of his father, Mr. H. McConathy. Apr. 19, 1849.
Mrs. Adelaide W. McConnell, from the residence of H. Lancaster. Aug. 23, 1865.
Mrs. Sallie A. McCoy, wife of W. W. McCoy; at the residence of R. McMichael. Dec. 13, 1873.
David, infant son of John McCracken. July 17, 1825.
S. D. McCullough. Jan. 14, 1873.
William Alexander, infant son of Thomas M'Quat. Sept. 11, 1826.
Mrs. Jennie E. McMeekin, wife of Mr. John McMeekin; from the residence of her father, Jeremiah McMeekin. Mch. 24 (no year date).
Dr. A. F. McMillan. June 16, 1870.
Mrs. Lucretia E. McMillan. Nov. 17, 1870.
Mrs. Louisiana McMurray, from the residence of her father, the Rev. Dr. Cloud. July 30, 1831.
Mrs. Jane McNair. July 16, 1825.
Mr. John W. M'Nitt, from the house of his father, Mr. Robert M'Nitt. June 29, 1831.
Mrs. Sophia Malone, wife of Rev. T. R. Malone; from the residence of Mr. James March. Jan. 31, 1844.
Mrs. Catherine March, from the residence of her daughter, Mrs. Emma Shaw. May 18, 1870.
Edward March, from the residence of his father, Mr. James March. June 20, 1849.
Mrs. Elenora March. Oct. 12, 1849.
Mr. John March, from his residence on Spring St., near that of Charles Humphreys, Esq. July 8, 1824.
Mrs. Nancy Markey. July 5, 1849.
Hon. Thomas A. Marshall. Apr. 18, 1871.
Mr. David Martin, from the residence of Mrs. Elizabeth R. Parker. Oct. 12, 1823.
Mrs. Ann Matheny, from the house of Dr. Thomas Satterwhite. July 22, 1824.
William C. May. Jan. 21, 1870.
Mr. William Medcalf. Jan. 23, 1853.
Mr. Patrick Meehan, from Megowan's Hotel. The members of the Lyon Fire Co. to attend. Oct. 2, 1851.
Annie, daughter of Lucretia and Louis Meglone. Dec. 5, 1862.
Prest. Robert Milligan. Mch. 21, 1875.
Mr. Christopher Misner. July 9, 1822.
Doct. Alexander J. Mitchell, at the residence of Mrs. Allen. July 27, 1822.
Mrs. Cordelia F. Mitchell, from the residence of her mother, Mrs. Mary Oots. Dec. 19, 1871.
Leonard Mitchell, son of T. D. and V. Mitchell, from the residence of Mrs. Leonard Taylor. Jan. 28, 1871.
Mrs. Ellen Norah Mixer, from the residence of Mr. Thomas B. McGowan. July 29, 1849.
Martha Montgomery, relict of the late Major W. Montgomery; from the residence of her son-in-law, Dr. J. B. Payne. July 5, 1870.

F. Montmollin, Jr. Dec. 31, 1871.

Mrs. Montmollin. June 11, 1874.

Mrs. Virginia Mooney, at the residence of her husband, C. E. Mooney. May 27, 1866.

Alex Moore. Apr. 13, 1871.

Mrs. Sarah Allen Moore, wife of D. T. Moore. May 2, 1872.

The body of Bro. Gen. John H. Morgan, late a member of Daviess Lodge No. 22, will arrive in this city this morning. The Masonic Fraternity are invited. Apr. 17, 1868.

Miss Sallie H. Morgan. Mch. 13, 1862.

Capt. Samuel D. Morgan and Lieut. Green Roberts, at residence of Mrs. Henrietta Morgan. Sept. 30, 1862.

Mrs. M. B. Morehead, at the residence of her son, Dr. Thomas W. Foster. July 14, 1869.

Mr. Richieson Morrison, from the residence of his brother, Mr. M. B. Morrison. July 14, 1852.

Mrs. Elizabeth H. Morton. Mch. 31, 1862.

Mrs. Mary, consort of George W. Mor—n (torn corner). May 23, 1826.

E. S. Muir. Apr. 10, 1901.

Mrs. Mary Muir, from the residence of her husband, William Muir. Sept. 13 (no year).

Mr. James Neal. The Lexington Light Infantry will attend. Oct. 26, 1824.

Mr. John C. Newcomb, from the residence of Mr. James W. Cochran. Jan. 21, 1862.

Mrs. Mary Nichols. July 1, 1806.

Mary Dewees Norris. July 25, 1867.

Mr. Guy Norris, from the residence of Major Fishel. Feb. 18, 1829.

Mr. Stephen P. Norton. Apr. 15, 1828.

William H. Norton, from the residence of George W. Norton. Apr. 1, 1871.

John R. Nutter. Fayette Co., Ky. Apr. 11, 1901.

Capt. Elijah O'Bannon. Oct. 2, 1851.

Mrs. Emma F. Offutt, wife of Dr. W. G. Offutt. Feb. 26, 1868.

Dr. W. G. Offutt, from the residence of Mrs. Jas. K. Thompson. Oct. 11, 1869.

Edward Oldham. The Odd Fellows and Masons to attend. Dec. 13, 1871.

Harriett Frances, infant daughter of Mr. William Oldham. Aug. 24, 1829.

Mr. James O'Mara. The members of the Lyon Fire Co. are requested to attend. Feb. 14, 1846.

Mr. Henry Owens, at the residence of his father-in-law, Mr. Wm. Hickey. Nov. 26, 1831.

Mr. Asa Park, from the residence of Mr. Thomas Studman on Short St., to the Garden of Mr. Edward West on High St. Jan. 30, 1827. He will be buried with Masonic Honors.

Mr. John Park. May 24, 1828.

Mrs. Elizabeth R. Parker. Jan. 23, 1850.

J. W. Patterson. May 28, 1877.

Daniel McCarty Payne, from the residence of his mother, Mrs. Daniel Mc. Payne. Mch. 15, 1869.

Edward Payne, from the residence of his mother, Mrs. D. M. Payne. Aug. 8, 1871.

Mrs. Mary E. Payne, wife of Wm. Payne of Scott Co. Jan. 18, 1876.

Orlando F. Payne, at residence of his mother on Broadway, tomorrow afternoon. Sept. 8, 1865.

Charles Clarendon, son of Doct. H. J. Peck, at residence of his grandfather, John Peck, Esq., on Mill St. July 10, 1846.

Miss Laura N. Peck, from the residence of Mr. A. F. Hawkins. Sept. 5, 1851.

Mrs. Agnes Perkins, from the residence of her husband, E. Perkins.

Oct. 18, 1839.

Mr. Felix Perrin. Jan. 2, 1852.

William Dallam Peter, son of Dr. Robert Peter. June 17 ,1849.

S. Pfeiffer. Aug. 18, 1871.

Sasimiro Pieri. Apr. 10, 1872.

William P., infant son of B. Pilcher. July 4, 1830.

Albin Pilkington, Jr., son of Albin and Kate Pilkington. Jan. 7, 1875.

Mr. George Pilkington, from the residence of Mr. Samuel Pilkington. Sept. 10, 1825.

Mary McNiell, infant daughter of Albin and Kate Pilkington, from the residence of her grandfather, Mr. John Pilkington. May 31, 1870.

Dr. Charles E. Pinckney, at the residence of William Elder. Aug. 24, 1845.

Mrs. Sarah E. Poindexter, wife of William Poindexter. Apr. 10, 1867.

Charles H. Poindexter, from the residence of Mr. E. H. Parrish. Sept. 2, 1868.

Mr. Nathaniel S. Porter. Aug. 31, 1827.

James, infant son of Gabriel Lewis Postlewaite; from the residence of William R. Morton, Esq. Sept. 22, 1833.

Gen'l. William Preston. Sept. 22, 1887.

John A. Price. May 3, 1875.

Alexander E. Prewitt, at Christian Church, in Athens, Ky. Feb. 12, 1877.

Thomas Quinn. Aug. 21 ,1871.

Ellen Quisenberry, from the residence of her father, Colby B. Quisenberry. July 25, 1871.

Boone Railey, from Phoenix Hotel. The Masonic Fraternity will pay the accustomed honors. Mch. 29 (no year given).

Mrs. Catherine Randall. Dec. 8, 1869.

Larkin C. Randall. Aug. 21, 1869.

Larkin Scott Randall, from residence of his father, Mr. L. C. Randall. July 20, 1851.

Mrs. Mollie V. Randall, wife of C. S. Randall. Mch. 13, 1871.

Mr. Philebert Ratel. The Masonic Fraternity to attend. Feb. 25, 1830.

A. J. Reed, Jr., from the residence of his mother, Mrs. H. W. Reed. Apr. 4, 1872.

John Isaac Reed, from the residence of his father, Henry W. Reed. Aug. 17, 1857.

Louis Cass Reed, from the residence of his father, A. J. Reed. Jan. 27, 1871.

Mrs. Lucy Reid, from the residence of her husband, Mr. Charles Reid. Feb. 20, 1865.

Mrs. Mary B. Reed. Apr. 22, 1863.

Mrs. Sabina Rice. Aug. 15, 1862.

Miss Catherine E. Richardson, from the residence of her brother, Mr. John C. Richardson, Jr. June 7, 1822.

Mrs. Louisa Jane Rice, consort of Mr. Wm. Rice. Oct. 5, 1864.

Dr. William H. Richardson. Sept. 15, 1845.

Mrs. Eliza Ridgley, from the residence of Dr. F. Ridgley. Mch. 19, 1822.

Henry A. Ridgley. May 29, 1876.

Sarah Jane, infant daughter of Mr. Charles Riley. Aug. 6, 1851.

Mrs. Lou Robbins, from the residence of her husband, John L. Robbins. Sept. 20, 1867.

Mrs. Margaret Roberts. Dec. 8, 1877.

James B. Robertson, from the residence of his father, Judge George Robertson. Feb. 27, 1867.

Mrs. Martha O. Rodes, from the residence of her husband, Mr. J. C. Rodes. June 5, 1822.

Waller Rodes. Sept. 9, 1868.

Julia F. Rogers, at the residence of her husband, R. C. Rogers. Dec. 2 (no year given).

Mrs. William F. Rogers, from the residence of her father, John Clark. Aug. 27, 1872.

Cora Lee, infant daughter of S. S. and K. E. Roszell, at the resident of Mrs. Tingle. Aug. 3, 1869.

John Scott Rousse, from the residence of Mrs. L. C. Scott. I. O. O. F. to attend. Apr. 10, 1849.

Garrett F. Rucker, from the residence of his father, Barnet Rucker. June 13, 1826.

Matilda Russell, daughter of Daniel Bradford, Esq. Jan. 23, 1851.

Col. Thomas A. Russell. July 21, 1846.

Dr. L. Sanders, from the residence of Mr. Winslow. June 13, 1849.

Mary Jane, daughter of Edward and Elizabeth Savill. July 18, 1870.

O. Orrin Saxton. Mch. 7, 1877.

Mrs. Abby V. Sayre. Mch. 10, 1871.

David A. Sayre. Sept. 12, 1870.

Sophia T., infant daughter of E. D. and Mary E. Sayre. May 22, 1852.

Mary Charlotte Schultze, infant daughter of Charles and Mary Jane Schultze; from the residence of Mrs. M. A. Delph. Sept. 22, 1863.

Henry Walter, infant son of Charles and Jennie Schultze; at the residence of C. Schultze. Dec. 6, 1869.

Ellen Scott, daughter of Persicles and Mary Ann Scott. July 27, 1849.

Mrs. Mollie E. Scott, from the residence of her father, P. Scott, Esq. June 3, 1871.

Sarah Hamilton Scott, infant daughter of Persicles and Mary Ann Scott. Nov. 10, 1848.

Mr. Clark Scrogins. Nov. 29, 1854.

James, infant son of James Scully, Sr. Sept. 28, 1850.

Harry, infant son of G. W. and M. C. Searcy. Dec. 5, 1870.

Mr. Benjamin Sharp. Apr. 7, 1838.

Mr. Charles Sharp, from the residence of Maj. John Tilford, on Main St. Feb. 9, 1827.

Mr. Marshall Sharp, from the residence of Mr. James Harrison. The Lexington Light Infantry will attend. Nov. 6, 1842.

Mrs. Emma Shaw. July 25, 1870.

Joseph M. Shaw. Jan. 4, 1875.

Mr. Evan Shelby. Fayette County. Jan. 24, 1853.

Gen. James Shelby. Aug. 16, 1848.

Mrs. Sarah B. Shelby, at the residence of her mother, Mrs. R. S. Mc-Clure. Aug. 19, 1866.

Maj. Thomas H. Shelby, Sr. Fayette County. Feb. 14, 1869.

Mrs. Nannie E. Shelton. (No date.)

Robert B. Shelton. Apr. 25, 1872.

Lucy W., wife of J. H. Shropshire. Nov. 5, 1876.

Miss Harriett Emeline Shy, in her 20th year, from the residence of her brother, Mr. Samuel Shy. Apr. 14, 1846.

Mrs. Margaret J. Sidener. May 30, 1871.

W. S. Simpson, and will be interred in the Cemetery at Paris, Ky. Dec. 24, 1866.

Mr. Joseph Singer, from the Powder Works of Samuel Trotter, Esq. Masonic lodges to attend. Sept. 26, 1823.

Mrs. Susanna Sinclair, from the residence of C. H. Woolums. Apr. 6, 1869.

Mrs. Elizabeth R. Skillman. Oct. 13, 1873.

Miss Mary M. Sloan, from the residence of her father, J. R. Sloan, Esq. Mch. 16, 1849.

Elisha Smith. Sept. 12, 1869.

Granville Smith. June 4, 1874.

Hallie Appleton Smith, infant daughter of J. Soule and Juliet G. Smith. Sept. 14, 1878.

Jacob Smith. May 28, 1875.

Jasper Smith, Sen. Nov. 27, 1868.

Jimmie H. B. Smith, infant son of J. and M. J. Smith. Apr. 11, 1870.

Mr. John Smith. July 29, 1826.

Mr. John R. Smith. June 19, 1849.

Mrs. Lizzie F. Smith, wife of Jasper Smith. Dec. 2, 1874.

Mrs. Margaret M. Smith, from the residence of her husband, Larkin B. Smith, Esq. Sept. 4, 1850.

Mary E. N. H. Smith, from the residence of her parents, J. and M. J. Smith. Mch. 27, 1870.

Miss Susan J. Smith, daughter of Elder Thomas and Mary S. Smith; from the residence of Dr. T. R. H. Smith. May 25, 1848.

Mr. John F. Smoot, from the residence of Mr. John Gordon. Nov. 6, 1848.

Thomas H. Sommerville. Mch. 30, 1872.

Mrs. Sarah E. Spotswood. June 19, 1868.

Mrs. Margaret Sprake. June 12, 1878.

Mary Winslow Stephens, infant daughter of Mr. Alvan Stephens. Mch. 22, 1830.

Sallie E. Stevenson, daughter of Rev. D. and Sarah A. Stevenson. Mch. 15, 1870.

Mr. George W. Stewart. May 15, 1876.

Jennie Stockdell, daughter of Dr. J. L. Stockdell. Mch. 15, 1866.

W. P. Stockwell. Feb. 21, 1876.

Mr. Benjamin Stout, Sen. July 14, 1822.

Mrs. Celeste B. Sutton. Apr. 14, 1870.

George W. Sutton. Oct. 12, 1870.

Mrs. Laura G. Sutton, relict of the late George W. Sutton. Feb. 18, 1875.

Prewitt Sweeny, son of Dr. and Mrs. W. O. Sweeny. Sept. 28, 1875.

Mrs. Sarah Swift, consort of Stephen Swift. May 16, 1827.

Thomas, infant son of Mr. Stephen Swift. July 11, 1826.

Mrs. Elizabeth Taylor. Nov. 26, 1828.

Mrs. Elvira Taylor, from the residence of her husband, Mr. James Taylor. Mch. 30, 1848.

Mrs. Sarah Tandy. Jan. 3, 1843.

Hon. Charles B. Thomas. Dec. 16 (no year).

Mrs. Sarah Ann Thomas; residence of her son, Judge Thomas. June 26, 1852.

Lemuel Thompson, infant son of T. T. and T. I. Thompson. Feb. 25, 1868.

Lewis B. Thompson, infant son of Butler F. and P. E. Thompson. Feb. 25, 1864.

Frank F. Thompson, from the residence of his father, P. Henry Thompson. June 26, 1866.

John F. Thorne, from the residence of his father, John Thorne. July 17, 1872.

Kate, infant daughter of John B. Tilford. Aug. 10, 1864.

Leslie Combs, infant son of John Tilford. July 25, 1829.

Mary Tilford, from the residence of her father, Thomas H. Hunt, Esq. Feb. 4, 1847.

Mr. George C. Timberlake. Jan. 24, 1849.

Mrs. Sarah Tingle. Mch. 11, 1866.

Mr. David Fayette Todd, son of General Robert Todd. Feb. 6, 1808.

Mrs. Eliza P., consort of Robert S. Todd, Esq. July 6, 1825.

Mr. James C. Todd, from the residence of Capt. James H. Allen. June 16, 1849.

Robert P. Todd, infant son of Mr. R. S. Todd. July 22, 1822.

Robert S. Todd. July 16, 1849.

Edwin M. Todhunter. Nov. 18, 1872.

Mrs. Sally Ann Toll, from the residence of her husband, Mr. Jonathan Toll. July 23, 1849.

J. D. Trapp. Nov. 23, 1877.

Robert Lee, infant son of J. D. and H. Trapp. Feb. 16, 1867.

Mrs. Catherine Trotter, from the residence of her husband, Samuel Trotter, Esq. Nov. 13, 1830.

General George Trotter, at the house of his father, Col. James Trotter. Oct. 14, 1815.

George Trotter, Jr., from the residence of Col James Trotter. Mch. 31, 1825.

George, son of George R. Trotter, Esq. Apr. 30, 1849.

Mr. James A. Trotter, from the residence of his father, Mr. Samuel Trotter. June 24, 1822.

Col. James Trotter. Aug. 6, 1827.

Mr. James G. Trotter, from the residence of his father, Col. James Trotter. The Lexington Light Infantry to attend. July 15, 1820.

Thomas Atchinson, son of Dr. R. T. and Eliza B. Tuggle. Oct. 14, 1870.

Mrs. Elizabeth Tweedie. Sept. 11, 1848.

Miss Laura C. Twyman, at the residence of her adopted parents, Mr. and Mrs. S. D. McCullough. Aug. 21, 1867.

Henry Ulrich, from the residence of Fred Guggisburg. Aug. 25, 1872.

Mr. Luke Usher. Dec. 24, 1829.

Addie Lovell, infant daughter of J. M. and Alice Y. Vanmeter, at their residence near Midway. Jan. 20, 1871.

Mrs. Elizabeth A. Vanmeter. Aug. 15, 1864.

Mr. Jacob Vanmeter. Aug. 4, 1864.

Mr. Solomon Vanmeter. Sept. 15, 1859.

Mrs. Sophia Vandorn, from the residence of P. A. Vandorn, Esq. Feb. 7, 1831.

Mrs. Anna Margaret Van Pelt, consort of William Van Pelt, Sr. Oct. 7, 1850.

William Van Pelt, Sr. Oct. 7, 1872.

Mrs. Elizabeth Vertner. Feb. 17, 1872.

Mr. William Virden. Apr. 1, 1833.

Mrs. Elizabeth Walker. May 16, 1870.

Mr. John S. Walker, from the residence of Thomas Raney. Mch. 31, 1833.

Mrs. Lucy R. Wallace. Nov. 21, 1875.

Mrs. Sue H. Walsh, wife of Mr. John T. Walsh; at the residence of her father, Mr. C. F. Lowry. May 12, 1867.

Benjamin Warfield. Oct. 18, 1866.

Caroline, infant daughter of Thomas B. Warfield. Feb. 3, 1851.

Elisha Warfield, of Pewee Valley. Aug. 15, 1872.

Robert Barr, son of Dr. E. Warfield. Oct. 27, 1825.

Debbie W. Warner, from the residence of her father, Col Wm. A. Warner. Dec. 17, 1862.

Henry C. Warner, from the residence of his father, D. Warner. June 29, 1869.

William Warner, Jr., infant son of Wm. Warner; from the residence of Mr. Joseph Wingate. July 29, 1851.

Mrs. Caroline V. Waters. Apr. 12, 1876.

Thomas H. Waters. Aug. 22, 1872.

Agnes C. ,infant daughter of B. P. and Mattie R. Watkins. June 23, 1875.

Miss Jane Watt, from the house of Mr. A. Gibney. July 24, 1825.

Richard Watts. June 19, 1851.

Mr. Alonzo H. Weaver. I. O. O. F. to attend. May 28, 1849.

Mrs. Catherine Webb. Aug. 21, 1871.

Mrs. Webster. July 23, 1827.

Wyall Webster. May 25, 1874.

Mrs. Mary Ann, consort of G. G. Weigert. Aug. 13, 1826.

Mr. Henry Weir. Sept. 23, 1833.

Mrs. West, from the residence of her husband, Mr. Edward West. Feb. 7, 1824.

John West, aged 83 years.   Apr. 23, 1868.
R. J. West.   Nov. 6, 1866.
Mr. Hichard P. Whitney, from the residence of his father, Dr. W. W. Whitney.   The Returned Volunteers to attend.   Aug. 26, 1847.
Charles Wickliffe.   Oct. 10, 1829.
D. C. Wickliffe.   May 15, 1870.
Mrs. Louisa Wickliffe, from the residence of her husband, Mr. Charles H. Wickliffe.   Sept. 7, 1850.
Mrs. Margaret P. Wickliffe, consort of Robert Wickliffe, Esq.   Feb. 24, 1825.
Robert Wickliffe, Jr.   Aug. 31, 1850.
Mr. William Wilgus, at the house of his father, Asa Wilgus.   Mch. 29, 1817.
Rev. W. T. Willet.   May 7, 1824.
Annie Kate, daughter of Benjamin M. and Elizabeth Williams.   Jan. 1, 1867.
Prof. S. R. Williams.   June 14, 1869.
Kittie Belle, from the residence of her uncle, Dr. W. M. Wilson.   Feb. 19, 1876.
Matilda J. Wilson, from the residence of her mother, Mrs. Nancy Wilson.   Jan. 15 (no year).
Mrs. Nancy Wilson.   Feb. 2, 1873.
R. S. Wilson.   Nov. 30, 1850.
Mrs. Susan Wilson.   July 6, 1868.
Joseph Wingate.   Aug. 1, 1871.
Mr. Elisha L. Winter, from Pheonix Hotel.   June 30, 1849.
Mrs. Margaret Woodhouse, from the residence of her daughter, Mrs. A. McMains.   Feb. 9, 1862.
William H. Woodhouse.   Feb. 22, 1870.
James E. Woodruff.   Aug. 15 (no year).
Mrs. Maria Woodruff, consort of Mr. Ezra Woodruff.   Apr. 10, 1828.
Mattie Craig, daughter of Joseph S. and Lucy Woolfolk.   Mch. 28, 1866.
Miss Joanna Wrigglesworth.   Feb. 22, 1822.
Mrs. Lucy Wyatt, consort of Maj. John Wyatt.   Aug. 25, 1816.
Mrs. Sue M. Yates, wife of James M. Yates; from the residence of her uncle, Sam'l D. McCullough.   Dec. 23, 1868.
Mr. Charles G. Young.   I. O. O. F. to attend.   Oct. 19, 1849.
Mary Elizabeth Young, from the residence of her husband, L. P. Young.   Dec. 10, 1846.
Mrs. Eliza Ann Young, wife of D. W. Young.   July 8, 1873.
(Donated by Miss Elizabeth Davis)
Henry Anderson, infant son of John C. and Catherine Young.   Mch. 20, 1848.
Mrs. Eliza E. Bryan, at residence of her husband, Gen. William Bryan.   Oct. 14, 1864.
Miss Mary Eliza, daughter of Daniel W. Young.   Jan. 14, 1850.
Mrs. Sarah Young.   May 19, 1875.
William H. Young.   Mch. 1, 1852.
Edward Allen, at South Elkhorn.   Aug. 9, 1872.
Mrs. Margaret Bryan, wife of the late David Bryan, Esq.; from the residence of her son, Gen. William Bryan.   June 26, 1856.
Mrs. Nancy Bowman, from the residence of her husband, Mr. Abraham Bowman.   Aug. 19, 1858.
Mrs. Nancy P. Bowman, consort of William Bowman, of Fayette Co.   Nov. 11, 1851.
Judith Bunn, from the house of Mr. John Elder, to Mr. James Wardlaw's burial ground.   Sept. 1, 1806.
Richard Cox, from residence of brother-in-law, John B. Wilgus.   Members of the Good Samaritan Lodge invited.   Apr. 25 (no year).
Mr. Allen Davis, from residence of Mr. George W. Stone.   Apr. 12, 1861.
Lucy, infant daughter of Mr. and Elizabeth P. Davis.   May 2, 1851.

Mrs. Mary Davis, from residence of her son-in-law, Joseph McAdams. Oct. 15, 1841.
Capt. W. P. Davis. Mch. 31, 1881.
Mrs. Elizabeth Eedge, from residence of P. P. Edge, Esq. Jan. 26, 1866.
Miss Julia A. Grinstead, from residence of her brother, James A. Grinstead. Feb. 14, 1881.
Mrs. Emily C. Hamilton. Jan. 19, 1857.
John J. Hunter. May 16, 1879.
Lucy, daughter of Edwin and Isabella Johnson. Jan. 17, 1875.
John Parker. Feb. 19, 1875.
Mrs. Joseph Ann Parker, from residence of her husband, John Parker, Esq. Dec. 16, 1858.
Mrs. Janna Talbott, wife of L. B. Talbott. Oct. 19, 1867.
Mrs. Elizabeth F. Schmidt. May 17, 1877.
Mrs. Nellie Todd, widow of Wm. L. Todd. Oct. 26, 1866.
William L. Todd. Mch. 10, 1865.

FUNERAL NOTICES IN COOPER BIBLE

Sophia Anna, daughter of I. F. Gasner, Georgetown, Ky. Oct. 20, 1860.
Mrs. Susan West, from residence of Mr. George Stifle. Georgetown, Ky. Aug. 10, 1860.
Dr. R. M. Dudley. Georgetown, Ky. Jan. 6. 1893.
Margaret Allen Payne; residence of her father, Judge G. V. Payne. Georgetown, Ky. Sept. 22, 1892.
Mrs. Delia A. Childers, wife of W. B. Childers. Mch. 15, 1894.
Mrs. Mary Hughes. Dec. 17, 1872.
Mrs. Martha M. Wood, from residence of husband, John T. Wood. Mch. 20, 1871.
Robert P. Kenney. Nov. 24, 1869.
Mrs. Drucilla Jones, wife of M. S. Jones. Dec. 16, 1878.
Mrs. Mary Muir; residence of her husband, William Muir. Sept. 13 (no year).
John T. Cantrill. Apr. 2, 1862.

FUNERAL INVITATIONS LYING IN THE TAYLOR-SNYDER-COOPER BIBLES

Mrs. Marion Herndon, from residence of Dr. S. F. Gano. Apr. 23, 1844.
Mr. James Sullivan. The Georgetown Artillery and Cadets of W. M. Institute will attend. Georgetown, Ky. June 7, 1847.
Mary B. Buck, infant daughter of J. W. and Mary B. Buck; at residence of Dr. W. L. Sutton. Georgetown, Ky. June 10, 1848.
Mrs. Mary Sullivan, from residence of Mr. Henry Moody. Georgetown, Ky. July 3, 1848.
Mr. Thomas Martin, from residence of Mr. David Nutter. Scott County. Dec. 10, 1848.
Dr. A. T. Cone. Georgetown, Ky. May 1, 1849.
James W. Grant. Georgetown, Ky. Mch. 26, 1849.
A. Campbell Elgin, son of Samuel Elgin. Georgetown, Ky. Apr. 1, 1850.
Dr. D. T. Humphreys. Georgetown, Ky. Mch. 21, 1851.
Mrs. Mary Lemmon, relict of Capt. John Lemmon. Georgetown, Ky. June 10, 1851.
Mrs. Eliza Burbridge, consort of Capt. Robert Burbridge. Apr. 14, 1852.
Susan Maria, from residence of her father, B. W. Finnell. Aug. 2, 1852.
Miss Ann Clint West. Oct. 11, 1852.
Fanny, daughter of James H. and Mary Daviess. Nov. 30, 1852.
Rev. Wm. G. Craig. Sept. 8, 1853.
Mrs. Harriett B. Wright, at residence of her father, Capt. Burbridge. Dec. 31, 1855.
Sarah Emma, daughter of E. W. and Mary La Rue. Jan. 8, 1855.
Jas. B. Crawford. Dec. 28, 1855.
Mortimer Price. Georgetown, Ky. Jan. 13, 1856.

Mrs. Mary Keene Elliott; residence of her father, Dr. W. B. Keene. Sept. 10, 1856.

Mrs. Ruth Offutt; residence of her father, John Downing. Scott County. Oct. 23, 1857.

George Madison, youngest son of George P. and Lutetia A. Peak. Feb. 13, 1859.

Nathan Payne. Scott County. Aug. 24, 1860.

James Richard, son of Mr. J. F. Lemon; residence of Mrs. Ellis. Georgetown, Ky. Oct. 18, 1860.

Eugene L., son of I. G. Gasner. Georgetown, Ky. Oct. 7, 1860.

Mrs. Sallie E. Johnson, from Cherry Spring Church. Feb. 6, 1862.

Mr. Thos. P. Johnson. Georgetown. Apr. 12, 1862.

Mrs. Elizabeth Varnon. Georgetown, Ky. Mch. 22, 1862.

Alice, daughter of Danford Thomas. Scott County. Sept. 12, 1860.

ADDITIONAL BIBLE RECORD

HUTTON BIBLE

(Owned by Mrs. Hannah Woods Hutton, with later additions by her daughter and granddaughter, Jane Miller Mastin.)

James Hutton was born April the 6th, 1761.
Hannah Hutton was born January the 20th, 1768.   Children.
    William Hutton was born January 20, 1793.
    Elizabeth Hutton was born June 21, 1795.
    Sarah Hutton was born December 24, 1798.
    John Hutton was born January 30, 1802.
    Henry Hutton was born August 16, 1800.
    Polly Hutton was born May 4, 1804.
    Patsy Hutton was born February 18, 1806.
    Nancy Hutton was born May 18, 1807.
Children of Elizabeth Hutton and first husband, John Miller:
    Jane Miller was born April 30, 1815; married John Gilbert Mastin as his second wife. Jane was a niece of his first wife, Sarah Hutton.
    Nancy Miller was born September 18, 1816.
    James H. Miller was born August 29, 1818.
    George Miller was born July 12, 1820.
    Sally Miller was born January 12, 1823.
    Hannah Hutton Miller was born December 16, 1823.
Children of Elizabeth Hutton (Miller) and second husband, Adam Reid:
    Michael Reid was born March 19, 1826.
    Henry H. Reid was born August 1, 1828.
    Rebecca Reid was born April 20, 1830.
    Peggy Reid was born April 8, 1832.
    ———— Reid was born May 2, 1834.
John Gilbert Mastin was born in Delaware, October 22, 1793.
Sarah Hutton, his first wife, was born December 24, 1822. Children:
    James Hutton Mastin—Born April 13, 1822.
    John William Mastin—Born October 16, 1823.
    Elizabeth Hannah Mastin—Born May 15, 1825.
Children of John Gilbert Mastin and second wife, Jane Miller:
    Sarah Jane Mastin—Born August 27, 1825.
    William Henry Mastin—Born March 12, 1836.
    Robert Gilbert Mastin—Born July 13, 1838.
    Anne Mary Mastin—Born September 9, 1840.
    George Hutton Mastin—Born April 4, 1843.
    Children: Presley, Emma, Fannie Bell and Martha Ann died

in childhood.

James Hutton departed this life June 13, 1833, aged 72 years 2 months and 7 days.

Hannah Woods Hutton, his wife, died Sept. 11, 1834, aged 66 years 7 months and 22 days.

John Miller died October 3, 1823.

James H. Miller died August 24, 1836.

George Miller died Feb. 3, 1846.

James Hutton and Hannah Woods were married January 11, 1790, in Madison County, Kentucky.

John Gilbert Mastin married Sarah Hutton, daughter of James Hutton, February 1, 1821.

John Gilbert Mastin married Jane Miller, daughter of John Miller and Elizabeth Hutton, September 22, 1833. Anderson County Records.

Sarah Mastin, wife of John Gilbert Mastin, died June 4, 1833, aged 33 years.

Martha Ann Mastin, wife of John W. Mastin, died January 25, 1845, aged 21 years.

John Gilbert Mastin died December 19, 1867.

Jane Miller Mastin, relict of John Gilbert Mastin, died February 28, 1894.

Elizabeth Hutton (Miller) Reid died in Preble County, Ohio, in 1878.

GENEALOGY SECTION

ALBERT (ALBRECHT) FAMILY

The above mentioned George Albert, Sr., had a sister, Mary Albert, who did not marry and who lived with her niece, Mary Ann Albert Beecher (Mrs. John), until she died, aged about 97 years and 6 months. Miss Mary Albrecht often told the story of her early life to the family and friends of Mrs. Mary Ann Beecher, and this was dictated by Lydia Beecher (the youngest daughter of Mrs. Mary Ann Beecher) to her grand-daughter, Annie Laurie Wilson. Miss Mary Albrecht said her father was a nobleman in Germany and next to the King in wealth and possessions, and had a large family of boys and two daughters. When Mary was 16 years old she and all of the brothers (except one small brother and her little sister) started for America in a ship belonging to their father, the father, mother, and the two small children remaining in Germany. The ship was attacked by pirates and all the brothers except George, the youngest (who surrendered) were killed and thrown into the sea. Mary had a deep sword cut on her head which she showed when she told the story. The ship was looted of the wealth and Mary and George were sold as slaves in Spain. They were well educated and Mary was made governess in a wealthy family and George was made clerk (or super-cargo) in a shipping business. After several years Mary and George escaped and returned to Germany, to find their father dead. George married Mary —— (her name forgotten). Later George and his wife, Mary; sister, Miss Mary Albrecht, and the remaining sister and brother again started for America, leaving their mother, who refused to leave Germany. They landed in Philadelphia, Pa., and as a citizen of America George discarded his title of Prince. Children of George and his wife, Mary:

Catherine (Katy) Albrecht married —— Brown.

Margaret Albrecht married —— Epler.

George Albrecht, Jr., died, aged 90, and had 5 or 6 children, and was buried at Elper Church.

Mary Ann Albrecht, who was born near Adamstown, Pa., Dec. 3, 1755; married John Beecher, Apr. 13, 1778; died Nov. 11, 1837. When the news came that their mother was dead and the estate waiting for the American heirs, none of the family were willing to go to Germany, except the husband of George's youngest sister. His name Lydia Beecher had forgotten, but knew that he was a lawyer in Philadelphia, and also owned a music store. He took the necessary documents and went to Germany, settled the estate and started for America, and was never heard from again and his fate is unknown.   George and his family lived near Adamstown, Lancaster County, Pa., near the family of John Beecher. Miss Mary Albert probably was born in 1713; died June, 1811; buried at Epler Church. George was buried at Adamstown, Pa., all dates and the name of his wife are unknown.

(I have no record of the grand-children of John Beecher, except two families—Jacob, 12th child, and Lydia, 16th child.)

Jacob Beecher, 12th child of John Beecher and Mary Ann Albert, married his cousin, Catherine Brown, of Jonestown, Lebanon County, Pa. She was a daughter of Catherine (Katy) Albert and Mr. Brown. (Katy's sister, Mary Ann Albert, married John Beecher.) Margaret Albert, another sister, married Mr. Epler (his family built Epler's Church). Children of Jacob and Catherine Beecher:

1. John Valentine Beecher—Died 1886; aged 65; married two times.
2. Jacob Franklin Beecher married Catherine Elizabeth Bracket, Mch. 28, 1844; had one son, Dr. A. C. W. Beecher, of Philadelphia, Pa.
3. Paris Epler Beecher.
4. Kaziah Beecher married Mr. Thompson.
5. William Lightner Beecher. (6, 7, 8, 9—no record.)

Lydia Beecher (16th child of John and Mary Ann Albert Beecher, daughter of George and Mary)—Born June 10, 1805, Reading, Pa.; died July 31, 1885, Cynthiana, Ky. Married Mch. 19, 1822, Stephen Beecher Cook, in New Holland, Lancaster County; Pa., by Rev. Peter Philbert. Stephen was born Mch. 1, 1798; died Mch. 10, 1874, Cynthiana, Ky. They celebrated their golden wedding in 1872. Both are buried at Battle Grove, Cynthiana, Ky. When Lydia died, aged 80, there were living five of her 12 children, 26 grand-children, and 24 great-grand-children. Stephen took the name of "Beecher" for a middle name, because when he married there was another Stephen Cook in the same town. Stephen B. Cook was son of Stephen Cook and Miss ————— Ayers, of Staten Island (where Mrs. Stephen, Sr., is buried). Stephen Cook, Sr., came over from England in a military band, during the Revolution, when he found what the Americans were fighting for, he deserted the English and joined the Americans, "Washington's forces"; no record of his services have been found, so he may have fought under another name. His brother, Dr. ————— Cook, visited him later and some of the family settled in Ohio. The wife of President Hayes was a descendant of this Cook family. Mrs. Stephen Ayers Cook (Sr.) was a daughter of Captain ————— Ayers, of the "India Tea Co.," and during the "Embargo" was not allowed to land his "tea" in Philadelphia, Pa., (see Abagail Adams' diary) from his ship, "Polly," Dec. 28, 1773. Several histories made mention of him. Miss Ayers was educated in a convent in Madrid, Spain and when her mother died, she came on her father's ship, and was married in America. They (Mr. and Mrs. Stephen Cook, Sr.) had 6 children, birth dates not known. Three daughters: Polly mar. ————— Turman (they had son, Edward, and 2 dau.); Margaret Cook married ————— Scott (he was a Mason, and was killed by a falling scaffold), they had 5 children, the oldest son was a potter in Lancaster Co., Pa.; Eliza Cook married ————— Disbell, and lived in Lancaster Co., Pa.; the three sons were James, Jacob and Stephen "Beecher" Cook, who married Miss Ayres. (Stephen Sr., married the second time and had a family.) Their children:

1. Cyrus Beecher Cook was born in the year of our Lord, 1832, March the 31st, at Forge Springs, Pa.
2. Benjamine Franklin Cook was born in the year of our Lord, 1825, September the 29th.
3. William Edmond Cook was born in the year of our Lord, 1827, May the 26th.
4. Mary Lucetta Cook was born in the year of our Lord, 1829, May the 1st.
5. James Albert Cook was born in the year of our Lord, 1830, September the 20th.
6. Casia Ann Cook was born in the year of our Lord, 1832, September the 4th.
7. William Augustus Cook was born in the year of our Lord, 1834, June 22nd.
8. Christeana Cook was born in the year of our Lord, 1836, August 23rd.
9. Anna Eliza Cook was born in the year of our Lord, 1838, June 19th, at Liverpool, Pa.
10. Lewis Paxton Cook was born in the year of our Lord, 1840, October 18th.
11. Martha Matilda Cook was born in the year of our Lord, 1843, February the 24th (Woodburn Farm, near Carlisle, Pa.).
12. Elizabeth Josephine Cook was born in the year of our Lord, 1845, June the 9th (Bricker Farm, near Newville, Pa.).

Martha M. (Cook), (Norris), Hedges—Born 1843; died July 3, 1901; buried at Cynthiana, Ky.

Elizabeth Josephine (Cook) Wolford—Born 1845; died Dec. 9th, 1912, in New York City; buried Cynthiana, Ky.

William Augustus Cook—Born June 22, 1834; died March 9th, 1912, buried Cynthiana, Ky.

Anna Eliza (Cook) Wilson died July 12th, 1926, Lexington, Ky.; buried at Cynthiana, Ky.

Benjamine Franklin Cook died in the year of our Lord, 1828, Oct. 21st.

William Edmond Cook died in the year of our Lord, 1828, Oct. 25.

Christeana Cook died in the year of our Lord, 1836, Dec. 19th.

Louis P. Cook died in the year of our Lord, 1865, March 25th; buried at Cynthiana, Ky.

James Albert Cook died A. D., 1873, June 22; buried at Cynthiana, Ky.

Stephen Cook died March 10th, 1874, aged 77 years; buried at Cynthiana, Ky.

Cyrus B. Cook died November 14th, 1880; buried at Cynthiana, Ky.

Mary Lucetta Swonger died July 7th, 1879; buried in Tiffin, Ohio.

Lydia B. Cook died July 31, 1885.

Casia Ann "Kate" Smith died March 3rd, 1894; buried at Cynthiana, Ky.

Mary Lucetta Cook (of Stephen B. Cook and Lydia Beecher) married Matthias Swonger in Carlisle, Pa. Children:

1. James Franklin Swonger—Born Nov. 13, 1847.
2. Louis Theodore Swonger—Born May 1, 1849; died Mch. 29, 1850.
3. Charles Augustus Swonger.
4. Mary Ellen Swonger—Born Feb. 17, 1853.
5. Annie Lydia Swonger—Born Feb. 16, 1855.
6. Frances Rebecca Swonger—Born Oct. 19, 1857.
7. Josephine Elizabeth Swonger—Born July 5, 1859.
8. Mattie Cook Swonger—Born Apr. 27, 1861.
9. Abbie Almena Swonger—Born Jan. 9, 1863.
10. Malinda Catherine Swonger—Born Oct. 22, 1865.

11. Florence Augustus Swonger—Born Aug. 28, 1869.
12. Etutra Blanche Swonger—Born Sept. 4, 1872; died Sept. 23, 1872.

Mary Lucetta Cook Swonger died July 7, 1879; buried Tiffin, Ohio.
James Albert Cook (of Stephen B. Cook and Lydia Beecher) married Sarah Wolford (daughter of Peter Wolford of Minneapolis, Minn.) Apr. 18, 1859. Children:

> (1) Mary Cook—Born Jan. 25, 1860; married James Frazer, of Cynthiana, Ky. (2) Charles Wolford Bates Cook—Born Aug. 31, 1861; died Sept. 23, 1918. (3) James Albert Cook—Born Dec. 25, 1864; died Sept. 9, 1865.

Casia Ann Cook (of Stephen B. Cook and Lydia Beecher) married Cornelius Smith, of York, Pa.; children:

1. John Calvin Smith—Born Jan. 9, 1853.
2. Virginia Smith—Born Aug. 22, 1863; died Feb. 5, 1865, White Pigeon, Mich.
3. Georgiana Smith—Born Feb. 10, 1867; married Evans D. Veach, Cynthiana, Ky.
4. Burt Wilson Smith—Born Dec. 24, 1871; married Sallie Shinbower, Lexington, Ky.

William Augustus Cook (of Stephen B. Cook and Lydia Beecher) married (1st) Annie Elizabeth Farrel; children (born Harrison Co. Ky.):

1. Albert Beecher Cook—Born Aug. 29, 1868; died Oct. 17, 1892.
2. William Cook—Born May 28, 1872; died Apr. 24, 1877.

Second wife Fannie Day. They adopted an orphan girl, Audrey. Third wife, Georgia ——— (widow).

Anna Eliza Cook (of Stephen B. Cook and Lydia Beecher) married William Henry Jenks Wilson Jan. 19, 1861, in Lexington, Ky. He was the son of Ranselear Jeremiah Jenks and Asenath Woodburn (of Moses Woodburn, Revolutionary soldier). W. H. Jenks ran away from home when a small boy and was adopted by Mr. Wilson, and was always known as Wilson instead of Jenks. He was a well known trotting horse owner, and built Abdallah Park, Cynthiana, Ky. Children:

1. Annie Laurie Wilson—Born Nov. 5, 1862; married R. B. James.
2. Stephen Henry Wilson—Born 1864; died July 26, 1865.
3. Martha Ednah Wilson—Born Feb. 25, 1866; married H. K. McAdams, Cynthiana, Ky. (D.A.R. No. 238379). Later moved to Lexington, Ky.

Lewis Paxton Cook (of Stephen B. Cook and Lydia Beecher) married Priscilla Kirkpatrick. No children.

Martha Matilda Cook (of Stephen B. Cook and Lydia Beecher) married (1st) Thomas Norris, Lexington, Ky.; one child, Frank Wolford Norris, who married his first cousin, Mattie Cook Swonger (of Mathias Swonger), no children. M. M. Cook Norris married (2nd) James Thompson Hedges (as his 2nd wife). No children.

Elizabeth Josephine Cook (of Stephen B. Cook and Lydia Beecher) married Jacob Albert Wolford, Nov. 14, 1867. Children:

1. Mary Lydia Wolford—Born Dec. 3, 1868; married James W. Megibben; two children.
2. Louis Carl Wolford—Born July 4, 1870; married Jessie Myers, of New York; six children.
3. Josephine Alberta Wolford—Born June 19, 1872; married Webb Stringfield. No children.

Children of James Albert Cook and Sarah Wolford Cook:

1. Mary Cook—Born Jan. 25, 1860; married James Frazer, of Cynthiana, Ky. Their children: (1) Charles Royal Frazer—Born Oct. 17, 1877; (2) Maymie Frazer—Born ———; died June 12, 1880; (3) James Cook Frazer—Born ———; died Jan. 26, 1884.
2. Charles Wolford Cook—Born Aug. 31, 1861; died Sept. 23,

1918; married (1st) Jeanette Orr, of Mayslick, Ky., who died ten weeks later. He married (2nd) Willie Conyers, of Covington, Newton Co., Ga. She was born Aug. 19, 1863; married Mch. 21, 1888. Their children: (1) son, born Feb. 4, and died Feb. 6, 1889; (2) Wolford Bates Cook—Born Jan. 1, 1890; (3) Charles Conyers Cook—Born July 16, 1892.

Children: John Calvin Smith (of Cornelius Smith and Casia A. Cook Smith)—Born Sept. 4, 1853; married (1st) Addie Bates, Mch. 1, 1872. She was born Mch. 20, 1853, died June 17, 1911. Their children: (1) Francis G. Smith—Born Jan. 26, 1874; (2) Mattie E.—Born July 12, 1878; (3) LeGrand—Born Sept. 7, 1880; (4) John C.—Born July 11, 1883; died May 20, 1893 at Sheldahl, Iowa; (5) Nettie A. Smith—Born May 6, 1887; (6) Milo E.—Born Feb. 5, 1889; (7) Luella—Born Feb., 1895; died July, 1906. John Calvin married (2nd) Mrs. Sadie (Redfearn) Potts, a widow with one son, Roy Potts.

Georgiana Smith (of Cornelius and Casia A. Cook Smith)—Born Feb. 10, 1867; married Evans D. Veach (son of Sam Veach and Priscilla Evans) Jan. 16, 1888. They had one son, Lamme Givens Veach—Born Dec. 20, 1888; died Sept. 17, 1892.

Burt Wilson Smith (of Cornelius and Casia A. Cook Smith)—Born Dec. 24, 1871; married Sallie Shindlebower, daughter of William Morton Shindlebower and Mary Winifred Adams. Wm. Morton Shindlebower was son of T. J. Shindlebower and Mary Robinson. Mary Winifred Adams was daughter of John Adams and Mary Sampson of Richmond, Va. (of Wm. Sampson, of England).

Children of Matthias Swonger and Mary Lucetta Cook:

3. Charles Augustus Swonger married Miss Jennie Shaw of Scotland; their children: (1) Mamie; (2) Carrie; (3) Jimmy; (4) Alma; (5) Wymo.

4. Mary Ellen Swonger married (as his 2nd wife) Cornelius Augustus Mathews, on Sept. 24, 1876. (His 1st wife was Sarah Catherine Whitmore, their children: (1) Allmamanda; (2) C. D. Mathews; (3) Earnest F. Mathews). Children of second marriage, all born in Seneca Co., Ohio:
   (1) Grace Manna Mathews—Born Oct. 21, 1878.
   (2) Ralph N. Mathews—Born Aug. 13, 1880.
   (3) Mabel V. Mathews—Born Oct. 3, 1886.

5. Annie Lydia Swonger—Born Feb. 18, 1855; married William Ashley, of Homer, Mich, Feb. 28, 1878; children: (1) Addie—Born may 18, 1879; (2) Alta Mary—Born Oct. 24, 1880; (3) Frank J.—Born Oct. 10, 1886; (4) Frances Louise—Born Oct. 20, 1890.

6. Frances Rebecca Swonger—Born Oct. 19, 1858; married G. G. L. Hollenbecker, of Marywell, Sutter Co., Cal., on Feb. 8, 1887.

7. Josephine Elizabeth Swonger—Born July 5, 1859; married Jacob A. Hamm.

8. Mattie Cook Swonger—Born Apr. 27, 1861; married her cousin Frank Wolford Norris, of Cynthiana, Ky., Sept. 2, 1886.

9. Abbie Almena Swonger—Born Jan. 9, 1863; married J. W. Paddock (died); married Rev. J. E. A. Peel, of Peoria, Ill., July 7, 1901. Married (3rd) Rev. C. T. H. Benton, of Peoria, Ill., Aug. 22, 1912.

Annie Laurie Wilson (daughter of William Henry (Jenks) Wilson and Annie Eliza Cook)—Born Nov. 5, 1862, at Louisville, Ky.; married Robert Bruce James on Jan. 19, 1889, in Oakland, Cal. R. B. James was born Nov. 3, 1858 (son of Oscar James and Ruth Calvert. Oscar James was son of Sam Thayne James and Annie K. Gillispie. Ruth Calvert was daughter of Robert Bruce Calvert and Olivia Arnold. Olivia Arnold was daughter of Thomas Arnold, of Connecticut, and Elizabeth Potter. Robert Bruce Calvert was son of Robert Calvert of

East Virginia, and Ruth Shelby of Maryland). Robert Bruce James and Annie Laurie Wilson had one son, Oscar William James—Born Nov. 6, 1889, who married Esther Anderson, of Salem, Oregon. Their children: (1) Roberta Mary James—Born Dec. 29, 1920, at Pocatello, Idaho; (2) Oscar Richard James—Born Oct. 16, 1922 at Eugene, Oregon. Oscar Wilson James was Lieutenant, Headquarters Co. 362nd Inf., in World War.

Martha Ednah Wilson—Born Feb. 25, 1866, at Cynthiana, Ky., (daughter of Wm. Henry Jenks Wilson and Annie Eliza Cook; married Harry Kennett McAdams at Cynthiana, Ky., May 23, 1888. He was born Dec. 18, 1865, at Williamsburg, Ohio (See McAdams History). Children: (1) Gladys Wilson McAdams, artist; (2) William Henry McAdams who married (1st) Helen Lucile Heckert (daughter of Mrs. Wm. Delmar Heckert of Tiffin, Ohio), who died; married (2nd) Miss Jean Estelle Dubbs (daughter of Mr. and Mrs. Carbon P. Dubbs) on Dec. 28, 1926. Their children: 1—Barbara Jean McAdams—Born Dec. 8, 1927, in Boston, Mass; 2—Nancy Ann McAdams—Born Jan. 31, 1929, in Boston, Mass.

W. H. McAdams is a professor of Chemical Engineering in Massachusetts Institute of Technology since 1927; consulting chemical engineer for several organizations; is a member of American Chemical Society and American Society of Mechanical Engineers. In 1924 he was elected a member of Alpha Chi Sigma (honorary chemistry fraternity). In 1926 he was elected a foundation member of Alpha of Kentucky, Phi Beta Kappa (honorary fraternity for arts and sciences). He served 14 months in the World War, as first Lieutenant of Chemical Service; later as Captain in Chemical Warfare Service, and later as Assistant Chief of Development Division, C. W. S. He designed the "narrow type" Flutter valve, adopted for U. S. Army gas mask.

O. K. McAdams served in the World War from Sept., 1917, to April, 1919. Enlisted in Barrow Unit No. 40; was Corporal, and was overseas for nine months. Is now a physician specializing in gynecology and obstetrics in Pittsburgh, Pa.

Annie Elizabeth McAdams married Walter Peter Clemmons (son of Robert and Alice Hifner Clemmons) Nov. 30, 1922. Their daughter, Jane McAdams Clemmons was born Nov. 14, 1928, in Lexington, Kentucky.

BIBLE OF FREDERICK AUSTIN OF ENGLAND.
Now Owned by Frederick G. Austin of Hattiesburg, Miss.

Frederick Austin, Mt. Holly, N. J., formerly of England, married Mary Z. Lippincott of Mt. Holly, N. J., Aug. 21, 1853. A. K. Street, Minister.

Francis G. Austin, Mt. Holly, N. J., married Lizzie Reeves, Mt. Holly, N. J., Oct. 2, 1877. G. K. Morris, Minister.

Mary E. Austin, daughter of Francis G. and Elizabeth Austin of Mt. Holly, N. J., and Julian Tilford of Frankfort, Ky., Jan. 19, 1903.

Frederick G. Austin, son of Francis G. and Elizabeth Austin of Mt. Holly, N. J., married Eva Woodward Barron of Louisville, Winston Co., Miss., Oct. 11, 1907. By Rev. T. B. Holloman, Hattiesburg, Miss.

Elizabeth Austin, daughter of Francis G. and Elizabeth Austin, of Mt. Holly, N. J., and Walter E. Skiles of Frankfort, Ky., July 3, 1912. Rodger Noye, Pastor.

Edith Lippincott, daughter of Daniel and Rachel Zelly, was born Mch. 11, 1778, in Jacksonville, N. J., on Zelly farm.

Mary E. Austin, daughter of Jonothan and Edith Lippincott, was born on the 9th day of the 11th month ,1815, on the farm called the Span, Mt. Holly, N. J.

Francis Gershom Austin, son of Frederick and Mary Z. Austin, was born Friday, Jan. 19, 1855.

Francis Gershom Austin, son of Francis and Lizzie Austin, was born Friday, Jan. 17, 1879.

Lizzie Reeves, wife of Francis G. Austin and daughter of Absolam and Pheobe Reeves, was born at Mt. Holly, N. J., Oct. 20, 1855.

Mary E. Austin, daughter of Francis and Lizzie Austin, was born on the 28th day of Mch., 1880; Mt. Holly, N. J.

Frederick Austin, son of Francis and Lizzie Austin, was born on the 10th day of Sept., 1882; Mt. Holly, N. J.

(The second) Francis Austin, son of Francis and Lizzlie Austin, was born Monday, the 6th day of Apr., 1885; Plattsburg, N. Y.

Pearl Austin, daughter of Francis and Lizzie Austin, was born on Oct. 20, 1888; Plattsburg, N. Y.

Lizzie Reeves Austin, dau. of Frank and Lizzie Austin, born June 20, 1892; Ardmore, Pa.

Annie E. Austin, dau. of Frank and Lizzie Austin, was born Feb. 10, 1894, at Mattoon, Ill.

Phoebe R. Austin, dau. of Frank and Lizzie Austin, was born Sept. 6, 1896, at Lacrosse, Wis.

Anna Page Tilford, dau. of Mary Austin and Julian Tilford, was born Nov. 8, 1903, at Frankfort, Ky.

Francis Joseph Austin, son of Frederick and Eva Austin, was born Nov. 19, 1908, at Hattiesburg, Miss.

Sarah Elizabeth Skiles, dau. of Lizzie Austin and Walter Skiles, was born Aug. 6, 1913, at Frankfort, Ky.

Alfred Gershom Austin, son of Frederick Austin and Eva Barron Austin, was born Sept. 6, 1913, Hattiesburg, Miss.

Frederick Austin departed this life 9th month, 27th day, 1856. Mt. Holly, N. J.

Mary Austin, wife of Frederick Austin, departed this life July 14, 1884.

Edith Z. Lippincott departed this life Dec. 30, 1859.

Anna Page Tilford died Nov. 6, 1911; age 8 yrs.

Lizzie Reeves Austin, wife of Francis Gershom Austin, departed this life June 21, 1919, at Lexington, Ky.

EMANUEL BEECHER HISTORY
(Pennsylvania, Kentucky and Ohio)

Compiled by descendants: Dr. A. C. Beecher in Philadelphia, and A. L. Wilson and sister, Mrs. H. K. McAdams, in Kentucky

Emanuel Beecher was born and married in Germany. The name of his two wives are not known. They were buried in Lancaster County, Pa. Dates of birth, marriage, emigration and death are unknown.

(Rupp's list of 30,000 names of Immigrants, gives one, "Immanuel Bager, Aug. 31, 1750—Ship Nancy, from Rotterdam, last from Cowes, landing at Philadelphia. This may be the German spelling of the name, as the two dots over the A makes an "E" sound, but we have no proof of this.)

Emanuel and first wife had one son, Henry, and two daughters. By his second wife two daughters (one of whom married a Mr. Loush), and four sons: Jacob Beecher who died at the age of 70, had two children; Peter Beecher, who died at the age of 92, in 1857, had four children: John Beecher (our ancestor)—Born Apr. 13, 1759; died Mch. 22, 1819; had 16 children; Benjamin Beecher died in 1841 at the age of 60; had four children.

John Beecher, son of Emanuel—Born Apr. 13, 1759; died March 22, 1819, and was buried at Eplers Church, near Reading, Burks County, Pa. He married on Apr. 13, 1778, Mary Ann Albert (or Albrecht), daughter of George and Mary Albert. John Beecher was a private in Col. Flowers Regiment, and was in a company of soldiers being formed in front of the house of John Adams (later President of the U. S.); Mary Ann Albert was on the porch of this house during this-time. She and John Beecher were married, either on the porch or in the house of John Adams. The soldiers from the street formed a lane with their swords for the couple to walk under. Immediately after the ceremony John marched with the company to Valley Forge; he was 19 years old that day. (See Albert history.) Mary stayed for some time with Mrs. Adams, and went with her to Valley Forge to care for the soldiers. Mary Ann Albert was born near Adamstown, Lancaster Co., Pa., on Dec. 3, 1755; died Nov. 11, 1837, and was buried at Piquea, Lancaster County, Pa. All of this family were Lutherans.

Copy of letter from U. S. Department of the Interior, Bureau of Pensions, received by Mrs. H. K. McAdams, 309 N. Broadway, Lexington, Ky.

"I advise you that from the papers in the Revolutionary War Pension Claim, S. 39982, it appears that John Beecher, or Becher, enlisted in Lebanon, in what was later Lebanon County, Pennsylvania, April, 1778, served as a Private in Captain Meng's Company, Colonel Benjamin Flowers Artillery Artificers Regiment and was discharged April 3, 1779.

"He was allowed a Pension on his application executed November 28, 1818, while a resident of Berne Township, Berks County, Pa., aged over fifty-six years. He died March 22, 1819.

"Soldier's wife, Mary Ann Beecher, died November 11, 1837. Her maiden name and date of marriage not stated.

"In 1854, Jacob Nyswender and Henry Carpenter stated in Columbus, Ohio, that the following were the children and only heirs of said John and Mary Ann Beecher:

"John Beecher, of Berks County, Pa.

"William Beecher and Barbara Nyswender, both of Franklin County, Ohio.

"Margaret Mulliner, of Philadelphia, Pa.

"Benjamin Beecher, Jacob Beecher and Catherine Paxon, all of Chester Co., Pa.

"Samuel Beecher, of Lancaster Co., Pa.

"Lydia Cook, of Clark Co., Va.

"There is no record in this bureau of land having been granted by the United States, on account of the service of the above named Revolutionary War Soldier, John Beecher, or Becher.

"Respectfully,

Rev. and 1812 Wars Section. "Winfield Scott, Commissioner."

Fifth Ser. Vol. 111, Page 1085 Pa. Archives, says: The Artillery Artificers Regiment. This Corps, as it was called first, was raised by the direction of General Washington, in the summer of 1777. Benjamine Flower, formerly Commissary of Military Stores, of the Flying Camp, in 1776, was made Colonel and Commissary of Military Stores. Very few of its records remain. Capt. Jesse Roe's Company was one of the original Companies. Companies were stationed at Carlisle and Philadelphia, and their duties were to cast cannon, bore guns and prepare ammunition for the Army.—Constitutional Line, Artillery Artificers. 1777-1779.

Children of John and Mary Ann (Albert) Beecher:

1, 2 and 3 died infants.
4. Betsy Beecher married Mr. Sagner, of near Columbus, Ohio. She died, aged 45, and had 13 of her own children at her funeral.
5. Catherine married Mr. Paxon, Chester Co., Pa.; died, aged 71; had 14 children.
6. Samuel married; lived at Lancaster, Pa.; had 7 or 8 children; died, aged 85 years.
7. Polly married Thomas Russell; died, aged 71; had 14 children.
8. John married; lived Berks Co., Pa.; died, aged 71; had three children.
9. George married; died, aged 40; had 5 children.

10. Peggy married Mr. Mulliner; died, aged 71; had one daughter. Lived at Philadelphia, Pa.
11. Barbara—Born Mch. 10, 1794; died Oct. 1, 1879; married June 11, 1811, at Reading, Pa. Married Michael Nyswender (also spelled Neiswender). He was born June 19, 1791; died Dec. 12, 1858. Lived Franklin Co., Ohio. They had 12 children. Buried on Fred Neiswender farm, later moved to Lutheran Church yard.
12. Jacob married Catherine Brown, his cousin. He died 1883. Had 9 children. They lived Chester Co., Pa.
13. Isaac—Died infant.
14. William married Julia Carpenter (of Pa.); lived near Columbus, Ohio. Had 6 children.
15. Benjamin married; lived Chester Co., Pa. Born 1797; had 6 children.
16. Lydia (our ancestor) married Stephen Cook; born 1805; died, aged 80, in 1885. Had 12 children. She was not 17 years old when married, and was born in her mother's 50th year, and Benjamin was 8 years old. Married in New Holland, Lancaster Co., Pa., by Rev. Peter Philbert. Both buried in Cynthiana, Ky.

THE BOARDMAN-CROSE FAMILIES
(Donated by Miss Minerva Lambert, Carlisle, Ky.)

The following statements are based on family tradition, United States Census and deed records of Bourbon and Nicholas Counties, Ky. The dates of births and deaths are taken from the family Bible of Benjamin Boardman, who was of the third generation who lived in America. The given name of the emigrant from England is unknown to the writer, but traditional statements are agreed that he came from England and lived first in New Jersey and later in Maryland. This pioneer had a son whose name was Joseph Boardman, born 1746; died 1818, but the place of his birth is stated to have been in Maryland as shown by letter from Mr. H. H. Boardman of Indiana to Abner Boardman, Jr., dated Apr. 3, 1892. This letter also states that Joseph Boardman moved to New Jersey when he married Elizabeth Parker (born 1844; died 1832). It is also stated that Joseph Boardman lived for a short time in Delaware and this statement is coraborated by his grandson, Abner Boardman, and Harry H. Boardman of Odon, in Graves County, Indiana, that Joseph Boardman passed through the town in which his father lived in Maryland on his journey to Kentucky.

The old deed records of Bourbon County, Ky., Book —, page 155, show that on Feb. 23, 1796, Henry Wilson and Francis Wilson sold to Joseph Boardman for a consideration of 45£ (pounds, equal to $218.70) 60 acres of land on the waters of Hinkston Creek in Bourbon Co., Ky. This 60 acres of land is now occupied by Finley Burris, a descendant of Joseph Boardman.

The same letter from Harry H. Boardman states that Joseph Boardman had five brothers, who left many children.

So far as known to me, Joseph Boardman had only one son, Benjamin Boardman, probably born in New Jersey, 1774; died Sept. 8, 1840. He married Keziah (Katie) Rice, born 1775; died Nov. 21, 1847. In History of Rice Family, see page 7. Benjamin Boardman had four sons as follows: Wm. Boardman, born Nov. 22, 1797, and died May 16, 1887; James, born Dec. 6, 1796; Eli R., born, died at Grapevine, Tex.; Abner, born Apr. 16, 1801, and died Aug. 29, 1875, and married Mary (or Polly) Crose, born Jan. 3, 1806; died Jan. 31, 1876. (See page 5.)

This brings to the passing of four generations of the Boardman family in America, three of which died in Ky.—but where?

On the 10th day of Dec., 1811, a Mr. David A. Graves gave to

Benjamin Boardman a bond for the title to 100 acres of land on the north bank of Somerset Creek in Nicholas County, Ky., six miles south of Carlisle, to which Benjamin Boardman moved, taking family. To this home Benjamin later brought his aged father and mother, Joseph and Elizabeth, and here in the same house lived and died all of the three generations mentioned above, and all are buried in the same graveyard near the original farm house, which is still standing.

From the United States Census of 1910 to 1950 and from the assistance of Mrs. Lute Squires Thompson. I have found that Michael Crose was born in Maryland in 1765, or earlier, and that his wife, Mary Crose, was born in Virginia in 1769.

They were both members of the German Baptist or Dunkard Church. They both spoke the German language and brought their German Bible with them to Kentucky about 1780.

In all probability their ancestors came to Pennsylvania with a colony of German Baptists in 1719 from near Kassel Hess, in Westfalia Province, Germany. This colony spread over parts of Pennsylvania, Maryland and Virginia, and finally a small community came to Bourbon and Nicholas counties, Ky. Among them were Blounts, Shrouts, Molars, Hahns and the Crose, or Kauses.

They built a church at the forks of Somerset Creek in Nicholas County, which they named East Union, and in which they preached in the German language.

The Crose family built their home on the south bank of Hinkston Creek, opposite the mouth of Long Branch. The house is still standing.

Michael Crose died in 1819 and an administration was taken out on his estate on Aug. 17, 1819. See Book F, page 288, old deed records of Bourbon County. Mary (Polly) Crose was living with her son-in-law, Covington Utterback, in 1850, aged 81 years, according to United States Census of that date.

Michael and Mary Crose were married in Virginia and probably came to Kentucky about 1796. They had 14 children, whose names are as follows:

1. Catherine (Katie)—Born Mch. 15, 1787; mar. Thomas Wilson.
2. Elizabeth—Born Oct. 2, 1788; married Benj. Utterback.
3. Jonathan—Born Feb. 2, 1791.
4. Rebecca—Born Aug. 26, 1794; married Philip Ross.
5. Andrew—Born Mch. 2, 1796.
6. Sarah—Born May 22, 1798; married Covington Utterback.
7. Barbary—Born Oct. 11; married Peter Ovenly.
8. Nancy.
9. George.
10. Michael.
11. Samuel.
12. Benjamin.
13. Adam—Died in Morgan Co., Ky.
14. May (or Polly)—Born Jan. 3, 1806; married Abner Boardman; died Jan. 31, 1876. (See Boardman History, page 3.)

BURBRIDGE AND BARNES BIBLE.

Thos. Barnes and Edith Rowland were married Oct. 7, 1795.
Thos. Barnes and Mary Bridges were married Mch. 2, 1815 or 1813.
John A. Barnes and Harriett Willis were married Feb. 27, 1825.
Nelson White and Martha Barnes were married Oct., 1813.
Sidney Burbridge and Susan Barnes were married June 18, 1813.
James Burbridge and Ann Eliza Barnes were married July 4, 1820.
Alfred T. Barnes and Catherine Crane were married Apr. 7, 1840.
Robert Burbridge of Scott Co., Ky., and Eliza Ann Barnes of Claiborne
Co., Miss., were married Sept. 22, 1819.
Oscar H. Burbridge of Scott Co., Ky., and Rebecca S. Matson of
Bourbon Co., Ky., were married Jan. 8, 1846.

Stephen G. Burbridge and Lizzie Garth of Scott Co., Ky., were married May 11, 1853.

Sallie E. Burbridge, Scott Co., Ky., and Hugh Brent of Louisville, Ky., were married Nov. 30, 1853.

Harriet B. Burbridge, Scott Co., Ky., and Governor James A. Wright of Indiana were married Aug. 15, 1854.

Thos. B. Burbridge, Scott Co., Ky., and Susan E. Henry of Hopkinsville, Ky., were married Oct. 3, 1855.

Eliza A. Burbridge (daughter of O. H. Burbridge and Rebecca S. Burbridge) and Byron O. Bollingsley were married in Covington, Ky., Oct., 1869.

Margaret Lemon Burbridge (daughter of Gen. Stephen B. Burbridge and Lizzie Garth) and Daniel Gilmore Hatch were married in Covington, Ky., Nov. 25, 1873.

Albert G. Burbridge and Ella Norbeck were married in Washington, D. C., Feb. 3, 1877.

Albert G. Burbridge married Clara, 2nd wife, in California.

Oscar Howard Burbridge married Mabelle.

Lillie Garth Burbridge and Edward H. Butler of Detroit, Mich., were married in Washington, D. C., Nov. 14, 1901.

Capt. Charles Burbridge Hatch, U. S. M. C., and Maude Embry of Portworth, N. H., were married Aug. 2, 1902.

Oscar H. Billingsley and Marion P. Johnson were married at Maytown, Pa., May 7, 1902.

Maude Billingsley and Geo. P. Gall were married in Washington, D. C., Aug. 29, 1899.

Louise Matson Billingsley and Paul W. Fishbaugh were married in Washington, D. C., Oct. 4, 1905.

James M. Burbridge and Ella Chew Pinkerton Ingels (nee Ella Chew) were married in Paris, Ky., Apr. 28, 1891.

Hattie W. Burbridge and Ed Shropshire of Bourbon Co., Ky.

Russell Clay married Marcie Webb, Kansas City, Mo.

Stephen Denny, not married; died Lexington, Ky.

Harriet Wrights children:
    Hattie, who married ———— Brinton, Philadelphia, Pa.
    Joseph (twin with Hattie), bachelor, Sparta, Wash.

Thomas Burbridge's children:
    Thomas, who married twice in Denver, Colo.
    Ewing, who married Miss Ware, Minneapolis, Wis.
    Charles, bachelor, New York.
    Mamie, who married Walter Cook, Hopkinsville, Ky.

Gen. S. G. Burbridge's children:
    Albert G. married in Los Angeles, Calif.
    Margaret, who married Gilman Hatch, Washington, D. C.
    Lillie, who married Mr. Butler, Detroit, Mich.
    Oscar H., who married Mrs. Whiting, Los Angeles, Calif.
    Stephen, who died infant, Lexington, Ky.

Mrs. Sallie Brent and children:
    Robert Brent, St. Louis, Mo.; Louis Brent, St. Louis, Mo.

BIBLE RECORDS AND BURBRIDGE HISTORY.
Certified by Mrs. Mary L. Burbridge Austin, Lexington, Ky.

Thomas Burbridge, her great-great-grandfather, came from England, settled in Spotsylvania County, Va., near the Potomac River. His wife was Sallie Sharp. Their children:
    Millie, who married, 1st Mr. Robinson, and 2nd Ellis, from Ky.
    Sally, who married Mr. Elly; lived in Scott Co., Ky.
    Money, who married Mr. Wm. Bullett, Louisville, Ky.
    Mary, who married Mr. Ellis, Virginia.
    Betsy, who married Garner Branham, Scott Co., Ky.
    Susan, who married David Branham, Virginia.

George, who married Mary Hord, Scott Co., Ky.
Thomas, who married ————, Springfield, O.
Linsfield married Mrs. Morton, Clark Co., Ky.
Fanny, who married Robert Smith, Louisville, Ky.

Our great-great-grandfather, George Burbridge, married Mary Hord, and moved to scott Co., Ky., lived and died on a farm near Stamping Ground. Children:
Sidney, who married Susan Barnes, Franklin Co., Ky.
James, who married Polly Smith, his cousin, Scott Co., Ky.
Thomas, who married Nancy Bradford, Scott Co., Ky.
Marion, who married Scott Herndon, Scott Co., Ky.
Willina, who married Thomas Blackburn, Scott Co., Ky.
Robert, who married Eliza Ann Barnes, Clayborn Co., Miss., Sept. 22, 1819. She was a sister of Mrs. Sidney Burbridge.

Linfield Burbridge moved from Clark Co., Ky., to Missouri.

Elijah Burbridge lived in Trig Co., and died a bachelor.

Eliza A. Billingsley had 5 children:
Oscar Henry, who married Marion Johnson, Falls Church, Va.
Maude B., who married George Gall, Philadelphia and Washington.
Hattie single; Louisa M., who married Paul Fishbaugh, Washington D. C.; Thomas, single.

Maude B. Gall has one daughter, Margurite.

J. M. Burbridge, no children; Robert O. Burbridge, bachelor; Oscar Henry, bachelor; Lucy M., single.
Mary L., who married Francis Gershom Austin, Lexington, Ky.

Hattie W. Shropshire's children, Afton, Iowa:
May B., who married C. E. Hend, Afton, Iowa.
Karl, single, Afton, Iowa.

John Burbridge had 4 sons and 4 daughters.
Roland, who married Elizabeth Jones, Mt. Sterling, Ky.
Richard, single, Bath Co., Ky.
Benjamine, who married Ellen Burnes, Bath Co., Ky.
James Walter, who married Mrs. Lillie Ann Glover, Bath Co., Ky.
Miranda, who married James Young, Bath Co., Ky.
Ann, who married James Stone, Bath Co., Ky.
Jane, who married Harry McKinervan, Bath Co., Ky.
Arleminia, who married 1st Wm. Dawson, 2nd James Ficklin.

Children of Robt. and Eliza Ann Burbridge:
Oscar H., who married Rebecca S. Matson (double wedding), Paris, Ky.
Harriett, who mar. Joseph A. Wright, Gov. of Indiana; died 1855.
Thomas, who married Susan Henry. He was killed by Rebel Guerillas, 1867, at Russelville, Ky.
Susan Mary, who died 1842.
Stephen Gano, who married 1st Elizabeth Garth, and 2nd Sallie McGarge, Philadelphia, Pa.

Sallie Eliza, who married 1st Hugh Brent; 2nd Mathews; 3d Caswell, and 4th McDonald.

Oscar H .and Rebecca S. Burbridge's children:
Eliza Ann, who married Byron O. Billingsley, at Washington, D. C.
Jas. M., who married Mrs. Ella Ingles, widow of Dr. E. Ingles and Wm. Pinkerton.
Robert O., who never married, Philadelphia, Pa.
Oscar Henry, married; died 1863.
Lucy Matson, who married ————, Hutchonson Station, Ky.; died.
Lizzie, twin to Mary L., who died in infancy.
Mary L., who married F. G. Austin of Mt. Holly, N. J., June, 1920; lives in Lexington, Ky.
Hattie W., who married Edw. Shropshire, Leesburg, Ky.

BOULWARE HISTORY
(Collected by Mrs. H. K. McAdams)

Ohio history says: "Jacob Boulware's father owned a plantation (maybe near Culpepper, Va.) and slaves. Jacob and a brother were sent to Ohio for an education. Jacob became an Abolitionist, and when he went home his father disinherited Jacob, who came back to Clearmont Co., Ohio, and taught school. He and Gen. Grant's father were warm friends." Jacob married Hannah Roodamar, a daughter of Mr. Roodamar and Miss VanDusan. Their children:

1. John. 2. Jacob.
3. Abraham (Twin)—Married Nancy Winters of New Harmony, O. (Had eight children.)
4. Benjamin (Twin)—Married Ann Peterson of Newton, O. (Had four children.)
5. Fyrman—Married Ruth Walker of Glen Este, O.
6. Hiram—Married Sarah Shotwell. (2nd, married Earhart.)
7. James—Married Catherine McAdams. (Her second marriage was to Jas. Porter.)
8. ————————.
9. William—Married Melinda Fisk. (Had eight children.)
10.
11. Andrew Van—Married Nancy Wright. (Had nine children.) Owned a chair factory in Williamsburg, O.
12. Joseph.

Of these Wm. and two sons were in the Civil War. Wm. and son, Wm. Livingston, were in Co. G., 153 Inft. Randolph in Reg. 89. Also Sidney McAdams in Reg. 89.

Wm. Boulware, ninth child of Jacob and Hannah. Children:

1. Randolph—Born at Bethel, O., Jan. 23, 1837; died Nov. 3, 1864; married Isabel Snell.
2. Mary E.—Born July 11 ,1839; died Oct. 29, 1884; married Oliver Perry McAdams (of John, of Ephrim, of John).
3. Melinda—Died infant.
4. William Livingston—Born Dec. 11, 1843; married Amanda Goff of Williamsburg, O. (2nd, married John Morford, Laurel, O.)
5. Corwin McLain—Born Sept. 9, 1846; died Dec. 1, 1907, at Williamsburg, O.; married Sarah Peterson.
6. Larella Susan—Born June 3, 1849; married Thomas Still, Williamsburg, O.
7. Lester—Born Jan. 5, 1852; married Judyth Blair, Williamburg, in 1875.
8. Charley—Born Jan. 4, 1855; died July, 1900, in Brooklyn, N. Y.; married Lida Miller of Warren Co., O., born Apr., 1857.

Abraham Boulware, 3rd child of Jacob and Hannah, married Nancy Winters (New Harmony, O.) Children: John, Cornelius, Hiram, Laura, Belle, Dr. Leonidas T. (of Midland City); Harvey and William.

Benjamine Boulware, 4th child of Jacob and Hannah, married Ann Peterson of Newton, O. (2nd, married Asa Smith of Smithville, O.) Children of 1st marriage: Marietta, Victoria, William and Angeline.

Fyrman Boulware, 5th child of Jacob and Hannah, married Ruth Walker, Glen Este, O. Children: Fyrman, Jr. (born Blanchester, O.), and Annie.

Hiram Boulware, 6th child of Jacob and Hannah, married Sarah Shotwell. (2nd, married Mr. B. Earhart.) Children 1st marriage: Elizabeth, Charlotte and Hiram, killed in Civil War.

James Boulware, 7th child of Jacob and Hannah, married Catherine McAdams. Children: A son and Louise. 2nd married James Porter. Children: Charlotte, who married Wm. Henter; Phoebe, who married Mr. Munsey, and Martha, who married Erastus Smith.

Andrew Van Boulware, 11th child of Jacob and Hannah, married Nancy Wright. Children: Mary E., Zella T., Charles H., Joseph C.,

Alva V. (lived at Gallipolis, O.), Harry E., Hiram Clifford, Clara Maude and Edgar W.

Charles H. Boulware, 3rd child of Andrew Van and Nancy, married Sarah Brown. Children: Jesse F., born Aug. 13, 1880; Clifford Van, born Nov. 16, 1881, Cincinnati, O. (Jesse F. married Mr. Scott, Waynesville, O.)

Randolph Boulware, 1st son of Wm. and Melinda, married Isabell Snell. Children: Everet and Mary.

William Livingston Boulware, 4th child of Wm. and Melinda, married Amanda Goff, Williamsburg, O.; 2nd married John Morford. Children: Edward, Bessie, George, Nora and Robert.

Corwin McLean Boulware—Born Sept. 9, 1846; died Dec. 1, 1907, at Williamsburg, O. Married Sarah Peterson, Williamsburg, Ohio. Children: Maggie P—Born Nov. 24, 1874; Anna Laura—Born Apr. 14, 1879; Stanley—Born Jan. 8, 1884; died July, 1884; Guy A.—Born Aug. 14, 1886; Lorena—Born Aug. 20, 1893.

Maggie P. married Wm. Cramer, live in Cincinnati; children: Geneva—Born Sept. 13, 1898; Lowell—Born Aug. 21, 1901; Verna —Born Mar. 26, 1904; Elda—Born Oct., 1905; William Russell—Born Dec. 21, 1909.

Anna Laura married Elbridge Snell (D. D. S.), lived at Bethel and Springfield, Ohio; also Miami, Fla. Children: Harold Elbridge—Born Aug. 11, 1903; Naomi Lorena—Born Jan. 9, 1907; Pauline Marie—Born Dec. 22, 1911.

Guy Albert married Olive Duckwall, reside in Williamsburg, Ohio.

Lorena married Benjamin McAfee, reside at Dayton, O. Child: Lawrence—Born Aug. 3, 1910.

Lester Boulware, 7th child of Wm. and Melinda, married Judyth Petterson Blair. Children: Robert Lester, born July 22, 1876; married Cora Hoyt (of Dr. Hoyt) on Dec. 24, 1903. Larella, born Sept. 8; married William Baumgartner on Dec. 31, 1903. Edith, born Dec. 8, 1880; died Sept. 20, 1891.

Larella, 6th child of Wm. and Melinda, married Thomas Still, Williamsburg, O. Children: Clifford and Edward.

Charley, eighth child of Wm. and Melinda, married Lida Miller of Warren Co., born Apr., 1857; died in Brooklyn, N. Y., and both buriea at Twenty Mile Stand, O. Children: William Lester, born Apr. 18, 1905; Marjorie Elizabeth, born Oct. 17, 1906; Sarah Blair, born June 30, 1909; Robert Hoyt, born Feb. 21, 1914.

Larella Boulware, 2nd child of Lester and Judy, married William O. Baumgartner of Mountain Lake Park, Maryland (now live in Chicago, Ill.) She was born Dec. 2, 1877. He is a post office inspector, headquarters at Chicago. One child: Mary Edith, born June 24, 1905, in Hillsboro, O.

Nina Boulware, only child of Charley and Lida (Miller), married Frank Hudson of Cincinnati, O. Own a farm near Mason, O. Children: Mary Elizabeth and Frances.

Other Boulwares Not Belonging to Above Family

Wm. Boulware, Fayette Co.. Will abstract Book A, page 77, mentions wife "Nuttie," sons, John, Wm. Jacob; daughters, Lucy Wortham, Frances Grubbs, Phebe Pemberton and Fannie. Grandson, Hyram Wortham. Dated Mch. 29, 1790.

Madison Boulware, Lt. Col. 7th Cal. Inft., 1861-1865.

1st cenus, Virginia, published in 1790, gives Jas. Boulware, Amherst Co.; Ritchie, Essex Co.; Samuel. Essex Co.; Younger, Essex Co.; Starke, Black, Halifax Co.

Franky Boulware married John Barker. Book 1, page 58. Apr. 21, 1814. Lexington, Ky.

Thos. Boulware, Comm. of Essex Co., Virginia, 1774. Ref. Wm. and Mary. Magazine No. 5, page 254.

W. E. Boulware's dau., Lilliam Jamison Boulware, mar. Jno. Spence.

Theodric Boulware married Susan Kelly. Ten children. (See Colonial Dames.)

Marriage register, Virginia, Mag. of Hist. and Biog. Muscoe Boulware married Elizabeth Spindle, Mch., 1810.

Gray Boulware, Jr., married Lilley S. G. Hudgins, Aug. 17, 1852.

Dr. Boulware of Carolina married Anne Tripp Slaughter. A. T. Slaughter was daughter of Reuben Slaughter and Emily Long of Baltimore. Reuben was son of John and Milly Coleman (daughter of Robert Coleman). Dr. Boulware was son of McCalla Boulware, who married Ada Jackson Miller. Children: Jackson Darious, Gideon Brown, Elizabeth Tripp. (Note on Culpepper Co.: Dr. Slaughter's list, St. Marks Parrish.)

ESTES FAMILY
(From History of Lewis and Kindred Families of Kentucky)
(By Mrs. Joseph B. Beard, Lexington, Ky.)

Estes ancestors came from Dover, England. The first one settled in Spottsylvania Co., Va.

1st John Estes married Nancy Montague. They had eight children:
1. Middleton Estes—Married Elizabeth Adams, in Lexington, Ky.
2. John Estes.
3. Abraham Estes—Born in Va. in 1787; died Sept. 11, 1825; married Dec. 24, 1813. Beulah Schooler, daughter of Wharton and Margaret Gatewood Schooler. Beulah was born Apr. 22, 1787; died Feb. 10, 18—.
4. Clement Estes—Married 1st Sarah Adams, 2nd Miss Wilson.
5. Bartlett Estes.
6. Elizabeth Estes—Married cousin, Spencer Estes.
7. Nancy Estes—Married Wililam Estes.
8. Polly Estes—Married Robinson.

Abraham and Beulah Schooler Estes. Children born in Ky.
1. Nancy Estes—Born May 1, 1815; married John Ballenger, Oct. 25, 1829.
2. Martha (Patsey) Estes—Born July 2, 1818; died June 8, 1859; married Aug. 8, 1833, to Preston Hedges, who lives at Hedges Station, Clark Co., Ky.
3. John W. Estes—Born Mch. 13, 1823; died Jan., 1895; married Mary J. Stipp Dec., 1850, Winchester, Ky. She was born June 26, 1823.

HOWARD HISTORY
(Contributed by J. M. Durbin, Mrs. Dennis Mulligan and Mrs. Charles Conner)

James Howard the 1st of England, settled in Maryland in 1770, married Margaret Wilson, of Washington Co., Maryland, near Hagerstown. They came to Ky. in 1790, and settled on land lying on left corner of Redmon and Maysville pike: Children: 1. Mathew Howard, married Mollie Hitt. 2. Elijah Howard the 1st married Miss Smith. 3. Paris Howard the 1st, born 1777; married Catherine Current. 4. Hannah Howard, born 1783; married William Ficher in 1800.

Mathew Howard and Mollie Hitt. Children: 1. Sam Howard, married Cassanda Howard, his 1st cousin. 2. Nancy Howard, married Joe Amos. 3. Rebecca Howard, married (in St. Louis). 4. Sally Howard. 5. Thomas Howard. 6. James C. Howard, married Delia Peck. 7. Mahala Howard, married Wills. 8. Mollie Howard, married Mattox Fisher. 9. Joe Howard, married Martha Berkley. 10. Ben Howard, married Minerva Dimmett.

Elijah Howard and Miss Smith. Children: 1. ————. 2. Sallie Howard, married Lear. 3. Rebecca Howard, married Lockwood. 4. Nancy Howard, married Rankin. 5. Cassanda Howard, married Sam Howard. 6. Westley Howard, married Widow Goddard.

Paris Howard the 1st mar. Catherine Current: Children: 1. Thomas Howard, married Sue Kimbrough. 2. Sallie Howard, married James Fisher, 1st cousin. 3. James Howard the 2nd married Miss Blackburn. 4. Polly Howard, married Isaac Night. 5. Margaret Howard, married John Stoker. 6. Elijah Howard the 2nd married (second) Sallie J. Dimmitt. 7. Mathew Howard 2nd. 8. Ely Howard married Hannah Isgrig. 9. John Howard married Betsy Turner.

James Howard the 2nd married Miss Blackburn. Children: 1. Paris Howard the 2nd married Mary George Dimmitt. 2. John Howard married Victoria Dimmett.

Polly Howard married Isaac Night. Children: 1. Elizabeth Night, married Jerome Sanford. 2. A son, married Miss Barton.

Margaret Howard married John Stoker. Children: 1. Vine Stoker. 2. Sallie Stoker. 3. Kate Stoker. 4. Alice Stoker. 5. Martha tSoker. 6. Ella Stoker. 7. Hattie Stoker. 8. Frank Stoker.

Ely Howard married Hannah Isgrig. Children: Two sons died infants. 3. Margaret Howard, married Frances Baird.

Paris Howard the 2nd married Mary George Dimmett. Children: 1. Bud Howard. 2. Walker Howard. 3. Nick Howard. 4. Cealy Howard. 5. Joe Howard. 6. William Howard. 7. Vine Howard. 8. Lena Howard. 9. Nannie Vic Howard.

John Howard married Victoria Dimmett. Children: 1. Frank Howard. 2. John Howard. 3. Jennie H. Howard, married Redmon. 4. Addie Howard, married Redmon. 5. Vic Howard, married Pugh.

A son of Isaac Night and Polly Howard married Miss Barton. Children: Mollie Night, married Fant, and had William Nelson Fant.

James Fisher, son of Wm. Fisher and Hannah Howard, married Sallie Howard, his 1st cousin. Children: 1. Thomas Fisher, married Emmarine Barton. 2. John Fisher married Louisa Jett. (They had children: 1. Cora Fisher. 2. Annie Fisher. 3. Lou Fisher. 4. John Fisher. 5. Claude Fisher. 6. Fred Fisher. 7. Pattie.

Sallie Howard Fisher, widow of James Fisher, married Colonel Dimmett. Children: 1. James Horace Dimmett. 2. Richard Dimmett.

Hannah Howard was born 1783; married, 1800, William Fisher. Children: 1. James Fisher, married Sallie Howard, 1st cousin. 2. Hannah Fisher. 3. Amanda Fisher. 4. Nancy Fisher, born 1821; died 1875; married Jacob Bowman, born 1807, died 1893. 5. Mattox Fisher, married Mollie Howard, 1st cousin. 6. John Fisher. 7. Peggy Fisher, married Sutton. 8. ———. 9. Sallie Fisher, married Mock. 10. Samuel Fisher, born 1809; died 1848; married Lucinda Talbott.

Nancy Fisher, 4th child of William Fisher and Hannah Howard, married Jacob Bowman Children: 1. Dock Bowman. 2. Joe Bowman. 3. Abe Bowman. 4. Will Bowman. 5. Mollie Bowman, married Henry. 6. Mary (?) Bowman, married Adenoram Allen. 7. Ella Bowman married Will Cason. 8. Dora Bowman, born 1852; married John Bowman.

Mary (?) Bowman married Admoram Allen. Children: 1. Annie Allen, married E. L. Martin. 2. Lena Allen. 3. Mary Allen.

E. L. Martin married Annie Allen. Children: 1. Grace Martin, married Denis Mulligan. 2. Lena Martin married Hupp Douglas (who had: 1. Jean Allen Douglas. 2. Marion Lee Douglas.) 3. Allen Martin. 4. Annette Martin. 5. Curry Martin. 6. Mary Martin.

History of this family Vol. 4, Kerr's "History of Ky."

DESCENDANTS OF DAVID HAMPTON, SR., OF CLARK CO., KY.
(Donated by Andrew Hood Hampton, Jr., Winchester, Clark Co., Ky.)

David Hampton, Sr., married Sarah Willson in South Carolina and came to what is now Clark Co., Ky., about 1785 or a little earlier. His mother-in-law, Mrs. Esther Willson, a widow, came to Kentucky with him. It is probable that several of his older children were born in South Carolina. Nine children of David Hampton, Sr.:

1. Willson Hampton married Susan Grigsby, who outlived him and afterwards married a Mr. Hieronymous. Willson Hampton has a number of living descendants.
2. Esther Hampton married Beverly Daniel and had a son, who married and left two or more children, one of whom was named Theisa. So far as I know this line is now extinct.
3. George Hampton married Catharine Routt, Dec. 17, 1807. Catharine, or Kitty, Routt, was the daughter of Daniel and Martha Stiglar Routt and was born in Fauquier Co., Va., near Warrenton on Mch. 13, 1791, and came to what is now Clark Co., Ky., with her parents in 1795, and died in that county Mch. 17, 1883, and is buried in the Winchester Cemetery. George Hampton is buried in the old Hampton Graveyard about five miles south of Winchester, near the Boonesboro Road.
4. Sallie Hampton married Martin Haggard and has many descendants in Clark Co. at the present time.
5. James Hampton. 6. William Hampton. 7. Joseph Hampton. These three sons are mentioned in the will of David Hampton, Sr., but I do not know anything further about them and do not think they have any descendants in this State. It is possible that they died at an early age.
8. Jesse Hampton (called "White-headed Jesse") married Nancy Jackson in the year 1813, and has many descendants in Clark Co. Mrs. James D. Lisle, Alfred Howard Hampton, Thaddeus W. Hampton and Mrs. Mollie Hampton Baldwin are the children of a daughter, Parthenia, who married Alfred Howard Hampton, Sr. Alfred Howard Hampton, Sr., was a distant kinsman of his wife and was the son of David Hampton, Jr. David Hampton, Sr., and David Hampton, Jr., were supposed to be related in some way, but the degree of relationship was not known when they came to Kentucky.
9. Wade Hampton, the youngest son, married and died when quite young. He left one child, James Hampton, who died a few years ago without descendants.

David Hampton, Sr., and Sarah Willson Hampton, his wife, are both buried in an old Hampton burying ground near the Boonesboro Road on the farm that formerly belonged to Braxton Lisle. David Hampton, Sr., as said above, was a South Carolinian, and was related in some way to Wade Hampton, the Revolutionary soldier, who was the ancestor of the Confederate general of the same name. Sarah Willson Hampton was the daughter of a British soldier, who died or was killed during the Revolution.

Eight children of George Hampton and Catharine Routt Hampton:
1. Patsey, a daughter born about 1808 and lived only a few months.
2. David L. Hampton, born July 29, 1810; married Lucy Gaines, and died about 187—. Has descendants in Missouri, but none in Kentucky that I know.
3. Daniel Hampton, born Sept. 13, 1812; married Mrs. Mary Jouett, who was a daughter of Beverly Daniel and his first wife, and was the step-daughter of Esther Hampton Daniel mentioned above. This Mrs. Mary Daniel Jouett Hampton was the grandmother by her first husband of Edward S. Jouett, Beverly R. Jouett and Mrs. James D. Simpson. Daniel Hampton had only one son, John Daniel Hampton, who married Rebecca Ritchie, and left surviving him a daughter, Clara, who died unmarried. This line is now extinct.
4. Lewis Hampton, born Aug. 17, 1814; married Fanny W. Hood, daughter of Dr. Andrew Hood and his first wife, Miriam White Hood, in the year 1847. Lewis Hampton (my grandfather) died in 1872, and left two children, Kate Hampton Bush and Andrew Hood Hampton, Sr.

5. Esther Hampton married Claiborne Lisle and has many descendants in Clark Co. She was the mother of James D. Lisle, Thomas Lisle, Mrs. Jesse N. Hodgkin, David Congreve Lisle, two other daughters now dead, and Marcus Lisle, formery a member of Congress from this district.

6. Mary Catharine Hampton, born 1829; was the first wife of Ambrose Bush, and has descendants in Clark Co.

7. Elizabeth Minerva Hampton, born Dec. 18, 1820; married John A. Hampton, a brother of Alfred Howard Hampton, Sr., Feb. 14, 1837. She and her family moved to Missouri about the time of the Civil War and she has many descendants in that State, but none that I know of in Kentucky.

8. Martha Jane Hampton (known as Patsey) was the 2nd wife of Ambrose Bush and has descendants in Ky. She was born in 1832.

(The above list probably doesn't give the children of George Hampton correctly, according to age, except the first four, as the entries were scattered through the old Routt Bible and some were almost illegible. The Routt Bible goes back to 1767 and is in possession of A. Hood Hampton, Winchester, Ky.)

Children of Lewis Hampton and Fanny Hood Hampton:

1. Kate Hampton, born June 6, 1848; married Valentine White Bush, and died in Apr., 1927. She had two sons, Lewis Hampton Bush, who died in 1916, and V. W. Bush, Jr., an attorney of Winchester, Ky.

2. Andrew Hood Hampton, Sr., born Sept. 15, 1849; married Amelia Moore, daughter of Major Thomas H. Moore and his wife, Maria Bright Moore, on the 15th of Sept., 1874, and died Oct. 14, 1920. His children were Fanny Hood Hampton, Thomas Moore Hampton (died Sept. 9, 1929), Marie Bright Hampton, Lewis Routt Hampton (died Nov. 3, 1918), A. Hood Hampton, Jr.

HAMPTON FAMILY
(Donated by Mrs. Alfred Howard Hampton, of Clark Co., Ky.)

David Hampton—Born Jan. 15, 1764; died Jan. 26, 1842.

Mary Hampton—Wife of David Hampton; born Aug. 1, 1771; died Sept. 4, 1818. Children:

John Hampton—Born July 23, 1788.

Sarah Hampton—Born Oct. 17, 1790; mar. Waller Pritchett, 1820.

Elizabeth Hampton—Born Mch. 4, 1793; married Adams.

David Hampton—Born Aug. 15, 1795; mar. Mary Johnson, 1819.

Cyntha Hampton—Born Feb. 8, 1798; mar. Claiborne Cox, 1814.

Mary Hampton—Born July 18, 1800; married Wm. Pigg, 1819.

Nancy Hampton—Born Mch. 8, 1803; married Jonathan Wooten, 1824.

Wade B. Hampton—Born May 30, 1805; mar, Rebecca Hodgkin.

Alfred Howard Hampton—Born Feb. 28, 1808; married Polly P. Hampton.

David Reed Hampton—Born May 22, 1810; unmarried.

George Washington Hampton—Born Sept. 9, 1812; mar. Jones.

John Andrew Jackson Hampton—Born Apr. 17, 1815; married Minerva Hampton.

David Hampton and Mary Jones were married Apr. 24, 1819.

David Hampton—Son of George Washington Hampton; born Feb. 15, 1835.

Mary Frances Hampton—Daughter of George Washington Hampton; born Nov. 14, 1837.

Nancy Hampton and Jonathan Wooten were married June 5, 1824. Home in Tennessee.

Jesse Hampton—Born Mch. 8, 1785; died June 17, 1870. He was the son of David Hampton.

Nancy Jackson, daughter of James Jackson, was born Mch. 10, 1797.

James Jackson was born Sept. 12, 1772.

Polly Embry Jackson was born Oct. 2, 1779. Polly Embry, daughter of Jos. and Milly Embry.

Jesse Hampton and Nancy Jackson were married in the year of Our Lord Jan. 12, 1813. Children:

Sallie Hampton was born July 14, 1816.

James Hampton was born Aug. 27, 1818.

Polly P. Hampton was born Aug. 26, 1820.

Emerine Elizabeth Hampton was born Aug. 5, 1829.

Joseph Wilson Hampton was born Mch. 10, 1831; died 22, 1862.

Emerine Elizabeth Hampton Quisenberry died Mch. 18, 1864.

Sallie A. Hampton was wedded to Lewis Hampton, Nov. 14, 1833.

Sallie Hampton later married Phil Hodgkin.

Sallie Hampton Hodgkin died Apr. 6, 1864.

Polly P. Hampton married John M. Reed, July 6, 1837.

Polly P. Hampton Reed married A. Howard Hampton, Sr., in 1841.

Children of Alfred Howard Hampton and Polly Panthier Hampton:

Henry Allen Hampton—Born July 29, 1842.

Jessie Mills Hampton—Born Sept. 5, 1844.

Nancy Jackson Hampton—Born Feb. 13, 1847.

David B. Hampton—Born Mch. 8, 1850; died June 24, 1916.

Thornton W. Hampton—Born Aug. 2, 1852.

Thaddeus Wardon Hampton—Born Apr. 10, 1855.

Molly C. Hampton—Born July 4, 1857.

Alfred Howard Hampton, Jr.—Born Feb. 21, 1860.

Henry Allen Hampton and Bettie Allen were married Mch. 22, 1877.

James D. Lisle and Nancy Jackson Hampton were married Sept. 26, 1871.

Dr. John D. Gilbert and Molly C. Hampton were married Nov., 1879.

W. T. Baldwin and Molly C. Hampton Gilbert were married July 4, 1897.

Thaddeus Wardon Hampton and Nancy Tucker were married Feb. 18, 1888.

D. B. Hampton and Mary C. Haggard were married Oct. 12, 1905.

A. Howard Hampton and Mattie Eades Griggs were married Feb. 6, 1907.

A. Howard Hampton, Sr., died Nov. 18, 1891.

Polly P. Hampton died Sept. 13, 1905.

JENCKES (JENKS) FAMILY

Chancellor L. Jenks, Jr., President (in 1827) of the Evanston, Ill., Historical Society, has compiled a complete history of the Jenks family, from Elyston Gladdrydd, the founder of the tribe of the "Marshes," the fourth royal family of Wales, to the American descendants, of this generation. This noted family of Jenckes traces its lineage in unbroken line to Vortigern, King of the Britons, in the year 449 A. D. The short account given below of three of the men is copied by Mrs. H. K. McAdams, a descendant, from the history written by Chancellor L. Jenks and from the National Cyclopaedia, Vol. X., and page 10.

Joseph Jenckes (first of the name, in America)—Born 1602; died 1683; came to America with the Winthrop Company in 1642. He was the first "inventor" in America, and settled at Lynn, Mass. His son, Joseph (2nd), 1632-1716, settled Pawtucket, R. I.; was "representative" of the Colony to Legislature for 40 years, and Assistant Lieutenant Governor at intervals, extending from 1680-1698. Four of his sons were noted men. Governor Joseph (3), Nathaniel, Major of Militia; Ebenezer, celebrated Baptist, and William, Judge of the Assembly for 40 years.

Joseph Jenckes (3) 1656-1740 was born at Pawtucket, R. I. His parents were the first white settlers of Pawtucket and their son, Joseph

(3), was probably the first white child born there. He was the eldest of ten children and by far the most prominent of the four noted brothers. He was "Councillor" almost continuously from 1680-1712; was elected to the "General Assembly" in 1679 when only 23 years old, becoming Clerk and Speaker of that body. He was the Speaker of the House of Deputies 1698-1699, and 1707-1708; was "Major of the Main," the highest military title of Colonial times, from 1707-1711. He was Deputy Governor from 1715-1727; Governor from 1727-1732, and declined re-election on account of his advanced age, 76, having given active and efficient service to his Country for a period of 52 years. He was Ambassador for the Colony of Rhode Island to the Court of St. James, for several years. In 1711, he was appointed on a committee to confer with the Five Nations. In 1705 he was appointed a member of the Boundary Commission to settle the disputes between Massachusetts, Connecticut and Rhode Island. In 1720 he was made joint agent with Partridge of Connecticut to lay the boundary disputes before the King. In 1717 he was appointed Chairman of a Commission to compile and publish the Laws of the Colony, and to make a "map" for the English Government.

Ransalear Jeremiah Jenks (of Caleb, of Capt. Joseph, of Dr. John, of Gov. Joseph, III, of Joseph II., of Joseph I.) Married first Asenath Woodburn (daughter of Moses Woodburn, Revolutionary soldier who served two enlistments, one as guard which conducted Andre to his execution, and in 1781 he was a marine on brig "Marquis Lafayette" and in 1782 he served on the "Randolph," when he aided in capturing prizes at sea. He was a descendant of John Woodburn, first settler of the name in Londonderry, and whose sister, Mary, married Zaccheus Greeley and became the mother of Horace Greeley. Moses was a descendant of Thomas Woodburn who fought in the war against King Edward, his estates were confiscated and he went to Ireland and married the daughter of Lord Carl; they came to America and settled at Greenfield, N. Y., and escaped in the Cherry Valley massacre with their two little boys.) Asenath Woodburn was born 1800 at Cherry Valley, Oslego Co., N. Y.; died Sept. 13, 1845, in Fulton, Whiteside Co., Illinois. Moses Woodburn married Asenath Wright (daughter of Edward Wright and Cloe Pomeroy.)

R. J. Jenckes—Born May 27, 1792, at Pawtucket, R. I.; died Oct. 16, 1872, at Wheatland, Iowa. Asenath Woodburn—Born May 3, 1800, at Cherry Valley, Ostego Co., N. Y.; died Sept. 13, 1845, at Fulton, Ill. They were married Dec. 25, 1816, at Wysox, Pa. Their children:

1. Abby Brown Jenks—Born Dec. 28, 1817, at Wysox, Pa.; died Feb. 3, 1887, at Fulton, Ill. Married Grover Rice, Nov. 12, 1839. Grover died Jan. 6, 1892, at Fulton, Ill.

2. Sarah Almena Jenks—Born Jan. 22, 1819, at Sheshequin, Bradford Co., Pa.; died at Fulton, Ill., 1898. Married first Knight S. Osgood, at Chicago, Ill., March 22, 1831; was divorced Sept., ˜1844, and married, June 14, 1846, Dr. John Johnson, a citizen of England. He died Aug. 5, 1856, at Panama, Central America. Almena and first husband had one son, Charles G. Osgood, born May 12, 1840; died in Paris, France, Oct. 22, 1876. This Charles Granville Osgood married Mary A. Baird, in San Francisco, Calif., April, 1865. Their children: Charles Raymond Osgood and Oscar Martin Osgood. Children of Almena Jenks and second husband, Dr. J. Johnson: Abby Jane Johnson, Sarah Asenath Johnson.

3. Moses W. Jenks—Born July 26, 1820, at Warren, Pa.; died 1906 at Oak Park, Ill.

4. Sena Wright Jenks—Born Oct. 10, 1821, at Warren, Pa.; married Martin Knox, Oct. 20, 1841, at Fulton, Ill. He died at Brownsville, Calif., in 1885, no children. Sena died at Brownsville, Calif., June 31, 1894.

5. Exie Smith Jenks—Born Warren, Pa., lived three years.
6. Charles Caleb Jenks (first)—Died at two and a half years.
7. John Brown Jenks—Born 1826; died Oct. 11, 1843, Fulton, Ill.
8. Ednah Shaw Jenks—Born Sheshequin, Pa., Mch. 2, 1829; died June 27, 1848, at Fulton, Ill.
9. Charles Caleb Jenks(second)—Born Sheshequin, Pa., Jan.,1831.
10. Edward Pelton Jenks—Born Sept., 1832, at Hambrook, Pa.; died at Beloit, Wis., June, 1857; married Matilda Fountain Feb. 15, 1854, in Beloit, Wis., and had children: (1) Clara Jenks, who married Mr. Middleton, Kalamazoo, Mich; (2) George Fountain Jenks. After death of E. P. Jenks, Matilda moved with her children to Indiana.
11. Charlotte Augustus Jenks—Born at Hornbrook, Pa., May 24, 1835; married James M. Harvey at Galena, Ill., Apr. 22, 1860; divorced in Cook Co., Ill. Children:
    (1) Edward Harvey—Born Jan. 28, 1861; married Nancy Whitaker and had a girl, born 1883, and James Edward, born Nov. 11, 1887.
    (1) Charles F. Harvey—Born Jan. 6, 1863; married Julia Gibson; children born (1) 1887 and (2) 1889.
    (3) Jessie L. Harvey—Born Dec. 12, 1864; married Henry Foss, Forbstown, Cal., in 1907; lives 3127 Mabel St., Oakland, Cal. They have four daughters and one son.
    4. Nettie Ednah Harvey—Married Sept. 15, 1893, Mr. Cuddyback, at Brownsville, Calif., and moved to Salt Lake City, Utah.
    (5) Ernest R. Harvey—Born Jan. 6, 1872; died Feb., 1872.
12. Nancy Woodburn Jenks—Born at Cass, Cook Co., Ill., Dec. 7, 1863; married James L. Gibson, Apr. 18, 1856, at Brownsville, Cal., and had:
    (1) Charles Caleb Gibson.
    (2) John Brown Gibson.
    (3) Edwin J. Gibson—Died at San Jose, Cal., at 22 years.
    (4) Frederick Wm. Gibson—Married Letie Pattie, Oakland, California.
    (5) Martin Knox Gibson—Born Dec. 13, 1868; lives at 612 Hyde St., San Francisco, Cal.
13. Wm. Henry Jenks Wilson—Born Nov. 5, 1838 at Round Grove, Ill., (near Fulton); married Annie Eliza Cook, at Lexington, Ky., on Jan. 19, 1861. He died in Cincinnati, Ohio, July 14, 1892. She was born June 19, 1838; died July 16, 1926, Lexington, Ky. Both were buried at Cynthiana, Ky. Children:
    (1) Annie Laurie Wilson—Born Nov. 5, 1862, Louisville, Ky.; married Robert Bruce James, in Oakland, Cal., and had (1) Oscar William James, born at Cynthiana, Ky., at Addallah Park, Nov. 6, 1889; married Ester Anderson, of Salem, Oregon, and had (1) Roberta Mary James, born Dec. 29, 1920; (2) Oscar Richard James, born Oct. 16, 1922, at Eugene, Oregon.
    (2) Stephen Henry Wilson—Born Aug., 1864; died July 26, 1865.
    (3) Martha Ednah Wilson—Born Feb. 25, 1886; married H. K. McAdams.
14. Ransallear Jeremiah Jenks—Born Sept. 18, 1840; died Oct., 1841, Fulton, Ill., aged 10 months.
15. Richmond Jerry Jenks—Born Sept. 23, 1842, in Bradford Co., Pa.; died at Spring Rock, Clinton Co., Ill., Mch. 7, 1868. R. J. Jenks and second wife, Mrs. Sarah Evans Bartlett (who died in 1852.) Children:
16. Josephine Jenks—Born at Toronto, Iowa, 1850; married Samuel Bell, and lives at Cedar Rapids, Iowa. Had 8 children.

17. ————.

R. J. Jenks third wife, no children.

LOGAN-MORRISON-HOCKER-REED-CAREY
(Donated by Mrs. Jos. Beard, Lexington, Ky.)

David Logan (immigrant), born about 1718; died 1757; married Jane ——— of Pa. Their children: 1. Hugh Logan, born 1745. 2. Benjamin Logan, born 1747. 3. John Logan, born 1749. 4. Nathaniel Logan, born 1751. 5. Mary Logan, born 1753. 6. Sara Logan, born 1755.

Hugh Logan married Sara Woods Mch. 10, 1780. Hugh died Dec. 25, 1816. Sara Logan died May 2, 1814; age 57 years. Their children: 1. Nancy Logan, born Feb. 1, 1783. 2. Jane Logan, born Feb. 7, 1785; married George Carpenter, July 4, 1806. 3. Dorcas Logan, born July 15, 1787; married Robert Lewis, Dec. 23, 1811. 4. Cyrus Logan, born Nov. 20, 1789; married Mahaly Lewis, Nov. 23, 1815. 5. Allen Logan, born Oct. 25, 1791; married Patsy Givins, Dec. 24, 1816. 6. Green Logan, born Feb. 14, 1794; married Francis McRoberts, Feb., 1823. 7. W. C. Logan, born July 12, 1796; married Sara B. Bell, Dec. 16, 1817. 8. Sara Logan, born Jan. 28, 1799; married John Ezra Morrison, Apr. 24, 1817. 9. Harriett Logan, born Apr. 4, 1801; married Hilton McRoberts, Apr. 4, 1826.

John E. Morrison, born about 1794, married Sara Logan Apr. 24, 1817. John E. Morrison died in Texas about 1836. Sara Logan (of Hugh and Sarah) Morrison died in Houstonville, Lincoln Co. Children: 1. Anna Eliza Morrison, born Mch. 27, 1818. 2. William Morrison, born 1820. 3. Ezra Morrison, born 1822. 4. Hugh Logan Morrison, born 1824. 5. Sara Woods Morrison, born 1827. 6. Harriett Jane Morrison, born Mch. 14, 1829.

Harriett Jane Morison married James M. Hocker, Oct. 24, 1844, Lincoln Co., Ky. Harriett M. Hocker was born Mch. 14, 1829; died Aug. 25, 1912, Lexington, Ky. James M. Hocker was born June 28, 1822; died Jan. 18, 1812, Lexington, Ky. Children: 1. Logan Hocker, married Bettie Laudeman. 2. Bettie Hocker, married Evan T. Warner. 3. White Hocker, married J. Henry Reed. 4. Wesley Hocker, married Annie Handy. 5. Monroe Hocker, married Nannie Little.

Henry Reed and White Hocker married Mch. 8, 1870. Henry Reed was born May 3, 1842; died Dec. 2, 1917, Lexington, Ky. White Hocker Reed was born June 14, 1851. Children: 1. James H. Reed. 2. Henry W. Reed. 3. Kate Jouett Reed, married George B. Carey, and had son, Burgess.

Green's History, pages 103 and 104, tells of marriage of Hugh Logan and Sara Woods. Hugh Logan's parents lived in James River Fork, Va.

"Harrison Morrison Hocker, directly related to Gen. Logan, who did active service for his country in the War of 1812." See Hist. of Fayette Co. (page 620), by Robert Peter.

BIBLE RECORD OF THOMAS MATSON OF BOURBON CO., KY.
Now Owned by Mrs. Mary L. Austin, Lexington, Ky.

Thomas Matson was born Oct. 13, 1778. Rebekah Spears Matson, his wife, was born Dec. 25, 1788. Died 1826. Their children: James S. Matson, born Sept. 17, 1805. (2) Louisa T. Matson, born Apr. 14, 1807. (3) Eloisa Peyton Matson, born July 7, 1808. (4) Mary Keller Matson, born Feb. 9, 1810. (5) Valentine Harrison Matson, born Jan. 16, 1813.

Lusey W. Webb was born Jan. 22, 1810.

Rebeckah Elizabeth Spears Matson, daughter of James S. Matson, was born 23rd of Apr. in the year of our Lord 1828.

Louisa Jane Matson was born Oct. 21, 1829.

James Matson Russell was born Dec. 29, 1846.

Elizann Burbridge, daughter of Oscar H. and Rebecca, was born Feb.

24, 1847.

James Matson Burbridge was born Mch. 7, 1849.
Robert Burbridge, Jr., was born Nov. 18, 1850.
Oscar Henry Burbridge, Jr., was born June 3, 1852.
(Same page, different writing.)
Isaac B. Matson, attorney at law, 39 Wiggins Block, Cin. O." John
Matson was born in Hamilton Co., O., in 1804. My grandfather's
name was Isaac. He came here with his father in 1790, died here
and was buried near Cin. My great-grandfather was John. He
came from Maryland, from there he entered the Revolutionary
War. He was captain of the Penny Regt. He had several sons,
John, James, Isaac, Enoch, Thomas. John, James and Isaac lived
in Hamilton Co., O., till their deaths."
Will Ferguson was born 1821. Noah Ferguson was born Sept. 23,
1823. Mary Eliza Ferguson was born 1826. Lucy Ellen Ferguson,
1828. Luie, 1831. Dr., 1834. Robert, 1837.
Louisa T. Matson departed this life Aug. 15, 1807.
Valentine Harrison Matson, departed this life Sept. 15, 1813.
Rebecca Matson departed this life Sept. 13, 1826. (Also a clipping.)
Louisa Jane Russell departed this life Apr. 22, 1847, in the 18th yr.
of her age.
Thomas Matson departed this life June 8, 1833, in the 54th yr of his life.
Robert S. Russell departed this life Sept. 24, 1852.
I. T. Matson departed this life Sept. 1, 1860, in the 55th yr. of age.
Thomas and Rebeckah Matson were married Sept. 10, 1804.
James Spears Matson was married to Lucey W. Webb July 5, 1827.
O. H. Burbridge and Rebecca Matson were married Jan. 8, 1846.
R. T. Russell and Louisa J. Matson were married Jan. 8, 1846. (Double
wedding, with Rebeckah S. Matson.)
Eloisa Peyton and Owing W. Grims were married Nov. 9, 1824.
Mary Keller Matson and Abm.(?) Lunsford Ferguson were married Nov.
15, 1826.
(John Crittenden Webb)—children:
Willis, born Nov. 16, 1794; John, born Sept. 16, 1796; Wyatt, born
Mch. 24, 1800; Mitchum, born Sept. 15, 1802; Garland, born Mch.
12, 1806; Jane, born Feb. 22, 1808; Lucy, born Jan. 22, 1810;
Charles, born Dec. 22, 1811; Frank, Apr. 16, 1813.
(Note: Data certified to and contributed by Mrs. Mary L. Bur-
bridge Austin.)
John Matson, father of Thomas (born Oct. 13, 1778), was born in
Hagerstown, Md., before 1756, and died in Hamilton Co., O., on
Oct. 1, 1804. He went to Ohio in 1790. He was a Lieut. in Col.
Hand's 1st Regiment, Pa., line in Oct., 1776. Jan. 16, 1777, he
was promoted to captain in the same reg. He resigned Jan. 1,
1778. His wife was Jane. (Pa. Arch. 5th Ser.) Children:
James Matson—Born 1776 or 1777; died Nov. 20, 1831.
John Matson—Born Nov. 16, 1769; died Jan. 10, 1847.
Thomas Matson—Born Oct. 13, 1778; died June 8, 1830.
Isaac, Enoch, Elizabeth and Mary Jane.

McADAMS FAMILY

John McAdams—Born in the extreme North Western county of Ire-
land, "Antrime," May 9, 1737, nearby the place of the famous
"Siege of Londonderry," where his wife, Ann, was born, in 1750.
Their children:
Ephraim—Born May 25, 1767; died May 11, 1842
John—Born Mch. 28, 1769.
James—Born May 7, 1771.
Katherine—Born Sept. 7, 1775.
Hamilton—Born Sept. 20, 1777.
William—Born Sept. 17, 1779.

Armstrong—Born Feb. 23, 1786.
Suter—Born Sept. 11, 1790.
Thomas—Born Nov. 20, 1793. (10th name ————.)
How many of these children were born in Ireland is not known, but the family lived in Northumberland Co., Pa., and moved to Williamsburg, Ohio, in 1800. Ephraim McAdams, "The Pioneer," has frequent mention in the early history of Clearmont County. In 1808, he and Charity, his wife, were in a little band of people that organized the Presbyterian church, that met for 22 years in the "Stone Court-house." He married Charity Britt, in Northumberland County, Pa., on Dec. 17, 1793. Children, first wife, Charity:

Nancy—Born Oct. 30, 1794.
Samuel—Born July 6, 1797.
Hannah—Born Feb. 7, 1799.
Ephraim—Born Oct. 13, 1800.
Hamilton—Born Feb. 10, 1802.
Julia A.—Born Dec. 2, 1803.
John A.—Born Nov. 14, 1805; married, Dec. 24, 1827, Mary Bryan, Williamsburgh, O.
James (twin of John A.)—Born Nov. 14, 1805.
Catherine—Born April 11, 1808.
Delilah—Born Feb. 15, 1810.

Charity died. Ephraim married (second) Catherine Hartman—Born Sept. 27, 1785, (one of 8 children), daughter of Christopher and Mary Hutchinson Hartman. (Christopher was born in 1750, Swintzburg Hesse Cassel, Germany, and came with 3 brothers and his father to Philadelphia, Pa. Christopher, Jr., was in Smallwoods Regt. in Revolution. Mary Hutchinson Hartman was born 1755.)

Children of Ephraim (second wife):
Mary Anne McAdams—Born June 8, 1812.
Thomas McAdams—Born June 6, 1813.
William McAdams—Born Jan. 5, 1815.
Andrew J. McAdams—Born Oct. 14, 1816.
Isaac Newton McAdams—Born Mch. 14, 1818.
Joseph Warren McAdams—Born Aug. 27, 1819.

Catherine died. Ephraim married (third) Martha Boyd. Children (third wife):
Manora McAdams—Born July 21, 1821.
Harvey McAdams—Born Jan. 24, 1826.
Riley McAdams—Born Mch. 19, 1828.

Of the children of Ephraim McAdams, 18 lived to have families. Isaac Newton McAdams, 5th child of Ephraim and second wife, Catherine Hartman, was born Mch. 14, 1818; married Dec. 28, 1842, Lavinchia Smith, of New York, daughter of John and Anna Lambkin White Smith. Children:

Harvey—Born Jan. 4, 1847. (Lived in Nevada.)
Albert—Born Apr. 4, 1849.
Amanda—Born Sept. 7, 1853; died Sept. 30, 1853.
Riley—Born Dec. 14, 1854. Married Ella McKibben.
Ephraim—Born Mch. 6, 1858.

Isaac McAdams was among the first to go to California (from Clearmont Co., Ohio.) in search of gold. The trip occupied 6 months traveling in ox-carts. He soon returned and enlisted on Sept. 30, 1861, in "Company F, of the 59th Ohio; was discharged Aug. 18, 1862, on Surgeons certf. of disability. He again went to California, taking his son, Harvey, who remained there. Isaac returned in 1867; and his wife died Dec. 3rd, 1880. Isaac died Sept. 28, 1891. His son, Albert, married Mary Gray Jones, at Hillesboro, O.; second wife, Catherine Friend O'Connor, of Portsmouth, O.

Oliver Perry McAdams—Born Jan. 31, 1836; died Aug. 7, 1870;

was son of John A. McAdams and Mary E. Bryant (who were married Dec. 24, 1827). John A. was son of Ephraim McAdams and first wife, Charity. Oliver P. McAdams married Mary F. Boulware, a daughter of Wm. and Malinda Fisk Boulware. She was born July 11, 1839; died Oct. 29, 1884. Oliver P. McAdams enlisted in 27th Reg. Ohio Inft., 1861-1862; re-enlisted in Co. G, 153rd Ohio National Guard until 1864. Children of O. P. and Mary Boulware McAdams:

1. Albert Clifford McAdams—Born Jan. 1, 1859; married Olive Gould, of Wyoming, O., and had two children, Julia, who married Frank Fogelman, and lives in Marion, Ark.; Alberta McAdams, who married Charles Stone and lives in Fayetteville, Ark.
2. Lorena Bell McAdams and Melinda McAdams—Died infants.
4. Harry Kennett McAdams—Born Dec. 18, 1865; married Martha Ednah Wilson, of Cynthiana, Ky., May 23, 1888. He is a member of McAdams and Morford, Wholesale and Retail Druggists, Lexington, Ky.
5. Lillian Florence McAdams.

Soldiers Named McAdams, Found in Different Histories

William Taggart McAdams, O. and Iowa Rebellion. Chaplain, 1861, 1880 and 1887; died 1893.

John Pope McAdams—Ky. Army Prvt. "B" 15th Reg. 4th Ky. Regt. May 29th, 1896-1899. Prvt. and Corp. 13th 1899-1901, 2nd Lieut.

James George McAdams—2nd Lieut. Ky., 1863. Mustered out, and each time re-enlisted. Capt. 6th Ky., 1865; 2nd Lieut. 1868; 1st Lieut. 1868; Capt. 1879; died 1890.

James C. McAdams—Capt. 3rd Inft. 1846.

Samuel G. McAdams—1st Lieut. 3rd Inft. 1846.

Robert McAdams—Prvt. Biggs Co., Jan., 1781; Rev. War Land Grant.

Robert McAdams—Prvt. Smiths Co. Land Grant.

McAdams in Virginia History—Soldiers

John McAdams—2nd Lt. 5th Va., 26th Feb., 1776; Capt. 1778. (Vol. 17). Land Grant, prior 1784.

Joseph McAdams—Hospital Surgeons Mate, 1778-1781.

Lieut John McAdams served in Confederate Army, 2 years. Married Jan., 1856, Frances H. Henner (of Alfred and Martha Henner) of New Orleans.

McAdams Marriages (in different histories)

Joseph McAdams married Janet Muir in 1712, in Scotland.

Dr. Joseph McAdams (son of Jos. and Janet), married Sarah Ann Gaskins in 1744. Their daughter married Wm. Brown, of Scotland (Gaskins history in Col.| Dames. Also in Conway history).

Henry McAdams married Mary Robbins, July 19, 1764.

Joseph McAdams married Pamita Shackleford, in Lexington, Ky., Feb. 16, 1837.

Joseph McAdams—Buried in Lexington, Ky., 1799.

Elizabeth McAdams married Andrew Hood, Apr., 1850.

John Loudon McAdams, Engineer, espoused the "Royal Cause," in 1775. Married in New York (first), Margaret Nicholl, of Islip, L. I.; she died. Married (second), Charlotte(sister of Bishop de Lancy). Inventor of Macadam roads.

David McAdams—Born in New York, 1838; died 1901. Jurist. Was son of Thomas and Janet, of Scotland. David married April, 1860, Carrie M. Crawford. (Had 4 sons.)

Clauric McAdams, son of David, Legislator, in 1901.

George Harrison McAdams, Lawyer—Born 1854; was son of James Graham McAdams and Phoebe.

George Hartly McAdams, Kewanee, Ills., son of Wm. and Adelaide (daughter of A. H. Ellinwood).

Clark McAdams (son of Wm. and Annie E. Curtis, daughter of Lama Baker, of Alton, Ills.)

Clark B. McAdams, Jersey Co., Ills., in 1874. Is a writer and lives in St. Louis Mo.

Dunlap Jamison McAdams (son of John and Susan M. Dunlap)— Born Morefield, Ohio, 1843. Educator and Engineer. Married Kate Wishart, of Washington. She was Born at Athens, O., 1862.

Hugh McAdams—Married Elizabeth Van Hurst, May 1739, Christ Church, Philadelphia, Pa.

Elizabeth McAdams—Married Jennings, July 26, 1774, Christ Church, Philadelphia, Pa.

Ann McAdams—Married Wm. Murray, Apr. 9, 1795, First Presbyterian Church, Carlisle, Pa.

MORTON HISTORY
(Donated by Mrs. Gertrude Vance, Lexington, Ky.)

1st gen.: Jacob Drog Morton, of Stockholm, Sweden.

2nd gen.: David Drog Morton—Born 1710; married Elizabeth Ankerstrom. Children: John, married, 1756, Hester Conway (of George and Mamie Pickett), (their son, Capt. John Morton, born 1757; died 1839). Elizabeth Morton, born 1736; married Thomas Fauntleroy (three sons, four daughters). Rebecca Morton, married Wm. Trousdale (children: 1. Wm., Jr. 2. Margaret. 3. Mary. 4. Susan. David, Jr. (twin brother), born 1743, in Bristol England. David, Revolutionary soldier, served 3 years Regt. Col. Glover; married Frances Ferrell (children: 1. John, born 1768. 2. Thomas, born 1773. 3. Richard, born 1775. 4. Abram, born 1778. 5. Elizabeth, born 1780. 6. Nancy, born 1786).

David Morton (married Sallie Wagner) was Rev. Sol. in regular army.

Capt. John Morton (son of John and Hester). Sons: 1. Elder William Morton, born Clark Co., Ky., 1790; died 1858. 2. Quinn Morton, died in Alabama, 1845. 3. Richard Morton, married Eleanor Petticord (they had son, Richard). 4. Elder John Morton, died Lexington, Ky., 1853 (his 1st wife was Elizabeth Rogers, 2nd wife Susan Christy). Elder John was born July 8, 1800.

Oldest son (of Capt. John) Elder Wm. Morton married 1st Rebecca Didlake (no children), and 2nd married Widow Davenport (no children).

Quinn Morton maried Elizabeth Hodges.

CHARLES RICE
Very little is known about Charles Rice. He was evidently an early settler in Madison Co., Ky.

On Aug. 31, 1797, Daniel Boone of Bourbon County deeded to Chas. Rice a one-half interest in the Settlement of Preemption of John Hart. The deed is recorded in Book D, page 293, of old deed records in Madison County.

Later Charles Rice moved to the Flat Rock Precinct in Bourbon County, where he raised three daughters.

The elder daughter married Gabriel Gillispie, the ancestors of the Bourbon County Gillispies. The second daughter, Mary, married John Noble, an English soldier who surrendered to Gen. Washington's army at York Town, Va. Both buried in Boonesboro graveyard. John Noble refused to be returned to England, but became a citizen of United States and later came to Ky. He and his wife are buried in the Boardman graveyard in Nicholas County.

John Noble's daughter, Mary, married James C. Bryan and they were the ancestors of the Boons Creek Bryans in Bourbon County. The third daughter, Kiziah or Katie, married Benjamin Boardman as stated on page 25.

Copy of John Noble's tax receipt, which was found when an old mantle was torn down in the home of one of his descendants, Anson Bryan, in Bourbon Co. This receipts is now in W. P. Thomas, possession.

The following is an exact copy: "Rec. of Isaac Turpin 89 cents, the full amount of John Noble's Taxes in the year 1807, this 8th day of May, 1809. Asa Guise, Dept.—James Turley, I. M. S."

When this tax receipt was written John Noble was in all probability living on Somerset Creek in Nicholas County, where he owned a small farm, which was afterward owned by my parents. This farm became the property of Charles Noble, a son of John, and an old maid sister. (See the will of Chas. Rice of record in Nicholas County.)

SPEARS' BIBLE RECORD.

Abraham, Noah, Solomon, Jacob. The daughter, Rebecca Spears, married Thomas Matson. Rachel married William Johnston, went to Mo. in the early 20, settled in Columbia. Sarah married Coleman. He died and she married Jones, went south, on a cotton farm, and died there.

EXTRACTS FROM TODD, PARKER, BOWMAN, TODHUNTER FAMILIES

United States Bureau of Pensions, Rev. and 1812 Wars sections * * * extracts from Revolutionary War claim, S. 14081 * * * "John Parker, Sr., was born Sept. 3, 1753, near Valley Forge, above Philadelphia. In 1774, he went to Louisa Co., Va., and while living with his uncle, Rev. Mr. Todd, enlisted as a Minute Man under Col. Samuel Meredith and was discharged Jan. 1, 1777 * * * was commissioned captain of a company of Artificers and from about Mch., 1777, assisted in the construction of the forts at Billingsport and Red Banks; after 6 months he resigned and was succeeded by Robert Megowan, who later married the soldier's sister, Mary Parker. In Sept., 1777, he served as substitute for his father-in-law * * * moved to Louisa Co., Va., and in 1778 he was appointed wagon master * * * and served thirteen month. * * * * Pension executed Nov. 26, 1832, while he was a resident of Fayette Co., Ky. He died May 28, 1837. * * * Children: John, Elizabeth, Mary, wife of Joseph Craig; Margaret Bryan, a widow; Nellie or Eleanor, wife of Wm. L. Todd; Nancy T., wife of Wm. Bowman. * * * Respectfully, E. W. Morgan." Tombstone inscriptions, John Parker, Sr., born in Pennsylvania, Sept. 3, 1753; died May 28, 1837. Was a soldier in Revolutionary War. Removed to Kentucky in 1784 and served the State of his adoption in many offices of trust and honor. Isabella Todd, wife of John Parker, Sr., born in Pennsylvania, Feb. 15, 1757; died Dec. 29, 1831.

Records from Bible of John Parker, Sr., William L. Todd, William P. Davis, and tombstone inscriptions in lots of Mrs. Eleanor Hood, William L. Todd, John Parker, Sr., and James Parker, Sr., in Lexington Cemetery. Some of these graves were removed from family burial ground, "Stoney Point," on Parkers Mills Road, Fayette Co., Ky.

(Donated by Miss Elizabeth Davis, Lexington, Ky.)

John Parker, Sr., and Isabella Todd married Sept. 7, 1777.
William L. Todd and Nellie Parker married Nov. 12, 1812.
Capt. W. P. Davis and Elizabeth P. Todd married Oct. 15, 1844.
Edwin H. Johnson and Isabel P. Todd married Apr. 3, 1856.
Edwin S. Davis and Somerville A. Neal married Dec. 25, 1870.
James Parker, Sr.—Born 1716; died Dec. 12, 1797. Married
Mary Todd—Born Mch., 1729. Their children:
    Jean Parker—Born Aug. 5, 1748.
    Isabella Parker—Born Apr. 18, 1750.
    John Parker, Sr.—Born Sept. 3, 1753.
    Mary Parker—Born Aug. 6, 1755.
    James Parker, Jr.—Born Dec. 5, 1758.
    Robert Parker—Born Oct. 12, 1760.
    Elizabeth Parker—Born Feb. 13, 1763.
    William Parker—Born 1765 (or 1766).
John Parker, Sr., born Sept. 3, 1753; died May 28, 1837; married

Sept. 17, 1777, to Isabella Todd, born Feb. 15, 1757. Children:
  Robert Parker—Born July 29, 1778.
  Mary Parker—Born Jan. 11, 1781.
  Margaret Parker—Born Feb. 13, 1784.
  Elizabeth Parker—Born Sept. 12, 1786; died Jan. 24, 1866.
  Eleanor Parker—Born Jan. 15, 1789.
  Nancy Parker—Born Feb. 4, 1793; died Nov. 11, 1851; married
    Wm. Bowman, Mch. 19, 1811.
  John Parker, Jr.—Born Apr. 2, 1797.
    Isabella, Daughter of Eleanor and Wm. Todd—Born Mch. 22, 1833;
married Edwin H. Johnson. Their seven children: Wm. Johnson, married Bland Stone, had one child, Nellie Johnson, born Aug. 6, 1857; died 1906; married Richard Arnspiger. Sallie Johnson, married Malcolm Brooks. Edwin Johnson, born Feb. 24, 1868; married Mary McKenna. Lewis Y. Johnson, born Aug. 27, 1872; married Elsie Cook. Lucy Johnson, died aged 13 years. Mildred Johnson, married Herbert McArdle.
  Joseph Ann Parker—Born July 11, 1832.
  Ann Maria Harrison—Born Sept. 13, 1806.
  Maria L. Saunders—Born Oct. 3, 1819.
  Dr. A. L. Saunders—Born Mch. 1, 1808.
  Joseph R. Megowan—Born Sept. 3, 1847.
  Martha J. Parker—Born Apr. 15, 1828.
  Sarah Parker—Born Feb. 13, 1814.
  Betsy Davis—Born Feb. 15, 1807.
  Allen Davis—Born Jan. 19, 1805.
  Edwin Davis—Born Apr. 4, 1846.
  Somerville A. Davis—Born Aug. 29, 1846.
  William P. Davis—Born Jan. 9, 1818.
  Mary Davis Grant—Born June 17, 1881.
  Elizabeth P. Davis—Born Nov. 22, 1821.
  Elizabeth Todd Davis—Born Jan. 19, 1859.
  Elizabeth Neal Davis and William Todd Davis married Oct. 4, 1871.
  Thomas D. Cassidy—Born July 1, 1856.
  Louise Davis Cassidy, wife of T. D. Cassidy—Born Mch. 17, 1873.
  Mary B. Davis—Born Aug. 14, 1785.
  William Davis Grant—Born June 17, 1881.
  Lucy Junkerson Davis—Born Apr. 1, 1849.
  Mary B. Davis—Born Feb. 12, 1855.
  George W. Grant—Born Oct. 7, 1822.
  Thomas Marshall Grant—Born May 18, 1844.
  Mary Louise Grant—Born Apr. 22, 1846.
  Richard M. Grant—Born Mch. 14, 1848.
  George M. Grant—Oct. 9, 1850.
  William M. Todd—Born Apr. 14, 1790.
  Nellie Parker Todd—Born Jan. 15, 1789.
  Elizabeth Todd Edge—Born Sept. 12, 1786.
  Jane L. Todd—Born June 3, 1818.
  David Bryan—Born Apr. 29, 1779.
  Margaret Bryan—Born Feb. 13, 1783.
  William Bryan—Born Sept. 8, 1806.
  Eliza E. Bryan—Born Nov. 19, 1816.
  Whitney Bowman—Born June 16, 1876.
  Lucy Johnson—Born Mch. 11, 1862; died 1875; age 13 years.
  Sallie J. Brooks—Born May 1, 1860.
  John W. Bowman—Born Sept. 26, 1836.
  John Madison Parker—Born Mch. 5, 1847.
  Isabella Todd—Born June 21, 1813.
  Robert Todd—Born Mch. 17, 1816.
  John P. Todd—Born July 5, 1823.
  Margaret Todd Brown—Born Apr. 14, 1826.

Betsy Davis died Dec. 3, 1885.
Allen Davis died Mch. 21, 1861.
Edwin S. Davis died July 2, 1879.
Somerville A. Davis died May 29, 1918.
William P. Davis died Mch. 30, 1881.
Mary Davis Grant died Mch. 22, 1904.
Eleanor Davis Hood died Sept. 17, 1873.
Mary Davis Stone died Apr. 11, 1876.
Elizabeth P. Davis died May 5, 1884.
Elizabeth Todd Davis died Mch. 11, 1929.
William Todd Davis died Sept. 14, 1873.
Mary B. Grant died June 13, 1889.
Joseph McAdams died Oct. 15, 1841.
George W. Grant died Dec. 30, 1863.
Anna Maria Grant died July 24, 1864.
Lucy J. Davis died May 1, 1851.
George M. Grant died Feb. 2, 1894.
William L. Todd died Mch. 9, 1865.
Nellie Parker Todd died Oct. 25, 1866.
Elizabeth Todd Edge died Jan. 24, 1866.
Jane L. Todd died Oct. 22, 1851.
David Bryan died Aug. 6, 1834.
Margaret Bryan died June 26, 1856.
William Bryan died Mch. 8, 1879.
Eliza E. Bryan died Oct. 14, 1864.
Sallie Bowman died Aug. 26, 1859.
Whitney Bowman died Aug. 25, 1876.
John Parker, Jr., died Feb. 18, 1875.
Sarah Parker died Dec. 24, 1850.
Lucy Johnson died Jan. 18, 1875.
Sallie J. Brooks died May 8, 1890.
John Parker, Sr., died May 28, 1837.
Isabella Todd Parker died Dec. 29, 1831.
Maria L. Saunders died Nov. 17, 1891.
Dr. A. L. Saunders died Dec. 8, 1868.
Joseph R. Megowan died July 27, 1852.
Martha J. Parker died Jan. 16, 1913.
John Madison Parker died July 10, 1849.
Robert P. Todhunter died Oct. 6, 1896.
Lydia C. Todhunter died Apr. 14, 1917.
Dr. Lewis C. Wagner died Feb. 14, 1895.
Sallie Henry died Aug. 24, 1874.
William Bowman died Apr. 6, 1847.
Nancy T. Bowman died Nov. 11, 1851.
Margaret Todd Brown died Jan. 9, 1872.
Edwin H. Johnson died July 2, 1891.
Eliza Berryman Bryan died Oct. 14, 1864.
Elizabeth Parker Edge died Sept. 12, 1786.
Isabella Bowman died Apr. 18, 1834.
Sallie Bowman died Aug. 26, 1859.
Thomas D. Cassidy died June 26, 1925.
James A. Grinstead died Oct. 9, 1886.
Robert Grinstead died Mch. 18, 1863.
Children of Wm. Bowman, Sr., and Nancy Parker Bowman:
   Robert Todd Bowman—Born Apr. 23, 1813; married Elizabeth
      Dickerson.
   Isabella Bowman—Born Feb. 22, 1815; married Thomas Pogue,
      Sept. 4, 1832; died Apr. 18, 1834.
   John Parker Bowman—Born Jan. 16, 1817; married Mary
      Elizabeth Chinn, Sept. 26, 1837; died from a wound received
      in Civil War.

William Bowman, Jr.—Born May 2, 1819; died Apr. 6, 1847. Was in Capt. Beards Co. 1848.

Sally Bowman—Born Aug. 31, 1829; married Henry Clay Bowman, Mch. 31, 1846; died Aug. 26, 1859.

Elizabeth Parker, daughter of James Parker, Sr., and Mary Todd Parker married Jacob Todhunter.

Parker Todhunter, son of above, married Catherine Ryland of Virginia. Children:

> Jacob Todhunter.
> John Todhunter—Married Mary Hart, dau, of Capt. Jack Hart.
> Joseph Todhunter.
> Robert Todhunter—Born Mch. 9, 1827; died Oct. 6, 1896; married Lydia Clark.
> Ryland Todhunter—Married Annie Neal, daughte of Maj. Neal of Warrensburg, Mo.

Robert Todhunter, son of Parker Todhunter and Catherine Ryland. Children.

> Susan Todhunter—Married Dr. Lewis Wagner (he was born Mch. 20, 1846; died Feb. 14, 1895).
> Lydia Todhunter—Married Knight.
> Jean Todhunter—Married Prewitt Payne.
> James Todhunter—Married Miss White.
> Katie Todhunter—Died.

BIBLE OF JOHN WEBB OF ORANGE CO., VA.

(Copied by Mrs. Mary L. Austin of Lexington, Ky.)

William C. Webb and Jane Vivian, both of Orange Co., Va., were married on the 23rd day of Feb., 1762. She died on the 25th day of Feb., 1783. He died on the 20th day of Dec., 1815. And they had the following named children: Augustine Webb, born the 6th day of Jan., 1763; no statement of when he died, but I believe in 1827 or 1828. (2) John V. Webb, born the 11th day of July, 1765; died Scott Co., Ky.; (3) Franky V. Webb, born 21st of Dec., 1767, died in Bourbon Co., Ky. (4) William C. Webb, born 20th day of Apr., 1769, and died the 17th day of Nov., 1845, in Orange. (5) Thacker V. Webb, born the 27th day of Dec., 1772, and died the 2nd day of Aug., 1843, in Orange. (6) Garland Webb, born the 19th day of Apr., 1775, and died the 4th Monday of Aug., 1814, at Ayletteware House, King William County, Virginia. (7) Charles Webb, the writer of this, born the 20th of Jan., 1778. (8) Wiatt Webb, born the 24th day of July, 1781, and died the 5th day of Oct., 1813, at Sumpterville, S. C. So that I am the only one of the eight children living. (Pasted below, a newspaper clipping.) "Died at his residence in the County of King William, on the 26th of July, Dr. Charles Webb, in the 74th year of his age. * * *"

William Crittendon Webb married Jane Vivian, 1762. Jane V. died Feb. 25, 1783, at the age of 43 yrs. William C. died 1815, aged 83. They had 7 sons and 1 daughter, Fannie, who married Branham, father of Webb Branham.

John and Margaret Vivian had one son, born Aug. 28, 1681. Married 1st Elizabeth Thacker, who died Jan. 12, 1732; 2nd mar. Jane Smith, Aug., 1733. Elizabeth, his child, born Aug. 17, 1717; died Oct. 23., 1717. (1) Richard. (2) Henry Thacker, married Elbonhead Conway, 1762. (3) Henry Thacker, married Elizabeth.

Elizabeth—Born 1694; married John Vivian 1712.

THE WINIFREE FAMILY OF POWHATAN COUNTY, VIRGINIA
Authority, Wm. Powhatan Winifree
(Donated by Misses Edna and Billy Whitlow)

The Winifree family were Huguenots, who came to America from

France after the St. Bartholomew massacre, 1572, and settled in Powhatan County at Bartholomew Springs, Va. The first of the name known to the contributor were John, William and another brother.

John lived in Powhatan Co., William in Chesterfield Co., and the brother in Western Virginia.

John Winifree was a Revolutionary soldier, married Miss Betsy Owens of Prince Edward Co., Va., and had, daughters, Sally, Nancy, and Mariah, who married Daniel Farley, and a son, Woodson.

Woodson Winifree, son of John and Betsy, was born in Powhatan Co., Va., in 1790, and married Serena Berry Farley in 1815. Woodson Winifree was in the War of 1812. He and his wife, Serena, had five sons and four daughters: Robert, who married Fannie Fitzpatrick and died May 16, 1919, in 95th year; William, born 1831, married Julia Nichols, and died in 1915, in 94th year; Alexander A., born 1823, married Mary Elizabeth Watkins, and died 1913, aged 90 years; Mathew died in 19th year; Mariah married Edward Farley, raised a large family and died in 77th year; Betsy died in girlhood; Nancy married A. Roberts of Georgia and had two sons; Susan was born 1830, married William Swinney, had seven sons and one daughter, and at 98 is sole survivor of children of Woodson and Serena Winifree.

Shurvin Trent Winifree was born 1819, married Elmira Atkinson in 1842, and had 14 children. He died in Kentucky, aged 84 years.

Children of Shurvin Trent Winifree and his wife, Elmira:

1. William P.—Born 1843; married Carrie Bradshaw in 1869, and had six children: Lulu, Virginia, William P., Jr., John Woodson, Benjamin Shurvin and James Bradshaw.
2. John Woodson—Married Mary Casky and had two children: Alice and James.
3. James Henry—Married Kate Sydnor, and had two children: Beulah and Henry.
4. George W.—Married Lucy F. Casky, and had eight children: Annie, Idah, Virginia, Georgia, Charles, Arthur Alexander, Irene and Floyd.
5. Virginia—Married Col. Ninian Edward Grey; no children.
6. Irene Serena—Married Richard Durrett, and had two children: Katie and Florence Durrett. 2nd daughter married Henry C. Whitlow, and had four children: Mary Katherine, Inez Digman, Edna Grey and Billy.
7. Florence—Married Eugene Callnon, and had one child: Dr. J. W. Callnon. (?)
8. Elizabeth—Married James Grey, and had one child: Harriett, who married Harry Wood.
9. Julius—Married Esther Faxon, and had three children: Douglas Woodson, Mabel and Edward Shurvin.
10. Thomas Shurvin—Married Fannie Breathitt, and had two children: Thelma and Gus.
11. Susan—Married P. H. Cunningham, and had three children: Francis William, Marie and Susan.
12. Mathew Forrest—Married Mabel Fallon, and has ten children: Forrest Fallon; Cunningham, George, Walter, Louise, Robert Trent, Mabel Elmira, Clara Irene, Susan Esther, Francis William and Shurvin Trent.
13. Alexander Arthur—Married Inez Digman, and has two children: Helen and Richard.
14. Caroline—Married John F. Boyle, and had one child: Virginia Rose.

(Note: See Winifree History, New York City Library, by Mrs. Stubbs.)

BIBLE OF ROBERT BARKLEY AND WIFE, MARY ADAMS

(Now owned by Dr. Harry Herring, Lexington, Ky.)

Children of Robert and Mary Barkley:
James E. Barkley—Born Apr. 15, 1807.
Samuel Barkley—Born Apr. 26, 1809.
Ann Barkley—Born Nov. 22, 1810.
Mathew Barkley—Born Nov. 9, 1812.
Mary Jane Barkley—Born Oct. 7, 1814.
Permelia Barkley—Born Dec. 13, 1816.
Hannah R. Barkley—Born Oct. 18, 1818.
(Dr.) Joseph Barkley—Born Sept. 18, 1820.
Robert Barkley (twin)—Born Sept. 18, 1822.
A. B. Barkley (twin)—Born Sept. 18, 1822, father of Mrs. M. B. Herring.
William Barkley—Born Jan. 27, 1825.
John H. Barkley—Born Feb. 6, 1828.
David Barkley—Born May 24, 1830.
Polly Cooper married Robert Barkley, 1806.
Elizabeth Cooper married Elisha Rice, Feb. 25, 1813.
Hannah Wright Cooper married John Sheley, May 20, 1813.
Samuel Cooper married Jane Tarleton, Dec. 23, 1813.
Sally Cooper married Henry Hann, Feb. 21, 1815.
Jane Cooper married Robert Wilson, Apr. 29, 1819.
David Cooper died Apr. 4, 1811; aged 23 years.
Samuel Cooper died Apr. 16, 1821; aged 39 years.
Samuel Cooper, Sr., died Oct. 23, 1823; aged 74 years.
Jane Cooper (daughter of Joseph Cooper)—Born June 7, 1822; died May 18, 1823; aged 11 months, 19 days.
Analiza Cooper—Born July 6, 1816; died Aug. 5, 1826; aged 10 years, (daughter of Joseph and Sally Cooper).
Joseph Cooper died Sept. 16, 1843, son of Joseph and Sally Cooper.
Elisha Cooper died Apr., 1845, daughter of Joseph and Sally Cooper.
Sarah Cooper died July, 1845, daughter of Joseph and Sally Cooper.
Wm. Montgomery Cooper—Born Apr. 6, 1818; died Aug., 1842.
Sally Cooper died July 15, 1846.
Elick Cise Cooper died Apr. 15, 1846.
Joseph Cooper—Born Aug. 27, 1796; married Sarah Rice Sept. 21, 1815. Sarah Rice was born Dec. 25, 1796.
Robert Henry Cooper—Born Nov. 8, 1819.
Samuel Cooper—Born July 8, 1824.
Elisha R. Cooper—Born Jan. 1, 1827.

ERRATA

Page 50—John Crow will: Jameson, instead of Jaeson.
Page 104—John Black-Janny Henderson, instead of —enderson.
Page 104—James Crump-Elizabeth Ballenger, instead of Ballengr.
Page 166—Nancy Jane Peck, instead of Jeck.
Page 197—John McClung, instead of MrClung.
Page 225—Wife of Thomas Odor, instead of Oor.
Page 226—Mary L., daughter of H. G. and A. E. Eals, instead of Earls.
Page 253—Charles Moore Gentry, married Mary Alice Bunton, instead of Bunston.
Page 253—Wm. Downing, Jr., married Charlotte Wymore, Nov. 2, 1820, instead of 1920.
Page 253—John Adams came to Kentucky from Maryland in 1791 and later married Mary Downing; date not given.
Page 275—M. R. McAdams, instead of M. R. Adams.
Page 317—Mary E. Austin and Julian Tilford married Jan. 19, 1903.
Page 322—Byron O. Billingsley, instead of Bollingsley.
Page 232—David Todd, born Apr., 1723; died Feb., 1785.

TABLE OF CONTENTS WILL BE FOUND ON PAGE 382

INDEX

151, 152, 156, 158, 159, 160, 161, 162, 163, 164, 167, 169, 170, 188, 192, 208, 209, 210, 214, 215, 221, 222, 223, 228, 231, 285, 317, 332.

Anderson Co.: Wills, 5-11; Marriages, 85-91. (Male names not indexed, but alphabetical.)

Andover, 126.

Andrews, 196, 237.

Ankerstrom, 337.

Annis, 155.

Antle, 109, 115.

Apperson, 266.

Arbuckle, 72, 117, 124.

Ardinger, 208.

Ares, 135.

Armstrong, 27, 63, 64, 70, 73, 94, 97, 112, 115, 124, 126, 129, 135, 136, 143, 144, 147, 151, 155, 156, 162, 167, 193, 195, 197, 199, 210, 211, 249, 277.

Arnett, 239.

Arnold, 29, 64, 103, 104, 107, 110, 112, 114, 115, 119, 124, 149, 158, 164, 264, 316.

Arnsparger (Arnspiker), 35, 210, 211.

Arthur, 107, 109.

Asbury, 221.

Ashberry, 129.

Ashbrook, 166, 167, 168, 169, 217, 221, 223, 240, 247, 266, 292.

Ashby, 38, 70, 71, 101, 126, 147, 213, 233, 235.

Ashcraft, 221.

Asher, 92, 137, 141, 155, 157.

Ashford, 83, 86, 89.

Ashley, 44, 128, 316.

Askew, 156.

Askins, 42.

Atchison (Atcherson), 30, 96, 237.

Atherton, 160.

Atkins, 134, 146, 239, 240, 284, 285, 289.

Atkinson, 104, 111, 162, 221.

Austin (Auston), 105, 123, 127, 139, 217, 317, 318, 323, 341.

Averil, 171.

Axton, 130.

Ayers (Ayres), 8, 30, 45, 58, 126, 191, 213, 313.

Ayles, 158.

Baber, 147.

Backer, 113.

Bacon, 98.

Badger, 145, 158, 159, 161, 163.

Badget, 153, 156.

Bady, 128.

Bagby, 159.

Bailey, 52, 100, 105, 110, 115, 118, 120, 121, 127, 140, 141, 146, 149, 159, 161, 203, 218, 237.

Baird, 191, 328, 331.

Baker, 17, 35, 48, 60, 62, 88, 103, 104, 130, 140, 150, 158, 242, 265, 336.

Baldridge 119, 161.

Baldrock, 101, 119.

Baldwin, 102, 221, 282, 328.

Bale, 55.

Balker, 108.

Ball, 27, 47, 48, 58, 93, 94, 101, 108, 117, 151.

Ballard, 159, 160, 242.

Ballenger, 326.

Ballew (Ballou), 103, 223.

Balling, 14.

Ballinger, 101, 102, 104.

Baltzelle, 226, 244.

Bands, 272.

Banford, 24.

Bangs, 169.

Banks, 39, 43, 100, 101, 103, 104, 115, 158, 169.

Banta, 72, 118, 130, 141, 142, 145, 148, 156.

Bantee, 129.

Banton, 106.

Barbee, 38, 82, 117, 190, 224, 251.

Barber, 71, 72, 76, 98, 131, 132, 286.

Barbond, 143.

Barbour, 13, 92, 94, 290.

Barclay, 156, 163.

Barintzer, 216.

Barker, 38, 94, 104, 159, 180, 241, 325.

Barkley, 168, 204, 229, 230, 294, 343.

Barlow, 221.

Barnard, 159, 160, 184, 219.

Barnes (Barns), 18, 45, 85, 104, 124, 132, 133, 135, 140, 143, 148, 154, 156, 162, 163, 164, 191, 255, 321, 333.

Barnett, 12, 30, 46, 48, 105, 112, 114, 115, 128, 130, 134, 136, 138, 141, 144, 148, 158, 181, 184, 268.

Barnor, 18.

Barnsides, 103.

Barr, 31, 38, 98.

Barrett, 47, 125, 192, 214.

Barrow, 81, 84, 158, 165, 317.

Barrs, 99.

Barry, 98, 115.

Bartlett, 158, 185, 332.

Barton, 28, 31, 168, 327.

Basey, 133.

Baskett, 140, 144.

Blanton, 39, 40, 100, 184.

Bledsoe, 17, 42, 51, 83, 102, 108, 172.

Blevins, 116, 130.

Blincoe, 97.

Bliss, 45.

Blount, 221.

Blythe, 27, 119, 193, 195, 200, 212.

Board, 126, 127, 145, 152, 154.

Boardman, 197, 198, 200, 320, 321, 337.

Boathe, 148.

Boatright, 211.

Boats, 146.

Bobb, 27.

Bodger, 238.

Bodgett, 93.

Bodkin, 17.

Bodley, 26.

Bogart, Boghart, 112, 143, 147, 151.

Bogee, 164.

Boggess, 6, 89, 90.

Boggs, 96, 222.

Bohannon, 64.

Bohon, 74, 127, 128, 130, 131, 133, 134, 136, 139, 142, 149, 151, 153, 154, 155, 197, 199, 204, 208, 209, 210, 211, 260.

Boice, 36, 149.

Boils, 87.

Bolds, Boles, 126, 140.

Boley, 101.

Bolling, 13, 64, 92, 145, 156.

Bolls, 163.

Bond, 5, 86, 87, 239, 267.

Boneham, 109.

Bonham, 124.

Bonneau, 278.

Bonnell, 153.

Bonner, 97.

Bonta, 106, 119, 124, 129, 131, 147, 152.

Booher (or Booker) 134.

Boon (Boone), 18, 23, 27, 31, 178, 184, 185, 186, 230, 241, 271, 285, 286, 337.

Booth, 134, 164.

Borden, 93.

Border (Borders), 133, 136, 141, Boslee, 102.

Bosley, 81, 125, 129, 136.

Boston, 5, 125, 136, 146, 150, 198, 222.

Boswell, 28, 47, 137, 178, 214.

Boswick, 92.

Bosworth, 34, 207, 213.

Bottom, 71, 75, 94, 125, 126, 127, 128, 129, 130, 132, 133, 134, 135, 137, 138, 139, 146, 149, 151, 152, 153, 155.

Botts, 158, 160, 161, 267.

Bouden, 99.

Boulware, 324, 325, 326, 336.

Bounds, 179, 187.

Bourbon Co. Wills, 11-13.

Bourn (Bourne), 42, 103, 163, 177, 236.

Bowdry, 48, 107, 108, 115.

Bowers, 132.

Bowles, 134, 152.

Bowlin (Bowling), 64, 91, 92, 100.

Bowman (Boman), 6, 48, 69, 74, 89, 90, 129, 131, 132, 133, 136, 141, 148, 149, 150, 213, 229, 235, 327, 338, 339, 340, 341.

Bowmar, 229.

Boxley, 158.

Boyce, 39, 142, 151, 156, 178, 279.

Boyd, 28, 46, 140, 147, 163, 167, 168, 170, 223, 261, 335, 342.

Boyer (Boyers), 46, 208, 209, 221, 277.

Boyle, 14, 43, 74, 100, 101, 108, 168.

Boyle Co.: Wills, 13-17; marriages, 91-95. (Male names not indexed, but alphabetical.)

Boyls (Boylls), 108, 182.

Boyrey, 106.

Brack, 6.

Brackenridge, 67.

Bracket, 313.

Bradford, 31, 191, 274, 277, 323.

Bradley, 99, 103.

Bradshaw, 25, 40, 134, 142, 144, 146, 147, 149, 158, 161, 342.

Brady, 101, 139.

Bramblett, 162.

Bramill, 158.

Bramlett, 164.

Brampton, 106.

Bran, 158.

Brand, 38, 231.

Branham, 322.

Brank, 56, 102.

Brannan, 102.

Brannock, 218.

Branson, 46.

Brants, 125.

Brashear, 130, 267.

Brassfield, 49, 96, 109, 184, 185.

Bratton, 25, 165.

Braxdell, 148, 151.

Breath, 78.

Breathitt, 342.

Brecken, 151.

Breckenridge, 143, 147, 163, 197, 203.

Breckinridge, 243, 244.

Breeding, 107, 122.

Breeze, 221.

Brennan, 98, 99.
Brennum, 200.
Brent, 322, 323.
Brewer (Brewar), 34, 62, 124, 125, 127, 128, 129, 132, 135, 136, 141, 144, 146, 149, 151, 153, 155, 244.
Brewington, 167, 168.
Brewsaugh, 46.
Brewster, 27.
Briant, 178, 180, 181.
Brice, 154, 237.
Brickey, 153.
Bridges, 38, 126, 127, 134, 149, 161, 162, 165, 177, 184, 321.
Briggs, 38, 49, 52, 232.
Bright, 104, 114, 115, 119, 120, 136, 141, 144, 151.
Briles, 143.
Briner, 147.
Bringer, 141.
Brinler, 104.
Brinton, 139, 322.
Brisby, 233.
Briscoe (Brescoe), 59, 92, 124, 129, 132, 139.
Bristol, 154.
Brite, 276.
Britt, 128.
Brittenham, 183.
Britton, 136.
Broadwell, 45, 192, 215, 216, 218, 225.
Brocaw, 132, 135, 147.
Brock, 80, 101.
Brockman, 28.
Brockway, 238.
Broiles, 93, 141, 155.
Bromfield, 125.
Bromley, 46.
Bronaugh, 18.
Bronston, 241, 242, 243, 249, 282.
Brooks, 46, 137, 159, 193, 246, 339, 340.
Brother, 159, 160, 163, 209, 210.
Brothers, 96, 158, 159.
Broughton, 199, 200.
Brower, 64.
Brown, 7, 28, 31, 40, 41, 44, 45, 46, 64, 72, 73, 96, 97, 99, 101, 102, 103, 104, 107, 111, 112, 117, 120, 124, 125, 126, 127, 128, 129, 130, 138, 139, 140, 141, 142, 143, 144, 146, 147, 148, 150, 151, 153, 155, 156, 157, 159, 161, 164, 176, 187, 221, 229, 230, 312, 313, 320, 325, 336, 339, 340.
Browning, 90, 113.
Broxdale, 144.
Broxdel, 148.

Broyles, 93, 137, 148.
Broys, 148.
Bruce, 56, 71, 72, 222, 224, 231.
Bruin, 5.
Brumager, 28.
Brumbarger, 39.
Brumet, 101.
Brumfield, 64, 71, 125, 129, 141, 142, 148, 153, 154, 156.
Bruner, 71, 124, 129.
Brunson, 53.
Brunts, 112, 119.
Bruston, 71, 162, 163.
Bryan, 107, 116, 162, 178, 182, 213, 215, 225, 230, 335, 337, 338, 339, 340.
Bryant, 28, 35, 39, 86, 94, 106, 116, 117, 118, 130, 141, 143, 161, 178, 179, 180, 181, 182, 186, 188, 189, 190, 193, 336.
Brynton, 125.
Bucanan, 136.
Buchannan, 49, 51, 113, 127, 130, 148, 153.
Buchannon, 60, 64, 70, 97, 122, 126, 144, 178.
Bucholts, 97.
Buck (Bucks), 81, 125.
Buckle, 149.
Buckley, 7, 89, 98, 147.
Bucknall, 116.
Buckner, 18, 181, 187.
Buford, 55, 107, 113, 115, 179, 187, 199.
Bulger, 49.
Bull (Bulls), 144, 147, 155.
Bullett, 322.
Bullock, 18, 117, 136, 138, 203, 226, 227, 232.
Bumbarger, 46.
Bunch, 18, 128, 131, 144.
Bunnell, 31, 126.
Buntain, 8, 132.
Bunton, 135, 141, 142, 149, 253.
Burbage, 184.
Burbridge, 321, 322, 333, 334.
Burch, 13, 49, 58, 83, 109, 113, 203, 227, 232.
Burcham, 125.
Burd, 115.
Burdett, 101, 104, 110, 294.
Burdette, 114.
Burford, 128, 131, 137, 151, 156.
Burgen, 197.
Burgess, 244, 245.
Burgin, 245.
Burk (Burks), 6, 130, 132, 135, 146, 152, 153, 154, 157, 159.
Burke, 97, 118, 125, 249.
Burkfield, 215.
Burkley, 158.

Burlingame, 31.
Burnon, 119.
Burns (Burnes), 45, 150, 219, 323.
Burnsides, 102, 109.
Burnum, 199, 200.
Burrass (Burriss), 5, 11, 17, 74, 76, 77, 103, 144, 154, 179, 186, 320.
Burrier, 203, 210, 211.
Burross (Burruss), 140, 141, 143, 144, 151.
Burroughs, 164.
Burrs, 112.
Burt, 236.
Burton, 13, 77, 93, 103, 106, 116, 121, 128, 129, 131, 132, 134, 142, 151, 241.
Busey, 5, 8, 16.
Bussey, 87.
Bush, 95, 157, 178, 184, 189, 200, 201, 202, 204, 328.
Bushall, 82.
Buster, 165.
Butler, 91, 110, 133, 134, 140, 142, 143, 144, 147, 158, 162, 322.
Butram, 165.
Butt (Butte), 71, 98, 160.
Butts, 87.
Byas, 120.
Bybee, 146.
Byers, 14, 49, 91, 126, 132, 154.
Byrnes, 31.

Cabbage, 143.
Cabbart, 138.
Cacurran, 99.
Cade, 23, 112.
Cahoon, 125, 127.
Cain, 112.
Caise, 40.
Calbert, 187.
Caldwell, 15, 49, 60. 66, 91, 93, 97, 109, 112, 113, 128, 139, 140, 148, 149, 151, 156, 159, 160, 251, 269.
Caleman, 225.
Calhoun, 222, 223.
Calk, 119.
Call, 83, 98.
Callahan, 98, 261.
Callaway (Calloway), 60, 110, 183, 238.
Callerson, 111.
Callnon, 342.
Cally, 98.
Calvert, 93, 213, 316.
Cammack, 147.
Campbell, 24, 26, 28, 47, 49, 52, 64, 79, 102, 107, 108, 111, 114, 121, 126, 128, 133, 142, 155, 158, 159, 161, 162, 164, 171, 194, 195, 197, 199, 233, 259.
Campdeno (or Campdexo), 103.
Camplin, 163.
Camron, 124.
Canab, 121.
Canady, 64, 65.
Candle, 123.
Candy, 97.
Canine, 130, 145.
Cannary, 150.
Canning, 99.
Cannon, 10, 127, 138, 150, 151.
Canton, 92.
Capell, 208.
Caperton, 60.
Cardwell, 10, 21, 89, 131, 135, 140, 143, 147, 156.
Caret, 163.
Carethers, 96.
Carey, 130, 136, 138, 141, 333.
Carington (Carrington), 84, 158, 163.
Carl, 331.
Carlisle, 25, 201.
Carlton, 129.
Carmale, 123.
Carmichael, 274.
Carmicle, 128.
Carns, 102, 103.
Carol (Carrol), 140, 192, 247.
Carpenter, 39, 49, 102, 115, 118, 285, 320, 333.
Carr, 6, 79, 80, 105, 124, 126, 141, 147, 148, 153, 196, 197, 232, 246.
Carrier, 122.
Carson, 28.
Carstaphron, 23.
Carteel, 103, 155.
Carter, 6, 84, 89, 141, 143, 144, 154, 159, 160, 161, 163, 174, 175, 181, 182, 188, 189, 190, 221, 222, 229, 250, 252.
Carthright, 107.
Cartmell, 163, 230.
Carty, 150.
Carver, 145, 147, 189, 190.
Cary, 147.
Casady, 150, 158.
Casatt, 153.
Casay, 110.
Case, 136, 159.
Casey, 68, 105, 127, 137, 141, 147, 222.
Cashman, 99.
Cashwiler, 124.
Casky, 342.
Cason, 65, 218, 327.
Cassall, 149.
Cassell, 271, 272.

349

Crane, 93, 135, 321.
Crase, 158.
Crasher, 115.
Cravens, 32, 118, 164, 202, 230.
Crawford, 21, 102, 103, 104, 119,
    120, 129, 133, 135, 136, 137,
    142, 146, 149, 156, 159, 160,
    161, 162, 188, 238, 336.
Creasey (Crecy), 124, 144.
Creason, 84, 159.
Creath, 103.
Crenshaw, 219, 222.
Crews, 96, 124, 141, 148.
Crigler, 123.
Crim, 160, 177, 178, 180, 181, 182,
    184, 185, 189, 190.
Crisman, 93, 165.
Crittenden, 81, 229, 279, 280.
Croak, 164.
Crocket (Crockett), 31, 104, 203.
Cromer, 102.
Cromwell, 23, 88, 156, 214, 227,
    247, 251.
Crooks, 159, 161, 174, 175, 176,
    218.
Crose (Krause), 320, 321.
Cross, 110, 166, 175, 189.
Crossfield, 90.
Croswit, 179.
Crouch, 129.
Croucher, 40.
Crow, 18, 43, 50, 51, 67, 70, 72,
    133, 156, 165, 187, 196, 250,
    251, 255.
Crowden, 39, 40.
Crowdis (Crowdus), 93.
Crowe, 129.
Crowswaite, 83.
Cruize, 92.
Crum, 91.
Crumbough, 154.
Crump, 100, 184, 149.
Crutchfield, 6, 93, 100, 110, 124,
    150.
Crutcher, 252.
Cubbage, 18.
Culberson, 106, 108, 110.
Cull, 70.
Culton, 148, 153.
Cummine, 99.
Cummings, 116, 137.
Cummins, 40, 102, 103, 120, 131,
    157, 221.
Cumpton, 110, 197.
Cunningham, 25, 82, 96, 123, 124,
    136, 137, 138, 149, 150, 151,
    153, 154, 156, 170, 193, 199,
    201, 212, 237, 266, 342.
Curby, 104.
Curd, 30, 105, 112, 117, 131, 132.
Curl (Curle), 158, 168, 222, 225.
Curran, 99, 217, 218.

Currens, 136, 140, 147.
Current, 221, 326, 327.
Currey, 124.
Curry, 13, 47, 63, 71, 93, 127,
    128, 129, 133, 134, 137, 143,
    146, 150, 151, 153, 157, 220,
    223.
Curtis, 23, 336.
Curtner (Kirtner), 145.
Curtrier, 152.
Cusanbary, 153, 177, 183, 184.
Cushion, 182.
Cuson, 223.
Cutright, 162, 183.
Cutter, 226.
Cuttings, 110.

Dabney, 159, 163.
Daggett, 156.
Dale, 5, 29, 135, 151, 158, 159,
    160, 221, 242.
Dallenhill, 133.
Dallingher, 98, 107.
Dalton, 99, 158.
Damaree, 128.
Dampson, 140.
Damron, 107.
Daniel (Daniels), 18, 19, 99, 132,
    144, 149, 158, 178, 184, 239,
    251, 328.
Daring, 93.
Darland, 124, 126, 143, 144.
Darnaby, 52, 79, 80, 128, 138, 165,
    177, 180, 181, 182, 183, 188,
    189, 190, 214, 246, 252, 288.
Darnal (Darnall), 141, 158, 159,
    160.
Darnell, 109.
Darosett, 221.
Darr, 86.
Daugherty (Dougherty), 67, 96,
    100, 107, 109, 111, 116, 124,
    130, 144, 145, 170, 172, 173,
    174, 175, 212.
Daughters, 282, 283.
Davenport (Devenport), 8, 25, 91,
    94, 124, 142, 146, 148, 155,
    337.
Davidson, 97, 100, 113, 135, 203.
Daviess, 10, 82, 125, 131, 147.
Davis, 5, 15, 31, 51, 52, 58, 65,
    70, 83, 84, 91, 94, 96, 97, 98,
    101, 107, 109, 113, 115, 117,
    119, 121, 124, 125, 127, 129,
    130, 131, 132, 134, 135, 136,
    137, 138, 139, 143, 144, 145,
    149, 151, 154, 156, 158, 159,
    160, 161, 162, 163, 164, 165,
    168, 182, 184, 185, 187, 217,
    230, 243, 252, 338, 340.
Davisman, 110.
Dawley, 159.

Dawns, 39.

Dawson, 8, 18, 19, 87, 105, 113, 144, 148, 149, 155, 178, 179, 186, 187, 189, 190, 276, 323.

Day (Days), 125, 126, 130, 135, 163, 214, 216, 217, 221, 223, 315.

Deal (Deale), 18, 57.

Deaman, 117, 154.

Dean, 124, 132, 137, 140, 142, 146, 152, 153, 154, 155, 157.

Deatherage, 79, 249.

Deavers, 78.

Debaun (Debaum), 151, 153, 155.

Debell, 272.

Debold (Deboll), 168, 169, 215.

Debond, 124, 131, 143.

Debord, 161.

De Camp, 288.

Decker, 127.

Dedman, 5, 10.

Deer, 14, 145.

Deering, 254.

Defo, 103.

Delam, 138.

De Lancy, 336.

Delaney, 61, 123, 124.

Delell (or Odel), 138.

Delf, 46.

Delling, 222.

Demaree, 64, 65, 124, 128, 129, 130, 131, 133, 139, 157.

Demmit (Demmitt), 128, 137.

Demott, 71, 72, 139, 142, 143, 145, 148, 149, 152, 156.

Dennis, 117, 126, 141.

Denny, 100, 103, 132, 134, 147, 157.

Denton, 44, 103, 104, 105, 106, 127, 128, 137, 254, 255.

Depaw, 92.

Derham, 72.

Dermin, 103.

Dermott (Dernott), 150, 153.

Desha, 215, 218, 222, 251, 252.

Deshazer, 153.

Devers, 105.

Devine (Divine), 124, 125, 134, 138, 141, 145, 149, 150, 152.

Dewees, 34.

Dewitt, 121, 164.

Diamond, 228.

Dick, 94.

Dicken (Dickens), 40, 63, 65, 104, 132.

Dickerson, 340.

Dickey, 61, 69, 133, 135, 160, 167, 168, 218, 222.

Didlake, 337.

Digman, 342.

Dilider, 133.

Dillard, 169, 210.

Dilling, 168.

Dillingham, 109, 110.

Dills, 169, 192, 214, 215, 216, 218, 219, 222, 223, 224, 292.

Diltz, 293.

Dimmett, 326, 327.

Dine, 132.

Dinsmore, 203.

Dinsmukes, 42, 142, 152.

Dinwiddie (Dinwiddle), 97, 171.

Dixon, 128, 145, 159, 186.

Doata, 136.

Dobbins, 158.

Dobe, 97.

Dobson, 119.

Dodd (Dodds), 51, 91, 113, 118, 190, 250.

Dodge, 131.

Dodson, 21.

Doggett, 164.

Doggins, 206.

Dohay, 101.

Doherty, 100.

Doke, 94, 126.

Dolan, 98, 99, 175.

Dole, 211.

Donahew (Donohew), 159, 163.

Donahoo, 99.

Donal, 137.

Donald, 136.

Donaldson, 118.

Donar, 116.

Donavan (Donovan), 135, 151.

Doneghy, 92, 93.

Donghy, 138.

Donnelly, 51.

Donnihue, 241.

Dooley (Dooly), 160, 163, 165.

Door (Doors), 14, 151.

Dority, 147.

Dorn, 153.

Dorrill, 103.

Dorsey, 62.

Doss, 117.

Doty, 130, 138, 152.

Douglass, 45, 103, 109, 112, 116, 135, 148, 207, 209, 211, 212, 243, 289, 327.

Dove, 117.

Downey, 6, 9, 18, 126, 129, 144, 145, 149, 151, 174.

Downing, 23, 38, 45, 65, 108, 117, 122, 139, 140, 144, 164, 190, 191, 225, 229, 230, 252, 253, 254, 265.

Downs, 83, 159, 282.

Downton, 29.

Doxy, 127.

Doyle, 276, 277.

Dozier, 114.

Flynn, 99.
Fogleman, 336.
Foker, 114.
Foley, 29, 129, 148, 155.
Followay, 106.
Fontain, 17, 62.
Forbes, 45, 100, 108.
Forbis, 54.
Forbush, 100.
Ford, 51, 99, 103, 116, 132, 134, 152, 159, 169, 177, 216, 218, 234.
Fordham, 243.
Forehead (Forehand), 149.
Foreman (Forman), 80, 119, 165, 216, 217, 257.
Forkner, 84.
Forrester, 226.
Forsythe, 77, 147, 156, 214, 223.
Fortner, 83.
Fortune, 6, 86, 89, 159.
Foster, 20, 65, 92, 94, 99, 135, 161, 162, 167, 168, 178, 180, 183, 185, 264.
Fouchee, 148.
Foulger, 95.
Fountain, 332.
Fountleroy, 15.
Fouquor, 22.
Fowell, 117.
Fowler, 158, 191.
Fowles (Towles), 131.
Fox, 59, 60, 83, 84.
Foxworthy, 244.
Fraiks, 115, 155, 156.
Fraizer, 287.
Frakes, 162, 237.
Frances (Francis), 24, 77, 160, 242.
Francisco, 163.
Frank (Franks), 32, 43, 79, 159.
Franklin, 42, 94, 99, 104, 109, 134, 144, 157, 177, 182, 184, 185.
Frazer, 29, 160, 167, 168, 169, 192, 205, 206, 215, 216, 217, 220, 222, 233, 257, 258, 293, 315.
Frazier, 24, 28, 85, 87, 143, 199, 201, 202, 203, 222, 223, 226.
Fredericks, 222.
Freeland, 163.
Freeman, 8, 11, 63, 66, 68, 72, 108, 128, 129, 136, 141, 147, 148, 152, 164.
Freer, 279.
French, 79, 84, 85, 109, 123, 126, 127, 144, 155, 162.
Fresh, 94.
Frey, 147.
Frick, 92.

Frier (Freer), 29, 32.
Frigate, 79.
Frisbee, 168, 247, 261.
Froman, 52, 65.
Frost, 15, 93, 94, 144, 154.
Fry, 92, 107, 109, 127, 129, 131, 153, 193.
Fugate, 43.
Fulkerson, 92, 94, 124, 125, 139.
Fullerton, 119.
Funeral Invitations, 294-311; not indexed but alphabetical.
Funk, 116, 238.
Furnish, 221.
Furr, 290, 291.

Gabbard, 135.
Gabbhart (Gabbert), 136, 141.
Gabhart (Gabhert), 133, 135, 149, 150, 153.
Gadburry, 92.
Gaddey, 100.
Gaines (Gains), 14, 91, 94, 105, 110, 120, 132, 134, 180, 188, 202, 207, 235, 237, 328.
Gaitskill, 158, 164, 245, 280.
Galbraith, 53, 108.
Gales, 131.
Gall, 322, 323.
Gallagher (Galligher), 124, 135, 139, 150, 157.
Gallop, 186.
Galloway, 117, 121, 130, 142, 233.
Gamble, 154.
Gano, 191.
Garden, 162.
Gardner (Gardiner), 15, 96, 97, 159, 161, 221.
Garghan (?), 114.
Garland, 23.
Garmony, 45.
Garnett (Garnet), 91, 113, 168, 169, 170, 190, 211, 215, 216, 217, 220, 222.
Garr (Garrs), 76, 136, 148.
Garrard, 29, 219, 269.
Garrard Co. Wills, 39-44; marriages, 99-105.
Garrett, 25, 57, 96, 102, 103, 158, 160, 161, 169, 205, 208, 210, 211, 212.
Garrick, 116.
Garrison, 158.
Garrot, 101.
Garshimler, 113.
Garshuiler, 117.
Garth, 322, 333.
Garvin, 104.
Gary, 110.
Gash, 133, 142, 145, 152.
Gashweiler, 130, 138, 141, 144.

Gaskins, 336.
Gasset, 165.
Gates, 124, 126, 133, 148.
Gatewood, 37, 104, 109, 162, 163.
Gatliff, 104.
Gaugh, 177.
Gault, 165, 236.
Gaunt, 126, 127, 156.
Gausney, 177, 184.
Gay, 48, 52, 112, 165, 194, 197, 199, 200, 204, 205, 206, 207, 208, 209, 210, 211, 212.
Gayle (Gale), 79.
Gee, 126, 127, 129.
Geiser, 93.
Gelespe, 19.
Gemblin, 103.
Gemeial (?), 203.
Genealogy, 312-342.
Gentry, 113, 123, 132, 244, 253, 265.
George, 11, 126, 177, 223.
Geter, 180.
Gettings, 154.
Gibbon, 98, 266, 267.
Gibbs, 99, 115, 122, 156, 180, 189.
Gibney, 99.
Gibson, 28, 42, 52, 72, 76, 112, 132, 133, 144, 148, 150, 151, 167, 258, 259, 332.
Gilbert, 52, 109, 177, 235, 330.
Gilbraett, 108.
Giles, 48, 52, 104.
Gilkerson, 91, 129, 130, 143, 153, 159.
Gilkey, 159.
Gill, 7, 65, 87, 92, 98, 100, 103, 114, 125, 139, 141, 143, 144, 147, 148, 153, 162, 259.
Gillas, 52.
Gilliam, 29.
Gillispie, 6, 32, 72, 96, 129, 133, 160, 161, 162, 316, 337.
Gillon, 84.
Gills, 163.
Gilman, 135.
Gilmon, 145.
Gilmore, 52, 63, 70, 107, 111, 117, 129, 160, 161.
Gilpin, 8, 126.
Gimble, 127.
Gist, 30, 95, 213, 254.
Givens, 52, 66, 111, 115, 138, 290, 333.
Givings, 51, 127.
Gladdrydd, 330.
Glasebrook, 126, 127.
Glass, 138, 171, 172, 173, 176.
Glave, 223.
Glazebrook, 129, 149.
Glover, 84, 85, 112, 159, 160, 162, 163, 164, 323.

Goard, 125.
Goddard, 326.
Godfrey, 132, 138, 142, 153.
Goff, 128, 324, 325.
Goin (Goings), 279, 280, 281.
Goldman, 137.
Goldsmith, 57.
Gooch, 104.
Good, 52, 221.
Goodbar, 84.
Goode, 92, 94, 114.
Goodknight, 153.
Goodlet, 146, 148, 250.
Goodloe (Goodlow), 60, 161, 163, 177, 178, 183, 185, 186, 187.
Goodman, 97, 163.
Goodnight, 15, 109, 117, 129, 134, 140, 152, 157.
Goodwin, 24, 47, 67, 99, 164, 182, 211.
Goolman, 136.
Goolrich, 98.
Gorden (Gordin), 118, 119.
Gordon, 15, 19, 52, 60, 66, 91, 97, 100, 109, 128, 129, 138, 143, 145, 197, 236.
Gore, 133, 136, 161, 164, 165.
Gorman, 99.
Gormly, 99.
Gostwick, 81.
Goudy, 225.
Gould, 336.
Gover, 92.
Gowes, 188.
Grabbs, 146.
Grabt, 161.
Grace, 90.
Grady, 15.
Grafton, 14, 92.
Gragg, 233.
Graham, 66, 75, 94, 109, 112, 115, 121, 128, 132, 134, 142, 146, 148, 193, 281.
Gramer, 42.
Granger, 235.
Grant, 14, 23, 24, 33, 129, 162, 240, 285, 339, 340.
Grant (or Gaunt), 137.
Grater, 218, 219.
Graves, 24, 29, 53, 115, 129, 134, 153, 156, 161, 176, 177, 182, 183, 187, 320.
Gray, 14, 15, 32, 37, 52, 90, 91, 92, 93, 94, 111, 117, 128, 131, 133, 139, 144, 147, 148, 149, 150, 151, 155, 184, 191, 192, 216, 342.
Grayham, 138.
Grayson, 79.
Greeley, 330.

Green (Greene), 7, 9, 21, 24, 42,
    47, 55, 57, 72, 92, 98, 103,
    107, 114, 119, 128, 130, 131,
    133, 135, 138, 141, 142, 143,
    144, 146, 148, 150, 151, 152,
    153, 154, 158, 161, 163, 197.
Greenen (Greenens), 178, 186.
Greenwood, 13, 34, 134, 142, 146,
    155.
Gregg, 221.
Gregory, 17.
Grey, 218.
Grider, 103.
Griffee, 247.
Griffin, 14, 88, 127, 141, 159, 164.
Griffith, 47, 186, 231.
Griffy, 90.
Grigg (Griggs), 110, 114, 188,
    330.
Grigsby, 95, 328.
Grimes, 16, 32, 102, 124, 163, 164,
    180, 184, 185, 186, 187, 188,
    190, 211, 255, 334.
Grinnan, 166, 169, 170, 218.
Grinstead, 32, 158, 165, 340.
Grisham, 125.
Grisholm, 126, 156.
Grithe, 135.
Gritton, 125, 127, 130, 131, 135,
    138, 142, 147, 150, 153.
Grixon, 66.
Groff, 275, 288.
Gromér, 104.
Groom (Grooms), 84, 95, 165.
Groves, 212.
Grubbs, 29, 162, 325.
Grundy, 128.
Gudgell, 143.
Guess, 5, 49, 185, 187.
Guff, 154.
Guilkerson, 294.
Guilliam, 252.
Guise, 338.
Gully, 103.
Gunsalley, 162.
Guthrie (Gutherie), 91, 98, 104,
    142, 149, 150, 152, 153, 260.
Gwinn, 153.

Hackett, 19.
Hackney, 129, 152.
Haden (Hadon, Haydon), 126,
    136, 138, 150, 162, 165.
Hadden (Haddon), 141; 158.
Hagan, 84.
Haggard, 95, 328, 330.
Haggerty, 98.
Haggin (Haggins), 99, 135, 142,
    149, 247.
Hahn, 250, 321.
Haines (Hains), 131, 133, 154, 155.

Hale, 66, 72, 77, 101, 118, 125, 126,
    128, 130, 132, 133, 136, 138,
    141, 145, 148, 151, 152, 156,
    203, 206, 207, 228.
Haley, 7, 30, 129, 130, 138, 180,
    181, 183, 186, 188, 189, 190,
    220, 247.
Hall, 15, 24, 45, 48, 94, 96, 112,
    118, 124, 125, 127, 128, 129,
    131, 135, 137, 138, 141, 143,
    145, 146, 149, 152, 159, 160,
    164, 181, 188, 206, 207, 208,
    210, 211, 224, 229, 287.
Halligan, 138.
Halloard, 100.
Halloway, 124, 130.
Halsey, 19.
Ham, 164.
Hambleton, 41, 51, 132, 142.
Hamilton, 15, 36, 44, 45, 47, 84,
    85, 96, 103, 118, 119, 140,
    143, 149, 150, 181, 187, 188,
    192, 198, 205, 222, 224.
Hamm, 316.
Hammer, 94.
Hammond (Hammonds), 120, 127,
    128, 148, 161.
Hamner, 14, 130, 137, 139, 146.
Hampton, 19, 22, 32, 95, 96, 125,
    158, 159, 160, 287, 327, 328,
    329, 330.
Hanberry, 7.
Hanbolt, 130.
Hancock, 86, 88, 105, 123, 142,
    281.
Hancy, 99.
Handback (Handbach), 177, 188.
Handy, 167, 333.
Haney, 147, 179, 187, 204, 206.
Hank (Hanks), 5, 122, 144, 163.
Hankla, 155.
Hankley, 91.
Hanlan (or Harlan), 125.
Hanley (Hanly), 97, 99, 161.
Hanline, 159.
Hann, 343.
Hanna (Hannah), 12, 53, 66, 97,
    111, 115, 125, 139, 162, 163.
Hannson, 110.
Hansbrough (Hansborough), 57,
    118.
Hanson, 203.
Hany (or Havy), 96.
Happy, 30.
Harbard, 101, 102.
Harbee, 142.
Harbeson (Harberson), 127, 135,
    149.
Harbison, 66, 72, 76, 105, 114, 134,
    136.
Harbour, 100, 101.

Harbson, 113.
Hardenbrook, 133.
Hardesty, 35, 154, 155, 156, 181, 189, 190, 193.
Hardgrove (Hargrove), 91, 118.
Hardin, 66, 123, 126, 127, 128, 142, 157, 219.
Harding, 217.
Hardwick, 273.
Hardy, 128, 223.
Hargrave, 116.
Harlan, 14, 15, 53, 92, 93, 105, 139, 146.
Harley, 151, 154.
Harlin, 131.
Harlow, 124, 150, 153, 154.
Harmon (Harmond), 101, 134, 143, 144.
Harnett, 99.
Harney, 234.
Harnshall, 44.
Harold, 133, 137.
Harp, 237.
Harper, 57, 132, 147, 150, 158, 159, 160.
Harrah, 84.
Harriett, 205.
Harring, 233.
Harrington, 110.
Harris, 9, 19, 43, 57, 66, 70, 86, 89, 102, 107, 110, 116, 117, 123, 125, 129, 134 135, 138, 142, 155, 159, 160, 162, 163, 179, 184, 186, 198, 254, 266.
Harrison, 32, 44, 47, 71, 72, 91, 92 93, 94, 125, 132, 133, 137, 144, 154, 214, 235, 240, 285, 339.
Harrison Co. Wills, 44-48.
Harrod, 15, 73, 124, 125, 128, 131.
Harrow, 19, 20, 158, 161.
Hart, 21, 53, 60, 94, 112, 120, 134, 136, 146, 152, 154, 160, 163, 164, 179, 188, 199, 201, 210, 211, 212, 337, 341.
Hartgrove, 136, 142.
Harthman, 178.
Hartley, 66.
Hartman, 335.
Hartridge, 116.
Harvey, 120, 139, 332.
Harwood, 190.
Haslette, 89.
Hatch, 322.
Hatchett, 94.
Hathaway, 7, 159, 160, 161, 162, 163.
Hatton, 20, 38.
Haughman, 104.
Haverin, 89.
Haviland, 217.
Havy (or Hany), 96.

Hawhimer, 101.
Hawins, 38.
Hawker, 113.
Hawkins, 10, 57, 80, 96, 106, 109, 124, 130, 133, 134, 135, 137, 140, 141, 143, 144, 146, 150, 151, 152, 153, 154, 220, 222, 226, 240.
Hawley, 84, 159, 161.
Haws, 34.
Hay, 23.
Hayback, 183.
Haydon (Hayden), 119, 126, 147, 163, 181, 189, 260.
Hayes, 104, 152, 161, 168, 179, 186, 220, 221, 250, 266.
Haynes, 7, 8, 10, 139, 141, 152, 248, 261.
Hays, 16, 131, 139, 150, 158, 160, 162, 241.
Haze, 36.
Hazel, 118.
Hazelrigg, 20, 23, 163.
Heachley, 86.
Head, 127, 153.
Heard, 102.
Hearne, 165, 166, 191, 280, 281.
Heaton, 165.
Hebb, 148.
Heben, 210.
Heber, 209, 210.
Heckert, 317.
Heddleson, 46.
Hedger, 89, 125, 132, 134, 160, 206, 208, 221.
Hedges, 87, 153, 164, 167, 168, 169, 186, 202, 203, 204, 205, 207, 216, 221, 223, 266, 314, 315, 326.
Hedrington, 177.
Hedwegs, 189.
Heflin (Hefling), 83, 158.
Heggins, 158.
Hehr, 222.
Heiber, 211, 212.
Heils, 97.
Heirogous, 154.
Helch, 94.
Hellicost, 111.
Helm, 108, 116, 121, 229.
Helms, 108, 149, 159, 161.
Hemphill, 145.
Hend, 323.
Henderson, 15, 45, 53, 92, 100, 104, 108, 124, 139, 140, 143, 145, 149, 163, 191, 192, 193, 204, 205.
Hendon, 81.
Hendricks, 113, 163, 192, 221, 266.
Hendrickson, 127, 135, 137, 139, 144, 177, 261, 262.

359

Houst, 141.
Houston, 45, 223, 247, 268.
Hover, 153.
Howard, 83, 159, 160, 161, 162, 164, 165, 193, 216, 271, 326, 327.
Howe, 161.
Howel, 158.
Howk, 220, 222.
Hoy, 119.
Hoyt, 325.
Hubbard, 102, 103, 112, 135.
Huddleson, 45.
Hudgens (Hudgins), 5, 10, 88, 108, 116, 326.
Hudson, 33, 39, 92, 177, 325.
Huey, 102.
Huff, 69, 125, 128, 132, 133, 136, 139, 140, 142, 143, 149, 155, 292.
Huffman, 40, 47, 111, 113, 153, 154, 193, 237.
Hufford, 237.
Huggins, 144, 221.
Hughart, 78, 159.
Hughes (Hughs), 12, 14, 15, 57, 100, 102, 116, 117, 122, 127, 128, 130, 133, 140, 153, 159, 160, 163, 164, 179, 186, 187, 193, 242, 243, 247.
Hukel, 20.
Hulbert, 20.
Hulet (Hulett), 177, 178, 179, 180, 182, 183, 184, 186, 187, 189, 214, 237.
Hull, 165, 236.
Huls, 237.
Hulse, 161.
Humble, 125.
Humphreys, 24, 33, 209, 221.
Hundly (Hundley), 48, 252, 253, 265.
Hungate, 124, 125, 126, 128, 129, 130, 136, 138, 143, 155, 156.
Hunt, 31, 33, 90, 154, 160, 161, 177, 178, 179, 180, 182, 184, 186, 188, 212, 226, 227.
Hunter, 18, 25, 45, 57, 90, 95, 126, 127, 136, 202, 203, 205, 231, 265, 266.
Hunton, 290.
Hurd, 43.
Hurst, 31, 91, 154, 157, 238, 337.
Hurt, 92, 161, 163, 165.
Husbands, 132.
Huston, 52, 110, 111, 119, 187.
Hutch, 116.
Hutchcraft, 179, 187, 266.
Hutchens, 145.
Hutcherson, 100.
Hutchings, 93, 148.

Hutchins, 52, 130, 133.
Hutchinson, 103, 216, 218, 219, 277, 278.
Hutchison, 25.
Hutsell (Hutsil), 33, 181, 189.
Hutton, 7, 156, 311, 312.
Hymore, 159.
Hysong, 245.

Ibrain, 220.
Igo, 168.
Iles, 163.
Ilsairy, 17.
Ingles, 322, 323.
Ingraham, 225.
Ingram, 103.
Inman, 92, 104.
Innis, 121, 217.
Innskeep, 39.
Inyart, 113.
Ioor, 278.
Ireland, 142.
Irvin, 113, 119, 137, 139, 146, 154, 155.
Irvine, 15, 60, 61, 70, 76, 114, 129, 203.
Irwin, 162, 164, 170, 171, 172, 173, 174, 175.
Isbell, 116.
Isgrig, 327.
Isom, 15, 39.
Iverson, 109.
Ivey, 238.

Jackman, 57, 92, 106, 111, 117, 122, 127, 129, 130, 147.
Jackson, 7, 13, 53, 93, 95, 98, 102, 109, 110, 111, 112, 114, 119, 121, 122, 145, 154, 162, 164, 193, 201, 203, 206, 216, 235, 255, 329, 330.
Jacob, 152, 243.
James, 8, 24, 49, 67, 111, 121, 126, 127, 141, 156, 159, 161, 164, 208, 211, 218, 315, 316, 317, 332.
Jameson (Jamison), 44, 96, 97, 104, 124, 140, 148, 158, 159, 160, 161, 162, 164, 215, 216, 251.
January, 96, 168, 169, 191, 221, 222, 224, 225, 226.
Jaquess, 45.
Jarman, 61, 162.
Jasper, 120.
Jeans, 159.
Jeffries, 41, 42, 67, 101, 104, 127, 129, 153.
Jemmison, 102.
Jenkins, 24, 33, 99, 104, 155, 157, 159.

Knight, 246.
Knode, 210.
Knots, 54.
Knox, 13, 15, 92, 139, 140, 146, 150, 154, 161, 331.
Knuckles, 146, 149.
Kombs (or Lambs), 139.
Koyd, 178.
Kreks, 274.
Kronchenaur, 125.
Kurtman, 127.
Kurtz, 249.
Kyle, 14, 134, 139, 143.
Kyler, 101, 103.

Laberton, 147.
Lacefield, 120, 139.
Lacey (Lacy), 55, 84, 163, 164.
Lacjland, 171.
Lackey, 16, 124, 182.
Lackland, 198.
Lacklen (Lacklin), 196.
Lad, 185.
Lafferty, 222.
Lafon, 209.
Lagrange, 151.
Lail, 215, 216, 219, 221, 223.
Lair, 170, 171, 192, 215, 216, 217, 219, 222, 223, 226, 227, 228, 286, 287, 292.
Lake, 168, 221.
Lalla, 166.
Lalyear, 100.
Laman, 103.
La Master, 277.
Lamb, 45, 105, 125, 126, 137, 157, 281.
Lambert, 92, 125, 132, 133, 137, 141, 152, 269.
Lambs (or Kombs), 139.
Lamine, 82.
Lamme, 30, 33, 45, 74, 177.
Lammons, 167.
Lampton, 95, 121, 150, 184.
Lancaster, 8, 98, 221, 238.
Lancurt, 94.
Land, 103, 223, 243.
Lander (Landers), 94, 164, 235, 268.
Lane, 7, 22, 27, 86, 88, 152, 159, 160, 161, 162, 163, 164.
Lanfield, 103.
Lanford, 128.
Lang, 195, 222.
Langford, 104.
Lanigore, 189.
Lankford, 54, 76, 110, 111.
Lapsley, 13, 54, 70, 91, 101, 106, 155.
Larrimore (Larimore), 45, 192, 217.

Lary, 183, 260, 270, 271, 284.
Lash, 101.
Lasley, 94.
Latheram (Lathram), 132, 134.
Latherice, 114.
Lathy, 74.
Latimer, 91, 92, 138, 149.
Latimore, 71, 124, 133, 146.
Laudeman, 97, 333.
Lauderdale, 251.
Laughlin, 102, 135, 164, 243.
Laurie, 211.
Laverty, 128.
Law, 141, 148, 181.
Lawell, 45, 188.
Lawhorn, 93.
Lawrence, 5, 72, 73, 96, 107, 120, 124, 125, 126, 144, 147.
Laws, 16, 127, 150.
Lawson, 43, 104, 132, 133, 149, 157.
Lay, 150.
Layer, 103.
Layton, 115.
Laywell, 183.
Lea (Lee), 53, 101, 104, 116, 120, 144, 155, 157, 164, 198.
Leach, 160, 184, 224.
Leachman, 128.
League, 126.
Lear (Leer), 11, 12, 105, 255, 268, 271.
Lease, 105.
Leathers, 7, 87, 144.
Leavell, 43.
Leayree, 148.
Lecht, 148.
Leckman, 143.
Leckteter, 142.
Le Compte, 257.
Ledgerwood, 20.
Leeds, 220.
Leeland, 5.
Leforce, 185, 189.
Legacer, 155.
Le Grand, 31.
Legrange, 124.
Lehrer, 227.
Leid, 97.
Leister, 101.
Lemon, 24, 33, 156.
Lennear, 138.
Leonard, 92, 132, 135.
Lepaw, 138.
Leslie, 94.
Lester, 96.
Letcher, 51, 146, 235, 236.
Lethgan, 65.
Letrell, 211.
Levea, 122.
Level (or Serel), 204.

Levett, 34.
Levi, 53.
Lewallin, 154.
Lewelling, 126.
Lewis, 20, 41, 94, 97, 111, 129,
135, 136, 139, 140, 141, 149,
157, 159, 164, 175, 191, 193,
213, 271, 333.
Lickester, 147.
Light, 149, 156, 221.
Lighter, 179, 187, 224.
Lightfoot, 126, 128, 134.
Lillard, 5, 8, 10, 11, 14, 72,
75, 76, 77, 90, 107, 124, 147,
150, 151, 154.
Lillyers, 154.
Lilly, 22, 221.
Lincoln, 238.
Lincoln Co. Wills 48-59; marriages
105-122. (Male names not in-
dexed but alphabetical.)
Lindsay, 54, 100.
Lineback, 155.
Lines, 103.
Lingenfelter, 199, 200.
Links, 113.
Linn, 54, 114, 170.
Linnett, 129.
Linney, 291.
Linyoir, 158.
Lion, 128.
Lipaun, 132.
Lippincott, 317.
Lipsey, 124, 125.
Lisle, 328, 329, 330.
List, 143.
Lister, 142, 143, 144, 150.
Liter, 193.
Litman, 126.
Little, 47, 67, 97, 134, 145, 152,
198, 205, 207, 333.
Littlepage ,76.
Littleton, 25.
Littrell, 100.
Liverston, 101.
Livingston, 102, 148.
Lizenby, 153.
Lobb, 92, 101.
Locke, 72, 124, 144.
Locker, 91.
Lockhard, 128, 136.
Lockhart, 136, 161.
Lockland, 198.
Lockman, 127, 137.
Lockridge, 50, 84, 161, 163, 215.
Lockwood, 326.
Loden, 111.
Loecher, 279.
Logan, 50, 52, 54, 96, 97, 106, 109,
111, 114, 119, 121, 127, 139,
151, 170, 171, 173, 174, 175,

176, 193, 201, 203, 204, 205,
206, 212, 221, 232, 272, 273,
333.
Logston, 103.
Loid, 160.
Loiseau, 97.
Loney (Looney), 100, 106.
Long, 16, 30, 45, 70, 99, 105, 112,
130, 138, 156, 160, 165, 171,
174, 177, 178, 185, 194, 219,
326.
Longdon, 97.
Longhead, 97.
Longly, 67.
Longmoor, 220.
Losson, 43, 105.
Lotter, 101.
Lounger, 100.
Loush, 318.
Lout, 151.
Love, 97, 222.
Low (Lowe), 107, 114, 117, 118,
122, 127, 130, 145, 146, 152,
157, 181, 182, 189.
Lowden, 131.
Lowler, 129.
Lowry, 22, 47, 67, 82, 83, 97, 132,
140, 169, 208, 224, 237.
Lucas, 124, 133, 219.
Luckett, 154, 158.
Ludowick (Ludwick), 94, 126, 156.
Ludwig, 168.
Lusby, 34.
Lusk, 185.
Luther (Louther), 294.
Luttrell, 100.
Lutz, 228.
Lychlyter, 137.
Lydig (Lydick), 30, 238, 247.
Lyle, 171, 176, 203, 269, 270.
Lynam, 108.
Lynch (Linch), 98, 99, 105, 140,
143.
Lyne, 264.
Lynn, 121.
Lyon (Lyons), 77, 99, 125, 128,
131, 133, 135, 138, 141, 144,
146, 150, 152, 154, 155, 181,
241.
Lyster, 134, 135, 143, 148, 151,
153.

McAbo, 94.
McAdams, 239, 273, 274, 275, 315,
317, 324, 330, 332, 334, 335,
336, 337, 340.
McAfee, 63, 64, 67, 70, 73, 75,
77, 124, 126, 128, 131, 137,
146, 151, 155, 156, 325.
McAlister (McAllister), 134, 140.
McAmy (or McKamey), 130.

McIsaac (McIsaach), 28, 97.
McKaber, 14.
McKamey, 131, 146, 154.
McKane, 31.
McKay, 114.
McKee, 25, 111, 124, 159, 160, 216, 218, 219, 223.
McKelsee, 111.
McKenna, 339.
McKenney, 39, 51, 86.
McKibben, 335.
McKinervan, 323.
McKing, 204.
McKinley, 48, 114, 222.
McKinney, 67, 73, 94, 113, 116, 119, 124, 127, 130, 131, 132, 136, 141, 143, 145, 154, 155, 163.
McKinzie, 155, 156.
McKitrick, 146.
McKnight, 129.
McKonky, 70.
McLain, 113, 120.
McLaughlin, 45.
McLean, 103, 105, 269.
McMahan, 194, 195.
McManies, 103.
McMeekin, 193.
McMichael, 5, 87, 135, 146.
McMickle, 139.
McMillan (McMillen), 20, 47, 97, 113, 160, 192, 201.
McMonigle, 163.
McMordie, 140, 142, 147.
McMullin, 112.
McMurray, 21.
McMurtrie (McMurtree), 130, 135, 146, 151, 156.
McMurtry, 44, 54, 67, 119, 132.
McNamara, 98, 99.
McNearney, 99.
McNeele, 106.
McNeely (McNelly), 48, 117, 208.
McNees, 121, 166, 168, 192, 291.
McNeil, 93.
McNutt, 127.
McPeake, 106.
McPheeters, 21, 26, 193, 194, 195, 196, 197, 204, 206, 212, 238.
McQuerry, 101, 122.
McQuinn, 99.
McRoberts, 14, 50, 91, 173, 333.
McShane, 168, 216, 221.
McWilliams, 101.
McWhorter, 116.
Macalester, 231.
MacCombs, 133.
Machan, 113.
Machir, 162.
Macinsey, 177.
Mackbee, 163.

Mackey, 266, 267.
Mack Intire, 129.
Macklin, 40.
Mackness, 118.
Madison Co. Wills 59-62; marriages 122-123.
Maddison (Madison), 8, 197, 198, 205, 223, 282, 283.
Maddox, 148, 173.
Magee, 157, 214, 216, 222, 226.
Magill (Magil), 59, 109.
Magoffin, 144.
Magowan, 245.
Magraw, 116.
Maguire, 222.
Mahan, 75, 125, 135, 150.
Maher, 160.
Maill, 129.
Mainard, 147.
Mallory, 99, 178, 182, 183, 185, 187.
Malone, 123.
Maloney, 221.
Manaway, 87.
Manelly, 130, 131.
Manier, 103.
Manire, 100.
Mankley, 94.
Manksfile, 105.
Mankspile, 108.
Manly, 97.
Mann, 76, 98, 131, 141, 142, 148, 153.
Manners, 55.
Mannon, 106.
Mansfield, 179, 186, 228.
Mansfile, 115.
Manuel, 34.
Many, 140.
Mardis, 153.
Margrove, 133.
Maritt, 159.
Markham, 161, 238.
Marksberry, 39, 43, 101, 106.
Markspile, 141.
Marney, 99.
Marr (Marrs), 29, 78, 92, 93, 179, 275.
Marriages, 85-165. Marriages by Rev. John Smith, 157-165; marriages St. Peter's Catholic Church, 97-99.
Marrow, 159.
Marsh, 81, 82, 162.
Marshall, 8, 23, 25, 34, 45, 55, 72, 81, 94, 97, 104, 108, 111, 116, 117, 132, 137, 143, 145, 155, 158, 160, 170, 172, 173, 174, 175, 176, 186, 192, 195, 196, 197, 198, 202, 203, 211, 249.

Martin, 15, 20, 47, 53, 92, 93, 101, 104,110,114,122,125,132, 133, 134, 137, 141, 142, 143, 149, 152, 153, 155, 156, 159, 160, 161, 163, 167, 168, 190, 192, 193, 194, 195, 196, 197, 198, 199, 200, 202, 203, 204, 205, 207, 216, 217, 219, 220, 221, 256, 327.

Masden, 143.

Masey, 138.

Mason, 34, 84, 85, 102, 104, 106, 109, 110, 120, 143, 147, 161, 213, 214.

Massee, 160.

Masterson, 84, 108, 110, 120, 121, 122, 160, 161, 162, 226.

Mastin, 7, 15, 311, 312.

Maston, 321, 323, 333, 334, 338.

Matheney, 155.

Matherford, 154.

Matherly, 134, 135, 139.

Mathers, 127.

Mathews (Matthews, Matheer), 83, 109, 129, 154, 186, 192, 203, 264, 316, 323.

Mathewson, 172.

Mattingly, 92.

Mattocks, 129.

Maupin, 61.

Maxe, 146.

Maxey, 121.

Maxwell, 79, 102, 103, 124, 132.

May, 14, 92, 94, 111, 114, 127, 132, 134, 135, 136, 137, 138, 140, 146, 148, 149, 150, 153, 155, 158, 163, 262.

Mayell, 5.

Mayfield, 39, 55, 112, 250.

Mayhall, 128.

Mays, 76, 126, 155.

Means, 114, 159, 162.

Meaux, 76, 144.

Meddey, 42.

Meek, 107.

Meekins, 34.

Megibben, 166, 168, 215, 219, 222, 247, 315.

Meglone, 276.

Megowan, 339, 340.

Mehey, 99.

Mehring, 209.

Melchor, 126.

Melear, 87.

Melon, 160.

Melvin, 12.

Menally, 112.

Menefee (Menifee), 104, 108, 114, 118, 238.

Meniway, 160.

Menzies, 197, 198.

Mercer Co., Wills, 62-77; marriages 123-157.

Merdiar, 219.

Meredith, 142, 148, 152.

Merrell (Merrill), 31, 261.

Messick, 50, 251.

Metcalf, 253.

Meudlow, 152.

Meyer, 93.

Michael, 144.

Middleton, 16, 90, 106, 113, 115, 121, 131, 229, 332.

Milbern (Milburn), 92, 157.

Miles, 34, 66, 162, 203, 204, 205.

Milfry, 133.

Miller, 7, 23, 26, 29, 45, 48, 55, 60, 62, 67, 88, 98, 101, 102, 103, 104, 110, 111, 112, 120, 122, 126, 128, 132, 133, 134, 135, 140, 143, 147, 148, 156, 158, 160, 165, 168, 178, 180, 191, 215, 216, 218, 219, 222, 235, 237, 252, 311, 312, 324, 325, 326.

Milligan, 144.

Mills, 8.

Millspaugh, 160.

Milner, 55, 116, 247.

Milton, 84, 197, 199, 200, 201, 202, 203, 204, 205, 206, 207.

Minor, 18, 64, 91, 92, 93, 127, 129, 133, 134, 140, 148, 152, 153, 154.

Miscellaneous Wills, 77-83.

Miscy, 154.

Miskel, 124, 148.

Mitchell, 7, 13, 14, 15, 24, 44, 68, 76, 84, 92, 94, 121, 123, 128, 131, 133, 137, 139, 142, 145, 150, 153, 155, 158, 162, 177, 178,179,180,181,182,183, 184, 186, 187, 188, 190, 211, 213, 294.

Mitchum, 177.

Mizner, 127.

Mobley, 100.

Mock, 91.

Modiloe, 111.

Moffett, 53, 161, 163, 293.

Moise, 158.

Molar, 321.

Molloy, 99.

Moloney, 99.

Monley, 154.

Monroe, 138, 158, 210, 257.

Montague, 184, 187, 326.

Montgomery, 16, 26, 34, 43, 55, 88, 91, 100, 101, 108, 110, 112, 114, 115, 116, 119, 122, 123, 128, 132, 137, 140, 150, 155, 156, 250, 251, 265, 269,

129, 133, 148, 158, 214, 222, 223, 225, 226, 252, 342.

Nicholson, 56, 102.
Nickels (Nickle), 159, 160.
Nickum (Nicum), 40, 101.
Nield, 16, 136.
Niell, 153.
Nifong (or Nisong), 131.
Night, 171, 327.
Niping, 149.
Nixon, 94.
Noaks (Nokes), 112, 122.
Noble, 118, 125, 126, 127, 337, 338.
Noe, 21, 35, 177, 179, 184, 186.
Noel (Noell), 42, 68, 103, 106, 116, 125, 131, 132, 137, 140, 146, 149.
Nolan, 123.
Noland, 78, 111.
Nold, 92.
Norbeck, 322.
Norman, 165.
Norris, 125, 167, 168, 169, 314, 315, 316.
North, 45.
Northcraft, 91.
Northcutt, 84, 93, 109, 110, 162, 182, 183, 221, 223.
Norton, 5, 79, 152, 188.
Nourse, 76, 134, 141, 146, 155, 269, 270.
Nouvell, 35.
Nowell, 103, 112, 147.
Nowland, 102, 148.
Nowlin, 100.
Nuckols, 175.
Nunley, 19.
Nuttle, 35.
Oakerson, 161.
Oakley, 159.
Oate (or Outes), 6.
Obannon, 108, 260, 273.
O'Brian (O'Brien), 76, 99, 149, 256.
O'Connell, 99.
O'Connor, 335.
O'Dell (O'Del), 9, 134, 138.
Oden, 160.
Odle, 152.
Odor, 45, 225.
O'Dougherty, 98.
Officer, 170, 172, 173.
Offitt, 203.
Offutt, 171, 173, 175.
Ogletharp, 113.
O'Harrow, 21.
Oldfield, 20.
Oldham, 18, 25, 59, 84, 92, 123, 157, 164, 243, 281, 282, 283.
Olds, 155.
Olive, 8.

Oliver, 8, 85, 95, 96, 122.
Ollaman, 154.
O'Neal (O'Neil), 80, 98, 117.
Orear, 159.
O'Regan, 99.
O'Reilly, 97, 98.
Orkeys, 130.
Ormsby, 223, 224.
Orr, 137, 199, 316.
Ortkes (Ortkies), 55, 144.
Ortkin, 124.
Osborne (Osbourn), 21, 95, 255.
Osgood, 331.
O'Shea, 99.
Otis, 243, 282.
Ott, 102.
Otwell, 165.
Oubay, 104.
Outman, 103.
Outs, 148, 151.
Ovenly, 321.
Overstreet, 93, 94, 102, 131, 132, 133, 140, 147, 148, 165.
Overton, 68.
Owens (Owen), 17, 91, 92, 118, 137, 140, 152, 177, 179, 279, 342.
Owings, 135, 137, 142, 144, 147, 157, 163.
Ownby, 121.
Owsley, 16, 42, 43 51, 104, 106, 111, 117, 118, 122, 164.
Oxley, 167, 168, 222, 224.

Paddock, 94, 316.
Paddox, 125, 127.
Padget, 131.
Page, 26, 29, 138, 145, 166, 167, 168.
Paget, 91.
Pagut, 159.
Paine, 105.
Palmer, 140, 153, 222, 226.
Pamers, 86.
Pancake, 14, 16, 130, 146, 148.
Pandergrass, 91.
Parberry, 47.
Parent, 139.
Parish (Parrish), 61, 140, 142, 151, 156, 177, 181, 182, 190, 220, 223, 244, 265.
Parker, 6, 62, 88, 105, 135, 145, 146, 154, 213, 222, 228, 233, 235, 252, 320, 338, 339, 340, 341.
Parkinson, 153.
Parks, 15, 91, 94, 104, 121, 139, 150, 161, 167, 219, 247,
Parmer, 163.
Parr, 137, 155, 156, 157.
Parsley, 141.

Parsons, 202, 204, 207.
Partlow, 277.
Pasley, 159.
Passmore, 68, 136, 147.
Pate, 221.
Patrick, 29, 176, 206, 209.
Patten, 174.
Patterson, 11, 41, 62, 97, 131, 132, 139, 147, 150, 152, 157, 177, 192, 214, 215, 216, 218.
Pattie, 332.
Patton, 21, 54, 58.
Paul, 92, 102, 191.
Pauling, 144.
Paush, 139.
Pawling, 43, 58, 149.
Paxon (Paxton), 77, 85, 163, 319.
Payne, 26, 30, 84, 98, 105, 121, 159, 163, 164, 184, 186, 189, 191, 193, 213, 224, 228, 233, 281, 283, 284, 341.
Peachey, 284.
Peak (Peake), 106, 178, 186, 284.
Pearce, 244.
Pearl, 111, 121, 122.
Pearson, 134, 138, 153, 157.
Peavier, 154.
Peavler, 141.
Pebboth, 178, 185.
Pebworth, 160.
Peek, 148, 149, 166, 168, 169, 170, 219, 222, 326.
Peckover, 168, 218.
Pedinger, 80.
Pedworth, 160.
Peebles, 163.
Peel, 26, 316.
Peirson, 127.
Pelham, 65, 72.
Pemberton, 30, 43, 325.
Pence, 116.
Pendergraff, 93.
Pendergrass, 92, 155, 156.
Pendleton, 149, 152, 165, 271, 284.
Penex (Penexes), 83, 110.
Penill, 23.
Pennell, 222.
Penney (Penny), 5, 8, 10, 11, 76, 77, 85, 92, 94, 140, 144, 151.
Pennington, 125, 133.
Perdnan, 277.
Perdue, 161.
Perkins, 100, 104, 140, 222, 244.
Perks, 158, 159.
Perreman, 109.
Perrin, 106, 108, 113, 165, 166, 167, 168, 169, 203, 204, 215, 217.
Perry, 93, 117, 169, 217, 277.
Person, 101.
Peters (Peter), 39, 113, 119, 129, 149, 156.
Peterson, 324, 325.
Pettett (Pettitt), 158, 160, 165.
Petticord, 337.
Pettig, 101.
Petty, 5, 21, 141, 148, 153, 155, 221.
Pew, 161.
Peyton, 27, 105, 110, 111, 114, 120, 121, 122, 334.
Pheamaster, 100.
Phelps, 101, 161, 164, 249.
Phemster, 25.
Pherigo, 94, 125, 127, 131, 137.
Phillips (Philips), 5, 15, 17, 46, 68, 85, 91, 92, 93, 94, 106, 109, 114, 119, 125, 129, 132, 133, 134, 135, 136, 137, 138, 140, 142, 143, 144, 147, 151, 152, 154, 155, 156, 159, 160, 167, 168, 202, 204, 221, 280.
Phipps, 161, 162.
Phonys, 147.
Piatt, 26.
Pickens, 45.
Pickett, 45, 98, 185, 337.
Pickleheimer, 159.
Picot, 284.
Pierce, 51, 144.
Piercy, 159.
Pieri, 230.
Pierson, 234.
Pigg, 117, 329.
Pile, 155, 156.
Pindar, 166.
Pindell, 34.
Ping, 106.
Pinkard, 81, 187.
Pinkerton, 322, 323.
Pipe (Pipes), 91, 92, 126, 129, 132, 135, 144, 150.
Piper, 16, 138.
Pitman (Pittman), 14, 126, 127, 133, 137, 150, 155, 156, 177, 178, 185, 187, 282.
Pitts, 152, 284.
Pixley, 219.
Pleasant, 139.
Plough, 127, 132, 134, 143, 151.
Plue, 148.
Plummer, 21.
Plunkett, 121.
Poage, 25, 26, 107, 113, 120, 204.
Pocher, 277.
Poe, 102.
Poff, 68.
Pogue, 54, 340.
Poindexter, 39, 179.
Pointer, 102.
Polk, 174, 175, 203.
Pollard, 39.

Pollock, 40.
Polsgrove, 253.
Pomeroy, 224.
Pond, 44, 101, 103, 104.
Pool (Poole), 79, 131, 178, 180, 185, 186, 187, 188, 256.
Poor, 40, 86, 164.
Pope, 27, 93, 94, 101, 105, 106, 117, 119, 157, 178, 217.
Pophan, 150.
Porter, 52, 94, 160, 164, 260, 324.
Posey, 8, 9.
Postlewaite, 232.
Poston, 179.
Potter, 115, 141, 316.
Potts, 155.
Poulter, 143, 149, 150.
Poulton, 42.
Pounter, 117.
Powell, 45, 54, 55, 58, 62, 94, 99, 106, 113, 119, 121, 125, 128, 137, 143, 144, 145, 149, 151, 152, 153, 155, 157, 162, 209, 211, 212, 259.
Power, 35, 97.
Poynter, 105, 112, 113, 118, 122.
Prall, 93.
Prather, 24, 63, 68, 71, 88, 89, 126, 127, 131, 155, 159, 177.
Pray (?), 99.
Presley, 24.
Preston, 56, 100, 102, 122, 126, 137, 139, 180, 189, 190, 203, 212, 231.
Prewett (Prewitt), 14, 17, 25, 26, 38, 64, 93, 94, 124, 128, 137, 138, 140, 141, 142, 144, 147, 148, 149, 153, 154, 178, 179, 186, 188, 234, 243.
Price, 30, 35, 56, 75, 77, 92, 110, 112, 114, 115, 147, 161, 178, 185, 201, 202, 203, 204, 205, 206, 212, 236.
Priest, 158, 159, 163.
Priestly, 63.
Pringle, 164.
Prior, 136.
Pritchard, 132, 140.
Pritchett, 15, 138, 158, 159, 329.
Procise, 155, 156.
Proctor, 56, 80, 92, 93, 100, 101, 102, 116, 121, 163, 180, 183.
Prosith, 107.
Pryor, 133, 134.
Puckite, 110.
Pugh, 158, 327.
Pullam, 134.
Pulliner, 107.
Pullum, 218.
Purkins, 123.

Quarles, 28, 177, 197, 201.
Quarrier, 167.
Quigley (Quigly), 68, 134, 138, 145.
Quinn, 104, 142, 144.
Quisenberry, 18, 61, 95, 330.

Rabourn, 158.
Radcliff (Radcliffe), 56, 100, 115.
Radford, 138.
Rafferty, 99, 158.
Ragan, 99, 159, 161, 162,
Ragland, 94, 161, 163, 234.
Rails, 158.
Railsback, 22, 78, 90.
Raily, 157.
Rainey (Rainy), 96, 141.
Rains (Raines), 81, 134, 136, 140, 143, 145, 147, 149, 150, 153, 155, 156, 157.
Raleigh, 198.
Rall (Ralls), 57, 164, 269.
Ralston, 20, 160.
Ramey, 10, 160, 161, 162, 163, 264.
Ramsey, 56, 108, 154, 176.
Randall, 161.
Randels, 103.
Randolph, 93, 139, 145, 151, 154, 160, 163, 171, 177, 184.
Ranes, 133, 154.
Raney, 129.
Rankin, 36, 45, 47, 96, 97, 137, 158, 179, 192, 199,, 200, 201, 212, 213, 221, 222, 224, 292, 326.
Ransdell, 126, 131, 146, 147, 151, 153, 155, 156.
Rarity, 41.
Rash, 182, 185, 262, 264.
Ratcliff, 117, 120, 182.
Rattan, 103.
Rawls, 102, 113.
Ray, 15, 100, 111, 128, 136, 145, 154, 155, 156, 165, 266.
Raymon, 192.
Read, 161, 162, 164.
Reader, 172.
Reading, 47, 89.
Reber, 221.
Redd, 103, 227.
Redding, 88.
Redds, 90.
Redfern, 256.
Redman, 87.
Redmon, 26, 158, 216, 218, 223, 228, 327.
Redout, 166.
Reed, 7, 8, 15, 29, 57, 66, 101, 103, 106, 107, 111, 120, 124, 127, 128, 131, 135, 140 143, 148, 155, 156, 160, 161, 164, 223,

226, 330, 333.
Reeder, 100.
Reely, 158.
Reese (Rees), 47, 159, 186, 211, 260, 261, 271.
Reeves, 317, 318.
Reid (Reids), 34, 112, 158, 161, 166, 203, 269, 311, 312.
Reiley, 99.
Reinhardt, 230.
Reins, 133.
Reland, 145.
Remington, 139, 222, 225.
Renaker, 218, 219, 220.
Rench, 250.
Renfro, 100, 102, 116.
Rennecks, 122.
Rennick, 118, 194, 196, 201, 203, 206, 209, 210, 211.
Rentfro, 101.
Reynolds, 88, 98, 99, 103, 104, 144, 151, 167, 285, 289.
Rhodes, 12, 211.
Riblin, 85.
Rice, 7, 15, 16, 54, 65, 94, 101, 102, 114, 118, 121, 131, 141, 142, 150, 151, 152, 158, 159, 160, 164, 234, 235, 271, 290, 320, 331, 337, 338, 343.
Richards, 82, 142, 147, 164.
Richardson, 5, 24, 29, 64, 87, 92, 114, 122, 127, 133, 135, 140, 145, 150, 151, 155, 156, 158, 161, 214, 269.
Richason, 255, 256.
Richerson, 18.
Richey, 5, 107.
Richie, 21.
Richmond, 23.
Rickenbaugh, 146.
Ricks, 79.
Riden, 159.
Ridge, 141.
Ridgeley, 133.
Ridgeway (Ridgway), 130, 135, 178.
Ridgley, 82, 169, 219, 220.
Ridon, 158.
Rieckel, 167, 168.
Riffe, 57.
Rigg, 86.
Riggs, 111, 135, 158, 160, 161.
Right, 108, 146, 151.
Righter, 222.
Riglett, 148.
Rignell, 220.
Rigway, 131.
Riker, 151.
Riley, 9, 32, 75, 99, 107, 126, 136, 140, 143, 146, 149, 152, 153, 155, 156, 204, 205.

Rinearson, 145.
Riner, 259.
Ringo, 157, 158, 159, 160, 161, 162, 163, 165.
Riperdan, 142.
Ripperdam, 13, 94.
Ripperdan, 13, 124, 131, 132, 133.
Ripperdon, 126, 154.
Rish, 159.
Risk, 173, 175, 176, 203, 238.
Riske, 174.
Ritchey, 168, 193, 194, 198, 200, 201, 203.
Ritchie, 206, 222, 328.
Roach (Roache), 77, 99, 128, 129, 130, 131, 136, 231.
Roachwell, 138.
Robards (Robard), 63, 68, 128, 129, 138, 141, 277.
Robason, 71.
Robb, 194, 231.
Robbins, 94, 336.
Roberson, 44, 110, 113, 121.
Roberts, 32, 81, 94, 97, 120, 123, 126, 156, 158, 159, 161, 162, 217, 219, 223, 259, 260, 271, 272, 342.
Robertson, 15, 50, 56, 57, 68, 73, 86, 101, 103, 108, 111, 124, 126, 127, 128, 140, 145, 148, 151, 152, 155, 172, 211.
Robeson, 93.
Robins, 154, 177.
Robinson, 19, 25, 35, 37, 44, 45, 47, 68, 94, 108, 110, 114, 117, 143, 149, 161, 162, 163, 164, 167, 173, 174, 177, 178, 180, 181, 182, 184, 185, 186, 188, 190, 191, 202, 217, 250, 279, 282, 283, 316, 322, 326.
Robison, 5, 57, 90.
Robitzer, 223.
Robnett, 268.
Robson, 131.
Rochester, 14, 72, 127, 139.
Rock, 132.
Rodes, 146, 227, 232.
Rodgers, 158.
Rodoker, 160.
Roe, 137, 164.
Rogers, 35, 43, 51, 74, 78, 84, 104, 109, 112, 138, 142, 143, 144, 148, 149, 155, 158, 161, 180, 181, 189, 213, 222, 226, 234, 238, 275, 337.
Roguskey, 98.
Roland, 137, 145.
Rolleland, 130.
Roman, 136.
Romine, 149.
Romley, 157.

207, 216, 217, 313, 325.
Scroggin (Scroggins), 96, 171, 199, 200, 201, 202, 225.
Scroggs, 163.
Scruggs, 160, 161.
Scully, 98.
Seamon, 148.
Searcy, 9, 88, 142, 229.
Seargeant, 226.
Seckester, 35.
Secrest, 163.
Seery, 61.
Seitz, 222.
Selch, 127, 140.
Self, 170.
Sellers, 101.
Selvin, 103.
Semon, 118.
Semonis, 92, 144.
Sennet, 137.
Serel (or Level), 204.
Servant, 152.
Settle, 56, 87, 205, 206, 210.
Settles, 9, 149.
Severe, 136.
Sevier, 93, 154, 155.
Seviers, 140.
Shackleford, 48, 53, 60, 102, 104, 105, '110, 111, 115, 116, 118, 120, 123, 135, 137, 144, 336.
Shad, 107.
Shafer, 161.
Shamlin, 183, 187.
Shannon, 41, 45, 93, 94, 99, 111, 130, 152, 160.
Shante, 140.
Sharp (Sharpe), 26, 45, 77, 97, 98, 101, 130, 132, 142, 144, 147, 148, 149, 152, 154, 155, 160, 184, 185, 276, 322.
Shattuck, 230.
Shaver, 124.
Shaw, 94, 96, 126, 135, 145, 198.
Shawhan, 46, 167, 168, 170, 215, 216, 218, 219, 222, 247.
Shearer, 56.
Shearley, 147.
Shears, 163.
Sheele, 112.
Shelby, 209, 210, 317.
Sheley, 343.
Shelly, 99.
Shelp, 113.
Shelton, 100, 110, 111, 127, 130, 133, 148.
Shely, 26.
Shepherd, 124, 126, 139, 147, 165, 240.
Sherman, 97.
Shewmaker, 152, 193, 212.
Shields, 47, 75, 131, 151, 157, 191.

Shiell, 57.
Shin, 17.
Shindlebower, 233, 316.
Shine, 99.
Shipman, 112.
Shipp (Ship), 179, 181, 189, 190.
Shirley, 164.
Shockey, 165.
Shockley, 104.
Shoonmaker, 229.
Shoot, 179, 180, 187, 188.
Short, 101, 102, 104, 136, 138, 140, 155, 177, 197.
Shortridge, 158.
Shotwell, 324.
Shouse, 5, 124, 158, 164, 177, 263.
Shrader, 98.
Shreve, 29.
Shrewsberry, 102.
Shropshire, 182, 183, 184, 247, 322, 323.
Shrout (Shroutt), 164, 321.
Shrum, 128.
Shryock, 186, 189.
Shuck, 47, 106, 154.
Shuff, 219.
Shults, 158.
Shumate, 222.
Shy, 136, 137, 263.
Sidebottom, 101, 109.
Sidener, 30, 36.
Sidner, 161.
Silcox, 150.
Silvers, 135.
Silvertooth, 68, 125, 130, 132.
Silvey, 131, 133, 135, 141.
Simmerson, 36, 144, 218.
Simmons, 115, 136, 221, 250.
Simms, 144, 218.
Simonton, 199.
Simpson, 25, 26, 36, 55, 87, 96, 100, 106, 107, 112, 116, 117, 118, 119, 126, 127, 128, 132, 133, 145, 148, 159, 160, 161, 162, 178, 328.
Simrall, 227.
Sims, 143.
Simson, 158.
Sinclair, 37.
Singer, 36.
Singleton, 51, 101, 102, 107, 112, 120, 152, 280.
Sinkhorn, 146.
Sinnett, 128, 134, 141, 144.
Skelon, 143.
Skelton, 142.
Skiles, 317, 318.
Skillman, 164.
Skinner, 123, 133, 152, 155.
Skomp, 91.
Slade, 58, 117, 122, 219, 221.

Stearman, 218.

Steel, 64, 98, 103, 157, 194.

Steele, 83, 91, 96, 97, 123, 128, 142, 147, 191, 196, 199, 236, 237.

Steels, 139.

Steen, 68, 74.

Steger, 104.

Stein, 128, 129, 134.

Stemmons, 133.

Stenshon, 133.

Stephens, 28, 37, 48, 58, 69, 101, 102, 103, 114, 189, 226, 229.

Stephenson, 45, 120, 122, 135, 170, 171, 172.

Stepp, 119.

Sterling, 127.

Stevens, 21, 43, 100, 102, 129, 153, 158, 162, 164, 169, 178, 181, 185, 190.

Stevenson, 112, 118, 127, 133, 162, 163, 164, 174, 176, 186, 192, 193, 194, 195, 196, 197, 198, 199, 200, 201, 202, 203, 204, 205, 206, 208, 209, 211.

Stewart, 12, 37, 44, 45, 58, 91, 92, 93, 96, 101, 104, 150, 157, 166, 177, 180, 184, 185, 200, 201, 202, 203, 221, 223, 258, 259, 264.

Sthreshley, 196.

Stiles, 203.

Still, 324, 325.

Stimmons, 142.

Stinnett, 126.

Stinson, 19, 172.

Stipp, 96, 252, 265, 326.

Stirman, 142, 217, 218.

Stith, 162.

Stivers, 30, 242.

Stockdale, 208.

Stocker, 327.

Stockton, 83, 91, 162.

Stofer, 161, 162.

Stogdill, 103.

Stogdol, 203, 204.

Stoghill, 101.

Stokely, 255.

Stoker, 102, 327.

Stokes, 59, 134.

Stone, 19, 22, 28, 61, 62, 91, 120, 126, 127, 132, 139, 141, 154, 164, 165, 177, 191, 287, 288, 323, 336, 339, 340.

Stoner, 152, 162, 163, 164.

Stopher, 142.

Storm, 151.

Story, 8, 25, 288.

Stott (Stotts), 5, 9, 121.

Stout, 7, 8, 37, 91, 147, 177, 191, 213, 261.

Stover, 81.

Strange, 102, 159.

Street, 131.

Stringer, 107, 158.

Stringfield, 315.

Strode, 264, 276.

Strong, 140.

Stuart, 58, 160, 164, 232.

Stuck, 124, 126, 154.

Stull, 155.

Stults, 107.

Stump, 47, 218, 223.

Sturman, 126, 129.

Sudduth, 162.

Sugden, 230.

Sullivan, 99, 123, 128, 135, 151, 152, 177, 203, 204, 222.

Summer (Summers), 18, 38, 105, 119.

Summitt, 121.

Sussell, 141.

Sutfield, 132, 136.

Sutherland, 91, 130, 143, 147, 154.

Sutterfield, 128.

Suttle, 155.

Sutton, 13, 41, 69, 101, 102, 103, 117, 129, 146, 153, 154, 239, 260.

Swan, 58, 178, 185.

Swaney, 21, 22.

Swann, 114.

Swartz, 219.

Swearingen, 74, 161.

Sweeny (Sweeney), 54, 94, 152, 215, 216.

Swier, 125.

Swindler, 155.

Swiney (Swinney), 116, 122, 342.

Swinford, 192.

Swingle, 7.

Swipe, 92.

Switzer, 117, 163.

Swonger, 167, 168, 314, 315, 316.

Sword, 118.

Sydnor, 342.

Sympson, 17 .

Tabee, 130.

Tabor, 138.

Tackman, 154.

Tadlock, 17, 91, 127, 130, 131, 140.

Talbert, 186, 218.

Talbott (Talbot), 37, 110, 126, 137, 157, 215, 222, 291, 292, 327.

Tally, 163.

Tapp (Tap), 28, 158.

Tarkington, 92.

Tarleton, 343.

Tarpin, 103.

Tash, 10.

Tates, 162.

Truea (?), 175.
True, 37, 116, 165, 177, 180, 182, 184, 185, 188, 190.
Tryer, 106.
Tucker, 50, 58, 115, 152, 157, 277, 278, 330.
Tuggle, 19, 22, 96.
Tulley (Tully), 100, 129, 285.
Tunget, 101, 103.
Tunning, 30.
Turley, 158.
Turman, 313.
Turnan, 47.
Turner, 37, 61, 62, 69, 82, 112, 143, 146, 149, 152, 156, 164, 191, 219, 221, 235, 286, 292, 327.
Turney, 93, 101, 139.
Turpin, 42, 74, 101, 102, 337.
Turrell, 168.
Turtoy, 216.
Tutt, 203.
Tuttle, 94, 215.
Twalt, 131.
Twemey, 152.
Twomey, 99.
Twyman, 7.
Tyburn, 121.
Tyler, 155, 156.
Tyner, 240.
Tyre, 177.
Tyson, 155.

Ubanks, 98.
Underwood, 65, 96.
Upton, 109.
Utley, 129, 134, 142, 230.
Utterback, 86, 159, 160, 321.

Valentine, 204, 205, 206, 207.
Vallandingham, 29.
Vamoy, 137.
Vanarsdale, 131, 143.
Vanarsdall, 92, 94, 124, 125, 126, 127, 128, 129, 130, 132, 140, 142, 143, 145, 146, 147, 149, 151, 152, 153, 154, 155.
Vanarsdallen, 129.
Vanarsdell, 91.
Vance, 8, 37, 45, 74, 101, 117, 130, 171, 172, 175, 176, 237, 238.
Vancleve (VanCleve, Vancleave), 70, 105, 112, 118.
Vandergraff, 172, 173.
Vanderipe, 144, 145.
Vandigrift, 281.
Vandike (Vandyke), 131, 139, 146.
Vandivere (Vandiver), 145, 146, 152.
Vandivier, 126, 128, 129, 130, 135, 138, 143, 148, 150, 157.
Vandivir, 153.
Van Dusan, 324.
Vanee (Vanie), 171, 176.
Vanfansen, 46.
Vanfleet, 150, 152, 153, 154, 157.
Vanhice, 127, 149.
Vanhook, 168, 215, 218, 222, 225.
Vanice, 124.
Vaniss, 136.
Vankice, 126, 149.
Vanleet, 148.
Vanmeter (Van Meter), 47, 210.
Van Metree (Van Metre), 58, 113.
Van Nays, 72.
Vannest, 141.
Vannice, 135, 144.
Vanoy (Vannoy), 92, 140, 141, 146, 149.
Vanpelt, 38.
Vanwinkle, 119.
Varbrike, 144.
Vardaman (Vardeman), 116, 117, 177, 178, 179, 180, 184, 187, 230.
Varval, 159.
Vaughn, 28, 78, 96, 157.
Vaughter, 144.
Veach, 168, 221, 224, 315, 316.
Veatch, 45, 138, 218, 222, 257, 258, 292, 293.
Vegus, 25.
Vemangan, 156.
Venable, 126, 140.
Venice, 154.
Verbryke, 75, 125, 130.
Verbyke, 72.
Vermilion (Vermillion), 93, 145, 148, 149.
Vert, 85.
Vest, 100.
Vestal, 158.
Vickers, 103.
Viles, 137, 138, 149.
Vincent, 132.
Vint, 164.
Vinvolkather, 119.
Violet, 157, 168.
Vistor, 167, 168, 169, 214, 217.
Vivian, 341.
Voirs, 34.
Vonhice, 151.
Vontress, 15.
Voorhies, 126, 128, 129, 136, 139, 141, 142, 143, 144, 146, 147, 149.
Vorbrike, 154.
Vorhees, 71.
Vorhis, 106.
Voris (Vooris), 126, 127, 128, 134, 151.

Vortigern, 330.

Wadde (or Waddle), 82.
Waddell, 19.
Waddle, 133.
Waddy, 62.
Wade, 14, 17, 146, 149, 152, 153, 161, 162, 163, 165, 294.
Wagers, 104.
Waggoner, 70, 141.
Wagland (or Wayland), 143.
Wagner, 337, 340, 341.
Wainwright, 37.
Wait, 285.
Waits, 168.
Walden, 102, 103, 104, 152, 162, 204, 209, 276.
Wales, 126, 129.
Walker, 5, 9, 10, 17, 45, 51, 58, 63, 72, 74, 77, 91, 92, 94, 100, 112, 114, 118, 120, 132, 135, 145, 146, 149, 150, 154, 155, 159, 165, 174, 191, 195, 206, 209, 223, 324.
Walkup, 135, 139, 142.
Wall, 47, 162, 169, 220, 225.
Wallace, 8, 10, 13, 27, 93, 96, 100, 104, 123, 131, 155, 199, 209, 238, 247.
Wallen, 108, 162.
Waller, 76, 96, 161, 185, 190, 293, 294.
Wallis, 58.
Walls, 21, 98, 148.
Walters (Walter), 92, 137, 139.
Walton, 57, 217, 222.
Waltop, 217.
Waltz, 199, 200, 202, 208.
Ward, 21, 47, 94, 137, 138, 140, 141, 143, 158, 191, 192, 221, 222, 223, 224.
Warder, 161.
Wardle, 212, 229.
Wardlow, 193, 194, 195, 196, 203.
Wardly, 96.
Ware, 22, 169, 198, 215, 322.
Warfield, 31, 45, 168, 169, 213, 215, 219, 220.
Waring, 278.
Warman, 130, 139.
Warmath, 44.
Warner, 110, 159, 160, 163, 333.
Warnock, 217, 218.
Warren, 28, 58, 106, 107, 110, 113, 114, 117, 119, 120, 122, 124, 126, 130, 144, 155, 160, 188, 243, 290.
Wasen, 202.
Wasg, 5.
Wash, 5, 119, 120.
Washburn, 112.

Washington, 42, 98, 174, 175.
Wason (Wasson), 37, 199, 201, 203, 204, 205, 206, 207, 208, 209, 212.
Waterfield, 6, 90.
Waterford (Wattersford), 136, 154.
Waters, 117, 140.
Watkins, 43, 128, 130, 212, 342.
Watson, 10, 47, 94, 129, 132, 198, 201, 238.
Watts, 6, 7, 9, 10, 30, 97, 124, 132, 137, 138, 139, 148, 151, 152, 181, 280.
Wayland, 77, 151.
Wayne, 158.
Wead, 259.
Weathers, 31, 103, 180, 181, 182, 183, 187, 190.
Webb, 14, 27, 93, 126, 127, 150, 216, 218, 219, 231, 248, 322, 333, 334, 341.
Webber, 96, 148, 216, 221, 222.
Webster, 75, 93, 126, 136, 149, 167, 219, 222.
Weeden, 16.
Weeks, 166, 256.
Weesburg, 218.
Weigan, 234.
Weighley, 114.
Welch, 29, 54, 167, 177, 178, 182, 186, 187, 188, 220.
Weldon, 181, 185.
Wells, 13, 55, 85, 114, 129, 138, 141, 144, 158, 159, 160, 161, 164, 235, 266.
Welsh, 48.
West, 37, 132, 147, 159, 165, 225.
Westerfield, 76, 105, 119, 124, 129, 130, 150, 151, 152.
Westerman, 118.
Whaley, 24, 34, 164, 291, 292.
Whalin, 222.
Wheat, 142, 148, 155.
Wheeler, 44, 62, 102, 103, 139, 144, 154, 161, 163, 186, 206, 207.
Whelan (Whelen), 14, 139.
Wherritt, 216, 218.
While, 159.
Whitaker, 278, 332.
White, 5, 22, 23, 78, 85, 87, 89, 96, 101, 119, 123, 125, 127, 130, 133, 140, 141, 143, 154, 157, 158, 160, 161, 162, 163, 171, 178, 179, 180, 181, 182, 183, 185, 187, 188, 189, 194, 195, 196, 214, 222, 230, 232, 255, 273, 294, 321, 341.
Whitehead, 217.
Whitehouse, 91, 92, 94, 124, 128,

130, 133, 136.
Whiten, 83, 183.
Whitenack, 144, 151, 152.
Whiteneck, 138, 140, 141, 145, 147, 155.
Whitenhill, 132.
Whitesides, 101, 178, 184.
Whithers, 120.
Whiting, 322.
Whitington, 163.
Whitlet, 272.
Whitley, 116, 119, 120, 124.
Whitlow, 342.
Whitman, 160.
Whitmore, 316.
Whitset, 159.
Whitsitt, 159.
Whitter, 129.
Whittinghill, 126, 138, 147.
Whittington, 194, 195.
Whittle, 54, 109, 110.
Whitton, 108.
Whoberry (Whooberry), 16, 126, 127, 128, 129, 137, 147, 150, 152.
Whooly, 112.
Wicker, 125.
Wickersham, 138, 139, 141.
Wickliff, 118.
Wicoff, 145, 147.
Wier, 31.
Wiett, 140.
Wigam, 92.
Wiggand, 76.
Wigglesworth, 222, 224.
Wiggs, 155.
Wigham, 128, 142, 148, 150, 153, 154.
Wight, 92.
Wigor, 135.
Wilcox, 117.
Wiley, 104, 108, 115, 119, 122, 128, 159.
Wilgus, 162.
Wilham, 138, 148, 153, 157.
Wilhite, 14, 152.
Wilhoit, 57.
Wilkersham, 132.
Wilkerson, 16, 111, 131, 159, 160, 162, 203, 204.
Wilkinson, 81.
Wilkison, 96.
Willard, 150.
Willcocks, 112.
Willett, 258.
Willey, 59.
Williams, 12, 14, 59, 69, 78, 91, 92, 94, 96, 102, 103, 107, 108, 111, 113, 123, 125, 128, 137, 140, 141, 142, 144, 150, 159, 160, 161, 162, 163, 164, 165, 168,

169, 186, 198, 199, 201, 203, 209, 213, 215, 216, 218, 219, 221, 222, 234, 266, 287, 288.
Williamson, 221, 233, 252.
Willis, 66, 68, 91, 92, 103, 129, 130, 131, 132, 142, 162, 321.
Wills, 23, 95, 158, 159, 326.
Wills and Deeds, 5-85.
Willson, 63, 77, 78, 95, 96, 164, 327.
Wilmot, 92.
Wiloughby, 165.
Wilson, 39, 45, 48, 59, 83, 92, 93, 96, 100, 113, 114, 121, 122, 125, 127, 128, 131, 132, 133, 134, 135, 138, 140, 142, 145, 148, 149, 151, 152, 153, 154, 155, 156, 158, 159, 160, 161, 162, 164, 167, 178, 180, 181, 182, 184, 185, 188, 189, 190, 213, 214, 222, 227, 237, 252, 271, 292, 293, 312, 314, 315, 316, 317, 320, 321, 326, 332, 336, 343.
Windsor, 172.
Wing, 163.
Wingate, 131, 141, 149, 152, 174, 175.
Wingfield, 227.
Winifree, 341, 342.
Winkfield, 200.
Winks, 81.
Winlock, 134.
Winn, 24, 37, 188.
Winston, 163, 218, 219.
Winter (Winters), 31, 191, 232, 233, 324.
Wirt (or Wurt), 88.
Wise, 18, 88, 158, 242, 337.
Withers, 56, 91, 122, 154, 222.
Witherspoon, 232.
Withrow, 145.
Witnesses not indexed.
Witt, 271.
Wolfe, 116, 221.
Wolford, 166, 168, 170, 314, 315.
Wolz, 274.
Wood, 18, 28, 60, 61, 78, 79, 80, 81, 95, 96, 101, 107, 118, 122, 123, 131, 133, 135, 137, 161, 238, 246, 256, 282, 283, 294, 342.
Woodard, 158, 161, 163.
Woodburn, 159, 315, 331.
Woodford, 162.
Woodfork, 131.
Woodgate, 239.
Woodram, 100.
Woodruff, 191, 224.
Woods, 47, 60, 61, 63, 70, 75, 89, 95, 97, 102, 111, 113, 114, 122,

ERRATA

Page 36—The "will of Gwynn R. Tompkins" is given on this page under the name of "Conrad Sidner." These wills both correctly given are as follows:

SIDNER, CONRAD—Will Book F, page 408, of Fayette County.—Written June 27, 1821. Names wife and "six children." "My dau. Peggy Jones." Wit: David Smith, J. H. Stewart, Daniel Sidener. Execx., wife, Jane. Probated October Court, 1824. Attest., James C. Rodes, Clerk.

TOMPKINS, GWYNN R.—Will Book F, page 408—Written August 22, 1823. Probated October Court, 1824. Names sons, John, Wm., and Gwynn R. Tompkins; dau. Powell and her children. "The rest of my children." Exrs., sons, John, Wm. and Gwynn R. Tompkins.

ERRATA PAGE 79

The will given as "William Wood," is the correct will of John Wood.

Omitted from this Book—Will of William Wood, of Louisa Co., Va., will Book 3, page 400, dated Feb. 12, 1791, names wife, Ursela, and grandchildren, and sons: Thomas, William and John, beneficiaries. In "John Wood, Estate," **Nancy married Joseph Fugate (not Frigate).

Omitted from the list of Deeds of Thomas Wood and wife, Martha— "Deed page 466. 100 acres of land to my son, John, of same parish, where John now lives. Dated Aug. 7, 1756." (Deed book number not given, but copied from "certified record.")

Additional information—"certified copy"—Nimrod Wood married first, Dryden Marsh; their children: (1) Eleanor, married ——— Payne; (2) Thomas, married Anne Elizabeth Clark; (3) Beale, married first, ——— Royse; second, ——— McClintock; (4) John, married Lydia Hawkins; (5) Susan, died; (6) Julia, married ——— Steele; (7) Dryden.

Nimrod Wood married second, Margaret McClintock; children: James, Susan, Nimrod, Nicholas and Anne.

ERRATA PAGE 81

Mrs. Effie S. Hobson (not Honson).
In will of Beale Marsh, of Bourbon County, Ky., **son, Benedict Beale Marsh (not Benedict Marsh, Beale Marsh). **Dau., Dryden Wood, wife of Nimrod Wood.

PAGE 223

July, 1930—Additional records of tombstones, in Old Graveyard on Main Street, at Cynthiana, Ky. These stones were found face down and buried under vines and soil. Secured by Mrs. H. K. McAdams.

David Morison. Died July 2nd, 1825, in 41st year of his life.
Willia W., son of Wm. and Sarah Werden. Died Nov. 13, 1856. Age 1 year.

Elizabeth Righter, wife of Thomas Hall. Died July 8, 1861.
Mary Hall and Mignionette, children of J. and G. Bruce. No date.
John H. Frazer. Born Oct. 30, 1799. Died Sept. 12, 1863.
Robert H. Gibbons. Born Feb. 5, 1833. Died May 13, 1857. I. O. O. F.
Leanahp, wife of Henry P. Irvin. Died May 1, 1852, in her 45th year.

Error Page 246. Nannie Clark Wood, born Feb. 5, 1859.

ERRATA

Page 272—Top line "Samuel Lewis and wife Miss Whitlet" was written in another hand than the rest of the record and has been found to be not the parents of "Jesse Lewis." No proof of Jesse Lewis' parents have been found, or where he lived before coming to Kentucky. The record of Jesse Lewis and his second wife is correct. No record of his first wife can be found.

Errata Page 332. Round Grove, not Round Grave.
Roberta Mary James, born 1920.

ERRATA

Page 339, line 33—Elizabeth Neale Davis and William Todd Davis, twins, born (not married) October 4, 1871. William Todd Davis died September 14, 1873.